Emerging Challenges, Solutions, and Best Practices for Digital Enterprise Transformation

Kamaljeet Sandhu
University of New England, Australia

IGI Global
PUBLISHER of TIMELY KNOWLEDGE

A volume in the Advances in Business Strategy and Competitive Advantage (ABSCA) Book Series

Published in the United States of America by
IGI Global
Business Science Reference (an imprint of IGI Global)
701 E. Chocolate Avenue
Hershey PA, USA 17033
Tel: 717-533-8845
Fax: 717-533-8661
E-mail: cust@igi-global.com
Web site: http://www.igi-global.com

Library of Congress Cataloging-in-Publication Data

Names: Sandhu, Kamaljeet, 1970- editor.
Title: Emerging challenges, solutions, and best practices for digital enterprise transformation / Kamaljeet Sandhu, editor.
Description: Hershey, PA : Business Science Reference, [2021] | Includes bibliographical references and index. | Summary: "This book offers new developments in digital enterprise transformation of business systems from a global perspective, demonstrating the far-reaching impact for digital enterprise transformation, and suggesting ways that digital businesses are global and are continuously evolving online faster than ever and into new ecosystems in different parts of the world via internet. "-- Provided by publisher.
Identifiers: LCCN 2021004486 (print) | LCCN 2021004487 (ebook) | ISBN 9781799885870 (hardcover) | ISBN 9781799885887 (paperback) | ISBN 9781799885894 (ebook)
Subjects: LCSH: Business enterprises--Technological innovations. | Technological innovations--Management. | Organizational change.
Classification: LCC HD45 .E3644 2021 (print) | LCC HD45 (ebook) | DDC 658.4/06--dc23
LC record available at https://lccn.loc.gov/2021004486
LC ebook record available at https://lccn.loc.gov/2021004487

This book is published in the IGI Global book series Advances in Business Strategy and Competitive Advantage (ABSCA) (ISSN: 2327-3429; eISSN: 2327-3437)

British Cataloguing in Publication Data
A Cataloguing in Publication record for this book is available from the British Library.

For electronic access to this publication, please contact: eresources@igi-global.com.

Advances in Business Strategy and Competitive Advantage (ABSCA) Book Series

Patricia Ordóñez de Pablos
Universidad de Oviedo, Spain

ISSN:2327-3429
EISSN:2327-3437

Mission

Business entities are constantly seeking new ways through which to gain advantage over their competitors and strengthen their position within the business environment. With competition at an all-time high due to technological advancements allowing for competition on a global scale, firms continue to seek new ways through which to improve and strengthen their business processes, procedures, and profitability.

The **Advances in Business Strategy and Competitive Advantage (ABSCA) Book Series** is a timely series responding to the high demand for state-of-the-art research on how business strategies are created, implemented and re-designed to meet the demands of globalized competitive markets. With a focus on local and global challenges, business opportunities and the needs of society, the **ABSCA** encourages scientific discourse on doing business and managing information technologies for the creation of sustainable competitive advantage.

Coverage

- Strategic Management
- Adaptive Enterprise
- Competitive Strategy
- Core Competencies
- International Business Strategy
- Strategic Alliances
- Value Creation
- Tacit Knowledge
- Value Chain
- Globalization

The Advances in Business Strategy and Competitive Advantage (ABSCA) Book Series (ISSN 2327-3429) is published by IGI Global, 701 E. Chocolate Avenue, Hershey, PA 17033-1240, USA, www.igi-global.com. This series is composed of titles available for purchase individually; each title is edited to be contextually exclusive from any other title within the series. For pricing and ordering information please visit http://www.igi-global.com/book-series/advances-business-strategy-competitive-advantage/73672. Postmaster: Send all address changes to above address.

Titles in this Series

For a list of additional titles in this series, please visit: http://www.igi-global.com/book-series/advances-business-strategy-competitive-advantage/73672

Competitive Drivers for Improving Future Business Performance
Carlos Martins (Lusíada University of Porto, Portugal) and Paula Rodrigues (Lusíada University of Porto, Portugal)
Business Science Reference • © 2021 • 267pp • H/C (ISBN: 9781799818434) • US $225.00

Entrepreneurial Innovation for Securing Long-Term Growth in a Short-Term Economy
Jorge Gamez-Gutierrez (Universidad de la Costa, Colombia) and Jose Manuel Saiz-Alvarez (Universidad Católica de Santiago de Guayaquil, Ecuador & Universidad Autónoma de Manizales, Colombia & CEIEF-Universidad de Santiago de Chile, Chile)
Business Science Reference • © 2021 • 256pp • H/C (ISBN: 9781799835684) • US $215.00

Global Perspectives on Military Entrepreneurship and Innovation
Sanya Ojo (Nigerian Defence Academy, Nigeria)
Business Science Reference • © 2021 • 357pp • H/C (ISBN: 9781799866558) • US $195.00

Handbook of Research on Sustaining SMEs and Entrepreneurial Innovation in the Post-COVID-19 Era
Neeta Baporikar (Namibia University of Science and Technology, Namibia & University of Pune, India)
Business Science Reference • © 2021 • 676pp • H/C (ISBN: 9781799866329) • US $325.00

Revolutionizing Institutional Theory Through Stakeholder Capitalism
Neslihan Aydogan-Duda (UC Berkeley Extension, USA)
Business Science Reference • © 2021 • 300pp • H/C (ISBN: 9781799844921) • US $235.00

Creating Social Value Through Social Entrepreneurship
Mine Afacan Fındıklı (Beykent University, Turkey) and Duygu Acar Erdur (Beykent University, Turkey)
Business Science Reference • © 2021 • 369pp • H/C (ISBN: 9781799847274) • US $195.00

Handbook of Research on International Business and Models for Global Purpose-Driven Companies
Rafael Ignacio Perez-Uribe (EAN University, Colombia) Carlos Largacha-Martinez (Fundación Universitaria del Área Andina, Colombia) and David Ocampo-Guzman (EAN University, Colombia)
Business Science Reference • © 2021 • 589pp • H/C (ISBN: 9781799849094) • US $345.00

Cases on Internationalization Challenges for SMEs
António Carrizo Moreira (University of Aveiro, Portugal)
Business Science Reference • © 2021 • 333pp • H/C (ISBN: 9781799843870) • US $185.00

IGI Global
PUBLISHER of TIMELY KNOWLEDGE

701 East Chocolate Avenue, Hershey, PA 17033, USA
Tel: 717-533-8845 x100 • Fax: 717-533-8661
E-Mail: cust@igi-global.com • www.igi-global.com

I dedicate this book to the memory of my mother and father.

Editorial Advisory Board

Ramkrishna Ghosh, *Haldia Institute of Technology, India*
Ayse Gunsel, *Kocaeli University, Turkey*
Farid Huseynov, *Gebze Technical University, Turkey*
Ashwini J., *BIMS, University of Mysuru, India*
Esha Jain, *The NorthCap University, Gurugram, India*
Danielle Kadlec, *Luiss Business School, Italy*
Fatma Sena Karal, *Turkish-German University, Turkey*
Bernice Kotey, *University of New England, Australia*
Jonika Lamba, *The NorthCap University, Gurugram, India*
Zakaria Lissaneddine, *National School of Business and Management, University of Moulay Ismail, Morocco*
Rajesh Many, *Mahatma Gandhi University, India*
Robert Marlin, *Queensland University of Technology, Australia*
Joana Maria Costa Martins das Dores, *University of Aveiro, Portugal*
Tlou Maggie Masenya, *Durban University of Technology, South Africa*
Diego Matricano, *Università degli Studi della Campania "L. Vanvitelli", Italy*
Zeynep Orman, *Istanbul University-Cerrahpasa, Turkey*
Fahri Özsungur, *Adana Science and Technology University, Turkey*
Samet Oztoprak, *Istanbul University-Cerrahpasa, Turkey*
Ranjith P. V., *CMS Business School, India*
Shailesh Palekar, *Queensland University of Technology, Australia*
Digvijay Pandey, *Department of Technical Education, India*
Nicholas Patterson, *Deakin University, Australia*
Francisco Xavier Pedro, *Universidade do Minho, Portugal*
Carla M. B. F. Pires, *CBIOS – Research Center for Biosciences & Health Technologies, Universidade Lusófona, Portugal & ISCTE, Instituto Universitário de Lisboa, Portugal*
Volkan Polat, *Yalova University, Turkey*
Sabyasachi Pramanik, *Haldia Institute of Technology, India*
Tansif Ur Rehman, *University of Karachi, Pakistan*
María-Mercedes Rojas-de-Gracia, *University of Málaga, Spain*
Debabrata Samanta, *Christ University, India*
Marisa Analia Sanchez, *Universidad Nacional del Sur, Argentina*
Deepak Saxena, *Birla Institute of Technology and Science, Pilani, India*
Sabrina Schork, *TH Aschaffenburg, Germany*
Plácido Sierra-Herrezuelo, *University of Malaga, Spain*
Mehmet Ali Şimşek, *Tekirdag Namik Kemal University, Turkey*
Murat Selçuk Solmaz, *Piri Reis University, Turkey*
Shahryar Sorooshian, *University of Gothenburg, Sweden*
Ayberk Soyer, *Istanbul Technical University, Turkey*
Halit Alper Tayali, *Istanbul University School of Business, Turkey*
Dhananjay Thiruvady, *Deakin University, Australia*
Aparna J. Varma, *GSSS Institute of Engineering and Technology for Women, India*
Nagarajan Venkatachalam, *Queensland University of Technology, Australia*
Rebecca Jen-Hui Wang, *Lehigh University, USA*
Atilla Wohllebe, *Szent István University, Kaposvár, Hungary*

Guy Wood-Bradley, *Deakin University, Australia*
Kamil Yagci, *Pamukkale University, Turkey*
Ibrahim Yikilmaz, *Kocaeli University, Turkey*
Mustafa Yılmaz, *Yalova University, Turkey*
Dina Ziadlou, *Colorado Technical University, USA*
Juana Ines Zuntini, *Universidad Nacional del Sur, Argentina*

Table of Contents

Detailed Table of Contents

This study aims to reveal the new generation banking product/service distribution channels that banks offer to their customers through fintechs and their perspectives on these channels in terms of both customers and banks. Today, the key issue for banks creates a unique customer experience. Accordingly, the study focused on customer experience for new generation banking product/service distribution channels and how to realize unique customer experience. Today, many bank customers are far from new generation distribution channels. However, as technology changes and develops very rapidly, the number of people reaching it is increasing day by day. In this regard, besides the suggestions that will enable the use of new generation banking distribution channels by wider audiences, suggestions were also made to banks in order to provide a unique customer experience for these applications.

Digital enterprise transformation is the amalgamation of digital techniques into the scopes of a business enterprise, fundamentally altering how one can employ and furnish ethics to clients. An organization can be authorized to take digital transformation due to several reasons. But the most important reason is that it is the survival issuance for many people. Digital transformation considers dissimilarity in every organization. Generally, it is the amalgamation of digital technology into all quarters of business. That consolidation brings about major alterations in how the business functions and conveys usefulness to its clients. Here, steganography and cryptography are used to facilitate digital transformation in any business.

highlight the existence of digital ambassadorship and e-reputation oversight practices. Finally, this chapter also provides some managerial recommendations and future research directions.

Recent advances in deep learning methodology led to artificial intelligence (AI) performance achieving and even surpassing human levels in an increasing number of complex tasks. There are many impressive examples of this development such as image classification, sensitivity analysis, speech understanding, or strategic gaming. The estimations based on the AI methods do not give any certain information due to the lack of transparency for the visualization, explanation, and interpretation of deep learning models which can be a major disadvantage in many applications. This chapter discusses studies on the prediction of precious metals in the financial field that need an explanatory model. Traditional AI and machine learning methods are insufficient to realize these predictions. There are many advantages to using explainable artificial intelligence (XAI), which enables us to make reasonable decisions based on inferences. In this chapter, the authors examine the precious metal prediction by XAI by presenting a comprehensive literature review on the related studies.

The digital trend for m-commerce has accelerated in recent years. M-commerce, which is referred to mobile commerce, is e-commerce delivered through handheld mobile devices. Mobile devices allow people and businesses to stay in touch around the clock. People are using their smartphones for the purpose of gaming, downloading videos and songs, watching television, doing video conferencing, and conducting other entertainment activities. The longer battery life, faster data processing capabilities, better screen resolution, connectivity, ubiquitous nature of the internet, personalization of customer behaviour and customer location, user-friendly software interfaces, mobile digital payment systems have led to increased acceptance of m-commerce. Mobile commerce faces complicated challenges such as small screen-size, limited memory, network issues, infrastructure, language, security issues of authenticity, confidentiality, and privacy. Digital biometrics will help increase the security of the phones and prevent any kind of data theft or fraud.

Web citation analysis is emerging as an important subject of research in web mining, information retrieval, library science, etc. Scientific publications form a significant part of the research. The quality of the publication is determined by the citation which is to a published or an unpublished source. Citation analysis is used to evaluate the corresponding significance or an impression of an author or publication which is assessed by several times that an author or publication has been cited by other related works. It is useful in ascertaining the impression of a research article. It is useful in learning more about an area of knowledge. The main objective of this chapter is to provide knowledge about web citation analysis. A brief overview of web citation index, citation styles, citation-based metrics, and research challenges are discussed.

Preface

In recent times many organisations of all sizes (e.g. small, medium, and large) are moving towards a digital enterprise. This has led to emerging challenges and to provide solutions, and identify best practices for Digital Enterprise Transformation. The business landscape has changed in the year 2020 and into the future, with the far-reaching global impact of COVID-19 pandemic, the demand and the necessity for digital enterprise transformation have accelerated exponentially. Management and strategies for the adoption and wider usage of newer digital technologies for the transformation of an enterprise through digital tools such as real-time video communications (e.g., zoom, skype, google meet, and many others) through which physical distance has disappeared, which has shown enterprise and people no longer required to be physically present in the same place having face to face interaction rather can be spread far away geographically. Large scale applications of artificial intelligence is being harnessed and increasingly being used widely across different platforms and apps, robotics taking over tedious and difficult jobs from humans through automated machine learning. Cloud computing is easily making on demand computing accessible from anywhere, integrated with block chain technology in which computers are autonomously managing and updating records. Digital payment and banking which has eliminated the need for cash and replaced by digital transactions, and cloud data in which the information can be accessed by the user from anywhere in the world. Inclusion of all these newer technologies have shown the fast pace at which the digital enterprise transformation is rapidly evolving, and new eco-systems are reshaping the digital enterprise model.

Three prominent players are leading the transformation, which are: people (e.g., senior leaders, managers, employees & customers), digital technology (e.g. artificial intelligence, robotics, cloud computing & data, and others), and digital enterprise (e.g. dealing in products & services which are being transformed digitally). The important roles played by these players is also leading to innovation. This book focuses on all the three prominent players. The process for management and strategies for digital enterprise transformation is not straight forward and is rather complicated. This study unravels the underlying process for management & strategies to fully incorporate new digital tools and technologies across all aspects of an enterprise undergoing transformation. The chapters in this book presents interesting research in which the authors have in depth studied digital enterprise transformation at different stages and across different settings, identified key issues, analysed and made sense of vast variety of data, that provides deeper insights and for unravelling the core problems under investigation and developing solutions and recommendations and suggesting future research directions for digital enterprise transformation.

On the road to digital enterprise transformation there are many successes, difficulties, challenges, and failures that an enterprise can learn from. Failures are not an end, rather are turning points for discovering newer innovations that can stem from such setbacks. Humans are constantly driving and at the centre of solving real world problems and driving the digital enterprise transformation and making important contribution through strategic thinking and focusing on core problems facing the enterprise. This also means modernising the management and the strategies around digital workforce as well as customers, and to fully understand their different roles and to make the interaction seamlessly simple, through digital platform interface. Digital business is not clearly understood at different levels of management as it passes through a very complicated process. The key areas of digitalisation and global challenges as shown during COVID-19 pandemic period are new and unique and requires new knowledge that is gained from a deep understanding of complex issues (technical e.g. technology related, & non-technical e.g. people related) that have been examined and reported in this book.

The journey for developing and completing this book is a long one in which all authors have made a valuable contribution to the body of new research knowledge, and adopted new research techniques to study the problems, and found innovative solutions to address those complicated problems. This study will be very useful for many researchers to build on new findings that have been reported in this book. This book will also serve as a valuable tool for many students, practitioners, government, managerial staff and other professionals to learn about new developments in digital enterprise transformation of business systems from a global perspective. International studies have been presented with important new findings from America, Australia, Asia, Europe, Africa & the Middle east, which demonstrates the far-reaching impact for digital enterprise transformation, and suggests that digital businesses are global and are continuously evolving online faster than ever and into new ecosystems in different parts of the world via internet.

ORGANIZATION OF THE BOOK

A brief description of each of the chapters follows:

Chapter 1 explores a new generation distribution channels and customer experience that are used in marketing financial products and services in digital transformation. This study aims to reveal the new generation banking product/service distribution channels that banks offer to their customers through Fintechs and their perspectives on these channels in terms of both customers and banks. Today, the key issue for banks creates a unique customer experience. Accordingly, the study focused on customer experience for new generation banking product/service distribution channels and how to realize unique customer experience. Today, many bank customers are far from new generation distribution channels. However, as technology changes and develops very rapidly, the number of people reaching it is increasing day by day. In this regard, besides the suggestions that will enable the use of new generation banking distribution channels by wider audiences, suggestions were also made to banks in order to provide a unique customer experience for these applications.

Chapter 2 describes techniques of steganography and cryptography in digital transformation. Digital Enterprise Transformation is the amalgamation of digital techniques into the scopes of a business enterprise, fundamentally altering how one can employ and furnish ethics to clients. An organization can be authorized to take Digital Transformation due to several reasons. But the most important reason is that it is the survival issuance for many people. Digital Transformation considers dissimilar in every organization. Generally, it is the amalgamation of digital technology into all quarters of business. That consolidation brings about major alterations in how the business functions and conveys usefulness to its clients. Here, steganography and cryptography are used to facilitate Digital Transformation in any business.

Chapter 3 presents a method for the storage of data organized in digital documents, which is proven in practice. The discussed method does not bear any disadvantages of the relational model used for data organization, such as the loss of data context and complications evoked by the lack of data redundancy. The method presented here can be used for data organization into documents (digital and paper) as classified aggregates and for data classification. The study also describes a new metamodel for the data structure which assumes that documents, being data structures, form compact aggregates, classified as objects or event descriptions, thus always assigning them a specific and unambiguous context. Furthermore, the study presents a design method for documents as context aggregates that allows leveling the disadvantages of the relational model and ensures efficient information management. The work also contains practical examples of the application of the described method.

Chapter 4 examines the digitalization of the education sector that has led to continuous learning that is beneficial for the students as well as teachers despite facing the medical emergency in the country due to the COVID-19 crisis. It was found that the impact of COVID-19 on the transformation of education has both positive and negative outlooks. The negative impact was that all educational organizations/ institutions shut down and examinations got postponed or delayed, but nothing stopped totally. It was also found that due to this pandemic, the educational system has taken a new turn and got evolved in an unimagined way. Teachers and faculty members are positively adapting and managing the digitalization strategy for education and make optimum use of digital media. COVID-19 has provided an opportunity for teachers to upgrade their skills and knowledge by joining multidisciplinary courses available online and it was also found that computer courses taught online were much more effective than theoretical subjects taught via online applications, but lengthy online lectures cause fatigue and boredom.

Chapter 5 demonstrates the role of ICTS, Digital Enterprise Transformation, and Banking Sector in Pakistan. Countries in the developing world, as well as the developed world, are now exploring different ways of facilitating their development process through deployment and exploitation of ICTs within their economies to gain optimum output. More and more facilities are being offered by banks to facilitate their costumers with ease as well as convenience regarding e-banking. While, Digital Enterprise Transformation facilitates financial services organizations via enabling them to be more secure, compliant, as well as being digital. It modifies the experience of employees, partners, customers, and stakeholders. But, in Pakistan, this is not the case. As, people still refrain from using ICTs and e-banking in Pakistan, because of various issues. In spite of the fact that the literature encompassing remittances and criminal offenses is limited. Remittances sent by relatives from overseas are an imperative source of domestic income in the South Asian region. But unfortunately, its influence on crime has mainly been unexplored.

Chapter 6 reports on the manufacturing scheduling strategy for digital enterprise transformation. Scientific research and mathematics are the driving forces of economic progress. Firms that can align themselves with the contemporary information and communication technology era through their decisions about the digital transformation and sustain their competitive advantage might have a higher chance of survival compared to those that cannot. The managerial decisions that revolve around manufacturing focus on production planning and control along with cost minimization. Scheduling and sequencing activities lie at the heart of production planning and control. This chapter provides a basic perspective for the transformation from the traditional batch processing type of short-term manufacturing scheduling to the single-piece flow type of scheduling while presenting a novel manufacturing scheduling model to minimize the manufacturing cost for varying setup times and job sequence.

Chapter 7 addresses the topic of digital management towards society 5.0 with emphasis on a review of the framework for Kurt Lewin theory during COVID-19 pandemic. Society 5.0, is human-centered social understanding, is defined as the period in which the technological opportunities offered by industry 4.0 will serve the welfare of people. However, Society 5.0 faces many factors in terms of resistance to social change. Both the commitment of individuals and organizations to the current social life practice and uncertainty slows down the path to Society 5.0. With The Covid-19 pandemic related digital solutions and applications on a world scale, life practices have radically changed. At this point, the process towards Society 5.0 has accelerated and the first stage of Kurt Lewin's 3-steps change model has started, "unfreeze". Decision-makers and managers need to initiate change, particularly in education and other fields, and contribute to social transformation by "refreezing" new practices and methods that will serve human well-being and Society 5.0. In this context, this process was discussed and recommendations were made in the scope of the study.

Chapter 8 aims to investigate the effect of customer relationship management (CRM) on digital enterprises focusing on their digital shopping process using the Agent-Based Modeling (ABM) in a digital store. In this regard, purposive non-probability sampling method was used to select 300 experts and descriptive and correlation coefficient with SPSS tools were used. The digital shopping process considered in this study include product review, product selection, payment, and receipt, and CRM dimensions include economic profitability, quality of optimal use of information, quality of information display, and customer satisfaction of digital shopping services. The research results based on the conceptual model, statistical analysis and use of ABM in Anylogic environment show that CRM system leads to improved digital enterprise performance and all dimensions of CRM system have a positive effect on digital shopping stages. Finally, the usefulness and accuracy of the results were confirmed based on the positive opinions of experts.

Chapter 9 illustrates on demystifying corporate restructuring strategy through digital transformation, and lessons learned from the banking sector of Zimbabwe. During the past two decades, corporate restructuring in the banking sector has gained much scholarly and public attention in both more developed and less developed countries as a strategic response to a decline in organizational performance. Surprisingly, there is fragmented and scant evidence on corporate restructuring through digital transformation in the banking sector, especially in the Zimbabwean context. With this in mind, this chapter aims at capturing worldwide issues and controversies linked to corporate restructuring through digital transformation, reviewing the success stories of corporate restructuring through digital transformation in the banking sector of Zimbabwe, identifying the challenges associated with digital transformation so that recommendations are proffered to top management and policymakers accordingly, and presenting suggestions for future research.

Chapter 10 provides insights to digital marketing best practices for management in tourist destinations. This work fills a gap that has existed up to now, proposing a series of specific indicators that serve as a manual of good digital marketing practices for the promotion of tourist destinations. According to the proposed model, the variables to take into account are those related to web metrics, SEO positioning and social networks. Likewise, the indicators and metrics proposed in the tourist destination Malaga (Spain) are applied. In this way, the model can serve as a guide for the managing institutions of tourist destinations that wish to measure the results of their efforts. This analysis facilitates the identification of the strengths of the strategy followed, as well as those that need to be improved. It can also be used to verify the positioning of tourist destinations with respect to their competitors.

Chapter 11 identifies emerging issues for connected societies through digital transformation. Converging, digitized, disruptive and globalized world is transforming the way society exists and human beings live. These changes have helped us to collaborate and contribute in exciting and unforeseen ways by creating connected societies world-wide. Technology drives growth across industries and connects people thereby promoting further opportunities & changing the standard of living. IoT has enabled connectivity among people exponentially and advancement in the speed of internet connections have improved accessibility among users to acquire information and services worldwide around the clock. In many parts of the world internet has established itself as the primary medium to connect the societies. Digital transformation has made it essential for enterprises for changing their strategies to make sure that they are connected all the time virtually. This has enabled development of new and innovative approaches in education, health care, public service entertainment, etc. The aim of this chapter is to provide an overview of the concept of connected societies and its importance.

Chapter 12 discusses using Internet of Things (IOT) technology in port management and strategies in the scope of Digital Business Transformation. Many businesses around the world have begun to take advantage of digital technology in recent years. Because, making use of digital technology enables one to do things in less time, need fewer employees, reduce costs, use information and resources effectively, produce the most products with the least resources and consequently increase the profitability of the enterprises. Ports are one of the building blocks of the maritime industry, which aims to increase its profitability by digitizing in today's increasingly competitive conditions. In recent years, IOT technology has been used extensively for digitalization in ports. This chapter introduces the current and potential uses of IOT technology in ports and to give an idea about how IOT technology will create an opportunity to develop the ports and to solve problems in ports.

Chapter 13 focuses on transforming digital enterprises towards web scale with machine learning. Digital enterprise transformation focuses on alignment of processes, products, services, business-models and technologies to perceive business value. Digital business integration in an organization utilizes information technology and its tools to drive and manage the life cycle of digital enterprise transformation. It utilizes the practices and approaches of IT governance with modern application tools and API's. The 2000 millennium brought many technological advancements over internet technologies and these technologies operate numerous applications and business services. The span of digital enterprises is expanding and continues to grow with their evolution on a Web Scale. This chapter is an effort to present understanding about Machine Learning and automation around businesses intelligence and analytics on a web scale. The chapter provides a brief summary of technologies used in digital enterprise transformation for all the domains of an organization.

Chapter 14 characterises digital employer branding through an exploration of the Moroccan customer relation centers. Digital transformation has become a key concern for many enterprises that social media now occupy an important place more than ever in the managerial strategies. The Human Resources (HR) function is considered as one of the organizational dimensions that have taken advantage of these digital platforms, especially for the employer branding purposes. This chapter aims to explore the practices that enterprises in Morocco use to manage their employer brand through social media to attract potential candidates, retain recruits and limit turnover. To achieve this research objective, a multiple case study was carried out with managers from four customer relation centers through semi-structured interviews. The findings highlight the existence of digital ambassadorship and e-reputation oversight practices. Finally, this chapter also provides some managerial recommendations and future research directions.

Chapter 15 investigates on precious metal prediction by using XAI in the perspective of digital transformation. Recent advances in deep learning methodology lead to artificial intelligence (AI) performance to be achieved and even surpasses human levels in an increasing number of complex tasks. There are many impressive examples of this development such as image classification, sensitivity analysis, speech understanding, or strategic gaming. The estimations based on the AI methods do not give any certain information due to the lack of transparency for the visualization, explanation, and interpretation of deep learning models which can be a major disadvantage in many applications. This chapter discusses studies on the prediction of precious metals in the financial field that need an explanatory model. Traditional AI and machine learning methods are insufficient to realize these predictions. There are many advantages to using explainable artificial intelligence (XAI) which enables us to make reasonable decisions based on inferences. In this chapter, the authors examine the precious metal prediction by XAI by presenting a comprehensive literature review on the related studies.

Chapter 16 presents a study about M-Commerce replacing E-Commerce. M-Commerce is E-commerce that is delivered through handheld mobile devices. Mobile devices allow people and businesses to stay in touch around the clock. People are using their smartphones for the purpose of gaming, downloading videos and songs, watching television, doing video conferencing, and conducting other entertainment activities. The longer battery life, faster data processing capabilities, better screen resolution, connectivity, ubiquitous nature of the Internet, personalization of customer behaviour and customer location, user-friendly software interfaces, mobile digital payment systems have led to increased acceptance of M-Commerce. M-Commerce faces challenges like limited screen-size, limited memory, network issues, infrastructure, language, security issues of authenticity, confidentiality, and privacy. Digital biometrics will help increase the security of the phones and prevent any kind of data theft or frauds. Due to the lockdown because of Covid-19, digital usage habits of people have changed. Users have become tech-savvy as it has become a necessity to take online education and business meetings as this is the only option available. With introduction of 5G technologies, the future of mobile commerce is very bright.

Chapter 17 reports on emerging challenges for digital resources transformation. Web citation analysis is emerging as an important subject of research in digital resources such as web mining, information retrieval, library science etc and in which universities and publishing outlets have strong interest. Scientific publications form a significant part of the digital research which is undergoing transformation but there are many challenges. The quality of the publication is determined by the citation which is to a published or an unpublished source. Citation analysis is used to evaluate the corresponding significance or an impression of an author or publication which is assessed by several times that an author or publication has been cited by other related works. Digital resources have become an easy access for search and use on the internet by the researchers. It is useful in ascertaining the impression of a research article. It is useful in learning more about an area of knowledge that is easily available digitally on the internet. The main objective of this chapter is to provide a knowledge about web citation analysis. A brief overview of web citation index, citation styles, citation-based metrics and digital research challenges are discussed.

Kamaljeet Sandhu
University of New England, Australia

Acknowledgment

I would like to acknowledge the help and contribution of all people, more specifically, to the authors and reviewers that took part in the review process. Without their support, this book would not have become a reality. All the authors have made valuable contribution by making many revisions to their chapters, presenting their interesting research to the readers of this book.

Reviewers provided continuous and important feedbacks to the authors for improvements in their chapters, coherence, and content presentation of chapters. I would like to personally thank all the authors and reviewers who have worked very hard to complete this book successfully. At every step we worked together as a highly coordinated and focused team.

In this journey we became very good and close colleagues, and this book has brought us all together from different parts of the world, and we have a valuable working relationship and I look forward to working with this great team again in another interesting book project to come soon. I would like to personally thank the staff at IGI-Global, development editors, who have provided the highest level of service and have been very helpful and supportive in this research at each stage of the book development process, without their persistent help this publication would not have been possible.

I would like to thank my family, including my father and mother who passed away leaving beautiful memories and the importance for higher education and new learning that was ingrained in my very early life and which later was built into my ability to provide this advanced scholarly work to the advancement of new scientific knowledge. This book is a tribute to my dear mum for all her love, support, belief, kindness, and trust, that I have received which transformed me into an author for scholarly research. I would not have achieved this book success without it. I also like to thank Jasper (my king charles spaniel puppy) for all the love, kisses, and support that I have received on writing this book. I also wish to thank Professor Brian Corbitt (RMIT University Melbourne, Australia), my research mentor and colleague, without him I would not have been here today writing this book.

Kamaljeet Sandhu
University of New England, Australia

Chapter 1
New Generation Distribution Channels and Customer Experience Used in Marketing Financial Products and Services in Digital Transformation

Berrin Arzu Eren
https://orcid.org/0000-0003-0839-5302
Ufuk University, Turkey

ABSTRACT

This study aims to reveal the new generation banking product/service distribution channels that banks offer to their customers through fintechs and their perspectives on these channels in terms of both customers and banks. Today, the key issue for banks creates a unique customer experience. Accordingly, the study focused on customer experience for new generation banking product/service distribution channels and how to realize unique customer experience. Today, many bank customers are far from new generation distribution channels. However, as technology changes and develops very rapidly, the number of people reaching it is increasing day by day. In this regard, besides the suggestions that will enable the use of new generation banking distribution channels by wider audiences, suggestions were also made to banks in order to provide a unique customer experience for these applications.

INTRODUCTION

The banking sector is an important sector for the economies of the country due to its contribution to the increase in investments and economic growth (Yüksel, Dinçer & Emir, 2017). The introduction of banking activities with a history of 4,000 years to the service of customers started to be implemented firstly through branches. At this point, the first distribution channel of the banking sector that still continues is bank branches. Although bank branches are decreasing in many countries of the world, especially

DOI: 10.4018/978-1-7998-8587-0.ch001

in financial centers, the main distribution channel role still maintains today. At this point, branches constitute the starting point of the customer experience. Banks provide not only banking transactions through branches, but also sales and after-sales services of many products such as life insurance, personal insurance. In the past 4,000 years, the banking sector has made critical strategic decisions such as transforming historical information into knowledge, taking the best technology, promoting change in customer channel usage, and managing new risks (Seenivasan, 2020).

Along with the technological developments, the business models and workflow processes of banks have also changed, and over time, ATMs, call centers, internet, and mobile banking have been added to product/service delivery and marketing channels. For many years, while the call center was the problem-solving point, ATM was the deposit (money) -withdrawal point, internet and mobile banking were channels where only monetary transactions are made, today these channels transformed into platforms where communication with customers is the forefront and advanced banking transactions are made and the products are sold. Moreover, these distribution channels started to be managed as separate organizational units in banks, and today they evolved to digital channel management.

One of the sectors where the developments in technology reflect most intensely is the banking sector. At this point, the distribution channels through which banks deliver their products and services to their customers have also changed over time. Although the traditional distribution channels mentioned today are in the first place for many customers in a large part of the world, the use of the artificial intelligence and cloud technology applications that have just been begun to be implemented and which will be accepted as future's traditional distribution channels is also becoming widespread (Jewendah, 2018). With the development of artificial intelligence, the banking sector has started to make extensive use of this technology in distribution channels in order to save time and cost. (Kaur, Sahdev, Sharma & Siddiqui, 2020). At this point, blockchain-based bitcoin, crypto money, mobile payment, and smart wallet applications continue to develop as a separate channel structure. Also, chatbots and robo-advisors are on the way to becoming the new generation channels. These applications provide services especially in subjects such as personalized product and service provision, financial consultancy and investment consultancy. Moreover, the intertwining of the world we live in with social media has also attracted the attention of banks, and over time, they have taken advantage of social media as a distribution channel and started product and service delivery and marketing activities. At this point, it is important for banks to work with coordinates with other channels on the platforms mentioned.

Strategies created for the management of business processes contribute to the review of the business processes of owners and employees as well as other stakeholders. Strategies for the management of business processes have also changed over time for banks (Baiyere, Salmela & Tapanainen, 2020). In fact, the level of use of technology is a management strategy for banks. So, technology plays an important role in the transformation and change process of banks. Intensive application of information technologies strategy in banks increases customer value and contributes to positive customer experience (Malar, Arvidsson & Holmstrom, 2019). In this section, as the technology is accepted as an important management strategy by the banks in the digital transformation process, the present situation and future of new distribution channels added to traditional banking distribution channels are tried to be revealed in terms of customer experience. At this point, the research question of the study is with which tools and to what extent banks integrate technology into their distribution channels as a strategy tool.

BACKGROUND OF THE STUDY

The research aims to deliver distribution channels used in the marketing of financial products and services to the reader with their current status and their' s future with rich literature infrastructure. At this point, the focus of the study is the customer experience in the digital transformation journey in the banking sector where technology is used as a management strategy.

Although it is known that today we are in the era of digital transformation and the banks in many countries' economies have also achieved the digital transformation, it is still at the beginning level in many developing countries. At this point, thanks to the information given in this section, it is thought to open a different window to the reader by revealing how technology is adapted to the banking sector as a management and change strategy and how it is used as a customer experience tool in the digital transformation process. For these purposes, the following questions are studied:

- What are the traditional banking product/service delivery and marketing channels?
- What are technology-intensive new generation banking product/service delivery and marketing channels?
- How can banks create a unique customer experience in the technological world?
- What are the problems encountered in customer experience and how can banks overcome this?

By answering these questions in this section, it is aimed to reveal the present and future of customer experience via the new generation distribution channels in the digital transformation process, which is provided to students and academicians who continue their academic education and studies in the field of banking and technology, as well as managers and employees in the banking sector.

RESEARCH METODOLOGY

The basis of the study is based on the theoretical framework. In order to contribute to the financial marketing literature, the new generation banking product/service delivery and marketing channels, as well as traditional distribution channels are included, and customer experience is focused. At this point, a descriptive research methodology was used in the study. Descriptive research ''is more concerned with what it is, rather than how or why it is something and aims to define a phenomenon and its properties'' (Nassaji, 2015, p.129).

ORGANIZATION BACKGROUND

Current Banking Service Distribution Channels

Banking, which dates back to 2000 BC, while it was a structure that managed the relationship between domestic capital and sustainable deposits and loans and financed the needs of individuals/institutions, and today it includes many products and services that contain global capital and face-to-face transactions have turned into a sector. As long as the economy models in the world continue, banks will be able to continue their activities, as well, by solving the financial needs of individuals or businesses through a structure that will keep up with the requirements of the age. The most important share in this structure is based on technological change as well as economic developments. Today, thanks to the fact that people from all segments of society have a certain level of technology, digitalization in the banking sector is gaining momentum. Technological innovations have brought some changes in the business models of banks, and even made compulsory deviations (Berz, Chin & Maguire, 2009).

The first presentation of banking activities in its traditional corporate form was made through bank branches. Over time, different service delivery channels have emerged thanks to technology due to reasons such as saving time, speed, 7*24 transactions, and cost of individuals and businesses. Even the materials used by banks have changed with technology. The material made up of paper in the past has been replaced by cloud technology. At this point, besides providing services from the branch, which is a traditional banking application, service delivery and product marketing activities were initiated through electronic banking applications. Electronic banking actually involves an electronic connection between the bank and the customer for the delivery, execution, management, and control of financial products and services, as well as online banking applications that offer customers the opportunity to make financial transactions on a secure website or platform through a 3rd party or institution (Daniel, 1999). Today, with the inclusion of artificial intelligence applications in the banking sector, ATM, call center, internet, and mobile banking applications, which we consider as new applications in the past, have turned into traditional distribution channels. At this point, the distribution channels of services offered by local or global banks to customers around the world can be listed as follows (Kashmari, Nejad & Nayebyazdi, 2016; Agwu, 2018; Felix, 2018):

- **ATM:** ATMs were first invented by Scottish inventor Shepherd-Barron and opened for use by Barclay's Bank in London on June 27, 1967 (Barclays, 2017). ATMs, which have been operating for half a century nowadays, have been an important service channel that has provided cash flow between individuals and businesses since the years it was invented. It is currently estimated that there are more than 3 million ATMs in the world, 70 thousand of which are in the UK (Reuters, 2017). ATMs provide services 24 hours a day, 7 days a week in many parts of the world, and cash flow transactions such as cash withdrawals/money transfers, as well as transactions such as credit card payment and taking passwords. In order to perform these transactions, a plastic card, or a smart card, in which personal passwords have been defined, has to be taken from bank branches beforehand (Adapa, 2011). ATMs have contributed significantly to the profitability and efficiency of banks by creating significant savings in branch and personnel costs since the day they were developed. For customers, it never loses its popularity thanks to facilities such as time-independent access and the expansion of the ATM network day by day. Moreover, common ATMs served by many banks at the same time are offered to customers.
- **Call Center / Telephone Banking:** Call center/telephone banking is one of the banking service channels that provide 24/7 service like ATM. Thanks to the high number of customer representatives, the call centers enable many transactions of their customers, except withdrawing/depositing money, through a pre-determined password and password transactions via phone. The first call centers were developed by Rockwell (the Rockwell Galaxy) in 1973 and opened for the reservation system of Continental Airlines. Its first application in banking was used by First Direct in England in 1989 (Callcenterhelper, 2018). Today, almost all banks serve their customers through call centers and effectively manage the human resources and marketing activities of the personnel serving through the call center channel.

- **Internet Banking:** After the internet was first used in the USA in 1995, internet banking is one of the most preferred service channels by customers today. Internet banking is a service channel that allows customers to perform almost all transactions, except for withdrawal and deposit, with the security settings set by individuals or institutions through a web browser. Internet banking can be defined as ''internet portal, through which customers can use different kinds of banking services ranging from bill payment to making investments'' (Pikkarainen, Pikkarainen, Karjaluoto & Pahnila, 2004, p. 224). The number of internet banking users is increasing day by day. Although the increase in the number of internet users positively affected the increase in the number of internet banking users, its use is more common in developed countries where security concerns are overcome by technological investments (Eren, 2020).
- **Mobile Banking:** The development of technology all over the world and the availability of technology by many income groups are rapidly increasing the sales of smartphones. The number of smartphone sales sold in the world in 2019 has reached 1.517.83 million from 172.4 million in the last 10 years (Statista, 2020a). The widespread use of smartphone sales and increasingly becoming a part of everyday life led banks to be carried the internet banking application to customers' smartphones, thereby creating a mobile banking application. Mobile banking ''[...] an interaction in which a customer is connected to a bank via a mobile device such as cell phone, smartphone, or personal digital assistant (PDA)" (Laukkanen & Kiviniemi, 2010, p. 373). Researches indicate that mobile banking has prevented the use of internet banking. According to the Deloitte Sights (2019), mobile banking is used more in all banking transactions except that detailed transactions.

New Generation Banking Product/Service Delivery and Marketing Channels in the Digital Transformation Process: Fintech Applications

Most of the economic activities in the world are carried out through banks. While this situation has increased interaction between banks and customers, human-computer interaction, which is an inference of the new world, has also led to a decrease in interpersonal contact. At this point, traditional banking applications have undergone an important evolution in the digital transformation process with Fintech applications. Thanks to innovation, digital transformation provides the development of new products and services that provide managerial and operational convenience (Nambisan, 2017; Baiyere, Salmela & Tapanainen, 2020). So, Fintech applications are one of the innovative products offered by digital transformation. Fintech applications have important contributions to the economies of the country besides individuals/businesses or financial services such as banks. The most important of these is that it decreases the circulation of informal money, especially by reducing the circulation of cash. This situation acts as a natural regulator especially for the economies of developing countries. Fintech is one of the most important agenda items in recent years. One of the most important reasons for this is the opportunities offered by the digital world to customers and banks. Innovation-oriented digital systems used in the delivery and marketing of financial services are implemented in line with the following principles (Travkina & Alexandra, 2019):

- Availability and operating speed of the technological products offered (Internet main service place);
- Scalability and openness of the products (Open-API interfaces)
- Distributable (distributed recording technology);

- Security and privacy of customer information about users (authentication technology, encryption, and cryptography);
- Standardization (validation conditions, data storage, use of cloud repositories for analysis, a large amount of information, and machine learning methods.

One of the sectors most affected by technological developments is the financial sector. Fintech was created by combining finance and technology to offer financial products and services or to carry out marketing activities easier and faster. The ways to improve customer relations in an increasingly competitive environment each day go through Fintech practices (Hernández-Nieves, Hernández, Gil-González, Rodríguez-González & Corchado, 2020). In fact, the use of technology in financial services is not a new application, it refers to the paradigm shift (Lukango, 2018). The number of Fintech companies is increasing day by day in developing and developed countries. Increasing and adopting Fintech practices mediate new opportunities by reshaping the financial sector in the world and developing customer-centered strategies. When Fintechs are analyzed around the world, it is seen that there are many Fintechs that provide services especially in payment systems, lending, personal financing, retail investments, corporate investments, crowdfunding, asset management, and money transfer. At this point, the main areas of interest of Fintech are:

- Reaching people who do not have an account in a bank yet
- Focusing on developing new products and services with personalized solutions
- In this way, to offer innovative products and services
- Lowering product and service costs
- Focusing on unique customer experience
- Making alternative product and service collaborations within the entire financial system.

At this point, the innovations offered by Fintech can be listed as follows:

- Blockchain
  - Bitcoin & Cryptocurrency & Smart Wallet
  - Mobile (digital) payment & Contactless Payment
- Artificial Intelligence Applications
  - Chatbot
  - Robo-advisor
- Open Banking
- Social Media Banking

Blockchain

Blockchain is a data structure representing account book entry or an account transaction record, it is digitally signed to prevent the authenticity of each account transaction and prevent interference by others (Sönmez, 2016). Blockchain can be defined as follows ''A blockchain is a magic computer that anyone can upload programs to and leave the programs to self-execute, where the current and all previous states of every program are always publicly visible, and which carries very strong cryptoeconomically secured guarantee that programs running on the chain will continue to execute in exactly the way that the blockchain protocol specifies.'' (Buterin, 2015). In fact, the blockchain system works on the principle of simultaneously approving the money flow from many sources as well as being fast and secure. At this point, blockchain is ''a network software protocol that enables the secure transfer of money, assets, and information via the Internet, without the need for a third-party intermediary such as a bank.'' (Swan, 2017, p.7). Blockchain is primarily a system on which many products such as Bitcoin and other crypto currencies are based. The main areas in which blockchain applications are used for financial institutions are currencies, stocks, bonds, and derivative products (Ledra Capital, 2014). The facilities provided by blockchain technology are as follows (Sönmez, 2016):

- It reduces costs and speeds up transactions without the need for authority and intermediary.
- Transactions are controlled by many different points, reducing the possibility of fraud in the system
- Blockchain is an ideal platform to track where an asset exits from which source, to which people pass and where

The advantages provided by blockchain application can be summarized as follows:

- Cryptocurrencies, bitcoin transfers, produced with blockchain technology, can be easily realized from one country to another, without having accounts in two countries, without conversion between currencies and with lower commissions.
- The purchase of abstract services (mobile application usage, movie watching, online education, software, softcopy books) will be easier and safer.
- Thanks to mobile wallet applications on smartphones, the need to move physical money elsewhere in the world is eliminated. With mobile wallet, transactions can be made from many stores as well as city food and beverage and hotel expenses. Also, cryptocurrencies can be cashed and cash can be withdrawn from ATMs via mobile application.
- Thanks to the blockchain, it is possible to make smart contracts for the purchase of securities or real estate by giving cash. Smart contracts are the applications that can act automatically when the conditions arise, take the money from one side and transfer the value of shares, deeds etc. to the other side.

Thanks to these conveniences created, banking products and services that entered our lives with blockchain technology can be listed as follows:

- **Crypto Money & Bitcoin:** Cryptocurrencies are virtual currencies just like credit cards or ATM cards. It is produced by a user-based, distributed data system. Bitcoin does not have a physical form. ''Bitcoin is a cryptocurrency based on protocols that work as a special irreversible payment mechanism in open source software and peer-to-peer networks, and is an internet-based payment protocol that works like a virtual currency.'' (Simser, 2015, p.157). It is limited to 21 million as per Bitcoin rules, and its price varies depending on demand due to the production of about 16 million (Barone & Masciandaro, 2019). While Bitcoin can be bought at prices lower than $ 0.1 when it starts to be sold on the first exchanges, it is traded at $ 11.600 as of August 2020 (Currency Rate Investor, 2020). Cryptocurrencies are still not considered legal or limited in many countries today.
- **Smart Wallet:** One of the important advantages that Fintech provides to customers is the smart wallet application. Smart Wallet is a software-based system that allows customers to make their

online purchases through computers, smartphones, or tablets, and where users' bank accounts or credit cards are integrated into the system (Marimuthu & Roseline, 2020). With this application, customers can turn their smartphones into a digital wallet and spend and use the money they have. Thanks to smart wallets, customers can collect their credit cards in the application on their mobile devices and shop. In fact, the system has further developed and it has become a technology that can be used for money transfer, tax, and telephone payments besides shopping. The most known and useful digital wallets today are PayPal and Google Wallet.

- **Mobile (Digital) Payment:** Mobile payment is the platform where cardholders can make secure digital payments with one click and one-touch via an online device, thanks to the agreement of businesses that sell with card organizations and the use of specified security technologies (Mastercard, 2020). Today, many businesses are among the mobile payment partners. It is highly applicable especially by telephone operators. In this way, spending can be made on digital exchanges to be made in the business itself or other contracted workplaces by uploading electronic money to the mobile phone number through operators. After the expenditures made, the system operates by deducting the amount of the expenditure from the first loaded amount. Also, if necessary, reloading and balance control can be performed. Similar applications can be made in many parts of the world by food and beverage businesses such as Starbucks and businesses that offer entertainment activities such as cinema, sport. Similarly, digital shopping is possible by getting digital code from the mobile application of banks and by getting code from Netflix, GooglePlay, App Store, and iTunes.
- **Internet of Things - Contactless Payment:** Thanks to the internet of things, billions of devices are connected to each other in the world today, so they can access the customers' accounts and access the accounts with smart devices by sharing the information in the cloud (Suseendran, Chandrasekaran, Akila & Kumar, 2020). Contactless payment, on the other hand, is the ease of payment offered to customers via the Internet of Things. Near field communication (NFC) is a system that enables mobile devices such as smartphones to communicate without touching each other, NFC devices have become available in contactless payment systems (Bhuvaneswari & Porkodi, 2014). In this way, it is ensured that the credit card is recognized by the pos and shopping is made by reading it only without entering the password.

AI Applications

In the changing world conditions, financial institutions within the service sector have adopted digitalization and they have assumed a leading role in many other service businesses. At this point, one of the most important reflections of technology in the banking sector is the presentation of new distribution/service channels to the user (Chedrawi, Harb & Saleh, 2019). In the 170 years since the first EFT transaction was carried out, banking transactions have been able to do with smartphones almost without face-to-face interaction, and the concept of money has become almost completely digital. In this context, there are two important reasons why digitalization has improved in the financial sector. The first one is that financial products and services are completely based on information, while the other reason is that many transactions do not require physical interaction (Wamba, Kamdjoug, Bawack & Keogh, 2020).

Since the basic demands of the bank customers are being able to perform their transactions in fast, easy, and flexible time frames, banks have started to benefit more from AI. In addition to the opportunities it offers, AI is also on the agenda with some concerns. AI use in the banking sector; in addition to the advantages it provides to its customers, such as flexibility in transaction fees, ease of use, offering personalized products and services, it also causes concerns about system bias, privacy, and security (Lui & Lamb, 2018, p.269). However, another important use of AI for banks is its ability to eliminate security risks. AI is an important tool especially in detecting fraud risks. In addition, voice, retina, and facial recognition features are also provided through AIs. At this point, the application of AI to bank products, services, and business models is as shown in Table 1 (Financial Stability Board, 2017).

Table 1. AI implementation in banking

Customer-focused	Credit scoring Insurance policies Client-facing chatbots Know your customer
Operations-focused	Capital optimisation Model risk management Stress testing Fraud detection
Trading and portfolio management	Trade execution Portfolio management
Regulatory compliance	Regulatory technology Macroprudential surveillance Data quality assurance Supervisory technology

Source: (Financial Stability Board, 2017)

AIs have become an indispensable element of banks and financial institutions in providing personalized products and services in marketing activities as well as data security. Today, customers receive services from AI, ranging from retina scanning and ATM transactions to chatbot customer representatives. In addition to the benefits that AI applications provide to banks and financial institutions in terms of cost, efficiency, it also includes advantages such as quick access to information to customers, quality responses, fun service delivery, and many transactions at zero cost. The most common AI applications that banks use today are chatbots and robo-advisors.

- **Chatbot:** The basis of managing the information and technology-oriented competition in the banking sector is based on the development of personalized products for the customers. In order to comply with this, banks' AI applications are designed to offer customers appropriate suggestions and preferences related to their past preferences (Hernández-Nieves, Hernández, Gil-González, Rodríguez-González & Corchado, 2020). The purpose of this is to match the preferences and trends of the customers and thus increase the efficiency and profitability of both individuals and the bank. One of the most important AI applications introduced at this point is chatbots.

"Chatbots are computer programs that simulate human conversations through voice commands or text chats and serve as virtual assistants to users" (Luo, Tong, Fang & Qu, 2019, p.937). Today, chatbots are extensively used by Santanderbank, HSBC, Bank of America (Erica), Capital One (Eno), BBVA, Unicredito, Société Générale, Swedbank, Swedish Bank (Aida), Bank Cler (Carl). The size of the chatbot market is forecast to reach around 1.25 billion U.S. dollars in 2025, a great increase from the market size in 2016, which stood at 190.8 million U.S. dollars (Statista, 2020b). One of the most important reasons for this is that especially customers under middle age prefer to use written or audio, technology interactive communication in other platforms they use in their daily lives as well as in their social lives. Since non-interactive communication eliminates emotional state, the success rate is high in standard service as well. However, there may be a concern for chatbots about product advice and security (Dietvorst, Simmons & Massey, 2018).

- **Robo-advisor:** Financial advice from humans within the traditional banking approach was thought to lead to corporate and customer conflicts of interest (Chalmers & Reuter, 2015; Linnainmaa, Melzer & Previtero, 2018). At this point, banks have started to use AI in this field in order to continue to provide financial consultancy services without shaking customers' feelings of trust. ''Robo-advisors require clients' information on their financial situation and their investment objectives and subsequently create an investment portfolio suitable to the clients' (risk)profile often using inexpensive exchange-traded funds (ETFs)'' (Brenner & Meyll, 2020, p.1). Robo-advisors today offer financial advice online with moderate or minimal human intervention.

In the changing world conditions, individuals' personal product suggestions and recommendation expectations are increasing day by day. At this point, customers are particularly interested in using digital tools in their complex decisions regarding retirement planning, retirement investments, and other investment tools (Lourenço, Dellaert & Donkers, 2020). This causes banks to review and further increase their investment in robo-advisors. The amount of investment made to robo-advisors in 2018 in the world is approximately $ 402.926 mn and this figure is expected to be $ 1.437.299 mn by 2022 with an increase of 37.5% each year (Bunmark, 2018, p. 11).

Open Banking (API)

Open Banking is the development of new financial services by allowing banks to share their data on permission through the interfaces of application programs through third institutions (Yazıcı, 2019). ''Open banking is the democratization of access to data previously exclusively owned by legacy financial institutions.'' (Kocianski, 2017). While this practice was applied as an option in the past, it has been applied in many countries today. There are many opportunities that open banking can create thanks to the enormous data it possesses. Thanks to the development of new business models through Open Banking, it is predicted that customers will be able to access many new and useful financial products more easily thanks to increased competition and transparent prices (Yazıcı, 2019). These applications are also an important opportunity for customers to purchase financial services more cost-effectively and quickly. It is also expected that open banking can offer personalized products to individuals through the data provided by banks from Fintech institutions (Kocianski, 2017). It is anticipated that banks will have significant profit potential for themselves, as well as developing sustainable business models for short markets, as well as providing customers with enhanced customer experience thanks to Open Banking practices (Brodsky & Oakes, 2017). Open Banking also makes it easier to reach new customers for banks. At this point, it can be concluded that open banking represents the future of the banking sector. Because open banking is an opportunity and it indicates that big fish can cooperate with agile small fish rather than swallowing small fish (Cerit, 2019). At this point, the opportunities created by Open Banking can be summarized as follows (Cerit, 2019):

- Giving information about the campaigns that will attract their attention by analyzing the consumption expenditures of the customers through the data obtained.
- Servicing investment suggestions and consultancy service for customers who want to save money by analyzing consumption expenditures
- Providing loan solutions suitable for the budget and need through the analysis of income and expense based on their expenditures.
- Providing life insurance advice and counseling to eliminate the insecurity of a borrowed life
- Providing simulation applications for possible situations in both investment and borrowing instruments
- Providing reminders and planners for regular payments etc.

However, Open Banking is likely to contain a number of threats as well as opportunities. The results of the research conducted in 2018 stated that the most important risk that can be experienced in the field of Open Banking is the misuse of the data obtained and the consequence of the problem of customer confidence (67%), while other concerns are the destruction that will occur as a result of data loss of the Fintech initiatives (52%) and there are fraud attempts (50%) that can be caused by possible cyber-attacks (Ernst & Young, 2019).

Open Banking can be implemented in various structures in banks. API models are classified by McKinsey as follows (Brodsky & Oakes, 2017):

- **Internal API Framework:** Within this structure, the bank only serves its own units. These API solutions have been developed in order to improve the bank's own processes, make them operable, and provide efficiency.
- **Business Partnership API Framework:** In this context, it is possible to prepare a common security system and action plan for the bank's business partners and other partners in order to create a holistic structure in the business processes of the activities carried out. In this way, a significant decrease in cost can be created.
- **Open API Framework:** This structure was created with the aim of creating new applications and business models by going beyond the bank's own borders. Therefore, the efforts of third-party enterprises that are not directly connected with the bank are supported in this way.

When evaluated within the framework of these applications, it is seen that open banking has four main components. These elements are ''regulatory environment, adoption potential, consumer sentiment, and innovation environment'' (Ernst & Young, 2018):

- **Regulatory environment:** This element checks the reliability of stakeholders to check the readiness for the implementation of open banking and to ensure that the implementation is adopted.
- **Adoption potential:** It includes examining users' technology vulnerabilities, digital banking, mobile banking products, and social media usage in order to reveal the potential of users to adopt the Open Banking application.
- **Consumer sentiment:** It includes users' thoughts and attitudes towards Open Banking applications and sharing personal data with other organizations. At this point, this information is tried to be obtained through consumer surveys and social forums.

- **Innovation environment:** FinTech VC investments are followed along with Global Innovation Index scores for countries' perspectives on innovation and their progress in this regard. In this way, the innovation dominance of stakeholders providing financial services is examined.

Open Banking is practiced in many developed and developing countries today, but compliance levels vary. Research covering England, China, Singapore, the USA, Australia, Hong Kong, the Netherlands, Canada, Germany and Spain ranked the countries' level of compliance with Open Banking between 1-10 scales. Accordingly, Canada (10), USA (9) and China (8) are the top three successful countries in ''regulatory environment'', Canada (10), Germany (9) and Australia (8) in ''adoption potential'', Netherlands (10), Germany (9) and Canada (8) in ''consumer sentiment'' and Germany (10), Spain (9) and Netherlands (8) are the top 3 successful in ''innovation environment''. At this point, it is seen that the countries take place in different scales in 4 categories according to their strong characteristics. Considering all the criteria in the table, it is seen that although the first Open Bank applications started in England, it lags behind other countries and Canada has a high level of compliance with Open Banking among other countries.

Today, the Open Banking application is used actively by financial institutions such as HSBC, BUD, BNP Paribas, Lloyds Banking Group, Spiir.

Social Media Banking

Social media can be defined as "a group of Internet-based applications that build on the ideological and technological foundations of Web 2.0, and that allow the creation and exchange of User Generated Content" (Kaplan & Haenlein, 2010, p.60). Social media is one of the most wasting time platforms of today. According to researches, daily social media usage of internet users, which was 90 minutes in 2012, increased to 136 minutes in 2018 (Clement, 2018). Assuming that active life outside of sleep will be 16 hours, this indicates that we spend approximately 15% of today on social media. This situation created an opportunity for many businesses and businesses started to carry out their sales and marketing activities from this channel. Today, social media has become a medium where current marketing activities are carried out effectively and up-to-date and customer interaction and connections are facilitated (Yasin, Liébana-Cabanillas, Porcu & Kayed, 2020). Many researchers also think that social media is the platform for self-expression of both consumers and businesses (Chen & Beaudoin, 2016). At this point, social media is also considered an opportunity for businesses that provide financial services. Social media is also an important tool for communicating with the young population, especially under the assumption that the young population will form the portfolio of future bank customers. The effectiveness and functions of banks on social media are important in reaching customers in these environments, which have become a wide marketplace.

Social media banking is the use of social media platforms for banks to market their products/services, understand customer complaints, and produce solutions, develop new products and services, receive product feedback and business partnerships. Researches indicate that banks accept social media as a necessary and important opportunity for their activities (MacKnight, 2017). While the quality of service in banking was evaluated with more physical factors in the past, the evaluation shifted to digital service quality thanks to the new technologies used. At this point, the researches point out that effective and widespread use of social media banking attracts new customers as well as ensuring customer loyalty and thus increasing the value of business assets (Ray, 2013). According to Accenture's research on the use of social media channels of financial institutions in the US, the positive results created by social media channels can be listed as follows (Accentur, 2013, p.3-8):

- ''60% have daily contact with clients through social media
- 77% affirm that social media helps with client retention
- 74% agree that social media helps them increase assets under management
- 73% say it has led to an overall increase in client interactions
- 40% indicate they have gotten new clients through Facebook
- 25% have developed new clients through LinkedIn
- 21% have earned new clients through Twitter''

At this point, the main opportunity that social media banking actually offers to banks is to perform customer analysis. By making the customer analysis correct, the existing information will be made available in the production of new information and a way can be achieved in accessing the unique experience targeted in the customer experience. In this way, it will be possible to get to know the customers more closely and to offer segment-specific service and customized products/services. In addition, social media is considered an important tool for banks to reach new customers.

CUSTOMER EXPERIENCE WITH NEW GENERATION BANKING DISTRIBUTION CHANNELS IN DIGITAL TRANSFORMATION

Customer experience has replaced the concept of customer loyalty with the contribution of technology in the digital transformation age. Customer experience is one of the most sensitive issues in the banking and finance world as in other service sectors. Econsultancy & Adobe (2017) 's researches point out that 63% of financial service providers' first priority is customer experience (Econsultancy & Adobe, 2017).

Today, banks provide customer experience through many platforms. In particular, new technology-based alternative distribution channels have become customer experience centers, where almost all transactions can be performed and provide a great advantage in terms of competition. As a result of this, the banks gain superiority in the competition thanks to their positive customer experience and turn to customer experience investments in order to focus on sustainable success. The ever-increasing investments in customer experience in the banking and finance sector clearly show how important the issue is. At this point, the way to create a unique customer experience for banks is to manage customer relations processes with a strong business partner with its technological infrastructure. When we look at it from the perspective of customers, it is seen that the customers use their choices in favor of the banks where they have the best experience. At this point, there are some indispensable elements at the heart of the customer experience. These can be listed as 6 C (Nicoletti, 2014):

- **Culture:** Customers are at the core of financial services, as in other service sectors. At this point, institutions have to develop customer-oriented strategies and act accordingly. This requires protecting the interests of shareholders and increasing their earnings. The common point of all stakeholders is speed. In the financial service industry, products, product-related returns, and dynamics can change very quickly. In this context, what is expected of the banks is that they can adapt to this change very quickly and can change flexibly.

- **Customers:** Financial institutions that are customers in the focus of activity have to manage and predict complex and changing customer demands at any time. Customer demands vary over time and from individual to individual.
- **Competition:** Competition in financial services shows itself not only among local businesses but also globally. With each passing day, the struggle of global competitors for financial products and services is intensified.
- **Computers:** Financial products and services are offered to users through intercontinental developments thanks to computer and information technology. Today, it is not possible to talk about financial products and services without computers, internet, and even AI applications.
- **Compliance:** As the technology intensity of financial services increases, the risks they carry an increase in parallel. The lack of face-to-face interactions question the security of products and services, and this situation is tried to be eliminated through both local and global legal regulations and legislation.
- **Cost:** For companies providing financial services, the equity ratio is the most important requirement for a sustainable business. According to Basel criteria, the minimum requirement is 12%, which is an important cost for financial institutions. Especially during the contraction periods, with the decrease in credit penetration, equity ratios increase and this affects profitability negatively.

Today, bank customers have entered into new expectations such as receiving credit/investment advice for their personal characteristics and preferences, as well as having a personalized experience as well as their expectations for 7*24 banking transactions. Because today's consumers perform four functions according to Service Encounter 2.0: an enabler, innovator, coordinator, and differentiator and these roles are not mutually exclusive and can occur at the same time (Larivière, Bowen, Andreassen, Kunz, Sirianni & Vossf, 2017). At this point, banks should have the ability to provide highly personalized and on-demand data and support for each customer by presenting their product/service contents through the right time and a suitable distribution channel in order to provide enhanced customer experience and gain a competitive advantage in customer service (Daqar & Smoudy, 2019). This forces banks to develop in the field of Fintech. Modern consumers are looking for hedonic benefits as well as a functional utility while consuming products or services. At this point, technological innovations are critical for businesses to provide real and different customer experiences to their customers (Trivedi, 2019). The expectations of customers surrounded by the Internet and smartphones from banks and financial institutions have adapted to this and focused on technological solutions. Thanks to these new applications, the aims to be achieved in the customer experience can be listed as follows:

- **Delivering a Personalized Experience:** Banks can collect extensive information from different sources for their customers through Fintechs, and they can get to know their customers more closely. So that they can provide new information to their customers in both product/service analysis and investment analysis.
- **Being practical:** One of the most valuable assets of today's customer is time and the convenience of technology in managing time also awaits from banks. At this point, Fintechs are solution partners in terms of creating time, managing time, and convenience.
- **Cost:** Branching is the highest fixed cost of banks. Although the most important advantage that Fintech will provide is the initially rising technology costs, it will contribute to the profitability of the banks as it will minimize the cost of branches and physical structures over time.

- **Wide range of products and services:** Thanks to Fintech applications, especially the development and increasing number of personalized and solution-oriented products and services will increase, and the research and development costs will be reduced thanks to the acceleration to be caught.

There are a number of determinants, especially confidence in the system, for banks to achieve these goals and thus create a unique customer experience. These elements can be listed as follows:

- **Trust in new practices:** In the past, the banking sector was a structure based on competition. However, the banking sector, which is based on trust with the effect of technological developments, has become a sector that requires more trust due to many factors such as differentiation of transaction diversity, digitalization of money and almost zeroing of face-to-face interaction. This situation reveals the need for trust rather than competition among financial service providers. In addition, it is very important to establish trust in the business partner that provides the application.
- **Access Security:** With the increase in the technology density of banking, it makes trust the most important factor among the stakeholders who are parties to the banking transaction of customers. At this point, it is a global perspective and action for the sector to constantly take security beyond them for the risk factors that try to take a step forward every day. In reality, security is an advantage. When customers enter the chat environment through the application or online branch they enter through multi-factor security stages of the bank or financial institution, they actually step into an extra secure virtual environment. At this point, the technology actually enables customers to do their transactions safely.
- **Data sharing security:** Most of the customer concerns regarding modern banking transactions are related to personal data sharing. While data sharing involves some risks in itself, banks are one of the protecting parties for the personal data security of their customers in new applications. In many countries, including developing countries, data security is protected by legal regulations in the financial service process. Although data sharing may seem intimidating for customers at the beginning, it will be positive for banks to be reflected on the customer as a result of developing customer-oriented strategies thanks to their professional processing and sharing under supervision. Although the researches have negative thoughts about sharing the personal data of the customers, they point out that their thoughts may differ when they are informed about the opportunities they will get when they share (Skinners, 2018).
- **Regulations:** The new generation banking distribution channels will be made possible by the customer's usage habit by establishing regulations and laws both by local governments and globally. Because there are many stakeholders in these application systems.
- **Human-Computer balance:** Today, banks and financial institutions are aware of customer needs and requests and plan their customer-oriented strategies in relation to technology. In fact, when we look at the difficulties mentioned above, we see that the common point is due to the fact that the service is not provided by the individual. At this point, the secret of the unique customer experience for banks and financial institutions is a combination of human/labor touch and technology. With each passing day, the scope of financial services is expanding and it is covering many instruments. At this point, key points in the customer experience are also changing.

Providing the privilege of unique customer experience will also create a unique opportunities and advantages for banks. Market share, protection of loyal customers, gaining new customers, and thus the reflection of profitability are the keys to the sustainable success of banks. This key can only be achieved through unique customer experience.

SOLUTIONS AND RECOMMENDATIONS

The banking sector is one of the leading sectors in many countries of the world with its intensive use of technology and visionary perspective. The integration of the new technologies mentioned in the department into the banking demand also requires an additional visionary perspective of both the banking system and bank management in the countries. At this point, the fact that banks are aware of the potential of these systems and take action will increase the speed of catching opportunities. When we look at the upcoming period, the diversity and developments in the channel structure make it even more important to capture and follow the holistic image of the customer. Today, bank products and services are offered and sales activities are managed through many distribution channels. Success in all distribution channels is important in terms of reflecting the bank's corporate image and reputation, managing customer relations with sustainable success, reaching new customers, and perfect customer experience. At this point, the recommendations for banks can be listed as follows:

- Banks are also required to adapt quickly to the rapidly developing and transforming Fintech world and to evaluate the opportunities that arise there, and to prepare action plans for this, in the short term. For this, they should approach all business processes with a strategic management perspective and actively participate in the digital transformation process.
- Banks' identification of the channels that customers communicate with and digitization of key points will contribute to improving the customer experience.
- Regulations should be based on the feasibility of business models, not competition for the stakeholders of the system, in order for the system of new generation banking applications to be healthy and sustainable.
- In order to create customer confidence in new applications and systems, regulatory agencies should follow not only the development process in their own countries but also the global development processes and accelerate the compliance process.
- In order to optimize the customer experience, financial institutions must first determine the common behavioral business processes that center the customers. This can be achieved not only by enhancing the professional competencies of the customer representatives who are in contact with the customer, but also by improving their communication skills and making them part of the business routine. Since our age is the age of technology, digital vehicle support should be provided to speed up the work processes of the personnel and strengthen their mobilization.
- It is always important to pay attention to customer feedback, whether the channel served is face-to-face or digital. Banks and financial institutions need to consider the feedback from their customers, identify areas of development, identify the right business processes, and use the feedbacks as strategies to create new applications.
- Today, considering the social media usage habits and usage times of individuals, it is important to position the social media channel as an important service delivery center. A customer who starts

communication via social media should be able to continue communication via phone, chat, or e-mail, and the process considering the previous call. This situation should not be overlooked for positive customer experience. In this way, banks will be able to serve wherever the customer is. Because one of the important needs of bank customers is to ensure uninterrupted communication with the bank.

- In our age, individuals prefer to use messaging platforms as communication channels rather than interaction by speaking in communication. At this point, the development of AI applications, especially for individuals who will become active bank customers of the future, will have a positive impact on banks' preference and market shares as well as their positive customer experience.

FUTURE RESEARCH DIRECTIONS

In this study, new distribution channels developed by Fintechs and used in the presentation and marketing of financial products and services and the contribution of these new applications to the customer experience are examined. Although the new generation distribution channels mentioned in the study are actively used in developed economies, they have started to attract attention in developing countries, too. The decrease in human interaction in banking services day by day is an important indicator of this. In future studies, conducting research using qualitative or quantitative methods in different countries will contribute to the literature in order to reveal the customer experience of new generation distribution channels and to contribute to the adoption of these practices by the wider audience.

CONCLUSION

Today, there are millions of individuals who still do not have a bank account. While only 69% of the world's population has a bank account, this rate is 94% in developed countries and 63% in developing countries, mostly men (World Bank Group, 2017). Therefore, the new practices mentioned in the study are far from individuals in the category of many underdeveloped and developing countries. However, the new generation banking product/service channels include applications that will become models for these countries over time, even if they are not realized within the first 10 years.

The key issue in banking is to reach new customers. Access to new data can be achieved by placing Fintech applications on bank marketing strategies correctly and developing customer relations. Fintechs are still in the process of maturation in many parts of the world, especially in developing countries. However, even though they do not have a 100% voice in the market in today's conditions, it is an undeniable fact that customers make their lives easier and add value. At this point, every contact with customers through blockchain products, AI applications, open banking, or social media applications provides valuable information about customer satisfaction, customer loyalty, communication quality, problem-solving, complaint resolution, efficiency, and business performance. Because banks have adopted these practices as a strategy in the digital transformation process. Today, thanks to interaction analytics, businesses can also derive different data from the data they provide through each interaction and customer contact. In this way, it has become possible to process data, use it as a marketing tool, have information about customer segments, and use this data to structure business models. Banks and financial institutions can use this data as the key to satisfying and loyal customers, who have unique customer experience, as well as a tool for employee satisfaction, loyalty, and motivation.

It is an undoubted fact that the decision mechanism will function correctly in the creation and processing of the target customer segment in blockchain, AI, open banking, or social media banking applications. In addition to this, thanks to the recognition and prevention of fraudulent actions, the customers' confidence in the bank will be prevented, as well as the loss of resources and income of banks. Including technology more in workflow processes not only reduces costs to banks but also facilitates/speeds up compliance with local or global regulations. At this point, directing the customers who receive service from the branch or the customers calling the call center to other distribution channels helps to manage the costs by using the number of customer representatives that provide service more efficiently. In addition to the increase in efficiency, these applications also make it easier to keep up with regulations.

REFERENCES

Accenture. (2013). *Closing the Gap HowTech-Savvy Advisors Can Regain Investor Trust*. Retrieved from https://www.accenture.com/t20150707t195225__w__/us-en/_acnmedia/accenture/conversion-assets/dotcom/documents/global/pdf/industries_5/accenture-cm-awams-pov-gen-d-advisor-summary-final-mar2013-web.pdf

Adapa, S. (2011). Global E-banking Trends. In M. A. Sarlak & A. A. Hastiani (Eds.), *E-Banking and Emerging Multidisciplinary Process: Social, Economical and Organizational Models* (pp. 1–16). IGI Global. doi:10.4018/978-1-61520-635-3.ch001

Agwu, E. (2018). The role of e-banking on operational efficiency of banks in Nigeria. *Basic Res J Bus Manag Acc*, *6*(1), 1–10. doi:10.2139srn.3122498

Baiyere, A., Salmela, H., & Tapanainen, T. (2020). Digital transformation and the new logics of business process management. *European Journal of Information Systems*, *29*(3), 238–259. doi:10.1080/0960085X.2020.1718007

Barclays. (2017). *From the archives: the ATM is 50*. Retrieved from https://home.barclays/news/2017/06/from-the-archives-the-atm-is-50/

Barone, R., & Masciandaro, D. (2019). Cryptocurrency or usury? Crime and alternative money laundering techniques. *European Journal of Law and Economics*, *47*(2), 233–254. doi:10.100710657-019-09609-6

Berz, K., Chin, V., & Maguire, A. (2019). *Come Out a Winner in Retail Banking*. The Boston Consulting Group BCG.

Bhuvaneswari, V., & Porkodi, R. (2014). *The internet of things (IoT) applications and communication enabling*. Paper presented at the meeting of the 2014 International Conference on Intelligent Computing Applications, Coimbatore, India.

Brenner, L., & Meyll, T. (2020). Robo-advisors: A substitute for human financial advice? *Journal of Behavioral and Experimental Finance*, *25*, 1–8. doi:10.1016/j.jbef.2020.100275

Brodsky, L., & Oakes, L. (2017). *Data sharing and open banking*. Retrieved from https://www.mckinsey.com/~/media/McKinsey/Industries/Financial%20Services/Our%20Insights/Data%20sharing%20and%20open%20banking/Data-sharing-and-open-banking.ashx

Bunmark. (2018). *Fintech Insights*. Retrieved from https://www.burnmark.com/uploads/offerings/Burnmark_Monthly_Fintech_Insights1.pdf

Buterin, V. (2015). *The Value of Blockchain Technology*. Retrieved from https://ethereum.github.io/blog/2015/04/13/visions-part-1-the-value-of-blockchain-technology/

Callcenterhelper. (2018). *The History of the Call Centre*. Retrieved from https://www.callcentrehelper.com/the-history-of-the-call-centre-15085.htm

Cerit, M. (2019). Dünyada ve Türkiye' de açık bankacılık: Bankacılığın geleceği. *Fintech Istanbul,* 11-40. https://bkm.com.tr/wp-content/uploads/2015/06/Dunyadaveturkiyedeacikbankacilik.pdf

Chalmers, J., & Reuter, J. (2015). Is Conflicted Advice Better Than No Advice? *NBER Working Paper Series*, 18158.

Chedrawi, C., Harb, B., & Saleh, M. (2019). The E-Banking and the Adoption of Innovations from the Perspective of the Transactions Cost Theory: Case of the Largest Commercial Banks in Lebanon. In Y. Baghdadi & A. Harfouche (Eds.), *ICT for a Better Life and a Better World The Impact of Information and Communication Technologies on Organizations and Society* (Vol. 30). Springer. doi:10.1007/978-3-030-10737-6_10

Chen, H., & Beaudoin, C. E. (2016). An empirical study of a social network site: Exploring the effects of social capital and information disclosure. *Telematics and Informatics*, *33*(2), 432–435. doi:10.1016/j.tele.2015.09.001

Clement, J. (2018). *Daily social media usage worldwide 2012-2018*. Retrieved from https://www.statista.com/statistics/433871/daily-social-media-usage-worldwide/

Currency Rate Investor. (2020). Retrieved from https://btc.currencyrate.today/usd

Daniel, E. (1999). Provision of electronic banking in the UK and the republic of Ireland. *International Journal of Bank Marketing*, *17*(2), 72–82. doi:10.1108/02652329910258934

Daqar, M., & Smoudy, A. (2019). The role of artificial intelligence on enhancing customer experience. *International Review of Management and Marketing*, *9*(4), 22–31. doi:10.32479/irmm.8166

Deloitte Sights. (2019). *The value of online banking channels in a mobile-centric world*. Retrieved from https://www2.deloitte.com/us/en/insights/industry/financial-services/online-banking-usage-in-mobile-centric-world.html

Dietvorst, B. J., Simmons, J. P., & Massey, C. (2018). Overcoming algorithm a version: People will use imperfect algorithms if they can (even slightly) modify them. *Management Science*, *64*(3), 1155–1170. doi:10.1287/mnsc.2016.2643

Econsultancy & Adobe. (2017). *Digital Intelligence Briefing: 2017 Digital Trends*. Retrieved from https://econsultancy.com/reports/digital-intelligence-briefing-2017-digital-trends/

Eren, B. A. (2020). The Role of Internet Banking in the Presentation and Marketing of Financial Services and Products in a Digital Environment. In K. Sandhu (Ed.), *Digital Innovations for Customer Engagement, Management, and Organizational Improvement* (pp. 162–183). IGI Global. doi:10.4018/978-1-7998-5171-4.ch009

Ernst & Young. (2018). *Open Banking Opportunity Index*. Retrieved from https://www.ey.com/en_gl/open-banking-opportunity-index

Ernst & Young. (2019). *EY- Eighth Annual global bank risk management survey*. Retrieved from https://www.ey.com/Publication/vwLUAssets/ey-eighth-annual-global-eyiif-bank-risk-management-survey/$FILE/ey-eighth-annual-global-eyiif-bank-risk-management-survey.pdf

Felix, P. (2018). Prospects and challenges of electronic banking in Ghana: The case of Zenith Bank Sunyani. *International Journal of Advances in Management, Economics and Entrepreneurship, 1*(1), 6–14.

Financial Stability Board (FSB). (2017). *Artificial intelligence and machine learning in financial services: Market developments and financial stability implications*. Retrieved from https://www.fsb.org/wp-content/uploads/P011117.pdf

Hernández-Nieves, E., Hernández, G., Gil-González, A. B., Rodríguez-González, S., & Corchado, J. M. (2020). Fog computing architecture for personalized recommendation of banking products. *Expert Systems with Applications, 140*, 1–10. doi:10.1016/j.eswa.2019.112900

Jewendah, S. (2018). How artificial intelligence is changing the banking sector –a case study of top four Commercial Indian Banks? *International Journal of Management, Technology and Engineering, 8*(7), 525–530.

Kaplan, A. M., & Haenlein, M. (2010). Users of the world, unite! The challenges and opportunities of Social Media. *Business Horizons, 53*(1), 59–68. doi:10.1016/j.bushor.2009.09.003

Kashmari, A., Nejad, A. H. G., & Nayebyazdi, A. (2016). Impact of electronic banking innovations on bank deposit market share. *Journal of International Bank Commerce, 12*(1), 1–12.

Kaur, N., Sahdev, M. S. L., Sharma, M., & Siddiqui, L. (2020). Banking 4.0: The influence of artificial intelligence on the banking industry & how AI is changing the face of modern day bank. *International Journal of Management, 11*(6), 577–585. doi:10.34218/IJM.11.6.2020.049

Kocianski, S. (2017). The Open Banking Report: How banks can leverage open APIs and maintain their retail banking dominance. *Business Insider*. Retrieved from https://www.businessinsider.com/open-banking-report-2017-4

Larivière, B., Bowen, D., Andreassen, T. W., Kunz, W., Sirianni, N. J., & Vossf, C. (2017). Service encounter 2.0: An investigation into the roles of technology, employees and customers. *Journal of Business Research, 79*, 238–246. doi:10.1016/j.jbusres.2017.03.008

Laukkanen, T., & Kiviniemi, V. (2010). The role of information in mobile banking resistance. *International Journal of Bank Marketing, 28*(5), 372–388. doi:10.1108/02652321011064890

Linnainmaa, J. T., Melzer, B., & Previtero, A. (2018). *The Misguided Beliefs of Financial Advisors*. Kelley School of Business Research Paper, No. 18-9.

Lourenço, C. J. S., Dellaert, B. G. C., & Donkers, B. (2020). Whose Algorithm Says So: The Relationships Between Typeof Firm, Perceptions of Trust and Expertise, and the Acceptance of Financial Robo-Advice. *Journal of Interactive Marketing*, *49*, 107–124. doi:10.1016/j.intmar.2019.10.003

Lui, A., & Lamb, G. W. (2018). Artificial intelligence and augmented intelligence collaboration: Regaining trust and confidence in the financial sector. *Information & Communications Technology Law*, *27*(3), 267–283. doi:10.1080/13600834.2018.1488659

Lukango, I. (2018). *Fintech, Inclusive Growth and Cyber Risks: A Focus on the MENAP and CCA Region.* IMF Working Paper. Retrieved from https://www.imf.org/~/media/Files/Publications/WP/2018/wp18201.ashx

Luo, X., Tong, S., Fang, Z., & Qu, Z. (2019). Frontiers: Machines vs. Humans: The Impact of Artificial Intelligence Chatbot Disclosure on Customer Purchases. *Marketing Science*, *38*(6), 937–947. doi:10.1287/mksc.2019.1192

MacKnight. (2017). *Banks say social media is important – but how many are engaging?* The Banker. Retrieved from https://www.thebanker.com/Transactions-Technology/Banks-say-social-media-is-important-but-how-many-are-engaging?ct=true

Malar, D. A., Arvidsson, V., & Holmstrom, J. (2019). Digital Transformation in Banking: Exploring Value Co-Creation in Online Banking Services in India. *Journal of Global Information Technology Management*, *22*(1), 7–24. doi:10.1080/1097198X.2019.1567216

Marimuthu, M., & Roseline, A. (2020). A study on Consumer Perception Towards e-wallet. *Our Heritage*, *68*(17), 283–288.

Mastercard. (2020). *Mobil ve Dijital Çözümler*. Retrieved from https://www.mastercard.com.tr/tr-tr/issuers/products-and-solutions/digital-commerce-solutions.html

Nambisan, S. (2017). Digital entrepreneurship: Toward a digital technology perspective of entrepreneurship. *Entrepreneurship Theory and Practice*, *41*(6), 1029–1055. doi:10.1111/etap.12254

Nassaji, H. (2015). Qualitative and descriptive research: Data type versus data analysis. *Language Teaching Research*, *19*(2), 129–132. doi:10.1177/1362168815572747

Nicoletti, B. (2014). *Mobile Banking, Evolution or Revolution?* Palgrave McMillian.

Pikkarainen, T., Pikkarainen, K., Karjaluoto, H., & Pahnila, S. (2004). Consumer acceptance of online banking: An extension of the technology acceptance model. *Internet Research*, *14*(3), 224–235. doi:10.1108/10662240410542652

Ray. (2013). *Four studies on the adoption of social media by financial advisors and investors*. Retrieved from https://www.socialmediatoday.com/content/four-studies-adoption-social-media-financial-advisors-and-investors

Reuters. (2017). *World's first ATM machine turns to gold on 50th birthday*. Retrieved from https://www.reuters.com/article/us-atm-anniversary/worlds-first-atm-machine-turns-to-gold-on-50th-birthday-idUSKBN19I166

Seenivasan, E. (2020). Retail banking services – role of channel of distribution in delivery system. *International Journal of Multidisciplinary Educational Research*, *9*(2-3), 93–99.

Simser, J. (2015). Bitcoin and modern alchemy: In code we trust. *Journal of Financial Crime*, *22*(2), 156–169. doi:10.1108/JFC-11-2013-0067

Skinners, C. (2018). *Open banking has arrived, whether you like it or not.* Chris Skinner's blog. Retrieved from https://thefinanser.com/2018/10/open-banking-arrived-whether-like-not.html

Sönmez, S. (2016). *Blockchain nedir?* Retrieved from https://www.dunyahalleri.com/blok-zinciri-blockchain-nedir

Statista. (2020a). *Global smartphone sales to end users 2007-2020.* Retrieved from https://www.statista.com/statistics/263437/global-smartphone-sales-to-end-users-since-2007

Statista. (2020b). *Size of the chatbot market worldwide, in 2016 and 2025.* Retrieved from https://www.statista.com/statistics/656596/worldwide-chatbot-market/

Suseendran, G., Chandrasekaran, E., Akila, D. & Kumar, A.S. (2020). Banking and FinTech (Financial Technology) Embraced with IoT Device. *Data Management, Analytics and Innovation*, 197-211.

Swan, M. (2017). Anticipating the economic benefits of blockchain. *Technology Innovation Management Review*, *7*(10), 6–13. doi:10.22215/timreview/1109

Travkina, E., & Alexandra, M. (2019). Modern types of Financial innovations in the conditions of digitalization of the global banking system. *Advances in Economics, Business and Management Research*, *85*, 18–22.

Trivedi, J. (2019). Examining the customer experience of using banking chatbots and its impact on brand love: The moderating role of perceived risk. *Journal of Internet Commerce*, *18*(1), 91–111. doi:10.1080/15332861.2019.1567188

Wamba, S. F., Kamdjoug, J. R. K., Bawack, R. E., & Keogh, J. G. (2020). Bitcoin, Blockchain and Fintech: A systematic review and case studies in the supply chain. *Production Planning and Control*, *31*(2-3), 115–142. doi:10.1080/09537287.2019.1631460

World Bank Group. (2017). *The Global Findex Database 2017.* Retrieved from https://globalfindex.worldbank.org/

Yasin, M., Liébana-Cabanillas, F., Porcu, L., & Kayed, R. N. (2020). The role of customer online brand experience in customers' intention toforward online company-generated content: The case of the Islamic onlinebanking sector in Palestine. *Journal of Retailing and Consumer Services*, *52*, 1–11. doi:10.1016/j.jretconser.2019.101902

Yazıcı, S. (2019). *Dünyada ve Türkiye' de açık bankacılık: Bankacılığın geleceği.* Fintech Istanbul. Retrieved from https://bkm.com.tr/wp-content/uploads/2015/06/Dunyadaveturkiyedeacikbankacilik.pdf

Yüksel, S., Dinçer, H., & Emir, Ş. (2017). Comparing the performance of Turkish deposit banks by using DEMATEL, GreyRelational Analysis (GRA) and MOORA approaches. *World Journal of Applied Economics*, *3*(2), 26–47. doi:10.22440/wjae.3.2.2

ADDITIONAL READING

Dubey, N. K., & Sangle, P. (2019). Customer perception of CRM implementation in banking context Scale development and validation. *Journal of Advances in Management Research*, *16*(1), 38–63. doi:10.1108/JAMR-12-2017-0118

Jakšič, M., & Marinč, M. (2019). Relationship banking and information technology: The role of artificial intelligence and FinTech. *Risk Management*, *21*(1), 1–18. doi:10.105741283-018-0039-y

Malar, D. A., Arvidsson, V., & Holmstrom, J. (2019). Digital Transformation in Banking: Exploring Value Co-Creation in Online Banking Services in India. *Journal of Global Information Technology Management*, *22*(1), 7–24. doi:10.1080/1097198X.2019.1567216

Parusheva, S. (2019). Social media banking usage from banks' perspective., *International. Journal of Business Research*, *15*(1), 38–54.

White, R., Marinakis, Y., Islam, N., & Walsh, S. (2020). Is Bitcoin acurrency, a technology-based product, or something else? *Technological Forecasting and Social Change*, *151*, 1–13. doi:10.1016/j.techfore.2019.119877

KEY TERMS AND DEFINITIONS

Blockchain: It is a system that connects the data blocks with encryption algorithms and thus enables the storage and distribution of data.

Chatbot: They are virtual assistants developed by artificial intelligence that banks use for product/service delivery and marketing to their customers.

Customer Experience: It is the evaluations of customers about their interactions with the businesses.

Digital Distribution Channels: It is that marketing activities and banking products/services are presented as electronic thanks to technology.

Digital Transformation: Digital transformation is the transfer of business processes to electronic environment as well as information thanks to the intensive use of information technologies.

Fintech: It is the combined use of finance and technology in the presentation of financial products and services to customers.

Open Banking: It is a system that enables bank customers to share their data with all other financial institutions on the network through secure interfaces, thus enabling customers to perform their transactions faster and more economically and to offer banks the most suitable products and services to customers' needs.

Robo-Advisor: It is that banks provide financial consultancy services to their customers through online channels using artificial intelligence.

Social Media Banking: It is that banks are using social media effectively in product/service delivery and marketing activities.

Chapter 2
Techniques of Steganography and Cryptography in Digital Transformation

Sabyasachi Pramanik
https://orcid.org/0000-0002-9431-8751
Haldia Institute of Technology, India

Ramkrishna Ghosh
Haldia Institute of Technology, India

Digvijay Pandey
https://orcid.org/0000-0003-0353-174X
Department of Technical Education, India & Institute of Engineering and Technology (IET), India

Debabrata Samanta
https://orcid.org/0000-0003-4118-2480
CHRIST University (Deemed), India

Soumi Dutta
Institute of Engineering and Management, India

Shawni Dutta
The Bhawanipur Education Society College, India

ABSTRACT

Digital enterprise transformation is the amalgamation of digital techniques into the scopes of a business enterprise, fundamentally altering how one can employ and furnish ethics to clients. An organization can be authorized to take digital transformation due to several reasons. But the most important reason is that it is the survival issuance for many people. Digital transformation considers dissimilarity in every organization. Generally, it is the amalgamation of digital technology into all quarters of business. That consolidation brings about major alterations in how the business functions and conveys usefulness to its clients. Here, steganography and cryptography are used to facilitate digital transformation in any business.

INTRODUCTION

Digital Enterprise Transformation is the amalgamation of digital techniques into the scopes of a business enterprise, fundamentally altering how one can employ and furnish ethics to clients. An organization can be authorized to take Digital Transformation due to several reasons. But the most important reason

DOI: 10.4018/978-1-7998-8587-0.ch002

is that it is the survival issuance for many people. Generally, digital transformation is the amalgamation of digital technology incorporating various quarters of merchandising. That consolidation brings about major alterations in how the business functions and conveys usefulness to its clients. Steganography and cryptography plays a vital issue in the security of a digital enterprise. The developing utilization of Internet among public masses and accessibility of public and private computerized information and its sharing has driven industry experts and analysts to give a specific consideration to data security. Web clients oftentimes need to store, send, or get private data and this private data should be secured against unapproved access and assaults. By and by, three principle techniques for data security being utilized: watermarking, cryptography and steganography. In watermarking, information is covered up to pass on some data about the spread medium, for example, proprietorship and copyright.

Cryptography methods depend on delivering the substance of a message distorted to unapproved individuals. Steganography procedures depend on concealing the presence of data by inserting the mystery message in another spread medium. While every one of the three is data security methods cryptography and steganography are having wide application as watermarking is restricted to having data especially about the spread medium. With the development of PC organization, security of information has become a significant concern and in this way information concealing method has pulled in individuals around the world. Steganography methods are utilized to address advanced copyrights the board, secure data, and disguise mysteries. This article combines technique of steganography and cryptography to secure a digital enterprise. Nowadays, every organizations look to digital enterprise to reshape and transform their business. CIOs (Chief Information Officer) understand that data and information technology is really an important issue to their organizations. The convergence of cloud is the first important step to make opportunities and to be in competition. Here, the authors use the concept of steganography (Pramanik et al. 2020) and cryptography to shift information from any node to other in an organization. Information reliability plays a vital role; the confidential data should not be interpreted by a third party. So, data security characterizes major criteria in the sphere of digital enterprise transformation. Concepts of steganalysis and cryptanalysis are introduced here and along with some steganalysis tools can interpret the presence of any secret data within a cover medium.

With the help of these tools the CIOs can interpret whether any confidential data is leaked from the organization or not. So, along with the concept of cloud and machine learning algorithms steganography and cryptography enacts a significant role regarding strategies of a change in digital enterprise. Steganography is an art of hiding secret data within any medium like text, image, audio or video. Thus, during a message transfer from the sender to the receiver there is little scope for the unauthorized users to intercept. Since the ascent of the web, the security of data has additionally been one of the most testing components of data innovation and correspondence. Enormous volume of information is moved each second in the web through messages, document sharing destinations, and long range interpersonal communication locales and so on. As the quantity of web clients rises, the worry on the believability of the administrations is additionally on rise, so the idea of web security has become the significant exploration point these days.

The serious nature of the PC business has constrained the web administrations into the market dangerously fast giving a very brief period for review of framework security. Then again, the tight work market causes web venture improvement to be dealt with less experienced work force, which may have no preparing in protection and security issues. This blend of market pressure and the low joblessness makes a condition with machines powerless against misuses, and pernicious clients to barge in those machines. Because of the quick advancement of correspondence innovations, it is advantageous to procure sight and sound information. Be that as it may, the issue of unlawful information access happens out of the blue without fail and all over. Subsequently, it is imperative to secure the advanced substance while guaranteeing the clients' security and the approved utilization of interactive media information.

Information encryption is fundamentally a system to make the information mixed up, imperceptible or unfathomable during transmission by scrambling the substance of information. Steganography is the workmanship what's more, study of concealing data by inserting messages inside apparently innocuous messages. It additionally alludes to the "Imperceptible" correspondence. The intensity of Steganography is in concealing the mystery message by indefinite quality, concealing its reality in a non-mystery record. Steganography works by supplanting pieces of futile or unused information in customary PC documents. This covered up data can be plaintext or ciphertext and even pictures. Here, in this article the authors use XOR and One Time Pad encryption process.

BACKGROUND

Poduval et al. (2020) proposed a hybrid methodology of steganography and cryptography in the cloud environment. Message is encrypted utilizing the Advanced Encryption Standard and 3DES encryption algorithms. The confidential key thus generated is further encrypted using the RSA algorithm. The secret key thus obtained is thus hidden in an image using the LSB technique. The combined techniques of AES, 3DES and RSA algorithms have made the system more robust and secure.

Bala and Kumar (2017) proposed a combined technique of cryptography and steganography to secure the MRI image in healthcare. The details of a patient are hidden in an image. The image is then encrypted and inserted in a database. Thus, third party other than the doctors would not be able to comprehend the confidential details of the patient. The images are stored in MIAS (Mammographic Image Analysis Society) database.

Younus and Younus (2020) developed a framework to hide data in AVI video files by the LSB technique and the Knight Tour approach. The confidential information is encrypted using an encryption technique. The experimental results show a better PSNR value of 71.36 dB and a low MSE value of 0.1366 resulting in a framework which is highly secured.

Abed et al. (2019) combined the concepts of steganography and cryptography to enhance the security in data that needs to be transferred. AES algorithm using Java language is used to encrypt the secret data. The ciphered data is hidden in video frames using FPGA implementation. The outcome of the results of hiding secret data in video frames shows that power dissipation and PSNR values of the proposed model outperform the similar methods.

Kumar et al. (2020) used the adaptive based watermarking algorithm using a chaotic secured layer. For the reason that this layer can be hacked, DCT is used to encrypt the image along with Arnold Transform and Chaotic encryption process. This model can be used in healthcare systems and e-commerce framework.

Pramanik et al. (2020) proposed a new model of steganography with cryptography depending on digital signature approaches. A digital signature approach identifies the genuineness of information. Signature picture message is embedded in a host image utilizing a private key of encoder and decoder. The framework has a high PSNR of 53.84 and a low MSE value of 0.203.

Verhoef et al. (2019) showed that digital alteration has a high impact on the consumers' expectations, thereby putting an enormous pressure on the conventional organizations. The growth strategies and the required assets and capabilities of an organization to efficiently transform it digitally is discussed.

Digital enterprise transformation facilitates any organization towards an adaptable, reliable and digitally validated operating model that transforms the way the employees, clients, associates and other collaborators encounter the business. Organizations that accept digital enterprise transformation can regain unparalleled competitive superiority, for e.g.,

1. Encountering the demand of future customers
2. Releasing innovation at speed and scale

Digital enterprise transformation is becoming an important topic for organizations worldwide (Von Leipzig et al. 2017; Kane 2015). It is predicted that the companies that cannot adopt the digital enterprise transformation strategies will soon perish and in the run for competition. In the current scenario there are many firms in the world that cannot keep in pace with current technologies and the managers lack clarity in dealing with strategic endeavors (Hess et al. 2016). Current work in relation to business strategic transformation has concentrated on the challenges and failures of past endeavors. Although there are many dedicated strategies the managers still lack the strategic considerations. The role of steganography and cryptography enacts a vital criterion for various spheres in a digital enterprise. In healthcare system, a medical officer can send an image embedded with text of some explanatory notes into it with the help of steganography to another medical officer.

Accepting Digital Transformation: The Destiny of Banking

The scope of banking has transformed in the last couple of years. Financial Technology firms have begun to obstruct the market situation with cryptocurrency (Pelosi et al. 2018), blockchain (Akter et al. 2020), bitcoin and much more. In UK, a new category of banks called "challenger banks" have come out. They focus on conveying digital-only assistance and client connection. Currently, in UK, there are more than 20 challenger banks. Advancing in the digital era has forced the banking personnel, with automation and thereby resulting in sacking and workforce reduction. There is an increasing request for data scientists with an exposure to banking experience—an expertise that is difficult to find in today's job market. It is thus necessary for the organizations to enhance a new manpower to teach the current workforce and hire new personnel.

Concept of Big Data and Its Consequences on the Client's Outcome

The banking industry is characterized by one of the most data-driven features. Loan facilities, insurance terms and mortgage facilities require the banks to store transaction data for many years. There is a provocation in transforming that information into relevant comprehension. Big Data allows various opportunities for banks to surpass their contest. Engrossing data to a cloud platform allows a customer to view a 360 degree of the data. This perception allows a bank to realize where they can put a higher level of insight and create more substance. Big data also facilitates to use technologies like artificial intelligence (Hanizan et al. 2017), blockchain (Xu et al. 2020) and IoT (Yin et al. 2015) to portray the customer insights into meaningful information.

Anchoring Technology to Recast the Banking Business Model

Innovative enhanced technologies authorize banks to reinforce customer meeting with customized, creative offerings. The banking industry grasps IoT with mobile apps, ATMs and card readers. It also offers a system for synchronized real-time asset financing. Several banks are heretofore using blockchain technology to modify their business procedures, as it offers reliable, appropriate to conventional banking activities. The blockchain technology has been in the limelight due to its capability to minimize deception in the financial world.

The blockchain technology is already used in the financial spheres of banking, which includes payment activities (interbank), mortgage and loan records, personal equity asset transfer and client service records. Glancing at cross-border payments, blockchain can minimize processing time from normal delay of two to seven days. This improves the client concern to an enhanced level with minimum cost real-time transactions. Stack procedures strengthened by blockchain are opening networks; international money transfers; auditing and asset proprietorship. Various different technologies, for e.g., machine learning can also automates various manual procedures which can help in trading and fraud management.

Banking Activities on the Cloud Environment

Banks take dominance of market opportunities prevalent via digital transformation. Banks also do need to supervise the risks obtained by the new digital economy. There is always a requirement or economical computing benchmarks that facilitate more adroitness. The newer digital technologies are enhancing the banking organizations. Banks that welcome innovation and adapt to newer technologies have many opportunities to improve the financial services, such as:

- Unite with financial technology brands to innovate digital platforms and products.
- Optimize business activities through optimization and collaborating cloud solutions.
- Innovate newer technologies like IoT, blockchain and artificial intelligence (AI)

Use of Steganography for Security of Biometric Data

Biometric systems are pattern recognition system that can uniquely identify a human being based on his/her biological characteristics like fingerprints, face recognition, voice recognition and iris pattern. Biometrics (McAteer et al. 2019) is used to reserve access to mobile phones, work places, laptops and bank machines. In healthcare, biometrics can be used by the healthcare persons and patients to have an access to health-related tools, without the need to remember complex passwords. Biometric authentication requires hiding an encrypted biometric data in a cover image. In a voting over internet on biometric and password security, the combined concept of cryptography and LSB steganography plays a major role.

What an Aggressor Can See?

An aggressor will just actually observe the media documents. The assailant will always be unable to perceive any inward framework state. Also, the aggressor will just actually observe the media documents once. Without this supposition, identifying the steganography would be an insignificant matter of checking for double contrasts in the two duplicates of the documents which the aggressor has. Clearly this necessitates the assailant doesn't see the first pictures to think about them.

What an Assailant Will Know?

Likewise with all steganography, it is accepted that an adversary won't realize that information is put away by any stretch of the imagination, yet this doesn't imply that the assailant won't be dubious that this framework is being used. In similarity to a ciphertext-just assault in cryptography (Pramanik et al. 2019), we accept that the aggressor will never know or have the option to pick what is put away.

What an Assailant Can Do?

It is accepted that any assault will be of the accompanying structure:

1. The client sets up the framework in a catalog of media records.
2. The client hands this catalog to the assailant.
3. The aggressor inspects or changes the registry somehow or another.
4. Whenever fulfilled, the aggressor restores the registry to the client.

There are not many suspicions about what an assailant will do once they have the records in their ownership:

1. They may include, eliminate, change or rename records trying to upset the plan.
2. They may endeavor to decide factually that the media documents certainly contain some concealed information.
3. They may endeavor to break the encryption.

One suspicion made is that the information is unmodified in a sensible number of documents. It would plainly be conceivable to upset the plan by overwriting all documents with irregular information, however this might disturb practically any type of steganography, so is accepted not to be a danger here.

Sorts of Steganography Tools

Different apparatuses are utilized to conceal message in interactive media information like content, picture, sound and video. A portion of the apparatuses that are examined underneath can be utilized in an advanced venture to conceal secret data and upgrade the security of the administration of a computerized undertaking.

MP3Stego

MP3Stego conceals data inside MP3 file at pressure cycle. Information is previously packed and scrambled. Later, it is covered up in the MP3 bit stream.

JPHide and JPSeek

JPHIDE and JPSEEK are tools that permit one to shroud a document in a jpg picture. Various heaps of renditions are there for comparative projects accessibility for the web however JPHIDE and JPSEEK are fairly exceptional.

BlindSide Cryptographic Tool

Blind Side is a case of the specialty of Steganography - the death of mystery messages in a structure with the end goal that any person will not speculate that the information is transferred. It is a cryptographic approach that is pulling in impressive enthusiasm lately. It can conceal a document (or records) regarding some assortment, inside a BMP document.

GIFShuffle

Gifshuffle tool is utilized to conceal information in GIF pictures before rearranging the color-map, and it abandons the picture obviously unaltered. gifshuffle functions during inclusion of every GIF pictures, incorporating straightforwardness and movement, and likewise gives pressure and encryption of the disguised message.

wbStego

wbStego is a mechanism which conceals various sorts of record in bmp pictures, text documents, HTML records or PDF documents. Records that are used to conceal the information aren't perceptibly altered.

StegoVideo

MSU StegoVideo permits concealing any record in a video arrangement. At the point when the tool was developed, many famous codec's broke down, thus a calculation was picked that gives little information misfortune during video pressure. One utilizes StegoVideo as VirtualDub channel or for independent .exe file, autonomous to VirtualDub.

Steganography Analyzer Artifact Scanner (StegAlyzerAS)

StegAlyzerAS provides one the capacity to check the whole document framework, or single indexes, on suspicious forum for the appearance of Steganography approaches. What's more, not normal for other mainstream criminological apparatuses, you can play out a computerized or manual inquiry of the Windows Registry to decide if any keys persist which are related to a specific Steganography implementation.

Steganography Analyzer Signature Scanner (StegAlyzerSS)

StegAlyzerSS enhances an individual to check each document on the suspicious multimedia data due to the existence of hexadecimal byte examples, or marks, consisting of specific Steganography approaches to be used. On the off chance that a realized mark is distinguished, it might be conceivable to extricate data covered up with the Steganography application related with the mark.

Advanced Invisible Ink Toolkit

Such an undertaking gives a straightforward Java-related steganography instrument which can shroud information in a 24-cycle shading picture so expressing the process how it seemed installed, or accomplishing measurable investigation, doesn't make it any simpler to locate the covered data.

Steganography is a likely danger. The most plausible utilization of Steganography is presumably to shroud illicit material, for example, youngster erotic entertainment. Steganography may likewise be utilized to shroud touchy data and move it starting with one spot then onto the next. For instance an unfamiliar army man might own a twofold specialist working for the US Military, the operator takes several touchy records, and he needs to duplicate by writing onto CD to bring in house and send email to individual bosses. He realizes that in the event that he consumes the records to the circle there is a plate of the circle being checked.

So what might he be able to do? Basic, conceal the reports inside picture documents that watch nothing strange. Individuals ought to zero in on the significant parts of Steganography, for example, what it is truly utilized for, rather than accepting publicity put out by the media. Organization information security has gotten one of the most significant fields in Information innovation. That is on the grounds that web innovation is being utilized all over and security has been a major concern. In such manner RSA calculation isn't particularly made sure about in light of the fact that RSA is a public key cryptography. On the off chance that plain content info message is past 11 character (letter or number) the product can't encode this message.

Issues, Controversies, Problems

Most of the respondents in a survey replied that they are going through a transition period of adapting to the digital transformation and have more jobs to be done. The survey was carried out in two types of organizations: one was a company with less than 100 employees and the other more than 5000 employees. The challenges were:

1. Employee rollback
2. Deficiency of proper manpower to lead the digital strategic combination.
3. Structure of the organization gets in-between
4. Budget limitation

This shows that the challenges of Digital Enterprise do not depend on the size of any organization.

RESEARCH METHODOLOGY

The proposed technique consists of a blend of steganography and cryptography. Fig 1 and Fig 2 are the encryption and decryption techniques respectively. Encryption is carried out in the sender side and decryption takes place in the receiver side. XOR cryptography is used in the encryption process. Information is scrambled using a key and XOR activity. Encryption happens by XORing the message and unscrambling happens by XORing the ciphertext. The plain content is first changed over to its ASCII esteem, which thus is changed over into its comparable twofold structure. The key can be a solitary character or a series of characters. Each information character bit is XORed with the pieces of the key. The result is the ciphertext of the message. Fig 3 is the flowchart for the age of keys. After the key age measure as appeared in Table 1, the XOR encryption procedure is applied. Fig 4 portrays the XOR encryption method. The plain content is changed over into its identical ASCII esteem, which thus is changed over into its comparable binary organization.

Figure 1. The encryption technique

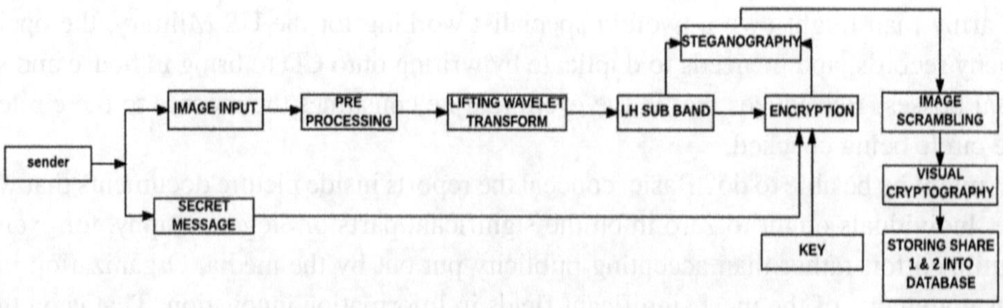

Figure 2. The decryption technique

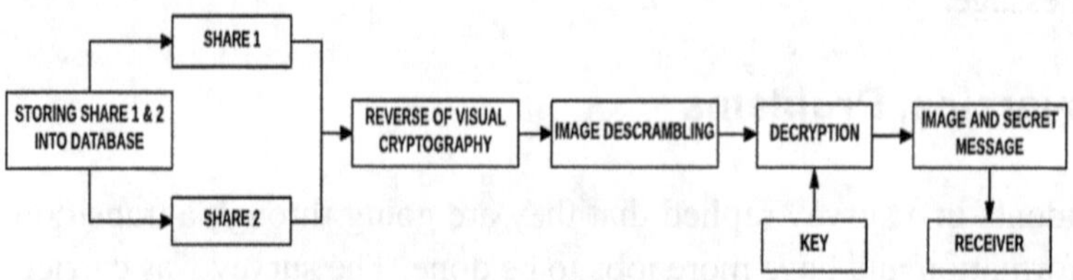

Encryption by the One Time Pad (OTP) Technique

OTP (Permana et al. 2019) is an encryption algorithm that can never be cracked. Here, a plaintext is paired with a randomly generated keyIn this article the writers utilize a 27 X 27 table in MS dominate sheet comprising of 26 english letter sets and the 27th character is a "space" character. An irregular key is produced. The OTP calculation is as per the following:

Info: Plain content and key Output: Cipher text

Stage 1: Scrutinize the excel table having 27 X 27 table
Stage 2: Find the key value in the column
Stage 3: Find the message character in the column
Stage 4: Acquire the convergence of row and column cell estimate
Stage 5: Repeat stage 2 to stage 4 for all the message characters

Figure 3. Key generation with XOR operation

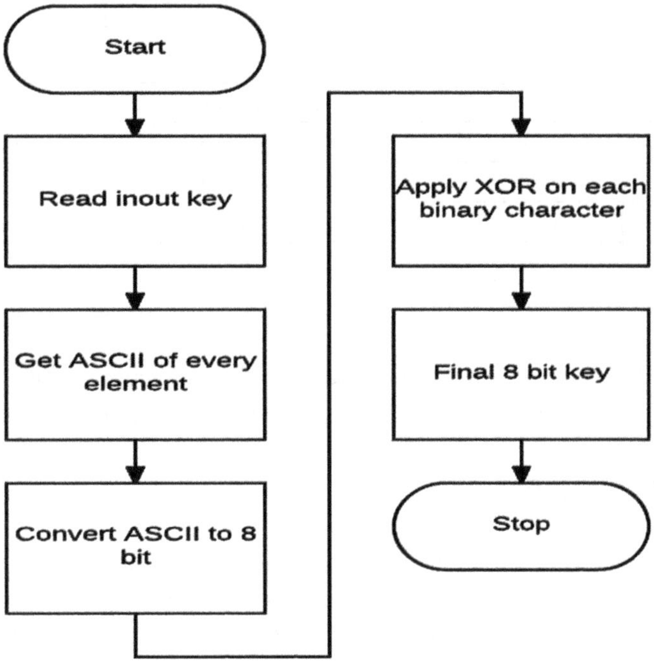

Figure 4. XOR Encryption Method

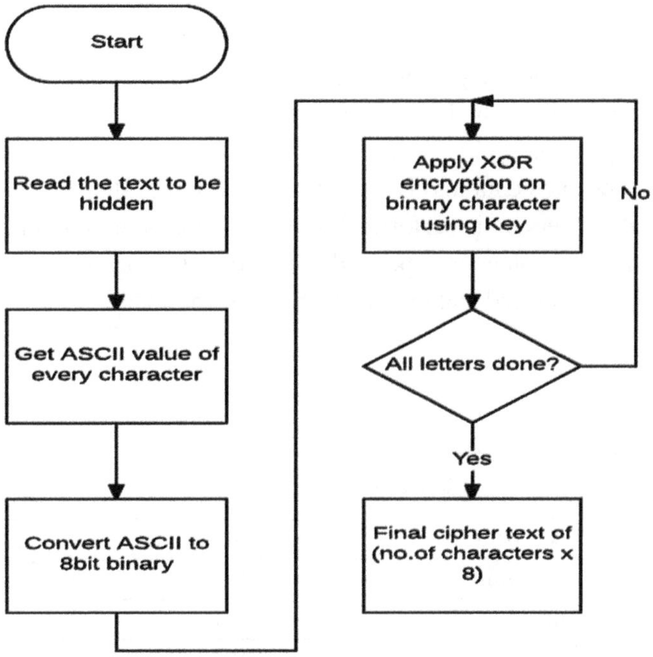

Table 1. Key generation using XOR operation

Key	ASCII Value	Binary Equivalent	Using XOR
delhi	d ------ 100	d---0110 0100	d------- 0110 0100
	e -------101	e----0110 0101	de----- 0000 0001
	l --------108	l---- 0110 1100	del----- 0110 1101
	h ------ 104	h----0110 1000	delh--- 0000 0101
	i ------- 105	i---- 0110 1001	delhi---0110 1100
			Key----0110 1100

Suppose, the text is "bengal", which is of 6 characters. The key length is also of 6 characters. Let the randomly generated key be "amazon". Then the encrypted text is "bqnfoy".

Steganography Technique

It is a data hiding technique of embedding the information in an image. Least Significant Bits of the image pixels are needed for embedding the message. Image has both high and low frequency variations. Discrete Wavelet Transform (DWT) (Pramanik, S. and Bandyopadhyay, S. K., 2014) is used to separate the two frequency bands. The frequency band obtained after DWT are the LH, HL, LL and HH sub-bands. The researchers in this article utilize the LH sub-band to insert data. Following steganography algorithm is used here:

Input: Cipher text Output: Stego Image
Step 1: The host image is read
Step 2: Perform the DWT operation to get four sub-bands
Step 3: The red plane is selected for the LH sub-band
Step 4: Constitute the red plane in digital equivalence
Step 5: Hide the digital encrypted data into Least Significant Bits in step 4
Step 6: Binary to decimal conversion is performed. It is then represented in matrix form
Step 7: Matrix of blue and green plane is appended with the matrix of step 6
Step 8: IDWT operation is performed and the stego image is obtained

Table 2. Encryption method using XOR

Plain Text	ASCII Equivalence	Binary Equivalence		
bengal	b ----- 98	0011 0010	Key—0110 1100	char_val1 0101 1110
	e ------ 101	0110 0101	Key—0110 1100	char_val2 0000 1001
	n ---- 110	0110 1101	Key—0110 1100	char_val3 0000 0001
	g ------ 103	0110 0111	Key—0110 1100	char_val4 0000 1011
	a ------ 97	0011 0001	Key—0110 1100	char_val5 0101 1101
	l ----- 108	0110 1100	Key—0110 1100	char_val5 0000 0000

Scrambling Technique

The stego image shown in Fig 6a has secret data hidden within it. Image scrambling which is used to make the system more secure is a technique in which the pixel locations are changed to make the image scrambled. It is shown in Fig 6b. Here, the authors initially change the pixels of column and thereafter the pixels of the rows. The scrambling process is shown below:

Input: Stego Image Output: Scrambled Image
Step 1: An Image size of 128 X 128 is read
Step 2: The first column of pixels is swapped with last column pixels
Step 3: The next set of pixels is selected. Step 2 is repeated until all the pixels are scrambled
Step 4: The first row of pixels is swapped with last row pixels
Step 5: The next set of pixels is selected. Step 4 is repeated until all the pixels are scrambled

Visual Cryptography Encryption Process

It is a technique where the visual particulars are encrypted by fragmenting the image into various portions depending on a certain threshold value. The image can be decrypted only if all the shares of the image are known. Threshold may be achieved by segregating the white and the black pixels. It may also be done by splitting the even numbering rows and the odd numbering rows. Here, the authors segregate the even numbering columns and odd numbering columns. Let the first set be column no1 and the second set is column no2. The algorithm is shown below:

Input: Stego Image Output: Two sets of the picture
Step 1: Stego picture as shown in Fig 5 is read
Step 2: Image is split in two parts. Part1 contains even numbering columns and part2 has odd numbering rows as shown in Fig 6.
Step 3: Two parts are stored separately

These two parts are then transmitted via a communication channel.

Visual Cryptography Decoding Technique

Two parts that are obtained in Fig 5 are integrated utilizing the similar threshold value which was taken in the encryption process. The two parts are attached to combine the scramble picture as shown in Fig 6. The decryption algorithm is shown below:

Input: Two parts of the picture Output: Scrambled picture
Step 1: Two picture parts are read
Step 2: The column wise values of both the parts are added and it is the distorted image is stored

Process of Descrambling

Descrambling is the opposite technique for scrambling. Here, the resultant picture after decryption of visual cryptography is used. Stego picture (Pramanik, S. and Bandyopadhyay, S. K., 2020) thus found is shown in Fig 7 a, and 7 b. The descrambling algorithm is shown below:

Input: Scrambled picture obtained after visual cryptography Output: Stego picture
Step 1: The picture obtained after the visual cryptography is read
Step 2: The first row for 8 pixels is swapped with the last row of 8 pixels
Step 3: The next set of the pixels are again swapped and step 2 is continued till all the rows are changed
Step 4: The first column of 8 pixels is swapped with the last column of 8 pixels
Step 5: The next set of the pixels are again swapped and step 4 is continued till all the columns are changed

Extraction of Message

In this article the researchers have embedded the data in the Least Significant Bits of the picture. After recovery of the data it is checked whether the message is plaintext or cipher text. If the message is a cipher text, the following algorithm allows it to convert it into plaintext.

Input: Stego picture Output: Embedded message
Step 1: The stego picture is read
Step 2: DWT operation is performed and sub bands are acquired
Step 3: Red plane for Low-High sub band is acquired
Step 4: Achieved plane is converted to its binary equivalence
Step 5: Binary cipher message that is hidden in LSBs is extracted
Step 6: The binary values are represented as 8 bits equivalent to 1 character

The XOR Decryption Technique

The decryption technique should know the key that was used in encryption. XOR of cipher text and key is carried out and the plain text is extracted. The process is given as in Table 3.

Decryption of OTP

OTP algorithm cannot be broken. Key is obtained by random generation. The decryption technique is shown below:

Input: Cipher message, key Output: Plain message
Step 1: Excel table consisting of 27 X 27 OTP table is read
Step 2: Find the key character present in the column represented by key
Step 3: Find the data character present in the row represented by key
Step 4: Find the equivalence of cell in the plain message row
Step 5: For each character, repeat processes starting from step 2

Table 3. XOR decryption technique

Key	ASCII Value	Binary Equivalence		
delhi	d ------ 100	d---0110 0100	char_val1 0101 1110	Key----0110 1100
	e -------101	e----0110 0101	char_val2 0000 1001	Key----0110 1100
	l --------108	l---- 0110 1100	char_val3 0000 0001	Key----0110 1100
	h ------ 104	h----0110 1000	char_val4 0000 1011	Key----0110 1100
	i ------- 105	i---- 0110 1001	char_val5 0101 1101	Key----0110 1100
		Decimal Scheme		Plain message
pvalue_1— 0011 0010		98—b		bengal
pvalue_2— 0110 0101		101—e		
pvalue_3— 0110 1101		110—n		
pvalue_4— 0110 0111		103—g		
pvalue_5— 0011 0001		97—a		
pvalue_6— 0110 1100		108---l		

RESULTS AND DISCUSSION

Experimental Peak Signal to Noise Ratio (PSNR) and Mean Square Error (MSE) metrics are obtained by MATLAB. Images after steganography operation are depicted below in Fig 5.

After scrambling the input stego image and the scrambled picture are depicted as in Fig 6a and 6b below.

Fig 7 a, and 7 b shows the descrambling process outcomes.

PSNR (Pramanik, S and Singh, R. P. 2017) indicates the ratio for the greatest conceivable intensity for a message and the intensity for unwanted noise that influences the level of precision of its portrayal. Let the pixels for host image be taken as C (i, j) and the stego picture pixels be denoted as S (i, j) for picture dimension of M x N. PSNR value is calculated by the following equation

$$PSNR = 10\log_{10}\frac{255\times 255\times M\times N}{\sum_{i=1}^{M}\sum_{j=1}^{N}\left(S_{ij}-C_{ij}\right)^2}$$

MSE is defined by the equation

$$MSE = \frac{1}{MXN}\sum_{0}^{M-1}\sum_{0}^{N-1}\left(S_{ij}-C_{ij}\right)^2$$

The PSNR and MSE (Pramanik, S. and Bandyopadhyay, S. K., 2014) values of the cover image along with stego picture is shown below in Table 4

Figure 5. a: Cover Image and b Stego Image

SOLUTIONS AND RECOMMENDATIONS

Every person, by their nature needs to follow a routine. This makes them feel in a comfort zone. Things look uncertain when uncertainty enters in anyone's life. Situations become fading. The advent of digital transformation makes them feel threatened. But it is feasible that change is sometimes riskier. Digital transformation is pivotal to any firm. One cannot minimize the doubts from the employees' minds but one can certainly minimize them. The employees must be well informed about the entire process to adapt to the digital transformation. The employees should be empowered to a bright future.

It takes both talent and infrastructure for any digital transformation. Digital transformation will have many technical challenges and the correct group of people is needed. Making investment at the correct time in the people can have a wonderful impact on the people's mind and the firms can stay a bit ahead. Internally, in an organization, there may not be the correct talent. So, an organization may think of recruiting many newer workforces and also collaborate with other business partners.

The embracing of digital transformation along with cutting-edge technologies may change a person's daily routine, from changing the responsibilities, changing of departments in a firm or a change in the organizational structure. Let us consider a case that a report will be made to an IT person only or a sales team may be designed in the same way does not mean that the entire situation cannot be changed. In fact, the change will give the employees a new life to breathe in with their new roles and careers.

Figure 6. a: Stego Picture and b Scrambled Image

(a)

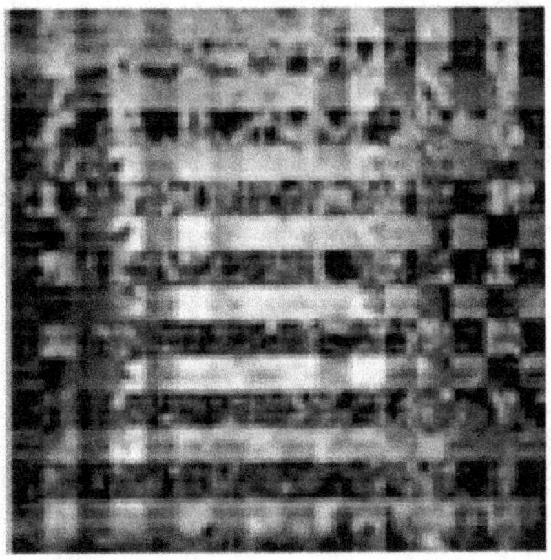

(b)

Budgetary constraints may act as a limitation to the entire journey of digital transformation. When the digital transformation needs anything substantial, then spending on employees, resources, clients and newer technology is not a serious issue. But, also the capability of the firm is also needs to dealt. One should not put the company into jeopardy, spending a lot. The concept of steganography and cryptography can enhance the security system of any digital enterprise and this will lift the management of an enterprise to an inflated level.

Figure 7. a: Shuffled Image and b: Stego Image

Table 4. Values for MSE and PSNR

	MSE	PSNR (dB)
XOR	0.2138	56.2351
OTP	0.2291	56.5249

FUTURE RESEARCH DIRECTIONS

Nearly 56% of companies with a robust digital eminence have an internal conflict between the departments to owe digital strategy. By 2022, to make business smarter, and more dependent on cutting-edge technologies, 48% of digital transformation technologies including 100% of IoT efforts must be backed by AI algorithms and features. Tech giants like IBM, Microsoft and Google are researching in the areas of quantum computing, which will be a big boost in the digital world in years to come. The concepts of

AI, cloud, IoT, machine learning and deep learning will make the enterprises more secure in the way data is communicated. More complex quantum computing algorithms including blockchain technology will enhance the security and privacy framework of the enterprises.

CONCLUSION

The aim of this chapter is to enlighten the current researches in digital transformation. It describes how an organization transforms to a digital trend. It exposes the ways by which an organization changes digitally. It also depicts the importance of steganography and cryptography in securing the network of an organization. In this article the authors have incorporated various encryption and decryption techniques like steganography, OTP, XOR, image scrambling and visual cryptography. All of these individual techniques can secure a framework. But when combined together, it enhances the security level to the highest level. Framework in a digital enterprise requires secured data and the combined concepts of steganography and cryptography makes an enterprise more secured during data transmission. OTP encryption technique is highly secured algorithm as it is unfeasible to decode the message due to the fact that random key is used. The image security is further enhanced with the use of scrambling and visual cryptography.

REFERENCES

Abed, S., Al-Mutairi, M., Al-Watyan, A., Al-Mutairi, O., AlEnizy, W. & Al-Noori, A. (2019). An automated Security Approach of Video Steganography–Based LSB using FPGA Implementation. *Journal of Circuits, Systems and Computers, 28*(5). doi:10.1142/S021812661950083X

Akter, S., Michael, K., Uddin, M. R., McCarthy, G., & Rahman, M. (2020). Transforming usiness using Digital Innovations: The Application of AI, Blockchain, Cloud and Data Analytics. *Annals of Operations Research*. Advance online publication. doi:10.100710479-020-03620-w

Bala, B. K., & Kumar, A. B. (2017). The Combination of Steganography and Cryptography for Medical Image Applications. *Biomedical & Pharmacology Journal, 10*(4), 1793–1797. doi:10.13005/bpj/1294

Hanizan, H. S., Din, R., Hafiza, A. S., Rukhiya, A., & Noor, M. S. (2017). A Review of Artificial Intelligence Techniques in Image Steganography Domain. *Journal of Engineering Science and Technology*, 106-116.

Hess, T., Matt, C., & Wiesbock, F. (2016). Options for Formulating a Digital Transformation Strategy. *MIS Quarterly Executive, 15*(2), 123–139.

Kane, G. C. (2015). Strategy, Not Technology, Drives Digital Transformation. *MIT Sloan Management Review*, 1–25.

Kumar, B. (2020). Secure Data Communication with Cryptography and Steganography. *International Journal of Electrical Engineering and Technology, 11*(3), 164–172.

McAteer, I., Ibrahim, A., Zheng, G., Yang, W., & Valli, C. (2019). Integration of Biometrics and Steganography: A Comprehensive Review. *Technologies, 7*(34), 1–22. doi:10.3390/technologies7020034

Pelosi, M. J., Poudel, N., Lamichhane, P., & Soomro, D. B. (2018). Steganography System with Application to Crypto-Currency Cold Storage and Secure Transfer, Advances in Science. *Technology and Engineering Systems Journal*, *3*(2), 271–282. doi:10.25046/aj030232

Permana, Tulus, & Situmorang. (2019). Combination of One Time Pad Cryptography Algorithm with Generate Random Keys and Vigenere Cipher with EM2B Key. *ICMASES*. doi:10.4108/eai.3-8-2019.2290723

Poduval, V., Koul, A., Rebello, D., Bhat, K., & Wahul, R. M. (2020). Cloud based Secure Storage of files using Hybrid Cryptography and Image Steganography. *International Journal of Recent Technology and Engineering*, *8*(6), 665–667. doi:10.35940/ijrte.F7227.038620

Pramanik, S., & Bandyopadhyay, S. K. (2014). Hiding Secret Message in an Image, - International Journal of Innovative Science. *Engineering & Technology*, *1*(3), 553–559.

Pramanik, S., & Bandyopadhyay, S. K. (2019). Image Steganography Using Wavelet Transform and Genetic Algorithm. *International Journal of Innovative Research in Advanced Engineering, 1*, 1-4.

Pramanik, S., Bandyopadhyay, S. K., & Ghosh, R. (2020). Signature Image Hiding in Color Image using Steganography and Cryptography based on Digital Signature Concepts. *2020 2nd International Conference on Innovative Mechanisms for Industry Applications (ICIMIA)*, 665-669.

Pramanik, S., & Raja, S. S. (2020). A Secured Image Steganography using Genetic Algorithm. *Advances in Mathematics: Scientific Journal*, *9*(7), 4533–4541.

Pramanik, S., & Singh, R. P. (2017). Role of Steganography in Security Issues. *International Conference on Advance Studies in Engineering and Sciences*, 1225-1230.

Pramanik, S., Singh, R.P., & Ghosh, R. (2019). A New Encrypted Method in Image Steganography. *Indonesian Journal of Electrical Engineering and Computer Science, 14*(3), 1412–1419. .v13.i3 doi:10.11591/ijeecs

Pramanik, S., Singh, R. P., & Ghosh, R. (2020). *Application of bi-orthogonal wavelet transform and genetic algorithm in image steganography*. Multimed Tools Appl. doi:10.100711042-020-08676-1

Verhoef, P. C. (2019). Digital Transformation: A Multidisciplinary Reflection and Research Agenda. *Journal of Business Research*. Advance online publication. doi:10.1016/j.jbusres.2019.09.022

Von Leipzig, T., Gamp, M., Manz, D., Schöttle, K., Ohlhausen, P., Oosthuizen, G., Palm, D., & von Leipzig, K. (2017). Initialising customer-orientated digital transformation in enterprises. *Procedia Manufacturing*, *8*, 517–524. doi:10.1016/j.promfg.2017.02.066

Xu, M., Wu, H., Feng, G., Zhang, X., & Ding, F. (2020). Broadcasting Steganography in the Blockchain. In H. Wang, X. Zhao, Y. Shi, H. Kim, & A. Piva (Eds.), Lecture Notes in Computer Science: Vol. 12022. *Digital Forensics and Watermarking. IWDW 2020*. Springer.

Yin, J. H. J., Fen, G. M., Mughal, F., & Iranmanesh, V. (2015). Internet of Things: Securing Data Using Image Steganography. *2015 3rd International Conference on Artificial Intelligence, Modelling and Simulation (AIMS),* 310-314.

Younus, Z. S., & Younus, G. T. (2020). Video Steganography using Knight Tour Algorithm and LSB Method for Encrypted Data. *J. Intell. Syst.*, *29*(1), 1216–1225. doi:10.1515/jisys-2018-0225

ADDITIONAL READING

Abbood, E. A., Neamah, R. M., & Abdulkadhm, S. (2018). Text in Image Hiding using Developed LSB and Random Method. *Iranian Journal of Electrical and Computer Engineering*, *8*(4), 2091–2097. doi:10.11591/ijece.v8i4.pp2091-2097

Altaay, A. A. J., Sahib, S. B., & Zamani, M. (2012). An Introduction to Image Steganography Techniques, *International IEEE Conference on Advanced Computer Science Applications and Technologies (ACSAT)*, DOI: 10.1109/ACSAT.2012.25

Arya, M. S. (2016). Improved Capacity Image Steganography Algorithm using 16-Pixel Differencing with n-bit LSB Substitution for RGB Images. *Iranian Journal of Electrical and Computer Engineering*, *6*(6), 2735–2741.

Bhowmik, S., & Bhaumik, A. K. (2016). A New Approach in Color Image Steganography with High Level of Perceptibility and Security", *2016 International IEEE Conference on Intelligent Control Power and Instrumentation (ICICPI)*, DOI: 10.1109/ICICPI.2016.7859718

Bhuiyan, S. S. N., Malek, N. A., & Khalifa, O. O. (2019). An Improved Image Steganography Algorithm based on PVD, Indonesian Journal of Electrical Engineering and Computer Science, Vol. 10, No. 2, May 2018, pp. 569~577. ρ ISSN: 2502-4752 Indonesian J Elec Eng & Comp Sci, Vol. 14, No. 3, 1412 – 1419 1418

Hussain, H. S., Din, R., Ali, M. H., & Balqis, N. (2018). The Embedding Performance of Stego SVM Model in Image Steganography. *Indonesian Journal of Electrical Engineering and Computer Science*, *12*(1), 233–238. doi:10.11591/ijeecs.v12.i1.pp233-238

Jain, R., & Boaddh, J. (2016). Advances in Digital Image Steganography", *International IEEE Conference on Innovation and Challenges in Cyber Security*, DOI: 10.1109/ICICCS.2016.7542298

Krishnaveni, N., & Periyasamy, S. (2018). A Novel and Innovative Approach for Image Steganography with Chaos. *Indonesian Journal of Electrical Engineering and Computer Science*, *11*(1), 263–267. doi:10.11591/ijeecs.v11.i1.pp263-267

Phadte, R. S., & Dhanaraj, R. (2017). Enhanced Blend of Image Steganography and Cryptography, *International IEEE Conference on Computing Methodologies and Communication (ICCMC)*, DOI: 10.1109/ICCMC.2017.8282682

Sabri, R. S., Din, R., & Mustapha, A. (2018). Analysis Review on Performance Metrics for Extraction Schemes in Text Steganography. *Indonesian Journal of Electrical Engineering and Computer Science*, *11*(2), 761–767. doi:10.11591/ijeecs.v11.i2.pp761-767

Soria L. A. and Berres, S. (2017). A Secure Steganographic Algorithm Based on Frequency Domain for the Transmission of Hidden Information, Hindawi, Security and Communication Networks, Article ID 5397082, 14 pages, Retrieved from: . doi:10.1155/2017/5397082

Trivedi, M. C. (2016). Analysis of Several Image Steganography Techniques in Spatial Domain: A Survey, *Proceedings of the Second International Conference on Information and Communication Technology for Competitive Strategies, Article No.* 84., 10.1145/2905055.2905294

Chapter 3
Digital Documents as Data Carriers and a Method of Data Management Guaranteeing the Unambiguity of the Recorded Information:
Ontology-Oriented Data Management and Document Databases

Jaroslaw Zelinski
https://orcid.org/0000-0002-8032-4720
Independent Researcher, UK

ABSTRACT

This study presents a method for the storage of data organized in digital documents, which is proven in practice. The discussed method does not bear any disadvantages of the relational model used for data organization, such as the loss of data context and complications evoked by the lack of data redundancy. The method presented here can be used for data organization into documents (digital and paper) as classified aggregates and for data classification. The study also describes a new metamodel for the data structure which assumes that documents, being data structures, form compact aggregates, classified as objects, or event descriptions, thus always assigning them a specific and unambiguous context. Furthermore, the study presents a design method for documents as context aggregates that allows leveling the disadvantages of the relational model and ensures efficient information management. The work also contains practical examples of the application of the described method.

DOI: 10.4018/978-1-7998-8587-0.ch003

INTRODUCTION

Numerous projects aiming at the management and digital processing of information have encountered the challenge of data model development. It is often assumed in advance that digital documents (hereinafter referred to as the document) are information organized as forms comprising specified fields and would be stored in a relational model. This model leads to the following condition: <document> = <dataset in relational model> + <SQL query to this set> (Shimura et al., 1999). In other words, documents can be considered as dynamically generated contents that do not exist as permanent entities (Umran Alrubaee et al., 2020). For comprehensive data models, the procedures entitled <SQL query to this set> are very complex, and their execution is time-consuming and demands high-processing power. In addition, the development and testing of procedures is costly due to a large amount of time dedicated by the specialists creating them. Moreover, introducing changes to these procedures in the software life cycle is equally costly.

The problem of many digital transformation projects is data ambiguity in the relational data model (Karnitis & Arnicans, 2015). The aim of this work was to develop a method that allows to organize data into structures as digital documents, so as to maintain their intelligibility and unambiguity.

RESEARCH METHODOLOGY

The source material used in this work is not large statistical data sets, but commonly available business document templates. In particular, in the field of finance and accounting, product management, property records and the archive of multimedia files. The key methods used in the work are conceptual models and object-oriented analysis. It is theoretical work. The application of the developed method is shown in the examples at the end of the study.

The methods described herein for the design of document data structures were previously applied by the author in several projects. The results of the projects demonstrated the advantage of this form of analysis and design of data structures in the process of knowledge management, in comparison to the methods that are based on the relational data model (Boumans, 2019).

Notional and object analysis and object modeling (Altan, 2020) were used as basic tools in the study. The following notation systems were used for documenting the results: Semantic Business Vocabulary and Rules (OMG.org, 2019), Unified Modeling Language (OMG.org, 2017) and Model Driven Architecture (Ambra Molesini et al., 2021; OMG.org, 2014). Furthermore, knowledge in the field of semantics (Sowa, 2000) and the notions of class, classifier, and object (OMG.org, 2017) were applied in the study. The aim of this paper is to describe the developed method, and not just present a review of the systems designed and implemented by the author.

BACKGROUND

Documents often contain a high volume of different data jointly forming multiple context datasets (aggregates). Application of relational model for the organization of such data leads to the generation of a comprehensive system of relational linked tables, while the removal of redundancies often results in the loss of content context of individual fields in the tables. This gives rise to a necessity to use the highly complex SQL queries so that these documents can be saved in and retrieved from this database. Thus, the database itself solely contains data deprived of the context present in tables, not the documents.

Many authors have pointed out the problem of complexity and the loss of uniform relational model context (Ślęzak et al., 2018). Those authors have suggested that contexts should be separated in large relational data models. However, recommendation of context separation (Evans, 2003; Fowler, 1997; Fowler & Rice, 2005), while maintaining the relational model, does not help to solve the issue completely (Awang et al., 2012, 2012, 2012).

Context change often alters the meaning of data (Danesi, 2004). Attempts made for maintaining the meaning of data frequently result in the formation of comprehensive relational data models, thus generating additional costs. Therefore, using one relational data model to save the contents of numerous different documents can make such a system an enormous and indivisible monolith, which is expensive to develop as well as maintain.

An approach has been utilized for this purpose, in which the software processes the document (its content) treating it as a standalone object, yet saving its content (individual fields) in a relational model (O'Neil, 2008). However, this results in increased work during the stage of system design and high demand for processing power at the time of reading and saving documents via an additional application layer; in this case, the layer is object-relational mapping (ORM). This issue is frequently referred to as the object-relational impedance mismatch (Ireland & Bowers, 2015).

The objective of the present study was to find an answer to the question why only approximately 10% of the IT system implementations are successful (The Standish Group International, Inc, 2015) and also to analyze whether a model different from the relational model of corporate data organization, which is often criticized for its inefficiency (Cook & Daniels, 1994), can help improve the efficiency of such projects. Author's field of study is the comparison of the models used for analysis and design and the metamodels used as a theory construction tool.

SOLUTIONS AND RECOMMENDATIONS

A system has been developed for standardizing the organization, storage, and processing of information. This allowed the development of a metamodel and a UML profile for the architecture of data modeling via the method designed for data organization into documents (Wei et al., 2018). Design methods for information gathering document structures were developed, based on the assumption that documents contain data aggregates (Papamarkos et al., 2015).

Information Processing

Information is always about something. In other words, it describes something that exists or could exist. If an information system is said to process information, it means that it processes data constituting the information saved. (Indeed, data may not carry any information, but this is not the subject of this study.)

Figure 1. Processing information about what exists and what happened

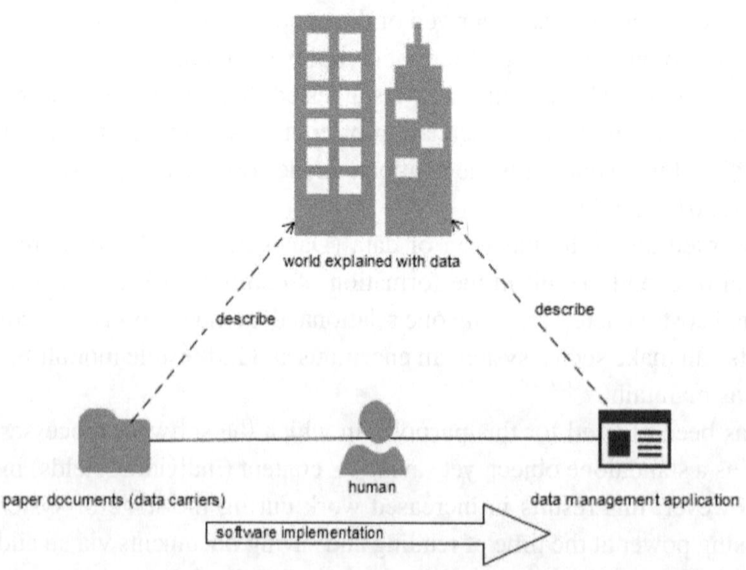

Figure 1 schematically represents the relationship between the real world (world explained with data), the data saved using traditional methods (paper documents which act as data carriers), and the data saved and processed with software (refers here to the data management application, see Computers, Models, and the Embedding World (B. C. Smith, 1985)).

In other words, paper documents (or data carriers) "carry" data that constitute specific information about the real world. Thus, they represent information on history—information about the state of the "real world" in the past. This can also be information about the future, for instance schedules or forecasts.

The aim behind the creation of software is to process the data comprising specified information that describes specified elements of the real world. The structure of these data should correspond to that of the described items (the information about the items being processed) (B. Smith, 1998; B. C. Smith, 1985). The invention of the computer opened up new possibilities for processing (implementation of software—direction of changes), but it does not alter the reality explained by the data processed therein, where the documents themselves also serve as the elements of reality.

Thus, it can be said that information describes an event or an object. Complex documents may contain numerous bits of information. However, it should be possible to assign the given document to one of the following types: object description or event description. This is because, as already said, one document may (should) have one context due to the required unambiguity of its content (context). Figure 2 presents explanation of this relationship.

Figure 2. Object and its history

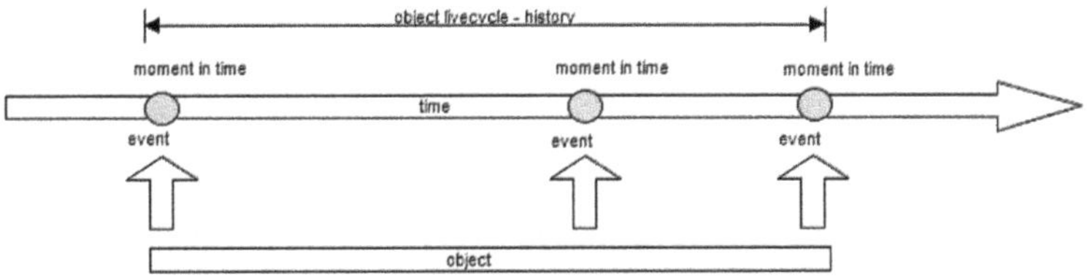

The figure shows one object and three events associated with it. This means that—as the author would like to postulate—four independent descriptions (documents) could exist: one describing the object and other three describing the events that took place. These four descriptions are four hypothetical documents; however, each would constitute a description of either an event or the object. The key is to assume that a document may have one of the two possible contexts: information on an object (object description) or information about an event (event description).

The notion of subject has been visualized and is explained in the "Expanded notion model." It has only two types: event and object, which agrees with Ackoff who indicated that "Data are symbols that represent the properties of objects and events. Information consists of processed data, the processing directed at increasing its usefulness. For example, census takers collect data. The Bureau of the Census processes that data, converting it into information that is presented in the numerous tables published in the Statistical Abstracts. Like data, information also represents the properties of objects and events, but it does so more compactly and usefully than data. The difference between data and information is functional, not structural." (Ackoff, 1999). This taxonomy is of key significance for the developed metamodel. Source of this division is the context of description, as shown in Figure 2. Object invariably exists over time and may be subject to change—it has a life cycle, but it lasts as a rule—and the changes are (maybe) the result of specific events, associated with the object. However, events do not have to alter the object and may only be "associated" with it. Objects and events are defined by their properties.

Specified time and place of an event is the factor that binds an event with an object. The object with which the event is associated constitutes an element of its description. Object invariably exists over time, and thus, the notion of life cycle is linked to it: object makes up its history. History of an object is a set of events associated with it (and participated by the object). Events and objects are described using properties. They must be unique (distinct from one another); however, the values of individual properties do not have to be unique (e.g. different events may have the same date, different events may have occurred in the same place). Values of properties are neither events nor objects, although they may bear a complex structure (e.g. full postal address is a value of a *location* property, yet it is neither an event nor an object), and hence, they are not subject type. Description subject is either an object or an event. If it is assumed that context determines the meaning of notions while description comprises notions, then a specific document may have only one context for its content to be unambiguous.

From the viewpoint of data processing, it does not matter whether the event is from the past or from the future, as both have the same properties (descriptive data: attributes). The notion of time is only important for the person interpreting the data (explained by A-theory and B-theory (Zimmerman, 2005)). Thus, an information system would chronologically sort the events, but determining whether a given event occurred in the past or will occur in the future requires correlating the date of the event (its property) with the date of the question. In other words, a question about "yesterday's events" will produce a different result every day, despite the fact that data on events are not subject to change.

Notion Model

During the study, documents that are commonly used in public and private entities, such as accounting documents, official letters, contracts, and memos, were also analyzed. The vocabulary that forms the content of these documents is very rich, yet the one used to describe the content (metadata, form field labels) is relatively less comprehensive. Furthermore, it has been determined that many bits of information are repeated on logically related documents, although the documents concern different issues and have different contexts.

Figure 3. Key notions

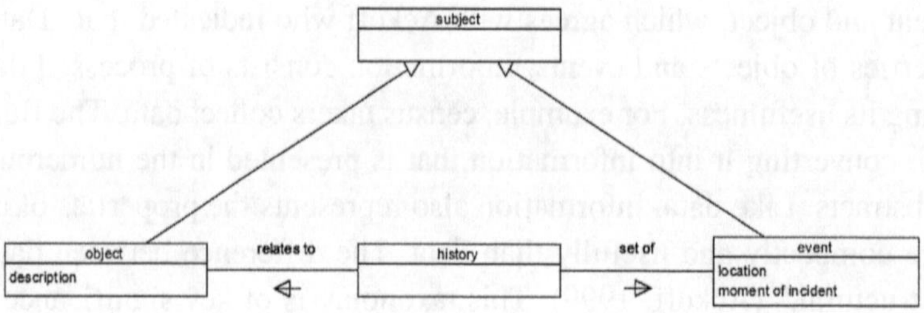

Figure 4. Expanded notion model

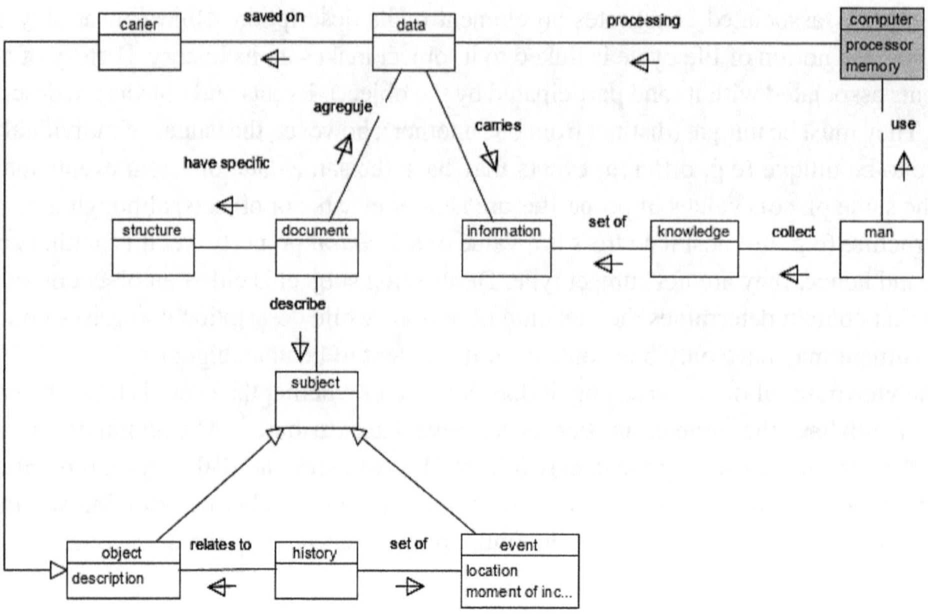

Each description, or description subject, independent of the form (structural or not), can be classified as an event description or as an object description. The defining property (i.e. constant) of an object is the fact that the object and its description exist, while the defining property of an event is the time and place of its occurrence. Both event and object may also have different properties (and this is normally the case). However, they do not determine the context classification of description subject.

The notion model is presented in Figure 3. Key notions have been expanded with additional notions from the problem area described herein. The expanded form of the notion model is presented in Figure 4. Furthermore, the model contains notions from the information processing area discussed above and the notion of a computer (also defined by properties: it has a processor and memory).

Data, as content, bear specified information (information means an understanding of the content). As described by the data, the real world consists of real, named elements of this world and its properties. Such data are considered as information on a specified subject. The specified subjects have been divided into two types: those describing objects and those describing events (Ackoff, 1999). Jointly, these notions form a concise namespace necessary to create the discussed metamodel. It is important to ensure that the introduction of the notion of a computer does not alter the meaning of the elements present in the remaining portion of the model, which can be considered as the "earlier" one. In other words, the addition of a computer (Figure 1) and its element (Data Management Application) should not alter the essence of collecting and processing information.

Figure 5. UML profile for document structure models

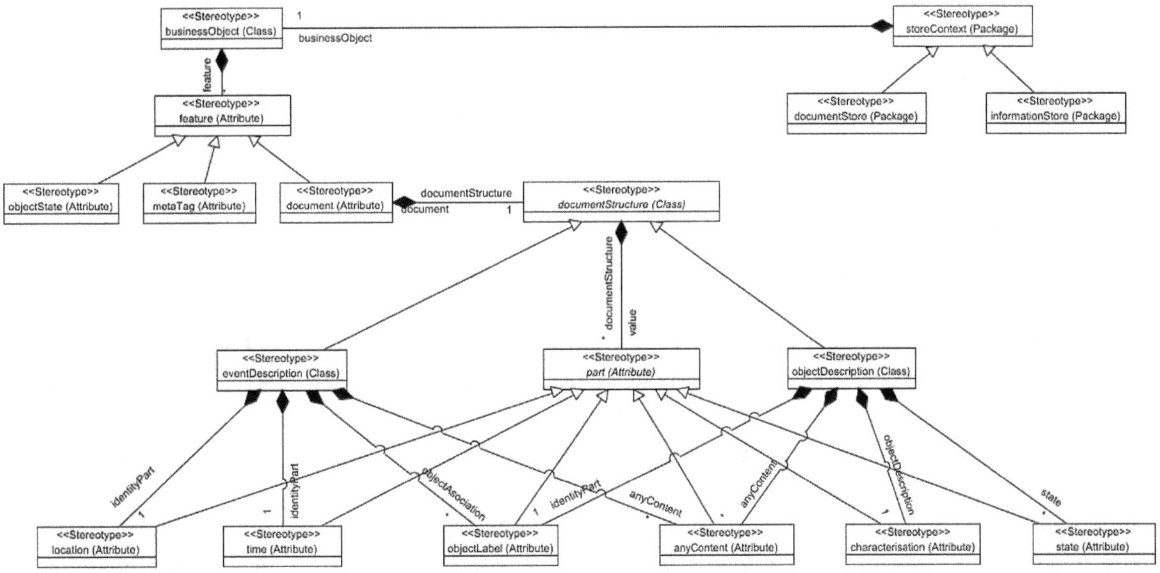

In the UML notation (OMG.org, 2017), the element structures are described via Structured Classifiers on Composite Structure Diagram. According to the specification of Metaobject Facility (OMG.org, 2016), additional intermediate layers are created in the M2 layer, which are metamodels comprising the so-called UML profiles. These are notional extensions (additional element types) of the standard notation elements. Based on the notion model (the "Expanded notion model" presented in Figure 4), a profile was developed for documents, which is illustrated in Figure 5.

Figure 6. Basic structure metamodel for two document classes

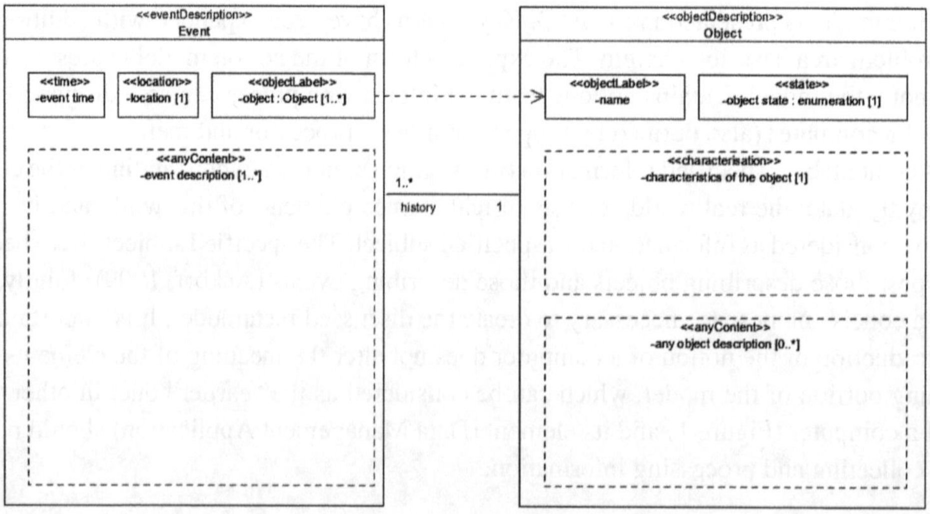

A document is a named data structure bearing an identity. Every document is classified as either eventDescription or objectDescription. A document classified as an eventDescription must contain two attributes, location and time, which as a pair forms the identifier of the event and at least one objectLabel attribute, thereby pointing to the objects associated with the event. On the other hand, a document classified as an objectDescription must possess the characterization attribute, which is its unique full description, and an identifier, which is an abbreviation of description or is assigned a unique objectLabel name. These identifiers determine the identity of documents. Object characteristics may be highly complex (long unique text, photograph, scheme, etc.), and thus each characteristic has its unique abbreviation or objectLabel.

Apart from these elements, documents may contain any additional content included in the anyContent attributes (Bézivin et al., 2011). This content can be of any type: text (string), unstructured, or structured (e.g. XML).

The content of a document may be determined (imposed) by its structure (fields and their names and content definitions). A set of documents should also have assigned context (storeContext). Each document is both an object as a content carrier (documentStore) and content with specified, classified type (informationStore). In other words, a document repository may contain all the documents of the given organization (company archives, records) or documents of the given class (e.g. property register).

Two Document Classes—Example

Key notions concerning the data organized in documents have been discussed, and a model was developed for their description and classification. It has been demonstrated that specific information constitutes either an event description or an object description. Furthermore, a UML profile was constructed enabling the modeling of those two structure types. In this subsection, the metamodels of the two document types are described.

Figure 7. Documents as attribute value

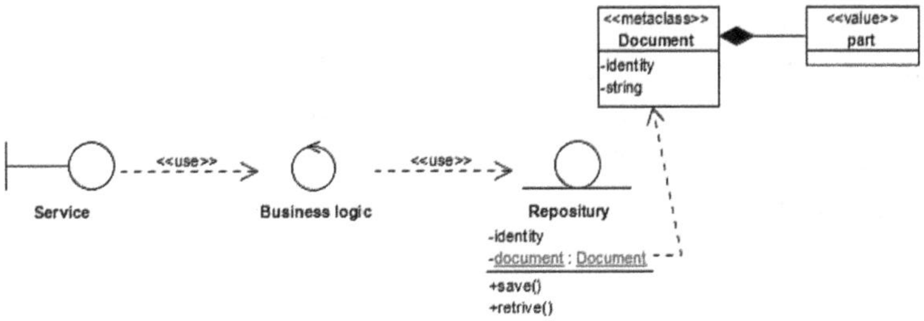

Figure 6 presents the metamodel for two document classes which determines the syntax for the profile depicted in Figure 5. The two document classes in the metamodel are labeled with appropriate stereotypes: eventDescription and objectDescription. Information structures of documents (documents) have been visualized with UML notation as composite structure diagram (Šilingas & Butleris, 2009).

Event description (signified with eventDescription stereotype) is identified via time and place of its occurrence and object (or objects) to which it refers. Object description (signified with objectDescription stereotype) is identified by its characteristics. In addition, it contains an abbreviation (identifier) of the characteristic (signified with objectLabel stereotype). This abbreviation is used as the unique object name instead of the long description signified as characterization.

The key property of event description (fact) is that it does not have a history status and such description does not have a life cycle. On the other hand, the key property of object description is that it lasts in time (exists) and has a life cycle (the object and the document constitute its description), a change history, and possibly the current status (signified with state stereotype). Object has a history, which is a collection of events related to it. The obligatory creation of the object is the key element of this history.

Apart from the aforementioned elements, every document may contain any amount of additional information resulting from the purpose of its creation. This information can be form fields, which are unstructured content that is either divided or not divided into sections. These elements have been signified with anyContent stereotype.

Therefore, each document, as a named and specified dataset, is unique and has an identifier (unique property). The elements of the content of a document (its properties) assume specified values referred to as VALUE. (Document property values do not themselves have an identity; instead, they belong to a document having an identity.) The structure of document content comprises elements that are properties of the described fact or object (unstructured description is also a property, an element of a document). Thus, document is the content (data) comprising notions arranged into sentences of natural language or form fields. The meaning of notions used in the document content provides the document context (meaning = word/character + context; (Danesi, 2004)).

The reason for introducing two document classes is related to their general rules of conduct (their processing). As a rule, documents containing descriptions of events (facts, histories) are not subject to modifications; they do not have a life cycle and describe the dynamics (facts) of the surrounding reality. By contrast, documents containing descriptions of objects may be modified, can have statuses, and represent real entities by existing in time.

These rules (event and object properties) are contrasting and thus cannot refer to the same dataset (document) simultaneously. This is the reason for the creation of the present metamodel which assumes that documents carrying content must be classified as one of those two (and only two) basic types.

The information management method discussed in the present paper is used to organize data into documents. A document can be any character string (e.g. XML or JSON) (Tomaszuk, 2010). Figure 7 presents the architecture for the implementation of application service using the BCE model (Jarosław Żeliński, 2019). The Repository component stores the complete document as the attribute value: Document (e,g, XML string). All business rules of the document content are realized by the Business Logic component.

Figure 8. Domain context vs. document classification

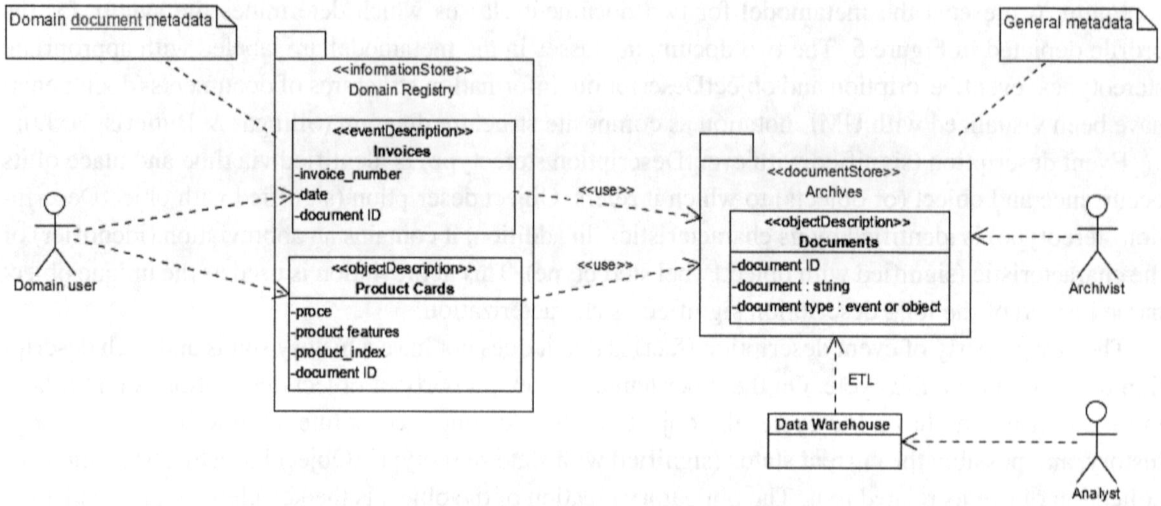

From the perspective of their content, documents have specified domain contexts and belong to a determined type: an object description or an event description. Domain systems require the separation of these contexts. However, a document archive has a specific context, where any content is an object. In an archive (records management), all the documents are stored objects and are described with one common set of general-purpose metadata (document classification). An example procedure is shown in Figure 8.

In the context of managing sales, Invoices are descriptions of events (who, to whom, when, at what price, what was sold), while Product Sheets are descriptions of objects (products). However, the company archive, or Document archive, comprises the Documents (records), where each document is considered an object (object in the archive). The discussed architecture, consisting mainly of Domain register and Documents archive, enables the designing and implementation of any information management system and ensures that any domain register can be created in the future without any changes to the current implementation and the retained data. Document archive stores physical documents that are classified using the general-purpose metadata, whereas domain registers comprise only the domain metadata. In the domain registers, documents are classified according to the established domain notions in the set context. One of the metadata contained in a domain register is the link to the physical archive. Moreover, domain registers are digital archives, which can be created and removed without damaging the physical documents. Thus, a new digital archive can be created any time, which shall require a one-time classification of historical documents. If one assumes that those documents (their content) have a structured form (e.g. XML), then this may take place automatically.

The architecture presented in Figure 8 contains the Data Warehouse component, which stores the collected data in a format that allows their mass processing for statistical purposes.

Figure 9. Architecture of sales system information

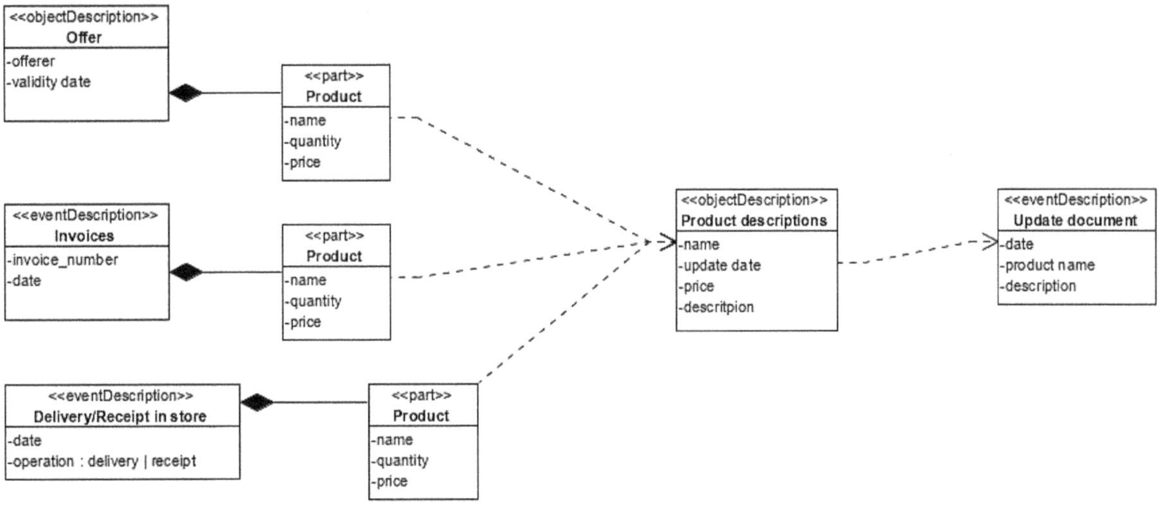

EXAMPLES FOR THE USE OF THE DISCUSSED THEORY

Many design patterns and known software implementations for business are associated with the successes and fails of their implementations. The so-called best practice is the effect of experience gathered, often based on numerous failures (The Standish Group International, Inc, 2015). This section shows in several examples how discussed theory aims at explaining the causes for such failures and successes. This is not a cross-sectoral study, but an attempt at assessing the efficacy of the proposed theory on selected examples, assumed as representative.

The key will be the definition explained in the text: an event is an entity which does not last in time understood as fact, object is an entity lasting in time. Formation and changes of an object are described by facts, object as such has its own description. Consequently, a "single information" may only concern only a fact or object. Information is a specified dataset called document. The basic stage of analysis of an information system is the classification of datasets for descriptions of events or objects. Dataset understood as a document has one context: description of an event or description of an object.

The most common applications on the business system market are Enterprise Management Systems, workflow, archival databases (Eden et al., 2014). The differences between the idealization discussed thus far and the actual implementation and the consequences of possible differences will be presented on examples of such systems.

Figure 10. Code architecture for sales supporting application

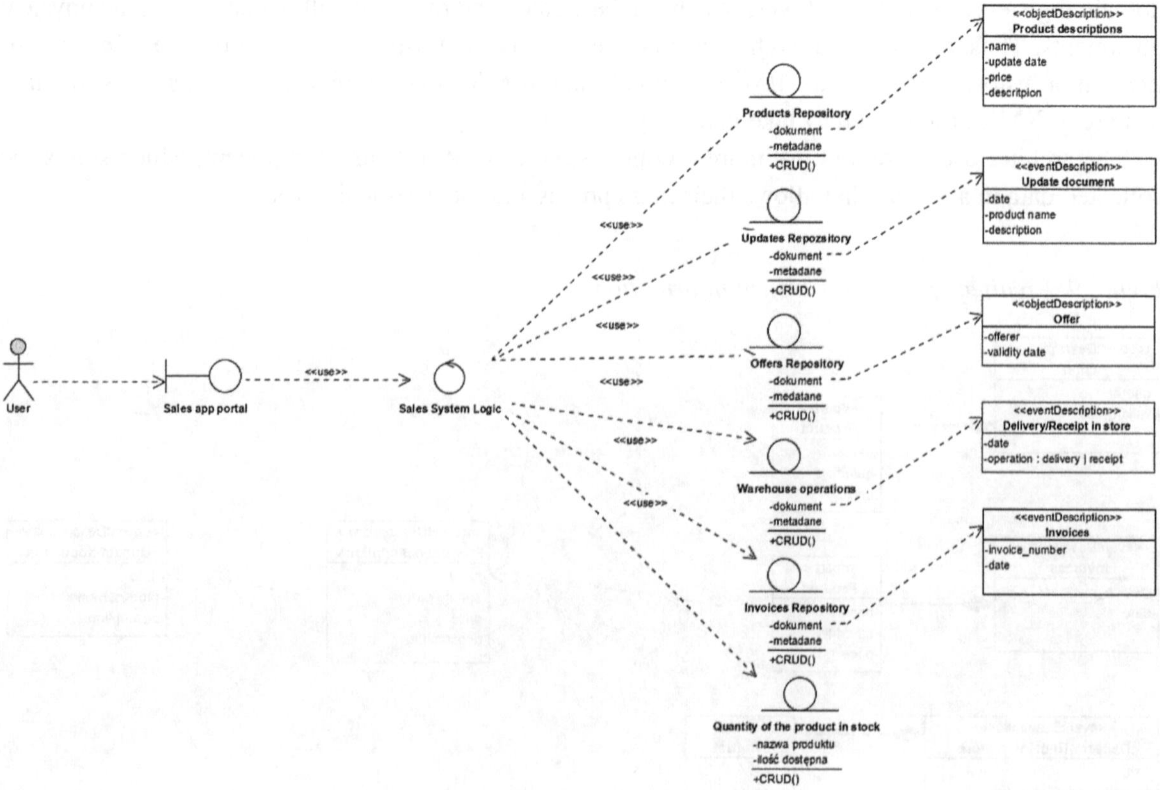

Sales System

Sales supporting systems, in their minimal form, manage such documents as product descriptions, offer, sales invoices. Therefore, there are three types of documents.

Sales support system is a set of information about what is offered, what was sold and when. Figure 9. Architecture of sales system information shows the architecture of sales system information created on the basis of the described metamodel. The diagram was developed using the UML notation. Classes represent documents (data sets). Documents were classified as objectDescription or eventDescription. This means that each document was attributed with one and only one context.

Offer is a document containing data of the offerer and a list (collection) of product names and their prices. These dates have been copied from Product Description documents. This document further includes e.g. validity date (for legal purposes). Offer, as a data set, is classified as object description, because its content constitutes a lasting in time description of what the company offers.

Invoices are documents describing events, that is the fact that a sales transaction has been made on the given day. Document contains data describing sold products, these are information copied from Product Description documents.

Here it should be noted that the relationship between using UML (the directed dotted line indicates the source) is not a relationship known from ER models describing data structures. None of the data here are shared. Documents retain full separation, and the selected data are copied from source documents.

Figure 11. Book rental system-notion model (SVBR, fact diagram)

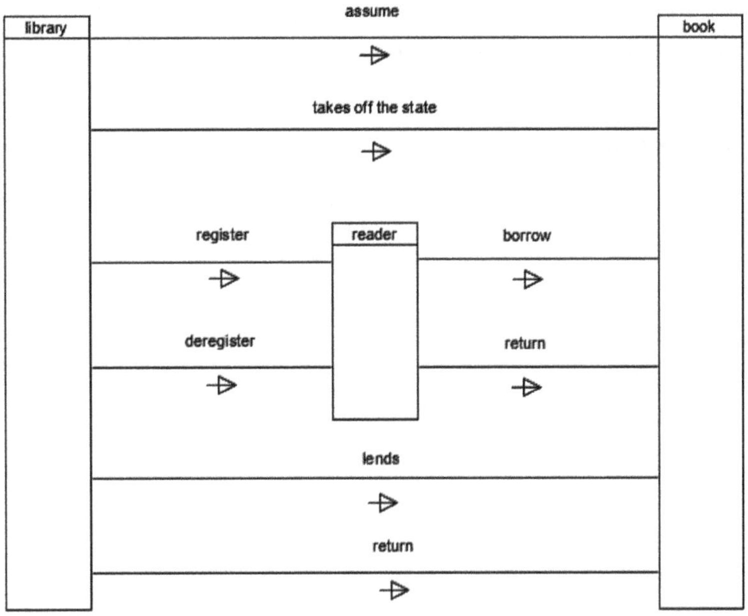

Thanks to this each document has an independent lifecycle, and its existence does not depend on the further existence of source documents.

Documents named Product Descriptions are product descriptions that last in time and are used on an ongoing basis to create offers and invoices. Product descriptions can be occasionally updated, each such update is an event described with Update document.

The elements marked on the diagram as objectDescription and eventDescription are documents. Some include collections of information on objects, to which they refer (Offer, Invoices). Such system for grouping and storing information allows creating and adding new documents and altering the structure of the existing ones throughout the lifecycle of the whole system, because each of the documents constitute a value of one object attribute that stores it. Retaining document classification into event descriptions and object descriptions guarantees that introducing changes to this structure would not be transferred into historical documents. These documents do not share any data. The guarantee of coherence of document structures is their common ontology (namespace) (Gomes et al., 2020).

Figure 10. Code architecture for sales supporting application presents the possible architecture of application code architecture used to manage sales information. The diagram utilized the pattern and symbols of BCE classes (Boundary, Control, Entity). The entity components in document attributes store documents (sets of data classified as eventDescription or objectDescription). Data saved as documents are encapsulated in repositories. The whole business logic is transferred outside of data, as an effect it is possible to change document structures (data) without the risk to harm the whole application. The use of the metamodel described will enable the proper distribution of information in documents and determination of their roles in the system: for instance, primary data describing products are not introduced in the offer, but in product description (and such descriptions shall be created). A common cause for management problems in PLM (Product Lifecycle Management) systems could be observed by the author in PLM systems, where offer fulfilled the role of product description, and as an effect it was not possible to properly manage historical contracts with offers as attachments. Repositories have typical CRUD (Create, Retrieve, Update, Delete) operations, attributes are the metadata and document, whose value is a document content (e.g. in the form of XML).

Figure 12. Library information architecture

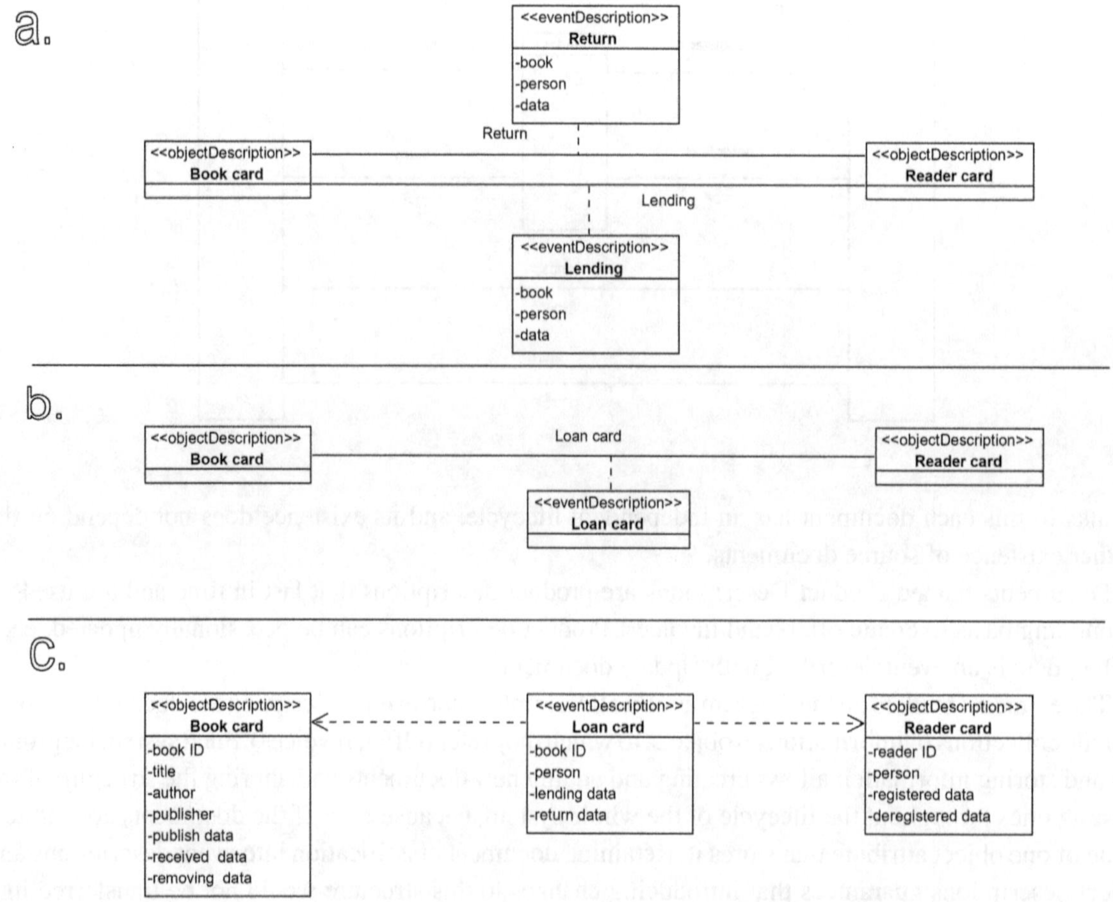

Book Rental System

The discussed Sales system is easy to design, because documents can be here easily classified as events or objects. The case of rental system is more complex because the classification of documents and what they describe (document) is not as obvious as in the above sales system. Here the question arises how many documents there will be and of what type?

Figure 11. Book rental system-notion model shows three key notions: library, book, reader. It is a simple notion model expressed with the use of SBVR (omg.org) notation as a fact diagram. These notions are connected with typical facts of the domain. In this case, which is more difficult than sales, it is significant to make a design decision concerning what data and how organized into documents shall be designed as implementation. The metamodel described earlier requires that such documents are either

description of event or object. The notion analysis, the product of which is this fact diagram assists in this: we have three notions classified as objects and eight facts associated with them. In a library context: assumes return and lends have their analogs in the context of reader borrows and returns.

Figure 13. Library application architecture

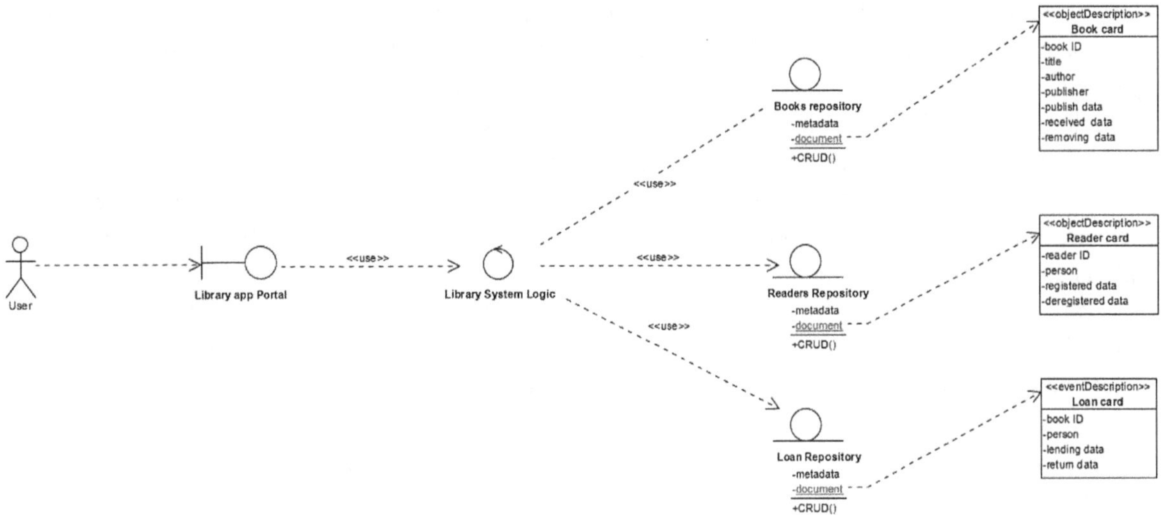

Based on the notion model, a structural model was created, which is illustrated in Figure 12. Library information architecture.

By analyzing the notion model in Figure 11. Book rental system-notion model we determine that lending and return concerns a book, so these are the same facts seen from the perspective of a library and reader. Thus, we deal with not eight but six facts.

Another thing in this analysis is the determination what constitutes (should be) a separate document. Problem domain analysis tells us that:

- Book can be received in the stock and removed from the stock of the library,
- Reader can be registered and deregistered,
- Book can be lent multiple times to various readers and the same reader multiple times.

Following the metamodel description, events concern different objects and they can be numerous and it is unknown how many. For this reason, data on an event are generally organized into separate documents. However, if a given object is associated with a predetermined number of facts and this is an immanent feature of these objects, it can be assumed that these facts are features of these objects and not separate entities. The next stages of work on the final information architecture models are shown in Figure 12. Library information architecture.

Objects and facts are represented by the documents that describe them. The relationship between reader and book are the facts of borrowing and returning the book by the reader. The facts are documented. In Figure 12. Library information architecture a. shows the first version of the information model (UML notation class diagram). Analysis of the domain allows the assumption that borrowing is strictly linked to book return (the number of returns is identical to borrowings, at this point we neglect the possibility for book loss), which gives us the right to combine these two facts in one document. This is shown in Figure 12. Library information architecture b. As stated before: dates of receiving and removing a book from the stock are book features, while dates of registration and deregistration of a reader are reader's features. Therefore, separate documents for these facts are not created, they are made attributes of book and reader, respectively.

However, every fact of borrowing a book is documented, so the loan cards will be numerous and it is impossible to predict how many of them will exist. Therefore, the borrowings will be documented on separate Cards. The final version of the information model is illustrated in Figure 12. Library information architecture c. This diagram (UML class diagram) shows a model of relationships, that is a Loan card utilizes the content of Reader card and Book card documents.

Figure 13. Library application architecture shows the possible architecture of the Library System application. The repositories are separate. None of the data here are shared as well. The Library System Logic is also responsible for their coherence.

Advantages of the method discussed in this study are primarily independence of documents and the possibility for their alteration during system operation. The independence of repositories allows conversion of each of them, at any time, into an integration adapter for a different, external application having an analogous repository. For example, if it were a university library, it is possible to easily resign from the local reader base and integrate with a university student base without the need to modify other components. The ability to freely change the structure allows adding new functionalities at any later time. For example, the charging and registering of a penalty for holding a book requires only adding the charging logic to the component Library System Logic and adding the attributes Actual number of days of borrowing and Penalty fee to the Lend card document (calculated in the component Library System Logic). As a result, the Loan Card document will always contain complete information about each borrowing, the retrieval of such information by the User requires only a simple Retrieve (document) command without the requirement to create a complex SQL query to the database, as is the case in the relational data storage model.

Workflow System

The third example to be discussed is workflow management software. In this case, tasks to be completed form the main context. Their management requires (may require) establishing task deadlines and the subject on which the work is to be done.

Figure 14. Workflow-key notions

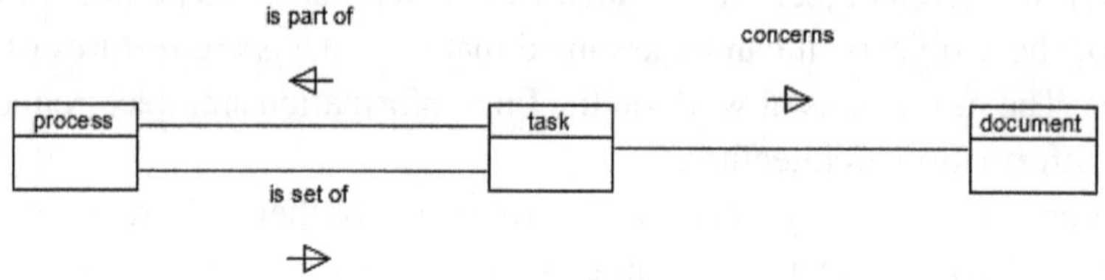

Figure 15. Workflow system-information architecture

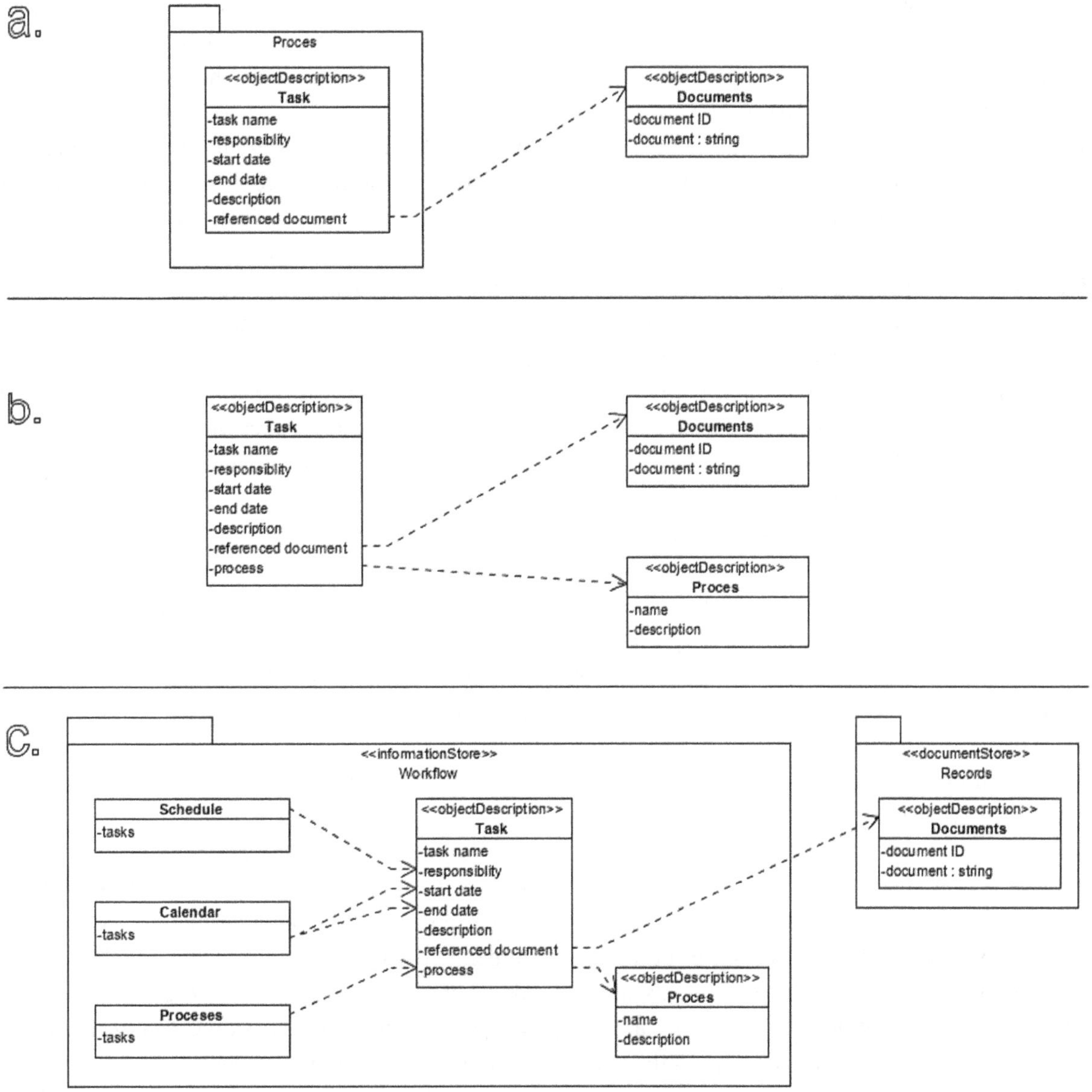

Workflow is another specific software system. In practically 100% it comprises of task management, yet in this case no independent events exist.

The most frequently mentioned process definitions, e.g. one in the BPMN notation specification, say that a process is a task or a specific sequence of tasks with a specific purpose. Due to the fact that information management is described, it is assumed that this goal is a specific content, i.e. a document (data carrying information).

Figure 14. Workflow-key notions present key notions included in process definition: process, task, document. In the chapter Book rental system it is shown that in some cases certain events are features of an object (it should be recalled here that object is here referred to as what lasts over time), so their description is an element of the content of a document classified as an object description. Task lasts in time, so it is an object, the events that are the beginning and end of the task are its features, therefore they are part of the content of the document describing the event. It should be recalled here that invoice is a document that describes one specific event, a sales transaction. On the other hand, task is defined as work (period) from its start to its end. As it can be seen, events are features of the task, the event described as "start of work" is by itself devoid of context: it is difficult to process information about the moments when work is commenced. Indeed, it can be envisaged that there are independent records of commencements of certain works and when they are completed, but no value is achieved apart from the complexity of managing such data. However, if, as discussed in the present study, it is determined that since the facts of the beginning and end of the work are inherent in this work, it can be recognized that the task and the time of its beginning and ending is one entity lasting in time, and so from the perspective of information about something it can be classified as an object.

The notion of processes in Figure 14. Workflow-key notions have a different nature. It should be recalled here that a term in the dictionary is the name of a class of designations which are specific occurrences of an ordered set of works. Developed offers and Product manufacture will constitute separate processes. Each of these processes will be realized multiple times. Thus, we have process name and perhaps its description which is its characterization.

The notion model presented in Figure 14. Workflow-key notions have been transformed into information architecture presented in Figure 15. Workflow system-information architecture. Its upper part, marked with letter a., shows preliminary version, that is tasks associated with documents to which they refer. These tasks are grouped as elements of a single process (it is possible that the process is one task). The central portion of the same diagram marked with letter b. shows the target version of the model: the package as a grouping element has been implemented as the value of the Process attribute of the Task classifier. Finally, three independent repositories of documents classified as objectDescription are obtained: Task, Document, Process.

In reference to the content of Figure 8. Domain context vs. document classification, the target version of the workflow system architecture can be created shown in the bottom part of the Figure 15. Workflow system-information architecture marked with letter c. Two separate components exist here: System archive and workflow. The former stores processed documents, the latter stores information about tasks related to the documents. These documents are the products of tasks and their inputs (e.g. a request from a client for a document in the archive, an offer prepared for a client is also a document in the archive). Document class objects store content as the value of the document attribute: string.

Such architecture does not have the disadvantage of workflow systems based on the state machine design pattern, which assumes that the tasks in the process are the statuses of the document processed within the process. This disadvantage consists in the inability to implement processes in which many different documents appear, e.g. the business process of handling inquiries processes the documents: request for proposal, price calculation, technical description, and combines the whole into one offer as a document constituting a product of the process. If the carrier of the process in state machine is e.g. an invoice, it is difficult to easily add documents constituting attachments to the process, such as e.g. acceptance protocol. The architecture model described here does not bear this disadvantage.

Figure 16. Workflow system-Application architecture

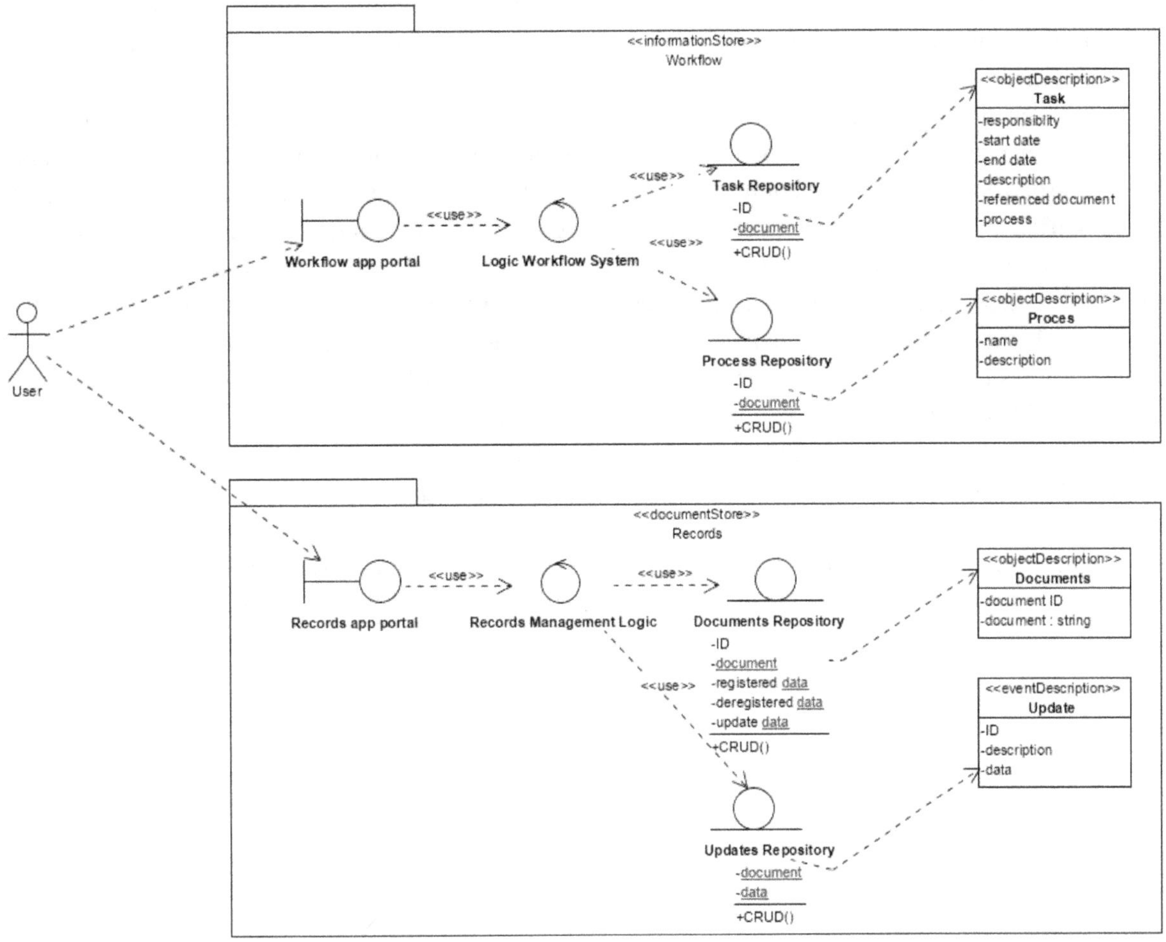

Figure 16. Workflow system-Application architecture illustrates the architecture of the Workflow application. This time there are two separate domain components, because each has a different context, which should be separated. The workflow component is a site where the data about tasks and processes exist. Both the process and the task are objects within the meaning of the meta-model described here. They are classified in this manner because, according to the given definition: an object is what lasts in time. Facts such as the start or end date of a task are elements of the definition of the task notion (attribute definition: a task is something that has a beginning and an end), thus these facts are not processed as separate entities as they would not have an identity (value object). As an effect, these two events form in principle the integral part of the Event object.

Process class objects only bear description, and they fulfill the role of a glossary (list) of processes: Each Task must be assigned to the given process, which is recorded as the process attribute value. It can be assumed that sets of tasks for each process are additionally stored as templates (this is not shown in the diagram so as not to add complexity). The planning scenario (process design) realized by the user can have two versions. The first one is the creation of new tasks and each assignment of them to the specified process (it is then as process occurrence, whose name and description contains a Process class object). The second version is the commencement of planning from selecting a specified process and creation of tasks in the context of this choice (then the value of process attribute is set automatically without the participation of the user). The second scenario is recommended because it minimizes the number of errors.

The System archive component bears a certain specificity. In a document archive the context consists of the documents as such, and not their content. Since each document has a date of creation, it may also have a date of destruction (e.g. deletion from the archive as part of the data retention management process), it is classified as an objectDescription because in the context of an archive, the document lasts in time.

A frequently required functionality of an archive is updating the content o af document. Two scenarios are possible here. A simple version is an update via overwriting (replacing) the old version with the new one. This is equivalent to inserting a new document into the archive in place of another one. Such functionality is highly hazardous because it allows for unintentional and irreversible damage of a document. This defect is removed by adding an Update Repository to the System Archive. This document is classified as a fact: update event, that is as eventDescription according to the definition: the event has one date. Figure 16. Workflow system-Application architecture does not present the details of an update. An example is the popular architectural design pattern, Event Sourcing, often combined with the architectural pattern known as CQRS. Authors describing these patterns mention their benefits and best practices as the source. The metamodel developed here explains the reasons for their efficiency.

Figure 17. Workflow system component architecture.

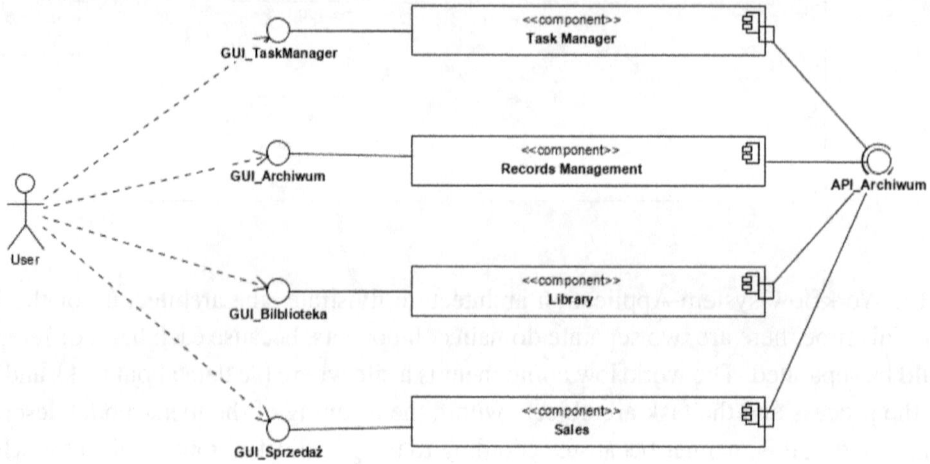

Figure 16. Workflow system-Application architecture presents the internal architecture of a workflow type system. It consists of two key context components: Workflow and System archive. These components should constitute separate structures.

Market has shown that workflow systems and archives are often offered as separate applications. This is highly convenient, as the document archive can be shared between functionally dedicated components. Figure 17. Workflow system component architecture presents architecture of an application of a hypothetical company, including applications described on the basis of examples. It should be noted here that applications also possess their main context. Workflow software, commonly offered on the marked as Task Manager bears the context of task management. Library often consists of internal systems of technical documentation management and the management of the information about who and when used it. Sales, often referred to as CRM (Customer Relationship Management) is the management of tasks related to customer service. However, all applications also require to work on specified documents (and files in the broader sense). Thus, sharing document repository, as shown in Figure 17. Workflow system component architecture is a good solution.

FUTURE RESEARCH DIRECTIONS

Numerous studies in the literature evoke the question of document structuralization; however, the author of this study was not able to find a generalized description in the form of a metamodel. Intuitive application of the XML format can be observed in some works, but such a method mainly consists in saving the content of XML documents in databases with the relational structure in the form of XML token mapping onto table columns (Shimura et al., 1999).

The essence of the discussed approach is to completely avoid treating documents and their fields as tables and their columns. This allows almost infinite freedom, both for data storage and for changing their structure after saving. Development of content access policies is considerably easier at the level of documents compared to their fields: instead of creating new rules for individual document fields, a new document with altered structure (information content) and rules for the entire document are created (determined name structure is a document class). Documents that are known for years (contracts, orders, invoices, warehouse releases, etc.) were often intuitively created as dedicated separate sets of redundant data. An example is an invoice, which contains data on product prices, and an almost identical order release document not having prices listed, which is needed to release sold goods from a warehouse and also orders the warehousemen to perform this operation without informing them about the transaction prices of the goods.

This form of data organization is used solely to manage data, and thus all calculations and statistics are performed using data copies organized differently in the Business Intelligence, BigData, Data Warehouse. Data storage in the form of documents with a well-structured shape, described in detail by means of dictionaries (namespaces) or embedded in a specific ontology (Musavi & Hashemi, 2018), allows for their smooth and quick transfer to the data warehouse using ETL (Extract, Transform, Load) processes. This process is much simpler than using the relational model.

The information management method presented in this paper has been successfully applied by the author to design and implement software for public administration and industry.

Further works are being conducted on the described metamodel and methods of its usage. These works are aimed at generalizing the knowledge management methods, constructing metamodels for decision-making systems based on the information gathered, and replacing the traditional relational data management models in Enterprise Resource Management systems with the model presented here. The planned next stage of work is to create documentation of contextual design patterns based on the concepts of event and object, based on the presented examples.

They also focus on the application of the discussed method in mechatronic device models with the use of the SysML notation (OMG.org). Internet of Things (IoT), replacing selected mechanical and electrical components with computers (drivers, information presentation systems, etc.) in many cases disable the use of a centralized relational data model (component separation is required). Transition to document model remains complies with message-based communication systems, where recognizing that each message is a document greatly simplifies analyses and design of heterogeneous (mechatronics) component systems.

CONCLUSION

The examples discussed herein: Sales system, Book rental system and Workflow system were aimed at presenting the utilization of the metamodel described in this study and the method of its use in the analysis and design of information management systems. It has been shown that organizing data into documents taking into account their context and assuming that this context can only be an event or an object enables solving the problem (or reducing the risk of its occurrence), which is the initial quick launch of the system and its future expansion without the need for any interference in historical records. The discussed metamodel enables a user to easily address the locations of new data in the structure of documents, because they are either a feature of an event or a feature of an object, and it is only necessary to determine which. The examples show that with the solutions and obtained positive effects, result of many years of experience, can be explained and used to consciously create data structures and application architectures in a way that gives a high probability of low maintenance and development costs.

REFERENCES

Ackoff, R. L. (1999). From data to wisdom. In *Ackoff's Best* (pp. 170–172). John Wiley & Sons.

Altan, Z. (Ed.). (2020). *Applications and approaches to object oriented software design: Emerging research and opportunities*. Engineering Science Reference, an imprint of IGI Global. doi:10.4018/978-1-7998-2142-7

Awang, M. K., Labadu, N. L., & Campus, G. B. (2012). Transforming object oriented data model to relational data model. *New Comput. Archit. Appl, 2*(3), 402–409.

Bézivin, J., Soley, R. M., & Vallecillo, A. (2011). Model-Driven Interoperability: MDI 2010. In J. Dingel & A. Solberg (Eds.), *Models in Software Engineering* (Vol. 6627, pp. 145–149). Springer Berlin Heidelberg., doi:10.1007/978-3-642-21210-9_14

Boumans, W. (2019). *A comprehensive meta model for the current data landscape*. Academic Press.

Cook, S., & Daniels, J. (1994). *Designing object systems: Object-oriented modelling with Syntropy*. Prentice Hall.

Danesi, M. (2004). *Messages, signs, and meaning: A basic textbook in semiotics and communication theory* (3rd ed.). Canadian Scholars' Press Inc.

Eden, R., Sedera, D., & Tan, F. (2014). Sustaining the Momentum: Archival Analysis of Enterprise Resource Planning Systems (2006–2012). *Communications of the Association for Information Systems, 35*. Advance online publication. doi:10.17705/1CAIS.03503

Evans, E. (2003). *Domain-Driven Design*. Pearson Education.

Fowler, M. (1997). *Analysis patterns: Reusable object models*. Addison Wesley.

Fowler, M., & Rice, D. (2005). *Architektura systemów zarządzania przedsiębiorstwem: Wzorce projektowe* (P. Koronkiewicz & P. Rajca, Trans.). Helion.

Gomes, S. B., Santoro, F. M., & Mira da Silva, M. (2020). An Ontology for BPM in Digital Transformation and Innovation. *International Journal of Information System Modeling and Design*, *11*(2), 52–77. doi:10.4018/IJISMD.2020040103

Ireland, C., & Bowers, D. (2015). *Exposing the Myth: Object-Relational Impedance Mismatch is a Wicked Problem*. http://oro.open.ac.uk/43318/1/download.php_articleid%3Ddbkda_2015_2_10_50020

Karnitis, G., & Arnicans, G. (2015). Migration of Relational Database to Document-Oriented Database: Structure Denormalization and Data Transformation. *2015 7th International Conference on Computational Intelligence, Communication Systems and Networks*, 113–118. 10.1109/CICSyN.2015.30

Musavi, S. A., & Hashemi, M. R. (2018). *A Method for Ontology-based Architecture Reconstruction of Computing Platforms*. ArXiv Preprint ArXiv:1811.02748.

O'Neil, E. J. (2008). Object/relational mapping 2008: Hibernate and the entity data model (edm). *Proceedings of the 2008 ACM SIGMOD International Conference on Management of Data*, 1351–1356. 10.1145/1376616.1376773

OMG.org. (2016, October). *MetaObject Facility*. https://www.omg.org/spec/MOF

OMG.org. (2017, December). *About the Unified Modeling Language Specification Version 2.5.1*. https://www.omg.org/spec/UML/

OMG.org. (2019, December). *About the Semantics Of Business Vocabulary And Rules Specification Version 1.5*. https://www.omg.org/spec/SBVR/

Papamarkos, G., Zamboulis, L., & Poulovassilis, A. (2015). *Xml Databases*. School of Computer Science and Information Systems, Birkbeck College, University of London. http://www.dcs.bbk.ac.uk/~sven/adm08/xmlDBs.pdf

Shimura, T., Yoshikawa, M., & Uemura, S. (1999). Storage and Retrieval of XML Documents Using Object-Relational Databases. In T. J. M. Bench-Capon, G. Soda, & A. M. Tjoa (Eds.), *Database and Expert Systems Applications* (Vol. 1677, pp. 206–217). Springer Berlin Heidelberg. doi:10.1007/3-540-48309-8_19

Šilingas, D., & Butleris, R. (2009). Towards implementing a framework for modeling software requirements in MagicDraw UML. *Information Technology and Control*, *38*(2).

Ślęzak, D., Glick, R., Betliński, P., & Synak, P. (2018). A new approximate query engine based on intelligent capture and fast transformations of granulated data summaries. *Journal of Intelligent Information Systems*, *50*(2), 385–414. doi:10.100710844-017-0471-6

Smith, B. (1998). *Basic concepts of formal ontology*. Academic Press.

Smith, B. C. (1985). The Limits of Correctness. *SIGCAS Comput. Soc., 14-15*(1-4), 18–26. doi:10.1145/379486.379512

Sowa, J. F. (2000). Ontology, Metadata, and Semiotics. In B. Ganter & G. W. Mineau (Eds.), *Conceptual Structures: Logical, Linguistic, and Computational Issues* (Vol. 1867, pp. 55–81). Springer Berlin Heidelberg. doi:10.1007/10722280_5

The Standish Group International, Inc. (2015). *Chaos Report 2015*. https://www.standishgroup.com/sample_research_files/CHAOSReport2015-Final.pdf

Tomaszuk, D. (2010). Document-oriented triplestore based on RDF/JSON. *Studies in Logic, Grammar and Rhetoric*, (22), 130.

Umran Alrubaee, A., Cetinkaya, D., Liebchen, G., & Dogan, H. (2020). A Process Model for Component-Based Model-Driven Software Development. *Information (Basel)*, *11*(6), 302. doi:10.3390/info11060302

Wei, B., Sun, J., & Wang, Y. (2018). A Knowledge Engineering Approach to UML Modeling (S). *SEKE*, 60–63.

Żeliński, J. (2019). Synthesis of MOF, MDA, PIM, MVC, and BCE Notations and Patterns. In *Applications and Approaches to Object-Oriented Software Design: Emerging Research and Opportunities*. IGI Global. https://www.igi-global.com/book/applications-approaches-object-oriented-software/235699

Zimmerman, D. W. (2005). The A-Theory of Time, The B-Theory of Time, and 'Taking Tense Seriously'. *Dialectica*, *59*(4), 401–457. doi:10.1111/j.1746-8361.2005.01041.x

KEY TERMS AND DEFINITIONS

Document Database: A class of non-relational, sometimes called NoSQL database, the document data model has become the most popular alternative to tabular, relational databases.

Notion Model (Also Fact Model, Conceptual Schema): Represented by a set of sentences, each of which connotes either a rule or a ground fact (OMG.org, 2019).

Object Paradigm: A paradigm that recognizes that the system is built of independent and encapsulated objects with specific responsibilities.

Chapter 4

Management and Digitalization Strategy for Transforming Education Sector:

An Emerging Gateway Persuaded by COVID-19

Esha Jain
https://orcid.org/0000-0002-0152-8566
The NorthCap University, Gurugram, India

Jonika Lamba
The NorthCap University, Gurugram, India

ABSTRACT

The digitalization of the education sector has led to continuous learning that is beneficial for the students as well as teachers despite facing the medical emergency in the country due to the COVID-19 crisis. It was found that the impact of COVID-19 on the transformation of education has both positive and negative outlooks. The negative impact was that all educational organizations/institutions shut down and examinations got postponed or delayed, but nothing stopped totally. It was also found that due to this pandemic, the educational system has taken a new turn and got evolved in an unimagined way. Teachers and faculty members are positively adapting and managing the digitalization strategy for education and make optimum use of digital media. COVID-19 has provided an opportunity for teachers to upgrade their skills and knowledge by joining multidisciplinary courses available online, and it was also found that computer courses taught online were much more effective than theoretical subjects taught via online applications, but lengthy online lectures cause fatigue and boredom.

DOI: 10.4018/978-1-7998-8587-0.ch004

INTRODUCTION

Digital transformation is the combination of improved innovation into all regions of a business, in a general sense changing how you work and deliver an enticement to clients. It is moreover a societal transformation that anticipates associations to persistently stir things up, explore, and get settle up with disillusionment. Education is one of the most important sectors in the economy that will decide the future of students in the country. India is moving towards the path of digitalization in every possible sector of the economy and using combinations of information and communication technology to ease the process of digitization such as e-commerce, e-governance, e-media, etc. The life of people has been moving at a fast pace and everyone wants to make optimum use of their time. The use of digital technologies has changed the face of education in our country. The learning of students has increased at a fast pace because they have the flexibility to access the educational materials when they require it. The usage of technology in the education sector has increased the interaction between a teacher and a student because teachers can focus on the weak points of a student with the help of assessment reports generated in online teaching software. Digitalization in education alludes to the utilization of workstations, cell phones, the Internet, programming applications, and different sorts of advanced innovation to show understudies all things considered. Test-taking utilizing a PC, online colleges, digital books, and edutainment are only a couple of instances of digitalization in instruction today. A few instructors and innovation evangelists accept that inevitably, training will be a completely computerized interest strengthened by man-made consciousness and augmented reality. The traditional method of teaching is now replaced with the help of computers, i-pods, mobiles, smartphones, tablets, etc. which have revolutionized the method of learning. With the help of digital learning experts and teachers from the diverse field can come together to a common platform and enrich the students about different cultures and values that are followed across nations this will help the students to grow in every aspect of life. Digital technologies have innovated the way of learning across nations. Information and communication technology have simplified the learning process with the help of online content development and management. There are two aspects of digital education one from the perspective of students and others from the perspective of teachers. The digital technologies have to lead to the emergence of learning online in the present scenario of COVID-19 where it's not possible to take classes physically in the school and colleges premises the information technology application such as Microsoft teams, Zoom classroom, Google teams, etc. have been used for taking classes online. These apps have eased the process of learning and ensure continuity of learning for the students. The learning is now not restricted to the school and college premises, but it is dependent on the accessibility to the internet and information and communication devices. The IT companies have developed software and applications that are used in Schools and Universities now a day to keep the process of learning uninterrupted. More and higher educational institutions are adopting information and technology-driven software to upgrade and keep their students and teachers up abreast of the latest technologies in the world. High profile schools have already shifted to virtual classroom platform they allow students to do their work on laptops and tablets but there are various private and government schools and colleges which still solely depend on physical infrastructure for learning. The objective should be to cope up with the changes in the progression of technology in the field of education.

We live in a developing economy where the digital revolution has been not fully acceptable to many so the need for the current situation is to make them aware of the benefits of Digitalization in the education sector. The use of digital textbooks, online classes, personalization in teaching, diversity in teaching, use of multimedia will lead to dynamic changes in the field of education and learning process. The online learning platform makes the learning process more innovative and interesting to the students; the teachers try to resolve the queries on a real-time basis. Now a day's learning is not restricted to the physical presence of students and teachers all the needed thing is access to internet and communication technologies. Various competitive examination preparation coaching centers have also adopted information and communication technology as they have started delivering lectures with the help of satellite classes and students will be provided a learning management system (LMS) and online doubts clarification session by the subject experts. It will lead to saving of cost, efforts, and money nevertheless students will be able to take classes from the subject experts located across the world. The process of digitalization in the education sector has its pros and cons therefore a balance needs to strike between both modes of learning. The online learning process may lead to health hazards as it will affect the eyes of the students as they will be staring at the screen for longer duration and students may develop the feeling of lethargic and skip the classes as they feel think they are not monitored.

BACKGROUND

Panel (2002) discussed a curriculum framework aimed at developing information and communication technologies for teachers. It has been seen that ICT bought changes in terms of social practice and a changing discourse about communication. The study reported how the framework of ICT has been applied in Japan curriculum. It was found in the study that many teachers were not aware of the ICT literacies and they were not able to integrate them into the curriculum. The data was collected from some schools in Japan. It was found that teachers have been shifted toward an awareness of ICT literacies made available to them.

Bowles & Bowles (2004) affirmed that e-learning contained three main areas of activity viz. content formation and management, knowledge management, and education activity. They also observed that superior network capacity and learning interactivity through CD-ROM, CBT, facilitator-led online content (e-books), data sharing – file transfer, videos, virtual classrooms, and two-way synchronous with datacasts/broadcasts.

Hong & Songan (2011) explored that senior instruction organizations are utilizing computerized advances to grow course materials, convey and share course substance, talks, and introductions, encourage correspondence among speakers and understudies, empower educational development, increment participation, and cooperation, lead inquire about, improve proficient turn of events, and bless with managerial and the board administrations.

Conole (2013) considered the instructional methods related to various sorts of Massive Open Online Courses (MOOCs). It contended that the present talk around the idea of MOOCs (fundamentally based around association with content and embracing a behaviorist learning approach), and MOOCs (which center around outfitting the intensity of computerized media and correspondence with peers, receiving a connective learning approach), is a deficient method of portraying the assortment of MOOCs and how learners engage with them.

Delgaty (2013) revealed that out of 75% of scholarly time happened out of typical available time, sixteen all out staff hours (12 arrangings and four conveyance) were required to help one hour of understudy online movement. Specialized obligations were fundamental all through, yet capricious. Colleges attempted to connect with staff with e-learning because of its unrecognized and (numerous scholastics accept) impractical remaining task at hand as well.

Tuomi (2013) described the recent developments in open educational initiatives and emerging revolution in education and learning and developed the foundation for the studies and policies on the open educational resource (OER). In the article, four different types of OER described, and they were in the field of learning theories and discussed how wide the adoption of OER accelerates the transformation of learning and education.

Marcum (2014) explored the changes in expectations that teachers and students had for gaining access to electronic information and how librarians were responding to those expectations. The digitalization of the education sector has transformed the learning process and examines how higher educational institutions were inculcating ICT in their learning process. It was found that the online learning landscape bought tremendous changes in the field of education and it could transform the learning process and made it more effective and student-friendly. The changes bought by electronic technology had made faculty, libraries, and universities to consider collaborative and consortium approaches to providing services and improve the whole phenomena of online learning.

Camilleri & Camilleri (2017) explored the educators' attitudes and perceptions about their exploitation of digital learning applications and found out that the higher educational institutions were committed to using digital technologies. The paper used a stepwise regression analysis that has shown, younger teachers were progressively more engaged in digital learning resources as compared to aged teachers.

Dube & Scott (2017) investigated the perspectives of the university students of Zimbabwe on the use of digital technologies as the tools and techniques for the learning and teaching process. It has been found that the limited use of digital technologies could lead to a second-order digital divide. The above problem harms the government and university efforts as their technological investment has not been effectively used. The quantitative data on the student's perspective was collected with the help of questionnaires and the sample size was of 100 students of Zimbabwe University. It was found that there was disappointment among the students about current traditional teaching methods and also there was frustration among the students because there was no connection between usually utilized showing techniques and the digital technologies effective for educating and learning.

Jain & Madan (2017) devised a suitable business model to exploit the opportunities in Indian video on demand industry for imparting online knowledge and found that responsiveness and empathy had not that much impact on the customer satisfaction as compared to other dimensions of SERVQUAL model but it doesn't mean that the institution will not focus on this factor as it may create indirect influence in another way. On the other hand, tangibility, reliability, assurance, and the product had a considerable impact on the satisfaction level of the customers which helps in boosting of sales and profits as increased customer's satisfaction level will lead to their intention to repurchase repeatedly and will recommend that product or service to other which will create potential customers for the company.

Jain & Yadav (2017) stated that technology is a major factor and tool for educators to reach the masses and the target audience for imparting quality education and digitalization is very helpful in achieving this target.

Machekhina (2017) stated that one of the logical inconsistencies genuinely obstructing the modernization of instruction is the error between the speed of digitalization of instructive assets and the speed at which the digitalization of the instructive procedure itself, which is still extremely low. The change of instruction is introduced in the article by the case of different types of curricular and extracurricular exercises focused on the dynamic utilization of computerized instructive assets including the audit of the citywide electronic diary and journal, which has been utilized for quite a while in Moscow auxiliary schools.

Yordming (2017) studied the requirement of including the internet in the teaching and need for using digital media in the traditional classroom. The study was based on a semi-structured interview and the interview protocol was being examined by the experts. The purposive sampling method was used to collect data from the five English language teachers working in Anthong and Phra Nakhon Si Ayuttaya Primary Educational Service Area. The findings of the paper suggested that teachers felt confident while using digital media in the traditional classroom set up, all participants understand the significance of using the internet in the classroom. Teachers acknowledged the efforts of school administrators who have initiated the shift towards the digitalization of education. It was also found that some schools in Japan did not provide the needed infrastructure for the digitalization of education.

Bond et al. (2018) described the perception of the students and teachers about the adoption of digital tools in German university classrooms. Two datasets were examined regarding the use and perceptions of students (n = 200) and teachers (n = 381) on the use of digital tools. Findings revealed that both students and teachers used LMS i.e. Learning Management System as the most useful tool. The study supported the broader use of educational technology for instruction and learning policies and policies for higher education departments.

Islam & Jahan (2018) focused on Effectiveness, Social Network, Gender, Education Time, and Helpful website and tools inside the classroom and showed the effect of social networking in the education site and future one can work with e-learning through Facebook that will more interactive and easy to access.

Marathe (2018) stated that India has exciting opportunities in the Education Technology sector with a rising young population, increasing internet penetration and acceptance of online learning as a cost-effective channel, and Digitalization in the education system will be a big success in future.

Reis (2018) provided insights regarding the state of the art of digital transformation and proposed avenues for future research. The paper studied 206 peer-reviewed articles to provide an overview of the literature. The findings indicated that managers should adapt their trade approach to a new digital reality. It has resulted in the alteration of processes and operations administration for digital transformation. Digital Transformation has expanded to all sectors of activity there are some areas with more projection of being urbanized in the upcoming time than others.

Bilyalova et al. (2019) studied the digital transformation in the education sector and how digital technology in the current situation had opened new opportunities and avenues for the learners. This must lead to continuity of the learning process, saving time, and effort. This article aimed to describe the present state of its implementation and predicted results and concerns in this regard. In this paper, the pros, and cons of the digitalization of education have been revealed. The implementation of digital education in the modern world has been studied and what kind of risk is associated with contemporary students have been also taken care of. In the paper statistical tools have been used to compare the success of the experiment on two types of learner one was the traditional students and the other one was the students who have been taught electronically. The results revealed that test group students of Naberexhnye Chelny Institute of Kazan Federal University had shown better results in comparison to the students of reference groups.

Chatwal (2019) described the digitalization in the education system in India. The basic changes faced by the higher education system in the country were the motivation level of students, resistance to change, technical skills of the students, student performance evaluation, etc. The education should be imparted to the students in a systematic manner to the students so that they can learn from the digitalization smoothly and effectively. The information collected in a digital form should be disseminated effectively to the students learning with the help of ICT enabled services. Digital education can be defined as the combination of information technology and communication devices, digital content management, and virtual classrooms to make learning more effective and affordable for the economically weak students. The paper attempted to understand the upcoming trends in the education industry that will shape the future of upcoming generations.

Gupta (2019) viewed that the greatest test is the place and how to apply new advanced advances to create and develop new wellsprings of economy, and the improvement of top-notch computerized instruction and preparing focuses are the arrangement. Notwithstanding, there are numerous obstacles and holes of the correspondence among the industry and instruction areas.

Ragalutu et al. (2019) showed that online learning based on digitalization implicitly and exponentially synergizes with character education, especially on character values of responsibility, independence, honesty, discipline, hard work, creative, independent, and curiosity.

Polikarpova et al. (2020) believed that the need heading of state arrangement in the field of education ought to be the preparation of exceptionally qualified educators, improving the level and nature of their life, just as expanding the eminence of instructor work.

Sousa et al. (2020) proved that advanced innovations are applicable and broadly utilized in different territories of society: the executives, financial relations, science, and training. Be that as it may, digitalization of the educational procedure is of specific significance, because the few factors such a development of the quality and pertinent involvement with this circle and significant change forms are occurring in the field of training: electronic reading material, Internet entries, databases of data needs are spreading, frameworks of online courses and separation learning are effectively creating.

MAIN FOCUS OF THE CHAPTER

The main focus of the chapter is stated as below:

Primary Focus

1. To examine the impact of COVID-19 on the digitalization of the education industry.

Secondary Focus

1. To study the e-learning initiatives taken up by the HRD Ministry.
2. To study student's and faculty's perspectives towards the adoption of e-learning in the school and college curriculum.
3. To study how the COVID-19 pandemic will redefine the standard of education and its methodology in the present situation.

Materials and Methods

The present research study strictly abides by the conceptual framework of the research process. The information gathered in this study has been taken from secondary sources of data collection including authentic sources as well as past studies such as the detailed information from publications, books, magazines, journals, web services. The primary data was collected to understand student's and teacher's perspectives towards the adoption of e-learning in the COVID-19 pandemic period with the help of the semi-structured interview method of data collection. The study is a descriptive analysis of the student's and teacher's perspectives towards the adoption of e-learning in the school and college curriculum. This study will be helpful for the education industry to understand student's problems and develop ICT enabled processes that capitalize the high-quality educational material and will help in bringing a new revolution in the education sector.

DIGITAL EDUCATION: TRANSFORMING THE FACE OF EDUCATION

With the advancement in technology, the process of interaction between a teacher and fellow student has completely changed in recent years. Digital education has redefined the process of learning, now learning is not restricted to the walls of schools and colleges. The learner just needs the ICT enabled technology at its disposal to learn and explore the new path of education. Classroom teaching has been replaced by online classes and distance education. Online blogs, video tutorials help the students to study and gain knowledge about their area of interest. This will help the students to enhance their knowledge and broaden their concepts and thinking potential. With the help of an online learning platform they can learn from the best faculty located in any part of the world, it has led to overcoming the problem of place hindrance. With the help of technology, education has become free and easily accessible.

1. **Digital Textbooks:** Physical textbooks have been replaced by digital textbooks. No longer students make notes of their learning they just access the study material available online and use them for their reading and practice purposes. Actual books are substituted by the e-books, e-magazines, pdf, etc. Textbooks have become extinct in a certain part of the world. The students carrying their heavy bags to school has become a thing of the past. They just carry their laptops, tablets, i-pods to the school, and enrich their learning experience with these ICT enabled technology only.
2. **Virtual Classroom:** The online classroom is the classroom where students and teachers located in their native place can interact and exchange their thoughts and experience. All they need is a good internet connection and information and communication devices. Teachers can give online assessments to the students and the online teaching experience will be even more effective with the help of a virtual whiteboard. Online quizzes, assignment keep the students engaged and they can be easily evaluated by the teachers.
3. **Diversity in Teaching:** The increased use of digital technology has also helped in bringing teachers from different cultures and subject domains from different parts of the world to come to a common virtual platform and share knowledge and experience with the students located in different parts of the world. Students can enroll in a multicultural classroom where the aim is to learn and explore the cultures of the country.
4. **Personalization in Teaching and Learning:** The technology has undergone several changes and the use of multimedia has catered to the needs of different groups of students. The online learning platform allows the teachers to personalize the teaching content according to the capability of the students. They can differentiate the students by making different teams according to the ability of the students and assign the content and study material accordingly. With the help of personalized lessons and projects, every student can learn and understand lessons at their own pace. Teachers can give online feedback to the students and results can be shared online itself after evaluation.

GOVERNMENT INITIATIVES IN TRANSFORMATION

The Human Resource Department Minister Ramesh Pokhriyal has ensured that there is no interruption in the learning process. Students are being motivated to carry on their studies with the help of e-learning platforms. The online classes provide them study material, online video tutorials, blogs, learning management systems so that learning continues. The e-learning platform provides opportunities to interact with the teachers and enhance their skillset and knowledge.

- **National Repository of Open Educational Resources (NROER):** It has provided an online platform for accessing e-resources such as e-books, e-courses, e-libraries, the opportunity to participate in online events, and content-based education. It is one of the most excellent Initiatives by the government of India that provides content in both Hindi and English language. It provides the opportunity for self-learning and establishing standards of quality education.
- **DIKSHA:** The government of the country has developed a portal that is useful for both the students and the teachers. It is beneficial for teachers to learn the working of online learning platforms and more they are equipped with these platforms more effective lessons they can deliver to students. The students have the option to scan the QR code and they will get access to the study material available in the repository. The distinguishing feature of this platform is that it is available in different languages.
- **E-Pathshala:** With the help of this online web portal, students from standard 1st to 12th get the right to use more than 1886 audios, 2000 videos, 696 e-books (e-Pubs) and 504 Flip Books. This web portal is also available in multiple languages. The online learning platform makes the learning process more innovative and interesting to the students.
- **SWAYAM:** It is one of the initiatives taken by the government of India to encourage students to learn with the help of ICT enabled services. The platform provides free courses to undergraduate and postgraduate students. It also provides a certificate after payment of nominal fees. This platform is connected to national corridors. The use of digital textbooks, online classes, personalization in teaching, diversity in teaching, use of multimedia will lead to dynamic changes in the field of education and learning process.

MANAGEMENT OF DIGITALIZATION STRATEGY

The Emergence of Digitalization in Education Sector During the Phase of COVID-19 Pandemic

The digitalization of the education sector has led to continuous learning that is beneficial for the students as well as teachers despite facing the medical emergency in the country, the digital world is standing uninterrupted due to the COVID-19 crisis. The academic calendar of the schools and colleges is changed with due regard to the guidelines issued by the human resource department. Having access to the information and communication technology, the students can have continuous classes and teachers can also evaluate their assignments and projects with the help of e-learning platforms such as Microsoft Teams, Google teams, Zoom, etc. The students have the option of uploading their work on their e-learning portal and teachers can evaluate them and return their marks after checking. The whole process of learning is simplified, and teachers try to make the learning process more interested and fruitful. Teachers organize quiz and online tests which keep students motivated to perform better. During the phase of COVID-19, the whole world is suffering and so their students, but educational specialists are organized webinars to address the issue of higher education during this hard time for the education sector. The school has adopted an e-learning platform for taking classes of all standards. The aim behind the digitalization of education is that process of learning remains unaffected due to the COVID-19 pandemic and students face this situation with courage and strength. The uninterrupted learning during this phase is possible only with the help of information and communication technology. So, digitalization in the education sector is need for the hour and to protect the future of education in the country it's the best way to adopt an e-learning platform and the process of learning continues amid this pandemic. The research and development of education demand the Digitalization of the education sector and the appraisal of e-learning activities and information technology.

Students are the future of the nation and their learning will determine the growth and prosperity of the country so, the information and technology resources should be exploited in the best possible manner for the betterment of students' life and nations' growth.

FINDINGS

The process of learning has undergone many changes since ancient times from the phase of learning in a gurukul where learners reside with their gurus and enrich their knowledge with the practical exposure to situations to the phase of physical infrastructure i.e. schools and university premises where students and teachers both come together to enlighten the process of learning. But now we have come far in the 21st century which is an era of technology advancement and automation. Digital technology has changed nearly every aspect of our lives. Education is an inevitable part of everyone's life and the mode of education defines how strong conceptual knowledge a learner would have. Today, students and teachers can contact each other in the virtual classroom with the help of information and communication technology. The physical presence of students and teachers is not the hindrance in the process of leaning anymore. Information and communication technology have simplified the learning process with the help of online content development and management. The use of digital textbooks, online classes, personalization in teaching, diversity in teaching, use of multimedia will lead to dynamic changes in the field of education and learning process. The COVID-19 has impacted all the sectors of the economy adversely and the education sector is not an exception. It has made us more creative and tech-ware. The virtual learning and ICT enabled processes to keep the learning process uninterrupted. COVID-19 could be an opportune time to grasp the potential of online learning. During the phase of a medical emergency, the government has approved various online training sessions and professional bodies have also started offering free online courses with the help of TCS ION application. The universities are conducting workshops and webinars so that process of learning remains unhampered by the havoc created by deadly disease corona. The findings of the study can be elaborate in two directions, one from the student's point of view and the other is from the teacher's point of view. The findings in both the directions are given as under: -

Student's Perspective Towards Digitalization of Education

The online learning platform has provided interactive and knowledge enhancing gateway to the students, but it depends on students how far they want to take it. Still, learners face problem-related to network connection, and the affordability of the information technology devices will always remain a major issue in the digitization of education. Students in the 21st century are technology prone but when it comes to studying there is an unwillingness among them to adopt online learning culture. The computer courses taught online are much more effective than theoretical subjects taught via online applications. Student wants that duration of the online class should be adequate. Lengthy online lectures cause fatigue and boredom. Students use to follow unethical practices during lectures they just logged in and keep the device and engage themselves in other activities. Teachers failed to monitor students effectively and students do whatever they like thinking that they are not being monitored. The digitalization of education can sustain in our country when students are interested in taking online classes. Various health issues are faced by students such as continuously staring at the screen may cause pain in the eyes and things become monotonous for them. Students often face the problem of headaches due to the long duration of online classes. The practical subjects are being found as difficult to learn online. The online learning platform can supplement the traditional classroom culture but cannot substitute it totally because students cherish going to Schools and carrying their school's bags. Studying in the school and college premises gives a unique feel to the students and they want to cherish them. Various competitive examinations have also started providing online coaching and provide all the study material online on the Learning Management System (LMS). They provide lectures on their indigenous applications such as AVA, the video application of Aldine Pvt ltd. For the students who live in rural areas, there is no benefit of online classes because they do not have good internet connectivity and failed to attend classes, therefore. As lectures and classes are being recorded by the faculty, students find it easy to recall and revise subjects when they face difficulty in understanding the concepts. But on the other hand, some of the students also said that they become careless due to recording lectures as they have the opinion that they will see video lectures during the examination time so they skip the current sessions of online classes. Some of the students accepted that they share their login Ids and passwords with friends and their friends attend the lectures on behalf of them. Students believe that online classes are effective during COVID-19 pandemic time as their studies are not affected much. The final year students are least happy with online classes because they want to enjoy their last year of college life. Students follow the practice of copying the content of the assignment from their classmates and upload the same in the assignment section. They felt that the assessment of the tests and quiz will not be authenticated and reliable because students resort to unfair means such as cheating. The hard-working students are suffering due to the unfair evaluation of assignments. On the other hand, the student acknowledged that their doubts are properly cleared in online sessions. Introvert students actively participate in online presentations and improving their presentation skills. Placement of the final year students will be affected due to the COVID-19 pandemic. The online classes are effective, but students do face challenges due to internet connectivity and lack of self-motivation to study in online classes. Various online courses are made available by the HRD Ministry and universities to upgrade the skills of the students. Students are attending workshops and webinars to enjoy the lockdown period and to stay up the breast of the latest things going on in the surrounding.

Teacher's Perspective Towards Digitalization of Education

Every problem comes up with opportunities which are needed to be identified and utilized optimally. The present situation due to the COVID-19 pandemic has posed challenges and opportunities both in the education domain. Their impacts on education are positive as well as negative both depending on the way one judges this. The negative impact is that all educational organizations/institutions shut down and examinations got postponed or delayed, but nothing stopped totally. There is a positive impact also due to this pandemic educational system has taken a new turn and got evolved in an unimagined way. Online classes have started, virtual summer internships are provided by reputed companies to the students and online examination is being conducted effectively to evaluate student's performance. Teachers and faculty members are positively adopting the digitalization of education and making optimum use of digital media. The admission process for the upcoming session has been shifted to the online platform. Teachers are attending online workshops and actively participating in the webinars. Teachers can make optimum use of time with the help of ICT enabled devices during online sessions as they can mute the students who create chaos in the class. COVID-19 has provided an opportunity for teachers to upgrade their skills and knowledge by joining multidisciplinary courses available online. Teachers are attending faculty development programs and increasing their research activities. Some of the teachers interviewed said that this COVID-19 pandemic has made them realize the significance of digital aids in the traditional classroom and they appreciated the efforts of universities and government in the online learning landscape. Teachers can understand the difference between the business of education and education of business. Faculty have realized that they do not need physical classrooms to teach students, learning is all the way more effective and fruitful in the virtual classrooms. Digital education material and content management will be more helpful for the students to prepare for their examinations. The online learning platform has made it easier to evaluate the student's assignment and test as teachers can give feedback online and return their marks as well. The virtual classroom provides innovative and interactive tools to make learning productive and enjoyable.

FUTURE RESEARCH DIRECTIONS

It was found that students use to follow unethical practices during lectures as they just logged in and engage themselves in other activities and teachers sometimes failed to monitor them effectively. This research can be extended in the future to experiment strategies for the effective execution of digital education. Also, it can be a base study for analyzing the impact of various pandemics or unavoidable events on the transformation of digitalization and its management.

CONCLUSION

Education is the most important part of one's life and the growth of the education sector will ultimately strengthen the base of our country. More educated and skilled people in the country there will be more contribution to the development and prosperity of the Nation. Digitalization of education with the help of IT-enabled devices to have to lead to study anywhere anytime with basic connectivity to the internet. The success of the online learning classroom depends on the corporation from the students. The students need to more attentive and focused while taking online classes. The phase of Digitalization has two aspects one from the angle of students and the other one is from the angle of teachers. The interaction between students and teachers during virtual classes will determine the success of education in the digital world. Students find it difficult to understand practical subjects like mathematics, accountancy, geometry, etc. in virtual classes. They understand practical subjects more effectively in the normal classroom. As far as the student's opinion is concerned digitalization of education can complement the traditional education system but it can never replace it. In basic elementary education, traditional classroom culture will be more effective. For the competitive examinations, online coaching will be beneficial as it can be accessed from the nation's best faculty. For school and college-going student's combination of both virtual and traditional classrooms can be used. The use of digital textbooks, online classes, personalization in teaching, diversity in teaching, use of multimedia will lead to dynamic changes in the field of education and learning process. The virtual classroom provides innovative and interactive tools to make learning productive and enjoyable.

A whole world is facing economic crunch and disturbance in the routine life structure and the pace of education is continuing and upgrading the skills of the students. As the country is facing a medical emergency the online classes are very much helpful and maintaining consistency in the learning process. At last, it can be said that there is no substitute for the traditional classroom but during the phase of COVID-19 pandemic ICT enabled processes to have proven to be very useful and the phase of learning continues.

ACKNOWLEDGMENT

This research received no specific grant from any funding agency in the public, commercial, or not-for-profit sectors.

REFERENCES

Armstrong, J., & Franklin, T. (2008). *A review of current and developing international practice in the use of social networking (Web 2.0) in higher education*. Retrieved from: https://arthurmckeown.typepad.com/files/web-2.0-in-higher-education.pdf

Bond, M., Marín, V. I., Dolch, C., Bedenlier, S., & Zawacki-Richter, O. (2018). Digital transformation in German higher education: Student and teacher perceptions and usage of digital media. *International Journal of Educational Technology in Higher Education*, *15*(1), 48. doi:10.118641239-018-0130-1

Bowles, M. S., & Bowles, M. S. (2004). *Relearning to e-learn: Strategies for electronic learning and knowledge*. Academic Monographs.

Brown, R. (Ed.). (2010). *Higher education and the market*. Routledge. doi:10.4324/9780203849002

Bulfin, S., Johnson, N. F., & Bigum, C. (2015). *Critical perspectives on technology and education*. Springer. doi:10.1057/9781137385451

Camilleri, M. A., & Camilleri, A. C. (2017). Digital learning resources and ubiquitous technologies in education. *Technology, Knowledge, and Learning*, *22*(1), 65–82. doi:10.100710758-016-9287-7

Chatwal, T. (2019). Digitalization of Higher Education in India: A Boon Or A Bane. *Research Journal of Humanities and Social Sciences*, *10*(4), 1083–1085. doi:10.5958/2321-5828.2019.00178.5

Clegg, S., Hudson, A., & Steel, J. (2003). The emperor's new clothes: Globalisation and e-learning in higher education. *British Journal of Sociology of Education*, *24*(1), 39–53. doi:10.1080/01425690301914

Conole, G. G. (2013). MOOCs as disruptive technologies: strategies for enhancing the learner experience and quality of MOOCs. *Revista de Educación a Distancia*, (39).

De Freitas, S., & Oliver, M. (2005). Does E-learning Policy Drive Change in Higher Education?: A case study relating models of organizational change to e-learning implementation. *Journal of Higher Education Policy and Management*, *27*(1), 81–96. doi:10.1080/13600800500046255

Delgaty, L. (2013). A critical examination of the time and workload involved in the design and delivery of an e-module in postgraduate clinical education. *Medical Teacher*, *35*(5), e1173–e1180. doi:10.3109/0142159X.2012.737963 PMID:23151211

Dube, S., & Scott, E. (2017). A Survey of the University Students' Perspectives about Using Digital Technologies in Education: Zimbabwean Case. *IAFOR Journal of Education*, *5*(1), 123–139. doi:10.22492/ije.5.1.07

Gupta, G. (2019, June). Education and Digital Economy: Trends, Opportunities and Challenges. In *Proceedings of the 2019 4th International Conference on Machine Learning Technologies* (pp. 88-92). 10.1145/3340997.3341013

Hiltz, S. R., & Turoff, M. (2005). Education goes digital: The evolution of online learning and the revolution in higher education. *Communications of the ACM*, *48*(10), 59–64. doi:10.1145/1089107.1089139

Hong, K. S., & Songan, P. (2011). ICT in the changing landscape of higher education in Southeast Asia. *Australasian Journal of Educational Technology*, *27*(8). Advance online publication. doi:10.14742/ajet.893

Islam, S., & Jahan, N. (2018). Digitalization and Education System: A Survey. *International Journal of Computer Science and Information Security*, *16*(1).

Jain, E. (2020). Digital Employability Skills and Training Needs for the Indian Healthcare Industry. In *Opportunities and Challenges in Digital Healthcare Innovation* (pp. 113–130). IGI Global. doi:10.4018/978-1-7998-3274-4.ch007

Jain, E., & Madan, M. (2017). An empirical study on acceptance of video on demand services in Indian market. *International Journal of Indian Culture and Business Management*, *14*(4), 375–392. doi:10.1504/IJICBM.2017.084353

Jain, E., & Yadav, A. (2017). Marketing and Technology: Role of Technology in Modern Marketing. *IOSR Journal of Business and Management*, *19*(5), 49–53. doi:10.9790/487X-1905064953

Lamba, J., & Jain, E. (2020). Covid-19 Pandemic–Bountiful for MSMES and Indian Economy. *Purakala Journal*, *31*(33), 89–94.

Machekhina, O. N. (2017). Digitalization of education as a trend of its modernization and reforming. *Revista Espacios, 38*(40).

Marathe, S. (2018). Digitalization in education sector. *International Journal of Trend in Scientific Research and Development,* 51-56.

Marcum, D. (2014). The digital transformation of information, education, and scholarship. *International Journal of Humanities and Arts Computing*, *8*(supplement), 1–11. doi:10.3366/ijhac.2014.0095

Munro, M. (2018). The complicity of digital technologies in the marketization of UK higher education: Exploring the implications of a critical discourse analysis of thirteen national digital teaching and learning strategies. *International Journal of Educational Technology in Higher Education, 15*(1), 11. doi:10.118641239-018-0093-2

Noble, D. F. (1998). Digital diploma mills: The automation of higher education. *Science as Culture, 7*(3), 355–368. doi:10.1080/09505439809526510

Panel, I. L. (2002). Digital transformation: A framework for ICT literacy. Educational Testing Service, 1-53.

Polikarpova, E. V., Shipelik, O. V., & Krylova, I. V. (2020, May). Digitalization of Education: Save the Human. In *International Scientific Conference "Digitalization of Education: History, Trends and Prospects" (DETP 2020)* (pp. 652-658). Atlantis Press.

Pradeep, H. G., Niranjanamurthy, M., Amulya, M. P., & Dayananda, P. (2020). Coronavirus – COVID-19 before and after solution through web application and App. *International Journal of Advanced Science and Technology*, *29*(5s), 27–41.

Ragalutu, H., Ibrahim, N., & Madokala, M. (2019). Existence and role of character education in the middle of digitalization of education 4.0. *Science Proceedings Series, 1*(2), 140–143. doi:10.31580ps.v1i2.802

Ragalutu, H., Ibrahim, N., & Madokala, M. (2019). Existence and role of character education in the middle of digitalization of education 4.0. Existence and role of character education in the middle of digitalization of education 4.0. *Science Proceedings Series, 1*(2), 140–143. doi:10.31580ps.v1i2.802

Raj, A., & Reshma, M. (2020). Impact of Digitalisation and Visual Communication on Education: A Study among Moodubidire City based Degree College Students. *CLIO An Annual Interdisciplinary Journal of History*, *6*(1), 465–473.

Reis, J., Amorim, M., Melão, N., & Matos, P. (2018, March). Digital transformation: a literature review and guidelines for future research. In *World conference on information systems and technologies* (pp. 411-421). Springer. 10.1007/978-3-319-77703-0_41

Sousa, R. D., Karimova, B., & Gorlov, S. (2020). Digitalization as a New Direction in Education Sphere. In *E3S Web of Conferences* (Vol. 159, p. 09014). EDP Sciences.

Tokareva, E. A., Smirnova, Y. V., & Orchakova, L. G. (2019). Innovation and communication technologies: Analysis of the effectiveness of their use and implementation in higher education. *Education and Information Technologies*, *24*(5), 3219–3234. doi:10.100710639-019-09922-2

Tuomi, I. (2013). Open educational resources and the transformation of education. *European Journal of Education*, *48*(1), 58–78. doi:10.1111/ejed.12019

Yordming, R. (2017). Teachers' perspective towards digital teaching tools in Thai EFL classrooms. *International Journal of Languages. Literatura y Lingüística*, *3*(2), 45–48.

Chapter 5
ICTS, Digital Enterprise Transformation, and Banking Sector in Pakistan

Tansif Ur Rehman
https://orcid.org/0000-0002-5454-2150
University of Karachi, Pakistan

ABSTRACT

Countries in the developing world, as well as the developed world, are now exploring different ways of facilitating their development process through deployment and exploitation of ICTs within their economies to gain optimum output. More and more facilities are being offered by banks to facilitate their costumers with ease as well as convenience regarding e-banking. Digital enterprise transformation facilitates financial services organizations via enabling them to be more secure, compliant, as well as being digital. It modifies the experience of employees, partners, customers, and stakeholders. But, in Pakistan, this is not the case. As, people still refrain from using ICTs and e-banking in Pakistan, because of various issues. In spite of the fact that the literature encompassing remittances and criminal offenses is limited. Remittances sent by relatives from overseas are an imperative source of domestic income in the South Asian region. But unfortunately, its influence on crime has mainly been unexplored.

INTRODUCTION

The respective work focuses on exploring the role of Information and Communications Technologies (ICTs), Digital Enterprise Transformation (DET), and banking sector in Pakistan with respect to socio-economic development. The objective of respective study is to highlight as well as critically analyze the significant role of remittances for the socioeconomic development and the contribution of ICTs, e-banking, and the use of Digital Enterprise Transformation to ensure the monetary flows in a secure manner. To an extent, this study will facilitate in filling previous gaps of other studies as it focuses on exploring multifaceted aspects of ICTs, Digital Enterprise Transformation, and banking sector with respect to socioeconomic development. Nations worldwide have recognized the developmental oppor-

DOI: 10.4018/978-1-7998-8587-0.ch005

tunities and challenges of emerging information age characterized by Information and Communication Technologies. These technologies are now driving national development worldwide. Pakistan is located at the crossroads of the Middle East and South Asia. It is bordered by Afghanistan and Iran in the west, India in the east, China in the north-east, along with the Indian Ocean in its south. These neighboring countries influence the economic, political, social, as well as cultural development of Pakistan. Pakistan's banks made a debut on internet banking in March 2005 (Abbasi, 2013) and during 2017-18 sector wise net FDI in the ICTs was $112.9 million. As most of the economic analysts had forecasted, Prime Minister' Special Assistant on Finance Hafeez Shaikh stated that as a result of economic downfall caused by Covid-19 world economy has suffered. As a result of a decline in the industrial, agricultural, as well as services sector of Pakistan. He was of the view that for the fiscal year 2020 the provisional GDP growth rate is estimated at -0.38 percent (The News International, 2020).

BACKGROUND

Information and Communications Technology (ICT)

According to the Free On-Line Dictionary of Computing (2020), Information and Communications Technology (ICT) is the study of technology used in handling information and facilitating communication. In 1997, Dennis Stevenson coined this phrase (ICT) in the report submitted to the government of United Kingdom. It covers the aspects already included in the wide domain of Information Technology, and further encompasses areas like, various types of video as well as audio processing and transmission, broadcast media, and telephony. ICT is usually used as a synonym with information technology, but Information and Communications Technology (ICT) is more broad and encompasses additional comprehensive aspects pertinent to digital technologies as compared to information technology (Rouse, 2019).

Digital Enterprise Transformation (DET)

Digital Enterprise Transformation is the incorporation of computerized technology into the domain of business. In a general sense, changing how a firm manages as well as deliver value to its consumers. In addition, it is the effect of ongoing sociocultural changes that require firms to repetitively challenge the existing parameters, experimentation, and become more comfortable with malfunctioning and even failure (The Enterprisers Project, 2020).

Stephanie Overby (2020) stated, "Ongoing digital transformation across industries became a given in 2019. At the same time, digital transformation fatigue also became very real." While, President of ISG (a global technology advisory as well as research organization), Steve Hall (2020) is of the view "2020 will still see the rapid scaling of digital initiatives across industries. In many areas, CIOs and organizations have prepped their organizations for change but haven't made the full leap to transforming their culture to fully embrace the change."

Recent Trends in Digital Enterprise Transformation (DET)

According to The Enterprisers Project (2020), there exists eight essential Digital Enterprise Transformation trends that IT as well as business leadership should be aware of:

1. A shakeout (because of the investments in big data governance and analytic progression by competitors).
2. Swift adoption of digital operating models, that includes integrated cross-functional units.
3. New Digital Enterprise Transformation success metrics.
4. Ongoing acquisitions and mergers in the information technology outsourcing sector.
5. New digital partnerships should be formed by consultancies.
6. Enlargement of public cloud adoption.
7. Attention to long-term value of digital initiative.
8. Enhance use of machine learning and artificial intelligence.

The Significance of ICTs in Digital Enterprise Transformation

For business organizations, progression within the domain of Information and Communication Technologies have surely provided ample opportunities, conveniences as well as cost savings. These benefits are cost cutting in highly automated businesses processes, data revolution in firms which are turning data generated by Information and Communication Technologies into insights that drive new services and products, Information and Communication Technologies-enabled transactions like, telemedicine, e-shopping, and social media that facilitates its consumers to have additional selection in how they interact, communicate, and shop (Rouse, 2019).

Digital Transformation in Banking Sector

Digital transformation is basically beyond just facilitating mobile as well as online functionality. Providers of traditional banking need to combine convenience along with digital speed that is compatible with human interaction. It should be contemplative and protective at critical points in a consumer's journey.

While, four out of five financial organizations have a firm belief that digital transformation will essentially modify banking sector and completely transform the respective competitive landscape. According to the Boston Consulting Group 43% admit that their organization has not even formulated a digital strategy. Surprisingly, when it comes to digital transformation one-in-five executives of banking sector consider their credit union as well as organization as "market leading" (The Financial Brand, 2018).

Boston Consulting Group suggests that in order to build a digital transformation strategy, credit unions as well as banks should focus on respective pillars:

1. Leveraging the power of data
2. Reinventing a consumer's digital journey
3. Building an organization that is digitally driven
4. Redefining the existing operating model (The Financial Brand, 2018).

Remittance

According to Merriam Webster Dictionary (2020), remittance is the transmittal of money (i.e. to a distant place), in accordance with Cambridge Dictionary (2020) "An amount of money that you send to someone". While, according to Collins Dictionary (2020) "A remittance is a sum of money that you send to someone".

Figure 1. Digital Transformation in Banking Sector

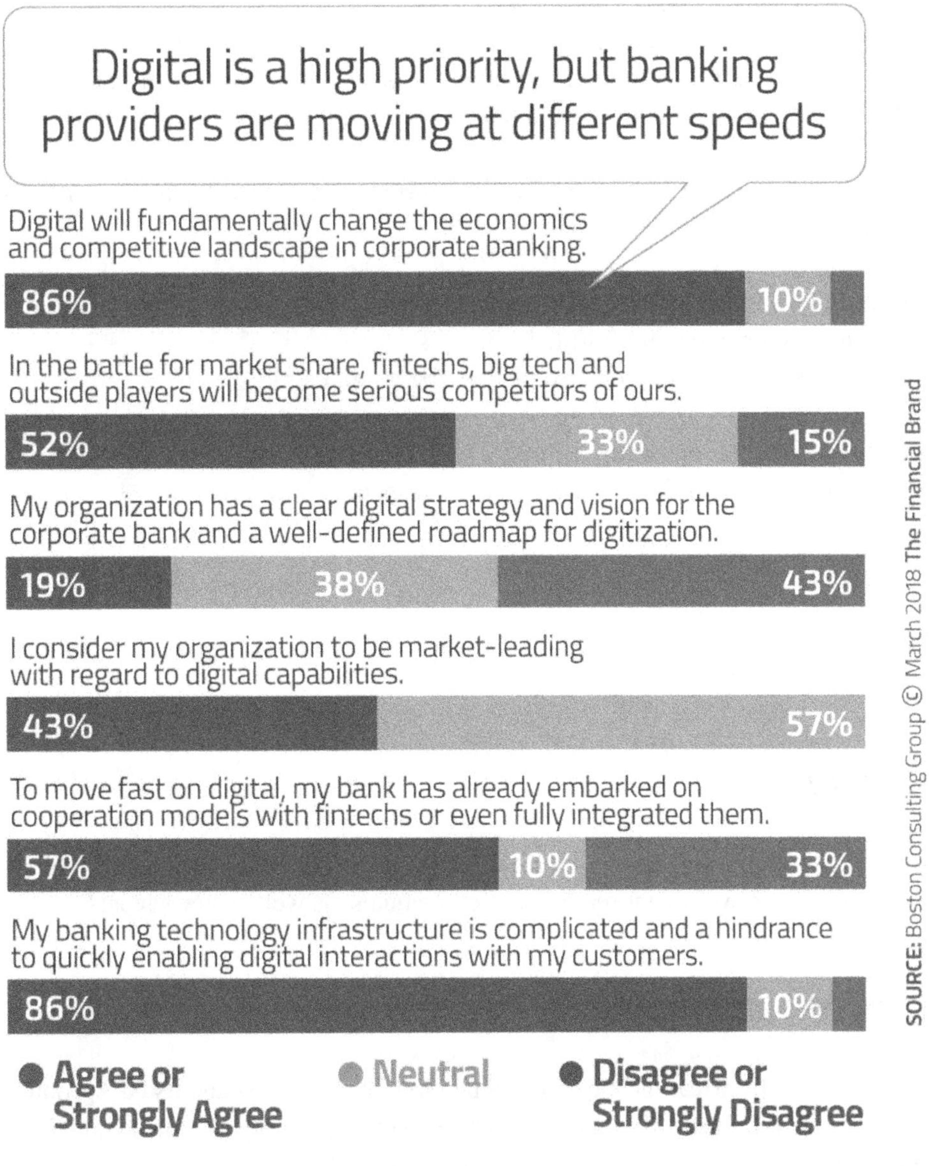

In a general sense, it is a money transfer by a foreign worker usually to his family in their country of origin. In case of developing countries, the sent money by respective migrants also contend with international economic aid as being one of the largest financial inflows (Al-Assaf & Al-Malki, 2014). With regard to labor-exporting countries like Pakistan, these remittances are an important component of international capital flows.

Related Issues to ICTs, E-Banking, and Remittance in Pakistan

General internet usage reveals that the average user is gaining experience as well as confidence online and is increasingly using the internet to perform tasks important to daily lives (Akhlaq, 2011). This includes conducting financial transactions and seeking information about finances (Chavan, 2013; Dannenberg & Kellner, 1998).

The Government of Pakistan plays a significant role in facilitating the usage of ICTs and all government institutions in Pakistan were pooled into the portal in the year 1997. Pakistan introduced e-government system in 2005 by incorporating the internet in internal public administration communications (Abbasi, 2013).

Those banks which utilize Digital Enterprise Transformation can possibly attain competitive advantages to a great extent:

1. It unleashes innovation at a broad scale and speed level.
2. Customer's upcoming needs are fulfilled.
3. Changing marketplace expectations are met by operational agility.

Saadullah Khan (2009) has discussed the major obstacles in low remittance, adoption issues of ICTs as well as e-banking in Pakistan. He has identified the respective elements:

1. Perceived (anticipated) risk
2. Registration process complexity
3. Security of the system
4. Transaction's reliability

METHODOLOGY

The respective study is qualitative and its nature is explanatory. Secondary academic sources have been used, i.e. past researches, government reports, policy manuals, as well as newspapers.

MAIN FOCUS OF THE CHAPTER

This research focuses on Information and Communication Technologies and its background with reference to Pakistan in general. In specific, it focuses on the banking sector of Pakistan and the relationship between remittance and crime with regards to Information and Communication Technologies. It also highlights the core issues encompassing ICTs and banking sector in Pakistan along with the role Digital Enterprise Transformation.

BACKGROUND OF INFORMATION AND COMMUNICATION TECHNOLOGIES IN PAKISTAN

Pakistan is an emerging global player in the telecommunications services and ICT. According to Economic Survey of Pakistan 2019-2020, more than 60% of current revenues from Pakistan's small and medium-sized ICT and telecommunication enterprises come from exports directly (The News International, 2020).

The Government tax reductions have also contributed to the increased growth in foreign call centers, which has resulted in more ICT firms in Karachi, as currently it is the top financial hub in Pakistan.

Table 1. Sector Wise Net FDI ($ Million)

Country	2009-10	2010-11	2011-12	2012-13	2013-14	2014-15	2015-16	2016-17	2017-18
Oil & Gas	740.6	512.2	629.4	559.6	502.0	300.5	248.9	146.0	192.5
Financial Business	(120.6)	155.8	(84.9)	26.8	71.4	282.2	1,159.2	700.0	400.3
Textiles	163.0	310.1	64.4	314.2	192.8	256.4	289.0	296.1	49.7
Trade	101.6	61.1	72.1	47.7	28.8	53.5	46.7	465.9	142.6
Construction	81.5	44.7	41.4	513.7	106.3	94.6	(14.1)	533.3	708.5
Power	132.0	104.6	18.7	44.1	2.7	6.2	70.2	57.6	997.0
Chemicals	112.1	30.5	96.3	(47.1)	94.9	60.3	88.5	5.4	48.9
Transport	117.0	53.0	25.3	5.1	(3.2)	50.5	26.8	32.7	56.9
Communication (IT&Telecom)	33.2	8.8	31.6	25.1	53.1	64.3	46.2	48.1	112.9
Others	790.4	354.0	(73.6)	(32.8)	649.8	(180.6)	343.9	461.6	382.7
Total	**2,150.8**	**1,634.8**	**820.7**	**1,456.5**	**1,698.6**	**987.9**	**2,305.3**	**2,746.8**	**3,092.0**

Note: Pakistan's Fiscal Year runs from 1st July till 30th June. The figures in brackets are in negative.
(Source: Board of Investment, Government of Pakistan, 2019)

Table 1: Over the past few years, a key focus of foreign investment in Pakistan has been the ICT (telecom) infrastructure, accounting for about 21% of 130 major investments. In previous years, Pakistan has undoubtedly established a thriving mobile telecommunications sector. During 2017-18 sector wise net FDI in the ICTs was $112.9 million, as previously (i.e. during 2016-17) it was just $48.1 million, and during 2015-16 it was $46.2 million.

Performance of Pakistani's ICT cluster is indeed based to a larger extent in the developments of telecom, as it provides substantial input to computer services and equipment production overall. This has been a prerequisite for the internet usage growth in Pakistan, as providing good quality internet connections are necessary for attracting the public towards the internet. Pakistan also proved to be one of the first countries in South Asia to get foreign investments into the telecommunications industry.

INFORMATION AND COMMUNICATION TECHNOLOGIES IN PAKISTAN

Total telecom investments in Pakistan will reach $ 2.4 billion by 2020, telecom sector revenues would cross Rs. 620 billion by the same year and mobile subscribers are expected to be around 161 Million, approximately 89% of the total population, said a report prepared by Pakistan Telecommunication Authority (ITCN Asia, 2019).

Pakistan is considered to be one of the successful examples of fast introduction of Information and Communication Technologies. A decade back, it was relatively technologically backward as compared to other Asian countries. New opportunities for mobile operators in Pakistan regarding revenue generation were initiated with the commercial launch of 3G and 4G in 2017-18. During the first two quarters of fiscal year 2017-18, revenues from telecom sector reached around Rs. 235.5 billion. While, the broadband penetration in Pakistan raised from 3.7 million to 52 million (ITCN Asia, 2019).

Today, it has become an attractive market for the Gulf states and Far East countries for doing business and investing. The conduct of monetary policy in Pakistan has undergone a paradigm shift in the aftermath of the reforms in financial sector that were initiated during the last decade. Pakistan in contemporary era is considered as one of the advanced emerging markets in Asia with a potential.

The financial services industry proved to be one of the first to recognize the potential of the internet as a mean of interacting with consumers (Eckenrode, 2006). But, unfortunately banks are falling behind other industries with respect to innovation within their internet channels (Fox, 2005).

BANKING SECTOR IN PAKISTAN

The State Bank of Pakistan (SBP) is the central bank of Pakistan which started its operation on 1st July 1948. The State Bank is not only responsible for issuing domestic currency and regulating foreign currency, but also aims at working for analyzing domestic economy. State Bank has been operating with a mission of promoting both the monetary and financial stability, as well as supporting the financial system for achieving sustainable growth by reducing inequality to all possible extent (State Bank of Pakistan, 2020).

History of Pakistani private banking industry goes back to the year 1985, when in Punjab the permission for the establishment of commercial banks was granted for the very first time. In 1992, a liberalization effort was taken advantage and there were already 14 banks working in Pakistan. In the start of 1992, setting up a bank was very popular, as there were no legislative restrictions to establish a bank then.

During its initial phase, the development in the financial sector has also been supported by OIC adapted legal framework. Foreign ownership also brought much influence into the management of the banks to a great extent in Pakistan.

In Pakistan there are 41 scheduled banks, six development finance institutions, and two micro finance banks. Their activities are regulated and supervised by the State Bank of Pakistan. While, commercial banks comprise of three nationalized and three private banks, along with 14 foreign banks, 15 private banks, four specialized banks, and two provincial scheduled banks. There are also three monetary agencies working in Pakistan, namely World Bank (WB), International Monetary Fund (IMF), and International Finance Corporation (IFC) (State Bank of Pakistan, 2020).

The relevant provisions which vest powers in the State Bank of Pakistan to carry out inspection of banks are derived from the enlisted acts and ordinance:

1. State Bank of Pakistan Act, 1956
2. Banking Companies Ordinance, 1962
3. Bank's (Nationalization) Act, 1974

While, the enlisted are the pertinent legislation which cover the activities concerning the banking sector and dealing with their various aspects.

1. Companies Ordinance, 1984

2. Financial Institutions (Recovery of Finances) Ordinance, 2001
3. Statutory Regulatory Orders (SROs)

The responsibilities and scope of work of the State bank of Pakistan has now increased. To cope-up with the ever-increasing workload and staff, the need for an integrated computer system has also enhanced. The State Bank of Pakistan ensures that new systems are installed, that will digitalize its work process and integrate all of its nation-wide branches into one computer network eventually.

According to the State Bank of Pakistan (2020). The banking sector in Pakistan comprises of:

1. Development Financial Institutions
2. Foreign Banks
3. Investment Banks
4. Micro Finance Banks
5. Nationalized Commercial Banks
6. Private Scheduled Banks
7. Provincial Banks
8. Specialized Schedule Banks

Under the existing legislative structure, the supervisory responsibilities in case of banks, development finance institutions as well as micro finance banks lies within the legal domain of the State Bank of Pakistan. The rest of the financial institutions are monitored and supervised by other authorities, like Securities and Exchange Commission of Pakistan (SECP) and Controller of Insurance respectively.

E-BANKING'S GLOBAL USAGE

Internet banking refers to the usage of the internet as a remote delivery channel for the banking services (Furst et al., 2004). Internet banking is becoming an ever increasingly important channel for banks to provide and facilitate banking services to individual customers and businesses.

Internet banking channel offers less waiting time with higher spatial convenience along with lower cost structure than traditional distribution channels used. The success of the internet banking can be gauged by identifying the number of current as well as the anticipated registered users (Hamilton, 1997).

INTERNET USAGE IN PAKISTAN

According to Bureau of Statistics - 6th Population and Housing Census, Pakistan's population is 212,742,631. According to Internet World Stats (IWS), in Pakistan, total number of internet users in October 2018 were 44,608,065, which is 22.2% of the total population.

THE RELATIONSHIP BETWEEN REMITTANCES AND CRIME

In spite of the fact that the literature encompassing remittances and criminal offenses is limited. Remittances sent by relatives from overseas are an imperative source of domestic income in South Asian region. But, unfortunately its influence on crime has mainly been unexplored.

Alcaraz, Chiquiar, and Salcedo (2012) argue that decrease in remittances causes absence in educational institutes attendance to a great extent and increased crime rate. Demirguc-Kunt et al. (2011) are of the view that remittances play an essential role in the development of the banking sector in a country. Woodruff and Zenteno (2007) argue that immigration networks alleviate capital restrictions (Vezina & Belanger, 2019). Thus, leaving a positive influence on profitability as well as investment level.

More educated people commit fewer crimes, because the formation of human capital enhances the opportunity cost of crime (Lochner, 2004, 2011). Economic downturns and non-economic shocks raises crime rate, and this rise may be felt long after the initial shock. As, deterrence as well as inequality are significant determinants of crime (Fajnzylber, Lederman, & Loayza, 1998). A negative macro-level income shock in France during the 19th century increased property crimes (Bignon, Caroli, & Galbiati, 2011).

There exists various evidences that remittances affect crime level. The direct income effect of remittances raises the cost of involvement in criminal offenses as well as reduces household poverty. Cash transfer in a housing voucher program reduced violent crimes in Chicago (Jacob & Ludwig, 2010).

An increase in household income via remittance can reduce the rate of crimes (Chioda, De Mello & Soares, 2012). Increased household income via remittances reduced property crime in urban areas of Colombia (Camacho & Mejia, 2013).

Increased income through remittances reduced the households' budgetary constraints, thus resulting in lower crime rates (Alcaraz, Chiquiar, & Salcedo, 2012; Antman, 2012; Dean, 2008; Theoharides, 2013).

The increase in years of education by means of remittances as support could also be related to a lower crime rate, i.e. both conventional and online crimes are reduced (Fella & Gallipoli, 2008). Being in an educational institute prevents individuals from engaging in conventional as well as online crimes (Berthelon & Kruger, 2011).

Remittances also enhances housing construction demand and this sector is labor intensive (Edo, 2019). Hence, it facilitates the benefits of having a formal job as well as self-employment (Figueroa & Veiga, 2019) and reduces the motivation to become involved in crimes (Kagochi & Kiambigi, 2012).

ROLE OF REMITTANCES IN PAKISTAN

Pakistan has the 6th largest diaspora in the world, as per the record of the UN Department of Economic and Social Affairs (Hamilton, 1997). According to the Ministry of Overseas Pakistanis and Human Resource Development, there are 7.6 million (approx.) expatriates, who send billions of dollars of foreign exchange to Pakistan each year. In first four months of the fiscal year 2019, the overseas Pakistanis remitted $7.4 billion (The News, 2018). The banks are also facilitating cellular users to check their balance, receive statements through SMS, and to carry out e-transactions.

It is evidently seen that developmental impact of these remittances is widespread (Amoros, et al., 2019). As it definitely affects different sectors of Pakistani economy and facilitate in improving living standards as well as they are non-debt creating inflows. Thus, helping in the development of financial sectors in recipient countries like Pakistan.

Remittances improve households' welfare by lifting recipient families out of absolute and relative poverty and backing them against income shocks and pertinent phenomena. Flows like these serve as means for increasing recipient families' income, along with ease credit, and liquidity constraints. Thus, allowing them in improving their living standards and consumption (Laudon & Traver, 2001).

On the other hand, such higher consumption along with more demand for goods and services may also increase tax revenues through determined consumption-based taxes. Such additional resources might be used up by the governments for allocating more and more resources for alleviating poverty and to strengthen country's physical infrastructure (Hamel, 2000).

Remittances also help in improving the country's debt sustainability level to a great extent. Recipient country of such remittances can sustain higher levels of future debt as empirical evidences have also suggested that such remittances play a positive as well as significant impact on economic growth and investment (Gao, et el., 2019).

Remittances also revive economic growth by its contribution to promote private consumption expenditures respectively (Choi & Whinston, 1999). One of the most eminent contribution of such remittances in Pakistan was definitely the poverty reduction during the last decade.

Remittances contribution in Pakistan's socioeconomic development has been throughout constructive as it has assisted for reviving economic activities, creating employment opportunities, reducing poverty, improving living standards of the recipient's family, and also secured balance of payment's (BOP) critical issue. It has also supported in building foreign exchange reserves and provided exchange rate stability, thus improving the country's credit rating.

As remittances are one of the most stable source of foreign exchange for developing countries like Pakistan, and has proven remarkably resilient in past trends during global economic adversities. More efforts have to be made for reducing cost and time for sending remittances. It also has to include removal of barriers to entry and competition in the remittance market respectively (Hamilton, 1997).

Table 2: During 2017-18 FDI from China were the highest, i.e. $1812.6 million, and lowest FDI was from Hong Kong, i.e. $4.1 million. This reveals the patterns of FDI inflow from China is increasing exponentially.

ROLE OF DIGITAL ENTERPRISE TRANSFORMATION

Digital Enterprise Transformation facilitates financial services organizations via enabling them to be more secure, compliant, as well as being digital. It modifies the experience of employees, partners, customers, and stakeholders. Those banks which utilize Digital Enterprise Transformation can possibly attain competitive advantages to a great extent:

1. It unleashes innovation at scale and speed level.
2. Customer's upcoming needs are fulfilled.
3. Changing marketplace expectations are met by operational agility.

Table 2. Country Wise Net FDI ($ Million)

Country	2009-10	2010-11	2011-12	2012-13	2013-14	2014-15	2015-16	2016-17	2017-18
China	(3.6)	47.4	126.1	90.6	695.8	319.1	1,063.6	1,211.7	1,812.6
UK	294.6	207.1	205.8	633.0	157.0	169.6	151.6	215.8	307.5
USA	468.3	238.1	227.7	227.1	212.1	223.9	13.2	44.6	136.3
Hong Kong	9.9	125.6	80.3	242.6	228.5	136.2	93.3	17.2	4.1
Switzerland	170.6	110.5	127.1	149.0	209.8	(6.5)	58.0	101.8	79.4
U.A.E	242.7	284.2	36.6	22.5	(47.1)	213.6	109.7	120.5	10.9
Italy	4.0	7.9	200.8	199.4	97.6	115.4	105.4	60.5	56.6
Netherlands	278.6	(48.5)	22.1	(118.4)	5.5	(34.5)	29.9	457.6	100.2
Austria	56.8	32.4	68.8	53.3	53.8	24.8	42.7	21.7	27.4
Japan	26.8	3.2	29.7	30.1	30.1	71.1	35.4	57.7	59.8
Turkey	0.8	1.8	0.3	0.5	7.9	43.4	16.8	135.6	29.8
Others	601.3	625.1	(304.6)	(73.2)	47.6	(288.2)	585.7	301.9	467.4
Total	**2,150.8**	**1,634.8**	**820.7**	**1,456.5**	**1,698.6**	**987.9**	**2,305.3**	**2,746.8**	**3,092.0**

(Source: Board of Investment, Government of Pakistan, 2019)

CORE ISSUES OF LOW REMITTANCE, ICTS AND E-BANKING ADOPTION IN PAKISTAN

Saadullah Khan (2009) in his Master's thesis "Adoption issues of internet banking in Pakistani' firms" has discussed the major obstacles in low remittance, adoption issues of ICTs as well as e-banking in Pakistan.

1. Perceived (anticipated) risk
2. Registration process complexity
3. Security of the system
4. Transaction's reliability

Perceived (Anticipated) Risk

In Pakistan, the development as well as use of ICTs and internet banking is still in very early stage. Like any other technology, it comes with a lot of perceived risks to the customers. To over come these risk issues, the bank's management should take initiatives to manage as well as control all its pertinent aspects.

They should also implement new and revised security polices, improvement in internal communication, evaluation and upgradation of their services as per customer's expectation. They must also develop innovative contingency plans to further minimize these perceived (anticipated) risks.

The banks can certainly enhance their ability to control as well as manage various risks inherent from e-transaction's activities. They should also implement more security to minimize the respective risks along with an increased customer authentication, like personal identification number and audit trials for the transactions.

Registration's Process Complexity

The registration process of ICTs and e-banking in Pakistan is though not very much complex, but it still needs some improvement. As, more convenience needs to be added to the customer's side and in return, the customers will associate themselves more with internet banking system vehemently.

Security of the System

Security is the most important issue for the customers while deciding the adoption of ICTs and e-banking services. Efforts must be taken by the government to ensure a more secured online environment to their customers and initiatives should also be taken to illustrate the authenticity along with confidentiality as well as integrity of online transactions. So, the customers feel it to be safe to transact via the internet. As, insecurity issues make it much difficult for the customers to develop their trust on ICTs and e-banking system in Pakistan.

Transaction's Reliability

The websites should also provide proper functioning to their customers as well as should be operative all time. As, it is also significant for the customers that their bank's website never freezes, especially after filling in all of the respective information. Because, it could create irritation as well as confusion.

It should be also be noted that accurate and problem free links, along with page download times are also of great concern to ICTs and e-banking customers in Pakistan. Transactions should be secured as well as paid more attention by e-banking service providers. E-banking websites must have accurate and updated information. These websites should also provide information about investments, stocks, as well as foreign exchange to gain attention of the prospective customers.

DISCUSSION

ICT is usually used as a synonym with information technology, but Information and Communications Technology (ICT) is more broad and encompasses additional comprehensive aspects pertinent to digital technologies as compared to information technology. Pakistan is considered to be one of the successful examples of fast introduction of Information and Communication Technologies. A decade back, it was relatively technologically backward as compared to other Asian countries. Total telecom investments in Pakistan will reach $ 2.4 billion by 2020, telecom sector revenues would cross Rs. 620 billion by the same year and mobile subscribers are expected to be around 161 Million, approximately 89% of the total population, said a report prepared by Pakistan Telecommunication Authority.

Digital Enterprise Transformation is the incorporation of computerized technology into the domain of business. In a general sense, changing how a firm manages as well as deliver value to its consumers. Digital Enterprise Transformation facilitates financial services organizations via enabling them to be more secure, compliant, as well as being digital. It modifies the experience of employees, partners, customers, and stakeholders. Those banks which utilize Digital Enterprise Transformation can possibly attain competitive advantages to a great extent. Digital Enterprise Transformation is basically beyond just facilitating mobile as well as online functionality. Providers of traditional banking need to combine convenience along with digital speed that is compatible with human interaction. It should be contemplative and protective at critical points in a consumer's journey. Credit unions as well as banks should focus on respective pillars like leveraging the power of data, reinventing a consumer's digital journey, building an organization that is digitally driven, and redefining the existing operating model.

Remittance is a money transfer by a foreign worker usually to his family in their country of origin. In case of developing countries, the remittance send by respective migrants also contend with international economic aid as being one of the largest financial inflows. With regard to labor-exporting countries like Pakistan, these remittances are an important component of international capital flows. Pakistan has the 6th largest diaspora in the world. There are 7.6 million (approx.) expatriates, who send billions of dollars of foreign exchange to Pakistan each year. In first four months of the fiscal year 2019, the overseas Pakistanis remitted \$7.4 billion. The banks are also facilitating cellular users to check their balance, receive statements through SMS, and to carry out e-transactions. In spite of the fact that the literature encompassing remittances and criminal offenses is limited. Remittances sent by relatives from overseas are an imperative source of domestic income in South Asian region. But, unfortunately its influence on crime has mainly been unexplored.

The State Bank of Pakistan (SBP) is the central bank of Pakistan which is not only responsible for issuing domestic currency and regulating foreign currency, but also aims at working for analyzing domestic economy. The State Bank has been operating with a mission of promoting both the monetary and financial stability, as well as supporting the financial system for achieving sustainable growth by reducing inequality to all possible extent.

Internet banking refers to the usage of the internet as a remote delivery channel for the banking services. Internet banking is becoming an ever increasingly important channel for banks to provide and facilitate banking services to individual customers and businesses. In Pakistan, total number of internet users exceeds 22.2% of the total population.

Major obstacles in low remittance, adoption issues of ICTs as well as e-banking in Pakistan are perceived (anticipated) risk, registration process complexity, security of the system, and transaction's reliability.

SOLUTIONS AND RECOMMENDATIONS

1. The Government of Pakistan should invite foreign investors via engaging them in bilateral contracts and investment plans.
2. Customers who are not be technologically sophisticated should be appealed by banks, as services should be simple enough to use.
3. More services should be offered by banks and online applications for new account opening, complaints, and corporate banking via the internet should be specially focused.
4. Huge liquidity is in the market during Muslim festivals, like Eid and Ramzan. E-banking can solve many liquidity problems, as it is a potential time to take advantage by the banks.
5. Private companies should develop a strong liaison with the Government of Pakistan regarding the swiftness of their internet approach.
6. Pakistani legal department should be equipped with the latest investigating technologies.
7. More customized and featured mobile banking services should be introduced. These services are not sufficient enough, as the usage of mobiles is on the rise so this area needs to be focused.

8. To conduct a research with the corporate customers and trade finance to investigate more of the external as well as internal issues of e-baking system and customer's adoption intention towards it.
9. Banks should install hardened operating systems, i.e. the system's software as well as firewalls should be configured to the highest security settings in consistency with the level of protection as per the customer's requirement.
10. Banks should conduct regular system as well as data integrity checks.
11. They must also implement a multi-tier application architecture which differentiates session controls, business logic, presentation logic, server side input validation, database access along with deploying stringent user authentication in wireless local area networks and protection of sensitive data with the help of strong encryption and integrity controls.
12. Banks should also increase their ability to control as well as manage various risks inherent from e-transaction activities.
13. Banks also need to implement more security to minimize the associated risks as to increase their customer's authentication, such as personal identification number and audit trial for transactions.

FUTURE RESEARCH DIRECTIONS

Significant areas for conducting future research encompassing ICTs and banking sector of Pakistan via engaging qualitative, qualitative, or eclectic approach can be:

1. Ease of doing business and the dilemma of cybercrime in Pakistan.
2. Foreign investments in Pakistani ICT sector and its effect on cyber behavior.
3. Identification of ICTs related issues and E-Fraud.
4. Issues encompassing online crimes and role of remittances in Pakistan.

CONCLUSION

Digital Enterprise Transformation facilitates financial services organizations via enabling them to be more secure, compliant, as well as being digital. It modifies the experience of employees, partners, customers, and stakeholders. The banking sector has been one of the leading spender on information communications technology (ICT). Many banks as well as exchange companies now offer online funds transfers from overseas, like workers remittances, etc. While, a few of the banks offer mobile phone banking, where customers can pay utility bills using their mobile phones. There are 7.6 million (approx.) expatriates, who send billions of dollars of foreign exchange to Pakistan each year. The State Bank has been operating with a mission of promoting both the monetary and financial stability, as well as to promote the financial system for achieving sustainable growth by reducing inequality to its extent.

In spite of the fact that the literature encompassing remittances and criminal offenses is limited. Remittances sent by relatives from overseas are an imperative source of domestic income in South Asian region. But, unfortunately its influence on crime has mainly been unexplored. Lack of system security concerns is the prime reason for slow adoption of ICTs and e-banking in the Pakistani context. Low reliability of transactions is also one of the most critical issues that include worries about the security of the system. The registration process of e-banking also needs improvement. There is a great level of concern regarding the security. Furthermore, the delivery of financial services via the internet should also be treated as a part of overall customer's service and distribution strategy. Thus, the relationship developed could then surely be used as a gateway for the delivery of product information. Firms that continue to undervalue the need for sociocultural changes will do so at their own risk.

REFERENCES

Abbasi, W. A. K. (2013, April 25). Pakistan's e-banking - past, present and future. *Business Recorder.* https://fp.brecorder.com/2013/04/201304251178401/

Akhlaq, M. A. (2011). Internet banking in Pakistan: Finding complexities. *Journal of Internet Banking and Commerce, 16*(1), 1–14.

Al-Assaf, G., & Al-Malki, A. M. (2014). Modelling the macroeconomic determinants of workers' remittances: The case of Jordan. *International Journal of Economics and Financial Issues, 3*(4), 514–526.

Alcaraz, C., Chiquiar, D., & Salcedo, A. (2012). Remittances, schooling, and child labor in Mexico. *Journal of Development Economics, 97*(1), 156–165. doi:10.1016/j.jdeveco.2010.11.004

Amoros, J. E., Ciravegna, L., Mandakovic, V., & Stenholm, P. (2019). Necessity or opportunity? The effects of State fragility and economic development on entrepreneurial efforts. *Entrepreneurship Theory and Practice, 43*(4), 725–750. doi:10.1177/1042258717736857

Antman, F. (2012). Gender, educational attainment, and the impact of parental migration on children left behind. *Journal of Population Economics, 25*(4), 1187–1214. doi:10.100700148-012-0423-y PMID:27616818

Asia, I. T. C. N. (2019). *ICT sector of Pakistan.* https://itcnasia.com/ict-sector-of-pakistan/

Berthelon, M. E., & Kruger, D. I. (2011). Risky behavior among youth: Incapacitation effects of school on adolescent motherhood and crime in Chile. *Journal of Public Economics, 95*(1), 41–53. doi:10.1016/j.jpubeco.2010.09.004

Bignon, V., Caroli, E., & Galbiati, R. (2011). *Stealing to survive: Crime and income shocks in 19th century France.* Cepremac.

Camacho, A., & Mejia, D. (2013). *Las externalidades de los programas de transferencias condicionadas sobre el crimen: El caso de familias en acción en Bogotá.* IDB Working Paper 406. Institutions for Development Sector. Washington, DC: Inter-American Development Bank.

Cambridge Dictionary. (2020). *Remittance.* Retrieved June 10, 2020 from https://dictionary.cambridge.org/dictionary/english/remittance

Chavan, J. (2013). Internet banking - Benefits and challenges in an emerging economy. *International Journal of Research in Business Management, 1*(1), 19–26.

Chioda, L., De Mello, J. M. P., & Soares, R. (2012). *Spillovers from conditional cash transfer programs: Bolsa família and crime in urban Brazil.* Department of Economics PUC-Rio.

Choi, S. Y., & Whinston, A. B. (1999). The future of e-commerce: Integrate and customize. *Computer, 32*(1), 133–138. doi:10.1109/2.738310

Collins Dictionary. (2020). *Remittance.* Retrieved June 10, 2020 from https://www.collinsdictionary.com/dictionary/english/remittance#:~:text=A%20remittance%20is%20a%20sum%20of%20money%20that%20you%20send%20to%20someone

Dannenberg, M., & Kellner, D. (1998). The bank of tomorrow with today's technology. *International Journal of Bank Marketing, 16*(2), 90–97. doi:10.1108/02652329810206743

Dean, Y. (2008). International migration, remittances and household investment: Evidence from Philippine migrants' exchange rate shocks. *Economic Journal. Revue Economique et Sociale, 118*(528), 591–630.

Demirguc-Kunt, A., Lopez, E., Martinez, M., & Woodruff, C. (2011). Remittances and banking sector breadth and depth: Evidence from Mexico. *Journal of Development Economics, 95*(2), 229–241. doi:10.1016/j.jdeveco.2010.04.002

Eckenrode. (2006). *Building a more responsive banking industry: The bell is ringing but are banks salivating?* The Tower Group.

Edo, A. (2019). The impact of immigration on the labor market. *Journal of Economic Surveys, 33*(3), 922–948. Advance online publication. doi:10.1111/joes.12300

Fajnzylber, P., Lederman, D., & Loayza, N. (1998). *Determinants of crime rates in Latin America and the world, an empirical assessment.* World Bank. doi:10.1596/0-8213-4240-1

Fella, G., & Gallipoli, G. (2008). *Education and crime over the life cycle.* Working Paper 630. London: Queen Mary University of London.

Figueroa-Armijos, M., & da Motta Veiga, S. (2019). Predictors of Early-Career Self-Employment among Millennials in the Digital Economy: The Role of The Great Recession. *Proceedings of the 52nd Hawaii International Conference on System Sciences.* 10.24251/HICSS.2019.546

Fox, S. (2005). *The state of online banking.* PEW Internet & American Life Project. http://www.pewInternet.org/pdfs/PIP_Online_Banking_2005.pdf#search='The%20State%20of%20Online%20Banking%20Pew

Furst, S. A., Reeves, M., Rosen, B., & Blackburn, R. S. (2004). Managing the life cycle of virtual teams. *The Academy of Management Executive, 18*(2), 6–20. doi:10.5465/ame.2004.13837468

Gao, J., Huang, C., Su, J., & Xie, Q. (2019). Examining the Factors Behind the Success and Sustainability of China's Creative Research Group: An Extension of the Teamwork Quality Model. *Sustainability, 11*(4), 1195. doi:10.3390u11041195

Government of Pakistan. Bureau of Statistics. (2017). *Provisional Summary Results of 6th Population and Housing Census - 2017.* https://bytesforall.pk/

Government of Pakistan. Board of Investment. (2019). *Foreign Investment.* http://boi.gov.pk/ForeignInvestmentinPakistan.aspx

Government of Pakistan. Ministry of Finance. (2019). *Economic Survey of Pakistan 2018-19.* http://www.finance.gov.pk/survey/chapters_18/overview_2018-19.pdf

Government of Pakistan. State Bank of Pakistan (2020). Retrieved from https://www.sbp.org.pk/

Hall, S. (2020). *What is digital transformation?* https://enterprisersproject.com/what-is-digital-transformation

Hamel, G. (2000). *Leading the revolution*. Harvard Business School Press.

Hamilton, S. (1997). E-commerce for the 21st century. *Computer, 30*(5), 44–47.

India has largest diaspora population in world: UN. (2016, January 15). *The Tribune*. https://www.tribuneindia.com/news/nation/india-has-largest-diaspora-population-in-world-un/183731.html

Information and Communication Technology. (n.d.). *Free On-Line Dictionary of Computing*. Retrieved June 10, 2020 from https://foldoc.org/Information+and+Communication+Technology

Internet World Stats. (2018). *World Internet Users and 2018 Population Stats.* https://www.internetworldstats.com/stats.htm

Jacob, B. A., & Ludwig, J. (2010). *The effects of family resources on children's outcomes.* Working Paper. Ann Arbor, MI: University of Michigan.

Kagochi, J., & Kiambigi, M. (2012). Remittances' influence on housing construction demand in Sub-Saharan Africa: The case of Kenya. *African Development Review, 24*(3), 255–265. doi:10.1111/j.1467-8268.2012.00321.x

Khan, S. (2009). *Adoption issues of internet banking in Pakistani' firms* (Unpublished Master Thesis). Lulea University of Technology, Lulea.

Laudon, K. C., & Traver, C. G. (2001). *E-commerce: Business, technology, society*. Addison-Wesley.

Lochner, L. (2004). Education, work, and crime: A human capital approach. *International Economic Review, 45*(3), 811–843. doi:10.1111/j.0020-6598.2004.00288.x

Lochner, L. (2011). *Non-production benefits of education: Crime, health, and good citizenship.* NBER Working Paper 16722. Cambridge, MA: National Bureau of Economic Research.

Merriam Webster Dictionary. (2020). *Remittance.* Retrieved June 10, 2020 from https://www.merriam-webster.com/dictionary/remittance

Overby, S. (2020). *What is digital transformation?* https://enterprisersproject.com/what-is-digital-transformation

Overseas Pakistanis remit $7.4 billion in first four months of FY19. (2018, November 9). *The News*. https://www.thenews.com.pk/latest/391754-overseas-pakistanis-remit-74-billion-in-first-four-months-of-fy19

Rouse, M. (2019). *ICT (Information and Communications technologies).* https://searchcio.techtarget.com/definition/ICT-information-and-communications-technology-or-technologies

The Enterprisers Project. (2020). *What is digital transformation?* https://enterprisersproject.com/what-is-digital-transformation

The Financial Brand. (2018). *The four pillars of digital transformation in banking.* https://thefinancial-brand.com/71733/four-pillars-of-digital-transformation-banking-strategy/

The News International. (2020, June 12). *Economic Survey 2019-2020.* https://www.thenews.com.pk/print/671294-economic-survey-2019-2020

Theoharides, C. (2013). Manila to Malaysia, Quezon to Qatar: International migration and the effects on origin-country human capital. Job Market Paper. Department of Economics and Ford School of Public Policy. Ann Arbor, MI: University of Michigan.

Vezina, S., & Belanger, A. (2019). Impacts of education and immigration on the size and skills of the future workforce. *Demographic Research, 41*, 331–366. doi:10.4054/DemRes.2019.41.12

Woodruff, C., & Zenteno, R. (2007). Migration networks and micro-enterprises in Mexico. *Journal of Development Economics, 82*(2), 509–528. doi:10.1016/j.jdeveco.2006.03.006

ADDITIONAL READING

Akhlaq, M. A. (2011). Internet banking in Pakistan: Finding complexities. *Journal of Internet Banking and Commerce, 16*(1), 1–14.

Allen, J. P. (2019). *Digital entrepreneurship.* Routledge. doi:10.4324/9780429506567

Benson, V., Morgan, S., & Filippaios, F. (2014). Social career management: Social media and employability skills gap. *Computers in Human Behavior, 30*, 519–525. doi:10.1016/j.chb.2013.06.015

Briley, D. A., Livengood, J., Derringer, J., Tucker-Drob, E. M., Fraley, R. C., & Roberts, B. W. (2019). Interpreting behavior genetic models: Seven developmental processes to understand. *Behavior Genetics, 49*(2), 196–210. doi:10.100710519-018-9939-6 PMID:30467668

Chavan, J. (2013). Internet banking - Benefits and challenges in an emerging economy. *International Journal of Research in Business Management, 1*(1), 19–26.

Chen, S. (2001). *Strategic management of e-business.* Wiley and Sons.

Eisenmann, T., & Trispas, M. (Eds.). (2002). *Internet business models: Text and cases*. McGraw-Hill Irwin.

Ford, D. H. (2019). *Humans as self-constructing living systems: A developmental perspective on behavior and personality*. Routledge.

Government of Pakistan. Ministry of Finance. (2018). *Economic Survey of Pakistan 2017-18.* http://www.finance.gov.pk/survey/chapters_18/overview_2017-18.pdf

Hamel, G. (2000). *Leading the revolution.* Harvard Business School Press.

Huang, R., Spector, J. M., & Yang, J. (2019). Learning in the context of technologies. In *Educational Technology* (pp. 33–48). Springer. doi:10.1007/978-981-13-6643-7_2

Hutchinson, D., & Warren, M. (2001). *A framework of security authentication for internet banking*. Paper presented at the 3rd International Conference on Information Integration and Web-based Applications & Services. Linz, Austria: Austrian Computer Society.

Kawai, N. (2019). Historical transition of psychological theories of fear: The view of fear in behaviorism. In *The Fear of Snakes* (pp. 1–18). Springer. doi:10.1007/978-981-13-7530-9_1

Kettunen, J., & Makela, J. P. (2019). Practitioners' conceptions of ethical practice in social networking in career services. *International Journal for Educational and Vocational Guidance*, *19*(3), 345–362. doi:10.100710775-018-9383-4

Kirkpatrick, R. (2009). *1969: The year everything changed*. Skyhorse Publishing Inc.

Komba, M. M., & Lwoga, E. T. (2020). Systematic review as a research method in library and information science. In *Handbook of Research on Connecting Research Methods for Information Science Research* (pp. 80–94). IGI Global. doi:10.4018/978-1-7998-1471-9.ch005

Krishnamurthy, S. (2003). *E-commerce management: Text and cases*. Thompson Learning.

Kuak, D., Dolezal, M., Kerous, B., Eichler, Z., Vasek, J., & Liarokapis, F. (2019). An interactive and multimodal virtual mind map for future workplace. *Frontiers in ICT (Lausanne, Switzerland)*, *6*, 12.

Nupur, J. M. (2010). E-banking and customers' satisfaction in Bangladesh: An analysis. *International Review of Business Research Paper*, *6*(4), 145–156.

Omar, S., & Tajudeen, F. P. (2020). The influence of career adaptability and career commitment to minimize intention to leave among ICT professionals. *International Journal of Human Capital and Information Technology Professionals*, *11*(2), 23–38. doi:10.4018/IJHCITP.2020040102

Pedro, C. P., Ramalho, J. J. S., & Silva, J. V. (2018). The main determinants of banking crises in OECD countries. *Review of World Economics*, *154*(1), 203–227. doi:10.100710290-017-0294-0

Rajenderan, M., & Zawawi, D. (2019). Leaky pipeline syndrome in information and communication technology (ICT) industry of Malaysia: A conceptual study on female career barriers and retention management. *International Journal of Academic Research in Business & Social Sciences*, *9*(2). Advance online publication. doi:10.6007/IJARBSS/v9-i2/5672

Rayport, J. F., & Jaworski, B. (2001). *Electronic commerce*. McGraw-Hill.

Schenkel, M. T., Farmer, S., & Maslyn, J. M. (2019). Process improvement in SMEs: The impact of harmonious passion for entrepreneurship, employee creative self-efficacy, and time spent innovating. *Journal of Small Business Strategy*, *29*(1), 64–77.

Vondracek, F. W., Lerner, R. M., & Schulenberg, J. E. (2019). *Career development: A life-span developmental approach*. Routledge. doi:10.4324/9781315792705

Zeithaml, V. A., Parasuraman, A., & Malhotra, A. (2000). *A conceptual framework for understanding e-service quality: Implications for future research and managerial practice*. Marketing Science Institute, Working paper report no. 00-115.

Zhang, J. H., & Lee, J. H. (2019). Beyond the Hawthorne research: Relationship between IT company employees' perceived physical work environment and creative behavior. In *International Conference on Software Engineering Research, Management and Applications* (pp. 147-159). Springer.

KEY TERMS AND DEFINITIONS

Banking: The services offered by a bank.

Digital Enterprise Transformation: Strategies by which organizations take advantage of information technology to develop digital capabilities.

E-Banking: Online banking (i.e., via the internet).

Enterprise: A business or company.

ICTs: Technologies that provide access to information through telecommunications.

Remittance: A transfer of funds by an expatriate to his country of origin.

Strategy: A plan of action designed to achieve a long-term or overall aim.

Telecommunications: It is the exchange of information over significant distances by electronic means.

Transformation: A marked change in form, nature, or appearance.

Chapter 6
Manufacturing Scheduling Strategy for Digital Enterprise Transformation

Halit Alper Tayali
https://orcid.org/0000-0002-2098-6482
School of Business, Istanbul University, Turkey

ABSTRACT

Scientific research and mathematics are the driving forces of economic progress. Firms that can align themselves with the contemporary information and communication technology era through their decisions about the digital transformation and sustain their competitive advantage might have a higher chance of survival compared to those that cannot. The managerial decisions that revolve around manufacturing focus on production planning and control along with cost minimization. Scheduling and sequencing activities lie at the heart of production planning and control. This chapter provides a basic perspective for the transformation from the traditional batch processing type of short-term manufacturing scheduling to the single-piece flow type of scheduling while presenting a novel manufacturing scheduling model to minimize the manufacturing cost for varying setup times and job sequence.

INTRODUCTION

The question of how to digitally transform the production function of an enterprise requires a multi-dimensional perspective for a satisfactory answer. All economic actors undergo the intangible and the inevitable process of globalization. Although the globalization aggravates the current affairs of income distribution gap, global climate change, and the culture of consumption -where all play a significant role in economic turmoil-, through supporting the flow of money, goods, services, and people, it is a natural growth factor. Setting aside the monumental concerns on globalization, it is the scientific research and mathematics that drive our well beings and economic progress.

This assumption dates to 17th century where the classical economics built upon the scientific approach along with Francis Bacon's empiricism, René Descartes' rationalism, mercantilists' foundation

DOI: 10.4018/978-1-7998-8587-0.ch006

of econometrics and William Petty's "Political Arithmetick". The economic liberalism that has emerged with the popular French term "laisse faire la nature" by Pierre de Boisguilbert, who implicitly referred to referring to leaving businesses alone and pointing out for minimal government, evolved into an ideology that supports the free-market economy where actors can decide freely on their choices (Kishtainy, 2018).

The theory of economics examines the interdependent relationships of actors with regards to different components such as interest rate, inflation, competition, growth, currency exchange, unemployment, social capital, technological leaps, and so on. Microeconomics, a branch of the economics theory, analyzes the decisions of the interacting actors and the managerial decisions of these actors revolve around the axes of supply and demand, or in other terms, production, and consumption. Production, along with finance and marketing is amongst the main functions of an enterprise. To manufacture goods or produce services, an entrepreneur aims for an optimal resource allocation while searching for ways to minimize cost or maximize profit.

At all economic levels, there have been infinitely many attempts to emphasize the importance of production planning and control activities. The practitioners of production planning and control, from almost every scientific field, have enjoyed a great application area since the First Industrial Revolution, by consulting mathematics, and optimizing for the total factor productivity of capital, labor, and other components of economics. This way, not only the enterprises gain advantage, but also our fledgling economic democracies: There is a growing need for implementing rational planning procedures and intelligent forecasting techniques to tackle globalization issues and to repair weaknesses of various aspects of our livings.

The contemporary approach in today's daily business practice is the digitalization and quantification of the production processes. Companies strive for insightful analysis to be able to compete in the global economy that promotes the concepts of big data, Industry 4.0, and the internet of things. The digitalization of operational processes in an enterprise addresses the business intelligence and decision support systems of that enterprise. A robust production planning and control solution must encompass all departments of the producing enterprise. The performance of the production planning and control activity depends on the digitalization level and the information obtained from the production processes. To achieve the challenging task of the production planning and control in a rational way, one needs to look deep into the enterprise for practical ways to model and optimize the operational processes.

This study poses two fundamental research questions for digitally transforming the manufacturing activities of an enterprise. The first one is about the advantage of this digital transformation since one should expect an increase in efficiency after digitally transforming the scheduling activities. The second question, as crucial as the first one, is then, how to achieve this digital transformation. This chapter tries to prescribe the basic and practical answers for these two questions.

The structure of the chapter is as follows: The background section defines the manufacturing environment and the corresponding layout arrangements for these manufacturing systems along with popular concepts and tools from the field of operations and supply chain management with emphasis on the continuous improvement programs. Then, the historical evolution of the manufacturing scheduling activity is explained through the traditional batch processing type of scheduling and single piece flow scheduling. The research methodology and the solutions and recommendations sections present the novel scheduling model as the significant contribution of this chapter for the single piece flow manufacturing scheduling literature. Finally, the chapter ends with emerging trends for future research directions and a further discussion of the overall coverage of the chapter with concluding remarks.

BACKGROUND

Manufacturing is the main activity of a goods' supplier. In a manufacturing environment the scope of an operation is limited to a person's or a machine's activity on product. The operations management literature presents many ways of classifying a manufacturing or a production system -for instance according to its type of manufacturing process and methods used, the type of end-product, the type of flow of products, the volume of the products. Furthermore, there are many attempts in the literature for specifying the differences in manufacturing and service processes and providing common definitions for factors of production. However, a brief classification for examining whether the system is working on a basis of make-to-stock, assemble-to-order, make-to-order, or engineer-to-order is usually preferable. Once the class of a manufacturing system is defined, then related layout strategies will be available to organize the processes in a shop floor. Possible layout strategies for manufacturing processes include project, work-center, manufacturing cell, assembly line, and continuous process. (Jacobs & Chase, 2018; Kasapoğlu & Tayalı, 2012)

The optimal allocation of resources within a manufacturing system is a critical decision to make. There have been many concepts developed since the First Industrial Revolution under the umbrella of continuous improvement programs to allocate the resources in an optimal way. Some popular concepts of operations management implemented for manufacturing systems since 1980s include but not limited to lean, just-in-time, total quality, six-sigma, business process reengineering, and the theory of constraints. Every conceptual framework has its own way of examining the enterprise's manufacturing and production processes.

The plans to reduce the cost, to improve efficiency, and to implement a continuous improvement program for the manufacturing processes of an enterprise, are also among the managerial decisions that require a thorough analysis of the manufacturing system. A deep perspective to the manufacturing environment is necessary for to mathematically model the operations and processes. Therefore, an entrepreneur might choose one from many well-known continuous improvement programs and follow its guidelines and implement the related quality tools to achieve the challenging task of the production planning and control task in a rational way. There is an extensive literature on comparing the advantages and disadvantages of the continuous improvement programs along with their implementation and application guidelines, assumptions and effects on the manufacturing systems (Nave, 2002) while a tailor-made approach that includes different aspects of several continuous improvement programs is also preferable (Tayalı, 2016).

The contemporary approach at the manufacturing environments is to adapt the digital twinning strategy to digitally transform and monitor the production planning and control activities of their enterprises (Lu, Liu, Wang, Huang, & Xu, 2020; Rasheed, San, & Kvamsdal, 2020; Zhou, Zhang, Li, Ding, & Wang, 2020). At the core of a digital twin, there is a decision support system for the manufacturing scheduling activity of the production environment (Jones, Snider, Nassehi, Yon, & Hicks, 2020; Wang & Wu, 2020). Therefore, the strategic decision of manufacturing scheduling plays a key role in the digital transformation of the enterprise (Liu, Chen, Zhang, Yang, & Cheng, 2020).

This chapter focuses on providing detailed information on the evolution of the manufacturing scheduling by explaining the basic principles of batch processing and single piece flow. Furthermore, this study equips readers with information on how to develop a novel manufacturing scheduling model using mathematical programming and create a decision support system.

The scheduling is the backbone of a manufacturing planning and control activity and the digital transformation of this activity requires a strategic perspective. This chapter aims to provide a basic perspective for the transformation from the traditional batch processing type of short-term manufacturing scheduling to the single piece flow type of scheduling, while at the same time presenting the solution of a novel model to minimize the cost of manufacturing where the setup times and job sequence vary. Furthermore, this chapter prescribes a way to convert this knowledge into a decision support system that will digitally transform the enterprise by satisfying the two research questions posed. The chapter broadly describes how to embed the mathematical model into a decision support system by the means of a computer programming language.

Next section outlines the production planning and control activities of an enterprise from an evolutionary perspective by following the selected continuous improvement program of lean manufacturing to provide content specific information on the concepts, tools and models used in scheduling and sequencing.

TRANSFORMATION OF MANUFACTURING SCHEDULING & SEQUENCING ACTIVITIES

The mathematical tools used in the ample production planning and control literature is vast and it is not feasible to go through and classify all the terminology, methodology or variables of the related tools. However, a broad classification with regards to the planning horizon is comprehensive enough: For short term horizons that encompass days or weeks, scheduling and sequencing methods are used, and for longer horizons that span months, the practitioners and scholars refer to the aggregate production planning methods (Chopra & Meindl, 2016). The optimization model of the aggregate production planning matches supply with demand in a time window specified by the production planning horizon and aims for minimization of costs recurring from the manufacturing activities of the enterprise. As mentioned previously, this chapter focuses on the evolutionary transformation of the traditional batch processing type of short-term manufacturing scheduling to the single piece flow type of scheduling suggested by the lean manufacturing approach.

Traditional Batch Scheduling

In a manufacturing system where the products to be processed, or jobs, move from one process to another in batches, all items in the batch must wait until all items in the batch have been processed. No single item in the batch can move to the next machine, process or operation until the ongoing process finishes its operation on all items of that batch. In other words, traditional batch manufacturing, avoids the completed items in the batch to proceed to the next operation, process, or machine, until all items in the batch complete their process. A manufacturing system that has digitally transformed its scheduling activities, on the contrary, has the capacity to move the items of a batch in a progressive way along the manufacturing processes without waiting for all items in the batch to complete their process. This type of movement is called the single piece flow. As the key element and successful application of the lean manufacturing approach, the movement of the single piece flow improves the quality performance of the enterprise (Cohen, Alhuraish, Robledo, & Kobi, 2020).

An explanatory model of a manufacturing system compares the performances of the traditional batch processing type of manufacturing and the single piece flow approach (Srinivasan, 2012). The basic single piece flow scheduling model explained in this section has four general assumptions:

1. Each machine requires a setup as jobs change.
2. Jobs follow a pre-determined route.
3. Jobs follow a pre-determined sequence.
4. Transportation cost of products are omitted.

The aim of this model is to create a production scheduling for the given production sequence and measure the scheduling performance where 3 dissimilar machines process 4 different jobs with a batch size of 10 units. The setup times for machines A, B, and C are 10, 15 and 20 units of time, respectively. Matrix $[T]$ represents the unit processing times for 4 different jobs at 3 machines:

$$[T] = \begin{bmatrix} 1 & 2 & 1 \\ 1 & 1 & 2 \\ 2 & 2 & 3 \\ 2 & 1 & 1 \end{bmatrix}$$

The rows represent the jobs, whereas the machines are at the columns. For example, the number at the intersection of the 3rd row and the 2nd column, which is 2, is the unit processing time of the 3rd job at machine B.

Two scenarios are examined within the framework of this manufacturing scheduling model. The first scenario schedules the traditional batch flow, whose transfer size is 10 units -the batch itself-, whereas the second case details the production scheduling for a transfer size of 1 unit, namely the single piece flow. Table 1 details out the manufacturing schedule of the first scenario as the jobs transfer to the next machine only after the machines complete processing the whole batch.

J1, the first job, whose batch and transfer size is 10, completes at the 20th time unit (t = 20), because it takes 10 time units for the setup of machine A, and the operation proceeds for 10 units of time since the unit processing time of J1 at machine A is 1 time unit -see $[T]$. Note that in this traditional case the machine setup starts as jobs arrive at the machines. The first batch of J1 proceeds to machine B and processing completes there at t = 55. Finally, J1 visits machine C to complete its manufacturing of the batch, at t = 85. This is the horizontal perspective of the scheduling constructed in Table 1. A vertical post-analysis for Table 1 explains that the second job, J2, cannot start on machine A, before machine A completes the first job, J1, as well. Note that all jobs complete at t = 205 which is the makespan value. As a commonly used performance measure in monitoring scheduling and sequencing activities for delivery promptness, the makespan denotes the time difference between the start and finish of a sequence of jobs. Therefore, a lower value of makespan indicates that the jobs are completed earlier, when compared to the makespan of another manufacturing schedule. (Srinivasan, 2012)

Table 1. Traditional batch transfer and manufacturing scheduling of 3 machines processing 4 jobs

	A	B	C
J1	20	55	85
J2	40	80	125
J3	70	115	175
J4	100	140	205

Single Piece Flow Scheduling

The concept of the single piece flow is a conjecture from the popular continuous improvement approach of lean manufacturing. It refers to an ideal manufacturing environment where items are transferred in unit sizes of one. Sometimes referred to as continuous flow in the operations management literature, the single piece flow defines a process where products proceed through various operations of the enterprise with the assumption that only a single piece, that is, an item of lot size one moves in a progressive way and flows through the operations without any interruption or backflows.

Previously explained scheduling approach is the traditional method for constructing the manufacturing schedule for the flow of the batch as can be followed from Table 1. The scenario depicted in Table 2, on the other hand, provides the manufacturing scheduling from the perspective of the single piece flow scheduling with the same quantitative measurements of setup times and batch sizes of the manufacturing environment of the traditional batch flow type of processing. There are only two differences between the model of the traditional manufacturing schedule of Table 1 and the single piece flow scheduling of Table 2. The crucial difference is that the transfer size is 10 units in batch flow schedule, but the single piece flow schedule proceeds with a transfer size of 1 unit. The other difference is that in Table 2 all the machines' setup take place at the beginning of the schedule, whereas in the traditional batch flow, machine setups take place as jobs arrive to the operation center.

The manufacturing schedule in Table 2 proceeds horizontally and vertically. The rows stand for the 10 pieces of each job, where each sub-job of a job moves as a single piece and flows through the predetermined sequence of machines. Note that some jobs must wait before being processed in the next machine. For instance, J1_1 starts its operation on machine A at t = 11, and because it has a unit processing time of 1 as can be seen from $\left[T\right]$, it finishes its operation at machine A at t = 11. If B were ready to process the incoming jobs, J1_1 would proceed to machine B and start operating at t = 12. However, machine B is undergoing a setup that completes at t = 15. Therefore, J1 can only start being processed at machine B at t = 16, the earliest. There are some manufacturing scheduling performance measures to minimize the idle time of jobs as well. Besides, note that in this schedule only the jobs are idle, and machines work at full capacity after their setup. Three dots in the schedules represent the sub-jobs in between. The manufacturing process ends at t = 159. Therefore, the makespan of the manufacturing schedule of the single piece flow outperforms the traditional batch process schedule and allows for a faster manufacturing.

Table 2. Single piece flow manufacturing scheduling of 4 jobs processed at 3 machines

Jobs	Machine A				Machine B				Machine C			
	Setup		Operation		Setup		Operation		Setup		Operation	
	Start	Finish	Start	Finish	Start	Finish	Start	Finish	Start	Finish	Start	Finish
J1_1	0	10	11	11	0	15	16	17	0	20	21	21
J1_2			12	12			18	19			22	22
…	…		…		…		…		…		…	
J1_9			19	19			32	33			34	34
J1_10			20	20			34	35			36	36
J1	*End batch*				*End batch*				*End batch*			
J2_1	21	31	32	32	36	51	52	52	37	57	58	59
J2_2			33	33			53	53			60	61
…	…		…		…		…		…		…	
J2_9			40	40			60	60			74	75
J2_10			41	41			61	61			76	77
J2	*End batch*				*End batch*				*End batch*			
J3_1	42	52	53	54	62	77	78	79	78	98	99	101
J3_2			55	56			80	81			102	104
…	…				…		…		…		…	
J3_9			69	70			94	95			123	125
J3_10			71	72			96	97			126	128
J3	*End batch*				*End batch*				*End batch*			
J4_1	73	83	84	85	98	113	114	114	129	149	150	150
J4_2			86	87			115	115			151	151
	…		…		…		…		…		…	
J4_9			100	101			122	122			158	158
J4_10			102	103			123	123			159	159
J4	End batch & process				End batch & process				End batch & process			

The two manufacturing scheduling examples presented above have investigated the makespan of these schedules under the conditions of the given assumptions of varying setup times (assumption 1) and fixed demand sequences (assumption 3). The 3rd assumption is critical in the horizontal approach of the schedule. In other words, one can relax this assumption to change the sequence of jobs whereas the 2nd assumption of the manufacturing scheduling models imply the vertical approach with regards to the route that the jobs must follow, which resembles the infamous travelling salesman problem.

The sequence of the jobs that will be taken into the manufacturing process relies mostly on the structure of the manufacturing environment. For instance, the 4th assumption of these two models points out the fact that this type of scheduling can be more useful in cellular manufacturing, where the machines are so close to each other that the transportation cost of products can be omitted (Srinivasan, 2012).

However, these schedules can easily be tailored for the needs of the manufacturing environment with the single piece flow approach.

There are many approaches for solving the job sequencing problem of the operations management, such as sequencing jobs according to their longest or shortest processing times (Kasapoğlu & Tayalı, 2012). The effort is for to find the best performing schedule in terms of a manufacturing schedule such as the minimization of the makespan, lateness or inventory levels (Winston & Albright, 2019).

The significance of the study stems from its novel methodological approach for the single-piece flow scheduling problem. To the author's knowledge, this chapter presents the first study that considers the varying sequence and setup times for the single piece flow scheduling problem. Furthermore, the study progressively elaborates on a manufacturing scheduling problem for different scenarios while introducing the fundamental concepts of the manufacturing scheduling and and shows that the novel methodology developed in this manuscript increases the efficiency compared to the traditional approaches of scheduling algorithms of traditional batch processing and single piece flow scheduling where the job sequence does not vary.

The next section provides the research methodology to solve the problem of fixed sequence and varying setup times in single piece flow type of manufacturing scheduling by changing the job sequence presented in Table 2.

Research Methodology

The first research question that this chapter is trying to find an answer to if it is possible to create a manufacturing schedule with an increased efficiency for the single piece flow scheduling. The novel methodology enables one to vary the sequence of jobs in the manufacturing scheduling using mathematical programming. Therefore, the first objective of this study is to examine the efficiency of the novel methodology with a manufacturing scheduling case.

The methodology introduces a novel approach to the manufacturing scheduling literature for the problem of single piece flow schedule with varying setup times. The mathematical optimization model is an extension of the models presented in the literature (Srinivasan, 2012; Winston & Albright, 2019) where the associated problems of the single piece flow scheduling do not include varying job sequence or setup times. The mathematical programming model developed and applied in this study relaxes the 3rd assumption to introduce job sequencing into the single piece flow manufacturing schedule developed in Table 2, but at the same time, holds on to the 1st assumption of setup times while aiming for the minimum makespan.

The next section provides the results of the novel methodology for the manufacturing scheduling case at hand. Furthermore, it tries to provide an answer for the second research objective of this study, which is to prescribe a decision support system using the novel methodology for the digital transformation of the manufacturing environment.

SOLUTIONS AND RECOMMENDATIONS

The research methodology of the mathematical programming model presents a solution as in Table 3 for minimizing the makespan of the single piece flow manufacturing schedule under varying machine setup times and job sequencing. The resulting quasi-optimal schedule given in Table 3 shows the increase in the efficiency of the manufacture schedule by obtaining %3.9 decrease in the makespan compared to the manufacturing schedule of Table 2. In other words, the novel methodology that integrates varying setup times and job sequencing into the single piece flow scheduling has the capacity to decrease the overall manufacturing costs occurring from the scheduling activity. Therefore, the primary research objective is satisfied as the novel methodology outputs a manufacturing schedule with an increased efficiency. Note that the solution, which has been obtained by Microsoft Excel's Solver add-in, is quasi-optimal since this type of a manufacturing scheduling problem belongs to the computationally NP-hard class and requires heuristics that do not guarantee optimality.

Today, many enterprises either use sophisticated digital enterprise resource planning software for the production planning and control activities or do not use any production planning and control system at all. A simple decision support system for manufacturing scheduling is a straightforward solution for managing the scheduling problems that cause delays in matching supply with demand and other problems in relation to the manufacturing structure (Rooney & Rooney, 2005). A common example of such problems is the inevitable increase in the inventory levels due to unbalanced manufacturing schedule, causing a physical distraction and consequently hiding away problems that need managerial attention.

Building a decision support system for implementing a manufacturing scheduling requires the following organizational steps taken by the managerial office:

Phase One: Create a cell in the manufacturing environment
Phase Two: Define machine setup times for the machines in the cell
Phase Three: Define job processing times in the cell
Phase Four: Create and implement the schedule for the cell

A manufacturing scheduling decision support system should consider all other cells in the manufacturing environment only after initiating the above hierarchic approach for a single cell in the shop floor as a pilot study. With the surveillance of a planning practitioner, the pilot study should point out the practical aspects of the implementation within a local cell, so that the combination of all cells in the manufacturing environment can then lead to a synchronous manufacturing schedule after initiating the decision support system.

The following question from the production planning and control practitioners' perspective is an important one: "Who" will create and implement this digital decision support system for the synchronous manufacturing schedule? From the computer science perspective "*a computer does two things, and two things only: it performs calculations and it remembers the results of those calculations*" (Guttag, 2013). From the enterprise perspective, on the other hand, communicating with the computer by writing a code for a repetitive task and make it do the tedious work is expected to be as efficient as the steam engine that named the First Industrial Revolution.

Knowing how to use a software or writing a piece of code in an arbitrary programming language to manage one's job is usually enough for daily business practice, although there is always room for improvement. One can always transcend the state of being familiar with using the software, especially with the vast information resources available on the world wide web. The mathematical and computer programming concepts are beyond the scope of this chapter but note that today there are hundreds of different computer programming languages. Theoretically, all of them possess the same computational power, but different languages can perform differently for different applications, while quantum computing is expected to create another paradigm shift within the digital era. Human resources, especially skillful in mathematical, statistical and computer programming areas, are the ones that meet the demand for implementing rational planning procedures and intelligent forecasting techniques. Therefore, the next question should answer how a capable person could create a decision support system.

Table 3. Sequencing of jobs in single piece flow schedule with varying setup times

Jobs	Machine A				Machine B				Machine C			
	Setup		Operation		Setup		Operation		Setup		Operation	
	Start	Finish	Start	Finish	Start	Finish	Start	Finish	Start	Finish	Start	Finish
J2_1	0	10	11	11	0	15	16	16	0	20	21	22
J2_2			12	12			17	17			23	24
…	…		…		…		…		…		…	
J2_9			19	19			24	24			37	38
J2_10			20	20			25	25			39	40
J2	*End batch*				*End batch*				*End batch*			
J1_1	21	31	32	32	26	41	42	43	41	61	62	62
J1_2			33	33			44	45			63	63
…	…		…		…				…		…	
J1_9			40	40			58	59			70	70
J1_10			41	41			60	61			71	71
J1	*End batch*				*End batch*				*End batch*			
J3_1	42	52	53	54	62	77	78	79	72	92	93	95
J3_2			55	56			80	81			96	98
…	…		…		…		…		…		…	
J3_9			69	70			94	95			117	119
J3_10			71	72			96	97			120	122
J3	*End batch*				*End batch*				*End batch*			
J4_1	73	83	84	85	98	113	114	114	123	143	144	144
J4_2			86	87			115	115			145	145
	…		…		…		…		…		…	
J4_9			100	101			122	122			152	152
J4_10			102	103			123	123			153	153
J4	End batch & process				End batch & process				End batch & process			

In today's information and communication technology era, decision support systems are one of those concepts that have initiated the industrial and digital paradigm shift towards Industry 4.0. Decision support systems are not only vital for manufacturing scheduling but are also used unwittingly in our daily lives for many useful and practical purposes, such as for being informed about weather and traffic, diagnosis of medical conditions, avoiding accidents, and for so many other aspects of our living.

A decision support system is at its best with its straightforward design for its user interface and experience. Decision support systems do not occupy the end users with technical details. It is defined as a user-friendly tool for an end user that can define inputs to a developed model by the help of simple instructions and notifications. As stated previously, there are many programming languages that one can use to write a computer code that can develop and run the decision support system for manufacturing scheduling. Therefore, a generic prescription is preferable in explaining the process of implementing a decision support system for manufacturing scheduling (Albright & Winston, 2015; Winston & Albright, 2019):

1. Explanation sheet for decision support system
2. Dialog box for obtaining user inputs
3. Optimal solution report

The backend of the decision support system might use a linear optimization method for a multiperiod production planning and control activity and the frontend of the decision support system might simply consist of the above three components. There are many open source and high-level computer programming languages that can be used for operating these backend and frontend processes. The wide eco-system around these programming languages allow not only scholars to model their mathematical approaches, but also enable software programmers, engineers, and practitioners to apply their programming skills for software production by the use of integrated software development environments. For instance, one can write the backend processes of the manufacturing scheduling decision support system with the R programming language and use extensions of the same programming language to design the frontend processes for publishing it on the world wide web.

FUTURE RESEARCH DIRECTIONS

The transformation in the manufacturing scheduling from the traditional approach to the single piece flow type of scheduling shows that there are many opportunities to increase the efficiency of the manufacturing environment. The trending approach of the Industry 4.0 promotes lean manufacturing methodologies within the manufacturing environment to focus on the elimination of all types of waste in the process. However, nearly all continuous improvement efforts towards the minimization of makespan, waiting time, work-in-process inventory levels, and unit processing times serve for the optimum allocation of resources and a fully automated manufacturing environment, which satisfy users and sustain businesses in the long run.

The development and production of a decision support system for manufacturing scheduling is an ongoing effort and it should be done in alignment with consistent insights from the scholars and practitioners of the production planning and control field as well as the related engineering departments. Therefore, a practitioner should constantly follow the emerging research on the integrated development environments for production planning and manufacturing scheduling algorithms.

The single piece flow scheduling of the lean manufacturing approach requires a transfer size of 1 unit between processes. The next step in tailoring a manufacturing schedule for the digital enterprise transformation is to determine the ideal batch size of the transported jobs in the manufacturing environment. The ideal batch size is 1 unit if the setup times are negligible, and it is possible to relax the assumption that a machine setup is required for each job. The idea of single-minute exchange of dies refers to this mathematical concept, by offering to decrease setup times under 10 minutes (Jacobs, Berry, Whybark, & Vollmann, 2011; Rooney & Rooney, 2005). Another probable future research direction is to apply the novel methodology of this manuscript for the multiple-piece-flow (Otto & Li, 2020) manufacturing environment.

In the 3rd manufacturing schedule presented at Table 3, machine setup is necessary when there is a change in the processed job. The schedule requires a machine setup only at the beginning so that the sub-jobs of the same job do not need any changeover or machine setup during the manufacturing. In other words, the novel scheduling model presented here for the single piece flow with varying setup times, may be adjusted to include not only the setup times for changing jobs but also the sub-jobs.

The lean manufacturing practices include but not limited to cellular layout, the single-minute exchange of dies and takt time (Amrani & Ducq, 2020). Takt, a Russian word, is the heartbeat of a lean manufacturing system referring to the rate of customer demand. To achieve the single piece flow, cycle time for every operation of a process needs to be reduced to equal takt time, calculated by dividing production time by the quantity of demand in that period. The production planning and control activity provides the link between quantities of supply and demand with regards to the manufacturing enterprise. Therefore, the enterprise needs to digitally monitor the manufacturing system to achieve the single piece flow status for equalizing the cycle time to the takt time. This requires another assumption to introduce into the novel model, which is the precedence relationships within the jobs.

The theory of constraints, also called constrains management, is a concept from the operations management discipline. It has been developed by Goldratt around 1980s as a systematic management tool to focus on removing constraints for increasing the efficiency of the manufacturing processes and decreasing inventory and related operational expenses (Goldratt, 1980). The scheduling algorithm of the theory of constraints, namely the drum-buffer-rope along with its mathematical definitions and preliminaries -e.g. synchronous manufacturing, capacity constrained resource, bottleneck, non-bottleneck, forward and backward scheduling- can be integrated within the findings, solutions and recommendations of this study for future research. To the author's knowledge, there is no study in the literature about modelling the single piece flow with the drum-buffer-rope scheduling of synchronous manufacturing and the theory of constraints. Defining dependent and independent jobs are critical, just as done in the methods of project management, such as the critical path. Therefore, the integration of the drum-buffer-rope and the theory of constraints with the single piece flow is a feasible approach for short-term manufacturing scheduling purposes, for the drum-buffer-rope manufacturing scheduling includes precedence relationships depicted by the activity-on-node graphics (Srinivasan, 2012; Tayalı, 2016). The hypothesis of the experimental study is going to examine whether there is an increase in the manufacturing scheduling performance or not, after developing the integrated model. Note that the drum-buffer-rope type of manufacturing scheduling focuses on inventories and carries the potential to treat inventories not in terms of physical manufactured items but in terms of units of time.

Finally, the last future research direction in relation to the production planning and control activity is to combine the long-term aggregate production planning models with the single piece flow manufacturing scheduling and sequencing. This kind of study also carries the potential to extend its findings to the problems that arise in the supply chain and project management frameworks. An open-source programming code might be presented for replication, modification, and testing of other production planning and control activities as well, to add value and prove useful for the digitalization and transformation efforts in the production planning and control activities within the manufacturing departments of the enterprises.

CONCLUSION

The current era of the information and communication technology challenges the companies to keep up with the hyper-competitive global economic environment and to allocate resources optimally. Firms that can align themselves with this environment through their know-how, the ability to use scientific research and mathematics and thus intelligent decisions, might have a higher chance of survival to sustain their competitive advantage, compared to those companies that cannot undergo a digital transformation to use computers and machines in tedious tasks.

Scheduling and sequencing activities lie at the heart of production planning and control. The mathematical models of these activities are the backbone of a decision support system built for manufacturing scheduling. This chapter explains the evolution of the manufacturing scheduling by the basic principles of batch processing and single piece flow and provides a wide perspective for the transformation from the traditional batch processing type of short-term manufacturing scheduling to the single piece flow type of scheduling, while presenting a novel manufacturing scheduling model to minimize the manufacturing cost for varying setup times and job sequence. By explaining how to develop a novel scheduling algorithm, this chapter contributes to the critical task of the production planning and control activity and the related operational research literature as the novel methodology solves the single piece flow scheduling problem of the lean manufacturing with varying job sequence and setup times.

This chapter depicts a framework for digitally transforming the manufacturing activities of an enterprise by proposing to develop a decision support system for overseeing the job scheduling in the manufacturing environment. Such efforts primarily target for an increase in the efficiency of the manufacturing system by reducing the makespan, which is the elapsed time between the start and finish of a sequence of operations. The novel methodology achieves to minimize the makespan of the single piece flow manufacturing scheduling problem under varying machine setup times and job sequences by %3.9, compared to the case with a fixed sequence of jobs. The chapter contributes to the literature significantly by examining the scheduling problem under varying setup times and job sequences.

An objective of this chapter is to equip readers with detailed information on how to create a decision support system for the novel manufacturing scheduling model and implement it across the enterprise to digitally transform the production environment. Therefore, while introducing the concepts related to the manufacturing scheduling and decision support system, the chapter guides the readers for how to practically develop a decision support system for the strategic production planning and control activity of the manufacturing scheduling.

The production planning and control activities create generic links that match the demand of the customers with the supply of the manufacturing enterprise. The business intelligence of an enterprise involves the digitalization of operational processes of the enterprise and the decision support systems are the components of this digital transformation. A digitally transformed enterprise can match supply with demand in a sustainable way as she has the required capability to oversee the incoming data from the shop floor.

The content in this manuscript equips the practitioners from the field of operations management with references for defining innovative ways to improve the manufacturing environment. The managerial decisions that revolve around manufacturing focus on production planning and control along with cost minimization. According to the lean manufacturing approach, an enterprise should strive to achieve the single piece flow status in her strategic manufacturing and production activities for a balanced, sustainable, and profitable process management.

REFERENCES

Albright, S., & Winston, W. (2015). *Business Analytics: Data Analysis and Decision Making*. Cangage Learning.

Amrani, A., & Ducq, Y. (2020). Lean practices implementation in aerospace based on sector characteristics: Methodology and case study. *Production Planning and Control*, *31*(16), 1–23. doi:10.1080/09537287.2019.1706197

Chopra, S., & Meindl, P. (2016). Supply Chain Management (Global Edition). Academic Press.

Cohen, A., Alhuraish, I., Robledo, C., & Kobi, A. (2020). A statistical analysis of critical quality tools and companies' performance. *Journal of Cleaner Production*, *255*, 120221. doi:10.1016/j.jclepro.2020.120221

Goldratt, E. (1980). Optimized production timetable: a revolutionary program for industry. *APICS 23rd Annual Conference Proceedings*, 14–17.

Guttag, J. (2013). *Introduction to computation and programming using Python*. Academic Press.

Jacobs, F. R., Berry, W. L., Whybark, D. C., & Vollmann, T. E. (2011). *Manufacturing planning and control for supply chain management*. McGraw Hill Higher Education.

Jacobs, F. R., & Chase, R. B. (2018). Operations and supply chain management. New York NY: McGraw-Hill/Irwin.

Jones, D., Snider, C., Nassehi, A., Yon, J., & Hicks, B. (2020). Characterising the Digital Twin: A systematic literature review. *CIRP Journal of Manufacturing Science and Technology*, *29*, 36–52. doi:10.1016/j.cirpj.2020.02.002

Kasapoğlu, Ö. A., & Tayalı, H. A. (2012). Transformation of Job Shop to Flow Shop in an Era of Global Crises. *Proceedings of the 10th International Logistics & Supply Chain Congress*, 112–116. Retrieved from https://papers.ssrn.com/sol3/papers.cfm?abstract_id=2919847

Kishtainy, N. (Ed.). (2018). *The Economics Book: Big Ideas Simply Explained*. Dorling Kindersley.

Liu, Z., Chen, W., Zhang, C., Yang, C., & Cheng, Q. (2020). Intelligent scheduling of a feature-process-machine tool supernetwork based on digital twin workshop. *Journal of Manufacturing Systems*. Advance online publication. doi:10.1016/j.jmsy.2020.07.016

Lu, Y., Liu, C., Wang, K. I. K., Huang, H., & Xu, X. (2020, February 1). Digital Twin-driven smart manufacturing: Connotation, reference model, applications and research issues. *Robotics and Computer-integrated Manufacturing*, *61*, 101837. doi:10.1016/j.rcim.2019.101837

Nave, D. (2002). How to compare six sigma, lean and the theory of constraints. *Toc-Cga.Org, 35*(3), 73–80. Retrieved from http://www.toc-cga.org/upload/reference/3.pdf

Otto, A., & Li, X. (2020). Product sequencing in multiple-piece-flow assembly lines. *Omega (United Kingdom)*, *91*, 102055. doi:10.1016/j.omega.2019.03.013

Rasheed, A., San, O., & Kvamsdal, T. (2020). Digital twin: Values, challenges and enablers from a modeling perspective. *IEEE Access: Practical Innovations, Open Solutions*, *8*, 21980–22012. doi:10.1109/ACCESS.2020.2970143

Rooney, S. A., & Rooney, J. J. (2005). Lean glossary. *Quality Progress*, *38*(6), 41–47.

Srinivasan, G. (2012). *Single piece transportation*. Retrieved from https://nptel.ac.in/courses/110/106/110106044/

Tayalı, H. A. (2016). A Literature Review on Production Scheduling with the Drum-Buffer-Rope Technique. *16th International Symposium for Production Research*, 1085–1090. Retrieved from https://papers.ssrn.com/sol3/papers.cfm?abstract_id=2919846

Wang, Y., & Wu, Z. (2020). Model construction of planning and scheduling system based on digital twin. *International Journal of Advanced Manufacturing Technology*, *109*(7), 2189–2203. doi:10.100700170-020-05779-9

Winston, W. L., & Albright, S. C. (2019). *Practical management science : includes Microsoft Office Excel 2007 applications* (6th ed.). Cengage.

Zhou, G., Zhang, C., Li, Z., Ding, K., & Wang, C. (2020). Knowledge-driven digital twin manufacturing cell towards intelligent manufacturing. *International Journal of Production Research*, *58*(4), 1034–1051. doi:10.1080/00207543.2019.1607978

ADDITIONAL READING

Alpaydın, E. (2020). Introduction to machine learning (Fourth edi). The MIT Press.

Atkinson, S., O'Hara, S., & Sturgeon, A. (Eds.). (2014). *The Business Book: Big Ideas Simply Explained*. Dorling Kindersley.

Cachon, G., & Terwiesch, C. (2020). *Matching supply with demand : an introduction to operations management* (Fourth edi). New York NY: McGraw-Hill Education.

Esen, H. Ö. (2008). *Applied Operations Research*. Caglayan.

Heizer, J., Render, B., & Munson, C. (2020). *Operations management: sustainability and supply chain management*. Pearson Education Limited.

Jones, D. T., & Womack, J. P. (1996). *Lean thinking*. Banish Waste and Create Wealth in Your Corporation.

Krajewski, L. J., Malhotra, M. K., & Ritzman, L. P. (2019). *Operations management processes and supply chains*. Pearson.

Pinedo, M. L. (2016). Scheduling: Theory, algorithms, and systems, fifth edition. In Scheduling: Theory, Algorithms, and Systems, Fifth Edition. doi:10.1007/978-3-319-26580-3

Strang, G. (2019). *Linear algebra and learning from data*. Wellesley-Cambridge Press.

Taha, H. (2017). *Operations research: An introduction*. Pearson Education Limited.

KEY TERMS AND DEFINITIONS

Back-End: Website development tasks regarding a server, an application, and a database.

Digital Twin: A virtual model of a production activity that monitors and controls the production environment for improved decision making by using data.

Front-End: The design and development of the interface that users interact when using an application or visiting a web site.

Lean Manufacturing: Body of system and techniques that focus and aim on the simplification of the manufacturing processes through waste management, cost reduction, increased customer satisfaction, being agile and accelerating cash flow by eliminating all kinds of waste that occur throughout the manufacturing and production processes. Lean refers to producing the maximum amount of sales of goods or services with the minimum operational cost, while maintaining an optimum inventory level. Waste refers to anything that does not add to creation of value for which the customer is willing to pay for and can be in form of inventory, waiting times, excessive production, defects, unnecessary tasks, and so on.

Makespan: The elapsed time between the start and finish of a sequence of operations in a set of machines. The completion time of the last job or task in an operation or process.

Operations: The transformation of physical material or abstract thinking into finished goods or completed product or service.

Single Piece Flow: A manufacturing process in which items are transferred in unit sizes of one from one operation to the next. Also referred to as one-piece flow or continuous flow.

Single-Minute Exchange of Dies: A term used for the techniques to reduce the setup times of machines during manufacturing to less than 10 minutes to eliminate the waste that occur in the flow of manufacturing.

Synchronous Manufacturing: A process or a set of processes of the manufacturing or production environment that operates in timely balance -or in synchronization- to achieve in supplying the demand.

Theory of Constraints (TOC): A management paradigm that identifies and resolves the barriers which prevent a business from achieving its goals. The theory finds the constraints and rebuilds the organization around them using focusing processes. According to the theory of constraints, a system is only as strong as its weakest link. Therefore, it tries to overcome the individual process inefficiencies as well as bottlenecks in the production system.

Chapter 7
Digital Management Towards Society 5.0:
A Review of the Framework for Kurt Lewin Theory During COVID-19 Pandemic

Bulent Akkaya
https://orcid.org/0000-0003-1252-9334
Manisa Celal Bayar University, Turkey

Ayse Gunsel
Kocaeli University, Turkey

Ibrahim Yikilmaz
Kocaeli University, Turkey

ABSTRACT

Society 5.0, human-centered social understanding, is defined as the period in which the technological opportunities offered by Industry 4.0 will serve the welfare of people. However, Society 5.0 faces many factors in terms of resistance to social change. Both the commitment of individuals and organizations to the current social life practice and uncertainty slows down the path to Society 5.0. With the COVID-19 pandemic-related digital solutions and applications on a world scale, life practices have radically changed. At this point, the process towards Society 5.0 has accelerated and the first stage of Kurt Lewin's three-steps change model has started, "unfreeze." Decision makers and managers need to initiate change, particularly in education and other fields, and contribute to social transformation by "refreezing" new practices and methods that will serve human well-being and Society 5.0. In this context, this process was discussed, and recommendations were made in the scope of the study.

DOI: 10.4018/978-1-7998-8587-0.ch007

INTRODUCTION

Today, above all, technological advances, for instance, the remarkable increase in computing power, are contributing to improvements in both business and society (Shiroishi et al., 2018). Digital transformation is generating new values and becoming a mainstay of industrial policy in many countries (Fukuyama, 2018). Simultaneously, the world is witnessing worldwide challenges, just like the lessening of natural resources, global warming, and rising economic inequality in general, an epidemic crisis –Covid-19- in particular. No doubt, we try to survive in a chaotic era of uncertainty, insecurity with complexity rising at all levels. Hence it is vital that human beings, now, have to leverage digital technologies to effectively and efficiently provide solutions for society to create better living standards and sustainable healthy economic growth. It is first the Japanese who look beyond Industry 4.0, at the same time as considering other countries' policies, such as Germany's Industry 4.0 and the United States' Advanced Manufacturing Partnership (Shiroishi et al., 2018; Fukuda, 2020).

Industry 4.0 consists of the incorporation of data flow amongst the partners, suppliers, and customers, in addition to the integration of the real world with the virtual world which leads to an updated information platform in real-time (Abreu, 2018). The technological and digital components, such as Artificial Intelligence (AI), Internet of Things (IOT), or Industrial Internet, are emphasized in Industry 4.0. At the same time, the human-centered focus is quite ignored (Ferreira and Serpa, 2018). Probably the only premise given concerning human resources is potential changes within the labor market as a result of automation, robotics, and AI. Above all, the world of work in Industry 4.0 is yet inconceivable without human beings. But what is the benefit of people and society from Industry 4.0? (Skobelev and Borovik, 2017) The technological uprising within Industry 4.0 can achieve its full potential just with the association of social innovation (Morrar et al., 2017). It is the Government of Japan's Society 5.0 proposal that tries to make use of digital technologies to create a "super smart" cyber-physical society that is more "human-oriented" (Harayama 2017; Fukuyama, 2018; Gladden, 2019) The main purpose of Society 5.0 is to create a technology integrated society in which all human beings can appreciate life minus all potential limitations. Even though Society 5.0 is initiated in Japan, its motivation isn't solely directed at the succeeding in one nation (Onday, 2019). The worldwide social trend now is the generation of Society 5.0., as it is compulsory to establish a better society, well-fare of everyone (Bryndin, 2018).

As mentioned above, Society 5.0 represents a paradigm shift from a traditional technology-driven approach to a more human-oriented one. It highlights a fundamental change regarding the role of technology: Technological development should be for the good of society (Carraz and Harayama, 2018; Bryndin, 2018). Just like any other change, no one doubts that this fundamental paradigm change will meet with powerful resistance. However, the world is now witnessing a huge crisis: Covid-19 pandemic. The world's greatest governments seem to be helpless. Giant companies are experiencing economic challenges. People are suffering from Covid 19; they are even dying. The rest is isolating themselves at home. But even at home, life is going on. Home office working becomes very common, even in very traditional companies. Best universities transformed their education style to distant learning. First level medical services are started being offered online. This pandemic crisis, which reminds the unfreeze, change and refreeze model of Kurt Lewin (1947), seems to break the resistance towards the use of digital technologies in many ways in business and social life for the benefit of the society (e.g., Society 5.0).

The aim of this paper is to examine the effects of pandemic crises on society 5.0 from Kurt Lewin's model of change. This paper is structured in three sections. The first section examines the Society 5.0 and the paradigm change underlying it. The second section presents Kurt Lewin's (1947) model of change and discusses the catalyst role of the covid-19 pandemic. The following third section shows the steps of how the worldwide pandemic crisis breaks the traditional rules of the game based on an example of the Turkish education system. The chapter concludes by arguing that if that transformation process towards Society 5.0 is sustainable in the long term or there will be a way back for organizations.

BACKGROUND

Industrial revolutions and technological developments as one of the main actors of social and economic changes have led to the formation of different social stages in the history of society (Yıkılmaz,2020). The Society 5.0, as a new period in the history of society, is first mentioned in Japanese strategic national political initiative in 2015 and proposed by the Japanese Cabinet in 5th Science and Technology Basic Plan in 2016 as: *"a society that is capable of providing the necessary goods and services to the people who need them at the required time and in just the right amount; a society that is able to respond precisely to a wide variety of social needs; a society in which all kinds of people can readily obtain high-quality services, overcome differences of age, gender, region, and language, and live vigorous and comfortable lives (*Government of Japan, 2016).

Society5.0 aims to establish a sustainable and high-quality living system in line with the technology and opportunities provided by industry 4.0 (Prasetyo and Arman,2017; Ferreira, and Serpa;2018). The technological and digital components, such as Artificial Intelligence (AI), Internet of Things (IoT), or Industrial Internet, are emphasized in Industry 4.0. while ignoring human-centered focus (Ferreira and Serpa, 2018). Probably the only premise given concerning human resources is potential changes within the labor market as a result of automation, robotics, and AI. Above all, the world of work in Industry 4.0 is yet inconceivable without human beings. But what is the benefit of people and society from Industry 4.0? (Skobelev and Borovik, 2017) The technological uprising within Industry 4.0 can achieve its full potential just with the association of social innovation (Morrar et al., 2017). It is the Government of Japan's Society 5.0 proposal that tries to make use of digital technologies to create a "super smart" cyber-physical society that is more "human-oriented" (Harayama 2017; Fukuyama, 2018; Gladden, 2019). In this vein, Japanese Prime Minister Shinzo Abe, at the CeBIT exhibition in Germany, claims that "technology and AI is not the source of fear and not a process that will take away people's jobs and fear. Growth and progress will all be possible with the innovation offered by this technological advancement" (Prime Minister Japan and his Cabinet,2017). The main purpose of Society 5.0 is to create a technology integrated society in which all human beings can appreciate life minus all potential limitations. Even though Society 5.0 is initiated in Japan, its motivation isn't solely directed at the succeeding in one nation (Onday, 2019).

We can find the same motivation in the 2030 Sustainable Development Agenda. United Nations has declared 17 goals on the "2030 Sustainable Development Agenda", basically targeting 5Ps (planet, people, prosperity, peace, and partnership) (Transforming our World: The 2030 Agenda for Sustainable Development,2015):

- End poverty in all its forms everywhere,
- End hunger, achieve food security and improved nutrition and promote sustainable agriculture,
- Ensure healthy lives and promote well-being for all at all age,

- Ensure inclusive and equitable quality education and promote lifelong learning opportunities for all
- Achieve gender equality and empower all women and girls
- Ensure availability and sustainable management of water and sanitation for all
- Ensure access to affordable, reliable, sustainable and modern energy for all,
- Promote sustained, inclusive and sustainable economic growth, full and productive employment and decent work for all,
- Build resilient infrastructure, promote inclusive and sustainable industrialization and foster innovation,
- Reduce inequality within and among countries,
- Make cities and human settlements inclusive, safe, resilient and sustainable,
- Ensure sustainable consumption and production patterns,
- Take urgent action to combat climate change and its impacts,
- Conserve and sustainably use the oceans, seas and marine resources for sustainable development,
- Protect, restore and promote sustainable use of terrestrial ecosystems, sustainably manage forests, combat desertification, and halt and reverse land degradation and halt biodiversity loss,
- Promote peaceful and inclusive societies for sustainable development, provide access to justice for all and build effective, accountable and inclusive institutions at all levels,
- Strengthen the means of implementation and revitalize the Global Partnership for Sustainable Development

The main goal of Society 5.0 is to produce sustainable solutions to environmental and social problems, with creating an ecosystem of systems that strive to serve the priorities of society based on the effective harmony of the virtual, real-world cooperation and IoT (Harayama, 2017). Hence we think that Society 5.0 has a similar vision to "2030 Sustainable Development Agenda" of the United Nations.

In order to understand the transformation of society to Society 5.0, one can find it useful to touch on the previous social stages. At the beginning of human history, Society 1.0 has the communities of hunters and gatherers in harmony with the nature they live in, while Society 2.0 has communities that are formed with farming, organization, and nation-building. Following Industrial Revolution Society 3.0 emerges as a society being industrialized and making mass production, Society 4.0 is "an information society that realizes increasing added value by connecting intangible assets as information networks." Beside the cumulative benefits of 4 levels; Society 5.0 is a sort of 'digital society;' nevertheless, it refers more specifically to new technologies of ICT with the goal of establishing 'a prosperous human-centered community (Harayama, 2017:10).

The technology that will serve the purpose of society 5.0 takes its roots from Industry 4.0 (Gladden, 2019). Industry 4.0, mentioned for the first time at the Hanover Fair in 2011, was a concept, attracted attention politically, sociologically and economically (Drathve Holch,2014:56). Industry 4.0 consists of the incorporation of data flow amongst the partners, suppliers, and customers, in addition to the integration of the real world with the virtual world which leads to an updated information platform in real-time (Abreu, 2018). Industry 4.0 period has started with Internet technology and the IoT which is transforming processes such as "value creation, business modeling, sub-services, and organizational structure" to reshape industry and production processes, and having impressive results such as smart factory, network systems that allow human-machine interaction (Kagermann, Wahlster, and Helbig, 2013; Kagermann, 2015:33). Industry 4.0 is an industrial and sociological period where "technology, virtual space, real-world and the human being" come together interactively (Hennies and Raudjärv, 2015) and smart factories are created (Ang, Goh, Saldivar and Li, 2017; Lin, Shyu and Ding,2017:4. But As McKinsey(2015) pointed out; The industry faces 4 issues that will come up with Industry 4.0 and must be overcome in its development. With the increased digitalization, the industry needs to improve its way of doing business and need to produce some alternative solutions for the increase in data, computing power and connection volume, wide range usage of the analytics and business-intelligence capabilities, new modes of human-machine interaction systems (augmented-reality systems e.g.). Overcoming these barriers is important for industry 4.0, the structures and service units that will emerge in this way will be capable of offering both social and economic benefits (Morrar, Arman and Mousa, 2017:18). Technological advances should focus on social benefit, otherwise, it will create both an economic and a social degradation. Technologies as IoT, industrial internet, and others should offer new opportunities and support to develop new jobs, training, and talents for people (Bryndin,2018). Although sharing a common ground with Industry 4.0 in some developmental processes, society 5.0 aims to find solutions to the problems of society (Skobelev and Borovik,2017:1). So Industry 4.0 paradigm focuses on the "smart factory" (Hozdi'c, 2015; Ferreira and Serpa 2018), but with a broader perspective, The Society 5.0 is focused on the "Super Smart Society" (Iwano et al. 2017:1; Harayama, 2017; Ferreira and Serpa 2018). The main differences between society 4.0 and Society 5.0 are shown in figure 1.

Figure 1. The Differences Between Industry 4.0 and Society 5.0
(Nakanishi, 2019).

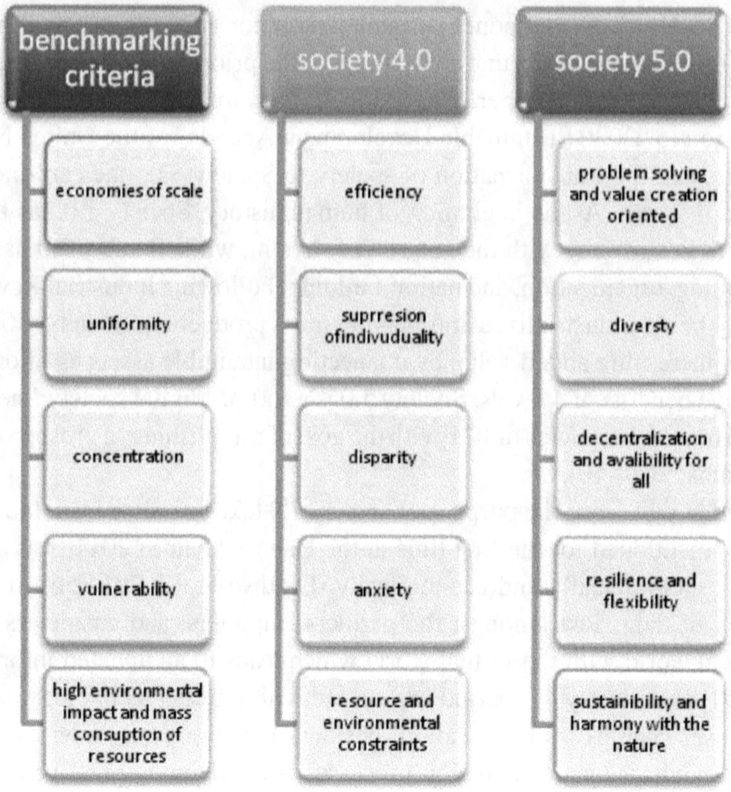

Even though the worldwide social trend towards is the creation of Society 5.0, there are still some issues being emerged at the stage of implementation. Especially old method technology and computer systems are a barrier to integrate and upgrade network interoperability, real-time process, and device synchronization, and, most importantly, security (Serpanos,2018:72). To deal with those issues, the construction of an integrated system, the development of the law infrastructure, the formation of the knowledge foundation, dynamic engagement in the new economy and society seems to be vital (Keidanren Japan Business Federation, 2016:149).

MAIN FOCUS OF THE CHAPTER

A number of preliminary studies for Society 5.0 have already started. For instance, a system (Science of Where), which is supported by AI, IoT, and aerospace Big Data for environmental and urban design, has been developed. For the implementation of Society 5.0, Sardinia 5.0 project was launched in Italy to evaluate the possible results and scenarios (Ratti, 2018). Some researchers explore the alternative ways of Society 5.0 paradigm at higher education(Sarif, 2017) and parent-child relationships (Romli et al., 2018). According to reports of The Royal Swedish Academy of Engineering Sciences (IVA) Tokyo visit, Japanese has already begun to offer solutions that will serve society 5.0, such as technologies interfacing harmoniously with human bodies, wearable sensors for monitoring and gathering data of the patient in an aging society, "Cybernetics" - an integrated technology of human, robot and information systems which can be helpful for a physically challenged person and improve the motor learning of cerebral nerves (https://sweden-science-innovation.blog/tokyo/iva15-visits-society-5-0/). Moreover, Hitachi's Business Unit for Healthcare extends its resources by incorporating artificial intelligence and other new innovations either (http://media.nature.com/).

Although Society 5.0 aims to serve well being of society, there are certain risks on the way of this goal. For instance, an accessible smart system based on technological developments can go beyond its intended purpose by creating an "addiction" similar to the experience in the previous "internet" and "smartphones" (Takahashi, 2018:119). There also might be cyberattacks as a major risk for Society 5.0, which has an advanced and integrated system built on the link between cyberspace and the real world (Government of Japan 2016:14). According to Salgues (2018); The ease of high-tech and integrated systems that will serve the purpose of Society 5.0 during the gradual development of the system can be integrated quickly to the existing industries, and this will cause to the destruction of many existing industries.

Creative Destruction

So social conflicts may cause social conflicts. Similarly, Gladden (2019:27) argues that integrating system and automation technologies (social robotics, ambient intelligence, virtual reality, cyberspatiality interfaces, neuroprosthetics, and other cyber-physical technologies) into the daily life may not be wide held accepted, or may not create the same beneficial effects on the psychological, social and cultural issues.

Society 5. has a promise to enhance the quality of life of all people through a super-smart society" (Bryndin,2018; Ferreira and Serpa, 2018). It is a dream where social problems on a global scale will be resolved, and everyone will have a healthy, comfortable, safe, and dream lifestyle (Keidanren (Japan Business Federation), 2016). However, the realization of this dream will probably be a challenge with the complex and diverse parties actively taking part in the process (Yousefikhah, 2017:38). Society 5.0, aiming for a human-centered and high-quality society that has started to be discussed and searched for solutions all over the world; is considered to indicate a period that unlike other social development processes, beyond all political-ideological ideas in the history of humanity, all the elements of society will experience a radical change and paradigm-shifting. Just like any other change, no one doubts that this fundamental paradigm change will meet with powerful resistance. This raises the question of how to manage that complex change as it involves social, technological, and economic facets. It may be useful to look at Kurt Lewin's model of change, as the Covid-19 pandemic crisis that all the world suffers from reminds the unfreeze, change and refreeze stages of Lewin's model (1947).

3 Step Model of Change

In this section, we will introduce Kurt Lewin's (1947) 3-Step model of change. Kurt Lewin, one of the modern pioneers of social, organizational, and applied psychology(Shein,2010:299; Burnes, 2004: 981). As "father of social change theories" (Kaminski, 2011), his ideas are at the heart of most theories in the field of change (Hendry, 1996: 624). Although there are various models in the change management studies such as "cultural excellence model for change" by Peters and Waterman (1982), "the processual approach" by Pettigrew (1973), "the emergent change model" by Weick and Quinn (1999) and "the self-organization/chaos model" by Thietart and Forgues(1995) and Lichtenstein (2000); Lewin's "3 steps model for change" offers a holistic view and model to the change process. Lewin states that the models of Field Theory, Group Dynamics, Action Research and the 3-Step model of change should be considered as a whole since they are complementarity to each other (Burnes; 2004: 981). So, to develop a better understanding of the 3 step model;, three other theories should also be mentioned. First, Field Theory which implies the group behavior. According to Field Theory, "group behavior" affects both the group and individual behavior together. Here, behavior is considered as a function of group environment or in other terms field (Lewin, 1947a.; Lewin, 1947b). Moreover, there is a quasi-stationary equilibrium (semi-fixed balance') mentioned in the model, implying that the changes in the conditions lead to a fluctuation in the balance (Burnes, 2004). In Group Dynamics, group behavior is considered to more dominant as individual behavior is directed by the group (Lewin, 1947b). In Action Research, change is a process of analysis and action (Bennett, 1983). Group members feeling and beliefs, in addition to group participation and cooperation, concerning the necessity of change, are the main determinants of the success of the change process (Burnes, 2004:984).

It is, after all those mentioned above, time to introduce the comprehensive 3-Step model of change. 3-Step model of change consists of three stages, as unfreeze, change, and refreeze," as shown in figure 2.

In the first step, "unfreeze," the quasi-stationary equilibrium (semi-fixed balance) mentioned in the field theory is disrupted (Schein, 1996). This can be accomplished by three stages: "disconfirmation of the validity of the status quo (feed the sense of "survival anxiety "to be changed), the induction of guilt or survival anxiety, and creating psychological safety" (Shein;2010:300). Here the group is facing anxiety. The possibility of loss of power, fear of inadequacy, exposure to negative consequences in case of failure, loss of identity and group membership (Shein, 2010: 304) begin to unravel the forces to initiate change. Following this step, comes the second phase, defined as the "change". In "change," new concepts, meanings, and standards replace the old ones; new roles are adopted, and new solutions are produced in terms of implementation and feedback (Lewin (1947a). In the third stage, refreeze; the learning process starts to have effective results, new behaviors are internalized, and this new quasi-stationary equilibrium is fixed and frozen, the group norms are permanently transformed and shape the behavior of individuals (Burnes, 2004).

Later on, in the field of organizational change and development, the theory was exposed to criticism. Especially the model of Lewin is considered as being static, simple, and linear (Kanter et al.; 1992: 10; Clegg et al., 2016: 376), and the "refreeze" phase, is not regarded as feasible (Child, 2015:350). Although such criticisms come to the fore, Lewin's (1947) 3-step model of change offers a comprehensive and holistic approach based on participation and collaboration instead of conflict (Burnes, 2004).

Figure 2. The 3 Step Model of Kurt Levin
(Swanson and Creed, 2014; Robbins and Judge, 2011: 632)

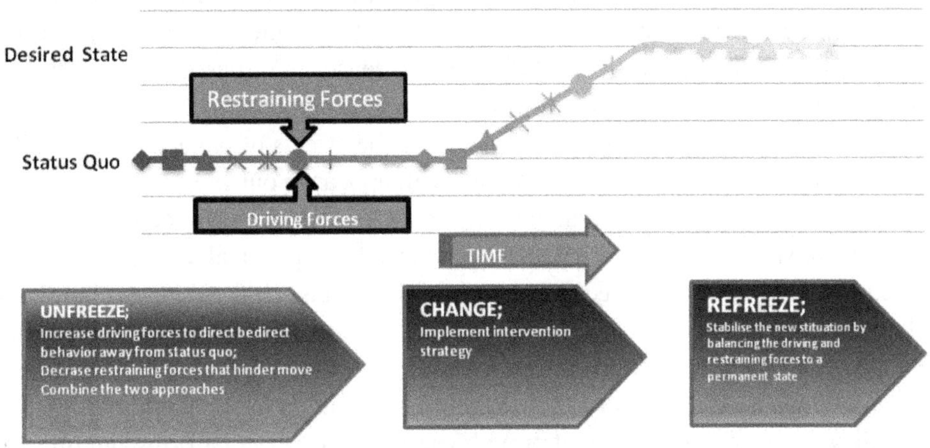

Issues, Controversies, Problems

Covid 19 pandemic started in Wuhan, China in December 2019 and quickly spread to the whole world and turned into a global health problem, caused significant changes in both social and economic field all over the world, and this change process continues. Also, the results of studies examining what COVID19 has changed in our lives are striking. Studying the behavior of consumers during the pandemic period, Sheth (2020) emphasizes that individuals' having to do everything from home triggers some very radical changes. He states that the use of complicated technology has become a valuable and indispensable actor in meeting both social life and physical needs. In addition, it is stated that staying at home brings about some changes in business life; the boundaries of work and life are blurred. The fact that both social and business life is in a same environment brings new experiences and uncertainties, but it has made it necessary for individuals to learn to carry out two basic responsibilities effectively, contrary to what they are accustomed to. The extra time that comes from staying at home without having to go anywhere has enabled the individual to gain new experiences and skills (such as making bread or pizza or musical instruments, which are the most shared on social media). Woodside (2020) emphasizes that expanding the boundaries of the marketing concept in the change people experience in their lives within the scope of public law and policy is important for local and national regulations. Carnevale and Hatak (2020) emphasizes that the pandemic has created radical changes in the workplace environment. In fact, it is mentioned that there is a radical change in how we socialize, consume, communicate and work, and probably that will not be the same as before. Individuals will have to adapt to "new normal", but the change in the needs and regulations for welfare and engagement will lead to the formation of misfits, especially for organizations. It is important for organizations to build a more virtual recruitment, training and workplace socialization to overcome those possible misfits.

As He and Harris (2020) stated, the culture of solidarity has increased in the uncertainty environment created by the pandemic. Large companies provide serious support and assistance to countries and people in need. Companies try to provide the necessary support and attention to both their employees and consumers. It has been observed that the existence of each actor of this multilayered social life practice is interdependent and better results can be achieved only by overcoming everything together. In practice, it is emphasized that it is important to have a more meaningful and permanent social support environment where the parties support each other. Such changes have enabled social responsibility strategies and practices to be implemented, companies to turn to social dynamics rather than profit margins and to read the needs of individuals through slightly different lenses. The pandemic has changed the way all organizations look at individuals and social practice and prompted them to reconsider their vision and goals. Krishnamurthy (2020), in his study evaluating the effects of pandemic especially under the title of education, emphasizes that spatial interaction will appear in our lives as "new normal" and the boundaries of individuals regarding virtual and physical environment will become very blurred. It is stated that the current situation will continue between virtual and physical after the pandemic and will transform education into a radical change. As a result of that change, individuals will probably begin to get educated through an algorithm instead of a faculty member on the long term, and that this artificial intelligence-based system will provide the individual with personalized learning. Educational institutions will switch to a continuous education mode, instead of an education understanding limited to a certain period of time, they will take a structure that provides services in every platforms and time in which the individual's need develops. More personalized and continuous education will affect the quality and form of the provided service. The increasing time people spend at home and reaching their needs through virtualized services has created pressure to question the structure of the supply chain and to increase its efficiency. The fact that the individual chooses the service provider in the virtual platform considering the sustainable environment and social responsibility has made it necessary to reconsider and develop the supply systems. Companies initially had to integrate artificial intelligence, the Internet of Things, and blockchain technologies (Sharma, Adhikary and Borah, 2020).). This change, albeit fast, has provided an important experience in terms of sustainability. Examining the effects of the pandemic in the field of education, Mhlanga and Moloi (2020) emphasize that the application of technologies based on the 4th Industrial Revolution in the field of education has effective results in solving the basic problems and making education accessible.

All these problems and solutions based on a virtual platform that came with the pandemic deeply affected the social life practice and initiated a necessary change and transformation. For the transformation of society 5.0, the pandemic has assumed the status of a catalyst in the transformation process of societies.

SOLUTIONS AND RECOMMENDATIONS

The Covid 19 pandemic started in Wuhan, China in December 2019 and quickly spread to the whole world and turned into a global health problem, caused significant changes in both social and economic field all over the world, and this change process continues. Covid-19 has dramatically affected various facets of life. Many businesses and public institutions were closed. Various sectors had to make serious economic disruptions and cease operations, especially the industrial sector. There was a need for radical changes and sudden innovations in the routine flow of business and life. Some regulations were made to meet the needs of the new situation in the field of health and social order. It has been experienced both intensity and change in the entire supply chain, especially the cold supply chain (Yıkılmaz, Sağbaş, & Karabal, 2020). Employees had to find some alternative ways of running their jobs away from their workplaces with digital-oriented solutions, and employers had to take structural and fundamental decisions for their employees to serve effectively and efficiently away from the work environment. Diversity and change occurred in individuals' understanding of consumption. The platform and form of sales and marketing have changed the paradigm. Various sectors have almost lost hope for the future (e.g. tourism, art). Contrary to this trend, online communication, entertainment, and shopping, which produces digital-based solutions in the digital platform, started to redesign daily life in a short time. The covid-19 pandemic has led to a faster realization of some expected future process of the Society 5.0 in social and economic facet of life.

Kurt Lewin's 3 Steps Change Model is an organizational change model used to manage change in the organization, and called "Force Field Analysis". In this model, Lewin adopts a dynamic perspective that focuses on the balance of forces acting in opposite directions rather than the traditional static perspective within the organization. Lewin believes that it should be approached in the context of forces or factors that force the current situation to change and forces or factors that resist change. While increasing the effect of forces that causes change is effective in some situations, it is generally more effective to weaken the forces that resist. These forces can arise from the internal and external environment of the organization as well as from the behavior of the tool of change. For example, education can be taken to identify the need for change.

Managers, especially school administrators, should play an active role in initiating change and easing resistance to change. School administrators should consider Covid-19 as a balance achieved as a result of the forces that lead to change and the forces that resist change to work against each other in current situation for their organization. As a matter of fact, in managing change, managers shape the change culture of the organization with their decisions and role-model behaviors. Therefore, it is necessary to get out of the current state of equilibrium. For this, resistance and pressures must be overcome. It is important to increase the driving forces that will ensure positive change and to decrease the limiting forces that prevent change. However, there are some factors preventing change in schools such as physical structure of the school (arrangement of school gardens, lack of branch classrooms, insufficient physical spaces), human resources (lack of permanent teachers, retired teachers, lack of morale and motivation in teachers) and inadequacy material resources (lack of technological equipment and equipment, traditional classroom system).

Nevertheless, it is seen that change in schools has many positive results due to Covid-19. Of the positive results, especially; the decrease in student absenteeism, the fact that schools are more hygienic, the communication between teachers and parents increases, students adopt their classrooms and develop a sense of responsibility, making teaching-learning activities more qualified, and using teaching tools, materials and materials more effectively are the positive results. In the world of change, education leaders and managers must also be experts in the field of change management. Today, schools that are adaptable, flexible, willing to change, are more successful than their peers. The main forces and resources of change that force schools to change; accountability, changing demographic structure, staff shortages, technological change and information explosion, processes and people. Participation in management in schools, support of senior management, the change process does not cause an increase in the workforce of teachers, active participation of the senior management in the change facilitates the change process.

In today`s chaotic era, technological advancements are contributing to improvements in both business and society, witnessing worldwide challenges, for instance Covid 19 pandemic. Digital transformation is generating new values and becoming a mainstay of industrial policy in many countries. Human beings, try to leverage digital technologies to effectively and efficiently provide solutions for society to create better living standards and sustainable healthy economic growth. It is first the Japanese who look beyond Industry 4.0 to create a new human-centered society so called "Society 5. 0. Society 5.0 is to create a technology integrated society in which all human beings can appreciate life minus all potential limitations. Technological development should be for the good of society. Worldwide Covid 19 pandemic also makes it necessary to use digital technologies more and more as people are isolating themselves at home. Indeed, world is already in a digital transformation process which meets resistance. This pandemic crisis, seems to break the resistance towards the use of digital technologies in many ways in business and social life for the benefit of the society Therefore this chapter aims to examine the effects of pandemic crises on society 5.0 from Kurt Lewin's model of change. Education industry of Turkey, which is moving to a more e-learning axis, is investigated to see the effects of pandemic crises. The findings show that higher education has also been influenced in Turkey. The academic timetable was interrupted, face to face teaching and studying has discontinued. Exams were adjourned and the method of assessment has been affected either. In higher education, undoubtfully there are some challenges, but those challenges can be addressed easily. Students, graduates, parents, university administration and higher education institutions are collectively responsible for coping with this situation. The requirement for new technology in the teaching phase of learning is growing faster and stronger. To improve the education process, the digital platform becomes a period of awareness that offers sound and unmatched viability for discovery, information sharing, collaboration, and exploration.

The forces of change in the organization as the driving forces for change are the resistance forces known as limiting forces that oppose change. The manager who wants to achieve change in the organization must be able to determine the limiting forces that both direct change and oppose change. Therefore, the process of change is a process of breaking the balance / status quo in the organization. The balance or status quo state refers to a steady state between the forces to support change and their forces to resist change. Only then can the managerial leader be integrated with change.

Finally, it can be stated that since it will be very difficult to realize change for institutions and organizations with a change-resistant management approach, institutions and organizations managers with an agile management approach will ensure that change is adopted and realized earlier. They should use their agile and dynamic capabilities to break the resistance against change. It is also important to inform and encourage those who resist change in their organizations. Because building an organizational agile climate that is open to innovation in institutions and organizations will result in the adoption of future changes faster, establishing organizations open to change at the establishment stage will have advantageous results.

FUTURE RESEARCH DIRECTIONS

Change makes itself felt in all areas of life and is included in social life practice as the only unchanging concept. Decision mechanisms should be aware of this continuous change process and contribute to taking the necessary steps in this regard. Educational institutions need to prepare for virtual, distant, and personalized education services, especially within the scope of the education of individuals, which is important for future generations in Society 5.0. Educational institutions should analyze the needs of the individual who will take place as the main actor in Society 5.0 with effective planning in the process that started with the pandemic period and bring some radical changes to the organization. Apart from education, it is considered that it is important to integrate the business manner and culture of other institutions into the virtual environment and improve their value chains and organizational agility capability. It is important to carry out various studies to sustain the radical changes experienced in both social and economic fields. Conducting studies that examine the integration of the individual into the virtual platform, evaluating the psychological and social reflections empirically, and analyzing the need of future possible members of Society 5.0 is important for the sustainability of the change process. Also, the future researches may focus on the relationship between agile management, reorganization, organizational climate and corporate performance and to create knowledge and synergy, especially, in Covid-19 pandemic.

CONCLUSION

Technological advances and industrial revolutions have played a key role in the historical process as the former of social stages. The new capabilities that emerged with the integration of the technological and virtual-physical platforms introduced by Industry 4.0 frightened individuals at first, but the Society 5.0 approach that started under the leadership of Japan changed this perspective. Although we are at the very beginning of reaching the Society 5.0 vision that is human-centered and caring for the welfare of all parties in the society, the Covid 19 pandemic has accelerated this process due to the radical changes it has created in our social life practice. In this context, the authors discussed the catalytic effect of the Covid 19 pandemic, Society 5.0 and Kurt Lewin's 3 Steps Change Model examined in detail. Decision-makers should seriously evaluate the effect of the pandemic which acts as a catalyst effect on the Society5.0 change process as an " unfreeze" step.In this pandemic period where we have to evolve into a more virtual and distant oriented life by eliminating the resistance in our social life practice and ways of doing business on the way to Society 5.0, the change should be deepened by the inclusion of various actors. For a social structure caring for Society 5.0 and human well-being, all stakeholders must be in view and cooperation. As a matter of fact, this consensus is important in ensuring the will to change the old balances that will be formed with the help of the "unfreeze" step at both organizational and social levels. For the change to take root, especially educational institutions should quickly implement serious changes. It is important to establish a more virtual oriented business and supply chain to serve the quality of life and welfare of individuals and to build virtual oriented lifelong learning systems. In this context, first of all, educational institutions should be the main actors in the process of change and should support individuals and organizations in issues that can resist change and eliminate uncertainty as much as possible. It is to update the education system for lifelong learning and personalized practices required for Society 5.0, abandoning more conventional methods and practices. The deepening in the phase of change provided by the contribution of various social actors should be followed by the meticulous steps taken during the "refreeze" step. In this context, Kurt Lewin's 3 Steps Change Model has been realized and the momentum caught on the way to Society 5.0 is evaluated in a meaningful way. It will be appropriate for decision mechanisms to manage change with co-operation, participation, entrepreneurial understanding, and human-centered perspective, considering these issues.

REFERENCES

Abreu, P. H. C. (2018). Perspectivas para a gestão do conhecimento no contexto da Indústria 4.0. *South American Development Society Journal*, *4*(10), 126. doi:10.24325/issn.2446-5763.v4i10p126-145

Ang, J., Goh, C., Saldivar, A., & Li, Y. (2017). Energy-Efficient Through-Life Smart Design, Manufacturing and Operation of Ships in an Industry 4.0 Environment. *Energies*, *10*(5), 610. doi:10.3390/en10050610

Bennett, R. (1983). Management Research. Management Development Series, 20. Geneva: International Labour Office.

Bryndin, E. (2018). System Synergetic Formation of Society 5.0 for Development of Vital Spaces. *Annals of Ecology and Environmental Science*, *2*(4), 12–19.

Burnes, B. (2004). Kurt Lewin and the Planned Approach to Change: A Re-appraisal. *Journal of Management Studies*, *41*(6), 977–1002. doi:10.1111/j.1467-6486.2004.00463.x

Carnevale, J. B., & Hatak, I. (2020). Employee Adjustment and Well-Being in the Era of COVID-19: Implications for Human Resource Management. *Journal of Business Research*, *116*, 183–187. Advance online publication. doi:10.1016/j.jbusres.2020.05.037 PMID:32501303

Carraz, R., & Harayama, Y. (2018). Japan's Innovation Systems at the Crossroads: Society 5.0. In Panorama: Insights into Asian and European Affairs. Digital Asia, 33-45.

Child, J. (2015). *Organization: Contemporary Principles and Practice*. Wiley. doi:10.1002/9781119176862

Clegg, S. R., Kornberger, M., & Pitsis, T. (2016). *Managing & Organizations: An Introduction to Theory and Practice*. SAGE.

Drath, R., & Horch, A. (2014). Industrie 4.0: Hit or Hype? *IEEE Industrial Electronics Magazine*, *8*(2), 56–58. doi:10.1109/MIE.2014.2312079

Ferreira, C. M., & Serpa, S. (2018). Society 5.0 and Social Development: Contributions to a Discussion. *Management and Organizational Studies*, *5*, 26–31. doi:10.20944/preprints201811.0108.v1

Fukuda, K. (2020). Science, technology and innovation ecosystem transformation toward society 5.0. *International Journal of Production Economics*, *220*(2), 107460. Advance online publication. doi:10.1016/j.ijpe.2019.07.033

Fukuyama, M. (2018) .Society 5.0: Aiming for a New Human-Centered Society. *Japan Spotlight*, 47-50.

Gladden, M. (2019). Who Will Be the Members of Society 5.0? Towards an Anthropology of Technologically Posthumanized Future Societies. *Soc. Sci*, *8*(148), 1–39. doi:10.3390ocsci8050148

Government of Japan. (2016). *The 5th Science and Technology Basic Plan*. Available online: https://www8.cao.go.jp/cstp/english/basic/5thbasicplan.pdf

Harayama, Y. (2017). Society 5.0: Aiming for a New Human-centered Society. Collaborative Creation through Global R&D Open Innovation for Creating the Future. *Hitachi Review*, *66*(6), 8-13. https://www.hitachi.com/rev/archive/2017/r2017_06/pdf/p08-13_TRENDS.pdf

He, H., & Harris, L. (2020). The Impact of Covid-19 Pandemic on Corporate Social Responsibility and Marketing Philosophy. *Journal of Business Research*, *116*, 176–182. doi:10.1016/j.jbusres.2020.05.030 PMID:32457556

Hendry, C. (1996). Understanding and Creating Whole Organizational Change Through Learning Theory. *Human Relations*, *49*(5), 621–641. doi:10.1177/001872679604900505

Hennies, M., & Raudjärv, M. (2015). Industry 4.0. Introductory thoughts on the current situation. *Estonian Discussions on Economic Policy*, *23*(2). Advance online publication. doi:10.2139srn.2708757

Hozdi'c, E. (2015). Smart Factory for Industry 4.0: A Review. *International Journal of Modern Manufacturing Technologies*, *7*. 28-35. Avaliable at: https://media.nature.com/full/naturecms/uploads/ckeditor/attachments/8431/InsideView_Display_-_Hitachi_-_Nature_-_Dec_21_2017_-_LH.PDF

Iwano, K., Yasunori, K., Yosuke, T., & Satoru, B. (Eds.). (2017). Future Services & Societal Systems in Society 5.0. Tokyo: Center for Research and Development Strategy, Japan Science and Technology Agency.

Kagermann, H. (2015). Change Through Digitization-Value Creation in the Age of Industry 4.0. In H. Albach, H. Meffert, A. Pinkwart, & R. Reichwald (Eds.), *Management of Permanent Change*. Springer Gabler. doi:10.1007/978-3-658-05014-6_2

Kagermann, H., Wahlster, W. & Helbig, J. (2013). *Securing the future of German manufacturing industry - Recommendations for implementing the strategic initiative Industrie 4.0.* Final Report of the Industrie 4.0 Working Group.

Kaminski, J. (2011). Theory applied to informatics – Lewin's Change Theory. *CJNI: Canadian Journal of Nursing Informatics*, *6*(1). http://cjni.net/journal/?p=1210

Kanter, R. M., Stein, B., & Jick, T. (1992). *The Challenge of Organizational Change*. The Free Press.

Keidanren (Japan Business Federation). (2016). *Toward realization of the new economy and society. Reform of the economy and society by the deepening of "Society 5.0"*. http://www.keidanren.or.jp/en/policy/2016/029_outline.pdf

Krishnamurthy, S. (2020). The Future of Business Education: A Commentary in the Shadow of the Covid-19 Pandemic. *Journal of Business Research*, *117*, 1–5. doi:10.1016/j.jbusres.2020.05.034 PMID:32501309

Lewin, K. (1947a). Frontiers in group dynamics. In D. Cartwright (Ed.), *Field Theory in Social Science*. Social Science Paperbacks.

Lewin, K. (1947b). Group decisions and social change. In T. M. Newcomb & E. L. Hartley (Eds.), *Readings in Social Psychology*. Henry Holt.

Lichtenstein, B. B. (2000). Self-organized transitions: A pattern amid the chaos of transformative change. *The Academy of Management Executive*, *14*(4), 128–141. doi:10.5465/ame.2000.3979821

Lin, K., Shyu, J., & Ding, K. (2017). A Cross-Strait Comparison of Innovation Policy under Industry 4.0 and Sustainability Development Transition. *Sustainability*, *9*(5), 786. doi:10.3390u9050786

McKinsey & Company. (2015). *Manufacturing's next act: Industry 4.0 is more than just a flashy catch-phrase. A confluence of trends and technologies promises to reshape the way things are made*. Available at: https://www.mckinsey.com/~/media/McKinsey/Business%20Functions/Operations/Our%20Insights/Manufacturings%20next%20act/Manufacturings%20next%20act.ashx

Mhlanga, D., & Moloi, T. (2020). COVID-19 and the Digital Transformation of Education: What Are We Learning on 4IR in South Africa? *Education in Science*, *10*(7), 180.

Morrar, R., Arman, H., & Mousa, S. (2017). The Fourth Industrial Revolution (Industry 4.0): A Social Innovation Perspective. *Technology Innovation Management Review*, *7*(11), 12–20. doi:10.22215/tim-review/1117

Nakanishi, H. (2019). Modern society has reached its limits. Society 5.0 will liberate us. *World Economic Forum Annual Meeting*. https: //www. weforum. org/agenda /2019 /01/ modern-society-has-reached-its-limits-society-5-0-will-liberate-us/

Onday, O. (2019). Japan's Society 5.0: Going Beyond Industry 4.0. *Bus. Econ. J.*, *10*(2), 2–7. doi:10.4172/2151-6219.1000389

Peters, T., & Waterman, R. H. (1982). *In search of excellence: Lessons from America's best run companies*. Harper & Row.

Pettigrew, A. M. (1973). *The politics of organizational decision making*. Tavis-took.

Prasetyo, Y. A., & Arman, A. A. (2017). Group management system design for supporting society 5.0 in smart society platform. *2017 International Conference on Information Technology Systems and Innovation (ICITSI)*, 398-404. doi:10.1109/icitsi.2017.8267977

Prime Minister Japan and his Cabinet. (2017). *Prime Minister Shinzo Abe at CeBIT Welcome Night*. Avaliable at:http://japan.kantei.go.jp/97_abe/statement/201703/1221682_11573.html

Ratti, B. (2018). Geographic Knowledge. Paradigm of Society 5.0. *Journal of Research and Didactics in Geography*, *1*, 123-26.

Robbins, S., & Judge, T. (2011). Organizational Behaviour. Academic Press.

Romli, A., Mazlina, A. M., Aziman, A., & Fatinatul, N. Z. (2018). *ePAL Apps: Enhancing Parenting Literacy in a Smart Society 5.0*. Paper presented at International University Carnival on e-Learning (IUCEL).

Salgues, B. (2018). *Society 5.0: Industry of the Future, Technologies, Methods and Tools*. ISTE Ltd.

Sarif, S. M. (2017). Society 5.0 Qalb with Tawhidic Paradigm. *Journal of Education and Social Sciences*, *8*, 208–217.

Schein, E. H. (1996). Kurt Lewin's change theory in the field and in the classroom: Notes toward a model of managed learning. *Systems Practice*, *9*, 27–47. https://doi.org/10.1007/BF02173417

Schein, E. H. (2010). *Organizational Culture and Leadership* (4th ed.). Wiley.

Serpanos, D. (2018). The Cyber-Physical Systems Revolution. *Computer*, *51*(3), 70–73. doi:10.1109/MC.2018.1731058

Sharma, A., Adhikary, A., & Borah, S. (2020). Covid-19's Impact on Supply Chain Decisions: Strategic Insights for NASDAQ 100 Firms using Twitter Data. *Journal of Business Research*, *117*, 443–447.

Sheth, J. (2020). Impact of Covid-19 on Consumer Behavior: Will the Old Habits Return or Die? Journal of Business Research. *Journal of Business Research*, *117*, 280–283.

Shiroishi, Y., Uchiyama, K., & Suzuki, N. (2018). Society 5.0: For Human Security and Well-Being. *IEEE Xplore*, *51*(7), 91–95.

Skobelev, P.O., & Borovick, Yu., S. (2017). On the way from Industry 4.0 to Industry 5.0: from digital manufacturing to digital society. *Internatıonal Scıentıfic Journal Industry 4.0*, *6*, 307-311.

Swanson, D. J., & Creed, A. S. (2014). Sharpening the Focus of Force Field Analysis. *Journal of Change Management*, *14*(1), 28–47. doi:10.1080/14697017.2013.788052

Takahashi, T. (2018). Behavioral Economics of Addiction in the Age of a Super Smart Society: Society 5.0. *Oukan Journal of Transdisciplinary Federation of Science and Technology*, *12*, 119–122.

Thietart, R., & Forgues, B. (1995). Chaos theory and organization. *Organization Science*, *6*(1), 19–31.

Transforming our World: The 2030 Agenda for Sustainable Development. (2015). https:// sustainabledevelopment.un.org/content/documents/21252030%20Agenda%20for%20Sustainable%20Development%20web.pdf

Weick, K., & Quinn, R. (1999). Organisational change and development. *Annual Review of Psychology*, *50*(1), 361–386.

Woodside, A. G. (2020). Interventions as experiments: Connecting the dots in forecasting and overcoming pandemics, global warming, corruption, civil rights violations, misogyny, income inequality, and guns. *Journal of Business Research*, *117*, 212–218.

Yıkılmaz, İ., Sağbaş, M., & Karabal, C. (2020). Pandemi Döneminden Çıkışta Çevik Soğuk Tedarik Zinciri Yönetimin Önemive Aşı Takip Sistemi Uygulaması, Anadolu 5. *Uluslararasi Sosyal Bilimler Kongresi*, 577-591.

Yousefikhah, S. (2017). Sociology of innovation: Social construction of technology perspective. *AD-Minister*, 31–43. doi:10.17230/ad-minister.30.2

ADDITIONAL READING

Akkaya, B. (2019). Leadership 5.0 in Industry 4.0: Leadership in Perspective of Organizational Agility. In Managing Operations Throughout Global Supply Chains (pp. 136-158). IGI Global.

Akkaya, B. (2020). Review of Leadership Styles In Perspective Of Dynamic Capabilities: An Empirical Research On Managers In Manufacturing Firms. *Journal of Administrative Sciences/YonetimBilimleri-Dergisi, 18*(36).

Akkaya, B., & Üstgörül, S. (2020). Sustainability of SMEs and Health Sector in a Dynamic Capabilities Perspective. In *Challenges and Opportunities for SMEs in Industry 4.0* (pp. 43–64). IGI Global. doi:10.4018/978-1-7998-2577-7.ch004

Alabbasi, Y., & Sandhu, K. (2019). The Framework for Blockchain Innovation and the Impact on Digital Economic Transformation. *International Journal of Innovation in the Digital Economy, 10*(4), 44–55. doi:10.4018/IJIDE.2019100104

Alhirz, H., & Sandhu, K. (2011). User Adoption and Acceptance of Enterprise Resource Planning (ERP). In *15th International Business Research Conference Proceedings*. World Business Institute Australia.

Guah, M. W. (2021). *Handbook of Research on Innate Leadership Characteristics and Examinations of Successful First-Time Leaders*. IGI Global. doi:10.4018/978-1-7998-7592-5

Harper, D. S. (2021). *Integration and Application of Business Graduate and Business Leader Competency-Models*. IGI Global. doi:10.4018/978-1-7998-6537-7

Sandhu, K., & Kaushik, J. (2014). Emotional suffocation, ventilation and interpersonal relationships in organizations. *ZENITH International Journal of Multidisciplinary Research, 4*(11), 104–112.

Tanniru, M. R., Xi, Y., & Sandhu, K. (2020). Leadership to Advance Innovation for Digital Healthcare Transformation. In Leadership, Management, and Adoption Techniques for Digital Service Innovation (pp. 1-24). IGI Global. doi:10.4018/978-1-7998-2799-3.ch001

Yıkılmaz, İ. (2020). New Era: TheTransformation From The Information Society To Super Smart Society (Society 5.0). Inbook Data, Information and Knowledge Management. Nobel: İstanbul Avaliable (https://www.researchgate.net/publication/347937634)

KEY TERMS AND DEFINITIONS

3 Step Change Model: It is a 3-step (freeze, change, unfreeze) model used by Kurt Lewin to explain the process of change.

Agile Leadership: It is a postmodern leadership style that provides organizational agility in firms where change and technology are very fast and leadership style in Industry 5.0.

Agility: It is the capability of organizations and institutional structures to develop procesess, and understandings quickly and at the proper time, taking into account the changing environmental dynamics

Dynamic Capabilities: It is the ability of a firm or organization to learn new methods occurred to produce and serve and to meet the needs of customers according to environmental and technological changes.

Industry 4.0: Industry 4.0, which was first mentioned at the Hannover Fair in 2011, is an industrial era and concept that takes advantage of the opportunities offered by information sharing and virtual-real world integration between various parties.

Innovation: Innovation means assessing the ability to alter and adapt of individuals or organizations.

Organizational Agility: It is about reaction and adaptation to changes which driven by customers, competitors, and technology. Being agile organizationally, not only in enterprise's production department but in other departments as well.

Society 5.0: Society 5.0 refers to the social level that caring for well-being of the human and that the needs and expectations of all segments of society will be met with help of the technological opportunities offered by Industry 4.0.

Chapter 8
Analysis of the Effect for Customer Relationship Management on Digital Enterprises:
Using Agent-Based Modeling

Maryam Ebrahimi
https://orcid.org/0000-0001-5837-8864
Independent Researcher, Germany

ABSTRACT

This study aims to investigate the effect of customer relationship management (CRM) on digital enterprises focusing on their digital shopping process using the agent-based modeling (ABM) in a digital store. In this regard, purposive non-probability sampling method was used to select 300 experts and descriptive and correlation coefficient with SPSS tools were used. The digital shopping process considered in this study include product review, product selection, payment, and receipt, and CRM dimensions include economic profitability, quality of optimal use of information, quality of information display, and customer satisfaction of digital shopping services. The research results based on the conceptual model, statistical analysis, and use of ABM in anylogic environment show that CRM system leads to improved digital enterprise performance and all dimensions of CRM system have a positive effect on digital shopping stages. Finally, the usefulness and accuracy of the results were confirmed based on the positive opinions of experts.

INTRODUCTION

Preserving a close relationship with customers and fulfilling their expectations are key issues in today's competitive market to promote business (Anshari et al., 2018). On the other hand, digital shopping in the field of electronic commerce is defined as shopping with the help of Internet technologies and tools.

DOI: 10.4018/978-1-7998-8587-0.ch008

The successful digital shopping requires that sellers can create more economic benefits for customers than the traditional way. It is not enough to simply display products on a beautiful site, and use attractive photos (Zhang, 2017; Duarte et al., 2018).

Investigating the effect of the Internet on businesses in today's world is a part of the growing body of digital marketing and business literature. However, despite extensive research on the impact of the Internet on business, there is little knowledge of the complex relationship between digital enterprises and the electronic markets function (Thakur, 2018; Duarte et al., 2018). Although several studies have been conducted in the field of customer satisfaction and loyalty in business, the impact of standardization and customization on these variables has received less attention (Piccoli et al., 2017).

The customer not only provides the main capital and financial resources of the business through deposits, but also is the buyer of all business services and therefore, the customer is very important to the business. As having customer guarantees the business survival, customer relationship is a key element in maintaining a stable and successful relationship with the customer and the success of small and medium enterprises (Ritter & Geersbro, 2018). On the other hand, customers' satisfaction with digital shopping and fulfilling their needs play a vital role in meeting business goals (Pozza et al., 2018). In other words, customer satisfaction with digital shopping services is the key to business growth (Ballestero et al., 2018). Hence, it is necessary to create an integrated departments of customer affairs in today's large business (Vanhanen et al., 2018).

The need for more accurate, faster and less risky decisions on the one hand and the complexity of issues, the diversity of decision-making criteria and the multiple choice of options on the other hand are caused by the current intense economic competition and increasing growth of technology (Fernández et al., 2018). Hence, more serious decision-making process is needed than ever before, and newer scientific techniques have been proposed in this regard. Customer relationship management systems clearly define all services and facilities and bring many benefits, including providing continuous information and services, reducing costs and increasing satisfaction. As a strategy of the process of gaining customers' data and their needs, customer relationship management causes maximizing profitability, income, customer satisfaction with digital shopping services, through customer selection and adopting behaviors that lead to customer satisfaction, customer focus, and closer relationship with them (Ritter & Geersbro, 2018; Ballestero et al., 2018).

On the other hand, a "high volume of data" is generated on a daily basis by expanding and prevailing the Internet. Therefore, a system with high processing power is needed for processing this amount of data because current common systems are not capable of processing such large volumes of data, and on the other hand, the provision of high-processing systems is not feasible for business due to high costs. Extracting repetitive patterns over the past two decades, including the collection of repetitive samples from transactions and the sequence of repetition sequences, has attracted the interest of several research.

Indeed, factors such as acceptance of product price, consumers' advertising susceptibility, consumers' following tendency, customer motivational performance, price sensitivity, price of commodity, quality sensitivity, quality of commodity, have a special impact on consumer's purchasing behavior (Zhang, 2017; Huiru et al., 2018).

The present study aims to investigate and analyze the effect of CRM dimensions on digital shopping in a digital store using statistical analysis and finally agent-based modeling (ABM) methodology. The dimensions of CRM examined in this study include the quality of information display and representation of CRM system, customer satisfaction with digital shopping services, the quality of optimal use of CRM system information resources, and the economic profitability of CRM system. Also, digital shopping stages include product review, product selection, payment, and receipt.

Because of the increasing progress of science and technology, as well as the complexity of human life, many people have been attracted to digital shopping for a variety of reasons, including saving time, buying a variety of items, etc. With the increase in the number of customers, the number and variety of digital stores has also increased, and hence, the issue of marketing has become very important for these stores (Zhang et al., 2018).

Since digital shopping plays an important role in the virtual communication of individuals in today's world, it is necessary to study the criteria affecting digital shopping from digital enterprises and digital stores. The reason for this is that paying attention to these criteria will lead to attracting customers, their satisfaction and, as a result, their loyalty to business (Sohn, 2017; Phan & Douglas, 2010) as well as profitability for digital enterprises. The present study investigates and analyzes the effect of customer relationship management on digital shopping stages in Anylogic with ABM approach in a digital store.

RESEARCH LITERATURE

CRM Basics

In order to succeed and survive in the long run in today's competitive market, enterprises have to use new methods of competition. In this regard, as a general business strategy, customer relationship management enables enterprises to effectively manage customer relationships. The customer relationship management system is a successful approach in the business and marketing world that integrates technology, process, and all customer-related business activities within a specific framework (Duarte et al., 2018; Phan & Douglas, 2010; Farooq et al., 2018). CRM emerged in the 1970s to manage and optimise sales-force automation within firms. Then, it has become one of the most common tools for enterprise information management, not only for sales and marketing purposes, but also for more effective customer interaction (Gil-Gomez et al., 2020).

CRM requirements include attracting the right customer, creating the right value proposition, institutionalizing the best revenue, motivating employees, and learning to retain customers. At the same time, the development of digital enterprises has doubled the importance of customer relationship management. Although the customer relationship management capability is well known, few have implemented this approach in practice (Bahrami et al., 2012). The influence of the Internet has dramatically changed the situation today, which is why the Internet is a good platform to integrate customer relationship management applications. This has led to the emergence of CRM. According to different definitions and concepts of the digital enterprises in CRM, it can be defined as the use of relevant networks and technologies to automate, improve, upgrade, complete, or redesign the business system to create more value for customers and business partners. Electronic CRM currently creates a new area for businesses to provide the best for their customers (Hasiri & Afghanpour, 2016). In other words, extensive changes in the business approach to the customer category, especially in marketing has been created with the advent of new technologies and the evolution of business attitudes towards the customer. The use of these technologies in CRM and its transformation into e-CRM has provided features that were previously unimaginable in traditional CRM, and no one was thinking of using them. On the other hand, as traditional strategies can no longer be effective, the need to use CRM is becoming more and more felt with the presence of various digital enterprises. CRM in its simplest form, equips businesses with tools for execution and implementation, and personalized customer interactions through traditional and modern Internet channels (Anumala & Kumar, 2007). On the other hand, by emerging a competitive market, customer relationships-based marketing has become one of the most prominent approaches. Customer information is consciously used by successful businesses to build relationships with customers (Wikhamn, 2019).

Creating customer loyalty is one of the goals of CRM. Therefore, it is necessary to create an integrated unit related to customer affairs in any business (Krishna & Ravi, 2016). On the other hand, new ways of business collaborations with customers and other businesses have been possible by increasing advances in information technology (Wikhamn, 2019; Norfazlina et al., 2016).

"Wining customer satisfaction" and meeting their needs play a vital role in succeeding today's businesses (Pozza et al., 2018). In other words, the key to business growth is to gain customer satisfaction (Ballestero et al., 2018). Therefore, it is essential to create an integrated unit related to customer affairs in large businesses (Ritter & Geersbro, 2018; Vanhanen et al., 2018).

CRM is a strategy for the process of obtaining information about customers and their needs in order to maximize profitable performance, income, customer satisfaction, through customer selection and adopting behaviors causing satisfaction, customer focus and strong relations with them (Ritter & Geersbro, 2018; Ballestero et al., 2018). CRM is one of the most important and vital points for businesses and is used to support marketing, sales and service processes (Ritter & Geersbro, 2018; Ballestero et al., 2018). In order to improve and develop performance in today's market, managers need to pay special attention to their most valuable assets, namely their customers.

Digital Shopping

Despite the rapid growth of digital shopping, not much research has been done in the field of internal relationship between risk factors, marketing effects, and their impact on the product and consumer confidence in retailers. The digital shopping stages include selecting a products/ services, pay for products/ services, and receiving and delivering products/ services. However, despite the growth of digital sales services, not much users and customers are eager to buy online, which shows the need to analyze the factors affecting the rejection of digital shopping for enterprises. On the other hand, users and customers who make digital shopping can easily analyze and compare the prices and services provided by different enterprises and commercial institutions and choose the best option in a short time. Accordingly, the bargaining power has been transferred from the sellers to the buyers, and therefore it is never easy for the retailer to maintain the effective behavioral factors on the acceptance of digital shopping by users. With its increasing growth, the Internet has found many applications in various industries. The Internet and related technologies have created new and different types of business, and the time spent on the Internet, social networks and digital shopping is rapidly increasing. Today, the Internet is a powerful medium available for the advertising industry and in a society in which it is important to have a competitive space, every business uses different strategies and the Internet to target their customers.

Huiru et al. (2018) in line with the research purpose namely investigating a agent-based modeling method to simulate consumer buying behavior in the Chinese beverage market, a simulation model was created based on an agent that combines the mixed motivational function with a recreational effect to simulate consumer buying behavior. A study of 976 valid samples was performed in China to estimate the key parameters in the simulation model. An obvious recreational effect was observed, and the agents that changed purchasing options showed similar motivations for the brands A and B. Agent-based modeling can model consumer buying behavior in different beverage markets by setting parameters in a similar model. Tests show that this is very evident in the Chinese beverage market. The findings provide valuable insights into consumer behavior in Chinese beverages market. It is expected that the modeling methods are used as a model for simulating consumer buying behavior in China. This is the first attempt to apply an agent-based model and calculate simulation parameters to simulate consumer buying behavior in the Chinese beverage market.

Aimed to implement CRM in business, Ritter & Geersbro (2018) concluded that managers' multi-skilling has a very important role in the implementation of CRM in improving business management. By offering a proposed framework, information technology tools are used as input to expand CRM, and ultimately, will provide useful outputs such as improving customer relationship, sustainable competitive advantage, and reducing business costs. The research findings show that CRM is desirable in small and medium-sized enterprises and finally, some practices are provided to improve customer relationship.

Pozza et al. (2018), in their study, investigated the role of CRM implementation on business performance and found that the rapid growth of wireless communication technology has led to more and more influence of CRM in electronic commerce and digital shopping. Examining the role of CRM implementation on the performance of businesses is very important in terms of awareness of perceptions and acceptance of electronic commerce and digital shopping by customers. CRM will increase the volume of transactions, profits, and revenue; however, despite these benefits, users are still unaware of the lack of infrastructure and act as a barrier to CRM and its acceptance.

Sohn (2017), in a study entitled "consumer processing from mobile online stores: resources and effects of processing method", examined the role of psychological perception of processing in consumer experiences of mobile internet shopping. Processing fluency refers to the ease of information processing and plays a pivotal role in short meetings and interactions that determine interactions with mobile devices. Findings from two experimental studies show that perceived visual complexity reduces mental comprehension, while perceived visual congruence (between a mobile online store and an online store available on a computer) has the opposite effect. No differences were found in the congruence perception of visual contact between mobile touch points. Fluency, in turn, affects both the satisfaction of the mobile online store and the satisfaction of the choice.

Zhang (2017) modeled consumer buying behavior according to the quality of the website. The main part of agent-based modeling is a corrective motivational function that considers the price of goods, the quality of goods, and the quality of the website. In addition, the study used Toolkit Repast Simphony as a corrective motivational function. Agent-based simulation method has been used to express dynamic in consumer behavior.

According to the results of the study by Shim et al. (2012), aimed to analyze CRM strategies on digital shopping behavior, it was found that in countries where communication has improved with the increase of mobile subscribers and Internet users, CRM and digital shopping behavior, as the backbone of any business for growth, has improved. Shim et al. (2012) concluded that due to their high role in adapting to CRM, electronic business and digital shopping providers should increase their adaptability to the different needs of users, previous experiences, lifestyles and their beliefs so that they can realize customers' expectations.

Phan & Douglas (2017) aimed to analyze CRM strategies on digital shopping behavior, it was found that in countries where communication has improved with the increase of mobile subscribers and Internet users, CRM and digital shopping behavior, as the backbone of any business for growth, has improved. Phan & Douglas (2010) concluded that business intelligence systems are the most important factor in customers '(users') decision-making to accept CRM and digital shopping behavior, and define it as the degree to which innovation is consistent with existing values and experiences. Due to the factors affecting customer relationship management and online shopping behavior, electronic business and digital shopping providers should emphasize the benefits and applications of using business intelligence systems in CRM and educate customers and motivate them to do their business through electronic commerce and digital shopping.

Ojelabi et al. (2018) gathered data related to social customer relationship management (CRM 2.0) in the business of Nigeria. They found that integrating social media management tools into the business environment can enhance the relationship between the constructor and the client in order to maintain a lasting and sustainable partnership. The target businesses included seventy-five active construction businessmen in Nigeria who were selected from a group of registered construction businesses and consultants using a random sampling technique. Descriptive statistics of Internet readiness of contracting and consulting businesses for acceptance of customer relationship management 2.0 and barriers to its absorption were analyzed. Also, inferential analysis was performed using Mann–Whitney U and independent t statistical tests on the obtained data. The data obtained from the construction business will support the need to participate in the management of social relations in ensuring the sustainable management of customer relations in the business environment.

In a study by Kubina & Lendel (2015), the successful application of social customer relationship management (CRM 2.0) in Slovakian electronic business was examined. The problems of successful application management of CRM in electronic business have not yet been well studied and is a weakly practices field in marketing management. Managers often do not know the modern techniques and criteria for evaluating social CRM implementation. The aim of this study was to create a system for the successful application of social customer relationship management (CRM 2.0) in electronic business based on detailed analysis of resources and existing research. Innovative approaches to relational marketing (E-CRM, CRM 2.0) and their applications in Slovak business acquisition (experimental research) were identified and evaluated for this purpose.

Harrigan et al. (2015) modeled CRM in the age of social media. Indeed, CRM is an ongoing and evolving field that has been particularly affected by social media, which has affected the way businesses and customers communicate. An Internet survey to collect data from the community of marketing professionals and to analyze the minimum squares was used to test the model. Findings show the importance of customer relationships orientation, how it affects the technology of social media and customer engagement initiatives, as well as the performance of CRM. Therefore, from a managerial point of view, one of our recommendations is that businesses should use the rich information of the customer to be able to guide future marketing decisions with any customer interaction through social media.

In a study by Norfazlina et al. (2016), with the aim of analyzing the user satisfaction with customer information system and work efficiency, the moderating effect of training was examined. Customer Information System (CIS) is a system used by a business to help employees to obtain effective customer information. User satisfaction with the system leads to improved productivity and allows employees to take full advantage of the system. This study investigated the relationship between user satisfaction factors and the productivity of the work of the Commonwealth of Independent States and the impact of training on this relationship. A total of 149 respondents, including call center staff in the Klang Valley answered the questionnaire. According to the research findings, all three factors (ease of use, content, and formatting) have a significant relationship with labor productivity of the Commonwealth of Independent States. The results also show that training significantly reduces the relationship between ease of use in the Commonwealth of Independent States and labor productivity. However, it does not reduce the relationship between user satisfaction (content and formatting) and labor productivity. Finally, some suggestions are also presented for future studies.

THE RESEARCH CONCEPTUAL MODEL

Table 1 presents the research theoretical framework.

Finally, after reviewing the research theoretical foundations and background, and considering the research gap in the field of multivariate relationships analysis between components of "customer satisfaction with digital shopping services", "quality of optimal use of CRM information resources", "quality of CRM information display and representation system", and "efficiency of economic profitability of CRM System", we can realize the contribution of the present study in eliminating the mentioned research gaps in order to improve the digital shopping process in Tehran's digital stores.

The research model is derived from the research by Zhang (2017), Huiru et al. (2018), Fernández et al. (2018), Pozza et al. (2018), Ritter & Geersbro (2018), Ballestero et al. (2018), Shim et al. (2012), Sohn (2017), Phan & Douglas (2010), Duarte et al. (2018), Farooq et al. (2018), Holm et al. (2018), and Platt & Gebbie (2018).

RESEARCH METHODOLOGY

Research Purposes

The main purpose of this study is to investigate the effect of customer relationship management on digital shopping processes using ABM methodology. Accordingly, the sub-objectives of the research are:

- Investigating the effect of customer satisfaction with digital shopping services on digital shopping with ABM methodology,
- Investigating the effect of display information quality and representation of CRM system on digital shopping stages with ABM methodology,
- Investigating the effect of economic profitability of CRM system on digital shopping process with ABM methodology,
- Investigating the effect of optimal use of information resources on digital shopping with ABM methodology

Research Techniques

Due to the use of ABM methodology in examining the effect of CRM on digital shopping in a digital store using Anylogic software, the statistical method is also used in the present study. In this way, before modeling and simulation in Anylogic environment, the effects of correlation research variables that provide the same results of linear regression in SPSS environment are first examined and analyzed.

Table 1a. Research theoretical framework

The quality of CRM information display and representation system and the optimal use of resources on the online shopping process (Zhang, 2017; Huiru et al., 2018; Holm et al., 2018; Platt & Gebbie, 2018)	
Accuracy and precision of information conversion; data storage; information processing; data transfer; and customer purchase information retrieval	Graphical analysis of information conversion
Database reliability	Satisfaction level of users from information conversion
Comprehensive (quantitative) information conversion	Utilization of information resources available in information conversion
The status of information transfer	Ease of data conversion analysis
Thematic (qualitative) diversity of information exchange	System flexibility in different information conversion conditions
Connection between information conversion	User-friendly information conversion environment
Analytical information conversion	alternatives for information conversion
The benefits of E-CRM for customer satisfaction with digital shopping services (Shim et al., 2012; Sohn, 2017; Phan & Douglas, 2010; Duarte et al., 2018; Zhang, 2017; Norfazlina et al., 2016; Pozza et al., 2018; Ritter & Geersbro, 2018)	
4. Faster customer service	1. performance of economic profitability of the CRM system
Rapid development of services and products to customers	Reduction of business costs in the field of hardware
Fast delivery of services and products to customers	Reduction of business costs in the field of software
Providing services independently or in groups	Reduction of business costs in the field of manpower
No delay due to hardware purchase and software	Reduction of business costs in the field of infrastructure updates
Increasing computational power	2. Improving flexibility and scalability
Presenting the latest solutions	Rapid business response to market changes
Use the Internet platform to provide business services at any time and place	Meeting customer needs on a variety of scales
5. Establish customer relationships	Meeting the needs within the business at various scales
Better insight from customers	3. Increase Productivity
Providing customized services	Easier use of new technologies
Facilitating payments between buyers and sellers	Integration of future applications
Sharing business plans	Eliminating the complexity of technology and business
Marketing and selling products and services in digital shopping (Zhang, 2017)	
A- Management of product marketing and sales team Interpretation of product marketing and sales team information Obtaining information about the product marketing and sales team The culture of learning of product marketing and sales team Distribution of product marketing and sales team information	B- Social characteristics of the electronic business website Website optimization (SEO) Ease of access to electronic product information Awareness of electronic products The attractiveness of an online business website
Digital shopping stages (Huiru et al., 2018; Shim et al., 2012; Sohn, 2017; Phan & Douglas, 2010; Duarte et al., 2018; Pozza et al., 2018) Product review / service in digital shopping, product / service selection in digital shopping Product payment / service costs in digital shopping Receive and deliver product / service in digital shopping	

Table 1b. Research theoretical framework

User / Customer Features in the digital shopping stages (Zhang, 2017; Huiru et al., 2018; Fernández et al., 2018; Pozza et al., 2018; Ritter & Geersbro, 2018; Ballestero et al., 2018; Shim et al., 2012; Sohn, 2017; Phan & Douglas, 2010; Duarte et al., 2018; Farooq et al., 2018; Holm et al., 2018; Platt & Gebbie, 2018)	"Environmental factors of electronic commerce" in the digital shopping stages (Zhang, 2017; Huiru et al., 2018; Shim et al., 2012; Sohn, 2017; Phan & Douglas, 2010; Duarte et al., 2018; Zhang, 2017; Huiru et al., 2018; Fernández et al., 2018)	"Product / Service Specifications" in the digital shopping stages (Zhang, 2017; Huiru et al., 2018; Shim et al., 2012; Sohn, 2017; Phan & Douglas, 2010; Duarte et al., 2018; Pozza et al., 2018; Ritter & Geersbro, 2018; Ballestero et al., 2018; Shim et al., 2012; Sohn, 2017)
Customer age	Economic factors affecting electronic commerce	Product price
Customer gender	Political factors affecting electronic commerce	Product quality
Marriage status	Cultural factors affecting electronic Business	product variety
Customer income	Technological factors affecting electronic commerce	Product weight
Customer education	Climate factors affecting electronic commerce	Product size
Customer living area	Considering customers in electronic commerce	Product color
Customer lifestyle	Considering competitors in electronic commerce	Product material
Customer attitudes and opinions	Considering colleagues in electronic commerce	Country of origin (COO) of a product
Customer activities and skills	Government economic policies	Product design and format
Customer tastes and interests	The country's Internet infrastructure	Possibility of product discount
Customer risk	Issues of justice and equality in electronic commerce	Product brand
Customer Internet knowledge	Privacy in electronic commerce	After-sales service of product
Customer online shopping experience	Sustainable existence in electronic commerce	Product utility
Effectiveness of third party evaluation	Creative work and effort in electronic commerce	Risk of product purchase
effectiveness of security infrastructure	Copyright in electronic commerce	Product customization
Satisfaction with online shopping	Function of the legal system in defining Internet crime and its pursuit	Meanings customers ascribe to a product
Internet loyalty	Network and telecommunication performance status	Ease of use of the product

ABM which is a form of Computational Social Science that offers a new analytical and computational approach, is one of the most flexible modeling methods. ABM has provided an interesting way to solve some complex problems in many research fields (Huiru et al., 2018; Zhang, 2017).

The basis of naming this methodology is that agents play a key role in the model. In this type of modeling, each of the real world factors are modeled as decision-making and fully automatic entities called agent. Each of these agents has a variety of areas for understanding the environment, analyzing it, and ultimately taking action. Indeed, in agent-based modeling, it is tried to simulate the decision-making process in the real world by similar factors.

Figure 1. Research model

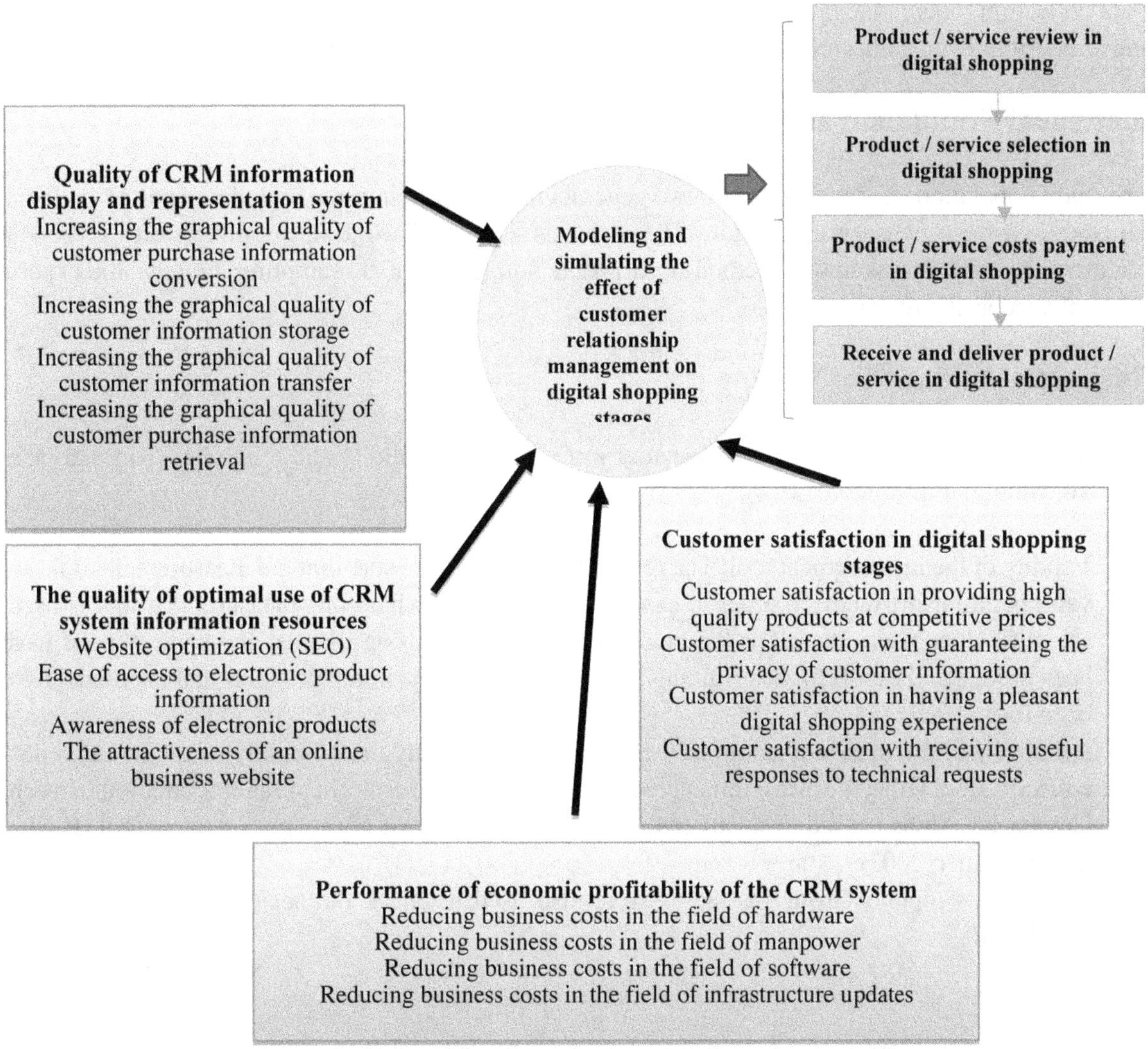

In the complex and dynamic market of communication, insurance, leasing and medical fields, customers make decisions based on various characteristics. In these systems, ABM can be easily utilized and data from statistical results can be used for model inputs. ABM is also widely used in Epidemiology systems like disease spread systems. This methodology is also widely used in the marketing process, competitors' analysis, and market share forecasting (Zhang, 2017; Huiru et al., 2018).

On the other hand, AnyLogic simulation software provides users with a wide range of possibilities for creating and analyzing ABM. Agent behavior can be plotted using the stateChart in the software.

AnyLogic simulation software manages each of the factors independently during execution based on the drawn behavioral logic.

Data Collection Methods and Tools

Data collection tools in the present study are research questionnaires made for digital shopping stages and dimensions of customer relationship management that have been used in the seven-point Likert scale.

Statistical Population and Sample

The study population can be divided into two general groups: the first group includes experts (academic experts), and the second group includes IT specialists and CRM working in online stores in Tehran (industry experts). The sampling method is purposive non-probabilistic sampling. Finally, 300 experts were selected as the research sample.

Research Validation

The two main criteria for measuring the accuracy of metrics are validity and reliability (Kirkpatrick et al. 2010, Blummer & Kenton. 2014):

1. Validity of the measurement tool: The researcher should make sure that the measurement tools are valid before using them. In order to examine the extent to which this measurement tool is used, scientific documents as well as the opinions of supervisors, consultants, and some experts have been used, and the tools for determining the components of the initial decision-making model have been formulated.
2. Reliability of the measurement tool: the reason for examining the reliability of the research data collection tool is that the measurement tool achieves the same results in the same conditions, so here Cronbach's Alpha is used to calculate the reliability coefficient of the measurement tool (Blaika, 2003; Cramer, 2003).
3. The experts' opinion in digital stores were also used to check the accuracy of modeling and simulation.

RESULTS

In the statistical analysis of this research, descriptive statistics including mean, standard deviation and correlation were used. Tables 2 and 3 show the descriptive information of the components of the customer relationship management effect on the digital shopping stages based on the number of data, minimum, maximum, average, and standard deviation. The data in this study are symmetrical and cumulative in the optimal situation, because the standard deviation of most of them is approximately one and has a suitable distribution.

Table 2. Descriptive information on the research variables importance

Research Variables	Research Indicators	n	Min	Max	Average	Standard Deviation
A. performance of economic profitability of the CRM system	Reducing business costs in the field of hardware	300	1	7	5.46	1.364
	Reducing business costs in the field of manpower	300	2	7	6.13	.937
	Reducing business costs in the field of software	300	1	7	6.26	1.097
	Reducing business costs in the field of infrastructure updates	300	2	7	6.11	.996
B- The quality of optimal use of CRM system information resources	Website optimization (SEO)	300	1	7	5.67	1.163
	Ease of access to electronic product information	300	1	7	5.59	1.342
	Awareness of electronic products	300	1	7	5.45	1.224
	The attractiveness of an online business website	300	1	7	5.57	1.368
C- the quality of CRM information display and representation system	Increasing the graphical quality of customer purchase information conversion	300	1	7	5.59	1.241
	Increasing the graphical quality of customer information storage	300	1	7	5.61	1.206
	Increasing the graphical quality of customer information transfer	300	1	7	5.34	1.178
	Increasing the graphical quality of customer purchase information retrieval	300	1	7	6.23	1.087
D- Customer satisfaction in digital shopping services	Customer satisfaction in providing high quality products at competitive prices	300	1	7	5.70	1.217
	Customer satisfaction with guaranteeing the privacy of customer information	300	1	7	5.69	1.216
	Customer satisfaction in having a pleasant digital shopping experience	300	1	7	5.68	1.233
	Customer satisfaction with receiving useful responses to technical requests	300	1	7	5.68	1.250

As can be observed, according to the organizational and academic experts' opinions and experience, which was measured on a seven-point scale, the most important indicator related to variable a (the efficiency of CRM's economic profitability) is to "reducing business costs in the field of software" with an average value of 6.26; the most important indicator related to the variable b (the quality of optimal use of CRM system information resources) is "website optimization (SEO)" with an average importance of 5.67; the most important indicator of the variable c (the quality of representation information of the CRM system) is "increasing the graphical quality of customer purchase information retrieval" with an average value of 6.23, and the most important indicator of the variable d (customer satisfaction with digital shopping) is "customer satisfaction in providing high quality products at competitive prices" with an average value of 5.70. While their performance status is lower, so that the indicator of "reducing business costs in the field of software" has an average performance status of 4.67; "website optimization (SEO)" indicator has an average performance status of 4.10; "increasing the graphical quality of customer purchase information retrieval" indicator has an average operating status of 4.39; and the "customer satisfaction in providing high quality products at competitive prices" indicator has an average performance of 4.68.

Table 3. Descriptive information on the research variables status

Research Variables	Research Indicators	n	Min	Max	Average	Standard Deviation
A. The economic profitability of the CRM system	Reducing business costs in the field of hardware	299	1	6	4.11	1.378
	Reducing business costs in the field of manpower	291	1	6	4.71	1.036
	Reducing business costs in the field of software	293	1	7	4.67	1.105
	Reducing business costs in the field of infrastructure updates	290	1	6	4.38	1.626
B- The quality of optimal use of CRM system information resources	Website optimization (SEO)	294	1	7	4.10	1.513
	Ease of access to electronic product information	297	1	7	4.22	.758
	Awareness of electronic products	298	1	7	4.72	1.061
	The attractiveness of an online business website	299	1	7	4.72	1.082
C- Quality of CRM information display and representation system	Increasing the graphical quality of customer purchase information conversion	300	1	7	4.53	1.036
	Increasing the graphical quality of customer information storage	299	1	7	4.71	1.163
	Increasing the graphical quality of customer information transfer	297	1	7	4.02	1.406
	Increasing the graphical quality of customer purchase information retrieval	294	1	7	4.39	1.186
D- Customer satisfaction in digital shopping stages	Customer satisfaction in providing high quality products at competitive prices	299	1	7	4.68	1.151
	Customer satisfaction with guaranteeing the privacy of customer information	300	1	7	4.55	.992
	Customer satisfaction in having a pleasant digital shopping experience	299	1	7	4.67	1.145
	Customer satisfaction with receiving useful responses to technical requests	299	3	7	4.17	1.392

Descriptive information on the importance and status of research variables shows that managers and experts of the online store should consider the performance status of the variable a (the efficiency of CRM's economic profitability) including the indicators like reducing business costs in the field of hardware, reducing business costs in the field of human resource, reducing business costs in the field of software, reducing business costs in the field of infrastructure updates; variable b (the quality of optimal use of CRM system information resources) including the indicators like website optimization (SEO), ease of access to information on electronic products, awareness of electronic products, attractiveness of the website of the online business; variable c (the quality of information representation of the CRM system) including the indicators like increasing the graphical quality of customer purchase information retrieval, increasing the graphical quality of customer information storage, increasing the graphical quality of customer purchase information transfer, increasing the graphical quality of customer information retrieval; and the variable d (customer satisfaction with digital shopping) including the indicators like customer satisfaction in providing high quality products at competitive prices, customer satisfaction with the guarantee of the privacy of customer information, customer satisfaction with having a pleasant digital shopping experience, customer satisfaction with receiving useful answers to technical requests as strategic considerations in organizational decisions.

Indeed, the main reason for the reliability analysis of the data collection tools of this research is to examine that to what extent the measurement tools achieve the same results under the same conditions and the correlation between a set of answers and another set of answers in an equivalent test that is independently obtained on one test group. The table related to the reliability statistics of research variables shows the high reliability of the data collection tools of this research:

Table 4. Reliability

Reliability	Cronbach's alpha	Items
	.939	16

Here, Cronbach's alpha for research variables is greater than 0.9, indicating that the reliability of the measurement tool to test the impact of customer relationship management on digital shopping processes is excellent.

Table 5. Questions related to the digital shopping stages

The research model components
A. Product review (E)
The appropriateness of product prices in the review of products (E1)
Appropriate product quality in products review (E2)
Comparing the product with similar products in the product review (E3)
B- the product selection (F)
Possibility to select the color of the product (F1)
Possibility of selecting required number when ordering (F2)
Ability to select a specific brand from the product (F3)
C- Payment of cost (G)
Possibility of payment at location (G1)
Ability to pay installments for special customers (G2)
Possibility to return the goods after receiving the cost (G3)
D- Receipt / delivery of product (H)
Proper packaging for product (H1)
Satisfaction with the time of receiving the product within the specified time frame (H2)
Possibility to deliver product by another person (H3)

Table 6. Correlation coefficients of digital shoping phases

			E	F	G	H
Spearman's rho	E	Correlation Coefficient	1.000	.499**	.474**	.589**
		Sig. (2-tailed)	.	.005	.008	.001
		N	300	300	300	300
	F	Correlation Coefficient	.499**	1.000	.600**	.526**
		Sig. (2-tailed)	.005	.	.000	.003
		N	300	300	300	300
	G	Correlation Coefficient	.474**	.600**	1.000	.528**
		Sig. (2-tailed)	.008	.000	.	.003
		N	300	300	300	300
	H	Correlation Coefficient	.589**	.526**	.528**	1.000
		Sig. (2-tailed)	.001	.003	.003	.
		N	300	300	300	300

**. Correlation is significant at the 0.01 level (2-tailed).

As can be seen, the correlation coefficient between product reviews with product selection is 0.49, product selection with payment is 0.60, and payment with receipt is 0.52.

Table 7. Correlation coefficients between the economic profitability of the CRM system and digital shoping phases

			E	F	G	H	A
Spearman's rho	E	Correlation Coefficient	1.000	.499**	.474**	.589**	.716**
		Sig. (2-tailed)	.	.005	.008	.001	.000
		N	300	300	300	300	300
	F	Correlation Coefficient	.499**	1.000	.600**	.526**	.545**
		Sig. (2-tailed)	.005	.	.000	.003	.002
		N	300	300	300	300	300
	G	Correlation Coefficient	.474**	.600**	1.000	.528**	.438*
		Sig. (2-tailed)	.008	.000	.	.003	.016
		N	300	300	300	300	300
	H	Correlation Coefficient	.589**	.526**	.528**	1.000	.445*
		Sig. (2-tailed)	.001	.003	.003	.	.014
		N	300	300	300	300	300
	A	Correlation Coefficient	.716**	.545**	.438*	.445*	1.000
		Sig. (2-tailed)	.000	.002	.016	.014	.
		N	300	300	300	300	300

**. Correlation is significant at the 0.01 level (2-tailed).

*. Correlation is significant at the 0.05 level (2-tailed).

Table 8. Correlation coefficients between the quality of optimal use of CRM system information resources and digital shoping phases

			E	F	G	H	B
Spearman's rho	E	Correlation Coefficient	1.000	.499**	.474**	.589**	.375*
		Sig. (2-tailed)	.	.005	.008	.001	.041
		N	300	300	300	300	300
	F	Correlation Coefficient	.499**	1.000	.600**	.526**	.807**
		Sig. (2-tailed)	.005	.	.000	.003	.000
		N	300	300	300	300	300
	G	Correlation Coefficient	.474**	.600**	1.000	.528**	.588**
		Sig. (2-tailed)	.008	.000	.	.003	.001
		N	300	300	300	300	300
	H	Correlation Coefficient	.589**	.526**	.528**	1.000	.630**
		Sig. (2-tailed)	.001	.003	.003	.	.000
		N	300	300	300	300	300
	B	Correlation Coefficient	.375*	.807**	.588**	.630**	1.000
		Sig. (2-tailed)	.041	.000	.001	.000	.
		N	300	300	300	300	300

**. Correlation is significant at the 0.01 level (2-tailed).
*. Correlation is significant at the 0.05 level (2-tailed).

As can be seen, the correlation coefficient of economic profitability efficiency of customer relationship management system with product review, product selection, payment, and receipt is 0.71, 0.54, 0.43, and 0.44, respectively.

As can be seen, the quality correlation coefficient of optimal use of customer relationship management system information with product review, product selection, payment, and receipt is 0.37, 0.80, 0.58, and 0.63, respectively.

As can be seen, the correlation coefficient of display information quality and customer relationship management system representation with product review, product selection, payment, and receipt is 0.40, 0.45, 0.89, and 0.51, respectively.

As can be seen, the customer satisfaction correlation coefficient with product review, product selection, payment, and receipt is 0.54, 0.53, 0.61 and 0.94, respectively.

Modeling and simulation

The following figure indicates the digital shopping stages drawn in the Anylogic environment.

As can be seen in Figure 2, each stage is related to the next stage by the determined correlation coefficient.

Check:

Table 9. Correlation coefficients between quality of CRM information display and representation system and digital shoping phases

			E	F	G	H	C
Spearman's rho	E	Correlation Coefficient	1.000	.499**	.474**	.589**	.409*
		Sig. (2-tailed)	.	.005	.008	.001	.025
		N	300	300	300	300	300
	F	Correlation Coefficient	.499**	1.000	.600**	.526**	.455*
		Sig. (2-tailed)	.005	.	.000	.003	.011
		N	300	300	300	300	300
	G	Correlation Coefficient	.474**	.600**	1.000	.528**	.890**
		Sig. (2-tailed)	.008	.000	.	.003	.000
		N	300	300	300	300	300
	H	Correlation Coefficient	.589**	.526**	.528**	1.000	.518**
		Sig. (2-tailed)	.001	.003	.003	.	.003
		N	300	300	300	300	300
	C	Correlation Coefficient	.409*	.455*	.890**	.518**	1.000
		Sig. (2-tailed)	.025	.011	.000	.003	.
		N	300	300	300	300	300

**. Correlation is significant at the 0.01 level (2-tailed).
*. Correlation is significant at the 0.05 level (2-tailed).

Table 10. Correlation coefficients between customer satisfaction in digital shopping services and digital shoping phases

			E	F	G	H	D
Spearman's rho	E	Correlation Coefficient	1.000	.499**	.474**	.589**	.547**
		Sig. (2-tailed)	.	.005	.008	.001	.002
		N	300	300	300	300	300
	F	Correlation Coefficient	.499**	1.000	.600**	.526**	.530**
		Sig. (2-tailed)	.005	.	.000	.003	.003
		N	300	300	300	300	300
	G	Correlation Coefficient	.474**	.600**	1.000	.528**	.612**
		Sig. (2-tailed)	.008	.000	.	.003	.000
		N	300	300	300	300	300
	H	Correlation Coefficient	.589**	.526**	.528**	1.000	.949**
		Sig. (2-tailed)	.001	.003	.003	.	.000
		N	300	300	300	300	300
	D	Correlation Coefficient	.547**	.530**	.612**	.949**	1.000
		Sig. (2-tailed)	.002	.003	.000	.000	.
		N	300	300	300	300	300

**. Correlation is significant at the 0.01 level (2-tailed).

Figure 2. Statechart of digital shopping stages

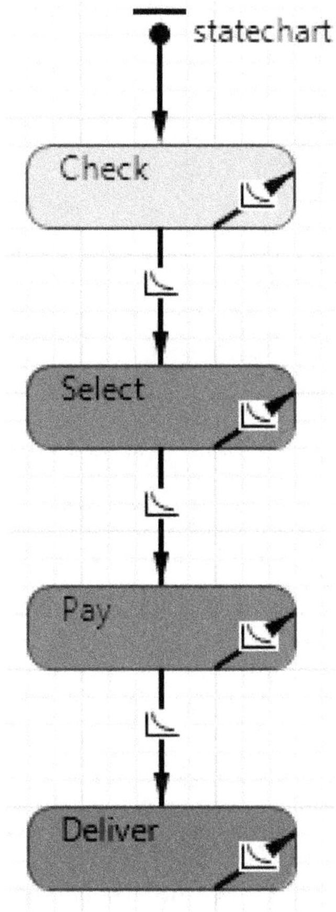


```
Entry action: get_Main().nCheck++;
color = GOLD;
Exit action: get_Main().nCheck--;
```

Select:

```
Entry action: get_Main().nSelect++;
color = RED;
Exit action: get_Main().nSelect--;
```

Pay:

```
Entry action: get_Main().nPay++;
color = MAGENTA;
Exit action: get_Main().nPay--;
```

Deliver:

```
Entry action: get_Main().nDeliver++;
color = GREEN;
Exit action: get_Main().nDeliver--;
```

Figure 3. Impact of the economic profitability of the CRM system on digital shoping phases after almost one month

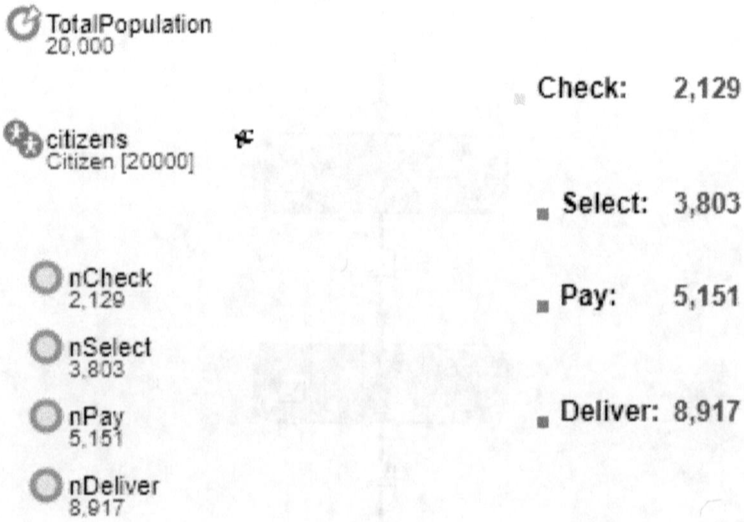

Figure 4. Impact of the quality of optimal use of CRM system information resources on digital shoping phases after almost one month

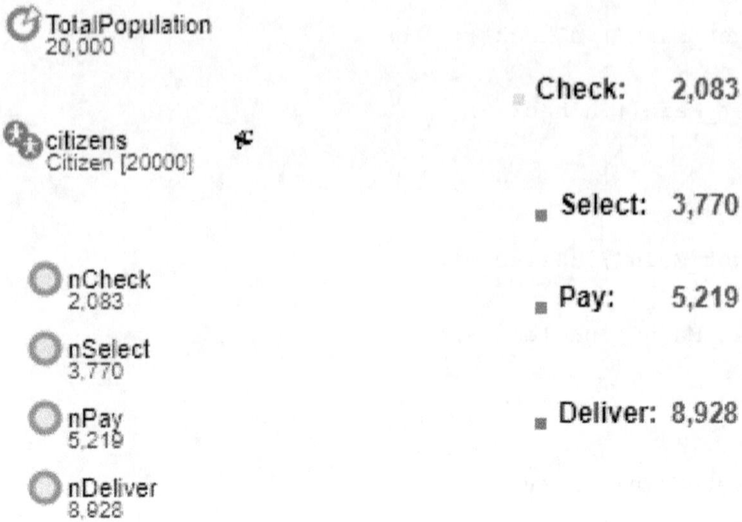

Figure 5. Impact of quality of CRM information display and representation system s on digital shoping phases after almost one month

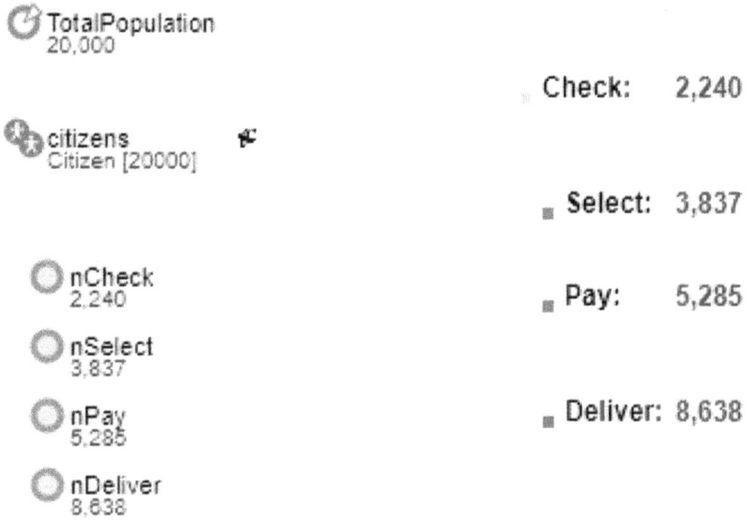

And the rates specified within each stage, in each run, are the correlation coefficient of one of the dimensions of the customer relationship management system.

The total population is considered 20,000.

Figure 6. Impact of customer satisfaction of digital shopping services on digital shoping phases after almost one month

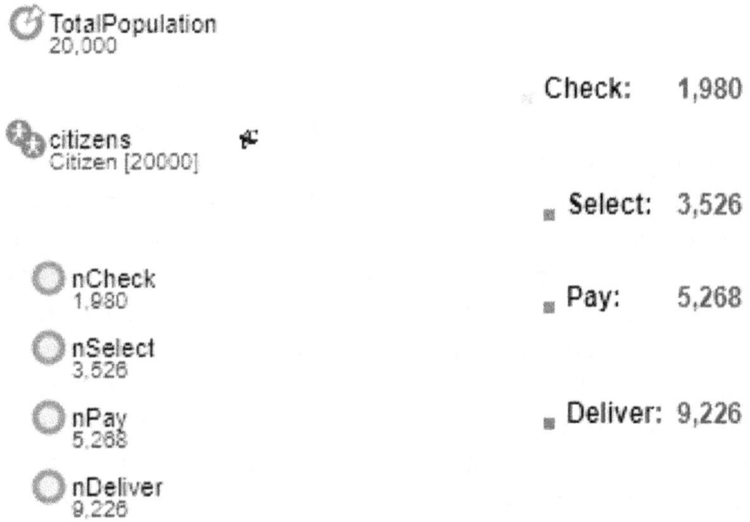

As the above results show, the digital store performance is better considering the customer relationship management system and all the dimensions and effects of the customer relationship management system have a positive effect on the digital shopping process. Due to the confidentiality of the digital store's information, only the hypothetical population of 20,000 has been used. However, the opinions of experts were used for the accuracy test, that all have positive views to the usefulness and correctness of the results.

Figure 7. Digital shopping results without CRM after almost one month

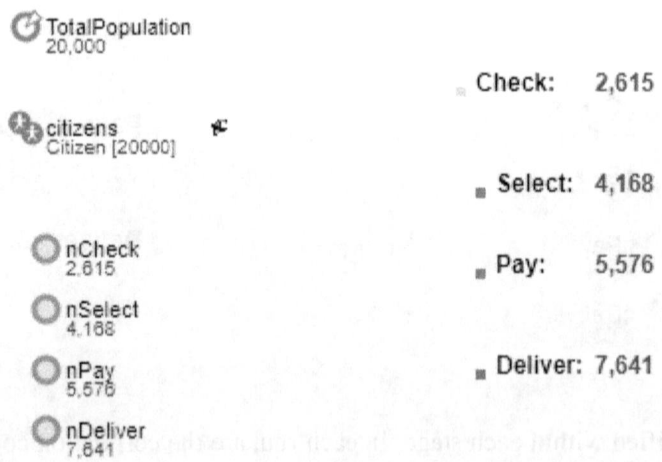

SOLUTIONS AND RECOMMENDATIONS

Since the quality of the optimal use of CRM system information resources has a positive effect on the digital shopping stages, factors such as website optimization (SEO), ease of access to electronic product information, and the attractiveness of an online business website affect easy purchase of customers. In this regard, website characteristics (ease of use, product availability, and visual appeal, among others) or e-store attributes (navigation, design, and content) influence buying behavior from digital shopping (Akram et al., 2018). Therefore, it is suggested to improve various attributes of a website, which might enhance its quality for the purpose of increasing digital store performance.

As the economic profitability performance of the CRM system has a positive effect on the digital shopping stages, cost reduction is recognized as an effective factor. However, a main focus of investments is on digital technologies like network, software, and hardware. Additionally, digital enterprises invest on training employees and driving required organisational change. Thus, it is recommended to reduce costs of technologies and human resources to have a better performance of digital stores.

It is shown that the quality of CRM information display and representation system has a positive effect on digital shopping processes. It means that increasing the graphical quality of (information conversion, information storage, information transfer, and information retrieval) is considered influencial on digital shopping processes. In this case, improving graphical quality of information related functions can be effective on individuals' intention to pass through online shopping phases.

Since customer satisfaction with digital shopping services has a positive effect on digital shopping processes, customer satisfaction as a customer's positive feeling about providing high quality products at competitive prices, guaranteeing the privacy of customer information, having a pleasant digital shopping experience, and receiving useful responses to technical requests would be benefiacial for digital shopping. For the sake of increasing market competition, customer experience has been broadly confirmed as the source of competitive advantage (Vakulenko et al., 2019). Therefore, working on digital services to improve customer satisfaction will direct Internet users through digital shopping phases.

FUTURE RESEARCH DIRECTIONS

Following the trend of digital shopping as a result of the presence of the Internet, the CRM factors that direct Internet users through online shopping phases are considered in this study. This investigation is therefore intended to underline the possible CRM factors responsible for their engagement in the digital shopping. To achieve this objective, a research model composing underlined CRM factors is established in the literature as key potential drivers for predicting individuals' intention to go through online shopping phases and statistical and simulation techniques are applied to predict the effect of CRM factor on digital shopping. Since the current research is about the domain of a digital store, it would be necessary if future researchers could explore other digital enterprises.

CONCLUSION

The present study, using statistical analysis and agent-based modeling methodology, modeled and simulated the effect of customer relationship management on digital shopping. According to the organizational and academic experts' opinions and experience, which was measured on a seven-point scale, the most important indicator related to variable a (the efficiency of CRM's economic profitability) is to "reducing business costs in the field of software" with an average value of 6.26; the most important indicator related to the variable b (the quality of optimal use of CRM system information resources) is "website optimization (SEO)" with an average importance of 5.67; the most important indicator of the variable c (the quality of representation information of the CRM system) is "increasing the graphical quality of customer purchase information retrieval" with an average value of 6.23, and the most important indicator of the variable d (customer satisfaction with online shopping) is "customer satisfaction in providing high quality products at competitive prices" with average value of 5.70.

While their performance status is lower, so that the indicator of "reducing business costs in the field of software" has an average performance status of 4.67; "website optimization (SEO) " indicator has an average performance status of 4.10; "increasing the graphical quality of customer purchase information retrieval" indicator has an average operating status of 4.39; and the "customer satisfaction in providing high quality products at competitive prices" indicator has an average performance of 4.68.

On the other hand, based on the results of the inferential statistics, product review with product selection has a correlation coefficient of 0.49, product selection with payment has the correlation coefficient of 0.60, and payment with receipt have a correlation coefficient of 0.52. The efficiency of economic profitability of customer relationship management system has the correlation scores of 0.71, 0.54. 0.43, and 0.44 with product review, product selection, payment, and receiving, respectively. Quality of optimal use of customer relationship management system has the correlation scores of 0.37, 0.80, 0.58, and 0.63 with product review, product selection, payment, and receipt, respectively. Quality of display information and customer relationship management system representation has the correlation scores of 0.4, 0.45,

0.89, and 0.51 with product review, product selection, payment, and receipt, respectively. Customer satisfaction has the correlation scores of 0.54, 0.53, 0.61, and 0.94 with product review, product selection, payment, and receipt, respectively.

According to the results of agent-based modeling and simulation, the performance of the digital store is higher when considering the customer relationship management system and all the dimensions of the customer relationship management system have a positive effect on the digital shopping stages. Due to the confidentiality of the digital store's information, only the hypothetical population of 20,000 has been used. However, the experts' opinions were used for the accuracy test and positive opinions were obtained about the results usefulness and correctness.

One of the most important results of the present study is that the performance of the digital store is higher when considering the customer relationship management system and all the dimensions of the customer relationship management system have a positive effect on the digital shopping stages.

All of the research hypotheses were confirmed so that we can say that:

- The quality of the optimal use of CRM system information resources has a positive effect on the digital shopping stages.
- The economic profitability performance of the CRM system has a positive effect on the digital shopping stages.
- The quality of CRM information display and representation system has a positive effect on digital shopping processes.
- Customer satisfaction with digital shopping services has a positive effect on digital shopping processes.

The research contributions are related to modeling the relationships between the efficiency of economic profitability of CRM system, quality of optimal use of CRM information resources, quality of CRM information display and representation system, and customer satisfaction with the digital shopping stages at the digital store.

REFERENCES

Akram, U., Kaleem Khan, M., Tanveer, Y., Mehmood, K., & Ahmad, W. (2018). How website quality affectsonline impulse buyingModerating effects of sales promotion andcredit card use. *Asia Pacific Journal of Marketing and Logistics*, *30*(1), 235–256. doi:10.1108/APJML-04-2017-0073

Anshari, M., Almunawar, M. N., Lim, S. A., & Al-Mudimigh, A. (2018). Customer relationship management and big data enabled: Personalization & customization of services. *Applied Computing and Informatics*, *15*(2), 94–101. doi:10.1016/j.aci.2018.05.004

Anumala, S., & Reddy, B. K. K. (2007). *Benefits of e-CRM for banks and their customers: case studies of two Swedish banks* (Master's Thesis). Industrial marketing and e-commerce, Lulea tekniska universitet, Sweden.

Bahrami, M., Ghorbani, M., & Arabzad, S. M. (2012). Information technology (IT) as an improvement tool for customer relationship management (CRM). *Procedia: Social and Behavioral Sciences, 41*, 59–64. doi:10.1016/j.sbspro.2012.04.008

Blaikie, N. (2003). Analyzing quantitative data: From description to explanation. *Sage (Atlanta, Ga.).*

Blummer, B., & Kenton, J. M. (2015). *Improving student information search, A metacognitive approach.* Chandos Publishing.

Cramer, D. (2003). *Advanced quantitative data analysis.* McGraw-Hill International.

Duarte, P., Costa e Silva, S., & Ferreira, M. B. (2018). How convenient is it? Delivering online shopping convenience to enhancecustomer satisfaction and encourage e-WOM. *Journal of Retailing and Consumer Services, 44*, 161–169. doi:10.1016/j.jretconser.2018.06.007

Farooq, M. S., Salam, M., Fayolle, A., Jaafar, N., & Ayupp, K. (2018). Impact of service quality on customer satisfaction in Malaysia airlines: A PLS-SEM approach. *Journal of Air Transport Management, 67*, 169–180. doi:10.1016/j.jairtraman.2017.12.008

Gao, Y. H. Z., & Chen, Y. J. X. (2018). Exploring hidden factors behind online food shopping from Amazon reviews: A topic mining approach. *Journal of Retailing and Consumer Services, 42*, 161–168. doi:10.1016/j.jretconser.2018.02.006

García-Fernández, J., Gálvez-Ruíz, P., Fernández-Gavira, J., Vélez-Colón, L., Pitts, B., & Bernal-García, A. (2018). The effects of service convenience and perceived quality on perceived value, satisfaction and loyalty in low-cost fitness centers. *Sport Management Review, 21*(3), 250–262. doi:10.1016/j.smr.2017.07.003

Gil-Gomez, H., Guerola-Navarro, V., Oltra-Badenes, R., & Lozano-Quilis, J. N. (2020). *Customer relationship management: digitaltransformation and sustainable business modelinnovation.* Economic Research-Ekonomska Istraživanja., doi:10.1080/1331677X.2019.1676283

Harrigan, P., Soutar, G., Choudhury, M. M., & Lowe, M. (2015). Modelling CRM in a social media age. *Australasian Marketing Journal, 23*(1), 27–37. doi:10.1016/j.ausmj.2014.11.001

Hasiri, S. M. A., & Afghanpour, M. (2016). Investigation of the factors affective on the loyalty of customers in banking industry in the framework of the model of personality characteristics of personnel (Case Study: Sepah Bank in Mazandaran Province). *Procedia Economics and Finance, 36*, 490–501. doi:10.1016/S2212-5671(16)30072-7

Holm, S., Thees, O., Lemm, R., Olschewski, R., & Hilty, L. M. (2018). An agent-based model of wood markets: Scenario analysis. *Forest Policy and Economics, 95*, 26–36. doi:10.1016/j.forpol.2018.07.005

Huiru, W., Jinhui, S., Jianying, F., Huiru, F., Zhijian, Z., & Weisong, M. (2018). An agent-based modeling and simulation of consumers' purchase behavior for wine consumption. *IFAC-PapersOnLine, 51*(17), 843–848. doi:10.1016/j.ifacol.2018.08.089

Kirkpatrick, L. A., & Brooke, C. F. (2010). *A simple guide to SPSS for version 17.* John- David Hague.

Krishna, G. J., & Ravi, V. (2016). Evolutionary computing applied to customer relationship management: A survey. *Engineering Applications of Artificial Intelligence*, *56*, 30–59. doi:10.1016/j.engappai.2016.08.012

Kubina, M., & Lendel, V. (2015). Successful application of Social CRM in the Company. *Procedia Economics and Finance*, *23*, 1190–1194. doi:10.1016/S2212-5671(15)00487-6

Nguyen, Q. C., Næs, T., Almøy, T., & Varela, P. (2018). Portion size selection as related to product and consumer characteristics studied by PLS path modelling. *Food Quality and Preference*, *79*, 1–10.

Norfazlina, G., Akma, A. S. S., Adrina, S. N., & Noorizan, M. M. (2016). Customer information system satisfaction and task productivity: The moderating effect of training. *Procedia Economics and Finance*, *37*, 7–12. doi:10.1016/S2212-5671(16)30085-5

Ojelabi, R. A., Afolabi, A. O., Oyeyipo, O. O., Tunji-Olayeni, P. F., & Adewale, B. A. (2018). Data exploration of social client relationship management (CRM 2.0) adoption in the Nigerian construction business. *Data in Brief*, *18*, 1471–1476. doi:10.1016/j.dib.2018.04.037 PMID:29900328

Phan, D. D., & Douglas, R. V. (2010). A model of customer relationship management and business intelligence systems for catalogue and online retailers. *Information & Management*, *47*(2), 69–77. doi:10.1016/j.im.2009.09.001

Piccoli, G., Lui, T. W., & Grün, B. (2017). The impact of IT-enabled customer service systems on service personalization, customer service perceptions, & hotel performance. *Tourism Management*, *59*, 349–362. doi:10.1016/j.tourman.2016.08.015

Platt, D., & Gebbie, T. (2018). Can agent-based models probe market microstructure? *Physica A*, *503*, 1092–1106. doi:10.1016/j.physa.2018.08.055

Pozza, I. D., Goetz, O., & Sahut, J. M. (2018). Implementation effects in the relationship between CRM & its performance. *Journal of Business Research*, *89*, 391–403. doi:10.1016/j.jbusres.2018.02.004

Ritter, T., & Geersbro, J. (2018). Multidexterity in customer relationship management: Managerial implications & a research agenda. *Industrial Marketing Management*, *69*, 74–79. doi:10.1016/j.indmarman.2018.01.019

Shim, B., Choi, K., & Suh, Y. (2012). CRM strategies for a small-sized online shopping mall based on association rulesand sequential patterns. *Expert Systems with Applications*, *39*(9), 7736–7742. doi:10.1016/j.eswa.2012.01.080

Sohn, S. (2017). Consumer processing of mobile online stores: Sources and effects of processing fluency. *Journal of Retailing and Consumer Services*, *36*, 137–147. doi:10.1016/j.jretconser.2017.01.008

Talón-Ballestero, P., González-Serrano, L., Soguero-Ruiz, C., Muñoz-Romero, S., & Rojo-Álvarez, J. L. (2018). Using big data from customer relationship management information systems to determine the client profile in the hotel sector. *Tourism Management*, *68*, 187–197. doi:10.1016/j.tourman.2018.03.017

Thakur, R. (2018). Customer engagement and online reviews. *Journal of Retailing and Consumer Services*, *41*, 48–59. doi:10.1016/j.jretconser.2017.11.002

Vakulenko, Y., Shams, P., Hellström, D., & Hjort, K. (2019). Online retail experience and customer satisfaction: The mediating role of last mile delivery. *International Review of Retail, Distribution and Consumer Research*, *29*(3), 306–320. doi:10.1080/09593969.2019.1598466

Vanhanen, J., Lehtinen, T. O. A., & Lassenius, C. (2018). Software engineering problems & their relationship to perceived learning & customer satisfaction on a software capstone project. *Journal of Systems and Software*, *137*, 50–66. doi:10.1016/j.jss.2017.11.021

Wikhamn, W. (2019). Innovation, sustainable HRM and customer satisfaction. *International Journal of Hospitality Management*, *76*, 102–110. doi:10.1016/j.ijhm.2018.04.009

Zhang, H., Zhao, L., & Gupta, S. (2018). The role of online product recommendations on customer decision making and loyalty in social shopping communities. *International Journal of Information Management*, *38*(1), 150–166. doi:10.1016/j.ijinfomgt.2017.07.006

Zhang, N. (2017). Agent-based modelling of consumer purchased behavior considering website quality. *5th International Conference on Mechatronics, Materials, Chemistry and Computer Engineering (ICMMCCE 2017)*. 10.2991/icmmcce-17.2017.105

Chapter 9
Demystifying Corporate Restructuring Strategy Through Digital Transformation:
Lessons Learned From the Banking Sector of Zimbabwe

Mufaro Dzingirai
https://orcid.org/0000-0002-1518-8275
Midlands State University, Zimbabwe

ABSTRACT

During the past two decades, corporate restructuring in the banking sector has gained much scholarly and public attention in both more developed and less developed countries as a strategic response to a decline in organizational performance. Surprisingly, there is fragmented and scant evidence on corporate restructuring through digital transformation in the banking sector, especially in the Zimbabwean context. With this in mind, this chapter aims at capturing worldwide issues and controversies linked to corporate restructuring through digital transformation, reviewing the success stories of corporate restructuring through digital transformation in the banking sector of Zimbabwe, identifying the challenges associated with digital transformation so that recommendations are proffered to top management and policymakers accordingly, and presenting suggestions for future research.

INTRODUCTION

During the past two decades, the banking institutions of both developed and developing countries have been subjected to corporate restructuring in the face of severe performance decline owing to various internal and external factors. This state of affairs heightened the need to advance our understanding of corporate restructuring from a digital transformation perspective. In this regard, banks around the world have embraced disruptive digital technologies and tools as a strategic move to ensure operational excellence.

DOI: 10.4018/978-1-7998-8587-0.ch009

Nonetheless, digital transformation is not only about change but encompasses issues related to corporate leadership and culture that sustain digital transformation momentum in an organization (Hesse, 2018). Notably, banks are undertaking restructuring in a manner that allows them to gain a competitive advantage. It is, therefore, not surprising to witness that banks are increasingly providing novel services such as bank-assurance, agency banking, mobile banking, faceless banking, and integrated banking services.

In light of the above, Girod & Karim (2017) stressed that the banks must be flexible and agile in a manner that ensures the adaptability of the organization to rapid changes in the operating environment so as to stay competitive in the current digital epoch. It is within this context that traditional banks are shifting towards the digitalization of business processes and systems. In essence, the banking sector appears to be significantly transformed by the digitalization process. With this in mind, it is salient to observe that the digital transformation of banks is not all about investment in new digital technologies but encompasses new markets, opportunities, and new ways of operationalizing the business.

Going forward, it is worth mentioning that digital tools and technologies are transforming the way banks conduct business in the 21st century. This is the major reason why digital transformation in the topical issue in the banking sector. From strategic management lens, it appears that digital transformation is viewed as a corporate restructuring strategy that can increase revenue, reduce operating costs, foster innovation culture, enhance information sharing and use, increase competitiveness, and augment customer engagement (Galazova & Magomaeva, 2019; Kaufman & Horton, 2015). In a similar vein, Kotarba (2018) underscored that concept of digital transformation has significantly influenced the survival and creation of modern organizations. With this in mind, it appears that digital transformation can be used as a response to a decline in organizational performance. This is substantiated by the fact that digital transformation necessitates restructuring and change of business models (Galazova & Magomaeva, 2019). Nonetheless, insufficient attention has been paid to corporate restructuring through digital transformation.

In the spirit of improving organizational performance, strategic managers are constantly looking for mergers with finance technology (FinTech) companies. The rationale behind mergers is that banks are aiming at acquiring new technologies that can be too expensive when developed in-house. In essence, these technologies include peer-to-peer lending, mobile payments, robo-advisory, and internet banking (Galazova & Magomaeva, 2019). In this regard, it is of great importance to mention that the digitalization of banking institutions must be consistent with other strategies so as to come up with digital technologies that contribute to maximizing organizational performance (Galazova & Magomaeva, 2019). More interestingly, Matt, Hess, & Benlian (2015) emphasized that digital strategy should encompass four major tasks, namely, financial aspect of digitalization, adoption of digital technologies, altering the organizational structure, and transformation of process.

There is no doubt that many banks are engaging in mergers and acquisitions with FinTech companies in order to revive their performance in this digital epoch. In this regard, it is widely accepted that digital transformation influences the performance of organizations (Chen, Jaw, & Wu, 2016). Admittedly, the banks that are effectively implementing new digital technology enjoy a big market share. It is imperative to note that established organizations transform their business models in order to stay afloat in the contemporary digital economy (Weill & Woerner, 2018; Scott, Van-Reenen, & Zachariadis, 2017). In the context of the banking sector, it is not surprising to witness that many banking institutions are embracing digital technologies through collaboration with Fintech companies in order to boost profit and sales (Chen et al., 2016).

It is of great importance to note that disruptive digital technologies and tools can lead to a change in leadership, a new business model, increased use of technology, and improvement in stakeholder engagement (Terrar, 2015). More importantly, the support from the leadership team is very crucial in inculcating digital culture in an organization (Rault, 2017). Notably, digital transformation can lead to a change in the organizational structure of banks. Nonetheless, to the author's best knowledge, there is fragmented and scant evidence on corporate restructuring through digital transformation in the banking sector, especially in the Zimbabwean context. Literature review methodology underpinned this research. The objectives of the current chapter are to review worldwide controversies linked to digital transformation in the banking sector, to capture the challenges associated with the digital transformation of banks in Zimbabwe, and to review the success stories of corporate restructuring through digital transformation in the banking sector of Zimbabwe.

BACKGROUND

It is well-known that a great deal of concerns linked to digital transformation in the banking sector has become more visible as from the 1950s (Heavin & Power, 2018). In this regard, it is of tremendous importance to highlight that digital transformation has been considered as a powerful tool for augmenting the performance of firms through disruptive changes in business models, processes, customer experiences, and operations (Heavin & Power, 2018). This suggests that a paradigm shift towards a digitalized enterprise demands a good combination of business model alignment, technology capabilities, digital culture, and organizational engagement and leadership skills. In the spirit of digital transformation, it is salient to observe that many banks worldwide are embracing digitally disruptive technologies. More interestingly, the implementation of digital technologies and tools appear to be increasing exponentially to attract new customers and increase sales revenue of banking institutions (Marakarkandy, Yajnik, & Dasgupta, 2017). In other words, digital transformation appears to be on the strategic agenda of many banks worldwide as a top priority given that the digital economy is gaining prominence in the 21st century.

Drawing from the available literature on digital transformation, it is apparent that there is no standard definition of digital transformation since digital transformation is a multi-dimensional, complex, and relative concept. Specifically, Haffke, Kalgovas, & Benlian, (2017) opined that digital transformation as a concept lacks a clear definition in the existing stock of knowledge. Digital transformation means different things to different scholars and researchers. In this regard, digital transformation refers to the alterations that happen in an organization owing to the adoption of disruptive digital technologies (Rojers, 2018; Martinez, 2019). More interestingly, Schwertner (2017) defined digital transformation as a journey associated with changes in business frameworks and models through the adoption of digital technologies and tools in an attempt to augment operations, processes, ways of communication, and customer experiences. Based on the above definitions, it is clear that investment in digital transformation provides avenues of new opportunities for firms especially banks as they can develop new products and services, decrease overhead expenses in the long-run, augment business efficiency and personalize customer experience. Admittedly, many scholars and researchers indicate that digital transformation is characterized by a major change in an organization brought about by digital technology (Brunetti et al., 2020; Hartl & Hess, 2017; Haffke, Kalgovas, & Benlian, 2017; Mueller & Renken, 2017).

In light of the above, it is of great importance to mention the drivers of digital transformation in the banking sector. In this regard, there is a plethora of drivers of digital transformation (Osmundsen, Iden,

& Bendik, 2018). It is within this context that globalization is one of the drivers of digital transformation. It is widely recognized that we are living in a global village that is supported by advancements in information and communications technology. In this regard, the banking sector is not excluded from the effects of globalization. Therefore, many banks in both developed and developing countries are embracing digital transformation in order to compete globally and restructuring for survival (Hartl & Hess, 2017).

More interestingly, upsurge in customer expectations mainly associated with advancements in disruptive technologies and tools has pressurized banks to make a transition from traditional banking to a digital enterprise. This state of affairs in the banking sector worldwide has forced banks to alter their business models. Notably, the digital natives have a high affinity for technology which is forcing banks to digitalize their operation and processes so as to effectively meet the expectations of these customers. It is with this context that Dahlström, Desmet, & Singer (2017) expressed that there is a dire need for strategic changes through disruptive technologies in an attempt to augment customer experiences. To this end, banks can maintain competitiveness through the adoption of digital products and solutions (Andriole, Cox, & Khin, 2018).

It is interesting to note that an increase in mobile penetration is another important driver of digital transformation in the banking sector. In this respect, banks are taking advantage of high mobile penetration rates when implementing disruptive digital technologies and tools. Mobile devices and broadband networks allow the management of banks to easily embrace digitalization (Rupeika-Apoga, Zaidi, Thalassinos, & Thalassinos, 2018). It is interesting to mention that mobile banking allows a banking transaction to be processed anytime.

Intense competition is widely accepted as one of the drivers of digital transformation in the banking sector. In this regard, the banking sector is mainly associated with stiff competition owing to the fact that banks offer similar products. Moreover, banks are encountering cut-throat competition from FinTech firms that are offering technology-based financial services at low cost (Galazova & Magomaeva, 2019; Kauffman, Liu, & Ma, 2015). Given this scenario, banks are now focusing on digital transformation as a major source of competitive advantage. Notably, some banks are collaborating with FinTech firms as a strategy to reduce competition and to embark on digital transformation.

Advancement in information and communications technology is another important driver of digital transformation when it comes to the banking sector (Kauffman, Liu, & Ma, 2015; Goh & Kauffman, 2013). It is apparent that advancement in technology has forced banks to adopt digital transformation since digital technology improves the provision of banking products and services. In this respect, banks can enjoy competitive advantage owing to the effective and efficient utilization of information and communications technology. In other words, rationalization of business processes and direct marketing can be easily done with the aid of information and communications technology. To this end, the major benefit that can emanate from the effective utilization of information and communications technology is cost reduction (Binuyo & Aregbeshola, 2014).

The above-mentioned developments in the banking sector have accelerated the adoption of disruptive digital products and solutions. In essence, this state of affairs puts into perspective the dire need for bank managers to successfully embrace a clear digital strategy. While the formulation and implementation of digital strategy require a deeper understanding of digital transformation within the context of the banking sector, little is known about corporate restructuring through digital transformation especially in Zimbabwe. Consequently, it is deemed necessary to cover this literature gap.

Digital Transformation and Banking Sector

It is widely recognized that investments in digital technologies and tools significantly affects the performance of banking institutions. Following the financial crisis of 2008, many banking institutions were in an arms race for digital transformation. The banking institutions across the world have witnessed a rapid increase in digital solutions and products which forced the banks to change their traditional business models (Veit et al., 2014). Many benefits can emanate from successful digital transformation implementation such as higher competitive advantage, an increase in revenue, expansion of digital capabilities, and an increase in operation efficiency (Rossato, & Castellani, 2020; Martinez, 2019; Herbert, 2017; Bazhair & Sandhu, 2015). With this in mind, many banks have managed to heavily invest in online and mobile channels given that many customers are now preferring digitalised banking services. This is not surprising since the young people of the 21st century are digital natives. A digital native has a high affinity for digital technology such as internet, tablets, and smartphones. (Kaufman & Horton, 2015). This means that a digital native has a digital mindset. Accordingly, it is deemed necessary for the banks to respond to the needs of the digital natives through the effective provision of digitalized banking services.

It is imperative to mention that banking institutions must adopt disruptive digital banking technologies and tools. Admittedly, some banking institutions are collaborating with FinTech firms as a digital strategy to effectively and efficiently execute digital transformation (Jun & Yeo, 2016). This suggests that the banking institutions should have a clear digital strategy in order to enjoy the benefits of digitalization (Cziesla, 2014; Lasi, Fettke, Kemper, Feld, & Hoffmann, 2014) Owing to an acceleration of change in technology and cut-throat competition in recent times, it appears to be a prudent approach for banks to collaborate with FinTech firms (Kaur & Bath, 2019; Scott, 2007). The rationale behind the collaboration of banking institutions with FinTech is to lower expenses, improve performance offer new commercial products, reduce cyber risks, and to solve other technological issues (Al-Halawani, 2019). However, the pursuit of digital transformation is mainly associated with resistance to change since digital transformation leads to a change of existing models of doing business (Butler & Hackney, 2015).

Going forward, drawing from the available literature on digital transformation in the banking sector, it is widely known that strategic perspective and customer perspective are mainly used to discuss the issue of digitalization in the banking sector. From a strategic perspective, scholarly debate on digital transformation in the banking sector is mainly linked to its effect on business models and business strategies (Kotarba, 2018; Schmidt, Drews, & Schirmer, 2016). The strategic perspective advocates for a paradigm shift from traditional business models towards digital business models in the current digital economy in order to achieve a strategic fit (Galazova & Magomaeva, 2019; Weill & Woerner, 2018). This suggests that digital transformation can affect not just the processes and operations only but also corporate strategies and business models of the banking institutions. The author takes this perspective in an attempt to assess corporate restructuring through digital transformation in the banking sector of Zimbabwe. The author reason that strategic managers of banks focus on coming up with a digital strategy with the purpose of ensuring a sustainable competitive advantage.

It is common knowledge that banks are operating in a dynamic and complex environment that is affecting their performance negatively. In this regard, rapid change in technology is being witnessed in the banking sector as substantiated by a rapid increase in FinTech start-ups. In order to achieve stellar performance, many banks across the world are implementing corporate restructuring strategy (Arham, et al., 2018). Restructuring can be defined as the change of the organizational structure and financial structure with the purpose of gaining a competitive edge (Waweru & Maina, 2019). With this in mind, it is apparent that the banks are mainly focusing on corporate restructuring so as to augment organizational performance. Notably, closure of some strategic business units and merging of departments as a result of the adoption of disruptive technologies and tools that promote the provision of novel products and services (Waweru & Maina, 2019).

Going forward, commercial banks in Kenya are offering new services like faceless and mobile banking in order to improve competitiveness and solvency (Kithinji, Mwangi, Litondo, & Ogutu, 2017). It is within this context that the commercial banks in Kenya have witnessed mergers and acquisitions in the mid-1980s and late 1990s that led to complex banking institutions. Despite the fact that some banks are engaging in restructuring in order to survive, it is worth mentioning that state of the art finance technology is a pre-requisite for successful bank restructuring (Hoenig & Morris, 2012; Ithiri, 2013). The main factors that are pressuring strategic managers to embark on corporate restructuring in the banking sector include low profits, losses, upsurge in non-performing loans, undercapitalized, depressed asset prices, and illiquid as well economic downturn (Hoenig & Moris, 2012; Vo & Nguyen, 2018).

In the Zimbabwean context, a myriad of factors has contributed to bank failures. Poor leadership, poor management, and poor corporate governance as well as the unconducive external environment are some of the factors that are linked to bank failures. It is discouraging to note that about 13 Zimbabwean banking institutions have shut down operations for the past 10 years. Some of the bank failures in Zimbabwe include United Merchant Bank, Zimbabwe Building Society, First National Building Society, Renaissance Merchant Bank, Royal Bank, Barbican, Genesis Investment Bank, Trust Bank, AfrAsia Bank, Interfin Bank, and Capital Bank. Although there is ample evidence on bank failures, not much scholarly literature is available on corporate restructuring through digital transformation in the banking sector (Nyoka, 2015). Consequently, it seems to be the most appropriate time to comprehensively analyze corporate restructuring through digital transformation in the Zimbabwean banking sector.

DIGITAL TRANSFORMATION IN THE ZIMBABWEAN BANKING SECTOR

In the past two decades, the banking institutions in Zimbabwe have embraced digital technologies and tools. It is within this context that Mavaza (2019) documented that the major drivers of digital transformation in the Zimbabwean banking sector are upsurge in the usage of mobile services and exponential growth of internet penetration rate. According to Postal and Telecommunications Regulatory Authority of Zimbabwe (POTRAZ) (2019), active mobile subscriptions registered a 4% increase to reach 12 853 615 in the third quarter of 2019 from 12 354 315 in the previous quarter and then the mobile penetration rate increased from 84.8% to 88.2%. More interestingly, internet usage recorded 3.2% in the third quarter of 2019, and internet penetration rate increased from 57.2% to 58.9% which indicates a 1.7% increase (POTRAZ, 2019). These developments provide a fertile ground for the adoption of disruptive digital banking technologies and tools in the banking sector of Zimbabwe.

The adoption of digital technologies and tools in the Zimbabwean banking sector has transformed traditional banking practices. It is interesting to observe that many Zimbabwean commercial banks have enhanced their banking services through the use of websites that allow customers to transfer funds, check account balances, and receive payments. Ndlovu & Siyavora (2014) emphasized that banks such as Central Africa Building Society (CABS), FBC Bank Limited, and Commercial Bank of Zimbabwe (CBZ) have managed to introduce the internet banking in 2008. These banks allowed their clients to do online transactions. Nonetheless, the uptake of digital technologies and tools in the banking sector of Zimbabwe is at a slow pace (Maswaure & Choga, 2016, Mavaza, 2019).

The Zimbabwean banking sector also adopted mobile banking. It is well known that rapid changes in technology have forced bankers in Zimbabwe to embrace mobile banking (Mavhiki, Nyamwanza, & Shumba, 2015). In this respect, mobile banking promotes the accessibility of banking services. The introduction of mobile banking in Zimbabwe allowed people who stay in remote rural areas to access banking services (Tapera, 2014). It is common knowledge that Zimbabwean banks are offering SMS banking to customers (Dube, Njanike, Manomano, & Chiriseri, 2011). However, Mavhiki et al., (2015) underscored that many banks in Zimbabwe did not fully benefit from the mobile banking business model since the banks did not collaborate with telecoms.

Despite the fact that digital transformation improves efficiency, the banking sector of Zimbabwe has witnessed an increase in the closure of banks. In this respect, it is worrisome to note that about 13 Zimbabwean banking institutions managed to shut down operations for the past 15 years. Drawing from the available literature on corporate restructuring in the banking sector, a myriad of factors contributed to bank failures were mentioned. Poor leadership, poor management, and poor corporate governance as well as the unconducive external environment are some of the factors that were linked to bank failures. Although many scholars suggest that a financial crisis is a major factor that can contribute to bank failures, it does necessarily lead to bank failures because some scholars perceived it as a situation that can allow the management to alter the existing out-of-date business model (Timmons & Spinelli, 2007). With this in mind, effective corporate restructuring appears to be a powerful tool for transforming the fortunes of poor performing banks. Nonetheless, there is fragmented and scant evidence on corporate restructuring through digital transformation in the banking sector (Nyoka, 2015).

RESEARCH METHODOLOGY

This study used a literature review methodology. Following the recommendations of Snyder (2019), a semi-systematic review was applied in conceptualizing corporate restructuring strategy through a digital transformation since numerous groups of scholars and researchers from diverse fields have studied issues related to digitalization. Semi-systematic review permitted the researcher to look at the progression of digitalization in the banking sector (Wong, Greenhalgh, Westhorp, Buckingham, & Pawson, 2013). The potential contribution of semi-systematic review is based on its suitability to detect theoretical lenses, themes, and common issues related to digitalization in the banking sector. More interestingly, semi-systematic review as a methodology enabled the researcher to amalgamate the fragmented extant body of knowledge and then capture the further research agenda (Snyder, 2019).

Success Stories of Digital Transformation in Zimbabwe's Banking Sector

It is deemed necessary to capture some success stories of digitalization in the context of banking institutions in Zimbabwe. In this regard, banks like CBZ, FBC, ZB, and Stanbic are at the forefront when it comes to digital transformation. The following are some of the success stories of banks that managed to embark on corporate restructuring through digital transformation:

Success Story One: ZB Sets Aside $20 Million for Augmenting I.T Programme

It is in the public domain that ZB has embarked on digital banking through the adoption of various digital technologies and tools in an attempt to revitalize organizational performance. Before 2015, ZB was registering losses which necessitated turnaround management through digital transformation as captured below:

In a separate interview, Ronald stressed that in this current technological environment, I.T expenditure is very critical to the Group has adopted a digitalization strategy which means the bank needs to modernize networks, equipment, and servers. Mutangagayi said the 5 Million that was recently spent was principally directed to Routers and Servers as well as surround systems and the Bank needed to spend at least 10 to 20 Million dollars on the digitalization exercise. He said the Group was aware it would obviously face challenges in raising that kind of money in this current market environment, so it would be done on a pismal basis as the bank was the first to go paper-less as far as the front office is concerned a few years ago and was now headed to the middle office to ensure that systems are optimized investment in document floor waiting for management to allow staff members to be more efficient. (Mhlanga, 2019).

Based on the above success story of ZB, it quite clear that the bank has managed to respond to rapid changes in the current technological environment through the adoption of a digitalization strategy. This implies that digital transformation requires managers that can execute the digital strategy in a manner that inculcates a strong digital culture. Moreover, the bank aimed at going paper-less which in line with the main tenets of digital transformation. It is with this context that Weill & Woerner (2018) accentuated that the adoption of digital transformation can lead to alteration of traditional business models. Notably, the digitalization strategy at ZB was focused on the enhancement of customer service and experience, and the improvement of the efficiency of workers. More interestingly, a digital strategy was used by ZB for turnaround purposes as indicated below:

We decided to increase the technological thrust. We were the first bank that added a mobile app in Zimbabwe. Our strategy is that we don't want customers coming to the branch unless they want to. They should be able to make transactions in their own homes and in their own offices. We upgraded our systems and conducted transactions on what we call ZIPIT which is faster than RTGS. You can transfer money from one account to another at the ATM, make card to card transfers and can move money from your account to an e-wallet and vice-versa. (The Independent, 2016).

As captured in the above quote, the bank managed to formulate a digital strategy that promotes convenience to customers since customers can access services 24/7. More interestingly, ZB also managed to come up with a mobile app the can permit customers to engage in mobile banking which a key aspect of digital transformation. This development has led to a dramatic turnaround of ZB in 2015 even though it was operating in a deteriorating economic environment in Zimbabwe. This suggests that the adoption of digital banking can lead to more non-income generated from technology driven-turnaround. The following success story focuses on Stanbic bank:

Success Story Two: Stanbic Enhances Digital Banking

Stanbic Bank in Zimbabwe has also embarked on the digitalization exercise. It is within this context that Stanbic managed to come up with a clear digitalization strategy in order to restructure its operations as captured below:

Stanbic Bank is stepping up the digitization exercise hot on the heels of being named Best Bank of The Year in 2019 by leading financial magazine, The Banker, at a gala in London. The bank will be closing its Chitungwiza and Beitbridge branches with effect from 31 March 2020 as the institution moves forward with its digitalization strategy, which allows customers to conduct their banking any hour of the day from any connected location. Stanbic Bank chief executive, Joshua Tapambgwa, said the digitalization strategy, which will leave the financial player with a physical footprint of 17 branches across the country, is being put to the test as they make such bold moves that rely on quality banking technologies (The Herald, 2020).

In light of the above success story at Stanbic bank on digital transformation, it is interesting to note that the bank is responding to changes in the external environment by embracing digital technologies and tools. As clearly indicated in the success story of Stanbic, the bank is aiming at providing quality banking technologies that are in line with the tenets of digital transformation. The following success story focuses on FBC Holdings:

Success Story Three: FBC Goes Digital

FBC Holdings is focusing on digital transformation so as to disrupt the banking sector in Zimbabwe. The bank is restructuring through digital transformation to eliminate or reduce paper-based transactions. This clearly shows that digital transformation is altering the traditional banking practices at FBC as captured below:

FBC Holdings will close five branches and has instructed the remaining branches to stop accepting paper-based transactions for selected services with effect from June 1 as the financial services group embraces digital banking. In line with our digitalization journey, five branches will be closed from June 1 2020. Our remaining branches across the country will also not be accepting [paper based] transaction for selected services. The branches to be closed are Beitbridge, Nelson Mandela, Samora Machel, Graniteside and FBC Building Society Centre. (The Business Times, 2020).

Based on the success story of FBC, it is of great importance to note that digital transformation is mainly associated with restructuring. In this respect, FBC closed five branches in accordance with its digital strategy. This means that digital transformation affects bank staff negatively. For instance, the closure of five branches of FBC leads to massive layoffs of employees. However, it can also lead to operational excellence of the bank.

Benefits of Digital Transformation

It is widely recognized that digital transformation in the Zimbabwean banking sector is associated with many benefits. Therefore, it is necessary to capture the benefits of digital transformation in the Zimbabwean banking sector as follows:

- **Cost Reduction:** This is one of the benefits of digital transformation in Zimbabwe's banking sector. Digital transformation can ensure the efficiency of business operations which is linked to cost reduction. Notably, Masvaure & Choga (2016) concluded that cost saving is one of the benefits of effectively implement digital technologies and tools in the banking sector of Zimbabwe.
- **Widen Customer Base**. Widening of the customer base is another benefit of digital transformation in the banking sector of Zimbabwe. It is within this context that many banks in Zimbabwe are a collaboration with FinTech companies so as to embrace advanced digital technologies and tools with the purpose of increasing the customer base. In this regard, Dube et al., (2011) expressed that an increased customer base is a major benefit of digital technologies and tools in Zimbabwe's banking sector.
- **Promote Innovation and Non-Core Business Services Development:** The effective adoption of digital technologies and tools can allow bankers in Zimbabwe to foster innovation culture and development of non-core business services. It is well known that most of the banks in Zimbabwe are currently relying on non-income. Therefore, by embracing digital technologies and tools, banks can develop more non-core business services (Dube et al., 2011).
- **Increase Customer Satisfaction:** Customer satisfaction is of great importance for any business. It is, therefore, necessary to mention that the successful adoption of digital technologies and tools in the banking sector of Zimbabwe can increase customer satisfaction especially those who are digital natives.
- **Marketing and Communication:** There is a general consensus that digital technologies and tools can be used by banks to market their banking services. It is within this context that Dube et al., (2011) underscored that digital technologies and tools can be used for marketing and communication in the banking sector. This means that banks can offer personalized services to customers.

Challenges Associated with Digital Transformation in the Zimbabwean Banking Sector

The banking institutions in Zimbabwe are facing a plethora of challenges when it comes to digital transformation. The challenges can be categorized into two groups, namely, internal and external challenges. The internal challenges are those that are controllable by the management. On the other hand, the external are those that are uncontrollable since they emanate from the external business environment. The formidable challenges faced by bankers in Zimbabwe when it comes to digital transformation are explained as follows:

- **Lack of Advanced ICT Infrastructure:** This is one of the challenges faced by bankers when it comes to digital transformation in Zimbabwe. It is within this context that the study conducted by Makanyeza & Makuwaza (2015) on the adoption of electronic banking technology in Zimbabwe's banking sector revealed that lack of infrastructure as a challenge faced by Zimbabwean bankers.

This shows that the banking institutions are not equipped with advanced ICT infrastructure that can support the effective implementation of digital transformation.

- **Limited Knowledge of Digital Business Models**: Given that digital transformation in the Zimbabwean banking sector is at its infancy stage, it is not surprising that the bankers have limited knowledge about digital business models (Musa, 2014). This is supported by Makanyeza & Makuwaza (2015) who stressed that digital business models are more pronounced in more developed countries than less developed countries like Zimbabwe. With this in mind, many bankers have limited knowledge of digital business models.
- **Customer Resistance**: This is another challenge faced by banking institutions when it comes to digital transformation. Worryingly, the study conducted in Zimbabwe on the adoption of electronic banking in Zimbabwe's banking sector by Makanyeza & Makuwaza (2015) showed that customer resistance is a challenge faced by banks and building societies. This means that the customer does not have trust in digital banking technologies and tools especially customers from rural communities.
- **Unstable Network Systems:** Unstable network systems is one of the challenges faced by banking institutions when it comes to digital transformation. In this regard, the study conducted in Zimbabwe by Tapera (2014) on the impact of mobile phone-based products on the provision of financial services revealed that inconsistency of network availability was a serious challenge faced by financial institutions.

SOLUTIONS AND RECOMMENDATIONS

As presented in the preceding section, it is salient to observe that the banking institutions are encountering a myriad of challenges when it comes to digital transformation. It is, therefore, of great importance to proffer recommendations for dealing with the above-mentioned challenges faced in digital transformation of banks. In this regard, the recommendations are detailed as follows:

- **Digital Banking Customer Awareness Programs:** In order to effectively deal with customer resistance, it is prudent that the management of banking institutions should invest in robust digital banking awareness programs. The programs could sensitize digital banking customers on the issues concerned with the importance of security measures when it comes to digital banking technologies and tools. This means that customer awareness programs should be on the agenda of banking institutions so that they can address the issue of customer resistance.
- **Mastering Digital Transformation Mindset:** The top management should master the digital transformation through learning in order to sustain digital transformation initiatives across the organization. The top managers could take executive courses on digital transformation that enable them to explore disruptive business models.
- **Mergers and Acquisitions:** In order to address the challenge of lack of advanced ICT infrastructure, it is recommended that the banking institution should merger with FinTech start-ups or engage in acquisition arrangements. These arrangements could lead to personalized products, talent acquisition, comprehensive service, access to new technology, expansion of customer base, and upgrade of aging ICT infrastructure.

- **Digital Transformation Training:** The banking institutions should come up with learning and development initiatives that are aimed at training workers on digital banking technologies and tools. This could foster a strong culture of knowledge sharing and life-long learning.
- **Provision of Reliable Electricity:** The government of Zimbabwe should ensure the provision of reliable electricity so that the banks cannot face the challenge of system downtimes. The main cause of system downtimes is linked to power outages.

FUTURE RESEARCH DIRECTIONS

The current research is a fertile ground for further research studies. The suggested areas of further studies with respect to digital transformation are explained below:

Provided that the current study has focused on digital transformation in the context of Zimbabwe's banking sector, it would be interesting for future studies to focus on digital transformation in the context of other countries in Southern Africa. Further studies are recommended using other financial institutions other than banks since the current study has focused on banks. For instance, it would be interesting to focus on digital transformation using microfinance institutions. It is suggested that further studies can be conducted on digital transformation in the manufacturing sector as comparative studies. Notably, further studies that are quantitative in nature are also encouraged.

CONCLUSION

This chapter consolidates the literature related to corporate restructuring through digital transformation in the banking sector of Zimbabwe. Three success stories of restructuring through digital transformation have been identified. Moreover, five benefits of digital transformation have been identified, that is, cost reduction, widen customer base, promote innovation and non-core business services development, increase customer satisfaction, and marketing and communication. Notably, four challenges faced by banks when it comes to digital transformation have been identified, namely, lack of advanced ICT infrastructure, limited knowledge of digital business models, customer resistance, and unstable network systems. The suggestions for addressing the above-mentioned challenges were proffered. The current research offers three major contributions. Firstly, it consolidates the fragmented literature on digital transformation in the banking sector of Zimbabwe. Secondly, it enlarges our knowledge base on the strategic perspective of digital transformation. Thirdly, it sets out the literature gaps to be addressed by further studies. The comprehensive insights on corporate restructuring through digital transformation assist policymakers and practitioners in making well informed digital transformation strategic decisions. Admittedly, strategic managers can formulate a digital transformation strategy on the basis of insights captured in this research. To this end, it is most appropriate to conclude that effective corporate restructuring through digital transformation can be used to turnaround the fortunes of banking institutions.

REFERENCES

Arham, A. F., Norizan, N. S., Khairuman, A., Hasim, M., Darson, M. D., & Faizal, N. S. M. (2018). Organizational restructuring: Lesson learned from tourism Malaysia. *International Journal of Academic Research in Business & Social Sciences, 8*(8), 42–49. doi:10.6007/IJARBSS/v8-i8/4431

Bazhair, A., & Sandhu, K. (2015). Factors for the acceptance of enterprise resource planning (ERP) systems and financial performance. *Journal of Economics Business and Management, 3*(1), 1–10. doi:10.7763/JOEBM.2015.V3.146

Binuyo, A. O., & Aregbeshola, R. A. (2014). The impact of information and communication technology (ICT) on commercial bank performance: Evidence from South Africa. *Problems and Perspectives in Management, 12*(3), 59–68.

Brunetti, F., Matt, D. T., Bonfanti, A., De Longhi, A., Pedrini, G., & Orzes, G. (2020). Digital transformation challenges: Strategies emerging from a multi-stakeholder approach. *The TQM Journal, 32*(4), 697–724. doi:10.1108/TQM-12-2019-0309

Butler, T., & Hackney, R. (2015). Understanding digital eco-innovation in municipalities: An institutional perspective. *Proceedings of ECIS 2015.*

Chen, Y. Y. K., Jaw, Y. L., & Wu, B. L. (2016). Effect of digital transformation on organizational performance of SMEs: Evidence from the Taiwanese textile industry's web portal. *Internet Research, 26*(1), 186–212. doi:10.1108/IntR-12-2013-0265

Cziesla, T. (2014). A literature review on digital transformation in the financial service industry. *Proceedings of BLED 2014.*

Dahlström, P., Desmet, D., & Singer, M. (2017). *The seven decisions that matter in a digital transformation: A CEO's guide to reinvention.* Retrieved May 28, 2020, from https://www.mckinsey.com/business-functions/digital-mckinsey/our-insights/the-seven-ecisions-that-matter-in-a-digital-transformation

Dube, T., Njanike, K., Manomano, C., & Chiriseri, L. (2011). Adoption and use of SMS/mobile banking services in Zimbabwe: An exploratory study. *Journal of Internet Banking and Commerce, 16*(2), 1–15.

Galazova, S. S., & Magomaeva, L. R. (2019). The transformation of traditional banking activity in digital. *International Journal of Economics and Business Administration, 7*(2), 41–51. doi:10.35808/ijeba/369

Girod, S. J. G., & Karim, S. (2017). Restructure or reconfigure? *Harvard Business Review*. Retrieved May 28, 2020, from https://hbr.org/2017/03/restructure-or-reconfigure

Goh, K., & Kauffman, R. (2013). Firm strategy and the Internet in U.S. commercial banking. *Journal of Management Information Systems, 30*(2), 9–40. doi:10.2753/MIS0742-1222300201

Haffke, I., Kalgovas, B., & Benlian, A. (2017). The transformative role of bimodal it in an era of digital business. In *Proceedings of 50th Hawaii International Conference on System Sciences* (pp. 5460–5469). 10.24251/HICSS.2017.660

Hartl, E., & Hess, T. (2017). The role of cultural values for digital transformation: Insights from a Delphi study. In *Proceedings of AMCIS 2017* (pp. 1–10). Retrieved May 28, 2020, from http://aisel.aisnet.org/cgi/viewcontent.cgi?article=1369&context=amcis2017

Heavin, C., & Power, D. J. (2018). Challenges for digital transformation - towards a conceptual decision support guide for managers. *Journal of Decision Systems, 27*(sup1), 38–45. doi:10.1080/12460125.2018.1468697

Herbert, L. (2017). *Digital transformation: Build your organizations future for the innovation age.* Bloomsbury Publishing Plc.

Hesse, A. (2018). Digitalization and leadership: How experienced leaders interpret daily realities in a digital world. In *Proceedings of the 51st Hawaii International conference on System Sciences* (pp. 1865-1863). 10.24251/HICSS.2018.234

Hoenig, T. M., & Morris, C. S. (2012). *Restructuring the banking system to improve safety and soundness.* Federal Deposit Insurance Corporation and Federal Reserve Bank of Kansas City.

Ithiri, M. D. (2013). *Corporate restructuring and its effects on Kenya Commercial Bank performance* (Master's Thesis). Kenyatta University, Kenya.

Jun, J., & Yeo, E. (2016). Entry of fintech firms and competition in the retail payments market. *Asia-Pacific Journal of Financial Studies, 45*(2), 159–184. doi:10.1111/ajfs.12126

Kauffman, R., Liu, J., & Ma, D. (2015). Competition, cooperation and regulation: Understanding the evolution of the mobile payments technology ecosystem. *Electronic Commerce Research and Applications, 14*(5), 372–391. doi:10.1016/j.elerap.2015.03.003

Kaufman, I., & Horton, C. (2015). *Digital marketing: integrating strategy and tactics with values.* Routledge Taylor & Francis Group.

Kaur, H., & Bath, A. K. (2019). Digital transformation strategies in different areas: A review. *International Journal of Scientific and Technology Research, 8*(12), 348–351.

Kithinji, A. K., Mwangi, M., Litondo, K., & Ogutu, M. (2017). Bank restructuring and financial performance. *International Journal of Economics. Commerce and Management, 5*(10), 84–98.

Kotarba, M. (2018). Digital transformation of business. *Foundations of Management, 10*(1), 123–142. doi:10.2478/fman-2018-0011

Lasi, H., Fettke, P., Kemper, H. G., Feld, T., & Hoffmann, M. (2014). Industry 4.0. *Business and Information Systems Engineering, 6*(4), 239–242.

Makanyeza, C., & Makuwaza, P. (2015). *The adoption of electronic banking technology: Challenges and opportunities in Zimbabwe's banking sector.* Paper presented at International Research Conference on Research, Technology and Innovation for Development in Africa, Chinhoyi University of Technology, Zimbabwe.

Marakarkandy, B., Yajnik, N., & Dasgupta, C. (2017). Enabling internet banking adoption: An empirical examination with an augmented technology acceptance model (TAM). *Journal of Enterprise Information Management*, *30*(2), 263–294. doi:10.1108/JEIM-10-2015-0094

Martinez, F. (2019). Process excellence the key for digitalisation. *Business Process Management Journal*, *25*(7), 1716–1733. doi:10.1108/BPMJ-08-2018-0237

Maswaure, F., & Choga, F. (2016). Electronic banking uptake in Zimbabwe. *Journal of Business and Management*, *18*(4), 80–82.

Matt, C., Hess, T., & Benlian, A. (2015). Digital transformation strategies. *Business & Information Systems Engineering*, *5*(57), 339–343. doi:10.100712599-015-0401-5

Mavaza, T. (2019). E-banking adoption by Zimbabwe banks: An exploratory study. *PM World Journal*, *8*(11), 1–10.

Mavhiki, S., Nyamwanza, T., & Shumba, L. (2015). Impact of mobile banking on traditional banking practices in Zimbabwe. *International Journal of Economics. Commerce and Management*, *3*(1), 1–13.

Mhlanga, K. (2019). *ZB embarks on $20 Million I.T boost programme*. Retrieved May 29, 2020, from https://www.eyetrodigital.com/2019/05/08/zb-embarks-on-20-million-i-t-boost-programme/

Mueller, B., & Renken, U. (2017). Helping employees to be digital transformers: The Olympus connect case. In *Proceedings of ICIS 2017* (pp. 1–19). Academic Press.

Musa, M. S. (2014). Customers' adoption of electronic banking: An investigation on the commercial banking industry in Zimbabwe. *International Journal of Economics, Commerce and Management*, *2*(7), 1–13.

Ndlovu, I., & Siyavora, A. (2014). Impact of internet banking on the Zimbabwean banking sector an application of the multinomial logit modelling. *International Journal of Economics, Commerce and Management*, *2*(8), 1–17.

Nyoka, C. (2015). Banks and the fallacy of supervision: The case for Zimbabwe. *Banks and Bank Systems*, *10*(3), 8–17.

Osmundsen, K., Iden, J., & Bendik, B. (2018). *Digital transformation: Drivers, success factors, and implications*, Paper presented at the 12th Mediterranean Conference on Information Systems (MCIS), Corfu, Greece.

Postal and Telecommunications Regulatory Authority of Zimbabwe. (2019). *Abridged postal and telecommunications sector performance report third quarter 2019*. http://www.potraz.gov.zw/wp-content/uploads/2019/12/Abridged-Sector-Performance-report-3rd-Q-2019-hmed-final.pdf

Rojers, J. P. (2018). Digital transformation, business model innovation and efficiency in content industries: A review. *International Journal of Computational Intelligence Systems*, *7*, 59–70.

Rossato, C., & Castellani, P. (2020). The contribution of digitalisation to business longevity from a competitiveness perspective. *The TQM Journal*, *32*(4), 617–645. doi:10.1108/TQM-02-2020-0032

Rupeika-Apoga, R., Zaidi, H. S., Thalassinos, E. Y., & Thalassinos, I. E. (2018). Bank stability: The case of Nordic and non-Nordic banks in Latvia. *International Journal of Economics & Business Administration, 6*(2), 39–55. doi:10.35808/ijeba/156

Schmidt, J., Drews, P., & Schirmer, I. (2016). End-users' perspective on digitalization: A study on work order processing in the German banking industry. *Proceedings of AMCIS 2016.*

Schwertner, K. (2017). Digital transformation of business. *Trakia Journal of Sciences, 15*(Suppl.1), 388–393. doi:10.15547/tjs.2017.s.01.065

Scott, J. E. (2007). An e-transformation study using the technology-organization-environment framework. In *Proceedings of BLED 2007* (p. 55). Academic Press.

Scott, S. V., van Reenen, J., & Zachariadis, M. (2017). The long-term effect of digital innovation on bank performance: An empirical study of swift adoption in financial services. *Research Policy, 46*(5), 984–100. doi:10.1016/j.respol.2017.03.010

Snyder, H. (2019). Literature review as a research methodology: An overview and guidelines. *Journal of Business Research, 104*, 333–339. doi:10.1016/j.jbusres.2019.07.039

Tapera, J. (2014). An analysis of the impact of mobile phone-based products on the provision of financial services to the individual Zimbabwean customer. *International Journal of Economics, Commerce and Management, 2*(5), 1–21.

Terrar, D. (2015). *What is digital transformation? Agile elephant.* Retrieved June 1, 2020, from http://www.theagileelephant.com/what-is-digital-transformation/

The Business Times. (2020). *FBC goes digital, closes five branches.* Retrieved May 30, 2020, from https://businesstimes.co.zw/fbc-goes-digital-closes-five-branches/

The Herald. (2020). *Stanbic enhances digital banking.* Retrieved May 28, 2020, from https://www.herald.co.zw/stanbic-enhances-digital-banking/

The Independent. (2016). *ZBFH: A turnaround success story for 2015.* Retrieved May 27, 2020, from https://www.theindependent.co.zw/2016/08/19/zbfh-turnaround-success-story-2015/

Timmons, J. A., & Spinelli, S. (2007). *New venture creation: Entrepreneurship for the 21st century* (7th ed.). Mcgraw-Hill/Irwin.

Veit, D., Clemons, E., Benlian, A., Buxmann, P., Hess, T., Kundisch, D., Leimeister, J. M., Loos, P., & Spann, M. (2014). Geschäftsmodelle: Eine Forschungsagenda für die Wirtschaftsinformatik. *Wirtschaftsinformatik, 56*(1), 55–64. doi:10.100711576-013-0400-4

Vo, X. V., Nguyen, H. H., & McMillan, D. (2018). Bank restructuring and bank efficiency: The case of Vietnam. *Cogent Economics and Finance, 6*(1), 1–17. doi:10.1080/23322039.2018.1520423

Waweru, S. W., & Maina, S. (2019). Corporate restructuring and organization performance of national police service in Kenya. *International Academic Journal of Human Resource and Business Administration, 3*(6), 55–70.

Weill, P., & Woerner, S. L. (2018). Is your company ready for a digital future? *MIT Sloan Management Review*, *59*(2), 21–25.

Wong, G., Greenhalgh, T., Westhorp, G., Buckingham, J., & Pawson, R. (2013). RAMESES publication standards: Meta-narrative reviews. *BMC Medicine*, *11*(1), 20. doi:10.1186/1741-7015-11-20 PMID:23360661

ADDITIONAL READING

Accenture. (2016). *Fintech and the evolving landscape: Landing points for the industry*. Accenture.

Belous, A., Lyalkov, P., & Yu, S. (2017). The vector of development of banks in the digital revolution. *Banking*, *10*, 16–19.

Faems, D., de Visser, M., Andries, P., & Van Looy, B. (2010). Technology alliance portfolios and financial performance: Value-enhancing and cost-increasing effects of open innovation. *Journal of Product Innovation Management*, *27*(6), 785–796. doi:10.1111/j.1540-5885.2010.00752.x

Maslenikov, V. V., Fedotova, M. A., & Sorokin, A. N. (2017). New financial technologies are changing our world. *Bulletin of the Financial University*, *22*(21), 6–11.

Omarini, A. (2013). Looking for strategies to re-launch retail banking: The mobile payment ecosystem. *International Journal on Business Review*, *2*(3), 192–197.

Osipovskaya, A. V., & Mikhaylin, A. V. (2017). The development of financial technologies in the field of banking services: The main directions. *Young Scientist*, *26*, 124–127.

Reydet, S., & Carsana, L. (2017). The effect of digital design in retail banking on customers' commitment and loyalty: The mediating role of positive affect. *Journal of Retailing and Consumer Services*, *37*, 132–138. doi:10.1016/j.jretconser.2017.04.003

Venkatraman, N. V. (1994). IT-enabled business transformation: From automation to business scope redefinition. *Sloan Management Review*, *35*(2), 73–87.

KEY TERMS AND DEFINITIONS

Corporate Restructuring: A process involved in altering a business strategy resulting in the closure of some units of the business, merging of departments, diversification with the purpose of increasing the long-term profitability of the organization.

Digital Competence: Encompasses a set of attitudes, knowledge, skills, awareness, and values that are of great importance when utilizing disruptive digital technologies and tools in an organization.

Digital Culture: Refers to shared values and norms emanating from the utilization of disruptive digital technologies and tools. Digital culture shapes how the organization interacts with its internal and external stakeholders.

Digital Mindset: It can be defined as a set of attitudes, behaviors, and beliefs held by people or a group of people that influence curiosity about disruptive digital technology in an organization. In the current digital era, managers must foster a digital mindset among employees.

Digital Transformation: Refers to a process whereby an organization embraces disruptive digital technologies and tools in order to improve organizational performance through the transformation of business models, processes, operations, and customer experiences.

FinTech: Refers to a plethora of newly developed disruptive digital technologies, solutions, and tools in financial and banking services.

Strategic Management: A process of formulating, executing, and evaluating business strategy in order to achieve sustainable competitive advantage. The process also encompasses the formulation of vision, mission, goals, and objectives of the organization. Environment scanning is very key when it comes to strategic management.

Chapter 10
Digital Marketing Best Practices for Management in Tourist Destinations

Cristina Callejón-Gómez
University of Malaga, Spain

María-Mercedes Rojas-de-Gracia
https://orcid.org/0000-0002-5006-039X
University of Malaga, Spain

ABSTRACT

This work fills a gap that has existed up to now, proposing a series of specific indicators that serve as a manual of good digital marketing practices for the promotion of tourist destinations. According to the proposed model, the variables to take into account are those related to web metrics, SEO positioning, and social networks. Likewise, the indicators and metrics proposed in the tourist destination Malaga (Spain) are applied. In this way, the model can serve as a guide for the managing institutions of tourist destinations that wish to measure the results of their efforts. This analysis facilitates the identification of the strengths of the strategy followed, as well as those that need to be improved. It can also be used to verify the positioning of tourist destinations with respect to their competitors.

INTRODUCTION

The current tourism sector can be considered a unique market in which each country, region or city competes with others to attract tourists (Assakeret et al., 2020; Manhasnet et al., 2016). This is due to the phenomenon of globalization. This fact worries the managers of the different tourist destinations, who are pressured to generate an attractive image that allows the destination to be in a competitive position within the tourism market. One of the most effective ways of promoting this competitive position is the construction of a recognized brand that can represent its identity in an attractive way for potential clients (Gallarza, Saura and García, 2002).

DOI: 10.4018/978-1-7998-8587-0.ch010

Tourist destination websites play a decisive role in this competitive and global context (Fernández-Cavia et al., 2013; Fernández-Cavia, Rovira, Díaz-Luque, & Cavaller, 2014). This implies that it is not enough that tourist destinations have a competitive image on the Internet. The large amount of information that the user can currently find on the net complicates the task of capturing the attention of tourists, who are increasingly demanding in terms of user-friendliness, speed and website design. This has given rise to a tendency of the different tourist destinations to give greater weight to the work of improving the website, in order to meet the demands and expectations of users and thus ensure that they have a satisfactory experience during their interaction with their portals. web (Martinis, Papadatou, & Kabassi, 2019; McCartney, Butler, & Bennett, 2008). That is, tourist destinations want to offer a promotional website that not only offers information about the destination, but that it is presented in the appropriate way so that it is useful and simple for the user who is looking for information or intends to plan a trip.

On the other hand, since the Internet began to increase in popularity and search engines were born, the volume of information has continued to grow. For this reason, techniques that aimed to classify and prioritize information according to its quality began to appear. This set of techniques is called SEO (Search Engine Optimization). As stated Yalçin and Köse (2010), SEO techniques allow a website to appear in the main search engine result lists for some specific keywords. Due to the large volume of information available on the Internet and, consequently, the difficulty of being in the top positions of search engines, SEO is strictly necessary for content to reach target users.

Finally, in this era it is essential to consider the role of social networks in the promotion of any company and also of tourist destinations. Social networks have not only changed the way in which companies exercise communication, but also the lives of people. These media are all those tools that allow us to speak, listen, dialogue and interact with other individuals, companies and institutions; those that put us in touch with a community made up of people with similar interests to ours or those of the company we work for; and those that destroy the traditional sender and receiver scheme and encourage interaction between all users, proposing a new communication paradigm (Gil, 2017). That is why social networks allow people to communicate with companies or institutions and vice versa. For companies, social networks can represent a window of communication with the user. In this way, you can easily reach people who fit within the profile of the company or institution, know what they like, have fun or dislike. It also allows to transfer different types of content related to the activity of the organism and to find out which one they like the most. Therefore, it is essential to develop a model of good practices for digital marketing of tourist destinations that serves as a guide for managers of tourist destinations and companies that want to take advantage of the opportunities offered by this new context.

BACKGROUND

The Web as a Basic Marketing Tool for Tourist Destinations

Certainly, the web is one of the most important marketing tools today. The main reason is the visibility it provides to any company or institution. If a company is not online, it does not exist. According to Álvarez, Pérez and Solana (2013), the use of web tools favors the reduction of marketing costs, increased sales and allows access to new market segments. In addition, it favors the improvement of service and customer service, which allows increasing customer loyalty and satisfaction. Specifically, according to these authors, the benefits can be summarized in three aspects: (1) The web can be a perfect means of distribution to reduce costs, since through the web, products and some services can be found anywhere part of the world and can lead to a significant increase in sales with a reduction in costs; (2) Users can meet companies they did not know before without the need for the company to be in the same country, since the Internet breaks any border; (3) Personalized and faster attention, since thanks to the web, customer complaints and suggestions can be dealt with quickly and comfortably for the customer, which increases consumer satisfaction and loyalty to the organization.

However, for these benefits to occur, the tourist destination must have a good website. And, in addition, the particular characteristics that the tourism website must possess must be taken into account. Therefore, the characteristics of a tourist portal must be studied specifically. In this sense, Fernández-Cavia et al. (2010) propose an analysis model for tourist destination websites that consists of 12 desired characteristics: accessibility, information architecture, positioning, quality and quantity of content, interactivity, presence in Web 2.0, brand image treatment, usability, distribution and commercialization, home pages, languages and discursive and argumentative analysis.

These authors understand accessibility as the set of strategies, recommendations and resources that make the web accessible or not, taking into account people with visual and / or hearing disabilities and access to web content through the use of devices of mobile phones with limited capacity, for example. In addition, they affirm that the web must be able to be used by everyone, regardless of the characteristics of each one, for which the letter must have an adequate size, the images must have the so-called ATL attribute, the video subtitles and the forms have to be prepared so that anyone can fill them.

Second, information architecture (AI) is defined as the art and science of organizing information spaces to help users meet their needs (Hassan, Martín, & Iazza, 2004). In other words, a website with a good architecture makes it easy for the user to access the content from a search engine and, once inside, find it easily. This can be achieved by allowing, on the one hand, the user to find information through indexes, classifications, taxonomies and information retrieval systems or search systems on the website, and on the other hand, allowing each element of information to be found through description by optimizing metadata and sites for search engines (Hassan et al., 2004).

On the other hand, SEO is a discipline that studies the process by which a web page obtains and maintains notable positions on search engine natural results pages, also called organic or algorithmic results (Ledford, 2009; Orense & Rojas, 2010). Thanks to this feature, you can take advantage of a website. If the positioning is not working properly, the web will not appear in the search engines. Therefore, all the work dedicated to the portal will not have been worth it.

Regarding the quality and quantity of the content, Fernández-Cavia et al. (2010) affirm regarding the quality and quantity of the content that the website of tourist destinations should provide information on all aspects of it. They establish that, in the first place, the user has to find general destination information, such as emergency numbers or ways of moving around it. Secondly, specialized tourist information, such as the type of tourism offered and the different options within it, must also be present. Finally, commercial tourist information such as different types of accommodation or restaurants should be included. Likewise, the information must be clear, complete, concise and well written and without misspellings.

Furthermore, practical and theoretical studies have shown that interactivity is one of the most outstanding characteristics of a website, since it influences the attitude of online consumers towards the site and their purchase intentions (Ghose & Dou, 1998). This interactivity must appear in different ways. Thus, user-message interactivity must be offered so that the former is able to personalize the information he wants to see on the web. Likewise, there must be user-brand interaction so that doubts can be resolved through means such as chats. Third, the option of brand-user interactivity should be included, so that the institution can learn more about the second, for example, through an online survey. Finally, it can be productive to enable user-user interaction, so that they can exchange opinions or advice, as is the case with forums.

Closely linked to interactivity is the feature called web 2.0 presence. or social web, which is defined by the social and communicative dimension that appears on the web, with blogs, social networks, forums or wikis being good examples of this (Aghaei, Nematbakhsh, & Farsani, 2012). The company or institution must have a presence on social websites, in addition to carrying out strategies that provoke a certain degree of interaction by users. It would also be desirable for the website to integrate content innovative enough to involve the user and provide an extra as a portal.

On the other hand, a good treatment of the destination brand image is necessary. This means that the destination must be faithfully represented to achieve a good brand image, considering for this, the combination of emotional and functional elements (Fernández-Cavia et al., 2010). It must represent what the destination offers in an objective and precise way, but also it must reflect what it can contribute as an experience in someone's life, that is, those experiences that the place can offer. Likewise, the design elements must be coordinated with the corporate image, including images and videos that adequately present the site, given its importance in the tourism field (Nicoletta & Servidio, 2012; Oliveira & Casais, 2019).

Usability refers to the ease of the web to be used and achieve the proposed objectives in an efficient, fast, pleasant, attractive and error-free manner (Maldonado, 2015). The use of the web must be simple and intuitive, so that the user is able to access the information they want without the help of anyone. For this, in addition to having a good architecture and a simple design, tracks must be thrown at the user during navigation. For example, it should be suggested what should be entered in the filters of a search engine when performing a search (Huertas & Fernández, 2006).

Regarding the ninth characteristic established by Fernández-Cavia et al. (2010), that is, distribution and marketing, these authors establish that it is made up of the different reservation systems of the different providers of tourist services on the websites. They also establish that it is very beneficial for the site to have its own reservation and payment system for accommodation, entertainment, events or restaurants. Or at least, tourism companies should facilitate redirection to websites that allow it.

The last three characteristics indicated by Fernández-Cavia et al. (2010), that is, those that refer to the start pages, the content in different languages and the discursive, argumentative and theoretical analysis have quite obvious implications. The way in which the home page is presented should cover such important aspects as the possible choice of language as soon as the user enters the web, or the immediate location of the logo. On the other hand, the presentation of the website in several languages is necessary given the global and intercultural nature of the destination. Finally, the discursive, argumentative and theoretical analysis of the texts and images is essential since the information is transmitted through them.

Apart from these these characteristics, whose analysis is essential to evaluate the quality of tourist destination websites, it is necessary to include the visibility and information that is poured through social networks. Without a doubt, social networks have changed many aspects of people's daily daily lives, with special emphasis on how they communicate. These emerged with the birth of web 2.0, when the user was included as a possible issuer and publisher of information. Since then, different social networks have not stopped emerging. Moreno (2015) defines them as all those tools that allow us to speak, listen, dialogue and interact with other people, companies and institutions; those who put us in contact with a community made up of people with interests similar to ours or to those of the company for which we work; and those that destroy the traditional transmitter and receiver scheme and promote interaction among all users, proposing a new communication paradigm. In fact, in addition to allowing communication between people, social networks allow them to communicate with companies or institutions and vice versa. For companies, these tools can represent a window of communication with the user. In this way, people who fit the profile of the company or institution can be easily reached, know what they like and what is fun for them, as well as transfer different types of content related to body activity according to the profile of the user.

However, as established by Moreno (2015), the creation of content on social networks should not be done under the rule of trial and error. For this, in the first place, this author states that the different networks and the majority profile of the users who use them must be well known to know how to take advantage of them. Secondly, it is essential to have a social media plan that includes aspects such as information about the competition, the buyer's personality or user profiles and the guidelines to follow in case of crisis. Finally, adequate planning must be developed to collect the content that will be included in the different social media profiles in the short or medium term. What seems clear is that among the social networks to consider in the case of tourism are Facebook, Instagram, Twitter and YouTube, the effects of which have been relatively important in tourism studies (Fatanti & Suyadnya, 2015; Forristal, 2012; Park, Ok, & Chae, 2016; Stankov, Lazic, & Dragicevic, 2010).

In summary, it has become clear that web design, SEO strategy and activity on social networks are basic tools that must be taken into account to assess the quality of digital marketing carried out by managers of tourist destinations. However, these managers do not have a manual of good practices that allows them to assess the adequacy of their actions in the digital context. It is here where this work wants to make its contribution: the proposal for a manual of good practices on digital marketing, in which the most representative variables are collected to measure the quality of a website, the most important characteristics of a good positioning strategy SEO, and the actions to take to carry out a good social media strategy. All this taking into account the differential characteristics of the tourism sector.

The Case Study

To achieve this objective, the chosen methodology has been the case study. This technique is appropriate when the investigator has no control over the issue and for those cases with a limited amount of previous experience or data compiled from studies. Specifically, as Yin (1994) affirms, the case study is an empirical investigation that analyzes a contemporary phenomenon in the context of real life. This allows taking advantage of previous theoretical proposals with the experience of practical cases whose development is known. More specifically, what has been done in the first place has been to consult various sources and academic publications in this regard. Based on this, a series of indicators are proposed to evaluate the quality of the digital marketing actions of tourist destinations based on the scientific literature, the academic and professional experience of the authors of this study, as well as the analysis of the sites website of various tourist destinations.

When choosing the model variables, several aspects were taken into account. To start, it was decided which digital marketing techniques and actions were to be included in the model. For this, the digital marketing actions that are organic were taken as a base, leaving aside the paid ones. The main reasons for selecting free actions are their popularity in destination marketing, since they are used by the vast majority and their greater accessibility for any enclave. The easiest way for a destination to obtain a good positioning is explained for two reasons. On the one hand, the official page of a tourist destination will always have greater domain and page authority, something that benefits a lot in SEO. On the other hand, non-commercial keywords on a destination tend to have less competition. To demonstrate this, we propose several examples collected in Table 1 of terms for a city like Malaga (Spain), in which it is observed that the competition, that is, the difficulty to dispute the words in no case reaches 0.3, which means the unit of the maximum degree of competence.

Table 1. Volume and competition of the search terms of Malaga

Search Term	Volume	Competition
Malaga temperature	22,200	25/100
Malaga what to see	14,800.	23/100.
Malaga tourism	5,400	27/100

Source: https://app.neilpatel.com/es/ubersuggest/

In this way, the chosen online marketing tools were: web metrics, SEO positioning and social networks. These instruments have been considered as the general variables of the model, which in turn are divided into indicators and sub-indicators. Because it is a somewhat unexplored topic, the compilation of the different indicators has been based on several criteria: the information collected in the scientific literature on the matter, the logic and the academic and work experience itself.

As a result, a measurement model of good digital marketing practices has been developed, consisting of the variables: web, SEO and social networks and their corresponding subdivisions. In addition, each variable has been associated with a score from 1 to 5, according to the criteria established, again, by the scientific literature, logic and professional experience. On the one hand, there are scores that require greater subjectivity, such as those of the degree of accessibility. For example, for this metric, 1 means that the font size makes reading comfortable and 5 that the font size is adequate, there is a contrast between it and the background, the ALT attributes are correct, the videos contain subtitles and the forms are suitable for anyone. On the other hand, there are other objective scores, of a numerical nature such as those of the number of likes on the Facebook page. For this metric, 1 is "0 to 1,000" and 5 means "more than 100,000". To establish these figures, the data in a wide variety of destinations have been previously explored with the aim of establishing a scale to serve as a guide, as established by the case study technique.

MODEL TO ANALYZE THE QUALITY OF DIGITAL MARKETING IN TOURIST DESTINATIONS

Metrics and Indicators

As can be seen in the literature on the subject, the model to analyze the quality of digital marketing in tourist destinations is made up of three variables that correspond to digital marketing tools: web, SEO and social networks. In turn, each of the variables is made up of indicators and sub-indicators. To definitively know the model, which is the subject of this study, we go on to detail each variable, its breakdown and the patterns of its scores.

For the measurement of the web variable, the following metrics have been considered: web architecture; usability; accessibility; the interaction; the content; brand image processing; distribution and marketing; and languages. Table 2 shows the composition of each one in detail. Secondly, Table 3 lists the sub-indicators used to measure the SEO positioning of the web pages of tourist destinations. Finally, Table 4 shows those that will be analyzed based on the corresponding social network (Facebook, Instagram, Twitter and Youtube).

Practical Application of the Model

Once the model is developed, it is applied to the chosen tourist destination, which is the destination of Malaga, in Spain. Specifically, the address of the analyzed website has been https://www.visitacostadelsol.com. The results of the application of the indicators are those shown in Table 5. It is observed that the average score for Malaga in the web variables, SEO positioning and Social Networks are 4.14, 3.00 and 3.23 respectively. As a general average, the destination receives a score of 3.46, which can be considered a medium-high score. As can be seen, the variable with the lowest score is the one corresponding to social networks, and within them, there are sub-indicators such as those that treat the interaction or content that have a lower rating. On the other hand, the best variable is the one that corresponds to the analysis of your website and the highest scores come from the content metrics "and brand image treatment". This analysis allows us to establish which aspects of the web and, consequently, of digital marketing should be improved. Clearly, in the case of the Malaga tourist destination website, this would be the management of social networks. On the other hand, the application of these metrics also allows comparing the websites of different tourist destinations, which would allow us to extract strengths and weaknesses, as well as draw positioning maps.

SOLUTIONS AND RECOMMENDATIONS

This work fills a gap that has existed so far in the literature, as it proposes a series of concrete and specific metrics and indicators that serve as a manual of good practices for digital marketing in tourist destinations. These variables represent the most popular organic tools of digital marketing, which deal with the Internet page, SEO positioning and social networks linked to the websites of tourist destinations. The result of this work has an eminently practical nature for those responsible for the marketing of these destinations, since it allows evaluating the performance of a very important part of digital marketing: its showcase on the Internet.

Table 2.

Metric / Subindicators	Score
Web architecture	
Structured menu without excess levels	1. The menu structure is not logical and has 10 to 12 levels. 2. The menu structure is logical, but it has 10 to 12 levels. 3. The menu structure is logical, but it has 7 to 9 levels. 4. The menu structure is logical, but has 4 to 6 levels. 5. The menu structure is logical and has 3 levels or less, which are the ones recommended.
Existence of breadcrumbs	1. There are no breadcrumbs on the web. 2. There are breadcrumbs on the web, but they are all wrong. 3. There are breadcrumbs on the web, but 100 to 50% of them are wrong. 4. There are breadcrumbs on the web, but up to 49% of them are wrong. 5. There are breadcrumbs on the web and they are all perfectly formed.
Visible and quality search engine	1. There is no search engine. 2. There is a search engine, but it is not easily visible or useful. 3. There is a visible search engine, but it does not segment the results well. 4. There is a useful search engine, but it is not easily visible. 5. There is a useful and visible search engine.
Usability	
Clear and accessible site purpose	1. The URL and menu give clues, but there is no description of the organization's activity. 2. The URL and menu clearly show the purpose of the website, but there is no description. 3. The URL and menu clearly show the purpose of the website, but there is a poor and misplaced description. 4. The URL and menu show the purpose of the site and there is a good description, but out of place. 5. The URL, the menu and the description clearly show the purpose of the site, and in addition, the latter is easily accessible within the web.
Purpose oriented menu	1. The menu options are not oriented to the purpose of the web, they are brief and confusing. 2. Some of the menu options are not entirely purpose-oriented and all are short and confusing. 3. All menu options are purpose-oriented, but are brief and confusing. 4. All menu options are purpose-oriented and offer a variety of information, but are concise. 5. All menu options are in line with purpose and provide complete and clear information.
Presence, visibility and image quality of the logo	1. The logo is present, but not up-to-date and not fully visible or of good quality. 2. The logo is present and updated, but without being visible and of good quality. 3. The logo is present, updated and visible, but poorly located and of low quality. 4. The logo is present, updated, easily visible, but of low quality. 5. The logo is present, updated, easily visible and of good quality.
Friendly URL that includes the name of the destination	1. The URL includes characters between the letters and contains a different name from the destination. 2. The URL does not contain rare characters but the letters are disordered and form a different name from the destination. 3. The URL forms words, but it is not friendly and does not contain the name of the destination. 4. The URL is friendly but does not contain the name of the destination. 5. The URL is friendly and contains the name of the destination.
Balance between design and content	1. Neither the design nor the content are well elaborated. 2. The design and content contain errors in their entirety and are not complete. 3. The design is well crafted, but the content is not complete and contains misprints. 4. The design is well crafted and the content is complete, but it has typos. 5. The content and design are well elaborated, complete and both are in harmony.
Consistent and attractive design	1. The design is not nice or homogeneous. 2. The design is nice, but it is not homogeneous in up to 80% of the pages. 3. The design is nice, but it is not homogeneous in a range of 79 to 50% of the pages. 4. The design is nice but it is not homogeneous in a range of 49 to 20% of the pages. 5. The design is nice and consistent on all pages.
Legibility of the text	1. The font is not nice, it does not use bold characters or bullets and it is not the right size. 2. The font is nice, but does not use bold or bullet characters and is not the right size. 3. The font is nice and well sized, but does not use bold characters or bullets. 4. The typography is beautiful, it is appropriately sized, it uses bold characters, but it does not use bullets. 5. The typography is nice, it is appropriately sized and the text contains bold characters and bullets.
Use of blank spaces	1. Blank spaces are not used to separate elements, paragraphs, or sections. 2. Blank spaces are used to separate only some elements, but not for all, nor to create sections or paragraphs in texts. 3. Blank spaces are used to separate all elements, but not to create paragraphs or sections. 4. Blank spaces are used to separate all elements and paragraphs, but not to create sections. 5. Blank spaces are used to separate elements and create paragraphs and sections.
Quantity of images with adequate size and quality	1. There are almost no images that accompany the content of the web and those that are have poor quality and an inadequate size. 2. There are many images that accompany the theme of the web, but they have poor quality and an inadequate size. 3. There are many images on the web with a good size, but low quality. 4. There are many images on the web that have a good size, but up to 50% of them are of low quality. 5. There are many images on the web and all of them have a good size and good quality.
Simple and intuitive interface	1. The interface is not simple and does not guide the user during navigation. 2. The interface is simple, but it only guides the user in 20% of the navigation route. 3. The interface is simple, but it only guides the user between 21 and 50% of the navigation. 4. The interface is simple, but it only guides the user between 51 and 80% of the navigation. 5. The interface is simple and intuitive.
Existence of broken links	1. 100 to 80% of web links are broken. 2. 79 to 60% of web links are broken. 3. 59 to 30% of web links are broken. 4. 29 to 1% of web links are broken. 5. There are no broken links on the web.

continued on following page

Table 2. Continued

Metric / Subindicators	Score
Footer menu with basic data	1. There is a footer, but it has no information. 2. There is a footer and it includes legal information and contact information. 3. There is a footer and it includes legal information, contact details and the navigation menu. 4. There is a footer and it includes legal information, contact information, navigation menu and link to social networks. 5. There is a footer with legal information, contact information, navigation menu, link to social networks and logo.
Responsive design	1. The web can be seen on mobile devices or tablets, but its design is not responsive 2. The web design is responsive, but in non-desktop versions there are more than 10 errors. 3. The web design is responsive, but there are between 5 and 9 bugs in the non-desktop versions. 4. The web design is responsive, but there are between 1 and 4 bugs in non-desktop versions. 5. The web design is completely responsive.
Clear and eye-catching calls to action	1. There are buttons with calls to action, but they are not flashy and do not contain an evocative message. 2. There are buttons with calls to action, but some are wrong or contain errata and are not flashy. 3. There are calls to action and they are correct, but the message does not ask you to click on them and they are not flashy. 4. Calls to action are correct and evocative, but they are not flashy. 5. Calls to action are clear, evocative, and eye-catching.
Loading speed	1. The homepage of the web takes too long to load, which generates a non-response error. 2. The homepage of the web takes more than 3 seconds to load. 3. Some of the web links take more than 3 seconds to load. 4. Some elements of the web take more than 3 seconds to appear. 5. Both the homepage and all the links and their elements take less than 3 seconds to load.
Accessibility	
Degree of accessibility	1. The size of the font makes reading comfortable. 2. The font size is adequate and the contrast between the background and the text makes the view of both comfortable. 3. The font size is adequate, there is a good contrast between the background and the font, and there is an ALT attribute. 4. The font size is adequate, there is a good contrast between the background and the font, there are ALT attributes and the videos contain subtitles. 5. The font size is adequate, there is a good contrast between the background and the font, there are ALT attributes, the videos contain subtitles, and the forms are suitable for anyone.
Interaction	
User-message interaction	1. The user has the option to customize the content they want to see just by browsing from one section to another. 2. The user has a search engine to find the desired information. 3. The user has a search engine that in turn incorporates a filter. 4. The user has a search engine for each section that in turn incorporates at least one filter. 5. The user has a search engine for each section, which in turn incorporates more than one filter.
User-brand interaction	1. The address of the institution is on the web. 2. There is a means of contact within the web. 3. There is more than one means of contact within the web. 4. There is information about all the means of contact on the web. 5. There is information on all forms of contact and also a help chat on the web.
Brand-user interaction	1. The only information received from the user is through cookies. 2. The company receives information from the user through cookies and a registration form. 3. The company interacts with the user through cookies, a registration form and landing pages. 4. The company interacts with the user through cookies, a registration form, landing pages and online surveys. 5. The company interacts with the user through cookies, a registration form, landing pages. online surveys and a support chat.
User-user interaction	1. Users cannot interact with other users. 2. Users can interact with other users through institutional profiles on social networks. 3. Users can only interact with each other through social networks, but they can also write and read opinions of other users in the forums. 4. Users can only interact with each other through social networks, but also write and read opinions of other users in forums, as well as publish and read opinions on the web. 5. Users can interact with each other through social networks, forums and opinion sections on the web.
Content	
General tourist information	1. The website includes information about the destination's location. 2. The website includes information on the destination's location and weather. 3. The website includes information on location, weather, how to get there and how to get around the destination. 4. The website includes information on location, weather, how to get there, how to get around the destination and other useful information such as language or visas. 5. The website includes information on location, weather, how to get there, how to get around the destination, useful information such as language or visas and other more specific issues such as emergency phone numbers.
Commercial tourist information	1. The website provides general information about the existence of some tourist companies in the destination. 2. The website offers detailed information on the existence of some tourist companies in the destination. 3. The website offers detailed information and the location of some tourist companies in the destination. 4. The website offers detailed information, location and contact forms of some tourist companies in the destination. 5. The website offers detailed information, location and contact of most of the tourist companies in the destination.
Specialized tourist information	1. There is general tourist information on what the destination can offer. 2. There is general tourist information and information on at least one of the special attractions of the destination. 3. There is general tourist information and information about some of the special attractions of the destination. 4. There is general tourist information and information about most of the special attractions of the destination. 5. There is general tourist information and information about all the special attractions of the destination.
Clear, concise and well written information	1. There is too much textual information, it is not clear and it contains spelling errors. 2. The textual information is not excessive, but it is not clear and contains spelling errors. 3. The amount of textual information is adequate, but it is not clear and does not contain misspellings. 4. The amount of textual information is adequate and clear, but contains spelling errors. 5. The amount of textual information is adequate and without spelling mistakes.

continued on following page

Table 2. Continued

Metric / Subindicators	Score
Brand image processing	
Representation of the destination through multimedia elements	1. The only graphic representation of the destination is the logo. 2. The destination is represented by the logo and a main image on the homepage. 3. The destination is represented by the logo and some images on the homepage. 4. The destination is represented by the logo and images of the destination on the homepage and on the rest of the websites. 5. The destination is represented by the logo, images and videos on the homepage and on the rest of the websites.
Coordination between the elements of the web and the brand	1. There is no coordination between the elements of the website and the brand. 2. There is general coordination of all the elements of the website and the brand, although it has defects in terms of color, typography and multimedia components. 3. There is general coordination between the elements of the website and the brand, although it has defects regarding the typography and the multimedia components. 4. There is coordination between the elements of the website and the brand, although it has defects in relation to the multimedia components. 5. There is complete coordination between the elements of the website and the brand.
Distribution and commercialization	
Reservation and payment system and degree of commercialization	1. There is no reservation or payment system, but commercial information about different hotels, tourist companies, shops and bars in the capital is included. 2. There is no reservation or payment system, but commercial information about different hotels, tourism companies, bars and shops in different parts of the destination is included. 3. There is no reservation or payment system, but it includes information on the location or the payment and reservation link of some tourist companies that appear on the destination's website. 4. There is no reservation or payment system, but it includes commercial information about the location, the contact or the direct link for the reservation and payment of all the tourist companies that appear on the destination's website. 5. There is commercial information on tourist businesses and a reservation and payment system for all of them.
Languages	
Versions of the web in different languages	1. The website only has a Spanish version. 2. The website has a Spanish version and in some dialects of Spanish. 3. The website has a Spanish version, at least one in a Spanish dialect, and one in English. 4. The website has a Spanish version, at least in a dialect of Spanish, another in English, and one in another international language. 5. The website has a Spanish version, at least in a dialect of Spanish, another in English, and at least two more in other international languages.
Correct use of each language	1. The website has grammatical errors in all the languages in which the website is available. 2. The website has grammatical errors in some of the languages in which the website is available. 3. The website has grammatical errors in half of the languages in which the website is available. 4. The website has grammatical errors in less than half of the languages in which the website is available. 5. The website does not have grammatical errors in any of the languages in which the website is available.

Source: Own elaboration

Table 3. SEO positioning subindicators for tourist destinations

Subindicators	Score
Traffic to the web	1. The average is from 0 to 10,000 monthly users. 2. The average is from 10,001 to 50,000 monthly users. 3. The average is 50,001 to 100,000 monthly users. 4. The average is from 100,001 to 500,000 monthly users. 5. The average is more than 500,000 monthly users.
Search engine positioning for the main keyword	1. By writing the name of the destination as a keyword, the web is positioned on the fourth page of Google. 2. By writing the name of the destination as a keyword, the web is positioned on the third page of Google. 3. By writing the name of the destination as a keyword, the web is positioned on the second page of Google. 4. By writing the name of the destination as a keyword, the website is positioned in the lower half of the first page of Google. 5. By writing the name of the destination as a keyword, the web is positioned in the upper half of the first page of Google.
Coincidence between the best keywords on the web and a good representation of the destination	1. The best keywords match in a range between 0-20% with good brand representation. 2. The best keywords coincide in a range between 21 and 40% with a good representation of the brand. 3. The best keywords coincide in a range between 41 and 60% with a good representation of the brand. 4. The best keywords coincide in a range between 61 and 80% with a good representation of the brand. 5. The best keywords coincide in a range between 80 and 100% with a good representation of the brand.
Quality of backlinks	1. Between 0 and 20% are follow links. 2. Between 21 and 40% are follow links. 3. Between 41 and 60% are follow links. 4. Between 61 and 80% are follow links. 5. Between 81 and 100% are follow links.
Domain score	1. The web score is between 0 and 20. 2. The web score is between 21 and 40. 3. The web score is between 41 and 60. 4. The web score is between 61 and 80. 5. The web score is between 81 and 100.
Trust score	1. The web score is between 0 and 20. 2. The web score is between 21 and 40. 3. The web score is between 41 and 60. 4. The web score is between 61 and 80. 5. The web score is between 81 and 100.

Source: Own elaboration

Table 4. Subindicators of social networks used by tourist destinations

Social Network / Subindicators	Score
Facebook	
Number of "likes"	1. From 0 to 1,000. 2. From 1,001 to 10,000. 3. From 10,001 to 50,000. 4. From 50,001 to 100,000. 5. More than 100,000.
User interaction	1. The interaction rate is less than 10% in proportion to followers. 2. The interaction rate is between 11% and 20% in proportion to the followers. 3. The interaction rate between 21% to 40% in proportion to the followers. 4. The interaction rate is between 41% to 60% in proportion to the followers. 5. The interaction rate is greater than 60% in proportion to followers.
Link to the web within Facebook	1. There is no link to the web. 2. There is a link to the web, but when clicking, it gives an error. 3. There is a link to the web, but only in 10% of the posts. 4. There is a link to the web in more than 50% of the posts. 5. There is a link to the web in more than 50% of the posts and in the contact section.
Updated, varied content, accompanied by multimedia and with hooked copys	1. There are no daily posts, they are not varied, they are not accompanied by multimedia and they are not good. 2. There are daily posts, but they are not varied, the pictures are not attractive, and the copys have no hook. 3. There are daily posts and they are varied, but they are not accompanied by attractive multimedia elements and the copys have no hook. 4. There are daily posts, they are varied, they are accompanied by attractive multimedia elements, but the copys have no hook. 5. There are daily posts, they are varied, the multimedia elements are attractive and the copys have hook.
Instagram	
Number of followers	1. From 0 to 1,000. 2. From 1,001 to 10,000. 3. From 10,001 to 50,000. 4. From 50,001 to 100,000. 5. More than 100,000.
User interaction	1. The interaction rate is less than 10% in proportion to followers. 2. The interaction rate is between 11% and 20% in proportion to the followers. 3. The interaction rate is between 21% to 40% in proportion to the followers. 4. The interaction rate is between 41% to 60% in proportion to the followers. 5. The interaction rate is greater than 60% in proportion to followers.
Link to the web within Instagram	1. There is no link to the web. 2. There is a link to the web in the biography, but clicking gives an error. 3. There is a link to the web in the biography and in the posts, but only in 10%. 4. There is a link to the web in the biography and between 11 and 50% of the posts. 5. There is a link to the web in the biography and in more than 50% of the posts.
Constant posts, good multimedia aesthetics and attractive copys	1. There are no daily posts and they are not good. 2. There are daily posts, but there is no good aesthetic and no copys are included. 3. There are daily posts, but there is a good aesthetic and although copys are included, they are not attractive. 4. There are daily posts and the multimedia aesthetic is good, but the copys are not attractive. 5. There are daily posts, the multimedia aesthetic is good and the copys are attractive.
Twitter	
Number of followers	1. From 0 to 1,000. 2. From 1,001 to 10,000. 3. From 10,001 to 50,000. 4. From 50,001 to 100,000. 5. More than 100,000.
User interaction	1. The interaction rate is less than 10% in proportion to followers. 2. The interaction rate is between 11% and 20% in proportion to the followers. 3. The interaction rate between 21% to 40% in proportion to the followers. 4. The interaction rate is between 41% to 60% in proportion to the followers. 5. The interaction rate is greater than 60% in proportion to followers.
Link to the web within Twitter	1. There is no link to the web. 2. There is a link to the web, but when clicking, it gives an error. 3. There is a link to the web in the biography and in the posts, but only in 10% of them. 4. There is a link to the web in the biography and between 11% and 50% of the posts. 5. There is a link to the web in the biography and in more than 50% of the posts.
Activity and varied, interesting content and accompanied by multimedia elements	1. There are no daily posts and they are not good. 2. The posts are varied, but they are not always accompanied by visual elements and the copys have no hook. 3. The posts are varied and are accompanied by quite attractive multimedia elements, but the copys have no hook. 4. The posts are varied and accompanied by attractive multimedia content, but the copys have no hook. 5. The posts are varied and both the copys and the multimedia elements are good.
Youtube	

continued on following page

Table 4. Continued

Social Network / Subindicators	Score
Number of subscribers	1. From 0 to 100. 2. From 101 to 500. 3. From 501 to 1,000. 4. From 1,001 to 10,000. 5. More than 10,000.
Activity and generation of interesting content	1. The content is sparse and uninteresting. 2. The posts are made less than 10 times a year, but the content is interesting. 3. At least one video is uploaded per month, but it's not interesting. 4. At least one video is uploaded per month and ît's interesting. 5. More than one video is uploaded per month and they are interesting.
Average views, likes and comments per video	1. The interaction rate is less than 10% in proportion to followers. 2. The interaction rate is between 11% and 20% in proportion to the followers. 3. The interaction rate between 21% to 40% in proportion to the followers. 4. The interaction rate is between 41% to 60% in proportion to the followers. 5. The interaction rate is greater than 60% in proportion to followers.

Source: Own elaboration

In summary, the main contributions of this work can be summarized in two. The first of these is the identification of the relevant variables to be taken into account to adequately evaluate the characteristics that the website of a tourist destination should have. This compilation of variables has been possible thanks to an exhaustive examination of the literature in this regard, the academic and professional experience of the authors of this study, as well as the analysis of different tourist websites. Secondly, an easy and detailed way of obtaining a score is proposed, which allows identifying the aspects of the strategy followed that are more solid and better elaborated, and those that must be improved. It can also be used to compare the websites of different competing tourist destinations. Both implications are of vital importance, since access to a large volume of destination information for users will depend on the quality of your website and, as a consequence, a greater probability that they will visit it. In this way, the model can serve as a guide for tourist destination institutions that want to measure the result of their efforts and be able to act accordingly.

FUTURE RESEARCH DIRECTIONS

Despite the fact that there are some computer applications that allow us to evaluate the quality of a website, we have not found any model that includes in such a complete way the different aspects of the quality of a tourist website. Likewise, since the active intervention of a person is necessary to apply this model, although it requires time, it allows a more exhaustive and personalized examination of the aspects to be evaluated. However, this does not mean that this work has no limitations. In fact, being a pioneering model, the foundations are laid for carrying out future research that will improve the guideline proposed in this work. Similarly, it would be desirable to expand the number of destinations to which it should apply. In this way, although the quality of the web is only one aspect that can influence the increase in the number of visitors to a destination, this comparison could provide indications of the relationship between the two variables. In short, all the variables that may influence the increase in the number of tourists deserve to be studied, so researchers are urged to follow the line of research proposed in this document.

Table 5. Application of the indicators to the tourist destination Malaga (Spain)

Subindicators	1 Point	2 Points	3 Points	4 Points	5 Points	Average
WEB METRICS	4.14					
Web architecture	4.67					
Structured menu without excess levels						
Existence of breadcrumbs						
Visible and quality search engine						
Usability	4.67					
Clear and accessible site purpose						
Purpose oriented menú						
Presence, visibility and image quality of the logo						
Friendly URL that includes the name of the destination						
Balance between design and content						
Consistent and attractive design						
Legibility of the text						
Use of blank spaces						
Quantity of images with adequate size and quality						
Simple and intuitive interface						
Existence of broken links						
Footer menu with basic data						
Responsive design						
Clear and eye-catching calls to action						
Loading speed						
Accessibility	3.00					
Degree of accessibility						
Interaction	2.75					
User-message interaction						
User-brand interaction						
Brand-user interaction						
User-user interaction						
Content	5.00					
General tourist information						
Commercial tourist information						
Specialized tourist information						
Clear, concise and spelling-free information						
Brand image processing	5.00					
Representation of the destination through multimedia elements						
Coordination of existing elements on the web with the Brand						
Distribution and commercialization	4.00					
Reservation and payment system and degree of commercialization						
Languages	4.00					
Versions of the web in different languages						
Correct use of each language						
SEO POSITIONING	3.00					
Traffic to the web						
Search engine positioning for the main keyword						
Coincidence between the best keywords on the web and a good representation of the destination						
Quality of backlinks						
Domain score						
Trust score						
SOCIAL NETWORKS	3.23					
Facebook	3.00					
Number of "likes"						
User interaction						
Link to the web within Facebook						

continued on following page

Table 5. Continued

Subindicators	1 Point	2 Points	3 Points	4 Points	5 Points	Average
Updated, varied content, accompanied by multimedia and with hooked copies						
Instagram	2.75					
Number of followers						
User interaction						
Link to the web within Instagram						
Constant publications, good multimedia aesthetics and attractive copys						
Twitter	3.50					
Number of followers						
User interaction						
Link to the web within Twitter						
Activity and varied, interesting content and accompanied by multimedia elements						
Youtube	3.67					
Number of subscribers						
Activity and generation of interesting content						
Average views, likes and comments per video						

Source: Own elaboration

CONCLUSION

Globalization and intense competition in the tourism sector forces destinations to compete with other countries, regions and cities to attract tourists. Therefore, those responsible for marekting of the different tourist destinations are concerned with generating an attractive image that allows them to establish themselves in a competitive position within the tourism market. One of the most effective ways to promote this competitive position is to build a recognized brand on the Internet through a quality website.

In this sense, this work fills a gap that has existed up to now, proposing a series of very specific and specific indicators that allow it to serve as a manual of good digital marketing practices in tourist destinations. Also, a practical example is shown applying it to the tourist destination of the city of Malaga, in Spain. This analysis facilitates the identification of the strengths and weaknesses of the strategy followed by the managers of tourist destinations. This model can serve as a guide for destination institutions that want to measure the results of their efforts.

REFERENCES

Aghaei, S., Nematbakhsh, M. A., & Farsani, H. K. (2012). Evolution of the world wide web: From web 1.0 to web 4.0. *International Journal of Web & Semantic Technology*, *3*(1), 1–10. doi:10.5121/ijwest.2012.3101

Álvarez, Y., Pérez, D., & Solana, P. (2013). Contribución de la web 2.0 al desempeño organizacional en las empresas del sector turismo. *Puente Revista Científica*, *7*(2), 7–13.

Fatanti, M. N., & Suyadnya, I. W. (2015). Beyond user gaze: How Instagram creates tourism destination brand? *Procedia: Social and Behavioral Sciences*, *211*, 1089–1095. doi:10.1016/j.sbspro.2015.11.145

Fernández-Cavia, J., Díaz-Luque, P., Huertas, A., Rovira, C., Pedraza-Jimenez, R., Sicilia, M., ... Máguez-González, M. I. (2013). Marcas de destino y evaluación de sitios web: Una metodología de investigación. *Revista Latina de Comunicación Social*, *68*, 622–638. doi:10.4185/RLCS-2013-993

Fernández-Cavia, J., Rovira, C., Díaz-Luque, P., & Cavaller, V. (2014). Web Quality Index (WQI) for official tourist destination websites. Proposal for an assessment system. *Tourism Management Perspectives*, *9*, 5–13. doi:10.1016/j.tmp.2013.10.003

Fernández-Cavia, J., Rovira, C., Gómez, L., Gascó, M., Pedraza, R., Bonilla, S., . . . Martín, S. (2010). Propuesta de diseño de una plantilla multidisciplinar para el análisis y evaluación de webs de destinos turísticos. In *VIII Congreso Turismo y Tecnologías de la Información y las Comunicaciones Turitec 2010* (pp. 1–18). Universidad de Málaga.

Forristal, L. J. (2012). Using YouTube videos of anthropology of tourism pioneer Valene Smith's work and philosophy to balance the tourism curriculum. *Journal of Teaching in Travel & Tourism*, *12*(1), 91–104. doi:10.1080/15313220.2012.650098

Gallarza, M. G., Saura, I. G., & García, H. C. (2002). Destination image: Towards a conceptual framework. *Annals of Tourism Research*, *29*(1), 56–78. doi:10.1016/S0160-7383(01)00031-7

Ghose, S., & Dou, W. (1998). Interactive functions and their impacts on the appeal of Internet presence sites. *Journal of Advertising Research*, *38*(2), 29–43.

Gil, E. (2017). Nuevos activismos sociales en la era digital: De las masas al crowd. *Politica y Sociedad*, *54*(1), 191–209.

Hassan, Y., Martin, F., & Iazza, G. (2004): *Diseño Web Centrado en el Usuario: Usabilidad y Arquitectura de la Información*. Retrieved from https://www.upf.edu/hipertextnet/numero-2/diseno_web.html

Huertas, A., & Fernández, J. (2006). Ciudades en la web: Usabilidad e interactividad de las páginas oficiales de los destinos turísticos. In *VI Congreso Turismo y Tecnologías de la Información y las Comunicaciones Turitec* (pp. 403–421). Málaga: Universidad de Málaga.

Ledford, J. L. (2009). *Search engine optimization bible*. John Wiley & Sons.

Maldonado, S. (2015). *Analítica web: Medir para triunfar*. ESIC.

Manhas, P. S., Manrai, L. A., & Manrai, A. K. (2016). Role of tourist destination development in building its brand image: A conceptual model. *Journal of Economics, Finance and Administrative Science*, *21*(40), 25–29. doi:10.1016/j.jefas.2016.01.001

Martinis, A., Papadatou, A., & Kabassi, K. (2019). An analysis of the electronic presence of national parks in Greece. In V. Katsoni & M. Segarra-Oña (Eds.), *Smart Tourism as a Driver for Culture and Sustainability* (pp. 433–449). Springer. doi:10.1007/978-3-030-03910-3_30

McCartney, G., Butler, R., & Bennett, M. (2008). A strategic use of the communication mix in the destination image-formation process. *Journal of Travel Research*, *47*(2), 183–196. doi:10.1177/0047287508321201

Moreno, M. (2015). *Cómo triunfar en las redes sociales*. Ediciones Gestión.

Nicoletta, R., & Servidio, R. (2012). Tourists' opinions and their selection of tourism destination images: An affective and motivational evaluation. *Tourism Management Perspectives*, *4*, 19–27. doi:10.1016/j.tmp.2012.04.004

Oliveira, B., & Casais, B. (2019). The importance of user-generated photos in restaurant selection. *Journal of Hospitality and Tourism Technology*, *10*(1), 2–14. doi:10.1108/JHTT-11-2017-0130

Orense, M., & Rojas, O. (2010). *SEO Cómo triunfar en buscadores*. ESIC.

Park, S. B., Ok, C. M., & Chae, B. K. (2016). Using Twitter data for cruise tourism marketing and research. *Journal of Travel & Tourism Marketing*, *33*(6), 885–898. doi:10.1080/10548408.2015.1071688

Stankov, U., Lazic, L., & Dragicevic, V. (2010). The extent of use of basic Facebook user-generated content by the national tourism organizations in Europe. *European Journal of Tourism Research*, *3*(2), 105–113.

Yalçin, N., & Köse, U. (2010). What is search engine optimization: SEO? *Procedia Social and Behavioral Sciences*, *9*(July), 487–493.

Yin, R. K. (1994). *Case study research : Design and methods*. SAGE Publications.

ADDITIONAL READING

Assaker, G., Hallak, R., & El-Haddad, R. (2020). Consumer usage of online travel reviews: Expanding the unified theory of acceptance and use of technology 2 model. *Journal of Vacation Marketing*, *26*(2), 149–165. doi:10.1177/1356766719867386

Bastida, U., & Huan, T. C. (2014). Performance evaluation of tourism websites' information quality of four global destination brands: Beijing, Hong Kong, Shanghai, and Taipei. *Journal of Business Research*, *67*(2), 167–170. doi:10.1016/j.jbusres.2012.10.008

Ip, C., Law, R., & Lee, H. A. (2011). A review of website evaluation studies in the tourism and hospitality fields from 1996 to 2009. *International Journal of Tourism Research*, *13*(3), 234–265. doi:10.1002/jtr.815

Law, R. (2019). Evaluation of hotel websites: Progress and future developments. *International Journal of Hospitality Management*, *76*, 2–9. doi:10.1016/j.ijhm.2018.06.005

Law, R., Qi, S., & Buhalis, D. (2010). Progress in tourism management: A review of website evaluation in tourism research. *Tourism Management*, *31*(3), 297–313. doi:10.1016/j.tourman.2009.11.007

Orlikowski, W. J., & Scott, S. V. (2014). What happens when evaluation goes online? Exploring apparatuses of valuation in the travel sector. *Organization Science*, *25*(3), 868–891. doi:10.1287/orsc.2013.0877

Vinyals-Mirabent, S., Kavaratzis, M., & Fernández-Cavia, J. (2019). The role of functional associations in building destination brand personality: When official websites do the talking. *Tourism Management*, *75*, 148–155. doi:10.1016/j.tourman.2019.04.022

Xiang, Z., Wang, D., O'Leary, J. T., & Fesenmaier, D. R. (2015). Adapting to the internet: Trends in travelers' use of the web for trip planning. *Journal of Travel Research*, *54*(4), 511–527. doi:10.1177/0047287514522883

KEY TERMS AND DEFINITIONS

Case Study: Research method based on a real case.

Copy Web: Set of persuasive texts found on websites whose main objective is to sell, communicate with users and build brand.

Domain Score: Measure of the importance of a page within a website based on the volume of links that point to that page or domain.

Organic Traffic: Visits of a user to a web page after making a conscious search, and not as a result of an internet advertisement.

Tourist Destination: Geographic area or zone frequently visited by tourists.

Trust Score: Measure of the trust of a website or domain, using for it the volume of links that come from other websites with great reputation.

Web Analytics: Set of techniques that analyze data on operations performed on a website.

Chapter 11
Connected Societies Through Digital Transformation

Ranjith P. V.
CMS Business School, Jain University, India

Aparna J. Varma
GSSS Institute of Engineering and Technology for Women, India

Ashwini J.
BIMS, University of Mysuru, India

ABSTRACT

The converging, digitized, disruptive, and globalized world is transforming the way society exists and human beings live. These changes have helped us to collaborate and contribute in exciting and unforeseen ways by creating connected societies worldwide. Technology drives growth across industries and connects people thereby promoting further opportunities and changing the standard of living. IoT has enabled connectivity among people exponentially and advancement in the speed of internet connections have improved accessibility among users to acquire information and services worldwide around the clock. In many parts of the world, the internet has established itself as the primary medium to connect the societies. Digital transformation has made it essential for enterprises for changing their strategies to make sure that they are connected all the time virtually. This has enabled development of new and innovative approaches in education, healthcare, public service entertainment, etc. The aim of this chapter is to provide an overview of the concept of connected societies and its importance.

INTRODUCTION

A hyperconnected society refers to a society in which there are large connections between people themselves, people to objects and between things and this is facilitated by digitisation and internet of things (IoT) (Chung et al, 2017). This is happening at such a rapid pace that all people and companies will be interconnected across the world which will make that information accessible across. Half of the world's

DOI: 10.4018/978-1-7998-8587-0.ch011

population, are internet users and the number of people using mobile devices is increasing at a fast pace every day. It is estimated that more than 5 billion people have mobile devises and the over half of these connections are that of smartphones (Silver, 2019). The main basis for connected community is Internet (IoT) of Things and Internet of People (IoP).

Connected society is the result of strategic intent from companies and individuals for connecting on a regular basis and this has happened due to digital transformation. Digital transformation is happening across the world. Concepts of artificial intelligence, industry 4.0 and technological advancements have helped to revolutionize the way we behave as a society. It has also helped to bring people together in real life. Enterprises are running digitally and especially in the last 6 months where Covid-19 has wreaked havoc in the world. We are meeting each other virtually, doing business virtually and growing virtually. In short doing everything in a connected society. Digital transformations and innovations in this area have helped us to be interconnected.

Some of the articles in the area of digital transformation are analysed here to get deeper insights into the applications and areas where there are gaps for further studies which can provide better understating of different issues..

Reis et al (2018) reviewed more than 200 cited articles and found applications of digital transformation. They found that digitisation is a key issue but it is a necessity in this world where technology is absolutely critical for any business process. They found that though digital transformation is happening in all industries and sectors. But this is rampant and more evident in some industries like healthcare and some sectors like public sector. This study gave output of more than 200 literatures and so can be used by future researchers.

A study by Ebert and Duarte (2018) suggested that the digital transformation goals can be viewed on social and economic perspective. The main objective of economic perspective is to increase income generation and productivity by implementing new and innovative business model. Whereas the objectives of social perspective can be of numerous reasons like foster a collaborative culture in industry and society, face lift the education industry through digital transformation, improve the digital accessibility of quality services to the population.

Manda and Backhouse (2018) investigated the adoption of digital transformation to promote inclusive growth in South Africa. The major challenges identified were poor coordination and fragmentation and poor cohesion among government, business and society. It was suggested that all the stakeholders should adopt a more integrative approach to create a connected society.

Hausberg et al (2019) in their article examined applications of digital transformation in areas like marketing management, innovation management and finance management. They studied different literature available in these functional areas as far as digital transformation is concerned. They found that in other functional areas of management, digital transformation research is less used. The main idea of the article was to make a model framework incorporating applications of digital transformation for future research insights.

Verhoef et al (2019) examined the way the digital transformation has changed the traditional business models and the customer expectations. The authors have identified digital technology, digital competition and digital customer behavior as the major external drivers of digital transformation. The study also discussed three different phases of digital transformation; Digitization, Digitalization, and Digital transformation with suitable examples. The paper concluded with a brief discussion on various strategic imperatives like digital recourses, organization structure, growth strategy, metrics and goals. The paper has provided a rich and timely dialogue on the external drivers, phases and strategic imperatives of digital transformation. Despite the fact that the study uncovers the different phases of digital transformation, the study impedes to elaborate how a firm goes through the phases of digital transformation. Also, the study has conducted only on the important assets and capabilities. It has not covered the areas like the development of such digital resources and its impact on shaping the success of digital transformation.

Chanias et al (2019) have echoed the relevance of crafting a digital strategy for the survival of many pre-digital organizations. The authors stressed on the point that digital strategy making is different and continuous in nature. The study proposed a process model for financial services provider and concluded that the digital transformation strategy is a highly dynamic process and how human agents have to continuously learn to transform the social structure. This paper proposes a process model for the digital transformation strategy for a pre-digital mid -sized financial services provider. The paper is confined to one case study of a pre-digital organization and doesn't discuss the evaluation process of digital transformation.

Davenport and Redman (2020) in their article talked about importance of data, technological advancements, organisational process and adaptability to change for implementing digital transformations in the respective companies. Without having real capability in these areas digital transformations will be difficult. This study gave the main components for digital transformations.

All these studies suggest that digital transformation is necessary. Digital transformation strategy facilitates connected society which will in turn help people and companies to be interconnected.

This is where the authors would like to focus, i.e., the relevance of digital transformation and connected society in the global scenario. It is an important study for future researchers to focus on and formulate methods to make the system to work efficiently.

BACKGROUND OF THE STUDY

Mobile connectivity is increasing across the world. But still it is hovering around 40% in the low-and middle-income countries. Whereas the high-income countries have almost 75% of its population with mobile internet connectivity (Bahia and Suardi, 2019). Increase of smartphones and technologies have made connected society a reality. Increased use of automation, digital technology, internet of things etc. have made life simpler for us to connect with each other.

According to researchers, Digital Transformation is more than a technical shift. This strategy can be defined as acceleration of business models, activities, models and activities to fully leverage the opportunities offered by digital technologies and also the impact they have in a strategic way. The digital transformation has made the society to get connected through technology.

A connected society through internet of things makes everything around us a bit smarter and a bit better. Internet accessibility and high-speed connectivity have created a platform to explore new ways of service delivery in different sectors like education, transportation, entertainment, energy and health care.

The chapter deals with the concepts, influencing factors, challenges and solutions for a smooth and efficient society connected virtually. There has been previous literature which is described in the chapter in this area but this chapter deals with challenges and solutions of connected society in detail.

FOCUS OF THE CHAPTER

The study mainly deals with the different concepts of connected society and how they are relevant now. The challenges and way forward is also discussed. The details of the chapter are discussed in the next paragraphs.

Purpose of the Study

The main purpose of this chapter is to understand past literature in digital transformation and connected society. The impact of industry 4.0 is also discussed. Also the study aims to give future directions for further research. The chapter gives directions for digital business transformation using internet of things and internet of people.

Justification of the Study

There have been studies in the past with respect to digitisation and its effect. But not much research has gone to connected society, its constituents and its impact. The role of social media and the challenges in this concept are given emphasis in the chapter. The concept is relevant in this world of pandemic of digitally connected businesses and society and hence this chapter is important.

Significance of the Study

The work is important for the practitioners to understand future direction of usage of technology and digitisation. This will also help academicians to prepare the content for courses of digitisation and connected society.

Research Methodology

The study here is qualitative with emphasis on literature review. Significant contributions in the world of connected society and digital business transformations are studied for the benefit of readers. Significant number of terminologies are explained in this chapter for the purpose of summarising key findings and suggestions.

Important Research Questions

1. What are the key concepts used to define connected society?
2. What are the challenges that are faced of connected society?
3. What is the role of social media in connected society?

Important Objectives of the Chapter

1. To understand the concept of 'Connected Society'
2. To study the important technological developments of connected societies.
3. To analyse the benefits of Industrial revolution 4.0 on connected society.

4. To understand and analyse main challenges in the implementation.
5. To explore the role of social media in connected society.

MAIN FOCUS OF THE CHAPTER

Issues and Challenges in Connected Society

The chapter focuses on the meaning of connected society, examples, advantages and disadvantages, new technological dimensions and the ethical dimensions. The study also proposes some solutions for the challenges.

Meaning and Definition of Connected Society

The Connected society means a society in which people and people, people and objects, things and things, online and offline, one to one, one to many and many to many are connected using digital technology or the digital based society that stores, analyses and manages data collected by sensors and mobile terminals through a network. This is possible only due to the digital transformation which is happening across the world.

Network society is the expression which was coined in 1991 related to the social, political, economic and cultural changes caused by the spread of networked, digital information and communications technologies. The intellectual origins of the idea can be traced back to the work of early social theorists such as Georg Simmel who analysed the effect of modernization and industrial capitalism on complex patterns of affiliation, organization, production and experience.

The term 'Network Society' was coined by Djik (1991; 2012). He defines the network society as "a society in which a combination of social and media networks shapes its prime mode of organization and most important structures at all levels (individual, organizational and societal)" . The wired society: a similar term was used by Martin (1978) as for the society which is connected by telecommunication and mass network.

Wellman et al (2003), Canadian social scientists, have argued that hyper-connected society is a concept derived from an announcement in "Networks of distance and media: A case study of a high-tech firm". It is a society in which people, and terminals are closely connected with each other through the development of IT technology and changes to the means of communication. Prior to that, Berry Wellman (2001) analysed and predicted connectivity and its social changes in his paper "Physical Place and Cyberplace: The Rise of personalized networking". Connectivity is a concept that encompasses all three connectivity features: place-to-place connectivity, person-to-person connectivity and globalized connectivity.

- Place to place connectivity: transforms from traditional door to door to interregional communities which are further consolidated through connection and communication via the internet.
- Person to person connectivity: enables private communication anytime, anywhere without restrictions in space, resulting in a change across society as a whole.

- Globalized connectivity: with network connectivity personal computers and servers are connected globally, and mobile phones and satellite communications accelerate this global increase in connectivity.

With advances in communications technology, the world is moving towards a connected society. Changes in network speed, improvements in accessibility and the pervasiveness of online connections means that people can access information and services around the clock irrespective of their physical location. This enables new approaches in education, health care, transportation, energy, and entertainment.

New media is the concept that new methods of communicating in the digital world allow smaller groups of people to congregate online and share, sell and swap goods and information. It allows more people to have a voice in their community and in the world in general. The most important structural characteristics of new media is the integration of telecommunications technologies. The second structural new media characteristics of the current communications revolution is the rise of interactive media. Interactivity is a sequence of action and reaction. The downloaded link or the supply of websites, interactive television and computer games is much wider that the uplink or retrieval made by their users. The third, technical, characteristics of new media is digital code. The new media are defined by all three characteristics simultaneously: "They are media which are both integrated and interactive and also use digital code at the turn of the technology driven century"

Table 1. Evolution of the concept of connected society

References	Concepts
Wellman, 2001	Concept of usage of computer networks which will help in being socially connected.
Fredette et al, 2012	Increased communication has made it an interconnected society which has made time and space irrelevant.
Choi, 2014	Role of Internet of Things on connected society with the help of lots of data.

The benefits of an increasing Connected Society are endless. The benefits depend on the speed of change, emerging anxieties and the risk of unintended consequences among other factors. Automation is improving company profitability, but putting traditional jobs at risk. Businesses using big data are coming under sustained attack from ever more sophisticated hackers. The Internet of Things is connecting cities, governments and communities, raising concerns about the risks posed by cyber criminals to critical infrastructure and also the national security. One of the top most concerns is the rise of fake news, cyber terrorism, online abuse, fraud, extremism, grooming and bullying, all of which are increasing because of ubiquitous and 24/7 connectivity.

We can notice that technology is moving at such a fast pace that society is struggling trying to keep up. The rise of unexpected threats is undermining the trust of both the institutions with which the public interacts and also the technology we are becoming increasingly dependent on in our day to day lives. This lack of trust will not only jeopardise the realisation of the benefits of the digital world, but also risks isolating those sections of population who will disengage or opt out. These issues are part and parcel of a Connected Society.

It is not the digital technologies themselves that will shape our future, but the ethical, social and political decisions taken about them and their use. These decisions taken by citizens, for citizens should be for the benefit of all within our connected societ

It is the shared responsibility of businesses, policymakers, academics and not-for-profit organizations to put the citizen at the heart of our connected society. Neither governments nor tech companies alone can claim to represent or understand the needs of the citizens in this fast-moving world. Individuals and communities should be given skills and tools needed to reshape their future. These skills and behaviours should promote safe, empowered and productive engagement like critical thinking, empathy, problem solving, resilience and civic and economic participation. Universal connectivity and the skills to use it are now considered fundamental to a citizen's participation in the world and we as a society have a duty to provide them. Technology is creating jobs as much as it is depleting them. But these are different jobs and without providing new skills, those jobs will never get filled.

The concept of network society are described by various researchers (Djik,2012; Castells,2006; Wellman,2001; Hiltz & Turoff,1978). Social networking sites such as Facebook, Twitter, instant messaging and email are prime examples of the Network Society at work. These web services allow people all over the world to communicate through digital means without face-to-face contact. This demonstrates how the ideas of society changing will affect the persons we communicate over time. Network society does not have any confinements and has found its way to the global scale.

Connected or Network society is developed in modern society that allows for a good deal of information to be traded to help improve information and communication technologies. Having this luxury connection to communication allows for globalization to take place. Having more and more people joining the online society and learning about different techniques with the world wide web. This benefits the users who have access to the internet, to stay connected at all times with any topic of discussion the use prefers. Individual without internet may be affected because they are not directly connected into this society. The connected society is constantly changing the "cultural production in a hyper connected world". This is seen as a global system that helps with globalization. It is beneficial to the people who have network with internet but the people without access actually do not get a sense of the network society. This society allows people to connect to each other quicker and to engage more actively.

Mobile internet is connecting people to new opportunities and life-enhancing services, driving economic growth. In 2018, almost 300 million people connected to mobile internet for the first time, bringing the total connected population to more than 3.5 billion people globally (Bahia & Suardi 2019).

While the reach of mobile networks has expanded significantly in recent years, there is still a 'coverage gap' of over 750 million people who reside in areas that are not covered by a mobile broadband network. In the twenty-first century, a network society is emerging. Fragmented, visually saturated, characterized by rapid technological change and constant social upheavals, it is dizzying, excessive, and sometimes surreal.

Technology is changing the world around us at a rapid pace and the capabilities of connected devices will continue to advance at break-neck speed. When we harness the ability to turn connections into data, and then into knowledge, we can empower. When we close the gap between data growth and data value – by ensuring that the right information is delivered to the right person at the right time – we will change the world. In today's world, with more than 10 billion connected devices, with a staggering 50 billion predicted devices for 2020. As the number of things connected to the global network increases – from data, voice, video and smart devices to new breeds of applications – the opportunities to realize much greater value from networked connection will also increase exponentially.

As the world transitions to the ***Internet of Everything*** – where people, processes and data are intelligently connected – we will be linked in even more ways. Billions and trillions of sensors around the earth and its atmosphere will send information back to machines, computers and people for further evaluation and decision making. This is truly Big Data. Gradually people will adopt products and services tied to the IoT – Internet of Things because it is their best life choice and at times in the world of connected society their only choice. Because they believe that opting out will not be an option in many situations, for example, in daily work and health care settings. As businesses, governments and other organizations begin to reap benefits from the IoT, people will be rewarded for their use and suffer consequences for nonparticipation. Even if there were no such carrot-stick motivations, network effects would leave the unconnected at a disadvantage.

'Disconnection and remaining in society are mutually incompatible'.

The Internet is the decisive technology of the Information Age, as the electrical engine was the vector of technological transformation of the Industrial Age. This global network of computer networks, largely based nowadays on platforms of wireless communication, provides ubiquitous capacity of multimodal.

Examples of Connected Society

- CISCO STORE: The connected store helps to connect employees, customers and stakeholders in an interconnected technological world.
- Connected home is another example where internet of things and artificial intelligence help in household appliance connectivity and devices like amazon echo and Alexa have changed entertainment inside home.
- The internet connections at home have also become better over the years with the help of technological advancements.
- Development of technology like augmented and virtual reality have helped companies to deliver innovative messages to the audience thereby making the society to become interconnected.
- E-Commerce platforms, Cloud computing, Automatic coding and artificial intelligence have made supply chain more agile which have helped products and services to reach customers faster and with more efficiency. Even products like smartphones, high end laptops etc. depend on this network. This has helped the concept of connected society immensely.
- Web platforms have helped businesses to be in regular touch with each other. This is applicable for personal connections also.
- Virtual conferences, Seminars and Workshops have become very common in the midst of COVID-19 pandemic and they are slowly replacing the need for physical connect due to their benefits.
- The use of technology is also used in different parts of the world during the pandemic for combating the disease by ways of creating awareness. The use of drones and other techniques help in disease management and making sure that people take adequate precautions while moving around in their respective places. The Arogyasethu app is just an example of how technology is used to

protect people from the pandemic and at the same time facilitate movement of common man for work and to be connected.

Connected Society: Impact on The Society

Two decades back only human intelligence helped people to do business. Now it is human intelligence and artificial intelligence combined together which is shaping the society. This has happened due to the wide digitization which has happened across societies. We live in connected society interwoven together by technology and internet of things. We are now a technology society using artificial intelligence, robotics and web technology. It is challenging for the society but the same time extremely rewarding as we see business excellence in all spheres of life. Mobile phone has now become smart phone and its impact on connecting people and businesses together is absolutely vital. Now people are connected together and are doing businesses even during the pandemic due to the advanced technologies and use of smart phone.

Zoom, Cisco WebEx, Microsoft Team and other online platforms are also helping us to be interconnected. These social connecting platforms are helping in business meetings and online education. They are also helping people to connect with each other especially during the prevailing lockdown situation in most of the countries. They are replacing the traditional systems of education and making it cheaper. It will not be long before education will go completely online. This is true with companies also and we will see more and more employees working online.

Online will become realistic if the organizations can make the technology better and make internet available at each and every corner of the world. This is the real challenge as in India for example, more than 75% of the people in India do not have internet connection. It is not easy as infrastructure in India is not conducive for the connection in rural and interior places. States in India are encountering these problems by providing internet connections wherever possible and involving private players to make connection. Countries are trying to go online for all transactions and businesses by improving their infrastructure and connectivity.

Important Technology Developments of Connected Society (Digital Transformation)

- Internet of Things-Trend which reduces the distance between physical and virtual worlds which has helped people to be connected.
- Artificial Intelligence-Theory and development of computer systems to perform tasks normally done by human intelligence used in business for improved agility and efficiency.
- Industrial Revolution 4.0-Innovation which substitutes human intelligence in some skills which has revolutionized the business.
- Internet of People – IoP consists of interconnect growing population of users while promoting their continuous empowerment, preserving their control over their online activities. In short it can be considered as merging people with IoT.
- Robotics- Design, Operation and Application of Robots used in business.
- E-Commerce and M-Commerce – Technology advancements which have helped to increase speed, agility and efficiency of transactions.

All these innovations and technology developments have helped people to connect better and faster. This has helped businesses to be more agile and also more profitable. This concept of connected society is evolving every day which is paving the way for more and more innovations in the area.

Internet of Things (IoT)

Internet of things is defined as a system by which data can be transferred over a network without any human to human intervention. The IoT Healthcare Market is estimated to contribute $158.07 billion and 50 billion connected devices are expected to be there by 2020. The use of technology is improving the service delivery and efficiency. It is expected to contribute to the advancement of healthcare by the following features.

- Remote Patient Monitoring & Telehealth-Use of remote monitoring and use of technology has helped to reach rural places also and provide healthcare which in turn has helped to save money.
- Healthcare Information-Real time data using IOT is being developed in most healthcare systems in most of the countries.
- Robotics& Healthcare Automation-Robots is helping surgeons to perform surgeries with utmost precision and they are expected to take more active part by reducing the workload of employees in healthcare systems.
- Preventive healthcare and IOT- IOT is helping in predicting diseases and controlling chronic diseases. In countries like Singapore hospitals are using wearable or smart devices to track real time data of behaviour or problems in patients to help in preventing serious health problems.
- Hospital Information Systems- IOT can help in understanding information about drugs, doctors, patients, staff etc. to make sure that errors are reduced and efficiency is maintained with respect to management system.

In short Internet of things helps in changing the healthcare into more agile and efficient one. But for this the healthcare system will have to maintain ethical and social dimensions by following different rules and regulations of internet safety. This will make sure that healthcare system will be world class and will be able to help mankind. The challenge for any system is to make the system full proof and at the same time maintaining the cost.

Cloud Computing

The use of internet for adjusting remotely hosted system by using mobile or other devices is defined as cloud computing. It is used for operational efficiency, to create a business model, to connect different parts of society and in short to create a better business model. It is useful for online education for students, for daily use, for data storage, for value creation and optimizing time. It is also useful for chatbots, communication, advertisements and for easy implementation of advanced technology. Cloud computing is also important to stop piracy. Companies like Netflix uses cloud computing to reduce cost of doing business. Productivity is another factor which can be improved by cloud computing which also helps in our daily life. This also helps for multiple storages of data and to improve the performance of business. E-Commerce platforms can be made more efficient by usage of cloud computing. The important application of cloud computing is that it creates more career options thereby helping the societal development. These technologies are helping the people to connect to each other and make businesses more efficient.

Internet of People (IoP)

Many academic researchers have substantiated that internet increases sociability and there is a direct significant relationship between the internet and social autonomy (Castells et al 2007; Cardoso & Araújo,2010; World Internet Project,2012; Rainie &Wellman,2012). While Machine to Machine Communication is taking momentum, the next phase of IoT is considered as Internet of People (IoP). Internet of People refers to the digitalization of relationships between people and the collection, processing and application of personal data. Since IoP focuses on personal information collection, it can be considered as a learning medium of how people interact with sensory data. Social Devices and People as a Service (PaaS) are the planforms that combine together to support IoP infrastructure.

People as a service (PeaaS) is a mobile centric application that creates an opportunity for a third-party service provider to provide software and hardware tools to the target audience through internet. This mode allows the third-party user to collect a variety of information about an individual like moods, social status, health habits, etc. to define their digital projection. With the help of various data analytics tools a company can build a rich sociological profile of its customers through PeaaS. Social devices, an IoT Model, provides a platform to promote proactive triggering of interactions with other devices connected to Internet of Things (IoT). Smartphones, which is one of the popular Social devices, have emerged as the most popular social devices to orchestrate interactions between devices of co-located people.

Industry Revolution 4.0

Industry revolution 4.0 uses traditional manufacturing in combination with latest technologies. The term is now called as I4.0 or I4 came in the year 2011 from a German high tech strategy which helped in digitisation of manufacturing. Some of the main technologies used in this are internet of things, smart factory, Artificial Intelligence and cloud computing. This is changing the way we look at our business. It will change our lifestyle, work pattern, social life, privacy, businesses and in short the culture. The use of automation, technology, Internet of things and artificial intelligence in different facets of business and life are just examples. Businesses like Health care, Social Media, Supply chain, Education, Information Technology, Online etc. are highly influenced by the changes brought about by the revolution.

A new research report by Deloitte Global, *The Fourth Industrial Revolution is Here—Are You Ready?* in the year 2018 finds answers to some of the questions which are interesting. Industry 4.0 uses physical touch, technological advancements and internet of things to connect employees, customers and stakeholders. The study finds that more than 85% finds that social and economic stability can be maintained even with the revolution. Another surprising fact is that most companies are still adopting older methods of talent management than innovative disruptive new methods. Most of the respondents of the survey said that they are doing everything to create and maintain an innovative talent driven workforce.

There was also lack of internal communication to the organisation and lack of collaboration to the external parties involved. These slow down the process of adaptation of the organisation to the environment. The study shows importance of adaptation to the changes happening in the technology so that workforce can be maintained in the organisation but at the same time business challenges are met.

Another study on 4th industrial revolution (Schwab, 2016) talks about the challenges and opportunities of the revolution. The author mentioned that this revolution is exponential as growth and speed of changes is rapid. The report talks about challenges and opportunities of the revolution on human life, society and business.

MAIN CHALLENGES FOR CONNECTED SOCIETY

Connected Society- Ethical Dimension

Now the world is moving towards virtual connection and to a society which is connected technologically. When this happens legal aspects will come into the system as well. When we work as a single society connected by technology and internet, privacy issues will also come which will pave way for unethical practices. The internet of things will bring a lot of benefits in the way we live. But it can bring out whole lot of unethical practices like hacking and cyber-criminal activities. The study done by business insider finds that there will be 64 billion IoT users by the year 2025 which will make things easier for business to connect virtually. But this will also make the users susceptible for cyber-attacks, security issues and invasion into private data. There are a lot of examples of invasion of applications.

A study by Rigby (2019) analyses the use of artificial intelligence in health care and its ethical dimensions. The advantages of the usage are too many but we cannot neglect the invasion of the technology into the privacy and safety of the patient. The major limitation of the usage is that its ethical dimensions are not yet developed till date. The future will be more forthcoming to the use of artificial intelligence if we can integrate AI into the medicine by taking into account policy changes required for ethical part of it. The risks like patient safety, consent and other factors have to be considered before AI can give viable solutions for patient treatment. Different studies have pointed out the usage of artificial intelligence for different treatments including surgery to make it more efficient. So judicious use of technology in combination of human intervention by keeping ethical factors into consideration is the way forward in healthcare.

Neaman (2017) has also spoken about the ethical and social aspects of automation and internet of things. He views that technology, automation, internet of things etc. are here to stay. But at the same time frauds, cyber terrorism, invasion of privacy is also going to increase. The need of the hour is to hone the critical thinking and problem solving skills of the human resource so that they remain empowered. They have to be re-skilled so that they are up to date with the environment and also able to manoeuvre technology for their benefit to the society. The important step here is to make sure that our workforce is skilled in digital platforms and technical advancements and organisations are able to implement digitisation ethically and without causing any social dilemma.

These observations of different authors highlight the importance of keeping intact the ethical part of technology and artificial intelligence so that we can be connected 24 hours 365 days without any fear of invasion or hacking. There is no denying that technology will replace human beings to an extent but at the same time it is imperative that we maintain our integrity and our privacy intact. The successful organisations of the future will be those who can sustain a balance between technology and human intervention.

Royakkers et al (2018) in their article mentioned that digitization is important but at the same time ethical dimensions are also equally important. It is important to have an understanding of these issues and privacy and data protection are important from the point of view of users. There should not be any discrimination or usage of power in digitisation and also human values have to be considered while implementing any sort of digitisation.

These articles mentioned in the chapter emphasize the importance of effective implementation and usage of ethical practices. Any digitisation techniques can be considered only when ethics is given due consideration.

Other Challenges

Another challenge is to penetrate technology into the urban and rural sector. For this social media is playing an important role. Social media is helping all innovations to penetrate into the market due to the widespread advertisements and promotions.

One more challenge is to make industries like education to be flexible to adopt technology for virtual learning and working.

Social Media as Medium of Connection

Social media has become the all-time favourable medium among all age groups. The first ever social media website Six Degrees was launched in 1997. This enabled any user to create a profile and facilitate sharing of ideas and thoughts through virtual communities. Though the primary objective of the social media sites were to provide a platform for the user to interact with friends and family, many of the businesses have explored its potential to reach out to a massive and engaged audience.

Soomro and Hussain (2019) researched that with smartphones and internet connectivity getting cheaper, more number of people are using social media network sites .The statistics shows that there are around 2.77 billion people enjoying the benefits of sharing faster electronic communication in the form of personal information texts, videos, documents and photos. The other tech enabled activities that can be done through social media are blogging, video sharing, virtual worlds, social gaming, business networks etc. The most influential social media tool is social networking sites. This has created significant impact on the way an individuals and groups communicate with each other. The most popular social media sites are Facebook, Instagram, Twitter, LinkedIn, Google+ and Blogger. The recent studies show that the application of social networking sites have grown beyond personal use.

ROLE OF SOCIAL MEDIA IN CREATING CONNECTED SOCIETIES

Industry

Companies take the advantage of this medium to do the background check of its prospective candidates before hiring them.

Host interviews, virtual meetings & brainstorming sessions.

Business meetings can be conducted through google hangout/meet, Zoom etc.

Business communication & co-ordination through Slack, Trello and Asana.

Education Sector

Discussion forums, Online interviews & counselling, Online classes, project discussions. Online mentoring, proctored exam software like Mettl, WeCP etc.

News & Journalism – Online news articles and top news stories are instantly available through social media by making the society much more knowledgeable of the worldwide news and affairs.

Customer Decision Making

The global reach and interactive nature of social media have created an avenue for people to talk with each other, make recommendations and suggestion on any topic under the sun. The reviews available in the social media platforms are influencing the customer decision making process. People are relying such reviews heavily while choosing educational institutions, restaurants, products, companies etc. Ex: Hopkins Interactive: Alumni of John Hopkins University designed and created a social media platform called Hopkins Interactive where current and previous students can share their experiences/opinions about the college/University on a common platform (Pidaparthy,2011). his platform can be used as a collection of reviews and has become an important tool for prospective students to understand whether the University is a good match for them or not.

Virtual Communities

A virtual community is a social network of individuals who join a forum to discuss topics of mutual interest, potentially crossing geographical boundaries. The virtual communities can be formed based on specific user characteristics like age, gender, alma mater, religion, specific product/service users etc. The other themes of VC are fantasy games and emotional support for patients suffering from any health issues. Ex: Caring Bridge is an NGO which allows people suffering from various medical conditions and their relatives to communicate and share their medical conditions on a regular basis.

The virtual communities can be evolved based on work related activities as well. Communities of Practice (CoP) is a term referred for professional virtual communities. Ex: A company can launch a customer based virtual community to encourage its customers to openly share their queries and feedback with the company representatives.

Make One's Own Online Presence

Social media has empowered individuals to create their own media channels. This inherently creates an opportunity for an individual to control the entire process of production and dissemination of communication from his/her end to the rest of the world.

Non-Profit Organization

Most small-scale nonprofit organizations thrive mostly on word of mouth and local activities. But they are increasingly using social media to spread their messages & initiatives. These organizations also form online communities through their own websites, blogs, social media handles and endorsements from celebrities or through similar other associations. They need to leverage these communities mainly for donations and outreach. For Example, Akshaya Patra Foundation was endorsed by actress Shraddha Kapoor and Sachin Tendulkar endorses Apnalaya, a Mumbai based NGO working to improve education, health and livelihood of the underserved communities. More and more such organizations are building online societies to gain more visibility and donations to serve their respective causes.

Politics/Political Organization

The authors see millions of protests worldwide as well as in the home country. It is visible that a lot of things happening on online social platforms mattered for politics. With the rapid growth of Internet, a lot of people are engaging in political debate and discussion on social networking sites. "Around half of Americans have engaged in some form of political or social – minded activity on social media in the past year"(Anderson et al, 2018). In the wake of current events that fueled the frequency of the hashtags #me-too and black lives matter around America, social media communities have spread the movements like wild fire across the globe. Evidently, the importance of social media is increasingly becoming crucial in politically charged movements. Another example of connected societies can be seen through the online campaigns and online channels to boost your party's candidate. Political leaders like Ex US President Barack Obama and Indian Prime Minister Narendra Modi have created a strong online presence through their personal social media platforms. Both these leaders have a huge follower base on their twitter and Facebook accounts.

Information Media and Entertainment

With the advancement of Internet connectivity, creating online channels of information and news, people do not really need to wait for print media anymore. Modern societies are subjected to an increasing amount of information on a daily basis and we get details of what is going around the world real time through various channels and these entities enable creation and development of many connected societies. These mediums bring together a community of people who either support or question the kind of information they share. Such connected societies consist of viewers who follow certain news channels, blogs & vlogs, YouTube, Twitter, Facebook Instagram etc. According to Bhatia et al (2020) due to the exponential growth in information and technology, connections in different forms get created. These connections can be people-people, people-things and things –things and through these connections, a hyper connected society is formed. One such example is the arrest of George Floyd which was broadcasted on all media and this has brought together enormous amount of people to flock together and fight against police brutality.

Entertainment

Entertainment is another area that has resulted in creating connected societies. Many Hollywood movies are released across the globe and at the same time a lot of American and British series/sitcoms are also made available for everyone to see. Due to the gaining popularity of subscription mediums like Netflix and Amazon Prime, everyone can watch anything that is available on these platforms, sometimes in their own regional language. Followers of Game of Thrones series by HBO formed multiple digital communities to discuss about the show, actors, storyline, locations and a lot of other aspects associated with the show.

Healthcare

Not just in the advancement of internet but the emergence of mobile technology has led patients and carers to increasingly search online about information on illness, symptoms treatments and providers. There exists a community of people who provide reviews, personal experiences which connect patients and providers to enable better health outcomes. According to a report by Taylor (2015),mental health apps have improved patient outcomes for example connecting people with similar issues, bringing together people with similar illness on a single platform etc to engage them better. Resorting to technology in cases of mental health problems can bring down the stigma of being physically present and seeking support. For example, there are multiple for new mothers to discuss, share advice and tips about raising children. In the UK, under the NHS (National Health Service) has created a community of agencies and professionals who can provide assistance and care for people at the end of their life. The information and wishes about the patients along with a carefully developed treatment/care plan are transmitted electronically to these agencies. This service is known to have a significant impact on palliative care in London.

Public Services

By enabling development in public services, participation of people in government operations has increased through E-government and M-government. This way it is easier to bring the government closer to its people. With better integrated communication and interaction through online portals and social media platforms, people form communities that help improve efficiency and services through problem sharing, tracking and resolution.

Some of the major public offices have a social presence like a Twitter profile or a Facebook page through which they share information, interact with their followers and promote their activities. @ PMOIndia is the official twitter handle of the Office of the Prime Minister of India. Many Indian cities have their own traffic police handles where they interact and share awareness with the people. This brings efficiency in governing since they are publicly answerable on these social platforms in case of any issues and simultaneously creates a link between the citizen and the Office. Such communities created also reduced the chances of officials getting corrupted as a result of their online and public presence.

DISCUSSIONS

The chapter discussed 6 major areas: Internet of People and Internet of Things, Industry 4.0, Technologies and Digital Transactions, Social Media Impact, Ethical Dimensions, Connected Society -Opportunities and Solutions.

Internet of People and Internet of Things

Future is digital and future is virtual. Automation and cloud computing are going to change the way world is looking into. Supply chain for example is now fully automated with robotics and artificial intelligence and with minimal human intervention. Similarly, business processes are now digitally transformed which is making them lean, profitable and nimble. At the same time people are connected digitally for interaction. For example, education is now virtual and technology is playing a big part in imparting knowledge. The major challenge faced by individuals and companies in connecting each other are cyber security problems which must be tackled by proper mechanisms of security and better education of concerned stakeholders.

Industry 4.0

Industry 4.0 has brought a revolution in terms of usage of automation and technology in manufacturing and service industries. These changes have resulted in digital transformation and through that the concept of connected society. This impact is discussed in the chapter.

Technologies and Digital Transformations

This era is different in terms of how the companies work. Digital transformations and technological advancements are reshaping the structure of the organizations. Data is becoming very important and concepts like big data and artificial intelligence are changing the way departments work. Strategy development is now incorporating digital transformations. How can we transform digitally? One way of doing this is to invest individually and as a company. If companies and employees are ready to embrace the changes then adaptation and adoption become easy. Here the role of government is equally important in terms of initiatives and investment.

Social Media Impact

Social media is important for all industries including nonprofit organizations for connecting all concerned stakeholders. We can't think about a world without twitter, Facebook, LinkedIn etc. These are important for connecting companies as well as individuals. Cyber-attacks are common in social media and maintaining security is going to be the challenge and both governments and companies have to work together for safe usage of these social media channels.

Ethical Challenges

Different articles indicted the importance of ethics and cyber-attacks. It is therefore important to consider strong laws and measures to curb these issues and keep human values and privacy intact. This is one area which requires utmost focus as an invasion into the privacy of individuals can jeopardize the benefits of digital transformation and connected society.

CONNECTED SOCIETY- CHALLENGES AND SOLUTIONS

Society is connected virtually and this is the future. The main challenges and solutions are discussed in the next section.

SOLUTIONS AND RECOMMENDATIONS

As mentioned in the chapter there are two broad areas of concern for connected society.

- One is ethical dimensions and the other is reach. Social media is helping to bridge the gap between consumers and technology whereas judicious use of technology in combination with proper education and implementation of safety measures will help in converting unethical practices to ethical way of doing things.
- Second concern is to make industries like education to be flexible to adopt technology to meet the needs of customers. This can be done by improving infrastructure and by educating the stakeholders especially students and teachers. Social media channels have helped in virtually connecting people from different cultures which is helping the growth of the society. The table below will summarize the discussion.
- Improving the reach of internet and how this can be penetrated to rural sector. Countries s like have a large rural population and internet connectivity is very less there. The challenge is to make sure that connectivity reaches in every village in the world.
- Interpreting the data and managing huge network requires usage of big data analysis and clod computing.
- This kind of data storage and handling will require the support of government and in a lot of countries priority is not there for digitalization. Also, proper designing of the network requires huge investment and manpower which is also a challenge.

Table 2. Challenges and solutions

Challenges	Solutions
Ethical and Safety Issues.	Education. Combination of technology with human intervention. Workforce Motivation. Stringent Measures of Safety.
Reach.	Better Infrastructure. Social Media. Investment.
Adoption.	Need Generation. Education of Stakeholders. Social Media impact.
Management of Data.	Big Data Analytics. Manpower Education.
Lack of Government Support &Investment.	Education of stakeholders in the benefits of digitization.

FUTURE RESEARCH

This chapter has focused on the main advantages of technology in connected society and main challenges.

- Future research can focus on the analytical side of this by using structured questionnaire and understand the independent and dependent variables and propose a model for Connected Society in practice.
- We have only considered some challenges and solutions but an empirical research will help in getting more focused approach in adopting technology and giving a true meaning to the concept of connected society.
- Future research can focus on analyzing impact of digital transformation on connected society and how strong is the relationship.
- Researchers can focus on understanding the effect of connectivity and infrastructure on the functioning of connected society.
- There will be a difference in the concept and its application based on culture and social parameters which can be studied
- Country specific studies can also be conducted for digital transformation and impact on connected society.

CONCLUSION

The chapter has given the basic elements of connected society and the challenges of the concept. Though technology has made it possible for us to be connected it has also made us vulnerable with respect to safety. There are a lot of benefits of connected society especially in this era of pandemic where everything is virtual. Individual or corporate connections are possible due to the impact of this digital transformation. Industries from healthcare to consumer durables to education are now dependent on digitization and connected society.

There are a lot of challenges. Internet connectivity and penetration (for example in a country like India it is roughly 40%) which is not very high is a major hurdle. Educating concerned stakeholders is another major stumbling block. Cyber-attacks and ethical issues are also very important. If we can manage the ethical dimensions and at the same time improve the infrastructure, then we as a society will benefit a lot especially during these times of pandemic and where everything is virtual.

The methods and improvements which we will implement now will help in aligning ourselves to an era where all enterprises will work virtually and physical proximity will no longer be required. It is vital for solving the major challenges in the future as trade is now global and culture is now integrated. Digital Transformation and through that interconnected society are the channels of growth globally and all of us should strive for this. Enterprises have to be ready with digital transformations and be connected virtually to make sure they remain competitive in this challenging era.

REFERENCES

Anderson, M., Toor, S., Rainie, L., & Smith, A. (2018). Public attitudes toward political engagement on social media. *Pew Research Center.* Retrieved from: https://www. pewinternet. org/2018/07/11/public-attitudes-toward-political engagement-on-social-media

Bahia, K., & Suardi, S. (2019). *Connected Society: The State of Mobile Internet Connectivity*. GSMA.

Bhatia, R., Kapoor, S., & Arai, K. (2020). Advances in Information and Communication*: Proceedings of the 2020 Future of Information and Communication Conference (FICC)*, Volume 1. Springer.

Cardoso, G., & Araújo, V. (2009). Out of information and into communication. Networked communication and Internet usage. *Worldwide internet: Changing societies, economies and cultures, 23.*

Castells, M. (2006). *The theory of the network society*. Great Britain by MPG Books Ltd.

Castells, M., Roca, M., Sancho, T., & Tubella, I. (2007). La transición a la sociedad red (No. Sirsi i9788434442719). Barcelona: Ariel.

Chanias, S., Myers, M. D., & Hess, T. (2019). Digital transformation strategy making in pre-digital organizations: The case of a financial services provider. *The Journal of Strategic Information Systems, 28*(1), 17–33. doi:10.1016/j.jsis.2018.11.003

Choi, A. J. (2014, November). Internet of things: Evolution towards a hyper-connected society. In *2014 IEEE Asian Solid-State Circuits Conference (A-SSCC)* (pp. 5-8). IEEE. 10.1109/ASSCC.2014.7008846

Chung, S. A., Park, S., & Lee, S. (2017). The era of hyper-connected society and the changes in business activities: Focusing on information blocking and acquisition activities. *International Journal of Management and Applied Science, 3*(4), 16–21.

Davenport, T. H., & Redman, T. C. (2020). *Digital Transformation Comes Down to Talent in 4 Key areas.* Retrieved from https://store.hbr.org/product/digital-transformation-comes-down-to-talent-in-4-key-areas/H05N4Y

Deloitte Touche Tohmatsu (Firm). (2018). *The Fourth Industrial Revolution is here: are you ready?* Author.

Dijk, J. V. (2012). *The network society* (3rd ed.). Academic Press.

Ebert, C., & Duarte, C. H. C. (2018). Digital Transformation. *IEEE Software, 35*(4), 16–21. doi:10.1109/MS.2018.2801537

Fredette, J., Marom, R., Steiner, K., & Witters, L. (2012). The promise and peril of hyperconnectivity for organizations and societies. *The global information technology report, 2012*, 113-119.

Hausberg, J. P., Liere-Netheler, K., Packmohr, S., Pakura, S., & Vogelsang, K. (2019). Research streams on digital transformation from a holistic business perspective: A systematic literature review and citation network analysis. *Journal of Business Economics, 89*(8-9), 931–963. doi:10.100711573-019-00956-z

Hiltz, S. R., & Turoff, M. (1978). *The Network Nation Reading*. Addison-Wesley.

Leberecht, T. (2012). *Shaping the values of our connected world.* Retrieved from https://www.weforum.org/agenda/2012/11/shaping-the-values-of-our-connected-world

Manda, M. I., & Backhouse, J. (2018). Inclusive digital transformation in South Africa: an institutional perspective. In *Proceedings of the 11th International Conference on Theory and Practice of Electronic Governance* (pp. 464-470). 10.1145/3209415.3209486

Martin, J. (1978). *The wired society*. Prentice-Hall.

Neaman, R. (2017). *Empowerment is the key to a connected society*. Retrieved from: https://www.computerweekly.com/opinion/Empowerment-is-the-key-to-a-connected-society

Panori, A., Kakderi, C., Komninos, N., Fellnhofer, K., Reid, A., & Mora, L. (2020). Smart systems of innovation for smart places: Challenges in deploying digital platforms for co-creation and data-intelligence. *Land Use Policy*, 104631. doi:10.1016/j.landusepol.2020.104631

Pidaparthy, U. (2011). *How colleges use, misuse social media to reach students*. CNN Tech.

Rainie, H., & Wellman, B. (2012). *Networked: The new social operating system* (Vol. 419). MIT Press. doi:10.7551/mitpress/8358.001.0001

Reis, J., Amorim, M., Melão, N., & Matos, P. (2018, March). Digital transformation: a literature review and guidelines for future research. In *World conference on information systems and technologies* (pp. 411-421). Springer. 10.1007/978-3-319-77703-0_41

Rigby, M. J. (2019). Ethical dimensions of using artificial intelligence in health care. *AMA Journal of Ethics*, *21*(2), 121–124. doi:10.1001/amajethics.2019.121

Royakkers, L., Timmer, J., Kool, L., & van Est, R. (2018). Societal and ethical issues of digitization. *Ethics and Information Technology*, *20*(2), 127–142. doi:10.100710676-018-9452-x

Schwab, K. (2016). *The 4th Industrial Revolution: What It Means, How to Respond*. Retrieved from: https://www.ge.com/news/reports/the-4th-industrial-revolution-what-it-means-how-to-respond

Silver, L. (2019). *Smartphone Ownership Is Growing Rapidly Around the World, but Not Always Equally*. Pew Research Center.

Soomro, T. R., & Hussain, M. (2019). Social Media-Related Cybercrimes and Techniques for Their Prevention. *Applied Computer Systems*, *24*(1), 9–17. doi:10.2478/acss-2019-0002

Taylor, K. (2015). *Connected health: how digital technology is transforming health and social care*. Deloitte Centre for Health Solutions.

Van Dijk, J. A. G. M. (1991). De Netwerk-maatschappij, Sociale aspecten van nieuwe media [The network society, social aspects]. *Digital Media*, 163.

Verhoef, P. C., Broekhuizen, T., Bart, Y., Bhattacharya, A., Dong, J. Q., Fabian, N., & Haenlein, M. (2019). Digital transformation: A multidisciplinary reflection and research agenda. *Journal of Business Research*.

Wellman, B. (2001). Physical place and cyberplace: The rise of personalized networking. *International Journal of Urban and Regional Research*, *25*(2), 227–252. doi:10.1111/1468-2427.00309

Wellman, B., Quan-Haase, A., Boase, J., Chen, W., Hampton, K., Díaz, I., & Miyata, K. (2003). The social affordances of the Internet for networked individualism. *Journal of Computer-Mediated Communication, 8*(3).

World Internet Project. (2012). *International Report* (4th ed.). Retrieved from: http://www.worldinternetproject.net/_files/_Published/_oldis /770_2012wip_report4th_ed.pdf

KEY TERMS AND DEFINITIONS

Connected Society: The connected society means a society in which people and people, people and objects, things and things, online and offline, one to one, one to many and many to many are connected using digital technology or the digital based society that stores, analyses and manages data collected by sensors and mobile terminals through a network.

Digitization: This is a process in which information is changed from physical entity to a digital format.

Enterprise: According to Cambridge dictionary, an enterprise is an organisation or a business entity formulated to earn money.

Industry Revolution 4.0: Industry revolution 4.0 uses traditional manufacturing in combination with latest technologies. The term is now called as I4.0 or I4 came in the year 2011 from a German high-tech strategy which helped in digitisation of manufacturing.

Internet of People: Internet of people refers to the digitalization of relationships between people and the collection, processing, and application of personal data. Since IoP focuses on personal information collection, it can be considered as a learning medium of how people interact with sensory data.

Internet of Things: Internet of things is defined as a system by which data can be transferred over a network without any human to human intervention.

Social Media as Medium of Connection: Social media has become the all-time favourable medium among all age groups. The first ever social media website Six Degrees was launched in 1997. This enabled any user to create a profile and facilitate sharing of ideas and thoughts through virtual communities.

Strategy: It is a general plan to achieve one or more long-term or overall goals under conditions of uncertainty.

Chapter 12
Digital Business Transformation in Ports:
IoT Applications in Port Management and Strategies

Murat Selçuk Solmaz
https://orcid.org/0000-0002-8528-2865
Piri Reis University, Turkey

ABSTRACT

This chapter discusses using Internet of Things (IoT) technology in port management and strategies in the scope of digital business transformation. Many businesses around the world have begun to take advantage of digital technology in recent years. Ports are one of the building blocks of the maritime industry, which aims to increase its profitability by digitizing in today's increasingly competitive conditions. In recent years, IoT technology has been used extensively for digitalization in ports. This chapter introduces the current and potential uses of IoT technology in ports and to give an idea about how IoT technology will create an opportunity to develop the ports and to solve problems in ports.

INTRODUCTION

As digital transformation offers a number of opportunities for organizations (Wessel, Baiyere, Ologeanu-Taddei, Cha, & Jensen, 2020), many businesses around the world have started to adapt to digital transformation and take advantage of digital technology in recent years. Because, making use of digital technology enables one to do things in less time, need fewer employees, reduce costs, use information and resources effectively, produce the most products with the least resources and consequently increase the profitability of the enterprises. The term transformation refers to a fundamental change in the organization that has a major impact on the organization's strategy, the structure of the organization, and the distribution of power in the organization (Berghaus and Back, 2016). The term digital transformation can be explained as organizational transformation in the digital age where market demands are driven

DOI: 10.4018/978-1-7998-8587-0.ch012

by developments in information technologies (Tanniru, Xi, & Sandhu, 2020). Information technology is the technology that includes the development, maintenance and use of computer systems, software and networks for data processing and distribution. (Al Amoush, & Sandhu, 2020a). Of course, the transition from a classical business to a digital business is difficult and time-consuming. However, the magnitude of the results to be obtained and the fact that it provides effective solutions to the problems faced by the business raises the appetite for Digital Business Transformation (DBT) in all sectors. DBT aims to achieve organizational change through the use of digital technologies to materially improve performance in a business. However, in order to achieve organizational change, systems consisting of digital technologies must first be integrated into the enterprises.

The philosophy of IOT technology can be defined as the fact that every object in the world is connected to the internet and each other. Mobile phones, tablets, and computers make up the largest proportion of internet-connected objects today. With the development of internet infrastructure and the increase in internet speed, the number of objects connected to the internet is increasing day by day. In this way, it is aimed to make all kinds of non-smart objects smart and to create a smart world as a result. This idea reveals the IOT concept. Nowadays, IOT has started to be used in many applications such as smart transportation and smart city (Singh, Rathore, & Park, 2020). Every object connected to the internet generates information and this information can be stored through the internet. This information is very valuable information in the commercial area. Because these reflect people's habits, behaviors, and desires. The most valuable aspect of smart systems is that they produce this valuable information. Information generated by objects that are not connected to the internet is lost. In the coming years, with the connection of all objects to the internet, the information produced by each object will be recorded and processed.

Ports have accelerated DBT in recent years in order to carry out all activities in the complex environment in the ports in the fastest, most practical and least costly way, to ensure good port management, and to determine the short, medium, and long term strategic plans accurately. In this context, they have started to benefit from various information technologies. IOT is one of the leading information technologies, which is being used in port management and determining port strategies, and its areas of use are increasing. Therefore, the research question in this study is, "Can IOT provide solutions to problems in port management and strategies to achieve digital transformation in ports?" determined as. As a result of the literature review, it has been determined that IOT has started to be used in many areas such as supply chain management and cargo tracking at ports, optimizing port traffic and port equipment, the transition from classical systems to digital systems, standardization, calculation of port performance indicators, green port applications, and port security. In the study, applications conducted with IOT technology in ports are examined under subgroups related to port management and strategies. The aim of the section is to introduce the potential uses of IOT technology in port management and strategies within DBT and to provide insight into how IOT technology will create an opportunity to solve current and potential problems in ports.

BACKGROUND

Digital Business Transformation (DBT)

DBT refers to the digital transformation that must be done in a business to meet today's needs. The reason why digital transformation is mandatory for all businesses is that businesses that cannot keep up with today's conditions are at risk of extinction in a brutally competitive environment. The transition speed of our world to digital systems gained speed with the COVID-19 pandemic that affected the whole world in early 2020. The vast majority of employees have begun to work in the home office system. Therefore, even the presence of empty stately buildings of companies has been questioned. Because the ability to access information from anywhere through the internet has removed the importance of the office. Pandemic has prompted many businesses that have already moved towards digitalization to think more about what they can do about more digitalization.

Businesses are trying to find the easiest and fastest solutions to the needs of their customers in our world, where all kinds of information can be reached from mobile phones in seconds. Instant access to customers' needs is now a deciding factor for customers' selection of the business they will receive services from, and businesses compete to deliver their services instantly and in real-time (Tanniru, Xi, & Sandhu, 2020). Manual operations in businesses quickly become history. Through many advantages such as the ease of processing, storing, and accessing information in digital media, saving paper and storage space spent for manual records, automation, e-commerce, ease of payment, digital signature, information security, providing managers with instant information about the status of the business, the DBT, which provides organizational transformation in enterprises, will inevitably occur.

Many authors have worked on DBT. Working on leadership to advance innovation in digital healthcare transformation, Tanniru, Xi, and Sandhu (2020) have combined Complexity Theory with HeXie Management Theory and multiple leadership processes (administrative, enabling, and adaptive) around four guiding principles and use them to discuss how these principles guide healthcare transformation. Al Amoush and Sandhu (2020a) have conducted a review of digital transformation in the higher education sector and have revealed students' perspectives on the factors affecting digital learning management system implementation. The authors also conducted research on how the implementation of digital learning management systems affects the learning perspective of educators in the higher education sector Al Amoush and Sandhu (2020b). Basole (2016) emphasized the importance of using four technological factors such as mobile, social, analytics, and cloud to reshape businesses with application programming interfaces to accelerate digital transformation. Reddy and Reinartz (2017) define DBT as the use of the internet and computers to reach economic value. Gölzer and Fritzsche (2017) argued that DBT can be explained in terms of Industry 4.0, which includes components such as the IOT and big data solutions for big data applications in industrial operations management. Ashwell (2017) approached the issue in terms of organized-based intelligence models to understand and counter organized crime networks and defined DBT as the relationship between data, digital technology, and people. Von Leipzig et al. (2017) stated that digitization shapes part of Industry 4.0, which overcomes the barriers to the digitization and shapes a business model for better efficiency and effectiveness. Li (2018) stated that DBT refers to converting traditional business methods into a digital format. Weill and Woerner (2018) argued that the purpose of digital transformation is to use digital capabilities to turn a traditional business into top performance. Choi et al. (2003) investigated the way to reduce development time and improve software quality through standardization in developing enterprise resource planning systems for container terminals. Heilig et al. (2017) analyzed the marine logistics environment with game theory to enable digital transformation in ports and evaluated that DBT can refer to the digitalization and transformation of an organization through various contexts such as cultural, technological, and governance strategy. They also state that the success of digital transformation lies not only in the use of advanced technologies and methods, but especially in the adaptation of organizational aspects according to the notion that "digital technology is not a goal, but a tool". Carlan et al. (2017) analyzed recent digitalization projects and initiatives to improve information flows, cargo flows, track vehicles, and cargoes. As the strategic values that contribute greatly to the economies of the countries, it is evaluated that ports can find solutions to many business problems, increase their customers, reduce their costs, and thus maximize their profits with the DBT. In order to understand the issue better, firstly information about Port Management and Strategies then IOT technology will be given.

Port Management and Strategies

Ports play an important role in the world economy as part of international trade. According to 2018 figures (Worldbank, 2019a), the gross domestic product of the world is approximately US $ 85,791 trillion. Considering the monetary value of the products exported in world trade, it is seen that the figure is the US $ 19.6 trillion (Worldbank, 2019b). It is known that seventy-five percent of this trade is carried out by sea (Solmaz, & Koray, 2020). When it is evaluated as weight, it is seen that the amount of cargo carried by sea is 11 billion tons (United Nations Conference on Trade and Development [UNCTAD], 2019). This cargo is loaded and unloaded in ships at ports; some cargoes are loaded and unloaded more than once by transfer. Ports carry the biggest burden of international trade on their shoulders.

The ranking of world ports by the amount of cargo handled is in Table-1. When the table is analyzed, it is seen that all of the ports in the first twenty places are located in Southeast Asia and Australia, except two. These two ports are Rotterdam from the Netherlands and South Louisiana from the United States. Among the 20 ports, 13 ports are the ports of the People's Republic of China. As can be seen from the table, most of the cargo transported by sea in the world is transported through these ports. The fact that this huge amount of cargo can be handled most effectively in ports requires very good port management. Good port management finds the most optimal solutions by using the data it has obtained. It uses operational research techniques to complete jobs in the shortest time, easiest and least costly. As a result, it tries to satisfy its customers and maximize its profits.

Ports are not only the places where the cargo is loaded and unloaded on the ships but also part of the logistics system. The basis of logistics is the integration and optimization of different processes and functions to increase customer satisfaction and reduce costs. Unlike the economic and commercial approach, the logistics approach combines transport with other components such as production, storage, inventory management, marketing, and procurement. Based on this, the ports are considered to be logistics and distribution centers where the services and goods movement in the entire transportation and logistics chain are optimized and added value is provided to the goods. It is an opinion accepted by everyone that ports are logistics centers. It is seen that the best and most efficiently managed ports in the world are the best logistics and value-added ports. For this reason, it is expected from the port manager to understand the different aspects of logistics management in the context of the port. (Institute of Chartered Shipbrokers [ICS], 2007)

Table 1. Global top 20 ports by cargo throughput (2017)

Rank	Port	Country	Cargo Throughput (Million tons)
1	Ningbo-Zhoushan	China	1007
2	Shanghai	China	706
3	Singapore	Republic of Singapore	626
4	Suzhou	China	608
5	Guangzhou	China	566
6	Tangshan	China	565
7	Qingdao	China	508
8	Hedland	Australia	505
9	Tianjin	China	503
10	Rotterdam	Netherlands	467
11	Dalian	China	451
12	Busan	Republic of Korea	401
13	Yingkou	China	363
14	Rizhao	China	360
15	South Louisiana	USA	308
16	Gwangyang	Republic of Korea	292
17	Yantai	China	286
18	Hong Kong	Hong Kong SAR	282
19	Zhanjiang	China	282
20	Huanghua	China	270
	Total		9354

Data Source: (UNCTAD, 2018)

Ports provide both cargo and ship-related services. Many complex operations within the port should be coordinated to ensure that these services don't fail. These operations should be planned in the most efficient way to provide port services effectively. Port management should make sure that all data are correct and reliable before planning. In classical methods, this data is obtained by entering the information collected at the ports into computers. During this process, mistakes can be made for various reasons during the data recording and entering the system, and as a result, the decision-makers can make false conclusions because the data is not correct. Excluding the geographical region where the cargo is to be transported, considering the shipowners who are among the most important customers of the ports, the most important of the port preference criteria is the shortest duration of the ship's stay in the port and the minimum port dues paid for the service it received. Shipowners also attach importance to the quality of the services they receive at the port. Port administrations try to minimize the duration of ships staying in the port without sacrificing quality and to reduce the port dues of their services compared to rival ports. In this way, they try to increase customer satisfaction and accordingly the number of customers. Today, ports have started to use digital technology to maximize their profits by planning the needs of ships, other transportation vehicles, cargo, and logistics systems in the best way, thus increasing the number of customers and customer satisfaction. Many ports around the world have begun to build their management and strategies on digital business management. While doing this, they make great use of IOT applications.

IOT Technology

IOT is considered as a network of physical objects. Objects connected to IOT can be machines, buildings, vehicles, appliances, animals, plants, and people. All physical objects are interconnected and can exchange data with each other without human intervention. These objects can be controlled remotely. Although IOT has become a remarkable concept in recent years, its first works date back to the 1980s. The first object connected to the internet in 1982 is a coffee machine at Carnegie Mellon University. But the term IOT was first introduced by British entrepreneur Kevin Ashton in his presentation to Procter & Gamble in 1999. At that time, the vision of IOT was based on RFID (radio frequency identification). IOT has become increasingly popular in recent years due to the combination of various technologies such as microcontrollers, sensors, wireless communication, embedded systems, and microelectromechanical systems. Today, IOT is seen as the next big thing, the future of the internet. It is estimated that there will be approximately 100 billion IOT devices by 2025. (Xiao, 2018)

IOT concept has been defined by many authors and institutions. IOT covers a world vision where billions of objects with built-in intelligence, communication tools, and detection and operation features will be connected over Internet Protocol networks (Cirani, Ferrari, Picone, & Veltri, 2019). IOT expresses the tight connection between the digital and the physical world (Ray, 2018). All devices that have the ability to connect to the internet and exchange data, from very simple sensor devices connected to the internet to devices with very complex cloud servers, constitute IOT (Ammar, Russello, & Crispo, 2018). IOT is a global infrastructure that is based on existing and evolving interoperable information and communication technologies, enabling advanced services by connecting physical and virtual things together (International Telecommunication Union [ITU], 2012). The elements that make up the IoT can be listed as follows. An internet network that can meet all the needs of the system; objects that can collect information through their sensors, connect to the internet, send the information they collect, and apply it by receiving commands sent to it. IOT makes objects smart by taking advantage of basic technologies such as widespread computer usage, communication capabilities, internet protocols, and applications so that objects can be remotely controlled with the ability to connect to the internet network, can be integrated with the real world easily and less human intervention can occur (Ammar et al., 2018). Data storage, processing, and analytical operations on data are essential requirements for enriching raw IOT data and converting them into useful information. Stored Big Data can be processed by new mechanisms, such as deep learning, to transform raw data generated by connected objects into useful information. Useful information will then be distributed to relevant devices and interested users or stored for further processing and access. (Cirani et al., 2019) Through the use of IOT, reliable data will be provided by analyzing the information received from the sensors. Using IOT technology instead of analog systems will provide real information. By compiling and analyzing this information with artificial intelligence programs, reliable data will be reached to help us make decisions. Reliable data is very important for making the right decisions. The most important benefits of IOT technology for us are the acquisition of reliable data. Through the right decisions, it will improve efficiency, safe working environment, and sustainability in enterprises.

The waiting period of forty years since the IOT concept first emerged in the 1980s can be considered too long. However, what is needed here is not only a ripening period for the idea to come to life but also the need to wait for the infrastructure to be ready for the system. To date, IOT technology could not be implemented at the designed concept level. The reasons for this are; insufficient internet infrastructure that is for all objects to be connected to the internet without any problems, to store information from objects, to create and process big data; lack of 5G cellular network technologies that support the speed at which objects connect to the internet; and the lack of technology to produce sensors that make objects smart. In addition, microchip technology has been expected to develop so that the sensors that would be put on them to make objects smart were as small as possible. Today, the number of internet-connected objects is estimated to be around 6 billion. With the transition to 5G technology in 2020, it is estimated that the number of devices connected to the internet will reach 100 billion in 2025. Another issue preventing the development of IOT was the concern caused by the security weakness of the system. To prevent abuse of the system by malicious people and to confirm that the system is completely secure, some security applications have been developed. It is evaluated that IOT can be used securely with its encrypted structure (Solmaz, & Koray, 2020) that blockchain technology, which has entered our lives in recent years, cannot be decoded. In his article, Kshetri (2017) states that, through its distributed, auditable and reliable structure, the blockchain can provide a solution to ensure IOT security. Blockchain technology will enable IOT devices to be reliably interconnected, creating secure networks by avoiding threats such as device counterfeiting and impersonation (Dickson, 2016). The decentralized distributed structure of blockchain provides a natural adaptation to the need for IOT protection, and the fact that the information recorded in the blockchain cannot be changed prevents the devices from trying to connect to the network with forged signatures to hide (Kumar, 2017). In addition, in their study, Singh, Rathore, and Park (2020) created the IOT network with a blockchain-based architecture and evaluated this structure as secure against cyber attacks.

RESEARCH METHODOLOGY

As the research question of the study, "Can IOT technology provide solutions to problems in port management and strategies to achieve digital transformation in ports?" has been determined. A qualitative research method was used in the research. In this context, firstly the studies about IOT technology in the world's ports have been examined through literature review and data have been collected. This data has been categorized under subgroups related to port management and strategies. The categorized information has been compared with the problems experienced in ports today. Then, IOT technology can find a solution to what kind of problems in port management and strategies in the future, and thus how IOT technology can contribute to digital business transformation has been evaluated.

INTERNET OF THINGS (IOT) APPLICATIONS IN PORT MANAGEMENT AND STRATEGIES

Ports have started to use digital technology in recent years in order to carry out all their activities in complex port environments in the fastest, most practical, and least cost, that is, to provide successful port management. IOT technology comes first among these digital technologies. In this section, examples of IOT technology, which have started to be applied in world ports, are examined and evaluations about what problems IOT technology in the future can solve in port management and strategies are made.

Supply Chain Management and Cargo Tracking

Supply chain management in maritime transport is the planning and management of the process from the time the logistics company takes cargo to delivery. Shippers' greatest expectation is to transport their goods at the lowest cost and safely. In increasingly competitive environment, reducing costs without reducing the quality and safety of transportation requires making the right decisions at every stage of transportation. Therefore, it is necessary to successfully observe every stage of transportation. (Solmaz, & Koray, 2020) Nowadays, various studies are being carried out to realize cargo tracking in real-time. Studies are generally focused on container tracking. With the signals sent by the IOT sensors placed on the containers, the containers can be monitored in real-time. By sharing this information, the owner of the cargo can also track the cargo.

An example of this is the joint initiative of IBM and Maersk. The aim of the initiative is to develop an open digitization platform designed to be used by the entire industry to enable digital tracking of goods. In this way, it will be ensured that the goods moving in the supply chain can be followed by all actors, and a very simple exchange of information and paperless trade will be provided. In this way, time and costs will decrease. (UNCTAD, 2018) Semtech Corporation, a semiconductor supplier in Cork port, Ireland's second busiest port, has started to use Wireless RF Technology to monitor containers by integrating it into the IOT network of Cork Port. The entire IOT network solution was designed by an IOT network service provider Net Feasa. The sensors placed on the containers allow the opening and closing of the doors of the containers to be detected, to monitor the temperature of the sensitive cargo, and to monitor the movement of the container from end to end. It transmits this information to both the cargo owner and the port staff. Sensors that don't require GPS use very low battery power and their battery life lasts 20 years. (Internet of Business, n.d.a) As another example, the Hyundai Merchant Marine Company and other consortium members in September 2017 may be given pilot studies for shipment reservation and cargo delivery, for blockchain applications using safe paperless processes. In this study, it is aimed to monitor and manage reefer containers on board in real time by using blockchain applications together with IOT. (Kang, 2017) A project called Container 42 was launched with the collaboration of Rotterdam port, IBM, Cisco, and Esri companies. With this project, it is aimed to make the containers smart. The container prepared for the project is equipped with sensors and communication technology and is left to travel around the world to collect data for two years. Data to be recorded includes vibrations, inclination, location, noise, air pollution, humidity, and temperature. (Weare42, n.d.) By making the containers smart as stated above, information such as the location of the container, security status, physical conditions, damage status, atmosphere, humidity, water in the container can be shared, online reservations of the containers can be made, and the payments are made automatically, transactions related to insurance and situations affecting insurance will be done much faster and fairer.

Optimizing Port Traffic

Traffic in the ports mainly consists of the sea traffic generated by the ships coming to the port for loading and unloading, the land traffic created by the trucks that bring goods to or from the port, and the railway traffic created by the trains coming and going to the port in the ports with railway connections. In addition, there is traffic generated by pilot boats, tugboats, port equipment such as mobile harbor cranes, straddle carriers, tractor and chassis, automatic guided vehicles, ship loaders, unloaders, reclaimers, stackers, as well as port workers moving inside vehicles. The movement of all these vehicles and equipment mentioned above creates a very large amount of traffic within the port. Failure to regulate this traffic well can cause chaos within the port.

In today's technologies, communication between ships, terminal operators, pilots, tugs, and employees in ports is based on traditional radio and radar communication. This type of communication both causes time loss and causes the information to not be used sufficiently. For this reason, decisions that can mostly be achieved with optimum results cannot be made, which can lead to time losses, money losses, and an unsafe working environment. With IOT technology, ship and land traffic can be arranged optimally in ports. When the ships arrive at the port, they can take their place in the docks without waiting. Once the ships are docked, the cargo can be ready at the dock and the ship can begin loading without any delay. Ships arriving for unloading can start unloading immediately, with the discharge equipment ready on time at the dock. IOT can provide synchronization between the port, ships, and cargo owners to optimize traffic flows and minimize congestion and operation time for all operators (Belfkih, Duvallet, & Sadeg, 2017).

The Port of Rotterdam, together with IBM, has started a project that aims to digitize the operational environment of the port using IOT technologies since 2018. The project also aims to prepare the Port of Rotterdam to host smart ships in the future. This project is aimed at safer and more efficient traffic management at the port. For this purpose, IOT sensors have been started to be equipped to cover all areas of the port. (World Maritime News, 2018) The first application of the IOT project in the Port of Rotterdam, containing sea and weather conditions, began to be used in early 2019. These sensors collect data about tides and currents, salinity, temperature, wind speed and direction, water levels, berth condition, and visibility conditions at the port. These collected data are analyzed by IBM's cloud-based IOT technologies and converted into useful information that can be used in decision making. Port of Rotterdam uses this information to reduce waiting times for ships, berthing the ships, finding optimal times for loading and unloading, and taking more ships into port using full capacity. With this technology, depending on the water level in the port, the times of the ship entering and leaving the port with the maximum loading can be estimated closest to the right. (World Maritime News, 2019)

Nowadays, studies on autonomous ships have gained speed. It is known that IOT technology is widely used in autonomous ship technology. For example, in the 60-meter-long ferry named Falco, which is currently being built autonomously, situational awareness is obtained with the data received from IOT. The route and speed of the ship are adjusted according the information obtained from the IOT, such as tidal currents, wind, and precipitation. For autonomous ships that can easily navigate in the high sea, their sensors can be sufficient. However, for ships moving in complex and narrow marine environments such as the Port of Rotterdam, additional situational awareness information should be provided from the port. (Horwitz, 2019) The port of Rotterdam is planned to host smart ships until 2025. Real-time data from IOT sensors related to the condition of the berths, the weather, the sea condition, the sea rise and fall due to tides will be collected, processed, and analyzed. Operating costs will be reduced through better communication and decision making. According to the information released by the Port of Rotterdam, a one-hour reduction in the duration of a ship in port saves companies operating ship $ 80,000 USD. In this way, more ships will be taken to the port every year. (Loftus, 2019) However, the use of these ships within the port limits depends on the good synchronization with the digital systems in the port. For this reason, it is inevitable for those working on autonomous ship technology and digital port technology to come together and work together. At the same time, studies should provide standardization around the world. This issue is explained in detail in the transition from classical systems to digital systems and standardization.

Optimizing use of Port Equipment

The vehicles such as mobile harbor crane, straddle carrier, tractor and chassis, automatic guided vehicle, ship loader, unloader, reclaimer, stacker in ports are used within a working day, excluding idle times, maintenance periods, and breakdown times. By using the IOT technology in these vehicles, they can be used optimally. The problems of the vehicles can be detected before the malfunction by means of the IOT sensors to be placed on these vehicles. Parts that need to be maintained can be identified and replaced before failure. In addition, idle times due to wrong planning can be prevented.

In Ijmuiden, at the entrance of the canal of the Port of Amsterdam, mooring piles were made for the purpose of unloading some of the ships before entering the canal. Before the ships enter the canal, they are moored to these piles and the ship is lightened by unloading some of its cargos. Thus, the ship does not have any problems due to her draft while entering the port of Amsterdam. These piles are deformed and bent over time as the ship's moor and lean. The Port of Amsterdam, together with the company named 30 Mhz, started a pilot project on this subject. The aim of the project is to check the status of the piles with IOT sensors and to proactively plan maintenance times according to the information sent by the sensors. As a result, it is aimed that potential maintenance periods will cause as little discomfort as possible for ships and operators. (Port of Amsterdam, 2016)

In addition, with the 5G technology, which is the infrastructure of IOT technology, it is possible to easily transfer three-dimensional information to augmented reality application. In this way, on-site maintenance teams can easily get help from a specialist while continuing their work. This will help those in the field during the breakdown and maintenance periods of the equipment in the ports. For example, the works for establishing the infrastructure of 5G technology have started in the port of Hamburg (Blackman, 2019). Once complete, it will easily support these applications.

Also, warehouses, depots, transit sheds, and storage areas can be used optimally with IOT technology. Through this optimization, waiting times for loading and unloading of ships arriving at the port can be reduced. With the planning that can be made instantly, land vehicles that bring cargo to the port and receive cargo from the port are prevented from waiting for each other, and possible time losses can be minimized. One of the best examples in this subject is the port of Hamburg. IOT technology in Hamburg Port is used effectively to coordinate ships and trucks and prevent congestion at the port and finds optimal solutions to the complexity of port logistics (Internet of Business, n.d.a).

Transition From Classical Systems to Digital Systems and Standardization

The use of classical systems has many difficulties in the collection, storage, processing, and use of information. Human involvement in the process of recording the obtained information in a computer system may cause the information to be recorded incorrectly or incompletely, to delete the recorded information accidentally, and to delay the time between obtaining and saving the information. Also, this time delay causes the information not to be used immediately. Failure to use the information in case of need may cause the decisions to be taken to be inaccurate or incomplete. For this reason, the system can be damaged. Instead, systems such as IOT technology that takes information from its source and save it directly to the computer system eliminates the mentioned problems. In the ports equipped with IOT, information from the sensors is immediately recorded in computer systems. The fact that the registration process is not interrupted confirms the accuracy of the information. At the same time, this information can be used immediately. The recorded information can be processed and made ready for use very quickly with software or artificial intelligence programs prepared according to the needs. One of the benefits of digitalization is that some analog information owned by staff leaving the port for retirement or other reasons eliminates the risk of loss (Horwitz, 2019). Those working in classical systems constitute the corporate memory of the enterprise. Because it is not possible to record every event in classical systems or it may be limited. This leads to a significant loss of information. For this reason, long-term experienced personnel in the enterprise become the corporate memory of the enterprise. When this experienced staff leaves work, this valuable information is also lost. The loss of information can be prevented since digitalization can be achieved with IOT technology and any information can be easily recorded.

Digitalization brings along standardization. The systems of ships coming from different countries of the world should be compatible with the IOT systems of the port so that the IOT systems of the ship and the port can easily communicate. Achieving this standardization, in the beginning, may pose enormous challenges, and perhaps international organizations such as the International Maritime Organization (IMO) may need to be engaged to achieve this standardization (Horwitz, 2019). Ensuring standardization can enable the maritime industry, which has an international characteristic, to work in harmony in the upcoming periods and minimize time losses. Naturally, in the beginning, each port will carry out its own work on IOT. The subject of standardization is considered after the studies reach a certain maturity. Therefore, there is the danger that initially an IOT application cannot improve its potential due to a lack of interoperability in other ports. Port administrations are aware that their future depends not only on infrastructure development but also on smarter approaches and seamless integration of the port community (Greenport, 2016). For example, the Fraunhofer CML firm, in I2PANEMA research project, Hamburg Port Authority along with other European project partners, in Hamburg Port, Gijon Port and Derince Port is developing IOT applications and they are trying to derive IOT reference architecture. It is planned that the standards, interfaces, and applications to be produced from this project will support the development of European ports-compatible IOT solutions and thus strengthens their competitiveness. (Hellenic Shipping News, 2019)

Calculation of Port Performance Indicators

The efficiency of the ports is measured by the calculations made with the data collected from the port and the evaluation of these calculations. In this way, a conclusion can be reached about the productivity of the port. If the productivity of the port is considered insufficient by the port management, the measures to be taken are determined by short, medium, and long term strategic plans and the improvements required by these plans are made. Port performance indicators are used to make this measurement.

Port performance indicators are control tools that help port managers to measure port or terminal performance and make corrective decisions when and where they are needed. Indicators are also useful for decision strategies of investments, port planning, and future projections. Port performance indicators can be categorized under three categories: Physical performance indicators measuring the outputs of vehicles and facilities available at the port, quality performance indicators covering the reliability, flexibility and application of the port, and financial performance indicators measuring the profit and loss contributions of each of the port operations and services. Port performance indicators need to be created in a measurable way to allow for objective analysis and comparison. (ICS, 2007) Reliable data are required for port performance indicators to provide accurate results. In today's technology, the data needed for the port performance indicators are obtained by entering the records kept manually into the computer systems. Entering the data received from many points into the computer one by one requires a great effort and sometimes it may cause the data to be entered incorrectly. IOT can eliminate manual data collection errors, increase collection efficiency and deliver instantly to every corner of the world over the internet (Dong, Gang, Li, Guo, & Lv, 2013).

With the use of IOT technology, much data needed for port performance indicators can be obtained automatically, saved in the system and the indicators can be calculated instantly. As a result of calculating the indicators with the correct data, accurate evaluations can be made and correct results can be reached. For example, the usage rate of a gantry crane can be tracked in real-time with information from an IOT sensor placed on the crane. Here, the IOT sensor will send information when the crane starts running and stops working. In this way, it can be observed immediately whether that crane is working efficiently. Also, if the usage rate of the crane has decreased in the last days, the reasons for this can be investigated immediately. If this situation is caused by the lack of maintenance of the crane, maintenance operation can be activated immediately. Thus, efficiency, safety, and sustainability can be achieved. In addition, with the information obtained from IOT sensors, indicators such as the waiting rate of ships, the occupation rate of the berths can be calculated immediately, and the problems in the berth allocation organization can be detected and precautions can be taken immediately. For example, it is aimed to turn the port into a smart port with a digital application called Pronto developed by the Department of Digital Business Solutions of Rotterdam port. In the pilot implementation, it was determined that the waiting time of the ships decreased by twenty percent (Port of Rotterdam, 2018).

Green Port Applications

The concept of green port reflects the ecological importance, environmental protection, and energy-saving perspective in port operations and the importance that countries place on the environment, safety, and human health. While the green port aims to increase its economic interests, it also supports sustainable development by meeting its environmental requirements. The main problem in the concept of the green port is to balance the environmental impact and economic interests. (Köseoğlu & Solmaz, 2019) Port administrations are increasing their profits by increasing the number of customers and reducing their expenses. In addition, the prevention of environmental damages caused by the port has also become the main subject of port managers. Environmental sustainability in the port industry is a growing concern for port authorities, policymakers, port users and local communities. Many national and international organizations have determined the green port criteria, and the ports have started to make arrangements according these criteria. It is observed that the green port criteria in the world are gathered under the titles of air quality, energy consumption, noise, public relations, ship wastes, port development, water quality, dredging, dust, and waste management (Köseoğlu, & Solmaz, 2019). Port management, by considering these criteria, tries to achieve sustainable development in order to minimize the harms that the port can cause to the environment.

Port administrations have started to use IOT technology to meet green port criteria. Many ports in the world have started to turn towards greener and more efficient applications through the technology provided by IOT (Greenport, 2016). For example, Hamburg Port Management started collecting and analyzing data on air quality with IOT sensors to combat air pollution. The project was carried out jointly with AQMesh, the manufacturer of air quality measurement devices. In this context, sulfur dioxide, nitrogen oxide, and fine dust emissions at various points of the port are measured with IOT sensors. With this system, data is collected in a regular and real-time manner and prepared for analysis. (Internet of Business, n.d.b) San Diego Port was among the first ports to launch an energy efficiency program with an energy efficiency digitization project launched in 2014 with Smart City San Diego Regional Cooperation. Within the scope of the project, it is aimed to make studies on energy efficiency by making use of IOT. The project aims to use smart sensors and reduce greenhouse gases to detect and stop wasted energy. In this context, based on 2006, a reduction of 10% in all greenhouse gases by 2020 and a reduction of 25% by 2035 are foreseen. (Greenport, 2016) Within the scope of the project, it was determined that the greenhouse gases decreased by 16% considering the activities of 2016 (Port of San Diego, n.d.).

Port Security and ISPS Code Applications

Growth in world trade and globalization in container transportation has revealed an increasing security threat in ports worldwide. The ports have their own security weaknesses, as they are located on areas easily accessible from land and sea, close to crowded cities, and intertwined with complex transportation networks (Solmaz, 2012).

The International Ship and Port Facility Security Code (ISPS Code) prepared by IMO to set international rules for detecting and deterring threatening actions in ship and port facilities and to ensure international cooperation in this field, came into force on July 01, 2004. As of this date, all ports in the world that serve ships engaged on international voyages have started to take measures within the scope of ISPS Code. One of the most important issues under these measures is the control of port facility security. For this purpose, the ports encircle the port borders with wire fences to control the entry and exit, prevent unauthorized people from entering the port area and take measures to ensure that only authorized people enter the security areas. They carry out the controls in the port area with security personnel and security cameras. In such classical security systems, security weaknesses may occur due to human errors made by security officers. For example, although the port is viewed with cameras, the desired security situation cannot be obtained due to the fact that these images cannot be watched carefully enough. By using IOT technology in port security systems, it will be possible to make port security independent from human errors. It will be possible to analyze the information received from motion detection systems, camera systems, or drones by means of algorithms. If the system detects a security breach, it will be possible to notify the port security units. In this way, the number of security guards working in the port can be reduced.

Of course, digitization will bring cyber risks with it. Digital information is more likely to be attacked. In order for the data obtained to be reliable, the cybersecurity system must be fully established and no one should doubt it. The reliable data will ensure that the decisions are correct. (Horwitz, 2019) The ISPS Code, which came into force in 2004, covers all security applications at the port facilities at that time. However, today, with the digitization, the importance of cybersecurity applications in ports has started to increase. Cyber-attacks on the maritime industry have started to increase in our recent history. These attacks cause time and money loss. For this reason, importance should be given to cybersecurity along with digitalization in ports. In addition, it is considered that the ISPS Code should be updated by IMO to cover cyber risks.

The cyber ransom attack on June 27, 2017, caused disruptions in computer systems in certain regions covering Europe and India. The Maersk Company, which handles one-seventh of the containers transported around the world, was also severely affected by this attack. Maersk stated that this cyber-attack affects all units including ship transport, port and tugboat operations, oil and gas production, drilling services, and oil tankers, causing $ 300 million damage. Maersk also stated that they took different and more protective measures to protect their systems against possible cyber-attacks from now on. (Solmaz, & Koray, 2020)

In this context, the emergence and development of blockchain technology have provided a light for closing the security gaps of IOT technology. One of the most important examples that can be given in this subject is Blocklab, which was established jointly by the Port of Rotterdam and the city of Rotterdam. The purpose of this organization is to implement blockchain technology as an "Intelligent Industries Field Laboratory". Pilot applications made by this organization proved that blockchain technology can be integrated with IOT technology (Port of Rotterdam, 2019).

SOLUTIONS AND RECOMMENDATIONS

In today's increasingly competitive environment, reducing transportation costs without reducing the quality and safety of transportation requires making the right decisions at every stage of transportation. Therefore, it is necessary to follow every stage of transportation. Now, the position of the cargo transported in the supply chain is wanted to be known instantly by all the actors in the transportation process. For this reason, studies have been started on the utilization of IOT technology to make containers smart and follow-up. By making the containers smart, information such as the location of the container, security status, physical conditions, damage status, atmosphere, humidity, water in the container will be obtained remotely, online reservations of the containers can be made, payments related to transportation can be made automatically, and situations affecting insurance and insurance-related transactions will be done much faster and much more fairly.

With IOT technology, the traffic generated by ships, trucks, trains, port workers, port equipment within the port can be regulated. Communication can be provided much well than conventional methods so that port employees can work in a more coordinated manner with each other and the decisions to be taken can be made more accurate. By providing synchronization between the port, ships, and cargo owners, it can be ensured that the ships are connected to the berth without waiting on arrival and the cargo-related operations can be started without delay. Meteorological and oceanographic conditions within the port limits can be monitored instantaneously, the waiting times of the ships can be minimized by sharing these data with the ships that will enter the port and leave the port, and the time of entering or leaving the port with the maximum load can be estimated.

In addition, IOT technology is planned to be used for information exchange and communication between autonomous ships which will be put into service in the near future and the port. However, it is inevitable to carry out a standardization work on digitalization projects related to autonomous ships and ports to serve these ships. Because maritime transportation is a global sector that requires standardization in ports and ships all over the world.

With IOT technology, port equipment such as mobile harbor crane, straddle carrier, tractor and chassis, automatic guided vehicle, ship loader, unloader, reclaimer, and stacker can be made smart. In this way, the problems of the equipment can be detected remotely, the parts that need to be maintained can be determined and replaced before the breakdown, and expert assistance can be provided to the teams in the field for repair or maintenance with augmented reality application. In addition, idle times due to wrong planning can be prevented. Thus, this equipment can be used optimally. In addition, with the IOT sensors, which can instantly detect the occupancy of warehouses, depots, transit sheds, and storage areas, they can be used in the most economical way.

The use of IOT technology at the ports will eliminate the difficulties and errors of classical systems in the process of collecting, storing, processing, and using information. It will also ensure that the information is used immediately. The institutional memory created by the presence of experienced personnel in classical systems is lost when the personnel leave the port for reasons such as retirement. Since all kinds of information can be easily recorded and digitized with IOT technology, the computer systems of the port will provide a perfect corporate memory and the acquired information will never be lost. Digitalization also brings standardization. Ensuring standardization can enable the maritime industry, which has an international characteristic, to work very harmoniously in the upcoming periods and minimize time losses.

Port performance indicators are used to measure the efficiency of the ports. In addition, these indicators form the basis of the port's short, medium, and long-term strategic plans. Port performance indicators are gathered in three categories: physical performance indicators, quality performance indicators, and financial performance indicators. In order to calculate these indicators, it is possible to obtain the required data automatically with IOT, upload it to computers, and calculate the indicators instantly. Thus, manual data collection errors can be eliminated, data collection can increase efficiency, and can be delivered instantly to every corner of the world over the internet. In addition, managers can be informed immediately. Accurate evaluations can be made and correct conclusions can be made by calculating the indicators with the correct data.

IOT technology has started to be actively used for the prevention of environment damages, namely green harbor applications, which has become the main subject of port management today. Information is collected from IOT sensors to meet the global green port criteria set under the headings of air quality, energy consumption, noise, community relations, ship wastes, port development, water quality, dredging, dust, waste management. Port management, by considering these criteria, tries to minimize the harms that the port can cause to the environment and to achieve sustainable development.

By using IOT technology in port security systems, it will be possible to make the port security independent from human errors, analyze the information received from the sensors with the algorithms to be created, and reduce the number of security officers working in the port. In order to eliminate the cyber risks that digitalization brings with it, it is considered that blockchain technology, with its almost impossible-to-decipher encrypted structure, will provide a solution for closing the security gaps of IOT technology.

FUTURE RESEARCH DIRECTIONS

As a result of this study, it is evaluated that IOT technology can find solutions to the problems in port management and strategies in order to provide DBT in ports. However, this study is a general study covering many subheadings within the scope of port management. IOT technology is a new technology that is being used in ports. The reason for this is that, as explained in the beginning parts of the study, developments in internet infrastructure have emerged in recent years. For this reason, the use of IOT technology in ports is still a pilot study on many projects. However, as a result of the study, it was seen that the potential capabilities of IOT technology are at a level that can solve many problems in port management and strategies. In the upcoming period, detailed and technical studies can be conducted on how to benefit from IOT technology in order to achieve DBT in areas under each sub-heading within the scope of port management.

CONCLUSION

DBT, which aims to achieve organizational change by using digital technologies to improve performance in business, has started to be preferred by many sectors. Because, making use of digital technology enables to do things in less time, need fewer employees, reduce costs, use information and resources effectively, produce the most products with the least resources and consequently increase the profitability of the enterprises. Ports are one of the building blocks of the maritime industry, which aims to increase its profitability by digitizing in today's increasingly competitive conditions. In recent years, IOT technology has been used extensively for digitalization in ports. When studies on IOT technology in ports are examined, it is evaluated that this technology can offer optimum solutions to ports on supply chain management, cargo tracking, optimizing port traffic, optimizing port equipment, the transition from classic systems to digital systems, standardization, calculating port performance indicators, green port, and port security applications. As a result of the study, it is evaluated that IOT technology can provide solutions to the problems in port management and strategies in many areas in order to achieve digital transformation in ports.

REFERENCES

Al Amoush, A. B., & Sandhu, K. (2020a). Digital Transformation of Learning Management Systems at Universities: Case Analysis for Student Perspectives. *Digital Transformation and Innovative Services for Business and Learning*, 41-61. doi:10.4018/978-1-7998-5175-2.ch003

Al Amoush, A. B., & Sandhu, K. (2020b). A Study of Digital Learning Management Systems in Developing Countries: Instructors' Perspectives. *Digital Transformation and Innovative Services for Business and Learning*, 80-101. doi:10.4018/978-1-7998-5175-2.ch005

Ammar, M., Russello, G., & Crispo, B. (2018). Internet of Things: A survey on the security of IOT frameworks. *Journal of Information Security and Applications*, *38*, 8–27. doi:10.1016/j.jisa.2017.11.002

Ashwell, M. L. (2017). The digital transformation of intelligence analysis. *Journal of Financial Crime*, *24*(3), 393–411. doi:10.1108/JFC-03-2017-0020

Basole, R. C. (2016). Accelerating digital transformation: Visual insights from the API ecosystem. *IT Professional*, *18*(6), 20–25. doi:10.1109/MITP.2016.105

Belfkih, A., Duvallet, C., & Sadeg, B. (2017). The Internet Of Things For Smart Ports Application To The Port Of Le Havre. *Proceedings of IPaSPort*, *2017*(May). https://www.researchgate.net/publication/316668793_The_internet_of_things_for_smart_ports_application_to_the_port_of_le_havre

Berghaus, S., & Back, A. (2016). Stages in Digital Business Transformation: Results of an Empirical Maturity Study. *MCIS 2016 Proceedings. 22*. Retrieved from https://aisel.aisnet.org/mcis2016/22

Blackman, J. (2019). Deutsche Telekom, Nokia proclaim 5G slicing for industrial IOT after Hamburg port tests. *Enterprise IOT insight*. Retrieved from https://enterpriseIOTinsights.com/20190626/channels/news/dt-nokia-proclaim-5g-slicing-for-industrial-IOT

Carlan, V., Sys, C., Vanelslander, T., & Roumboutsos, A. (2017). Digital innovation in the port sector: Barriers and facilitators. In Competition and regulation in network industries (pp. 1–23). doi:10.1177/1783591717734793

Choi, H. R., Kim, H. S., Park, B. J., Park, N. K., & Lee, S. W. (2003). An ERP approach for container terminal operating systems. *Maritime Policy & Management*, *30*(3), 197–210. doi:10.1080/0308883032000089549

Cirani, S., Ferrari, G., Picone, M., & Veltri, L. (2019). *Internet of things : Architectures, protocols and standards (First)*. John Wiley & Sons Ltd.

Dickson, B. (2016). How Blockchain Can Change the Future of IOT. *Venture-Beat.* Retrieved from https://venturebeat.com/2016/11/20/how-blockchain-can-change-the-future-of-IOT/

Dong, X., Gang, X., Li, Y., Guo, X., & Lv, Y. (2013). Intelligent ports based on Internet of Things. *Proceedings of 2013 IEEE International Conference on Service Operations and Logistics, and Informatics, SOLI 2013*, 292–296. 10.1109/SOLI.2013.6611428

Gölzer, P., & Fritzsche, A. (2017). Data-driven operations management: Organisational implications of the digital transformation in industrial practice. *Production Planning and Control*, *28*(16), 1332–1343. doi:10.1080/09537287.2017.1375148

Greenport. (2016). 'Smart' and sustainable ports. *Greenport.* Retrieved from https://www.greenport.com/news101/Projects-and-Initiatives/smart-and-sustainable-ports

Heilig, L., Lalla-Ruiz, E., & Voß, S. (2017). Digital transformation in maritime ports: Analysis and a game theoretic framework. *NETNOMICS: Economic Research and Electronic Networking*, *18*(2–3), 227–254. doi:10.100711066-017-9122-x

Hellenic Shipping News. (2019). Internet Of Things On Course To The Ports. *Hellenic Shipping News.* Retrieved from https://www.hellenicshippingnews.com/internet-of-things-on-course-to-the-ports/

Horwitz, L. (2019). Autonomous shipping charts new waters on the intelligent edge. *Cisco.* Retrieved from https://www.cisco.com/c/en/us/solutions/internet-of-things/autonomous-shipping.html?dtid=osscdc000283

Institute of Chartered Shipbrokers (ICS). (2007). *Port and Terminal Management.* London: Witherbys Publishing Limited.

International Telecommunication Union (ITU). (2012). *Overview of the Internet of things.* Retrieved from https://handle.itu.int/11.1002/1000/11559

Internet of Business. (n.d.a). Semtech LoRa geolocation helps Irish Port of Cork track shipping assets. *Internet of Business.* Retrieved from https://internetofbusiness.com/semtech-lora-irish-port-cork/

Internet of Business. (n.d.b). Port of Hamburg turns to Internet of Things to track pollution. *Internet of Business.* Retrieved from https://internetofbusiness.com/port-hamburg-IOT-pollution/

Kang, T. J. (2017). *HMM completes pilot blockchain voyage with reefer-laden boxship*. Retrieved from https://lloydslist.maritimeintelligence.informa.com/LL111275/HMM-completes-pilot-blockchainvoyage-with-reeferladen-boxship

Köseoğlu, M. C., & Solmaz, M. S. (2019). *Green Port Approach: A Comparative Assessment Criterion of Turkey and the World Green Port.* doi:10.18872/0.2019.2

Kshetri, N. (2017). Can Blockchain Strengthen the Internet of Things? *IT Professional, 19*(4), 68–72. doi:10.1109/MITP.2017.3051335

Kumar, S. (2017). Not Just for Crypto- cash: How Blockchain Tech Could Help Secure IOT. *IOT Agenda.* Retrieved from https://internetofthingsagenda.techtarget.com/blog/IOT-Agenda/Not-just-for-cryptocash-How-blockchain-tech-could-help-secure-IOT

Li, F. (2018). The digital transformation of business models in the creative industries: A holistic framework and emerging trends. *Technovation.* Advance online publication. doi:10.1016/j.technovation.2017.12.004

Loftus, A. (2019). How Industrial IOT will Disrupt the Shipping Industry. *IOT Evolution.* Retrieved from https://www.IOTevolutionworld.com/smart-transport/articles/442702-how-industrial-IOT-will-disrupt-shipping-industry.htm

Port of Amsterdam. (2016). A mooring pile that tells you how it's doing. *Port of Amsterdam News.* Retrieved from https://www.portofamsterdam.com/en/news-item/mooring-pile-tells-you-how-its-doing

Port of Rotterdam. (2018). The port is getting smarter and smarter. *Port of Rotterdam News.* Retrieved from https://www.portofrotterdam.com/en/news-and-press-releases/the-port-is-getting-smarter-and-smarter

Port of Rotterdam. (2019). How Rotterdam is using blockchain to reinvent global trade. *Port of Rotterdam News.* Retrieved from https://www.portofrotterdam.com/en/news-and-press-releases/how-rotterdam-is-using-blockchain-to-reinvent-global-trade

Port of San Diego. (n.d.). On Track to Meet 2020 Goal. *Port of San Diego What we do.* Retrieved from https://www.portofsandiego.org/environment/energy-sustainability/climate-action-plan

Ray, P. P. (2018). A survey on Internet of Things architectures. *Journal of King Saud University - Computer and Information Sciences, 30*(3), 291–319. doi:10.1016/j.jksuci.2016.10.003

Reddy, S., & Reinartz, W. (2017). Digital transformation and value creation: Sea change ahead. *GfK-Marketing Intelligence Review, 9*(1), 10–17. doi:10.1515/gfkmir-2017-0002

Singh, S. K., Rathore, S., & Park, J. H. (2020). BlockIoTIntelligence: A Blockchain-enabled Intelligent IoT Architecture with Artificial Intelligence. *Future Generation Computer Systems, 110*, 721–743. doi:10.1016/j.future.2019.09.002

Solmaz, M. S. (2012). *In the context of the maritime security, evaluation of the ISPS Code port security implementation's effectiveness and Turkey's implementations* (Doctoral dissertation). Retrieved from Council of Higher Education Thesis Center. (318754)

Solmaz, M. S., & Koray, M. (2020). Blockchain Technology in Maritime Transportation and Management. Handbook of Research on the Applications of International Transportation and Logistics for World Trade, 483-499. doi:10.4018/978-1-7998-1397-2.ch026

Tanniru, M. R., Xi, Y., & Sandhu, K. (2020). Leadership to Advance Innovation for Digital Healthcare Transformation. *Leadership, Management, and Adoption Techniques for Digital Service Innovation*, 1-24. doi:10.4018/978-1-7998-2799-3.ch001

United Nations Conference on Trade and Development (UNCTAD). (2018). *Review of Maritime Transport*. Retrieved from doi:10.18356/fd502c06-en

United Nations Conference on Trade and Development (UNCTAD). (2019). *Review of Maritime Transport*. Retrieved from https://unctad.org/en/PublicationsLibrary/rmt2019_en.pdf

Von Leipzig, T., Gamp, M., Manz, D., Schöttle, K., Ohlhausen, P., Oosthuizen, G., Palm, D., & von Leipzig, K. (2017). Initialising customer-orientated digital transformation in enterprises. *Procedia Manufacturing*, *8*, 517–524. doi:10.1016/j.promfg.2017.02.066

Weare42. (n.d.). The smartest container this planet has even seen. *We are 42*. Retrieved from https://weare42.io/about/

Weill, P., & Woerner, S. L. (2018). Is your company ready for a digital future? *MIT Sloan Management Review*, *59*(2), 21–25. https://sloanreview.mit.edu/article/is-your-company-ready-for-a-digital-future/

Wessel, L. K., Baiyere, A., Ologeanu-Taddei, R., Cha, J., & Jensen, T. B. (2020). Unpacking the Difference between Digital Transformation and IT-enabled Organizational Transformation. *Journal of the Association for Information Systems*.

World Maritime News. (2018). Port of Rotterdam Teams Up with IBM to Build Smart Port of the Future. *World Maritime News*. Retrieved from https://worldmaritimenews.com/archives/242383/port-of-rotterdam-teams-up-with-ibm-to-build-smart-port-of-the-future/

World Maritime News. (2019). Port of Rotterdam: New IOT Platform Put into Operation. *World Maritime News*. Retrieved from https://worldmaritimenews.com/archives/270275/port-of-rotterdam-new-IOT-platform-put-into-operation/

Worldbank. (2019a). *Databank*. Retrieved from https://data.worldbank.org/indicator/NY.GDP.MKTP.CD

Worldbank. (2019b). *Databank*. Retrieved from https://data.worldbank.org/topic/trade

Xiao, P. (2018). *Designing embedded systems and IOT with the ARM Mbed*. John Wiley & Sons Ltd.

KEY TERMS AND DEFINITIONS

Cargo Tracking: Tracking by the sender and the recipient of the entire route from the point where the cargo is sent to the point where it is received.

Digital Business Transformation (DBT): Transformation from classical systems to digital systems in a way that all functions of a business can be carried out on digital media.

Green Port: The port designed to reflect the ecological importance, environmental protection measures, energy saving, safety, and human health in port operations.

Internet of Things (IoT): Internet network of smart objects connected to the internet.

Port Performance Indicators: The indicators revealed by the measurements and calculations made at the port in order to measure the efficiency of the port, to make corrective decisions when necessary, to make predictions and plans for the future.

Smart Object: A device that can generate information through its sensors, share this information over a network it connects to, communicate with other smart objects, and execute commands sent to it over the network.

Supply Chain Management: The planning and management of the process from the time the logistics company takes cargo to delivery in maritime transport.

Chapter 13
Transforming Digital Enterprises Towards Web Scale With Machine Learning

Tasneem Aamir
Rajiv Gandhi Proudyogiki Vishwavidyalaya, India

ABSTRACT

Digital enterprise transformation focuses on alignment of processes, products, services, business models, and technologies to perceive business value. Digital business integration in an organization utilizes information technology and its tools to drive and manage the life cycle of digital enterprise transformation. It utilizes the practices and approaches of IT governance with modern application tools and APIs. The millennium brought many technological advancements over internet technologies and these technologies operate numerous applications and business services. The span of digital enterprises is expanding and continues to grow with their evolution on a web scale. This chapter is an effort to present understanding about machine learning and automation around businesses intelligence and analytics on a web scale. The chapter provides a brief summary of technologies used in digital enterprise transformation for all the domains of an organization.

INTRODUCTION

Digital technologies have made our world a digital globe. Each individual interacts with technology and digital devices in some way or the other. With regard to digital enterprises of varied extent, their in-house and outward business operations are carried over automated platforms. Businesses excel and enhance their customer experiences by adopting innovative ways and delivering automated solutions through technology strengthened business practices. This also opens a window of opportunity to keep business management flexible and agile.

Distributed data processing has been applied so far in developing web-oriented digital platforms. With significant advancements and recent developments in deep learning methods, there is much to offer to digital enterprises. Artificial intelligence, machine learning and cloud computing provide personalized

DOI: 10.4018/978-1-7998-8587-0.ch013

experiences to a varied customer base and tackle ongoing enterprise data, applications and services for a competitive edge. The implementation of machine learning solutions increments the customer value of enterprise and boosts the internal operating models. Machine learning is the most powerful tool to achieve automation and it could afford limitless applications and tools. The view proposed by Jasney (2020) explains that the operational efficiency of DBMS increases with machine learning in a digital enterprise transformation.

Echo from Amazon, Google Home, Siri from Apple are interactive apps and tools were only possible through machine learning technology. With NLP uniting the prominent features of these applications, it has made text and GUI old fashioned. Machine learning makes decisions faster. The work of Obukhova et al. (2020) explains that latest tools and models of computing with machine learning in digital enterprises leads to faster production and enhances scalability of the system. Businesses get help through machine learning in innovation and to elevate the right kind of services and products. Machine learning advocates minimum human error and stronger cyber security to transform digital enterprises. Key elements of a digital enterprise are -

1. Product - The unique component of a business platform which is sold or which caters to the needs of customers and the range of outcomes which are offered by the enterprise.
2. Services - Set of physical, hardware, software, goods or assets and custom-tailored solutions by the enterprise.
3. Work process - Products and services along with the revenue generation and customer interaction dimensions comprises the work process of a digital enterprise.
4. Business models - The technologies and tools, workflow process, life cycle and management of products and services are studied under business models.

Figure 1. Salient features in Digital Enterprise Management (Sucoso)

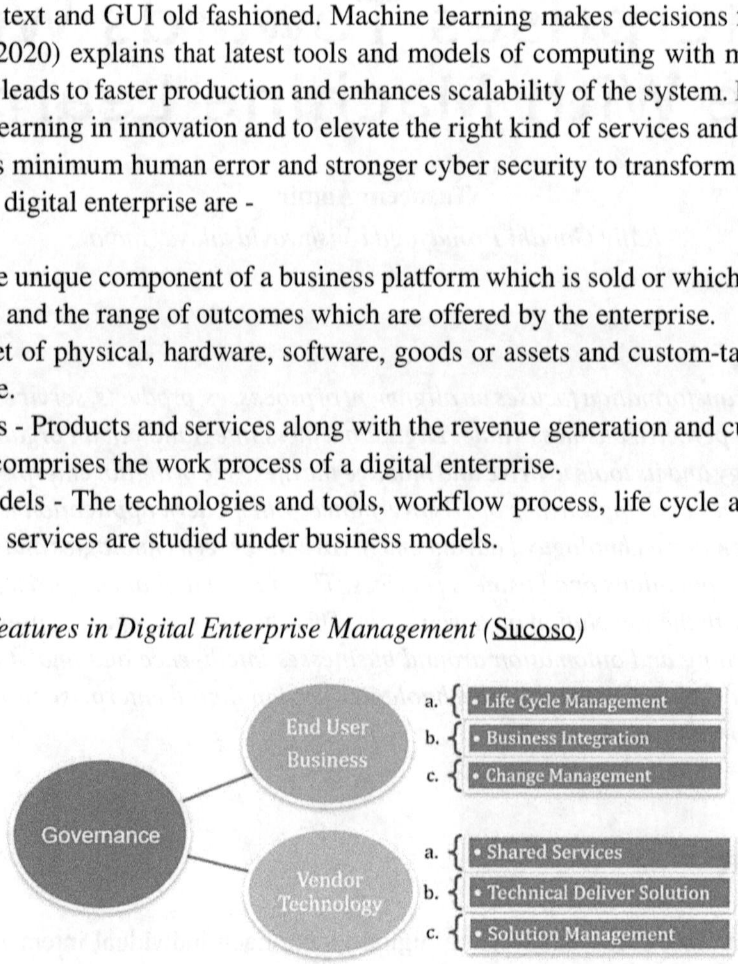

The Figure 1 illustrates features in Digital Enterprise Management. These are the major underlying components of an enterprise. Each feature is discussed below:

Governance:

It is the process of monitoring and managing an entire enterprise and all of its elements. It encompasses management of end user business and vendor technologies. Governance takes into consideration all the four elements, that is, product, services, work processes and business models. It is further classified in following categories:

1. End User Business: This deals with the scenario which concerns end users. Its major domains are:
    a. Life Cycle Management: This concerns the life cycle of the business product. Strategies are developed for continuous monitoring of the product at various stages.
    b. Business Integration: It is the digital strategy of integrating and optimizing the major business processes, like sales, supply, logistics, etc.
    c. Change Management: Change management and version control is an essential technique in any enterprise for its products, services and tools. This concerns up-to-date versions and timely updates as per requirements.
2. Vendor Technology: Vendor technology refers to the proprietary technology including tools, services, interfaces or any other intellectual property licensed to the vendor. It comprises of following elements:
    a. Shared Services: It includes services shared among various departments and groups in a digital enterprise. These services are the driver of digital transformation engines.
    b. Technical Deliver Solutions: To deliver new solutions aligning business requirements for growth and transformation of digital enterprise.
    c. Solution Management: Solution management focuses mainly upon the product of enterprise. It also deals how the product interacts with other elements within an enterprise.

BACKGROUND

The management strategies for digital enterprise transformation primarily focus on the existing applications and data. They need to be initially connected in a cloud environment so that their integration with evolving technologies is flexible and they could be skilfully managed. The API's and tools are created later to publish the services. Rangone (2020) in his research discussed innovation and technology as the major elements in a digital enterprise. The transformation strategies are hugely impacted with powerful computing and technological tools. He emphasized that the latest trends of innovation revolutionize strategic management of digital enterprises. Hou et al. (2019) in their work presented an improved C4.5 machine learning algorithm. They showed remarkable growth in the learning curve and reduced errors in prediction. The transformation should offer an easy to use ecosystem to developers, end users and should be open to sustainability in an evolving technological era. Its performance and quality of service should excel and remain unaffected. The optimized services must also not compromise the security concern. Enterprises trading assets are extensively using the Blockchain platform to achieve security. With the dawn of machine learning, the scale of digital enterprises is growing. Machine learning gave birth to automation and various tools and technologies emerged along with it. In the later sections of the chapter, web scale IT is discussed. The abstract view of Web Scale IT is to target millions of users by scaling up the existing digital enterprise scale. According to Liu et al. (2020), the web scale applications need to maintain elasticity when users demand responsiveness. It must operate upon pressure or when there is volatile behaviour in the application environment.

In current times, employees, customers, managers and end-users, all are bonded in an invisible link which is traversed through digital tools. Hence to ace business growth to an even better position, digital enterprises rely on effective operations and advanced strategies. Hussain (2020) explains how these operations are a dashboard of Machine Learning, Artificial Intelligence and Business Intelligence. The major steps in machine learning are termed as- learn from training data, build models based on learning, and classify unseen data based on models.

Machine learning strategies and algorithms are broadly classified as:

1. Supervised Learning:
   a. Classification Method: Support Vector Machines, Decision Trees, Naïve Bayes, Random Forest.
   b. Feature Selection Algorithm: Based on Component Analysis, Consistence, and Correlation.
2. Unsupervised Learning:
   a. Classification Method: DB Scan, K-Means.
   b. Feature Selection Algorithm: Fast Correlation based filter, Principal Component Analysis, Consistency and Correlation.

The following table gives a description of Machine Learning algorithms:

Table 1. Machine Learning Algorithms

Types of Machine Learning	Description	Algorithms	Web Scale IT Application Areas
Supervised Learning	Classification: Predicts the class of samples Regression: Value estimation for the continuous variable.	Linear regression, Logistic regression, Bayesian classifiers, Neural networks, SVMs, k-nearest neighbors, decision trees and random forests.	Classification is carried out in pattern recognition, diagnostics, image processing. Regression involves predictions, weather forecasting, stock market estimates.
Unsupervised Learning	When the training data is without labels, then the inferences are drawn using unsupervised learning. Clustering helps to deduce patterns in data.	k-means or hierarchical clustering, t-SNE, latent class analysis.	Big Data, target marketing, segment marketing.
Reinforcement Learning	This is similar to AI. The behavioral actions and responses are maximized.	Markov Decision Process, Q Learning	Gaming with AI, Robot Navigation, Simulation, Sensor networks, aircraft control.

IT enterprises are consistently transforming their infrastructure and operations to leverage market consistency as well as to meet their client's requisites. The world is swiftly observing more and more digital advancements. Major industries underneath digital enterprises are– electronic and print media, advertisement, banking, education, healthcare, manufacturing and entertainment. To a significant extent, every small or big business gets converged with digital technologies inevitably.

The Internet settles at the core of digital operations. Every access to a single web page, every query on a search engine, each second on a social networking site produces a huge volume of data. Approximately, 2.5 Quintillion bytes of data is generated every single day, as per forbes.com. Appearance and captivity of a web page leaves lasting impressions on its users. Web designers efficiently play their roles for outlook and presentation. But the architecture or the website design with the details of data presented to the users and customers brings more opportunities in business's expansion and with data, comes the terms of statistics, algorithms, business intelligence, analytics, data science and machine learning.

Following are the essential goals of Digital Business Transformation with Machine Learning-

1. To optimize applications and business models thus leading to cost reduction: The fusion of machine learning and artificial intelligence results in decreasing cost reduction of various enterprise elements. The speed of operation increases thus the faster delivery of results and outcomes is achieved.
2. To increase the opportunities for cloud-based operations for a rapid growth in business value: Cloud computing is another approach for significant cost reduction and for flexibility of enterprise operations. It minimizes the burden of maintenance and administration of resources, and boosts business value and market competency.
3. To furnish customer experiences across multiple applications: The power of pattern recognition and decision making is a key feature of machine learning in a digital enterprise. Machine learning systems learn the preferences of customers to drive customized services for easy and convenient delivery of enterprise solutions.
4. Enhance marketing and reach to a large extent of customers by high cost reduction and rapid deployment of services: With the magic of machine learning, the digital enterprises streamline their processes to outreach large numbers of customers. The recommendation engines bring personalized and accurate experiences.
5. To gain higher revenues by revolutionizing business processes with the latest technologies: Machine learning aid in digital enterprise transformation by strengthening decision making in key areas such as CRM, operations management, sales and finance strategies. The customer acquisition and customer retention further increase market capital and revenue of an enterprise.
6. To balance workload on employees and offering of flexible technologies and tools: Machine learning reduces time of operations and various everyday tasks in an enterprise. This benefits employees by shedding the burden of routine tasks and enhances their job satisfaction.
7. To offer fast delivery of services with automation, cloud computing, machine learning and artificial intelligence: Machine learning integrated with AI and other computing methodologies improves enterprise growth with increased sales and profitability. IBM WebSphere Application server is an excellent example of a strategic business environment on cloud computing offering great many opportunities for digital enterprise transformation.

ERA OF MACHINE LEARNING IN DIGITAL ENTERPRISE TRANSFORMATION

Figure 2. Key Areas in Machine Learning (Bramasol)

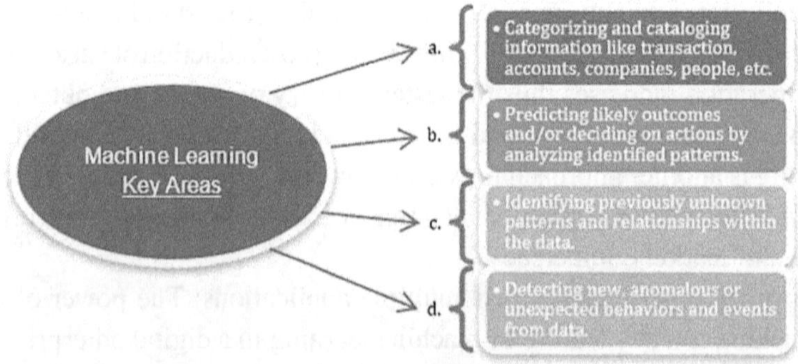

Figure 2 illustrates key areas of machine learning which drives the strategies for digital enterprise transformation. These elements carry following functions:

1. Qualitative analytics: Business analytics helps enterprises to realize conceptualization and advocate upgraded business models. Data is the fundamental element and its quality is assessed during data mining.
2. Preliminary data reports: Data reports provide business insights and are helpful in decision making. These become the foundation of predictive business analytics.
3. Reporting with visuals: Data collected from reports is graphically presented for better understanding of insights. This uses graphs and charts to display reports.
4. Creating dashboards: Dashboards are further addition to data visualization. These could be interfaces and integrated applications of a business analytics system.
5. Sales forecasting: Sales forecasting is the data science approach of machine learning. It is a prediction and decision-making stage in machine learning.
6. Client retention: The knowledge of customer behavior helps in client retention. Enterprises offer special offers, rewards and discounts to customers to continue branding and retain their customers.
7. Fraud prevention: Fraud prevention is an enterprise wide strategy for enhanced security. It is concerned with cyber security, data theft, masquerade attack and other threats.

Machine learning algorithms take input data points and metrics (bad, good, satisfactory, excellent) and perform inferences of how customers behave upon those metrics. This helps enterprises to serve better to their customers and improve the sales by sorting out the odds. Majority of corporate giants have a drift towards the use of Machine learning. The major areas in digital enterprise transformation which exploit machine learning algorithms as discussed by Shende et al. (2020) are:

1. Image Classification - Internet content is growing exponentially. It's important to have a sharp surveillance over it. Image classification is used to restrict unwanted and spam content travel around the internet and also blocking it from getting viral.

2. Recommendation engines - Once an application or a website has been accessed or used for quite a number of times by the user, she confronts suggestions based upon her interests and choices. These recommendation engines as present in Pinterest and Expedia, produce ideas collectively through AI and deep learning. For example:
   a. Digital enterprises of marketing and shopping domains will suggest products to customers based on their previous purchases.
   b. The entertainment provider Netflix recommends watch lists to viewers based on their taste.
   c. Websites offer customized homepages to users of different categories.
3. Customer Service- Customer services are now being offered by virtual assistants who are indeed fast and accurate in execution. Machine learning offers NLP (Natural Language Processing) solutions to let customers interact with enterprises. There are Chatbots available as an interface for customer service. RPA is discussed in further sections which explains automation and chatbots.
4. Information Security Through Machine Learning- Machine learning algorithms work by feature selection to detect unauthorized access points and to protect information. Immeasurable understanding of machine learning tools is the masterstroke for productive management of digital enterprises. Machine Learning is used in internet traffic classification by software defined wireless sensor networks. Machine learning algorithms have solutions for classifying legitimate and malicious attack activities. It can distinguish internet traffic from distinct networks and detect traffic anomalies. Machine learning has offered time efficient solutions for traffic classification, especially in DPI (Deep Packet Inspection). Any encountered change in pattern of internet traffic is automatically detected and reported to the network controller. Machine learning algorithms extensively used for information security according to Issong et al. (2018) are:
   a. SVM - It performs classification and finds boundaries with the largest data set.
   b. C4.5 - Classification and prediction is made by decision tree.
   c. KNN (k nearest neighbors) - Stored patterns and new patterns are classified upon a similarity measure that is, distance functions.
   d. MLP (Multi-Layer Perceptron) - This supervised learning algorithm can distinguish non linearly separable data. It uses backpropagation for training.
5. Business Intelligence Analysis- This is the process of explaining past performance of business activities, derived through data skills, business intelligence and intuition. According to Wanga et al. (2016) the strategic transformation with big data analytics helps to gain business insights and also in formulating data driven business models. The specialist in this process termed as Business Analyst is the person who strengthens the business through power of data. He aims to gauge the business performance and progress by presenting data in the form of reports and dashboards. Business Analyst keeps track of KPI's and is used on price optimization, sales forecasting and inventory management. Business analytics on a web scale involves predictive analysis. Business Intelligence is primarily the process of analysing and reporting past events business data. It attempts to:
   a. Analyses past data: The value of a business lies in its potential data. Insights gained from past data help in decision making and in creation of right products.
   b. Extract useful insights: Useful insights helps enterprises to understand customers better and to condition themselves as per changing requirements of business.
   c. Create appropriate models: With the improved understanding of customers interest, it is easier to build strategies and models which would increase revenues and market competency.

6. Machine learning helps to bring solutions of analytics in a business. Predictive analysis over data is carried through traditional data science. Businesses do not merely work with data but rather with Big Data. These analytics includes the approaches of:
   a. Regression- This model is used to quantify casual relationships among distinct variables included in analysis. It is of two types-
      i. Linear Regression- variables obey y=mx rule.
      ii. Logistic Regression- variables here use a nonlinear model also non as binary regression.
   b. 6. b. Cluster Analysis- This model breaks the large populations from data set into small groups. Clustering can be termed as the process of breaking down a large population or data-set into smaller groups. This is also termed as factor analysis. Functions are of the form:

y= a+b1x1+b2x2+.......bnxn where x= predictor variable.

7. Sentiment Analysis: Digital Enterprises are doing their business expansion and evaluating business operations through Sentiment Analysis. The real time opinions of customers, their feedback, reviews, and suggestions experts influence on the decision making for any business. Sentiment Analysis is carried under data mining and is also a sub field of computational linguistics. The entire process of Sentiment analysis comprises of the following steps:
   a. Data gathering: Under the work proposed by Alasadi and Bhaya (2017), they focused that quality of data must not be compromised after data collection. Data gathered from web scale enterprises is used to find patterns and in decision making.
   b. Text cleaning and preprocessing: According to Alasadi and Bhaya (2017), the missing values, outlier data, inconsistent and noisy data must be processed out of the raw data to enhance data efficiency.
   c. Sentiment recognition: Jain and Kumar (2020) in their book explained deep learning models for sentiment analysis. This helps to determine customer reviews. Convolution Neural Networks (CNN) is an example of a machine learning algorithm used to extract reviews.
   d. Sentiment classification: Akaichi (2017) in their book focused on learning models integrated with artificial intelligence for sentiment classification. They discussed methodologies for classifying sentiment in reviews from text data.
8. Data entry- Data comes with two troubles. Data inaccuracies and data duplication. Moreover, raw data cannot be analysed straightaway. Hence data entry with machine learning comes into action. Thomas et al. (2020) emphasizes that missing data is the result of error in human data entry. Therefore, data entry by humans is an unviable option for future and we need a shift towards machine learning for effortless data entry to eradicate common errors, to save time and precious man hours. Automated data entry has now become an industry compliant standard and in future it would help companies to stay on top with their competitors. It works using predictions and recommendation engines. It remembers past inputs and offers suggestions of what might a user need to enter. Automated data entry reduces cost and has faster turnaround, it is accurate and its end result is increased client satisfaction. Automated data entry has also been a great option for discovering trends by generating different scenarios and to identify patterns in data. It presents detailed forecasts by detecting patterns in purchase and sales, bills and invoices. It further helps business managers to identify engrossing dependencies and take business decisions.

9. Enterprise Content Management (ECM)- It is an on-premise enterprise management approach. The information management system of an enterprise is further explored and termed as Enterprise Content Management. The focus of ECM is laid on use of digital technologies and operations. The data which is gathered through the end users and applications, governance processes that is web content, records and assets management, and the sustainable approaches for their storage and distribution comprises ECM. Enterprise Content Management efficiently manages structured and unstructured data. Machine learning and Artificial Intelligence collaboratively is the best solution for cloud deployment as well for Enterprise content management.
10. IoT in Business- In recent years, 90% of data was generated by flourishing IoT (Internet of Things). According to Hussain et al. (2020), machine learning and deep learning solutions in IoT devices will aid to cope with security problems of the network. The Internet of Things has given birth to Green Technology, SMART GRID, big data, cloud technology, cognitive technologies, nano materials, biomedical technologies and are important discoveries of the current millennium. These technologies altogether are the frontiers on the flagship of digital enterprises. The research work proposed by Deepa et al. (2020) portrays the perspective of enterprise IoT and the importance of advanced machine learning algorithms which are the backbone of IoT in decision making and pattern matching.

The abstract advantages of IoT with machine learning offers complete automation. IoT facilitates real time business processes. It lays a complete and independent framework in digital enterprise and boosts automation. This further leads to expansion in the global economy by aiding in price formation and merchandising. The goal of IoT focuses on standardization and strategic development of solutions which are created using machine learning models. They drive the operations concerning demand predictions, logistics, personalized offers, fraud detection, sentiment analysis etc.

ADVANTAGES OF MACHINE LEARNING FOR DIGITAL ENTERPRISE MANAGEMENT

In the view of Chauhan et al. (2020), following are the major advantages of machine learning:

1. Extraction of meaning information from text data, example as used in sentiment analysis.
2. Detect objects on images or finding hidden knowledge from graphic data. This includes pattern recognition in spam and unwanted content.
3. Search and understand web data for business intelligence. This process is done using predictive analytics.
4. Automate expert tasks and make predictions by using chatbots and recommendation engines.
5. Increase revenues and profit by finding new business opportunities through curated information received from sources with unstructured data.
6. Machine learning models are a time and cost-effective solution for key employees since customary tasks engrossed 50% of the workforce.
7. Unleash the creative dimension among employees of enterprise. They get freedom from monotonous and tiresome work of data processing operations and thus could bring out innovations.

8. Proliferate Client Retention because AI and deep learning recommends ideas and gives customized outcomes.
9. Digital Capability Maturity Model is used for meta management in a digital enterprise.
10. Insurance sector utilizes machine learning methodologies for claim handling
11. Healthcare sector is revolutionizing toward intelligent healthcare. Machine learning offers models for electronic health records, predictive analytics is used for diagnosis and treatment strategies.

NEGLIGENCE AREAS OF MACHINE LEARNING

1. Machine learning when integrated with Artificial Intelligence offers high performance computing but also brings computationally intensive workloads.
2. Machine learning requires fast CPUs, large datasets and accelerated networking.
3. Management of hardware resources is difficult, tedious and expensive.
4. The Governance standards are essential for thriving e-business and strengthening the digital economy. These standards have a role to play in -
    a. Database creation on websites.
    b. Monitoring Payment transactions.
    c. Deliveries of goods and digital content.
    d. Digital marketing
    e. Mechanisms for Information Security.

Enterprises need to prepare themselves for the best position to keep competence in future. Employment opportunities, income and prosperity have taken a leap and the number of megacities and smart cities have been continuously growing. Digital enterprises are also consistently evolving and upgrading themselves with revolutionary technologies and tools. Tech giant Apple has revised its hardware, software and music marketing to a great extent since its inception. Amazon has revolutionized the logistics industry. Google has stirred up its enterprise for research, archiving, learning and navigation tools. Facebook is helping in transforming a lot of small and big scale enterprises through its community options. Digital enterprises are playing a crucial role in the corporate world. Twitter, WhatsApp, Instagram, all have succeeded to reach hundred million of active users in a very short span of time.

The business models are apparently transforming with the modern trends of big data, machine learning, data science, artificial intelligence and cloud computing. Digital enterprises have wired their entire promotions and advertisements with each other. For example, Google YouTube, Twitter, Facebook etc. are dashboards to showcase the operations of various digital enterprises.

WEB SCALE IT AND MACHINE LEARNING

The architectural approach of Web scale IT is to innovate business models in major services of global enterprises. The digital enterprise has achieved a significant jump through Web Scale IT specially in the Cloud Computing domain. Data center technology, virtual servers and business critical applications are relying on web scale information technology especially for complex and inflexible operations. This approach enhances scalability, storage issues are resolved with the presence of an innovative and creative environment for employees. Web Scale IT enterprises have emerged in support of e-commerce, social networking, big data and other corporate activities. Provisioning of cloud services has also been a major initiative. It has successfully offered resiliency with asynchronous and stateless communication. The reach of Web Scale applications is vast and among a variety of devices, such as mobile apps and those without GUI's used under other applications.

The need for software defined systems which are scalable and simple to implement with the ease of carrying operations have given birth to Web Scale. Business models for commodity-based enterprise as well as IT firms involving demand-supply chains, deployment services and management functionalities utilize the features of Web Scale IT. Existing digital enterprise infrastructure often fails to meet the needs of Web Scale IT and operation environments to deploy applications. Before proceeding on the path of agile digital enterprise transformation through Web Scale IT, it is important to realize the principles of transformation -

1. Digital enterprises need to have a clear perception of business processes and future growth plans.
2. To build infrastructure with rigid policies and best models for ease of use to customers.
3. To get insight of metrics for estimating an idea of consumption, costs and usage.
4. To understand data quality and figure out the completeness to align operations with business services.

Transforming digital enterprises to a web scale requires modifying architectural infrastructure, operational process, technologies, structure model organization and skills of employees. Web scale technology and its products offer huge potential for servers and storage and are a source of high competency business model. The dimension of modification and upgradation has certain risks associated with it but if they could be proactively mitigated, they provide a scalable and agile enterprise solutions. The exposure of Big Data gave birth to tools like Hadoop Ecosystem, MapR, Apache Spark, NoSQL Database, Blockchain etc. are the tools committed in capturing, analysis and processing of huge volumes of data and generating actionable business insights.

Web scale as a whole extends accessibility and acceptability to the existing conventional enterprise. The different and radical environments of digital enterprises need proficient skills to acquire web scale infrastructure and thus arises the need of learning as well as managing web scale tools and technologies. The digital environment of enterprise is converged with computational, storage, hardware and networking solutions of web scale IT to deliver efficient business solutions. The storage layer is a software defined module which works among multiple platforms and reflects as a large cloud enterprise. Thus, neither the legacy and compliance issues are affected nor the expert deployment or management is required. Simple GUI and API competently manage on-site and off-site resources from one place. Web-scale brings distributed computational resources, storage and network resources and the virtual resources dispersed at distinct multiple nodes in the networks to a single data centre and delivers cost effective solutions.

The entertainment industry is significantly utilizing web scale approach. The cloud services provide entertainment content be it music, drama, or movies rapidly to a large population of customers. Media and Entertainment industry are undergoing a massive transformation through digital enterprises. The digital solutions are revolutionizing entertainment firms to offer personalized user experience. Custom tailored digital solutions are increasing revenue growth and offering high performance.

Web scale IT attempts an innovative and dynamic architectural approach to deliver high performance, personalized and quick services to users at the global standard scale. In a nutshell, its offerings are similar to that of cloud services along with customized experience and reduced costs. Google, Microsoft's Azure, Amazon Web Services (AWS) are the large cloud service providers which represent a flexible, agile and efficient route to Web Scale IT. The incorporation of web scale IT into the business operations strategically intensify the efficiency and proficiency of digital enterprises. It is essential to realize the implementation challenges associated with the adoption of technological shift towards Web Scale IT. The resilient infrastructure of Web Scale IT offers speed, scale, and consistency for meeting business demands. Web scale IT has become an integrated component contributing in the digital enterprise transformation and giving a thrust to the digital economy. It offers customers a 24x7 online operations service with location and device independence. Speed, reliability and scalability of Web Scale IT is way ahead of its coexisting technology and tools. The online breadth of services through Web Scale IT practices are extremely fast. The digital presence of enterprises around the globe has indeed accelerated their business growth but also bears the timely pressure to embrace innovative and mission critical transformations by web innovators. The transition to the Web Scale automation environment needs to be stable to ensure consistent legacy workloads. In the work carried out by Fankhauser et al. (2016) the dimensions of scale are manpower, server and storage capacity, complexity and time to reach end users.

Web Scale IT as devised by Gartner, is the utilization of computing resources and IT infrastructure in an enterprise for large scale cloud services. The urge of Web Scale Machine Learning has emerged due to ever growing big data of IT enterprises such as Uber, Google, Facebook etc. The exponential growth of data sets demands scalable solutions in Machine Learning. Memory and CPU time are the prime constraints in dealing with Machine Learning solutions for Web scale.

DEFINING WEB SCALE

Web scale is an IT term which defines computing as a globally spanning approach. In the context of architecture, it has the potential to offer services as offered by huge cloud providers. Speed and agility provided by Web Scale architecture is beyond the scales in terms of building, designing, and managing large data centres. The social media tycoon Facebook, e-commerce giant Amazon, media services provider Netflix, and several others when integrated together, lays down the framework for Web Scale enterprise. Web scale aims to deploy, design and manage IT infrastructure at varied scales and it is so flexible that it can be conveniently enhanced with any category of business. Sjardin (2016) in their book titled, "Large Scale Machine Learning with Python" discussed the Machine Learning concepts along with the algorithms of supervised and unsupervised learning that are significant for large scale databases.

Large data sets have been there even before the concepts of Big Data and Machine Learning have evolved. Enormous collection of text documents in archives, medical diagnosis data, DNA sequences, data collected in world summits, data collected by scientists and researchers, astronauts, poses challenges to data analysts, and business Intelligence systems. A large datasets and scalable data sets are distinct in a fundamental way that for a large data set, the Machine Learning algorithm will work on a large number of cases or variables, but for scalable data sets, the algorithms must also perform efficiently with its running time in accordance with the size of the problem.

Dong et al. (2014) proposed a Web scale Knowledge Vault methodology, which withdraws data from large datasets from Web content. The web content can be existing in any structured or unstructured form, for example, text, tabular, graph, human annotations etc. They implemented Supervised learning algorithms of Machine Learning to derive information. The service-oriented architecture of web services is not strictly coupled; instead it leverages the API's to promote reuse and sharing among customers. Programming languages, application runtime environment, and operating systems are operationally independent to achieve a high degree of reliability and uptime. They also support dynamic workloads with high speed and agility. Operational efficiency and automation goals of Web Scale IT helps achieve the business goals while maintaining the stability of web services architecture. It enabled companies to develop an infrastructure which responds to changing market and users' expectations. IT developers work over heterogeneous models to create a unified business process which focuses on automation, networking and communication and legacy compliance standards.

The power of Web Scale IT gives web innovators the ability to develop practices which aim to hold up quick deployments and effectively respond to changing business requirements being resilient in nature. The complex infrastructure potential also scales up. Attempts are made to create faster and agile business models without affecting roots and principles of enterprise. Enhancement in personalized customer experience is also a focus area for web innovators. Investments are made in productive innovations and effective technologies. Successful digital enterprises allow their development teams to try new ideas and creative products. They use an incremental software design approach as used by Google, Amazon, Facebook of implementing an immature version and then they perform alpha beta tests and build the potential product incrementally. Various development teams maintain transparency and keep sharing information for the strong release of the product. Digital enterprises business services have become an integrated scenario of SaaS, PaaS and hybridized cloud computing services. The enterprise data with Web Scale leverages automation with predictive analytics technology. This cuts down the costs of critical business services and creates a 'n' tier application setting which eliminates the need of making probabilistic calculations for system management. This brings along the need of automation, monitoring and management to map the enterprise to a higher and greater scale. The quality metrics of capacity, speed and performance must remain unaffected and the enterprise system should be capable of making autocorrections and restoration in event of failure. And ensuring the system runs 24x7.

It has been observed that conventional IT applications and monitoring systems fail to scale proportionally in Web Scale environments. This takes place when resources are added to meet the needs of upscaling environments. The decision-making potential of Web Scale IT is affected by lack of granularity in data collected by business solutions and it has to derive the enriched data as per contextual requirement

AUTOMATION FOR WEB SCALE IN DIGITAL ENTERPRISE TRANSFORMATION

Automation is the underlying strength of Web Scale IT. It reduces the manpower workload and gives reach to the same patterns that could be brought and developed manually. Automation provides time and cost-efficient infrastructure with less dependence on hardware and configured resources. It can handle heterogeneous platforms. Linux, Windows, AIX operating systems are all supported in the same network. Cloud computing resources are expertly managed by a good automation platform. The migration of on premises resources to cloud resources is efficiently taken care of with consistency and structure. Automation enables sustainability and scales up the enterprise operations. Chauhan et al. (2020) explains AutoML (Automated Machine Learning) with its practical applicability in a digital enterprise context. Management of enterprise infrastructure becomes efficient and the rate of deployment of business processes increase on premises and on cloud. Automated business models carry testing of deployment modules with ease and consistency. Automation helps in predicting patterns for future digital marketing without investing significant amounts of time and money. Thus, giving ample time and opportunities to enterprises to plan for the future. Enterprise could quickly respond to changing business trends. Automation offers dynamic provisioning of infrastructure services at different scale among heterogeneous business environments

Automation gives ability to enterprises to work in compliance with legal policies and standards. Version control and configuration drift are controlled by an automation base. Consistency provides a robust infrastructure and monitors risk prevention and mitigation work process. Consistency also offers ease of migration of applications to the cloud. Automation platforms are easily recoverable in event of disaster. Hence making the digital enterprise a fault tolerance infrastructure. It allows the network connections of an enterprise system to go offline during system boot and recovery. It could handle complex interdependence among servers which require distributed coordination. Hence the policy-based convergence about multiple networks in the network is achieved and the automation platform brings a distributed architecture. In the view of Gartner (2020) automation also ensures secure communications among resources and security controls on specific nodes facilitating access control. It guarantees protected access between nodes and servers. Automation platforms are the forthcoming must haves of a digital enterprise. The automation of essential business configuration tasks gives opportunities to digital enterprises to excel in business by creating a consistent delivery pipeline. In due course of time this boosts the growth of business and revenue.

Limits on Analysing Data Without Machine Learning

1. CPU computation is affected by the time required to analyse the data.
2. Memory constraint for processing since input/output affects the size of data units taken into memory from storage.
3. Memory is also affected by the size of scalable data that can be processed at any given time.

Advantage of Web Scale IT With Machine Learning

IT giants are gaining a horizontal expansion as well as vertical growth with the advent of Web Scale algorithms. Google and Facebook have achieved Business Agility, because Web Scale algorithms could efficiently handle millions of data in TB. Even the data centre's technology is being greatly impacted by Web Scale. Digital transformation in the view of Martins et al. (2020) aims not only to flood the existing enterprise system with technology and automation but to create a journey in a digital environment with speed and agility. The system should be flexible to undergo timely changes and rapid modifications, should perform every slight operation with automation and it should free people from doing complex tasks and bring out their creativity and innovation. The strategies of digital enterprise transformation often create panic of replacing jobs and manpower through Artificial Intelligence, automation, and RPA. But the only point of technological advancements since the beginning is only to accelerate the growth and speed and turn the concerns and focus on other business processes and things. Technology does not affect jobs practically; it creates some and replaces some. It indeed will give birth to even more dynamic education and learning systems to train and prepare people for other significant jobs and roles.

ROBOTIC PROCESS AUTOMATION THROUGH MACHINE LEARNING ON WEB SCALE

This recent technology automates business processes through software robots, bots or chatbots and digital workers (AI). It uses specialized software robots which basically are computer programs which assists in automation and standardize repeated business processes. The software robots impersonate human actions through interacting apps. Martins et al. (2020) in their work explains how these bots are virtual assistants in business and they improve employee morale and productivity. The digital enterprises efficiently manage their revenue generation, productivity and accuracy through robotic process automation. The bots automate various business processes such as they could work with distinct application user interfaces, copy paste data, open attachments in emails, form filling, login and logout. Bots increase their intelligence with changes in business processes and thus automate tasks by interplaying with different applications. This beauty of robotic process automation will give assistance in driving digital business transformation and future work.

Under the work published by Romao et al. (2019) following benefits of RPA are discussed-

1. Less technical hurdles- Configuring a software robot does not need efficient programming skills. It extensively uses a drag and drop designer approach and automates the business model through a process recorder feature.
2. Accuracy- The consistency and accuracy of bots is much higher thus they produce error free results and they don't make mistakes. Information and record keeping are excellently managed by RPA.
3. Compliance with regulations and standards- Bots meet and follow the instructions through which they have been configured and they also keep an audit trail log in case a business process needs a review. The suitable meet the strictest compliance standards.
4. Interruption free work- Software bots can autonomously and tirelessly perform operations 24x7 without any need of medical staff to begin the business process. RPA doesn't clash with underlying systems and integrates with multiple applications. Thus, making RPA a reliable solution in digital business transformation.
5. Increases employee involvement and employee morale- The staff members can engage themselves in productive work and strategic management. The offloading of manual tasks to bots lets employees to focus on revenue producing activities. This eventually increases productivity.

RPA helps to optimize business process automation in an online manner and is an efficient tool for project handling. This powerful technology increases productivity and leads to cost reduction. Machine learning helps bots to identify patterns in data and integration of machine learning with artificial intelligence allows robotic process automation to work across multiple interfaces, in error handling and to cognitively work in bringing and elevating more value to business. According to Romao (2019), the employees could use RPA as a personal productivity tool. They are able to discover extra opportunities in routine tasks with the help of a bot assistant. It enables employees to narrow their monotonous tasks by offering self-serving automation solutions. Enterprise wide deployment of RPA is not essential and need not demand for intensive resources.

Maintenance of bots is also very flexible since they are audited and monitored on top of a centralized server. This way the employees could deploy their customized solutions in a digital enterprise. The shift in digital efforts towards RPA is a pragmatic approach as automation rapidly increases digital transformation and is indeed an alternative for digital transformation. RPA applications also need to integrate with legacy systems. This promotes a rapid growth in the initiatives of digital transformation and also keeps the investments balanced. The usual transformation that companies seek to carry out requires big operational and structural challenges. But RPA can begin with existing legacy systems and user interfaces without a need to change much and the enterprise would continue to evolve as it grows. The application only needs to be configured to work along with RPA. With Robotic Process Automation, the enterprise system is blessed with the ability to perform repetitive tasks and gradually learn and do more.

The studies and business reports have found the wide use of Robotic Process Automation in departments of finance and accounting as these departments encounter repeated tasks of cut and paste the spreadsheet fields. With automation, a bot saves a lot of employees' time as it could do these repetitive actions in a fraction of time and without raising a moment of issue against its intelligence and potential. Thus, making RPA the most sought-after technology. Leshob et al. (2018) suggests how machine learning and artificial intelligence are making the digital business process self-sustained and intelligent. Bots can also learn conversational intelligence to chat and interact with customers (Chat-Bots) and they could understand human intent to react and perform actions. Bots have also played a key role in dealing with raw and unstructured data to help in business analytics and decision making. They could decipher unstructured data content and RPA bots then take actions upon the pre-processed data. The automation ability of RPA makes it a prominent tool for bridging the gap in system integration. The bots work among applications and bring out solutions for data syncing, complying with legacy systems and third-party sites without human interruption. With RPA the Digital Transformation voyage is swiftly sustained by carrying automation of routine repetitive tasks challenges and assistance in business activities to achieve higher potential.

SOLUTIONS AND RECOMMENDATIONS

Machine learning is undoubtedly an extremely powerful tool for horizontal business expansion as well as vertical revenue growth. The decision-making potential of machine learning provides quick responsiveness, accurate and consistent results upon predictive analysis. Pattern recognition and rules application in accordance to the algorithm is the essence of machine learning. Decisions and outcomes are predicted by analysis of information for example, user data, accounts and transactions, sales data etc. Equally significant is to identify previously unknown patterns to detect threat and unexpected events from data. Digital enterprises incorporate machine learning to derive business centric understanding of data and to implement relevant actions to improve business processes. Machine learning algorithms drive data observations and analyses events, responses and account shifts in the data environment. Thereby it refines existing business processes and improves the performance of business activity. In this way the enterprise system learns and consistently improves its quantifiable results. By incorporating machine learning in web scale digital enterprise transformation has several benefits. The essence of Machine Learning lies in pattern recognition, estimation, data extraction, harnessing non textual data, AI and prediction. The dynamic and rapid growing nature of data exclusively in Web Scale IT demands learning algorithms to be efficient in: Processing nonlinear and non-quadratic programs. Memory requirements and CPU computation of algorithms should be tractable. Classification, prediction and analysis should be carried out efficiently in distributed applications. Although only insignificant automation exists in this process because software systems do not bring out the creative actions and solutions on its own. Digital enterprises deploy machine learning platforms not only to identify solutions of targeted processes and activities but also to intrinsically recognize the unidentified and unexplored business areas. Machine learning can efficiently handle larger datasets and grant a power to digital enterprises to function at a faster pace and deliver the accurate solutions to raise the business revenue and competence. The complex models and learning algorithms are dedicated to optimizing the automated technology through machine learning. Large numbers of repetitive tasks are handled by machine learning models.

FUTURE RESEARCH DIRECTIONS

Digital enterprises adopting machine learning at web scale have gained remarkable growth in their business and operations. IBM's Watson leveraged digital enterprise with machine knowledge and artificial intelligence capabilities. At web scale with machine learning, it is expected to observe a significant improvement in business processes and decision making. In future, the digital enterprises will solely rely on automated management tools for effective data management and for customization. Machine learning integrated with artificial intelligence enhances business collaboration of digital enterprises. Industry 4.0 has its foundations based on essential ingredients such as machine learning, automation, artificial intelligence, cloud computing and distributed computing. In the near future, enterprises will use their acquired "knowledge" as a service. The issues of knowledge ownership will be resolved by machine learning strategies.

Machine learning automates models to work with complex data and provide insights without the need of explicit programming of the system. This will help in transformation of digital enterprises to bridge the gap between products and users. Change is the only constant in life and also in business. The recent COVID-19 pandemic caused terrible disruptions across the globe. Remote access and offsite business processes were designed to cope and adapt this new reality. The journey of digital enterprise transformation is continued and profitable if enterprises are equipped with potential tools and technologies. Machine learning and artificial intelligence ensures in building a strong system for digital enterprise transformation which would address the needs of a changing business environment. Machine learning for digital enterprises at web scale accelerates deployment and operational efficiency to very high percentage. The speed and scale of processes are the key elements in assessing the impact of digital enterprise transformation. There are some challenges linked with machine learning workflows. Digital enterprise transformation requires operational support for machine learning tools and technologies. Effective deployment of machine learning and artificial intelligence models is essential. Digital enterprises need to upskill their workforce towards data science, data analytics and machine learning.

The transformation of digital enterprises is like the metamorphosis of a butterfly. It's in the hands of an enterprise management to anticipate the future of services and transform itself towards being in the market and be a butterfly freely achieving heights with superpowers or stay stuck at being a Caterpillar. The digital economy is revolutionizing around the world with fast growing and changing business strategies. Though the Web Scale and automation is still being not utilized by many of the companies. Most caterpillars crawl while only a few butterflies fly. The marketplace competence among digital enterprises has promptly increased the pressure upon enterprises to keep a pace with business and sales growth, reduce the operating costs and development time along with meeting customers' expectations and satisfaction. A case study found that 68% of companies turned their operations towards machine learning and artificial intelligence to scale up and speed up their digital transformation.

CONCLUSION

Rome was not built in a day. Analogous to this digital transformation also goes down the lane with strong plans and right strategies. It involves senior management of enterprises to ensure that employees understand their capacities and responsibilities and adopt smart technology by identifying their roles in various environments and platforms. Then only an enterprise will achieve extremely powerful acceleration in its transformation process. The initial drive of digital transformation is carried with "data". Data pre-processing through piles of data from various business domains and to gain the insights from real time data is the primary step. Machine learning algorithms perform data analysis and deliver predictive solutions which will be vital for enterprise and give the power to organizations to linger in industry competencies. In a web scale IT, with the strength and influence of IoT, RPA, and machine learning applications, businesses will constantly advance and expand their digital capabilities, infrastructure and transformation further for effective data analysis. The integration of artificial intelligence with machine learning is used by development quality assurance, predictive maintenance and sentiment analysis of customers. The capability of machine learning algorithms to study patterns and behaviours on a network helps to alert the corresponding teams and also indicate if the behaviour is tolerable and stable. If any anomalies take a long time, then machine learning tries to insert fixes on its own.

The human perception towards technology and digital tools, the social behaviour and inclination of their lifestyle towards the digital world affects the management of digital enterprises. The anti-revolutionary social movements, political outrage and workflows and digital divide amongst people impacts the business in a digital enterprise. The recent COVID-19 is the most suitable example of how digital enterprises are affected by environmental factors. COVID-19 pandemic will impose a long-lasting global impact for humanity as well as for the economy. It has caused digital marketing out stay supply chain disruptions and thus has radically affected most businesses. There is a solution for every problem. Eventually COVID-19 brought about the promotion of online marketing and work from culture to digital enterprises. E-learning, streaming, online gaming and shopping has exponentially increased. The businesses which evolved with time and shifted their technology potential to digital platforms are running smoothly and have mitigated the influence of this outbreak.

The digitized documentation, audits, contracts, legal policies, legacy compliance standards and lawsuits helps businesses to digitally transform as a whole. The enterprise overcomes the slow, tedious and manual record keeping system and becomes a digital enterprise with a speedy and automated environment. The automation of manual documentation efficiently analyses data for business insight and helps customers and businesses in making better and smarter decisions. Digital transformation enhances the customer expectations and their interactions with digital enterprises. They are in a unified framework with business services and with the company revenues they want to elevate their economy as well. In the final analysis, for automating the journey of digital enterprises transformation, the businesses will have to establish certain challenging and costly operations and platforms, prepare themselves for technology readiness, understand technology impacts on digital products, and ultimately have to monetize their data assets.

REFERENCES

Akaichi, J. (2017). *Sentiment Classification ch076.* . doi:10.1155/2020/7403128

Alasadi, S., & Bhaya, W. (2017). Review of Data Preprocessing Techniques in Data Mining. *Journal of Engineering and Applied Sciences (Asian Research Publishing Network)*, *12*, 4102–4107.

Chauhan, K., Jani, S., Thakkar, D., Dave, R., Bhatia, J., Tanwar, S., & Obaidat, M. (2020). *Automated Machine Learning: The New Wave ofMachine Learning*. ICIMIA. doi:10.1109/ICIMIA48430.2020.9074859

Deepa, B. (2020). *Advanced Machine Learning for Enterprise IoT Modeling*. Springer. doi:10.1007/978-3-030-44407-5_5

Dong, X., Gabrilovich, E., Heitz, G., Horn, W., Lao, N., Murphy, K., Strohmann, T., Sun, S., & Zhang, W. (2014). Knowledge vault: a web-scale approach to probabilistic knowledge fusion. *Proceedings of the 20th ACM SIGKDD international conference on Knowledge discovery and data mining*. 10.1145/2623330.2623623

Gärtner, C. (2020). *Smart HRM*. Springer. doi:10.1007/978-3-658-29431-1

Hou, W., & Perkowski, M. (2019). *A Novel Machine Learning Algorithm to Reduce Prediction Error and Accelerated Learning Curve for Very Large Datasets*. IEEE. doi:10.1109/ISMVL.2019.00025

Hussain, F., Hussain, R., Hassan, S. A., & Hossain, E. (2020). *Machine Learning in IoT Security: Current Solutions and Future Challenges*. IEEE. doi:10.1109/COMST.2020.2986444

Jain, V., & Kumar, S. (2020). *Sentiment Recognition in Customer Reviews Using Deep Learning*. doi:10.4018/978-1-7998-0414-7.ch077

Jasny, M., Zeigler, T., Kraska, T., Roehm, U., & Binnig, C. (2020). DB4ML - An In-Memory Database Kernel with Machine Learning Support. *Sigmoid ACM Conference*. 10.1145/3318464.3380575

Leshob, A., Bourgouin, A., & Renard, L. (2018). *Towards a Process Analysis Approach to Adopt Robotic Process Automation*. IEEE. doi:10.1109/ICEBE.2018.00018

Liu, B., Guo, W., Niu, D., Luo, J., Wang, C., Wen, Z., & Xu, Y. (2020). GIANT: Scalable Creation of a Web-scale Ontology. *Proceedings of the ACM*. 10.1145/3318464.3386145

Liu, C., Feng, Y., Lin, D., Wu, L., & Guo, M. (2020). *Iot based laundry services: an application of big data analytics, intelligent logistics management, and machine learning techniques*. International Journal of Production. doi:10.1080/00207543.2019.1677961

Lockard, C., Shiralkar, P., Dong, X., & Hajishirzi, H. (2020). Web-scale Knowledge Collection. *Proceedings of the 13th International Conference on Web Search and Data Mining*. 10.1145/3336191.3371878

Martins, P., Sá, F., Morgado, F., & Cunha, C. (2020). *Using machine learning for cognitive Robotic Process Automation (RPA)*. IEEE. doi:10.23919/CISTI49556.2020.9140440

Obukhova, A., Merzlyakova, E., Irina, E., & Karakulina, K. (2020). *Introduction of digital technologies in the enterprise*. IEEE. https://ui.adsabs.harvard.edu/abs/2020E3SWC.15904004O/abstract

Olifrov, A., Makoveichuk, K., Zhytnyy, P., Filimonenkova, P., & Petrenk, S. (2018). *Models of process for governance of enterprise IT and personal training for digital Economy*. IEEE. doi:10.1109/PTES.2018.8604166

Rangone, A. (2020). *Innovation and Technology: The Age of the Digital Enterprise*. Springer. doi:10.1007/978-3-030-31768-3

Romao, M., Costa, J., & Costa, C. J. (2019). *Robotic Process Automation: A Case Study in the Banking Industry*. CISTI. doi:10.1109/ACCESS.2020.2974934

Shende, V., & Kulkarni, M. (2020). Application of Machine Learning in Cryptography. *International Journal of Advanced Trends in Computer Science and Engineering*. doi:10.30534/ijatcse/2020/149932020

Sjardin, B., Massaron, L., & Boschetti, A. (2016). *Large Scale Machine Learning with Python*. Academic Press.

Thupae, R. (2018). *Machine Learning Techniques for Traffic Identification and Classification in SD-WSN*. IEEE.

Wanga, Y., Kung, L., & Byrd, T. (2018). *Big data analytics: Understanding its capabilities and potential benefits for healthcare organizations*. Elsevier. doi:10.1016/j.techfore.2015.12.019

ADDITIONAL READING

Wilaisakoolyong, N. (2018). *The essential factors that improve organization to be Digital enterprise Thailand 4.0*. IEEE. doi:10.1109/ICSEC.2018.8712785

Chapter 14
Digital Employer Branding:
An Exploration of the Moroccan Customer Relation Centers

Zakaria Lissaneddine
https://orcid.org/0000-0003-2263-6459
National School of Business and Management of Meknès, Morocco

Younès El Manzani
https://orcid.org/0000-0002-4529-9953
ISM-IAE, Versailles Saint-Quentin en Yvelines University, France & Paris-Saclay University, France

Mostapha El Idrissi
https://orcid.org/0000-0003-0989-6539
FSJES Marrakech, Cadi Ayyad University, Morocco

ABSTRACT

Digital transformation has become a key concern for many enterprises that social media now occupy an important place more than ever in the managerial strategies. The human resources (HR) function is considered as one of the organizational dimensions that have taken advantage of these digital platforms, especially for the employer branding purposes. This chapter aims to explore the practices that enterprises in Morocco use to manage their employer brand through social media to attract potential candidates, retain recruits, and limit turnover. To achieve this research objective, a multiple case study was carried out with managers from four customer relation centers through semi-structured interviews. The findings highlight the existence of digital ambassadorship and e-reputation oversight practices. Finally, this chapter also provides some managerial recommendations and future research directions.

DOI: 10.4018/978-1-7998-8587-0.ch014

INTRODUCTION

Human capital is a key source of competitive advantage that determines the success or failure of any enterprise (Brymer, Molloy, & Gilbert, 2014; Carpentier et al., 2017; Ha & Luan, 2018). Many industries are facing hostile competition between enterprises to attract and retain the most talented employees (Carpentier et al., 2017). In this context, to supply their needs in terms of human labor, enterprises rely mainly on the employer branding as a distinctive weapon to overcome this extremely fierce "war of talents" (Ha & Luan, 2018). Practitioners as researchers all agree that employer branding has gained in popularity as a managerial strategy (Eger, Mičík & Řehoř, 2018), combining two substantial organizational areas, branding and human resources (Gilani & Cunningham, 2017; Lievens & Slaughter, 2016). In this sense, HR professionals apply branding principals to HR management to promote their enterprise, both within and outside the organization as an outstanding and desirable employer (Backhaus, 2016; Backhaus & Tikoo, 2004; Bondarouk et al., 2014).

In parallel, social media have become an integral part of daily life for people all over the world. They cover a wide variety of platforms and services (e.g. social networking sites, Wikis, blogs, podcasts, and video-sharing sites) which facilitate interaction, creation and the sharing of content between the internet and social users (Kissel & Büttgen, 2015). According to Digital 2020 reports[11], social media encompassed 3.80 billion users in January 2020, an expansion of more than 9% (321 million new users) compared to last year. At present, 60% of the world's population is online, and new projections suggest that over half of the total population of the world is about to use social media by the middle of 2020. Over the coming years, it will be noticed that the world population will be more and more involved in the use of social networks to seek national or international work opportunities.

The rapidly evolving social media are expanding the way of doing business, especially in marketing and brand management (Otken & Okan, 2016). Indeed, social media are no longer seen as a fad but a real competitive tool, organizations that are conscious of this reality are exploiting social networking sites for creating awareness and networking in terms of employer branding (Ha & Luan, 2018; Otken & Okan, 2016; Sharma & Verma, 2018). Compared to conventional media channels, social media are more effective since they are a promising new medium not only for direct communication with employees but also to interact with job seekers to advertise the brand meaning of the employer (Kissel & Büttgen, 2015; McFarland & Ployhart, 2015).

Despite the intensification of the use of social media in the employer branding, the majority of previous studies have focused more on the implication of social media use in supporting organizational employer brand attractiveness (Carpentier et al., 2017; Carpentier, Van Hoye, & Weng, 2019; Eger et al., 2019; Kashive, Khanna, & Bharthi, 2020; Kissel & Büttgen, 2015; Mičík & Mičudová, 2018; Otken & Okan, 2016; Sivertzen, Nilsen, & Olafsen, 2013; Tanwar & Kumar, 2019), beside the enhancement of the job application intention (Ha & Luan, 2018; Sivertzen et al., 2013). The literature on the relationship between employer branding and social media still fragmented and lacks studies that are interested in the whole process of employer brand management in the context of social media networks.

To fill this gap, the purpose of this chapter is to explore the way the process of employer branding occurs by using social media. The authors tried to better understand the practices undertaken by enterprises in terms of HR marketing in the digital era. Their ambition is therefore to provide clear insights about the use of digital social media by enterprises to shape their employer brand and how this latter can be beneficial in retaining current employees and attracting potential ones in the Moroccan organizational context, and more particularly in the customer relation centers. The research question of this chapter is formulated as follows: how do customer relation centers in Morocco manage their employer brand via digital social networks?

To bring answer to this question, the study reported in this chapter has mobilized an exploratory fieldwork interview to explain in which particular way the four call centers studied use social media to appeal to potential employees, implicate and retain their employees to deal with the complexity of the turnover problem. In Morocco, the turnover[22]rate in call centers varies between 15% and 25% depending on the nature of the firm's activity (making or receiving calls). A high turnover rate would be a factor of dysfunction and a source of significant additional costs necessary for the replacement of departures and the training of recruits.

This chapter will, in the first place, introduce the topic of the employer branding and its relationship with social media. Secondly, a full section is dedicated to the methodology used in the study. Thirdly, results and discussion will be exposed. Finally, research implications, limits and future research directions are given in the conclusion.

THEORETICAL BACKGROUND

Employer Brand

Customers are not the only targets of marketing activities. Marketing can also apply to all the situations in which offers are presented to stakeholders who undertake exchanges of tangible and/or intangible values with the organization. Employees, therefore, represent another group of stakeholders with whom organizations carry out these value transactions and with whom information exchanges must be established.

The employer brand was born as the result of the branding principles from marketing to human resource management. Beyond being an outstanding topic in the HR management field, it has become one of the emerging concepts of business management in general. Ambler & Barrow (1996, p. 187) were among the earliest academics to define this concept as "*the package of functional, economic and psychological benefits provided by employment, and identified with the employing company*". After its introduction, the employer brand gave rise to other related concepts such as *employer brand capital* (Ewing et al., 2002), *employer brand attractiveness* (Berthon, Ewing & Hah, 2005), and *employer's brand image* (Knox & Freeman, 2006).

There is a consensus that the role of the employer brand is to make the firm the ideal place to work in (Ambler & Barrow, 1996; App et al., 2012; Berthon et al., 2005; Kapoor, 2010). Employer branding is primarily based on the idea that human capital is crucial for companies' value creation, and companies who invest in qualified human capital have an enhanced performance (Backhaus & Tikoo, 2004). Given the importance of human capital, organizations must distinguish themselves from their rivals by building an appealing employer brand (Lievens & Slaughter, 2016). Having a superior employer brand supports the company in the war for talent. It gives it a long-term strategic competitive advantage and represents a key success factor in an era where competitiveness is increasingly based on human capital as a source of innovation and differentiation (App et al., 2012; Mangold & Miles, 2007).

Employer Branding Strategy

In the literature, two terms coexist and sometimes refer to the same concept, namely "*Employer Brand*", and "*Employer Branding*" which means management of the employer brand (Lissaneddine, 2019). Lloyd (2002) describes the employer branding as the '*sum of a company's efforts to communicate to existing and prospective staff that it is a desirable place to work*'. It represents the efforts that a firm makes to promote, both internally and externally, a clear vision of what makes it different and desirable as an employer (Backhaus & Tikoo, 2004). According to Edwards (2009), the management of the employer brand is a process that brings together marketing and HRM techniques to create an employer brand. Therefore, the employer brand management brings together the tools and techniques that the firm applies to ensure that current and potential employees recognize, experience and believes in the essential values defined by the same company. For Backhaus & Tikoo (2004), this is a process that consists of three stages:

- The first stage consists of *the value proposition*, where the company uses information concerning its identity, organizational culture, management style, and brand image, to design a specific employer brand intended to be presented to current employees and potential candidates. Building this unique employer brand begins with the identification of the target image that one wishes to give to current and potential employees. The value proposition refers to the image with which the company hopes to be perceived. It describes the main qualities with which the firm hopes to be associated as an employer. An effective value proposition must be clear, focused and easy to understand (Mosley, 2014).
- The second stage represents *external marketing*. It is based on communication on the employer brand with targeted potential candidates. Thus, the challenges of the employer brand externally are to improve organizational attractiveness, to ensure a long-term continuous flow of quality candidates (Charbonnier-Voirin & Vignolles, 2015).
- The third and final stage involves *internal marketing* which is the most crucial of this process. It consists of respecting the promises made to recruits during their hiring. This stage is crucial for the firm in the sense that it would be continuous marketing that does not end with the signing of an employment contract. Also, the recruited candidates can become ambassadors of their own business (Kapoor, 2010).

Employer branding has become a top management priority for companies that consider HR to be one of the most valuable intangible assets (Kissel & Büttgen, 2015). This strategic dimension given to the management of the employer brand is also explained by the desire of companies to obtain a sustainable competitive advantage through a quality employer brand. Moroko & Uncles (2008) argue that several firms from different industry sectors have formally defined their employer brand and manage it strategically.

Digital Employer Branding via Social Media

Social media can be described as digital platforms on which users can create a profile, connect with other users, generate and exchange content and engage in interactive communication (Boyd & Ellison, 2007; Carpentier et al., 2017; McFarland & Ployhart, 2015). Previously, organizations used social media to market their brand image to external stakeholders such as customers, suppliers, and shareholders.

However, more recently, organizations have used social media in their employer brand management to retain their employees and attract competent employees.

Digital transformation has become a key concern for many enterprises (Chanias, Myers & Hessa, 2019). Therefore many studies have proved that the use of social media in employer branding enhances a firm's organizational attractiveness and stimulates job seekers' intention to apply (Carpentier et al., 2017; Ha & Luan, 2018; Kissel & Büttgen, 2015; Sivertzen et al., 2013). The use of social media raises the firm's social presence (Short, Williams & Christie, 1976) by giving a feeling of humanness, interpersonal warmth, and proximity when interacting with potential employees. Thus, social media can be perceived as informal communication channels that allow adopting a personal and friendly communication style (Carpentier et al., 2017). Social media can act as a relationship-building tool to create and maintain a strong linkage with candidates. Individuals, including job candidates, can interact with the employer by sending private messages, liking, sharing or writing a reaction on the organization's posts (Carpentier et al., 2017).

Social media provide the firm with the opportunity to build a positive employer brand and a good organizational attractiveness when it shares accurate and complete information with job applicants on its culture and work atmosphere, career progression, business ethics, and growth perspectives (El Zoghbi & Aoun, 2016; Turban & Cable, 2003). For example, organizations deploy their Facebook or Twitter accounts to promote themselves regularly using tweets, posts or instant messages or propose subjects of discussion with its followers (Bondarouk, Ruël, Axinia & Arama, 2014). Such information will be gathered by job applicants to form an image of the firm and will constitute the basis for their processes of assessing the attractiveness of the organization to estimate their fit with it (Kissel & Büttgen, 2015). Firms that use social media to convey the relevant information sought by job applicants have an employer brand image that looks more persuasive and more attractive which increases the job applicants' attitudes, intentions and behavior associated with joining the organization (Carpentier et al., 2017).

Beyond potential employees, the use of social media in employer branding is also advantageous for the empowerment and loyalty of firms' current and newly recruited employees. Indeed, firms have to face the complex task of harmonizing internal beliefs with the brand's external message disseminated through social media (Edwards, 2009). The challenge of this task is to retain employees without creating a gap between their perceptions of the company's employer brand and the experienced reality within the organization. As long as the gap is very small, there will be an establishment of trust between the employee and the employer. Several authors state that respecting the promises made by the firm before recruitment helps in retaining recruits (Kapoor, 2010).

Social media are a space where current employees can see and feel the notoriety scale of their organization's employer brand. Alike customers, employees like to be identified in remarkable organizations. According to social identity theory, when employees possess a high level of organizational identification, then it is likely that they will also have a high level of organizational-based self-esteem (Tajfel & Turner, 1987). Hence, their values and beliefs will be intermixed with the values of the organization (Brunetto & Farr-Wharton, 2002) which will strengthen their sense of loyalty towards the organization. Studies have shown the positive association of employer brand with job engagement and organizational commitment (Rana & Sharma, 2019). According to Parry & Solidoro (2013), an effective interaction through social media might enhance positive workplace culture and improve employee satisfaction and engagement along with reinforcing a favorable external reputation. Moreover, employer branding enhances employee's morale, and it has been noted that employees subconsciously become brand ambassadors when they appreciate working and being part of an organization (Holbeche & Matthews, 2012).

The Employer Brand Digital Ambassadorship

Brand ambassadorship is a very recent phenomenon in the business world (Andersson & Ekman, 2009; Quaratino & Mazzei, 2018). The expressions "*live the brand*", "*brand champions*" and "*brand ambassadors*" are terms used in the literature to refer to high-performance employees who bring the employer brand to life through their attachment to it (Wallace & de Chernatony, 2009). The brand ambassador concept is used more and more in the marketing literature and can be implemented according to several scenarios (Marler & Fisher, 2013): (i) employees as brand ambassadors, (ii) celebrities as brand ambassadors, (iii) customers as brand ambassadors (the fanatic customers).

For this research, the authors will focus on the first case, which refers to employees as employer brand ambassadors. Electronic word of mouth and digital traces generated by employees on social media are crucial in firms' communication policies (Fueyo, 2015). Nowadays, each employee creates and disseminates content. He can give his opinion, comment, interact about his firm, without prior approval of the latter. Everyone thus participates in shaping the image that the firm sends back in terms of the employer brand. Exchanges with current and potential employees, therefore, become faster, more frequent and above all more transparent. The consistency between the employer brand offer and the reality experienced in the firm leads to the strengthening of the credible spread network made up of employees ambassadors, who create more direct and less institutional communication. Graham & Cascio (2018) studied the impact of the employer branding on the organizational reputation, focusing on the role of employers' brand ambassadorship. They reported that social media is used by employees as a channel for positive word-of-mouth about their employer. Thus, employee ambassadors tend to express their satisfaction, loyalty, and pride in belonging to their firms in social media (Parry & Solidoro, 2013).

Generally, organizations can mobilize their employees to act as powerful brand ambassadors who shape their reputation and increase credibility to the values publicized by its employer brand among key audiences (Dreher, 2014). The implementation of an employer brand ambassadorship strategy provides many advantages for the firm because this strategy contributes to the recruitment and retention of the best talent, which translates into better service and better productivity. In addition to creating a substantial employer brand, it reduces recruitment difficulties and costs and increase the number of suitable candidates (Parry & Solidoro, 2013).

E-Reputation

The advent of digital technologies (especially social media) and the appearance of virtual communities have led enterprises to worry about their online reputation. This new aspect of reputation can be managed by the enterprises themselves, but also by other stakeholders. E-reputation has been defined by Fueyo (2015) as the judgment made on any digital platform by the stakeholders, according to their expectations, their beliefs, their values and the information exchanges (electronic word of mouth), judgment resulting from their perception, the sum of the actions, the performances and behavior of an enterprise since its creation. In order to avoid unpleasant surprises (bad buzz, rumors, etc.) that external stakeholders can create thanks to digital technologies, enterprises have only one choice, which is to take care of their e-reputation continuously. In this sense, digital employer branding can be one of the fundamental aspects of e-reputation management.

METHOD

Context and Research Design

To understand the way the process of employer branding occurs through social media, the authors have chosen to conduct multiple case studies of four Moroccan call centers. The choice of these firms belonging to the customer relationship management segment, which is among the most successful Offshoring activities, has been motivated by two main reasons. First, call centers have posted positive performances for several consecutive years despite a difficult economic context. The main problem of these companies being the loyalty of their employees, it is not uncommon for the turnover rate to reach 70% (Pierre & Tremblay, 2012). Second, to overcome this situation, several customer relation centers have adopted HR marketing strategies to attract and retain recruits. Aware of the importance of their image as an employer, those firms are increasingly inclined to use social media to develop and communicate their employer brand with their current employees and potential candidates.

The authors adopted a qualitative case study design that provides a better understanding of complex social phenomena such as the management of the employer brand through social media (Yin, 2009). They believe that case studies will serve as an illustration of the process that occurs when firms decide to manage their brand as an employer by using social media. The case study seems particularly appropriate to the investigation of a new subject as it the case in this research (Eisenhardt, 1989; Miles, Huberman & Saldana, 2014). For the replication objective (Eisenhardt, 1989), the authors utilized a multiple case study design to create analytical rather than statistical generalization (Yin, 2009). Indeed, multiple case studies offer a broader exploration of the subject studied and enable more robust findings (Eisenhardt & Graebner, 2007). Furthermore, great insight would be gained from investigating the process as it occurs in a variety of firm contexts (Yin, 2009). Consequently, to draw up a detailed understanding of how the use of social media in the employer brand management works, authors choose to focus and explore the research question in four leading firms in the customer client's relationship sector.

Case Selection

In qualitative research based on case studies, researchers choose their cases for the potential that they offer in getting new theoretical vision, revelation, replication of the results or the development of an emerging theory (Eisenhardt & Graebner, 2007; Glaser & Strauss, 1967). So, in contrast to quantitative studies, qualitative ones are based rather on theoretical sampling than statistical representativeness (Eisenhardt & Graebner, 2007). In this chapter, the selection of the four cases was driven by the research question, not by any concern for representativeness (Miles et al., 2014). Indeed, the four companies interviewed were well known on the Moroccan job market for job seekers and belonged to the same activity segment, namely customer relationship management. The four firms also share several common points, such as digital presence on social networks, the practice of HR marketing, labeling in terms of employer branding and internalization. Table 1 gives a summary of the characteristics of the four studied cases.

Table 1. Characteristics of the cases

Case / Characteristics	WH	IN	AS	PG
Nationality	Multinational	Moroccan	Multinational	Moroccan
Year of introduction in Morocco	2002	2000	2002	1999
Number of employees	9.500	10.000	5.000	6.000
Number of settlements in Morocco	17	11	8	10
Presence in Social Media	Facebook LinkedIn Twitter Instagram	Facebook LinkedIn Instagram	Facebook LinkedIn Twitter YouTube	Facebook LinkedIn Instagram YouTube

Source: author's own contribution

Data Collection and Analysis

Due to the exploratory nature of this research, data were collected mainly through semi-structured interviews, consisting of semi-open questions allowing greater freedom to the respondents to express themselves freely on topics that it deems more important to them (Denzin & Lincoln, 2018). Yet, an interview guide was developed to serve as an orientation of discussions and ensure that all relevant topics were covered (Gioia, Corley & Hamilton, 2013).

Questions of the interviews are focused on the deployment of an employer brand strategy by the call centers and how those enterprises implement such a strategy. The authors asked the respondents to specify the role played by digital social media in shaping an employer brand and a good e-reputation, and how employees are encouraged to become ambassadors in social media to enhance the image of the company as a great place to work in. The questions are also focused on the feedback of potential employees and their reactions to such employer branding development.

In this research, interviews include people that are actively involved in the management of the employer brand. In this sense, the interviewees are generally HR managers, HR marketing managers, employer brand sourcing, communication and marketing officer within the four selected firms. Their function and affiliation are specified in more detail in Table 2 (their functions and companies are intentionally anonymous for ethical reasons).

Table 2. List of the interviewed managers

Interviewee	Function	Seniority	Duration	Firms Acronyms	Location
LK	HR Marketing & Social Media Manager	15 years	2H 05	WH	Rabat
YA	HR Project Manager	11 years	1H 10		
SM	HR Marketing Officer	10 months	1H 35		
IK	Sourcing & Employer Brand Officer	2 years	55 Min		
SB	Recruitment Officer	6 years	1H 05	IN	Casablanca
KH	Social Media Manager	6 months	55 Min		
HB	Internal Communications Officer	2 years	1H 45		
ME	Communication Manager	1,5 years	1H 15	AS	Casablanca
SS	HR Development Manager	4 years	1H 25		
JS	Communications Officer	7 years	55 Min		
MB	Deputy Director of Communication	3 years	1H	PG	Casablanca
AM	Digital Communication Project Manager	10 months	45 Min		

Source: author's own contribution

The interviews were recorded and fully transcribed, the average interview lasted about one hour and ten minutes. The authors keep making interviews until reaching information saturation in which material began to replicate itself and certain patterns appeared. According to Eisenhardt (1989), reaching information saturation gives a sign that the data collection process could be finished.

The data analysis follows an abductive approach since it relies on both the deductive and the inductive coding process (Miles et al., 2014). Therefore, the authors started with deductive coding by creating primary general codes from the concepts identified in the literature review. As coding progressed, authors inductively create new codes based mainly on the material gathered from the research field. Authors repeated the process until no codes can emerge, the final result of this process was to obtain a classification of data into key codes and main aggregate themes that allow better interpretation and extraction of fruitful results (Gioia et al., 2013; Miles et al., 2014).

Research Validity and Reliability

In order to increase the validity and reliability of the research, certain steps were taken according to four criteria mentioned by Gibbert et al. (2008) and Yin (2009). These criteria are commonly used to assess the rigor of case studies' research, it is about internal validity, construct validity, external validity and reliability.

In addressing internal validity, the authors tried to reflect the true picture of the deployment and impact of digital social media in building an employer brand and how its influence to attract potential employees and retain the current employees. To achieve this, the authors built the argument and conclusion mainly on data by using respondents' words and verbatim. The authors tried to report the reality as it was evoked by the interviewees. In order to achieve construct validity, the authors carried out multiple interviews in each company to verify the accuracy of the information provided. Snowball technique was used to interview informants who were an appropriate source of information. Fields notes and full transcriptions of interviews was accomplished to preserve all the information provided by the respondents.To enhance the external validity of the research, the authors used multiple case study design to establish more generalizable findings. The replication between cases allows authors to compare and contrast insights across cases and identify patterns to the phenomenon under study. Reliability of research is closely linked to the way in which the data were collected. The description of the data collection tools and the protocol of data analysis in the method section can ensure the transparency of the approach used and guarantee the reliability of the research.

RESULTS AND DISCUSSION

Overview of Findings

The employer branding occupies a very important place in the managerial jargon of the companies observed in this study, the interviewees attribute to the employer brand a strategic aspect which equals the overall reputation of the company given the nature of the activity sector judged very sensitive. Within these companies, the tasks of the employer branding are mainly assigned to the Human Resources department, but this does not prevent close collaboration with other departments such as communication and marketing departments. The Human Resources department of call centers is generally divided into several workgroups, centered on different axes, such as HR marketing, HR projects, sourcing, and employer branding.

"Digital employer branding is a part of the HR department, but there is also another department in the game, we work closely with the communication department, the only difference between us is that we are more focused on the outside: the e-recruitment, digital communication, and social networks, while the communication department is interested in employees inside and clients outside the company" (Sourcing & Employer Brand Officer – WH).

Companies are increasingly vigilant about all the sources of information to which potential candidates go to obtain information about their future employer, even before applying. They use social media to find information about the quality of life in the company and the job vacancy. The proactivity of the enterprises studied in this research has led them to manage their employer brand through social media. They mobilize these digital channels to communicate on all the advantages that their current employees benefit from, thus, making potential candidates wanting to join them. The managers of the observed companies underlined the importance of social media in their communication strategy, in particular in the promotion of their employer brand.

"For me, the employer brand is the image that the company can reflect, it is the word-of-mouth effect too because if someone has already had an experience here within AS, they will certainly tell his entourage and his family, that's where the influence on the perception of the employer brand begins in my opinion" (HR Development Manager – AS).

The process of employer branding in call centers begins with the value proposition and the enhancement of the work image. The value proposition represents a packaging which can include a fair remuneration, a good working climate, social and economic benefits, all this to satisfy the needs of the employee and guarantee him good working conditions within the company.

"An attractive employer brand is a pleasant working climate, well-appointed premises, and equipment, understanding managers, first of all, it is the human aspect that makes a good company and not only the working conditions, you can have the best of companies, but if your manager is not good or if you are not comfortable in your work you will not like the company" (Social Media Manager – IN).

Based on the conclusions of the interviews carried out, the managers interviewed wanted to assign that their companies were a pleasant workplace with a good atmosphere, good working conditions and numerous opportunities for professional development. This, of course, goes hand in hand with the literature. When these companies wish to demonstrate that they are a good place to work in and thus promote their employer brand, they communicate their values and their culture and try to disseminate the daily experience of their employees during work to create a coherent image between their employer brand and reality (Backhaus & Tikoo, 2004; Edwards, 2009).

The second step in the process of employing branding in call centers is the federation of employees, their retention has become an absolute priority for the top management of call centers, more and more of these structures are realizing that human capital is now one of the most precious intangible assets they own. Employee engagement is an important objective for managing the employer brand, the factors that motivate employee engagement must be taken into account when developing the value proposition (Mosley, 2014). Giving meaning to the tasks performed by employees can make their work attractive. Thus, the achievable challenges, the creativity at work, the training of staff, the reward for the efforts of employees would lead to organizational involvement. The employer branding must start inside the company before going to its outside, it would first have to satisfy the needs of its collaborators to be able to attract others thereafter.

"A good employer brand is a brand that manages to be attractive to its employees first before being attractive to its customers, for me a brand always starts from the inside, regardless of its field, environment or customers it serves, the most important, first of all, is to serve its employees. I often say that what is experienced internally is seen externally" (Communication Officer – AS).

The retention of employees within the firm is based on the absence of differences in perception before and after recruitment. In other words, before joining the company potential candidates conceive a certain image concerning their future employer thanks to the information collected mainly on social media. The adequacy of this perception conceived by future employees with the reality experienced within the company facilitates their integration and their retention.

Finally comes the stage of attracting potential candidates as a result of an external HR marketing campaign where social media is used extensively. Social media allow the organization to be presented as a good employer to a large and highly segmented audience at a low cost. The technological features of social networks make this possible due to the information and characteristics of users: age, region, level of education, area. Thus, the organization can select specified characteristics according to these criteria and target a segmented category of users of a social network.

So, we are already present in four social media, we are on Facebook, LinkedIn, Instagram and YouTube, I will talk about the first two networks ... So our approach consists of having two messages between Facebook and LinkedIn, on Facebook we have a funny, playful and offbeat message... we target young people who may have the profile of a customer adviser, so we will talk a lot about our daily life inside the company, events such as challenges, meetings, small lunches, birthdays, celebrations ... on LinkedIn we adopt another editorial line, we publish all our job offers and career prospects, we have a more corporate message on LinkedIn than on Facebook, that's how we deploy our employer brand on social media we reflect our daily life internally within the firm, we are not talking about artificial speech, we are reflecting what is happening on our work site. (Digital Communication Project Manager – PG).

Managers deploy their company's digital strategy through a digital presence on various social media. The operationalization of this strategy is carried out according to communication styles specific to the social network used: mass communication on Facebook, which targets young job seekers who have the profile of call center advisers, corporate and segmented communication on LinkedIn, which targets middle management profiles. The content of this communication mainly deals with aspects related to daily life within the company and its working conditions.

Social media is mobilized to attract candidates and communicate with them throughout the recruitment process, they serve to share the daily experience of employees with potential candidates through direct and spontaneous dissemination in images and videos, these actions introduce future employees to the working climate within the firm while highlighting financial advantages such as remuneration and bonuses. This allows the employer branding specialists to communicate and broadcast online messages to a specific group of potential candidates who best meet the company's recruitment needs. In this sense, proximity and active listening to potential candidates can make the company an attractive employer, furthermore, and thanks to social media, call centers promote their notoriety as employers through the promotion of their strengths such as the management style, social commitment and meeting the needs of their employees to become responsible social actors, corporate citizens and above all, prime employers. This allows the employer branding specialists to communicate and broadcast online messages to a specific group of potential candidates who best meet the company's recruitment needs. In this sense, proximity and active listening to potential candidates can make the company an attractive employer, as well, and thanks to social media, call centers promote their notoriety as employers through the promotion of their strengths such as the management style, social commitment and meeting the needs of their employees to become responsible social actors, corporate citizens and above all, prime employers.

When we say that we are the leader of customer relation centers in Morocco, it is that we absolutely must, through our daily actions, prove that we are number 1 in Morocco, through our social responsibility, through our charter diversity, through our HR policy, our management style ... after that, we can accept dissatisfied people, and that is what makes our employer brand strong, it is to listen to people who are dissatisfied, who criticize, but represent only a minority, and this confirms that our employer brand has been attractive and has been attentive to suggestions for improvement. (HR Project Manager – WH).

SPECIFIC FINDINGS

Employees as Employer Brand Ambassadors

Organizational loyalty is achieved by meeting employee needs and by fulfilling the promises contained in the employer brand. Employee commitment and loyalty translate into a pride of belonging to the organization. Thus, employees tend to identify with their company by sharing their experience within it with their entourage on social media. The dissemination of the "employee experience" on social media then becomes a spontaneous means for promoting the employer brand of a company. The ambassadorship can also take the form of a proposition of recruits, which facilitates the hiring, integration and retention of these.

The managers interviewed in this research claim to have participated in promoting the employer brand of their firm in different ways. The recommendation of the company to its entourage and the participation in social and philanthropic activities are the main forms of promotion of the employer brand of the company by the collaborators.

"When I set up an e-recruitment site and I put it online, the first population to communicate with before I share it on Facebook are my collaborators, I will send a nice email to all the staff saying " good news, today I am announcing the birth of our career site, your role is to share this information with those around you as much as possible ", our watchword is like and share because it is a thousand times more credible than a marketing or communications agency work" (HR Marketing & Social Media Manager – WH).

The use of social media could also promote the effect of Inbound marketing (Megargel, Shankararaman & Reddy, 2018) for the dissemination and promotion of the employer brand. This strategy consists of attracting internet users to the company's website and official pages and accompanying them in a communication tunnel to transform:

- The internet user to a potential candidate.
- The potential candidate to an employee.
- The employee to an employer brand ambassador.

In this sense, Schlager, Bodderas, Cachelin & Maas (2011) argue that the employer brand would have a positive impact on employees' satisfaction which could influence the customer experience and potential candidates. The initiatives of employee ambassadors can generate a feeling of attachment to the organization among other employees (Sahu, Pathardikar & Kumar, 2018) and help spread a positive image of the employer to potential candidates (Schlager et al., 2011). This deduction can be applied in the case of employees in the customer relationship sector, who can improve the attractiveness of their activity and develop their work image positively. Customer relation centers that practice this strategy can be the exception and become employers of choice while promoting the profession of the teleoperator.

Employer Branding as a Solution to Employees' Turnover

The war for talent, visible in several fields, is prompting many organizations to look after their employer brand to be more attractive and reduce their turnover rate by retaining the most competent employees.

Having an attractive and credible employer brand makes it easier to target and attract suitable profiles for the customer relationship management profession, which limits "casting errors" in call centers. Maintaining a positive image of the company as being an employer of choice can be considered as a solution to fight turnover among customer relation centers in Morocco.

Digital employer branding would be a process of continuous improvement, it should not stop after reaching a given purpose, but it is the capitalization of attributes, incessant care of the employer's reputation to make the image of the firm more attractive on social media. Finally, an employer brand that meets the expectations and ambitions of employees in terms of benefits and working conditions would minimize departures and establish pride in belonging to the organization. Once satisfied, they would become ambassadors for their employer brand, which is a sign of credibility for potential candidates wishing to join the organization. With this in mind, the authors support the idea that the management of the employer brand can limit the shortage of job applicants.

"You must know how to retain the people you have because they are the ones who have this ability to propel you forward, if each time you train collaborators, you insert them into production, they get experience, but after you can't keep them loyal, they will leave and it will generate a cost to redo this process and the results will not be good, so better keep the resources we have as staff, keep them loyal, after that when we have other recruits it will be to progress towards other objectives and avoid turnover and not to replace those who have left "(Recruitment Officer – IN).

E-Reputation Oversight on Social Media

Social media acts as a barometer to assess the digital reputation of the company and probe the expectations of potential applicants. Thus, the care and maintenance of the employer brand is part of the oversight e-reputation process, making contact with Internet users on social media as part of community management allows HR managers to measure the basis of criticisms and objections. To process them on the web or notify the service concerned via reporting in a way to fix the problems raised during these online exchanges. The oversight e-reputation on social media is also used to benchmark competitors to discover new good practices and above all avoid bad situations by taking advantage of the experience of rivals in the field, social media can be mobilized to collect the information necessary to carry out this competitive benchmarking in HR marketing all with the aim of continuous improvement of the employer brand. The above tasks are carried out through reporting containing information collected from the official company pages on social media. This report is then analyzed to obtain lessons and useful implications for the care and promotion of the company's reputation.

We really follow very closely everything that is said about us, it already is a basis of study for us, it allows us to know how we are followed, what do job applicants ask, we have monitoring tools in case there is a reputation crisis or a bad buzz. We are there, we are alerted, we don't let things explode in front of us, we also work with a communication agency that allows us to follow the news and benchmark ourselves with the competitors every day, we have what we call a "daily alert" to follow up on negative social media posts. (Communication Officer – AS).

It seems that most of the companies observed were at least at a certain level of the avant-garde in terms of the use of digital social networks, more precisely, regarding the strategy of the employer brand.

All of these companies are among the employers of choice in their industry at least nationally, which means that their employer brand is already strong.

Figure 1. Management of the employer brand through social media at customer relation centers in Morocco (author's own contribution)

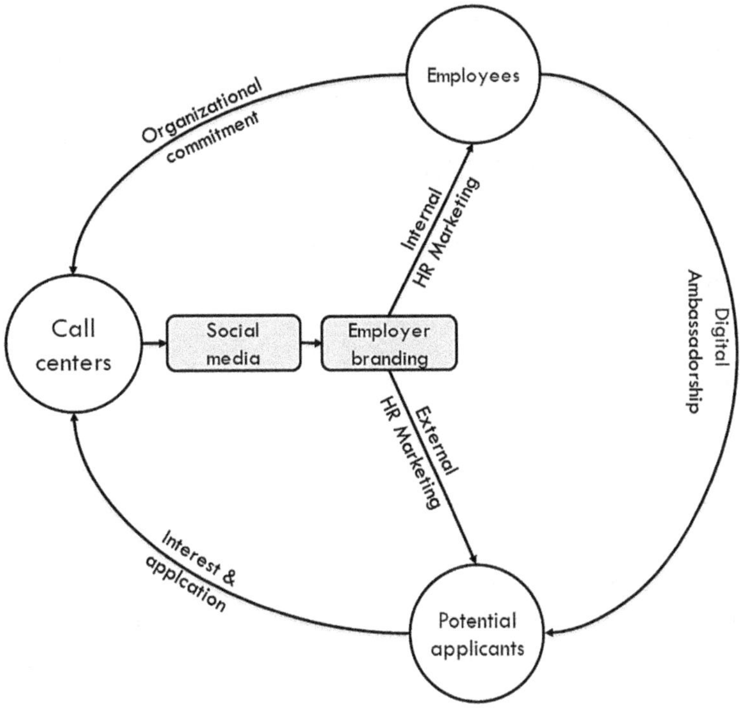

As shown in Figure 1, the management of the employer brand at customer relation centers begins with the proposition of values of the employer brand and the enhancement of the image of the profession. Then comes the stage of the loyalty of the current employees and their mobilization as part of a digital ambassadorship strategy while attracting potential candidates through an external HR marketing campaign where digital social networks are widely used. Digital ambassadorship practices generally result in recruiting by sponsorship. The employee ambassador can recommend a referral to his company, which makes it easier to hire and integrate the latter. Organizations use employees as the most credible ambassadors of their employer brand (Lissaneddine, 2019). They, therefore, expect a reflection of the internal attributes of their employer brand outside the organization (Mangold & Miles, 2007). Organizations consider offering a good "employee" experience as the cornerstone of their management of the employer brand. They combine internal organizational loyalty practices with external attraction policies by offering a package of concrete and realistic benefits that can be disseminated on social media.

SOLUTIONS AND RECOMMENDATIONS

This research tends to make Moroccan managers more aware of the benefits of using social media in the development of the employer brand. To better manage their employer branding, they should elaborate on an efficient digital communication strategy to adjust themselves to the digital native generation. This generation is a challenge to HRM managers who are brought to develop innovative strategies to attract, recruit and manage them efficiently. By doing so, Moroccan call centers managers must develop an action plan relating to the management of the employer brand according to the following four fundamental aspects (i) promotion and dissemination of the employer brand via social media, (ii) the revaluation of the business image according to the sector of activity, (iii) monitoring e-reputation and benchmark with rivals and employee mobilization for digital ambassadorship perspectives. Considering all these implications, the Human Resources function plays a major role in the employer branding strategy. Its mission is to involve employees in a global employer brand ambassadorship strategy and to ensure that they become real ambassadors for the firm.

FUTURE RESEARCH DIRECTIONS

This research work has some limitations to be considered. The first limit of this research lies in the research field, which is restraint and consists only of four firms. This small sample only allows authors to explore some of the practices of digital management of the employer brand in companies operating in the customer relationship management segment in Morocco without embracing all the existing practices in that sector. Second, the gathered qualitative data was solely based on the declarative of some managers. For some reason of feasibility, the authors have not been able to study the feelings of employees to compare their testimonies with those of managers. In light of the evoked limits, several research perspectives can be considered to comprehensively understand social media strategies that firms implement to manage their employer brand. A first perspective would consist of carrying out a study with a broader sample of large firms operating in different sectors that actively use social media. Second, this research can be extended by focusing more on employees to measure the degree of their engagement in the ambassadorship strategy and their loyalty towards their employer. Finally, it is necessary to question the impact of the employer brand and employees' ambassadorship strategies on potential employees' intention to apply according to different social media platforms (LinkedIn, Facebook, etc..). These perspectives will be more relevant if they are especially conducted in sectors characterized by a war of talents and suffering from turnover issues.

CONCLUSION

The evolution of digital technologies is bringing about a profound transformation within the company in terms of HRM. Job advertisements are posted on Facebook and Twitter, recruitment and sourcing are done with headhunters on LinkedIn and Viadeo. The deployment of an HR marketing strategy on social media offers companies many perspectives, particularly in terms of promoting their employer brand, enhancing their business image, e-reputation monitoring, and digital ambassadorship. The main purpose of this research is to understand the way the management of the employer brand utilizing social media is carried out in customer relation centers in Morocco.

Through qualitative interviews with managers of four renowned call centers involved in social media, the results of this research show that to attract potential candidates, firms communicate on a daily basis within the organization. They look after their reputation on the benchmark with competitors and they mobilize ambassadors on social media. Indeed, to retain employees, they try to respect the promises made on social media and during recruitment.

The majority of researchers study the impact of the employer brand via social media on organizational attractiveness or application intent of job seekers. Few are interested in the relationship between the use of social media in promoting the employer brand and employee loyalty. In this sense, an important contribution of this research resides in the exploration of the employer brand management using social media in the attraction of prospective applicants and the retention of current employees of the organization. The study contributes to the employer brand and social media literature by offering a synthesizing framework that explains the interaction between the two fields. Likewise, this research was interested in a particular sector of activity barely studied in the literature, which refers to the customer relation centers in Morocco. The study of the employer brand in this sector is very relevant because it suffers from a high turnover rate. This puts companies belonging to this sector in a delicate situation since their process of creating value is largely based on the human factor.

ACKNOWLEDGMENT

The authors gratefully thank Dr. Lalla Amina ALAOUI for her help in proofreading the chapter.

REFERENCES

Ambler, T., & Barrow, S. (1996). The employer brand. *Journal of Brand Management*, *4*(3), 185–206. doi:10.1057/bm.1996.42

Andersson, M., & Ekman, P. (2009). Ambassador networks and place branding. *Journal of Place Management and Development*, *2*(1), 41–51. doi:10.1108/17538330910942799

App, S., Merk, J., & Büttgen, M. (2012). Employer branding: Sustainable HRM as a competitive advantage in the market for high-quality employees. *Management Review*, *20*(1), 53–69.

Backhaus, K. (2016). Employer Branding Revisited. *Organizational Management Journal*, *13*(4), 193–201. doi:10.1080/15416518.2016.1245128

Backhaus, K., & Tikoo, S. (2004). Conceptualizing and researching employer branding. *Career Development International*, *9*(5), 501–517. doi:10.1108/13620430410550754

Berthon, P., Ewing, M., & Hah, L. L. (2005). Captivating company: Dimensions of attractiveness in employer branding. *WORLD (Oakland, Calif.)*, *24*(2), 173–192. doi:10.1080/02650487.2005.11072912

Bondarouk, T., Ruël, H., Axinia, E., & Arama, R. (2014). What Is the Future of Employer Branding Through Social Media? Results of the Delphi Study into the Perceptions of HR Professionals and Academics. In Social Media in Human Resources Management (pp. 23–57). doi:10.1108/S1877-6361(2013)0000012006

Boyd, D. M., & Ellison, N. B. (2007). Social network sites: Definition, history, and scholarship. *Journal of Computer-Mediated Communication, 13*(1), 210–230. doi:10.1111/j.1083-6101.2007.00393.x

Brunetto, Y., & Farr-Wharton, R. (2002). Using social identity theory to explain the job satisfaction of public sector employees. *International Journal of Public Sector Management, 15*(7), 534–551. doi:10.1108/09513550210448571

Brymer, R. A., Molloy, J. C., & Gilbert, B. A. (2014). Human Capital Pipelines. *Journal of Management, 40*(2), 483–508. doi:10.1177/0149206313516797

Carpentier, M., Van Hoye, G., Stockman, S., Schollaert, E., Van Theemsche, B., & Jacobs, G. (2017). Recruiting nurses through social media: Effects on employer brand and attractiveness. *Journal of Advanced Nursing, 73*(11), 2696–2708. doi:10.1111/jan.13336 PMID:28494103

Carpentier, M., Van Hoye, G., & Weng, Q. (2019). Social media recruitment: Communication characteristics and sought gratifications. *Frontiers in Psychology, 10*, 1669. doi:10.3389/fpsyg.2019.01669 PMID:31379686

Chanias, S., Myers, M. D., & Hess, T. (2019). Digital transformation strategy making in pre-digital organizations: The case of a financial services provider. *The Journal of Strategic Information Systems, 28*(1), 17–33. doi:10.1016/j.jsis.2018.11.003

Charbonnier-Voirin, A., & Vignolles, A. (2015). Marque employeur interne et externe : Un état de l'art et un agenda de recherche. *Revue Française de Gestion, 41*(246), 63–82. doi:10.3166/rfg.246.63-82

Denzin, N. K., & Lincoln, Y. S. (2018). The SAGE Handbook of qualitative Research. SAGE.

Dreher, S. (2014). Social media and the world of work. *Corporate Communications, 19*(4), 344–356. doi:10.1108/CCIJ-10-2013-0087

Edwards, M. R. (2009). An integrative review of employer branding and OB theory. *Personnel Review, 39*(1), 5–23. doi:10.1108/00483481011012809

Eger, L., Mičík, M., Gangur, M., & Řehoř, P. (2019). Employer Branding: Exploring Attractiveness Dimensions in a Multicultural Context. *Technological and Economic Development of Economy, 25*(3), 519–541. doi:10.3846/tede.2019.9387

Eger, L., Mičík, M., & Řehoř, P. (2018). Employer branding on social media and recruitment websites: Symbolic traits of an ideal employer. *E+M. Ekonomie a Management, 21*(1), 224–237. doi:10.15240/tul/001/2018-1-015

Eisenhardt, K. M. (1989). Building Theories from Case Study Research. *Academy of Management Review, 14*(4), 532–550. doi:10.5465/amr.1989.4308385

Eisenhardt, K. M., & Graebner, M. E. (2007). Theory building from cases: Opportunities and challenges. *Academy of Management Journal, 50*(1), 25–32. doi:10.5465/amj.2007.24160888

El Zoghbi, E., & Aoun, K. (2016). Employer Branding and Social Media Strategies. In F. Ricciardi & A. Harfouche (Eds.), *Information and Communication Technologies in Organizations and Society Past, Present and Future Issues* (pp. 277–283). Springer International Publishing Switzerland.

Elving, W. J., Westhoff, J. J., Meeusen, K., & Schoonderbeek, J.-W. (2012). The war for talent? The relevance of employer branding in job advertisements for becoming an employer of choice. *Journal of Brand Management, 20*(5), 355–373. doi:10.1057/bm.2012.21

Ewing, M. T., Pitt, L. F., de Bussy, N. M., & Berthon, P. (2002). Employment branding in the knowledge economy. *International Journal of Advertising, 21*(1), 3–22. doi:10.1080/02650487.2002.11104914

Fueyo, C. (2015). *E-réputation corporate : influence de la voix digitale des employés via l'e-contenu de leur « Profil » sur les réseaux sociaux professionnels ; application au secteur automobile.* Université Toulouse 1 Capitole.

Gibbert, M., Ruigrok, W., & Wicki, B. (2008). What Passes As A Rigorous Case Study? *Strategic Management Journal, 29*(13), 1465–1474. doi:10.1002mj.722

Gilani, H., & Cunningham, L. (2017). Employer branding and its influence on employee retention: A literature review. *The Marketing Review, 17*(2), 239–256. doi:10.1362/146934717X14909733966209

Gioia, D. A., Corley, K. G., & Hamilton, A. L. (2013). Seeking Qualitative Rigor in Inductive Research. *Organizational Research Methods, 16*(1), 15–31. doi:10.1177/1094428112452151

Glaser, B. G., & Strauss, A. L. (1967). *The discovery of grounded theory : strategies for qualitative research.* Aldine Transaction.

Graham, B. Z., & Cascio, W. F. (2018). The employer-branding journey : Its relationship with cross-cultural branding, brand reputation, and brand repair. *Management Research: Journal of the Iberoamerican Academy of Management, 16*(4), 363–379. doi:10.1108/MRJIAM-09-2017-0779

Ha, N. M., & Luan, N. V. (2018). The effect of employers' attraction and social media on job application attention of senior students at pharmaceutical universities in Vietnam. *International Journal of Business and Society, 19*(2), 473–491.

Holbeche, L., & Matthews, G. (2012). Engaged: Unleashing your organization's potential through employee engagement. San Francisco, CA: Jossey-Bass.

Kapoor, V. (2010). Employer Branding : A Study of Its Relevance in India. *IUP Journal Of Brand Management, 7*(1/2), 51–75.

Kashive, N., Khanna, V. T., & Bharthi, M. N. (2020). Employer branding through crowdsourcing: Understanding the sentiments of employees. *Journal of Indian Business Research, 12*(1), 93–111. doi:10.1108/JIBR-09-2019-0276

Kissel, P., & Büttgen, M. (2015). Using social media to communicate employer brand identity: The impact on corporate image and employer attractiveness. *Journal of Brand Management, 22*(9), 755–777. doi:10.1057/bm.2015.42

Knox, S., & Freeman, C. (2006). Measuring and Managing Employer Brand Image in the Service Industry. *Journal of Marketing Management*, *22*(7–8), 695–716. doi:10.1362/026725706778612103

Lievens, F., & Slaughter, J. E. (2016). Employer Image and Employer Branding: What We Know and What We Need to Know. *Annual Review of Organizational Psychology and Organizational Behavior*, *3*(1), 407–440. doi:10.1146/annurev-orgpsych-041015-062501

Lissaneddine, Z. (2019). *Management de la marque employeur via les réseaux sociaux numériques : Cas des centres de la relation client au Maroc*. Cadi Ayyad University.

Lloyd, S. (2002). Branding from the inside out. *Business Review Weekly*, *24*(10), 64–66.

Mangold, W. G., & Miles, S. J. (2007). The employee brand: Is yours an all-star? *Business Horizons*, *50*(5), 423–433. doi:10.1016/j.bushor.2007.06.001

Marler, J. H., & Fisher, S. L. (2013). An evidence-based review of e-HRM and strategic human resource management. *Human Resource Management Review*, *23*(1), 18–36. doi:10.1016/j.hrmr.2012.06.002

McFarland, L. A., & Ployhart, R. E. (2015). Social media: A contextual framework to guide research and practice. *The Journal of Applied Psychology*, *100*(6), 1653–1677. doi:10.1037/a0039244 PMID:26052712

Megargel, A., Shankararaman, V., & Reddy, S. K. (2018). Real-Time Inbound Marketing: A Use Case for Digital Banking. In Handbook of Blockchain, Digital Finance, and Inclusion, Volume 1 (pp. 311–328). doi:10.1016/B978-0-12-810441-5.00013-0

Mičík, M., & Mičudová, K. (2018). Employer Brand Building: Using Social Media and Career Websites to Attract Generation Y. *Economia e Sociologia*, *11*(3), 171–189.

Miles, M. B., Huberman, A. M., & Saldana, J. (2014). Qualitative Data Analysis: A Methods Sourcebook. In The SAGE Handbook of Applied Social Research Methods. SAGE.

Moroko, L., & Uncles, M. D. (2008). Characteristics of successful employer brands. *Journal of Brand Management*, *16*(3), 160–175. doi:10.1057/bm.2008.4

Mosley, R. (2014). *Employer brand management : Practical lessons from the world's leading employers*. Wiley.

Otken, A. B., & Okan, E. Y. (2016). The Role of Social Media in Employer Branding. In Entrepreneurship, Business and Economics (Vol. 13/1, pp. 245–260). doi:10.1007/978-3-319-27570-3_20

Pierre, X., & Tremblay, D.-G. (2012). Améliorer l'implication et la rétention des agents dans les centres d'appels: Agir sur les pratiques de gestion. *Recherches En Sciences de Gestion*, *91*(4), 17. doi:10.3917/resg.091.0017

Quaratino, L., & Mazzei, A. (2018). Managerial strategies to promote employee brand consistent behavior. *EuroMed Journal of Business*, *13*(2), 185–200. doi:10.1108/EMJB-02-2017-0008

Rana, G., & Sharma, R. (2019). Assessing Impact of Employer Branding on Job Engagement: A Study of Banking Sector. *Emerging Economy Studies*, *5*(1), 7–21. doi:10.1177/2394901519825543

Sahu, S., Pathardikar, A., & Kumar, A. (2018). Transformational leadership and turnover. *Leadership and Organization Development Journal, 39*(1), 82–99. doi:10.1108/LODJ-12-2014-0243

Schlager, T., Bodderas, M., Cachelin, J. L., & Maas, P. (2011). The influence of the employer brand on employee attitudes relevant for service branding: An empirical investigation. *Journal of Services Marketing, 25*(7), 497–508. doi:10.1108/08876041111173624

Sharma, S., & Verma, H. V. (2018). Social Media Marketing: Evolution and Change. In Social Media Marketing (pp. 19–36). Academic Press.

Sivertzen, A.-M., Nilsen, E. R., & Olafsen, A. H. (2013). Employer branding: Employer attractiveness and the use of social media. *Journal of Product and Brand Management, 22*(7), 473–483. doi:10.1108/JPBM-09-2013-0393

Tajfel, S., & Turner, S. (1987). The social identity theory of intergroup behaviour. In S. Worchel & W. Austin (Eds.), *Psychology of intergroup relations* (2nd ed., pp. 7–24). Nelson-Hall.

Tanwar, K., & Kumar, A. (2019). Employer brand, person-organisation fit and employer of choice: Investigating the moderating effect of social media. *Personnel Review, 48*(3), 799–823. doi:10.1108/PR-10-2017-0299

Turban, D. B., & Cable, D. M. (2003). Firm reputation and applicant pool characteristics. *Journal of Organizational Behavior, 24*(6), 733–751. doi:10.1002/job.215

Wallace, E., & de Chernatony, L. (2009). Exploring brand sabotage in retail banking. *Journal of Product and Brand Management, 18*(3), 198–211. doi:10.1108/10610420910957825

Yin, R. K. (2009). Case study research : design and methods. In Applied social research methods series: 5 (4th ed.). SAGE Publications, Inc.

ADDITIONAL READING

Bissola, R., & Imperatori, B. (2014). The unexpected side of relational e-HRM. *Employee Relations, 36*(4), 376–397. doi:10.1108/ER-07-2013-0078

Hillebrandt, I., Ivens, B. S., Rauschnabel, P. A., Hartmann, C. O., & Krey, N. (2016). Social Media: Harming or Enhancing Your Employer Brand Attractiveness? An Empirical Investigation. In: Groza M., Ragland C. (eds) *Marketing Challenges in a Turbulent Business Environment. Developments in Marketing Science: Proceedings of the Academy of Marketing Science*. Springer, Cham. 10.1007/978-3-319-19428-8_98

Theurer, C. P., Tumasjan, A., Welpe, I. M., & Lievens, F. (2018). Employer Branding: A Brand Equity-based Literature Review and Research Agenda. *International Journal of Management Reviews, 20*(1), 155–179. doi:10.1111/ijmr.12121

Van Zoonen, W., Bartels, J., van Prooijen, A.-M., & Schouten, A. P. (2018). Explaining online ambassadorship behaviors on Facebook and LinkedIn. *Computers in Human Behavior*, *87*, 354–362. doi:10.1016/j.chb.2018.05.031

KEY TERMS AND DEFINITIONS

Digital Ambassadorship: It is the act of representing or defending the interests of a brand in a spontaneous or administered way on the web and social media mainly. This role can be played by several stakeholders (employees, customers or celebrities).

Employer Attractiveness: Benefits envisaged that a potential employee, influenced by the image of the employer, sees while working for a specific organization, these benefits can be conceptualized through instrumental and symbolic characteristics.

Employer Brand: The image that a company reflects as an employer, it consists of all the advantages or benefits that this company can offer to its employees.

Employer Branding: The process of managing an employer brand, it is composed of three main stages, the shaping of the content of the employer brand (value proposition), the promotion of this employer brand outside the company (External HR Marketing) to attract potential candidates, retaining recruits by fulfilling the promises of the employer brand (Internal HR Marketing).

Organizational Commitment: A behavior and an attitude characterized by a strong belief in the goals and values of the organization, by a will to exert significant efforts for the benefit of the latter and by a strong desire to remain one of its members.

Social Media: It is a group of internet-based applications that allow the creation and exchange of user-generated content. They are generally very accessible and bring together very varied socio-technical configurations in terms of the dynamics of participation (by interest, by friendship) and visibility (nature and purpose of the data published online). Social media are classified into six main types: blogs, collaborative projects, content communities, social networking sites, virtual game worlds, and virtual social worlds.

Turnover: It is usually an employee's decision to end an employment relationship, which is one of the forms of employee turnover. Voluntary departure corresponds to an initiative by the individual to leave the organization because of his working conditions or in the case of other employment opportunities elsewhere. As for involuntary turnover, it occurs when a company terminates an employee's employment contract because of their incompatibility or underperformance. In other cases, this can happen due to the choice of the company to cease its commercial activity or to outsource one of its activities.

Work-Image: It is the perception that an individual form in his mind on a profession from his exposure to different backgrounds, and to which he refers when he wants to make a judgment regarding this profession.

ENDNOTES

1 https://wearesocial.com/blog/2020/01/digital-2020-3-8-billion-people-use-social-media consulted on 02.04.2020

2 Survey of the Moroccan National Agency for Communication Regulation, available on the following link: https://www.anrt.ma/sites/default/files/Etudes_dev_centres_appel_maroc_2007_0.pdf

Chapter 15
Precious Metal Prediction by Using XAI in the Perspective of Digital Transformation

Samet Oztoprak
Istanbul University-Cerrahpasa, Turkey

Zeynep Orman
https://orcid.org/0000-0002-0205-4198
Istanbul University-Cerrahpasa, Turkey

ABSTRACT

Recent advances in deep learning methodology led to artificial intelligence (AI) performance achieving and even surpassing human levels in an increasing number of complex tasks. There are many impressive examples of this development such as image classification, sensitivity analysis, speech understanding, or strategic gaming. The estimations based on the AI methods do not give any certain information due to the lack of transparency for the visualization, explanation, and interpretation of deep learning models which can be a major disadvantage in many applications. This chapter discusses studies on the prediction of precious metals in the financial field that need an explanatory model. Traditional AI and machine learning methods are insufficient to realize these predictions. There are many advantages to using explainable artificial intelligence (XAI), which enables us to make reasonable decisions based on inferences. In this chapter, the authors examine the precious metal prediction by XAI by presenting a comprehensive literature review on the related studies.

INTRODUCTION

Artificial intelligence (AI) becomes one of the indispensable parts of human life day by day (Iansiti and Lakhani 2020). It is crucial from image and face recognition systems that occur in all kinds of applications to predictive analytics, speech usage, autonomous use, and hyper-personalized systems. AI is heading towards a wide range of sectors such as education, construction, healthcare, manufacturing, law

DOI: 10.4018/978-1-7998-8587-0.ch015

enforcement, and finance. Decisions and predictions are made by AI-powered systems that are mainly used in unmanned cars, healthcare, and even the use of warfare.

Many of us need to know how the decisions are made while artificial intelligence is in progress. Many of the algorithms used for machine learning cannot be studied specifically to understand how and why a decision is made (Iansiti and Lakhani 2020). This is especially true for the most popular algorithms currently used – e.g. deep learning neural network approaches. As humans, we must be able to fully understand how decisions are made so that we can rely on AI decisions. The lack of clarity and trust hampers our ability to fully trust AI systems. Therefore, people expect such systems to produce transparent explanations and reviews of the decisions they make. This is known as Explained AI (XAI).

Explained AI is a fresh field in computer science and machine learning that intends to address how black box decisions are made by artificial intelligence systems. This area examines and tries to understand every single step and models involved in decision making. XAI is expected to answer some hot questions by most business owners, operators, users, and even experts such as: Why did the AI system make a specific estimation or decision? Why did not the AI system do anything else? When did the AI system succeed, and when did it fail? When do AI systems give enough confidence to the decisions you can trust, and how can the AI system correct the errors that occur in the decision making process?

Until now, there has been early, yet new researches and studies in the field of making deep learning approaches to machine learning explicable. However, it is hoped that as well as having both transparency and openness, adequate progress can be made to ensure that we have both strength and accuracy. AI actions should be observable to a certain level. These levels should be determined by results that may result from the AI systems. Systems with more important, fatal or significant consequences must have necessary clarification and transparency requirements to know everything when something goes wrong.

Every single system does not need the same levels of transparency. While it is not possible to standardize algorithms and even XAI approaches, it may be possible to standardize levels of transparency according to requirements. For example, book recommendation systems need a little transparency, and therefore a lower level of transparency may be acceptable. On the other hand, military, juristical systems or autonomous vehicles may require higher levels of clarity and transparency. These levels of transparency have attempted to achieve common understandings of transparency to maintain and sustain communication between users and engineers through their standard organization.

This study will be a comprehensive literature review on the prediction of precious metals. It is seen that most of the studies have been estimated the gold value by using various AI approaches. The reason why gold is in great demand can be shown to be one of the most used and most valuable mines in the industry. Various artificial intelligence algorithms have been used on the gold prediction, but it is not known how the prediction is made due to the black-box approach. In this chapter, the authors took on the prediction of precious metals based on artificial intelligence methods. All studies point out that the prediction of precious metal based on artificial intelligence creates a much more precise prediction. The main aim is to understand whether or not there is an explainable model to convince investors to make reasonable investments and predict more precisely the value of precious metals in the related papers in the literature. Therefore, a systematic mapping study is conducted to survey the studies between the years 2017-2019.

The chapter is organized as follows: The Background section presents general information about precious metals, artificial intelligence (AI) and explainable artificial intelligence (XAI). The acquisitions of explicable artificial intelligence are emphasized. The Literature Review section includes a summary of the novel and valuable papers which are the main context of the information discussed throughout the chapter. Solutions and Recommendation section introduces an insight into the work that has taken place so far. The studies are classified according to the country and method distribution of the year. Finally, the last section states the conclusion of this chapter.

BACKGROUND

What Are the Precious Metals?

The precious metal is a term for the classification of metals that are rare or have a high economic value. The rise values of these metals are affected by some factors, such as rarity, uses in industrial processes and investment vehicles. A few of the most popular precious metals among investors are gold, platinum, and silver, and precious metals used in industrial processes include iridium, used in specialty alloys, and palladium, which is used in electronics and chemical applications.

What Causes the Gold Price to Fluctuate?

It is not easy to estimate precious metal prices. Precious metal trading takes place in a global market and is therefore influenced by a wide range of different economic, social and political factors. This makes fluctuations in the value of precious metal challenging to attach to a single event or situation. Politics can play a major role in fluctuating precious metal prices as well as the economy.

However, there are some patterns that become apparent when we analyze fluctuations in the value of precious metals. One of the most common themes we may be concerned with changes in the value of precious metals is one of the main reasons of the investors buying precious metals - security. In the simplest terms, there are a few things that affect the price of gold.

Supply - The amount of precious metals removed can be affected. Mining companies are closed, the mines reach a point where the amount of precious metals remaining is not worth the cost of extracting it, or new laws mean that operations cannot continue. In contrast, new deposits can be discovered, mining methods can be improved, or investment can be increased.

Demand - Consumer demand increases and decreases for financial or social reasons. Precious metals also have many uses in technology; new technology can see that demand has increased. If the supply cannot meet the demand, the price will increase, and if the supply demands, the price will decrease.

Economic and Political Changes - The economy has a huge impact on the price of precious metals, as discussed below, and policy affects the economy sometimes in a subtle and sometimes obvious way.

What Is Artificial Intelligence?

The artificial intelligence system to be pre-programmed, instead they use algorithms that can work with their own intelligence. It includes machine learning algorithms such as reinforcement learning algorithms and deep learning neural networks.

Depending on their capabilities, AI can be classified into three types:

1. Artificial narrow intelligence (ANI), which has a narrow range of abilities.
2. Artificial general intelligence (AGI), which is on par with human capabilities; or

3. Artificial superintelligence (ASI), which is more capable than a human.

Artificial narrow intelligence (ANI), also called weak AI or narrow AI is the only type of artificial intelligence we have successfully achieved so far. Narrow AI is targeted, meaning it is designed to perform singular tasks such as face recognition, speech recognition/voice assistants, driving or searching the Internet and is very clever to complete the scheduled task it will perform.

Artificial general intelligence (AGI), also called strong AI or deep AI is a machine concept with a general intelligence that can learn and apply intelligence to solve a problem, imitating human intelligence and/or behavior. AGI can think, understand and act in any way indistinguishable from a person.

Artificial super intelligence (ASI) is a theory AI that doesn't only mimic or understands human intelligence and behavior; ASI is where machines recognize themselves and exceed the capacity of human intelligence and ability.

What Is Machine Learning?

Machine learning works on a self-learning algorithm using historical data. If we are creating a machine learning model for detecting pictures of dogs only, it will only work for dog images, but if we provide new data such as cat images, it will work in certain areas such as not responding. Machine learning is used in various places such as online learning systems, Google search algorithms, Email spam filters, Facebook Automatic friend tagging suggestions, etc.

It can be divided into three types:

1. Supervised learning
2. Reinforcement learning
3. Unsupervised learning

Using supervised learning is plentiful in the general of practical machine learning. Supervised learning is where there are input variables (x) and an output variable (Y) and you use an algorithm to learn the input-to-output mapping function. The goal is to get so close to the mapping function that when you have new input data (x), you can estimate the output variables (Y) for that data.

Reinforcement learning takes appropriate measures to maximize the reward in each situation. It is used by various software and machines to find the best possible behavior or path that it should take in a situation. Reinforcement learning is different from supervised learning, so that it has the answer key next to the training data, so there is no answer in learning the reinforcement, while the model is trained with the correct answer itself, but the reinforcement agent decides what to do to fulfill the given task. In the lack of a training dataset, it must learn from experience.

Unsupervised learning is only required if there is an input variable (X) and the corresponding output variables. The purpose of unattended learning is to model for the underlying structure or use it to learn more about it. These are called unsupervised learning because, unlike controlling learning, there are no correct answers and no teachers. Algorithms are left to their own devices.

What Are the Differences Between Artificial Intelligence AI and ML?

Table 1. Comparison of AI and ML

Artificial Intelligence	Machine Learning
Artificial intelligence enables a machine to simulate human behavior.	Machine learning is a subunit of AI which allows a machine by itself to learn from data without programming evidently.
The aim of AI is to make an intelligent computer system like the human capacity to solve complicated problems.	The aim of ML is to allow machines to learn from data to produce precise output.
It is made by intelligent systems to fulfill any task like a human being in AI.	It is taught machines with data to fulfill a specific task and give an accurate result in ML.
Machine learning and deep learning are both essential subcategories of AI.	Deep learning is an essential subcategory of machine learning.
The scope of AI is very wide.	Machine learning has a smaller working area.
AI systems are interrelated about maximizing the ratio of success.	Machine learning is chiefly interested in accuracy and patterns.
Some examples of AI are Siri, Expert System, Online game playing, an intelligent humanoid robot, etc.	Some examples of machine learning are Online recommender systems, Google search algorithms, Instagram auto friend tagging suggestions, etc.
AI utterly takes care of Structured, semi-structured, and unstructured data.	Machine learning takes care of Structured and semi-structured data.
It contains learning, reasoning, and self-correction.	It contains learning and self-correction when introduced with new data.

Table 1 shows the explanation of artificial intelligence and machine learning more clearly and understandably because there is often confusion about the differences between AI and ML.

Understanding Artificial Intelligence

When people often hear the term artificial intelligence, what they usually think of is robots. Because big-budget films and novels consist of stories about human-like machines that harm the Earth.

Artificial intelligence is based on the principle that human intelligence can easily imitate a machine and perform tasks from the simplest to the more complex. The objectives of artificial intelligence include basic principles such as learning, reasoning, and perception.

Technology advancement, previous criteria defining artificial intelligence are becoming outdated. For example, machines that calculate basic functions or recognize text through best character recognition are no longer thought to embody artificial intelligence, because this function is now considered a natural computer function.

The Evolution of AI is to benefit many different industries. Machines are cabled with an interdisciplinary approach based on mathematics, computer science, linguistics, psychology and more.

Machine Learning Methods in AI

It is called a machine learning algorithm, or in other words, a model, a mathematical expression that represents data in a business problem. The aim is to draw a certain prediction from the data. For example, if a vendor wants to set a sales quantity for the next quarter, he must use a machine learning algorithm that predicts these sales based on past sales and other relevant data. Similarly, a car manufacturer can monitor the visual data that matters and identify the video data by feeding it with a trained algorithm to identify scratches on the car.

Regression

It is the simplest machine learning method, the machine learning method using the mathematical equation of the line ($y = m * x + b$) to model any data set is regression. All data points train a linear regression model with many data pairs (x, y) by calculating the position and slope of a line that minimizes the total distance between the line. In other words, the slope (m) and the intersection y (b) are calculated for a line that best approximates the observations in the data.

Classification

One of the supervised ML methods, classification methods predicts or explains a class value. For example, they can help estimate whether an online customer will receive a product. The output can be yes or no: the recipient or not. However, classification methods are not limited to two classes. For example, a classification method can help assess whether a given image contains a cat or dog. In this case, the output will be 3 different values: firstly, the image contains a cat, secondly, the image contains a dog and thirdly, the image contains neither a cat nor a dog.

Clustering

The clustering method is included in the unsupervised ML category because their purpose is to group or cluster observations with similar characteristics. Clustering methods allow the algorithm to define output instead of using output information for training. In clustering methods, we can only use visualizations to control the quality of the solution.

Dimensionality Reduction

It is the Principal Component Analysis (PCA) that reduces the size of the feature area by finding new vectors that maximize the linear diversity of the data. This is one of the most important dimensional reduction methods. PCA can reduce the size of the data greatly and without losing much information when the linear correlations of the data are strong. (In fact, you can also measure the true size of the loss of information and adjust it accordingly.)

Ensemble Methods

Ensemble methods use the idea of combining several prediction models (supervised ML) to achieve a higher rate of prediction success than each model can provide on its own. For example, Random Forest algorithms are a community method that combines many Decision Trees trained with different data set instances. As a result, the quality of the estimates of a Random Forest is higher than the estimated rate achieved by a single Decision Tree method.

Neural Networks and Deep Learning

Unlike linear and logistic regressions, which are considered linear models, the purpose of neural networks is to capture nonlinear models in the data by adding parameter layers to the model. In fact, the structure of neural networks is linear and flexible enough to form our logistic regression. The term deep learning comes from a neural network with many hidden layers and covers a wide range of architectures.

Transfer Learning

Transfer Learning is used to reuse part of a previously trained neural network and adapt it to a similar and new task. In particular, after training a neural network using the data of a task, it can transfer some of the trained layers and be combined with several new layers that can train them using the data of the new task. By adding a few new layers, the new neural network can adapt to it by learning its new task quickly.

The main advantage of the transfer learning approach is that less data is needed to train the neural network, which is very important because training is expensive in time and money for deep learning algorithms - it is often very difficult to find tagged data for training.

Reinforcement Learning

As with the mouse maze game, it reflects what we do with Reinforcement Learning (RL) to train a system or game. Generally, RL is a machine learning method that helps an agent learn from experience. By recording actions both using a trial and error approach in a particular setting, RL can maximize a cumulative reward. In our example, it is the mouse and labyrinth environment. Possible actions for the mouse are moving front, back, left or right. The reward is bread.

XAI Applications

Medical

One of the XAI applications is the Clinical Decision Support System (CDSS), in health care, where a system is built to predict a diagnosis for patients by looking only at the medical records. If the CDSS has a credible positive predictive value and the clinician's question "How and why did the application reach the possible diagnosis?" If he answers his question, it becomes much more valuable and logical. For example, A person is diagnosed with type 2 diabetes because his head complaints are unexplained weight loss, increased hunger, and fasting blood sugar is 126 mg / dL (7 mmol / L) or higher and random blood sugar is 200 mg / dL (11.1). mmol / L) or above.

Defense

XAI gains importance in military applications because deadly autonomous weapon systems can cause less damage if they can distinguish between a civilian and a fighter.

Banking

In banking, sector regulators want to look at overall business volumes and the number of suspicious activities reported. Any rate outside the industry norm will need regulatory investigations. In such cases, XAI will help reduce false positives.

Finance

About 40 million Americans cannot get credit because simple AI models refuse applicants with little or no history in their records. Rather, XAI uses more data and improved algorithms to identify valuable borrowers that older models could ignore.

As the decision-making process becomes more transparent with XAI, they serve an important ethical filter on decisions. Data are the key to any financial, defense and medical decision making, as regulatory laws must be followed. With more efficient models working in the cloud at XAI, these institutions will be able to provide explanations about why a decision has been made and effectively meet regulatory and compliance requirements.

How XAI Works?

XAI has a much more transparent structure. The human factor, which interacts with artificial intelligence, is not only informed about what decisions it has made and the actions it will take, but also how it came to these results based on the available data. It aims for high learning performance.

The existing AI incorporates data into the machine learning process and generates a learned function and leaves the user with a series of questions such as: Why did it do this? Why didn't he do anything else? When will it be successful? And when will it fail? How can I trust it? And how do I fix an error?

On the contrary, XAI uses a new machine learning process to produce an explicable model with an explicable interface. This should answer all the questions above.

This issue carries its own risks. Any decision made by an AI is only as good as the data used to do this. While XAI increases confidence in the decision, this trust is misplaced if the data is untrusted.

Another problem is AI's ability to explain its decisions. If it could not be understood by the user who could be a member without technical infrastructure, the explanation would be worthless. Solving this would involve complex studies on explanation psychology as well as scientists working with AI specialists.

Figure 1 shows that XAI not only produces results but also shows why it has made this decision. There are two basic questions about making this decision. One of them is "Why is it?" and other is "Why is it not?" These two basic questions can be further elaborated if needed and the number of questions can be increased. It can be determined which data set will be more useful within the scope of the answers to the questions we encounter. It can be observed how the newly added data sets change the results and the data set can be changed or removed accordingly.

Risk, Trust and Regulation: Why Do We Need XAI?

Risk factors are high in "big ticket" decisions such as military, finance, security-critical systems in autonomous vehicles and diagnostic decisions in health services. Therefore, it is very important to explain their decisions in order to increase confidence in the ability of artificial intelligence. However, there are many advantages to businesses in other industries.

Figure 1. General Scheme of XAI

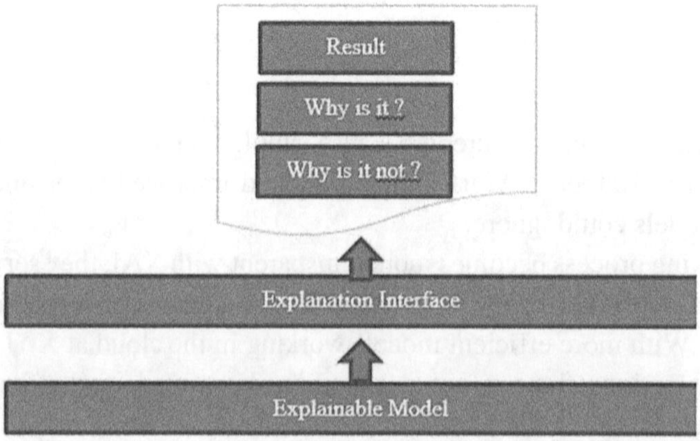

XAI can handle pressures such as regulation, as it will provide full transparency in the audit situation. It will encourage best practices and morality by explaining why each decision is the moral, social and financially correct decision. It will also strengthen trust in the company, which will give trust to shareholders.

It will also put businesses in a stronger position to promote innovation because the more advanced AI is, the more talented it is for innovative uses and new capabilities. Interaction with artificial intelligence will soon become standard business practices in many industries, including marketing. For this reason, it is very important for users to invest comfortably and safely.

Experts think this will empower marketers and effectively transform AI into a colleague rather than a vehicle. "To rely on artificial intelligence, people need to know what artificial intelligence is doing," says Appier Chief Data Scientist Hsuan-Tien Lin. "Just like AlphaGo's board game shows us new insights on how to play Go, it can show explainable AI marketers' new ideas about how to market. For example, AI can reach the right audience at the right time, but if future XAI can explain this decision to people, it helps marketers understand their audience more deeply and plan better marketing strategies. "

In addition, marketers can reveal a new way of working by accepting or rejecting XAI's explicable suggestions to help AI learn. "Today, people are ignoring their strength, because the rejection of many great suggestions has not been announced," says Appier Chief AI Scientist Min Sun. However, these days may end soon ...

The Defense Advanced Research Projects Agency is currently running an XAI program by 2021. The program understands the context of the machines and the working environment. Other experts also predict that XAI will become a reality in three to five years. XAI is undoubtedly the next step for AI, enhancing trust, confidence, and transparency. It is wise not to ignore the potential of businesses.

LITERATURE REVIEW

Many expert practitioners and researchers have developed various models using various techniques, basic and analytical techniques to predict the stock market model. Ruchira et al. (Ruchira et al., 2018) introduced Artificial Intelligence (AI) techniques that give promising results in stock market prediction based on Artificial Neural Network (ANN). Jianwei et al. (Jianwei et al., 2017) represent implementing gate recurrent unit neural network GRUNN to independent components (ICs) to achieve the predicted series of independent components (ICPs) and the forecasting result of the gold price is the combination of ICPs. Ehsan et al. (Ehsan et al., 2019) have proposed a CNN-based framework that can be applied to a collection of data from various sources, including different markets, to gain features to predict the future of these markets. Essentially, Zhanhong et al. (Zhanhong et al., 2019) have aimed at a new gold price estimation method based on the integration of Long-Term Memory Neural Networks (LSTM) and Convolution Neural Networks (CNN) Attention Mechanism (indicated by the LSTM-Attention-CNN model). Manjula et al. (Manjula et al., 2019) have found that random forest regression had better predictive accuracy for the entire period, and gradient enhancing regression provided better accuracy for two periods taken separately. Ufuk et al. (Ufuk et al., 2017) concentrate on data which includes gold, silver, palladium, platinum, Brent Petrol, natural gas prices, 30 years' bond, 10 years' bond, 5 years' bond, S&P 500, Nasdaq, Dow Jones, FTSE100, DAX, CAC40, SMI, NIKKEI, HANH, SENG and Euro/USD within the period of 4th of January 2010 to 14th of December 2015. D. Richard et al. (D. Richard et al., 2018) have shown that their approach is particularly useful in classification problems, where the goals are to determine membership in a cluster based on their characteristics. Ruth (Ruth, 2019) has shown that counterfactuals can aid the provision of interpretable models to make the decisions of inscrutable systems intelligible to developers and users. Alberto et al. (Alberto et al., 2019) have intended to include a position document that develops a comprehensive analysis of the evolutionary fuzzy systems research area. Daniel et al. (Daniel et al., 2018) have highlighted how Multi-run Subtree Encapsulation can provide equivalent white box solutions to facilitate Explainable Artificial Intelligence (XAI). Wojciech et al. (Wojciech et al., 2018) have offered two approaches to explain deep learning prediction models, a method that calculates the sensitivity of the estimate for input changes, and an approach that refutes the decision in terms of input variables. David (David, 2017) gives the main questions which humans need to understand explainable artificial intelligence concepts and put forward the main principles of explainable artificial intelligence. Dominik et al. (Dominik et al., 2019) have included a fusion system that uses the intermediate outputs of state-of-the-art CNNs to recognize whale sounds in spectrograms. Hereby They use Explained Artificial Intelligence (XAI) to evaluate the relevance assessments of each feature in the representations obtained. Based on these eligibility values, we create new masking algorithms to extract important subsets of related representations.

Studies using machine learning algorithms in the literature for precious metal prediction are common. However, due to the black-box machine learning approach, the use of XAI systems can be more explained and enables convincing results. Since XAI is a newly introduced concept, its work in the literature is rather limited. XAI studies will increase soon for the reasons the authors have mentioned.

SOLUTION AND RECOMMENDATIONS

This chapter surveyed all studies that used machine learning methods and AI in the prediction of precious metals the toughest side of these studies is the determination of the exact parameters which influence the value of precious metals. It is not easy to determine because political and global issues have a great impact on precious metals. It is highly required to define sentimental parameters. Determining sentimental parameters is not easy and always in change. It requires reading and understanding central bank reports and newspapers daily. Therefore, it requires a great source of the server to ensure data interpretation. It will be a costly process.

Table 2. Comparison of studies by years

Year	Publishing	Total
2017	(Ufuk et al., 2017), (Wojciech et al., 2017), (David, 2017)	3
2018	(Ruchira et al., 2018), (Amina et al., 2018), (Regis et al., 2018), (Daniel et al., 2018),]	4
2019	(Jianwei et al., 2019), (Ehsan et al., 2019), (Wesley et al., 2019), (Zhanhong et al., 2019), (Manjula et al., 2019), (Chanida et al., 2019), (Dennys et al., 2019), (Alberto et al., 2019), (Dominik et al., 2019), (Alejandro et al., 2019), (Bernhard et al., 2019), (Blen et al., 2019), (Gerald et al., 2019), (Richard et al., 2019)	14

Table 2 presents the studies are entirely up to date. The reason for this is that XAI is a very new field and artificial intelligence prediction is obscure about how the decisions were taken. Although there are old articles for the prediction of precious metals, research has been done through further studies.

Table 3 shows that it is seen that all countries work intensively on artificial intelligence and explainable artificial intelligence. In the field of artificial intelligence, it is seen that America is ahead as in many other fields. It is seen that it belongs to the USA in the highest quality and leading publications. European publications offer new solutions to existing algorithms.

Table 4 shows the papers by classifying them based on conference, journal, and workshop. It is seen that mainly journal publications are selected here. Gold prediction is the most popular asset among the other precious metals. Therefore, the content of these publications appears to be on the estimate of gold value. Table 4 also illustrates various artificial intelligence methods that have been used to estimate precious metals. The most prominent of these methods is the Neural network, but in recent publications can be seen the very different methods. The gradual increase of these different approaches is the desire to predict more precisely the gold forecast.

FUTURE RESEARCH DIRECTIONS

In this chapter, we presented a broadly applicable approach to XAI implementation in knowledge-intensive domains. Because XAI is a new field in computer science. This chapter surveyed a considerable amount of work carried out between the years of 2017-2019 about explainable artificial intelligence by using artificial neural networks and other artificial intelligence algorithms. In order to understand more deeply new explainable artificial intelligence approaches, studies were compared according to classification methods, years, success rates. Future work is about adding the sentimental parameters which influence the value of the precious metals on an instant basis and make more broadly search about the prediction of precious metals.

Table 3. Comparison of studies by countries

Country	Publishing	Total
Brazil	(Dennys et al., 2019)	1
China	(Jianwei et al., 2019)	1
France	(Alejandro et al., 2019), (Regis et al., 2018)	2
Germany	(Wojciech et al., 2017), (Dominik et al., 2019)	2
India	(Ruchira et al., 2018), (Manjula et al., 2019)	2
Iran	(Ehsan et al., 2019)	1
Ireland	(Ruth et al., 2019)	1
Italy	(Alberto et al., 2019)	1
Korea	(Alberto et al., 2019)	1
Malaysia	(Wesley et al., 2019)	1
Morocco	(Amina et al., 2018)	1
Norway	(Zhanhong et al., 2019)	1
Spain	(Alberto et al., 2019), 15]	2
Thailand	(Chanida et al., 2019)	1
Turkey	(Ufuk et al., 2017)	1
USA	(David, 2017), (Bernhard et al., 2019), (Blen et al., 2019), (Ruth et al., 2019), (Dominik et al., 2019), (Gerald et al., 2019)	6

Table 4. Methods used in studies using AI method

Year	Reference No	AI Method	Publication Type
2018	(Ruchira et al., 2018)	Neural Network	Conference
2017	(Ufuk et al., 2017)	Neural Network	Journal
2019	(Jianwei et al., 2019)	Neural Network	Journal
2019	(Ehsan et al., 2019)	Convolutional Neural Networks	Journal
2019	(Wesley et al., 2019)	Time Series	Journal
2019	(Zhanhong et al., 2019)	Convolutional Neural Networks	Conference
2019	(Manjula et al., 2019)	Machine Learning	Journal
2019	(Chanida et al., 2019)	Deep Learning	Journal
2019	(Dennys et al., 2019)	Neural Network	Journal
2019	(Alberto et al., 2019)	Fuzzy Systems	Journal
2017	(Wojciech et al., 2017)	Deep Neural Networks	Workshops

CONCLUSION

In this study, artificial intelligence applications in the financial sector are examined and their results are observed. The impact of artificial intelligence algorithms on the financial sector is gradually increasing. On the other hand, the application of artificial intelligence in the financial sector is expected to make the market more stable. Explained artificial intelligence has a wide range of uses. As a result of this research, it is unlikely that artificial intelligence will be an openable guide rather than a black box. These areas of use include critical and sensitive areas such as defense industry, transportation, finance, security, medicine, and law. While explanatory intelligence provides strong advice for the investor, it can also help investors make a more logical and risk-free step.

ACKNOWLEDGMENT

This research received no specific grant from any funding agency in the public, commercial, or not-for-profit sectors.

REFERENCES

Alberto, F., Francisco, H., Oscar, C., Maria, J. J., & Francesco, M. (2019). Evolutionary Fuzzy Systems for Explainable Artificial Intelligence: Why, When, What for, and Where to. *IEEE Computational Intelligence Magazine*, *14*(1), 69–81. doi:10.1109/MCI.2018.2881645

Alejandro, B. A., Natalia, D. R., Javier, D. S., Adrien, B., Siham, T., Alberto, B., Salvador, G., Sergio, G. L., Daniel, M., Richard, B., Raja, C., & Francisco, H. (2019, December). *Explainable Artificial Intelligence (XAI): Concepts, Taxonomies, Opportunities and Challenges toward Responsible AI. IEEE International Conference on Fuzzy Systems*, New York, NY.

Amina, A., & Mohammed, B. (2018). Peeking Inside the Black-Box: A Survey on Explainable Artificial Intelligence. *IEEEE Access*, *6*(1), 52138–52160.

Bernhard W. & Roland V. (2019, October) *A Survey on Explainable Artificial Intelligence (XAI): towards Medical XAI*. IEEEE Access.

Blen, M. K., Devinder, K., Ali, A. B., Vijaya, K. D., Ahmad, Y. J., Jack, D. Z., & Robert, P. M. (2019). Evolving Rule-Based Explainable Artificial Intelligence for Unmanned Aerial Vehicle. *IEEEE Access*, *7*(1), 17001–17016.

Chanida, P., & Vichai, R. (2019). Material Cost Prediction for Jewelry Production Using Deep Learning Techniqu. *Engineering Journal (New York)*, *23*(6), 145–160.

Daniel, H., & Mark, A. E. (2018) *Explainable A.I.: the promise of Genetic Programming Multi-run*. 2018 International Conference on Machine Learning and Data Engineering (iCMLDE), Malvern, UK.

David, G. (2017). *Explainable Artificial Intelligence (XAI)*. Retrieved from https://www.darpa.mil/attachments/XAIProgramUpdate.pdf

Dennys, C. A. M., & Ricardo, A. S. F. (2018, December). Predicting the direction, maximum, minimum and closing prices of daily Bitcoin exchange rate using machine learning techniques. *Applied Soft Computing*, *75*(1), 596–606.

Dominik, S., Tobias, H., Florian, L., Michael, D., Andreas, S., & Elisabeth, A. (2019, September) *Relevance-based Feature Masking: Improving Neural Network based Whale Classification through Explainable Artificial Intelligence*. INTERSPEECH, Graz, Austria.

Ehsan, H., & Saman, H. (2019, March). CNNpre d: CNN-based stock market prediction using a diverse set of variables. *Expert Systems with Applications*, *129*(1), 273–285.

Gerald, F., & San, J. (2018, November) *Developing Transparent Credit Risk Scorecards More Effectively: An Explainable Artificial Intelligence Approach. International Conference on Data Analytics*, Athens, Greece.

Iansiti, M., & Lakhani, K. R. (2020). *Competing in the Age of AI. Strategy and Leadership When Algorithms and Networks Run the World*. Harvard Business Review Press.

Jianwei, E., Jimin, Y., & Haihong, J. (2019, May). A novel hybrid model on the prediction of time series and its application for the gold price analysis and forecasting. *Physica A*, *527*(1), 1–16.

Manjula, K. A., & Karthikeyan, P. (2019). Gold Price Prediction using Ensemble based Machine Learning Techniques. *Proceedings of the Third International Conference on Trends in Electronics and Informatics*. 10.1109/ICOEI.2019.8862557

Regis, P., Jean-Philippe, P., & Celine, H. (2018, July) *Learning Fuzzy Relations and Properties for Explainable Artificial Intelligence*. *IEEE International Conference on Fuzzy Systems*, Rio de Janeiro, Brazil.

Richard, K. & Raghu N. K. (2019, May) *An Application of Combinatorial Methods for Explainability in Artificial Intelligence and Machine Learning*. National Institute of Standards and Technology, Gaithersburg, MD.

Ruchira, R., & Prakhar, K., & B., B. (2018) *A Survey on Stock Market Prediction using Artificial Intelligence Techniques*. *International Conference on Smart Systems and Inventive Technology (ICSSIT 2018)*, Kattankulathur, Chennai.

Ruth, M. J. B. (2019). Counterfactuals in Explainable Artificial Intelligence (XAI): Evidence from Human Reasoning. *Proceedings of the Twenty-Eighth International Joint Conference on Artificial Intelligence (IJCAI-19)*.

Ufuk, Ç., & Çağatay, B. (2017, June). The Prediction of Precious Metal Prices via Artificial Neural Network by Using RapidMiner. *The Journal of Operations Research, Statistics, Econometrics and Management Information Systems*, *5*(1), 45–54.

Wesley, G. Y. Y., & Suliadi, S. (2019, January). Data Mining Technique in Precious Metal Price Forecasting. *Advances in Computing and Intelligent System*, *1*(1), 1–16.

Wojciech, S., Thomas, W., & Klaus-Robert, M. (n.d.). Explainable artificial intelligence: Understanding, visualizing an interpreting deep learning models. *ITU Journal: ICT Discoveries*.

Zhanhong, H., Junhao, Z., Hong-Ning, D., & Hao, W. (2019). *Gold Price Forecast based on LSTM-CNN Model*. International Conference on Cyber Science and Technology Congress, Gjøvik, Norway.

KEY TERMS AND DEFINITIONS

Artificial Intelligence (AI): Development of computer systems that can perform tasks that require human intelligence and ability, such as visual perception, speech recognition, translation between languages and voice recognition.

Convolutional Neural Network (CNN): Convolutional neural network is an evolution-based math operation that works to perform feature selection and classification tasks through data information.

Explainable Artificial Intelligence (XAI): Explained artificial intelligence is artificial intelligence programmed to define its purpose, decision-making process so that it can be understood by the average person.

Machine Learning: Machine learning is an artificial intelligence (AI) application that gives systems the ability to automatically learn and develop from experience without being explicitly programmed.

Precious Metals (PMs): The precious metals are used in industry and as ornaments, they have high economic value, they are metallic elements that exist in nature.

Chapter 16
The Digital Edge for M-Commerce to Replace E-Commerce

Bhavna Taneja
Amity University, Jharkhand, India

ABSTRACT

The digital trend for m-commerce has accelerated in recent years. M-commerce, which is referred to mobile commerce, is e-commerce delivered through handheld mobile devices. Mobile devices allow people and businesses to stay in touch around the clock. People are using their smartphones for the purpose of gaming, downloading videos and songs, watching television, doing video conferencing, and conducting other entertainment activities. The longer battery life, faster data processing capabilities, better screen resolution, connectivity, ubiquitous nature of the internet, personalization of customer behaviour and customer location, user-friendly software interfaces, mobile digital payment systems have led to increased acceptance of m-commerce. Mobile commerce faces complicated challenges such as small screen-size, limited memory, network issues, infrastructure, language, security issues of authenticity, confidentiality, and privacy. Digital biometrics will help increase the security of the phones and prevent any kind of data theft or fraud.

INTRODUCTION

The term “M-Commerce” is derived from the union of two words “mobile” and “commerce.” It was first used in 1997 by Kevin Duffey and refers to any transaction of monetary value taking place over a wireless mobile telecommunications network. M-Commerce is also about delivering services online without physically going to geographical locations such as banks, shopping malls etc. M-Commerce is the subsequent generation of e-commerce which facilitates the user to access internet without requiring a place for plug-in. M-Commerce is defined in many ways in literature; the main understanding from many studies suggests that M-Commerce is “E-commerce that is delivered through handheld or mobile devices”; it refers to the ability to do a monetary transaction anywhere through internet-enabled mobile

DOI: 10.4018/978-1-7998-8587-0.ch016

devices (Clarke, 2008). Tiwari and Buse (2007) suggests that M-Commerce as a subset of E-Commerce. Further, as a subset of E-Commerce, all the aspects involved in E-Commerce can be extended and applied to M-Commerce. Initially Mobile phones were used for communication but now they have become a sign of personality and individuality (Persaud and Azhar, 2012). Smartphones have widened its reach and has introduced innovation in information exchange and transactions through mobile applications. M-Commerce enable users to access Internet-related services such as purchasing, selling, and searching for information, without being tethered to a wired desktop. From selling home-made chocolates to selling apparels online, this has an impact on all products and services.

Prior studies suggest that E-Commerce and M-Commerce are not only leading edge for doing global business and trade but also offers multiple benefits to the business, government, and consumers on substantial scale. The main forces behind the success of M-Commerce today are rapid proliferation of mobile handheld devices, growth of Internet companies and other telecommunication networks, advancement to 4G, the development of highly personalized content, context aware, and location sensitive applications, development of mobile applications, advancements in mobile payment systems, and development of back-end systems of the Internet (Sadeh, 2003).

The objective of this study is to understand the concept of E-Commerce and M-Commerce by a comparison. All the related aspects of M-Commerce like technologies, features, advantages, disadvantages, and challenges have been discussed. Finally, the growth factors and the recent trends have been analysed.

BACKGROUND

Electronic commerce offered the possibility to reach new markets at a relatively low cost, in a convenient way for both buyers and sellers, generating increased revenues since its inception. The benefits of E-Commerce such as efficiency, 24X7 services, competitive pricing, variety in item selection etc. has outnumbered the resources required in the initial setup of the E-Commerce websites. The advances in modern Internet E-Commerce, including advertising, shopping, investing, banking, and other online services (e-mail, information seeking, etc.) has facilitated people to interact with the Internet in their daily lives (Wu & Wang, 2005). All these activities provide new opportunity for marketers to develop their brand identity.

Tarasewich (2003) suggests that E-Commerce is made up of two components: information and transaction. Information represents the content available on the website and transaction represents how smoothly and effectively the payments are made. Cotlier, (2000) is of the opinion that E-Commerce and M-Commerce should be considered as two different tools of technology. Their roles must not be understood in isolation because they vary in their own advantages and disadvantages. Kourouthanassis and Giaglis (2012) differentiate between M-Commerce and E-Commerce as "M-Commerce services are accessible on the move through devices (such as smartphones and tablets) with fundamentally different processing, presentation, and interaction modalities compared to a desktop computer. Such services enable a whole new set of unprecedented service capabilities, including location awareness, context sensing, and push delivery. Kaur and Singh (2016) in their studies highlighted that the growth of M-Commerce is because of its mobility such as mobile marketing, mobile entertainment, and mobile banking. Earlier companies had to keep geographical limitations while making strategies, but M-Commerce has led everyone to a global market without any boundaries. M-commerce has superseded all demographical, geographical, sociological boundaries in the world. Online response time, 24 hrs availability, page loading speed and visual appearance have led to a preference of M-Commerce over E-Commerce. M-Commerce aims to provide ease, convenience, comfort to its users. M-Commerce being an extension of E-commerce has more features which provide more advantages. Mobiles have made movies downloading, series uploading, online movie tickets booking so convenient. Mobiles provide vast variety of entertainment which is not dependent on indoor connection (Kuoppamaki et al., 2017). The new digital users of today do not want to wait to log on to a site. They find their mobiles as the most convenient option to shop, make payments, transfer funds by the fastest mode (Vanathi et al., 2016).

After the emergence of M-Commerce, E-Commerce has expanded to newer digital markets because it has increased its accessibility, portability, and connectivity. Now, a digital user does not need to search a place to plug-in because it just needs a wireless handheld digital device. Even though M-Commerce is a subset of E-Commerce, it has many more advantages over E-Commerce. Many factors contribute to the inclination of society towards M-Commerce such as wireless communication technology, coupled with high quality Internet; smart phones within the purchasing power of a digital user, availability of internet over mobile phones, availability of services at economical rates and many other benefits. Mobile digital devices allow people and businesses to stay in touch around the clock. The major reason for the popularity of M-Commerce is its distinguishing feature of using and accessing the desired digital information while moving (anywhere, anytime). Moreover, it is more secure and convenient digital platform for a vast range of digital activities. These latest digital technologies have enabled new forms of digital learning, digital health care, digital economic development, and digital governance innovations. People are using digital smartphones for the purpose of gaming, videos, songs, TV, video conferencing and entertainment on their smart devices and this leads to steady growth in digital activities such as mobile advertising and apps industry (Batra, 2013). Smartphones can now digitally connect to Internet at superior speeds starting from 50 Mbps. The longer battery life, faster processing capabilities, larger screens, and high-speed net capabilities offered by affordable smartphones have led to increased acceptance of M-Commerce. Mobile phones are compact in size and so convenient that they always accompany a person whether he is going for work or leisure, whether he is with friends or family. For some people, daily life without M-Commerce, shall be so chaotic that their survival without it cannot be imagined.

WHAT IS E-COMMERCE?

E-Commerce (also known as electronic commerce) is the process of buying and selling of products or services, making money transfers, and transferring data over an electronic medium like the Internet. This network allows people to do business without the constraint of distance and time. Simply put, it is online shopping as we commonly know it. There will be no face-to-face interaction between the parties. The trading is carried out with the help of wired and wireless media. It includes all the activities like transportation, banking, insurance, warehousing, advertising, etc.

Electronic commerce offered the possibility to reach new markets at a relatively low cost, in a convenient way for both buyers and sellers, generating increased revenues since its original. The benefits of E-Commerce such as efficiency, 24X7 services, competitive pricing, variety in item selection etc. has outnumbered the resources required in the initial setup of the E-Commerce websites. The advances in modern Internet E-Commerce, including advertising, shopping, investing, banking, and other online services (e-mail, information seeking, etc.) has facilitated people to interact with the Internet in their daily lives (Wu & Wang, 2005). All these activities provide new opportunity for marketers to develop their brand identity.

How Do E-Commerce Businesses Function?

Online business works on the same principles as an offline/retail store does. The whole E-Commerce process can be broken down into three main components or work processes:

- Receiving orders: This is the first step where customers place the order through the E-Commerce platform (website or an online portal), and the seller makes a note of it.
- Processing order information: The second step where all the details of the order are processed and completed. It is now ready for delivery.
- Shipping: The last step wherein the delivery process is carried out. All the logistics components play a significant role in this step to ensure timely delivery to the customer.

Types of E-Commerce business models based on their functions are:

- Business-to-Business (B2B): Electronic transactions of goods and services between companies. Example: A business sells its products to other businesses.
- Business-to-Consumer (B2C): Electronic transactions of goods and services between companies and consumers. Example: A person buys a new t-shirt from an online store.
- Consumer-to-Consumer (C2C): Electronic transactions of goods and services between consumers, mostly through a third party. Example: A person sells his old smartphone on eBay or Olx to another consumer.
- Consumer-to-Business (C2B): Electronic transactions of goods and services where individuals offer products or services to companies. Example: A Social media influencer offers exposure to their online audience in exchange for a fee.

ADVANTAGES OF E-COMMERCE BUSINESS

Since last few years, E-Commerce has gained tremendous importance due to the increase in the internet users (Surbhi, 2018). The main advantage of an E-Commerce business is that it allows a person to conduct his business flexibly and at the same time is very useful in reaching a full range of target audience within seconds. Nowadays, internet home business has also become a prevalent means of earning money in the form of E-Commerce. One needs to have a computer and internet connection, and the user can easily conduct the marketing and business tasks with just a click of the mouse. Another significant benefit of an E-Commerce business is that it helps you to identify the target audience very quickly and reach them easily too. For example, if you are trying to sell some goods or products, you can easily identify your niche market. Accordingly, you can send emails or promotional brochures to prospective customers who will be interested in your product or service. Compared to conventional promotional methods, this is cost-effective as you do not have to approach the customers on an individual basis. These advantages can be summed up as-

- Flexibility-Online stores can be opened in a short time as compared to physical stores. Physical stores will require furnishing and décor whereas online sites can be opened sitting at home.
- Cost effective- A online store is less expensive than a physical store because one does not have to furnish it or pay rent for it.
- Immediate reach- A person can get the best deal by ordering goods after comparing two three sites. The characteristics and the features of the product are mentioned with detail.
- Elimination of middlemen- which leads to cost saving.
- Twenty-four hours a day, seven days week, and three sixty-five days a year accessibility as there is no time limitation. A person does not have to worry about the opening or closing time of shop. E-Commerce is available all the time.
- Less overhead cost- as a person can save on rent, electricity, furniture, fixtures less salespeople etc.
- Simple, safe, fast, and convenient as you do not have to travel, and a person saves on commuting time.
- Personalized Online Experience-With the advent of AI the shopping experience has changed. The past browser history and choices are kept in mind when online portals show related products.
- Easier to Encourage Impulse Buy- Repeated ads are shown to tempt customers to buy a product. These sites offer a lot of discount and schemes to prompt customers to buy a product.
- Able to Process a High number of Orders-Since computers are doing the work it is possible to execute many orders in a short span of time.
- Can Scale Business Quickly as costs are lower and geographical boundaries are absent.
- Prospective consumers can review existing customer's experiences through feedback and understand if he should buy the product or not.

DRAWBACKS OF E-COMMERCE

However, E-Commerce is accompanied with some drawbacks like there are chances that if some customers have a bad experience, then they will provide negative feedback to others. In addition to this, E-Commerce is not right for perishable goods, the cost of shipping the goods, etc.

No one can buy during a site crash, whereas in a physical store people can go in the shop and buy goods but in an online store if your site crashes people will not be able to make purchases. That is why it is necessary that a website is hosted on the right platform.

Customers cannot try goods before they buy- This is a major drawback as people cannot get the feel of the object that they want to purchase. They must rely on supplier's description of the product.

E-Commerce is highly competitive- Competition is high as there are many sites offering the same products, so suppliers must reduce their margins or give discounts to attract customers.

Business faces added cost of shipping their products- As goods must be delivered to the doorstep of the consumer, this is an additional cost which is not present in a physical store.

E-Commerce lacks personal touch- Everyone likes a suggestion from the salesperson when in a fix. But in online mode there is no one to help a person. The connection between the seller and the buyer is missing.

E-Commerce delays goods – Usually FMCGs are delivered the next day. So, if a person must use a pen today, he must wait till the product is delivered.

Security problems-Online trade means online payments which can pose a threat as a person enters his debit/credit card details in the site.

DEFINITION OF M-COMMERCE

M-Commerce or mobile commerce is an upgraded version of E-Commerce. Mobile Commerce refers to wireless electronic commerce used for conducting commerce or business through a handy device like cellular phone or tablets. Mobile Commerce is a term to describe any commercial activity on a mobile device, such as a mobile phone (iPhone, Android, Blackberry) or a tablet (iPad, Galaxy Tab, Surface). It needs no wire and plug-in devices. It includes browsing, buying, selling, dealing, ordering, paying and many other activities. This includes all steps of the customer journey; reach, attract, choose, convert, and retain. Hence mobile commerce is probably best described as shopping that takes advantage of unique properties of mobile devices. One of the first uses of M-Commerce was in 1997.

After the emergence of M-Commerce, E-Commerce has reached new heights because it has increased its accessibility, portability, and connectivity. Now, a person does not need to search a place to plug-in because it just needs a wireless handheld device. Surbhi (2018) and Kyaw (2020) reports that despite M-Commerce being a subset of E-Commerce, it has many more advantages over E-Commerce. Moreover, it is more secure and convenient.

Many factors contribute to the inclination of society towards M-Commerce such as wireless communication technology, coupled with high quality Internet (Pascoe, 2002; and Rupp, 2002), smart phones within the purchasing power of a common man, availability of internet over mobile phones, availability of services at economical rates etc. Mobile devices allow people and businesses to stay in touch around the clock. The major reason for the popularity of M-Commerce is its distinguishing feature of using and accessing the desired information while moving (anywhere, anytime).

Mobile commerce technologies mean how producers and service providers connect with customers and vice versa. Kaur and Singh (2016) explain the main technologies supporting mobile commerce as-

- High Speed Circuit Supported Data (HSCD) - is circuit-switched wireless data transmission for mobile users at data rates up to 38.4 Kbps, four times faster than the standard data rates of the Global System for Mobile (GSM) communication standard in 1999.
- Global System for Mobile Communication (GSM) GSM uses GPRS, a packet-based communication service, to transmit data, such as through web browsing.
- General Packet Radio Services (GPRS)- GPRS is an expansion Global System for Mobile Communication. It is basically a packet-oriented mobile data standard on the 2G and 3G cellular communication network's global system for mobile communication. GPRS overrides the wired associations, as this framework has streamlined access to the packet information's network like the web (Ashushrma, 2019)
- Enhanced Data rate for Global Evolution (EDGE): is a digital mobile phone technology that allows improved data transmission rates as a backward-compatible extension of GSM
- Wireless Application Protocol (WAP): A WAP browser is a web browser for mobile devices such as mobile phones that uses the protocol.
- Universal Mobile Television System (UMTS)- UMTS (Universal Mobile Telecommunications Service) is a third generation (3G) broadband, packet -based transmission of text, digitized voice,

video, and multimedia at data rates up to 2 megabits per second (Mbps). UMTS offers a consistent set of services to mobile computer and phone users.

- Bluetooth: With proximity of 10 m range, this method is used only by small businesses and shopkeepers such as mall owners and restaurant and café houses (Kaur and Singh, 2016).
- Area-based marketing (GPS): It focused on customers of specific area or locality. Companies locate their customers with the help of Global Positioning System (GPS) and provide goods and services as per requirements of people in that area.
- Short message services (SMS): This is the simplest, cheapest, and widely used method adopted by business houses to sell their products and services. These business houses have data bank of their existing and potential customers and they send bulk messages to their customers with product description and other details such as payment, outlets, and offers.
- Multi-media message services (MMS): Colour screen mobile phones are basic requirement for the use of multimedia services. Audio, video, and text are used in it. This method of mobile marketing is more convenient than SMS. The reason behind is that product demonstration is possible which proves to be more convenient to customers.
- Interactive voice response (IVR): Being a latest one, this method is now widely accepted to provide various services to users. In this system, recorded instructions are there, and a customer can benefit by obeying the instructions.
- Web pages/websites: With internet connectivity, mobile users can go through various company or product web pages/websites by searching various search engines such as Google and Yahoo, etc. These search engines also provide paid space for advertisement of product and collect handsome amount from these services.

These latest technologies have enabled new forms of learning, health care, economic development, and governance innovations (West, 2014). People are using smartphones for the purpose of gaming, videos, songs, TV, video conferencing and entertainment on their smart devices and this leads to steady growth in mobile advertising and apps industry (Batra, 2013). Smartphones can now connect to Internet at speeds starting from 50 Mbps. The longer battery life, faster processing capabilities, larger screens, and high-speed net capabilities offered by affordable smartphones have led to increased acceptance of M-Commerce. For some people, without M-Commerce, their daily life shall be so chaotic that their survival without it cannot be imagined.

Comparative Analysis of M-Commerce and E-Commerce

With the emergence of new trends of doing business, nowadays people need not wait in queue for a long time just to buy a single article. However, traditional commerce is still in vogue, but every second person uses electronic commerce (E-Commerce) and mobile commerce (M-Commerce). The use of mobile devices is a convenient way to quickly act online in the offline world. These three ingredients (convenience, speed, location) are essential to understand the differences between traditional online and the quickly growing mobile behaviour. Mobile users perceive their devices to quickly assist them in their offline activities, such as rapid communication, price checking or location-related services. When comparing mobile commerce to E-Commerce, these differences become more evident. When following an E-Commerce customer journey, all activities such as price and product comparison, user reviews and purchasing are performed using the computer. Complex operations are easy and there is enough time. For M-Commerce physical sources and time are much more important.

Table 1. Comparison Chart of E-Commerce and M-Commerce

Basis for Comparison	E-Commerce	M-Commerce
Definitions	Any kind of commercial transaction that happens over the internet using electronic system is known as E-Commerce	M-Commerce refers to the commercial activities which are transacted with the assistance of wireless computing devices like mobile phones or laptops
Which device is used?	Laptops and Computers	Mobiles, tablets, PDA's, iPad etc.
Developed	In 1970's	In 1990's
What is it?	Superset	Subset
Scope	Scope of E-Commerce is wider than M-Commerce	M-Commerce is the extended form of E-Commerce that involves more innovative technology
Ease of carrying device	No	Yes
Use of internet	Mandatory	Not mandatory
Reach	Narrow i.e., it is available only in places having internet and electricity.	Broad due to its portability.

CHARACTERISTICS OF M-COMMERCE

- Effective time management: Due to connectivity feature, products and services are provided by producer in time. In the same way, consumers also get benefited by real-time availability of products.
- Wireless: In case of mobile commerce, customer need not sit at one place with a fixed infrastructure. But in this form of commerce, he can avail anywhere and anytime business transaction facility. So, it is very convenient for users to operate it.
- All time internet: With new form of mobile technology, user can enjoy all-time internet facilities with Wi-Fi or 3/4g data and can enjoy facilities such as online shopping, online payments, and online service facilities.
- High-speed: Affordable Internet access is increasingly common in many regions across the world and instantaneous access to real-time information leads to use of M-Commerce in time-critical applications such as stock quotes, and traffic updates, etc
- Ubiquity: Mobile handheld devices of today are lightweight and portable and are near users during entire day. Real time information is critical for many business decisions.
- Convenience: Instantaneous access to a variety of options to choose from adds to this convenience. Communication thus takes place irrespective of the user's location, and hence mobile devices offer the capability of sending and receiving information on an anywhere, anytime basis.

- Immediacy: It is the availability of M-Commerce services that facilitate an instant action and reaction to changing demand. It can provide real-time information to clients anywhere, regardless of their location. They gain instant connectivity to their customers who can interact with brands regardless of location or time (Pavel and Vlad, 2016).
- Personalization: Personalization is a key factor in the success of mobile commerce. Marketers have realized that getting consumers to buy a product or service is not as important as providing a tailored experience that gives them exactly what they want and need. Nowadays, consumers crave contextually relevant and targeted information (Kats, 2017). Businesses can use push strategies and track consumer behaviour and use his location data to personalise messages.
- Localization: With the advent of GPS technology location-based services such as information on nearby ATMs, restaurants, hospitals, or turn-by-turn navigation services are possible using location data. Thus, information on a few applications relevant to the consumer's position can be provided in real time.
- Mobile app availability: Several mobile apps are now available which makes use of mobile commerce easier. These apps are related with online payments, online education, online booking, and online shopping.
- Browsing data: Now many upgraded mobile browsers are available, and mobile users can browse World Wide Web at any time and place. They can shop online by operating these browsers. Further, they need not be in present in person to shop goods online.
- Online digital stores: Presently, the lifestyle of the people is extremely busy especially in cities as male and female both are working. As both are busy with their work and commitments, they are left with only a little spare time. With the availability and usage of smart phones, people find internet the easiest medium to fulfil their needs and requirements. M-Commerce makes the digital user shopping experience much easy as all the sites are available there on mobile, just one touch away, which gives users' facility to shop online anything, anytime, a Speed facility: One of the unique features of mobile commerce is that it speeds up transaction process and provides instant satisfaction and contentment to customers. It involves urgency in transaction and speeds up sales through business tactics such as short-term discount, etc.
- Affordability feature: Due to technology development, now smartphones are in reach of lower income group people also. These smartphones can easily be used as internet device for online shopping and payments (Panneerselvam, 2013).
- Identifiability: M-Commerce can identify user of a service, as mobile devices are typically used by an individual, as opposed to a Personal Computer (PC) where the identity of the user is ambiguous. A mobile phone also has an inbuilt identifier to facilitate secure transactions, whereas a desktop is anonymous. Using GPS technology, it is possible to identify and locate a customer to provide personalized content and/or services.
- Independent of geographical location: In mobile commerce, consumer can buy product and services directly by use of their mobiles anywhere. Producers and customers need not be at same place. Further, producers can sell their products anywhere in the world without any regional boundaries.
- Possibility of future innovation: Mobile commerce market is continuously developing over time and thus, will provide opportunity for development in mobile phone market also. Possibility of potential innovation is very high in mobile commerce such as there is need of new mobile apps and innovative payment system.

APPLICATIONS AND ADVANTAGES OF M-COMMERCE

- M-Commerce has several major advantages over its fixed counterparts due to its specific inbuilt characteristics like digital personalization for users, flexibility, and distribution. Mobile commerce promises exceptional business, market potential and greater efficiency. It has been widely seen that people nowadays make use of various applications.
- Digital entertainment: Digital entertainment is also one of the important applications of M-Commerce. Playing online games, watching online videos, and listening songs on smartphone devices played an important role in development not only for entertainment industry but also for M-Commerce industry. Entertainment applications are a segment with maximum share in M-Commerce market, and it is predicted to become the leading part of M-Commerce.
- Digital mobile banking: Convenience is one of the key drivers for growth of digital mobile banking. Mobile banking services can be classified in two categories: transaction based and non-transaction. Today, most of the leading banks have developed their own mobile banking applications which offer a wide range of services such as checking account history, notifications on account activity, review of card/loan statements, fund transfers between linked accounts, bills payments, real time stock quotes, Micro payment, Tax payment, Request for mini statement etc. Mobile banking saw a growth of 92% according to the Reserve Bank of India Annual Report (2017-2018).
- Digital mobile wallets: Mobile wallet is mobile payments mechanism under which mobile user opens a mobile wallet account in a partner bank and deposits some money in the account which can be used for making online payments. Issuing bank, registers the mobile number and gives a mobile wallet account number to the user. While making payment, bank checks available balance in mobile wallet account. If balance is sufficient account is debited for the requested amount. Mobile wallets are gaining popularity. One important feature of mobile wallets is that user does not need a bank account, especially in developing countries where still many citizens do not have a bank account. They can open their account in mobile wallet partner banks and can make easy online and offline payments.
- Digital news/Information updates: All important information related with news, stock, traffic, and sports updates which were initially available on Personal Computers, can now be availed on mobile phones.
- Digital mobile ticketing: Today mobile ticketing is used in several parts of the world for booking tickets in airlines, tourist attractions, zoos, museums, cinema, and public transport. In India, many passengers use the IRCTC (Indian Railway Catering and Tourism Corporation) mobile application to book and pay for tickets using their mobile phones (Kapoor et al., 2013)
- Digital Information services: Information on stock prices, sports scores, weather updates, emergency alerts, flight information, news, and traffic information can be delivered to handheld devices in real time. This is especially advantageous for highly time-sensitive data such as stock quotes.
- Digital mobile vouchers: Vouchers, coupons, and loyalty cards are represented by virtual tokens. These can be sent to mobile phones and users can avail benefits of these virtual tokens by just showing them to the concerned person.
- Digital brokerage services: Stock market services can easily be provided via mobile device. Mobile brokerage and user can take timely and accurate decision related with the stock by using this mobile brokerage service.

- Digital content purchase and delivery: Due to high speed and uninterrupted connectivity of internet, mobile users can purchase full audio/video contents online. Ring tones, wall papers, and games are mainly sold.
- Digital e-auction: Now, electronic auction can be possible with the help of mobile commerce. In it, bidding for goods and services can be performed with the help of electronic implementation. This method of auction is less time consuming and convenient for both suppliers and buyers.
- Digital education services: It is now possible to browse all type of information related with students, academicians, researchers, NGO's, and funding agencies with the help of mobile devices. Online journals and books are also available easily. Further, online access to libraries is also possible by subscribing to these. One can access lot of contents without any time and location constraint using handheld devices. Many of the online journals, books, research papers, and articles have their dedicated applications and help the students in their education and learning (Sharma, 2016). M-learning is an advanced tool that helps students and teachers to navigate the options available in the distance-learning world. This application has helped many schools, colleges, and universities to complete their courses on time during the Covid-19 pandemic times.
- Digital electronic grocery market: This service was of utmost importance during covid-19 lockdown. Electronic grocery permits the consumers to buy grocery online through various payment mediums such as cash on delivery and online payments without any constraint of time and location. These e-grocery vendors provide home delivery of various products including staples, edible oil, beverages, milk, and dairy products and constitutes nearly 46% of the market shares in the e-grocery market.
- Digital mobile marketing and advertising: Marketing and advertising of product and services with the help of mobile commerce is in trend. The sellers get instant connectivity to their customers regardless of location or time (Pavel & Vlad, 2016). Social media advertising has low cost and broad reach. This is very convenient and less expensive method for business houses to expand their brand.
- Digital location-based services: Through the development and integration of GPS technology in mobile phones in the late 1990s and early 2000s, location-based services have become very popular. Location Analytics can be merged with Business Intelligence to bring in Intelligence Analytics which can enhance the user experience by verifying the optimal site of the nearest restaurant or gas station, or ATM etc (Rybarczyk et al., 2018). Today, these services include location-based real-time weather reports, traffic updates, and requesting a nearest service.
- Digital relationship: Due to full time connectivity with customers, companies using mobile commerce can easily maintain better relationship with customers. Further, they are also able to get timely feedback for their services and use this information for future reference, after sales services, and customer data maintenance.
- The growth of digital wearable devices such as smartwatches is expected to aid further development of applications in M-Commerce. Social buy buttons which enable users to purchase a product without exiting social media platforms is predicted to grow in popularity.

ISSUES, CONTROVERSIES, AND PROBLEMS

M-Commerce: Disadvantages

Based on the findings of Schwiderski-Grosche and Knospe (2002) and Niranjanamurthy et al. (2013), the following list summarizes the main disadvantages of M-Commerce:

- Limited functionality and screen size of mobile phones as compared to traditional desktops or laptops.
- Limited memory available on mobiles as compared to a desktop.
- Absence of user-friendly keyboards. (Davis, 1989 TAM)
- Wireless communication between mobile device and the network makes way for additional security threats such as eavesdropping.
- Mobile devices are liable to loss by theft or misplacement. According to a study by IDG Research and Lookout, 44% of stolen phones were taken after being forgotten at a public place. High security standards must be in place to protect mobile devices due to the increasing amounts of personal and confidential information stored in it.
- Additional cost of setting up mobile and wireless broadband infrastructure.
- Security-related risks concerning data moved across mobile devices and wireless networks.
- Mobile phones do not have sufficient memory as compared to a desktop.
- The absence of common wireless networking standards, which might lead to low internet connectivity.

M-Commerce: Challenges

Several challenges faced by M-Commerce include -

- Limited bandwidth available for wireless communication.
- Willingness of the people to search for information and compare information, as well as responsibility (Carey & Helfert, 2016).
- Lack of knowledge of internet for some people- If people will not know how to use a smart phone, they cannot avail the services provided by M-Commerce. Technology can bring resistance from the users (Heinz et al., 2017).
- Lack of infrastructure- On the level of infrastructure good roads, mobile networks with good coverage and high-quality broadband are required (Popomaronis, 2016). At times there is no connectivity or no towers especially in rural areas (Khokhar, 2016).
- Beliefs (the opinions held by the nonusers)- People in rural areas believe that they do not require internet, or such activities are for the young people. Such belief can be because of illiteracy. (Singh & Agarwal, 2019).
- Language barrier-If the people are not versed with English, they will have problems executing the transactions.
- Higher dependency on text-only services with limited interactivity and visual appeal, and user interfaces that are hard to deal with.

- Security issues-Security issues can be of security and privacy. India is number one in COD (cash on delivery) transactions (Nielson report, 2016). COD MEANS that when goods are delivered to a person's doorstep, payment will be made then. This proves that people are still apprehensive to use their debit/credit cards online. Security will also come from privacy. Privacy means to keep the information of the customers private.

Though M-Commerce has come a long way but, it still faces challenges such as privacy and security which affect consumer trust. According to the LexisNexis report, (2016), M-Commerce companies experience 880 fraud attempts each month of which 66%, that is, 581 attempts are successful. Majority of the people are unaware of whether their information is being collected, stored, and used for questionable purposes. As a result, consumers are becoming more wary of divulging sensitive information to online vendors (Kim et al., 2011). This stems from a lack of trust in, and the subsequent perceived risk of using M-Commerce services.

According to Laudon and Traver (2006), security of online transactions deals with the concepts of:

- Integrity: ability to ensure that information transmitted via Internet is not altered by unauthorized third party.
- Nonrepudiation: ability to ensure that a party cannot deny an action undertaken online.
- Authenticity: ability to know and identify with certainty the party with whom one is dealing with online .
- Confidentiality: ability to ensure that the information provided by one party is only viewed by authorized person(s).
- Privacy: ability to control the use of one's information provided online 6. Availability: ensuring that the online service continues its operations as intended.

The decision to conduct transactions online involves an evaluation of the risks involved in doing so. These risks depend on the nature of purchase and vary from one service to another. M-Commerce transactions involve purchases, without personal interaction and without the touch and feel of products. This leads to customers feeling insecure. Unlike the purchase of tangible goods where only minimal personal information is required, the purchase of services online requires a significant amount of personal information (Featherman et al., 2010). This risk associated with M-Commerce is due to a lack of trust in M-Commerce security. Trust in M-Commerce can be divided into two categories—trust in mobile technology and trust in mobile vendors. Distrust in availing M-Commerce services can be due to several factors. These include unreliability of payment gateways, fraudulent sellers, loss of personal information and potential misuse of the same, phishing attacks, pharming attacks, mad ware (mobile adware), and cyber laws, to name a few. However, studies suggest that consumer trust in M-Commerce transactions can be increased through aesthetically designed websites (Li & Yeh, 2010) and mobile applications, with greater interactivity and customization. Brand image as well as responsiveness of M-Commerce suppliers affects consumer inclination to perform M-Commerce transactions.

SOLUTIONS AND RECOMMENDATIONS

The year 2007 was marked by the launch of Apple's iPhone which revolutionized the cell phone industry and thereafter ushered the era of mobile applications. Subsequent competition between various phone manufacturers and supporting software led to Apple (iOS), Google (Android), and Microsoft (Windows Phone) developing hardware and engaging customers through mobile applications. The huge market success of mobile applications can be attributed to a large customer base that in turn attracts many developers who compete to develop and provide the best features. Mobile apps today are highly personalized, context aware, user friendly, and location sensitive. Overall, smartphones accounted for 64 percent of global E-Commerce traffic and for 46 percent of E-Commerce orders.

It is evident that M-Commerce has certainly seen a marked transformation. The evolution and growth of M-Commerce was supported by parallel advancements in Internet, wireless communication technology, handheld devices, Internet companies, mobile applications, mobile payment systems, and Internet back-end systems. Progress in all these domains supported one another and led to the development of M-Commerce. Today, the number of apps available on Google Play Store is over 2.8 million, while the number of mobile app downloads worldwide in 2019 was over 204 billion, while in 2018 it was 192.45 billion (Statista, 2020).

With its growing influence on individual consumers and large economies alike, it has become a crucial part of our day-to-day lives. Clement (2019) reports that China has the biggest online population at 829 million users, followed by India at 560 million and the United States at 293 million. Notwithstanding East Asia's 1 billion internet users, English is the most popular language online, representing 25.2 percent of global internet users, followed by Chinese.

Online shoppers are spending more time on mobile apps (applications) than laptops or desktop computers. In 2019, internet users worldwide spent a daily average of 150 minutes on their mobile devices, over three times the global internet consumption via desktop, which was 39 minutes daily (broadband search). Around 70% of Amazon shoppers used mobile devices to browse for products and make transactions (Clement, 2020). M-Commerce has a promising future for mobile internet usage, as global mobile data traffic is projected to increase nearly seven fold between 2017 and 2022.

WhatsApp is the most popular mobile messaging app in the world with 1.6 billion monthly active users, followed closely by Facebook Messenger at 1.3 billion monthly active users. Facebook was found to be the leading social network with 2.4 billion monthly active users. As of 2020, covid-19 times, Videos account for more than half of downstream internet traffic volume, with Netflix representing the largest share of global internet bandwidth usage (Clement, 2020). Figure 1 shows that the mobile traffic is more than double in mobile phones as compared to desktop traffic.

Amid the COVID-19 crisis and the looming economic recession, the M-Commerce market worldwide will grow by US$5.1 Trillion, driven by a revised compounded annual growth rate (CAGR) of 23.8%. M-Commerce is forecast to grow at over 23.8% and reach a market size of US$6.6 Trillion by the end of the analysis period forecasts by Globe Newswire (2020). An unusual period in history, the coronavirus pandemic has unleashed a series of unprecedented events affecting every industry. The M-Commerce market will be reset to a new normal which going forward in a post COVID-19 era will be continuously redefined and redesigned. Staying on top of trends and accurate analysis is paramount now more than ever to manage uncertainty, change and continuously adapt to new and evolving market conditions.

Figure 1. Distribution of retail website visits and orders by device.
Distribution of retail website visits and orders worldwide as of 1st quarter 2019, by device (Press Release by DUBLIN, May 28, 2020 /PRNewswire/)

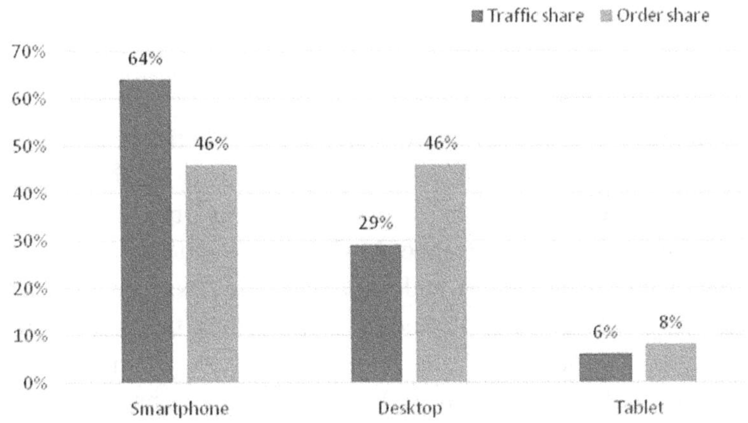

Mobile applications today take advantage of improved hardware in terms of mobile device screen size, processing power, screen resolution, and battery life; connectivity in terms of fast and ubiquitous nature of the Internet; personalization through tracking of customer behaviour and customer location; and user-friendly software interfaces. Mobile commerce adoption has increased significantly in the country due to multiple factors such as enhanced 3G penetration and availability of affordable smartphones.

Skourletopoulos et al. (2016) discuss the transition toward fifth generation (5G) mobile networks. The research on fifth-generation mobile-enabled services will conceptualize by 2020 with the one thousand times more network traffic than it is today. Internet access and web browsing on mobiles have become an inseparable part of mobile. Mobiles come with an added advantage of touch screen technology, which makes it easy to handle anywhere and anytime. It also incorporates all the comforts and conveniences satisfying the needs of the consumers. Changes in the technology have given the M-Commerce world a better push and a great support to carry on transactions more smoothly. One of the important driving forces for the M-Commerce technology is the easy access of internet on mobiles.

FUTURE RESEARCH DIRECTIONS

The sudden lockdown due to covid-19 has changed a lot of habits of people. Many people have become tech savvy as it was a necessity to attend online business meetings. Also, the free time has been used to browse and indulge in their hobbies. A lot of people have learnt music, dance, yoga, meditation, exercise etc online. So, a lot of apps have been developed and used. Study can be done on what device the consumers were using during this time. Once the lockdown is over will they continue pursuing their hobbies and online browsing and social connecting. The M-Commerce market will reset to a new normal in the post COVID-19 pandemic era.

A study can be done on what devices are used for final purchase of goods and services. For people who own both a desktop and mobile what device is used for browsing and what for final purchase as mobiles are always with the users and can lead to price scrutiny and impulse purchases. Staying on top of trends and accurate analysis is of paramount importance now, to manage uncertainty, change and continuously adapt to new and evolving market conditions.

CONCLUSION

Worldwide, mobile commerce is growing rapidly. Increased competition, customer awareness, and different market strategies are certain factors those directly contribute to mobile commerce growth. Major Internet companies of today include Amazon, Alibaba, eBay, and Uber. Personalized services offered by these companies have led to the development of M-Commerce and encouraged more people to adopt the same. It is very much customer friendly and gives opportunities to customers to shop anytime at any place. Moreover, with introduction of 4G and 5G technologies, the future of mobile commerce is very bright. It provides value for money to the users by providing convenience, timely, and personalized services. It is evident from marketing experiences that ever-growing technology will boost mobile commerce market if proper marketing techniques are clubbed with strategic initiatives.

Telecom and internet penetration worldwide have been on a rise. Decreasing mobile internet tariffs and availability of smartphone at prices as low as INR 5000 add to this growth. Due to mobile internet penetration, the primary shopping instincts of the consumer has been modified as instant information access is available to the consumer.

The internet service providers on the one end, the application developers on the other end, and most importantly, the users of the M-Commerce technology should be encouraged to play a participative role (Schneiderman, 2001). Latest smartphones have fingerprint recognition system software. Therefore, unless the user itself tries to access the phone, no one else can do so. Digital biometrics will not only increase the security of the phone, but such software will also prevent any kind of data theft or frauds. The success of M-Commerce will depend on the effective merging of the stakeholders, incorporating marketers, as well as telecommunication companies (Schwartz, 2000). Value-added services will be an added advantage to effectively satisfy the stakeholders and create high-end brand loyalty among the users.

It is user friendly, accommodating, economical, and has bypassed all the barriers of communication. A technology which provides solution to all communication deterrents, language barriers, and above all, it wins over all the special needs. The latest software's have incorporated the demands of the people born with special needs. The technology is not only supporting them but also complementing their requirements. People with different learning disabilities can make use of the technology and many apps, which instil confidence in their abilities.

Mobile technology, due to its ease, accessibility, and convenience has taken over all the other electronic and other gazettes from us. Whether it is a diary, calendar, clock, alarm, calculator, camera, Walkman, radio, albums, newspapers, or contacts collection, it has taken over almost every other thing. The mode of communication now remains mobile, whether through chat, messenger, mails, social media, video calling, or anything else; Gordon and Gutiorrez, (2007); Clarke, (2008).

ACKNOWLEDGMENT

This research received no specific grant from any funding agency in the public, commercial, or not-for-profit sectors.

REFERENCES

A Global Perspective of Mobile Commerce. (2016). IAB-Global-Mobile-Commerce-Report.

Arora, J., & Narang, B. (2016). *Present and Future of Mobile Commerce: Introduction, Comparative Analysis of M Commerce and E Commerce, Advantages, Present and Future*. IGI Global.com.

Ashushrma. (2019). *Information security*. Geeks for geek. Retrieved from https://www.geeksforgeeks.org/e-commerce/

Balasubramanian, S., Peterson, R. A., & Jarvenpaa, S. L. (2002). Exploring the Implications of M-Commerce for Markets and Marketing. *Journal of the Academy of Marketing Science*, *30*(4), 348–361. doi:10.1177/009207002236910

Barnes, S. J. (2002, April). The Mobile Commerce Value Chain: Analysis and Future Developments. *International Journal of Information Management*, *22*(2), 91–108. doi:10.1016/S0268-4012(01)00047-0

Batra, S., & Juneja, N. (2013). M-Commerce in India: Emerging Issues. *International Journal of Advanced Research in IT and Engineering, 2*(2).

Bhalla, P. (2020). *What is ecommerce and how it operates*. Retrieved from https://www.shiprocket.in/blog/s

Bhatti, T. (2015). Exploring Factors Influencing the Adoption of Mobile Commerce. *Journal of Internet Banking and Commerce*, *12*(3).

Carey, K., & Helfert, M. (2016). Improving the Front End of Innovation: The Case of Mobile Commerce Services. In *International Conference on HCI in Business, Government and Organizations*. Springer International Publishing.

Clarke, I. (2008). Emerging Value Propositions for M-Commerce. *The Journal of Business Strategy*, *25*, 2.

Clement, J. (2019). *Largest online population Countrywide*. Statistia reports.

Clement, J. (2020). *Number of mobile app downloads*. Statista reports.

Clement, J. (2020). *Statistics & Facts, Internet usage worldwide*. Statistia reports.

Cotlier, M. (2000). *Wide Wireless World, Catalog Age*. New Canaan.

Davis, F. D. (1989). Perceived usefulness, perceived ease of use, and user acceptance of information technology. *Management Information Systems Quarterly*, *13*(3), 319–340.

Deshmukh, S. P., Deshmukh, P., & Thampi, G. (2013). Transformation from E-Commerce to M-Commerce in Indian Context. International Journal Computational Science, 10(4).

Electron, J. (2012). *Introduction to the Special Issue Mobile Commerce: The Past, Present, and Future of Mobile Commerce*. Research Int.

Featherman, M. M., Wells, J. D., & Campbell, D. E. (2010). *The Effect of Perceived Novelty on the Adoption of Information Technology Innovations: A Risk/Reward Perspective*. Elsevier publications.

Ferreira, N. M. (2019). *Ecommerce-advantages-and-disadvantages*. Retrieved from https://www.oberlo.com/blog/20-

Firdausi, A., Shaik, N., & Tiwari, G. (2020). *What is E-Commerce and how it operates*. Emerging Trends in Business.

Globe Newswire. (2020). *Global Mobile Wallet Industry to 2028 - Flourishing m-Commerce Industry, Proliferation of Smartphones and Internet Penetration, Driving Growth*. Research and Markets.

Hayden, T., & Webster, T. (2014). *The Mobile Commerce Revolution: Business Success in a Wireless World*. Que Publishing.

Heinz, J., Thomann, M., & Fischer, P. (2017). Ladders to M-commerce Resistance: A Qualitative Means-end Approach. *Computers in Human Behavior*, *73*(2), 362–374.

Huang, S. M. (2003). Mobile Commerce: The Convergence of E-Commerce and Wireless Technology. *International Journal of Services Technology and Management*, *4*(3), 302–322.

Kapoor, K., Dwivedi, Y. K., & Williams, M. D. (2013). In Role of Innovation Attributes in Explaining Intention and Adoption: A Case of the IRCTC Mobile Ticketing Application in the Indian Context. *UK Academy for Information Systems Conference Proceedings*.

Kats, R. (2017). *Mobile Commerce Daily*. Academic Press.

Kaur, R., & Malhotra, H. (2016). *Securing Transactions and Payment Systems for M-Commerce*. IGI Global Publishing.

Kaur, R., & Singh, S. (2016). Mobile Commerce: Indian Perspectives. *International Journal of Innovative Research in Computer and Communication Engineering, 4*.

Keen, P. G., & Mackintosh, R. (2001). *The Freedom Economy: Gaining the M-Commerce Edge in the Era of the Wireless Internet*. McGraw-Hill Professional.

Khokhar, F. (2016). *E-Commerce challenges: The Story of Online Groceries*. Academic Press.

Kim, D., & Adler, H. (2011). *Student's use of hotel mobile Apps: Their effect of brand loyalty*. Retrieved from: http://scholarworks.umass.edu/cgi/viewcontent.cgi?article1/41242&context1/4gradconf hospitality

Kourouthanassis, P. E., & Giaglis, G. (2012). Introduction to the Special Issue Mobile Commerce: The Past, Present, and Future of Mobile Commerce Research. *International Journal of Electronic Commerce*, *16*(4), 5–18.

Kuoppamäki, S. M., Wilska, T. A., & Taipale, S. (2017). Ageing and consumption in Finland: The effect of age and life course stage on ecological, economical, and self-indulgent consumption among late middle-agers and young adults between 1999 and 2014. *International Journal of Consumer Studies*, *41*(5), 457–464. doi:10.1111/ijcs.12353

Kyaw, N. Y. (2020). Next Generation of E-Commerce's Impacts on Myanmar Business Era. *International Journal of Scientific and Research Publications*, *10*(05), 690–699. doi:10.29322/IJSRP.10.05.2020.p10179

Laudon, K., & Traver, C. (2006). *E-Commerce Essentials*. Pearson Publication.

Lexis Nexis. (2016). *True Cost of Fraud Study.* Annual Report.

Li, Y. M., & Yeh, Y. S. (2010). *Increasing trust in mobile commerce through design aesthetics*. Computer Human Behaviour.

Madden, G., Banerjee, A., Rappoport, P. N., & Suenaga, H. (2017). E-Commerce Transactions, the Installed Base of Credit Cards, and the Potential Mobile E-Commerce Adoption. *Applied Economics.*

Neelam. (2020). *Mobile Commerce - Its Advantages, Limitations, Future, Case study*. Retrieved from www.geocities.ws/neelam21582

New York. (2020). *Global Interior Car Accessories Industry*. Globe Newswire Report. Retrieved from https://www.reportlinker.com/p05899775/

Nielsen. (2016). *Securing Transactions and Payment Systems for M-Commerce*. IGI Global.

Nielson. (2016). *The Science Behind What Will Happen Next*. Annual Report.

Niranjanamurthy, M., Kavyashree, N., Jagannath, S., & Chahar, D. (2013). Analysis of E-Commerce and M-Commerce: Advantages, Limitations and Security Issues. *International Journal of Advanced Research in Computer and Communication Engineering*, 2360–2370.

NPD. (2020). *Distribution of retail website visits and orders worldwide as of 1st quarter, by device.* Press Release by Dublin/PRNewswire.

Panneerselvam, M. K. (2013). Mobile Commerce – A Mode of Modern Business. *Asia Pacific Journal of Marketing & Management Review*, *2*(7), 141–149.

Pavel, C., & Vlad, F. (2016). Trends in the Evolution of Mobile Commerce. *Quaestus*, *8*, 38.

Persaud, A., & Azhar, I. (2012). Innovative mobile marketing via smartphones. *Marketing Intelligence & Planning*, *30*(4).

Popomaronis, T. (2016). Think Great Innovation Drives Mobile Commerce? It's Actually This. *Forbes.*

Reserve Bank of India Annual Report. (2018). Retrieved from https://www.rbi.org.in/Scripts/AnnualReportPublications.aspx?year=2018

Rybarczyk, G., Banerjee, S., Starking-Szymanski, M. D., & Shaker, R. R. (2018). Travel and Us: The Impact of Mode Share on Sentiment Using Social Media And GIS. *Journal of Location Based Services.*

Sadeh, N. (2003). *M-Commerce: Technologies, Services, and Business Models* (C. A. Long, Ed.). John Wiley and Sons.

Schneiderman, C. (2001). Are you billing in real-time. *Telecommunications*, *35*(7), 71–72.

Schwartz, E. S., & Mark, M. (2020). Rational Pricing of Internet Companies. *Financial Analysts Journal*, (January), 2019.

Schwiderski-Grosche, S., & Knospe, H. (2002). *Future mobile networks: Ad-hoc access based on online payment with smartcards.* Conference paper of Personal, Indoor and Mobile Radio Communications.

Senn, J. A. (2000). The Emergence of M-Commerce. *Computer*, *33*(12), 148–150.

Sharma, C. (2016). *Mobile Commerce Statictics.* Retrieved from hhttp://www.ecbilla.com/blogs/mobile-ecommerce-statistics-2016.html

Singh, N., & Agarwal, S. (2019). *Encumbrances in M-Commerce: A Demographic context*. Taylor and Francis Group.

Skourletopoulos, G., Mavromoustakis, C., Mastorakis, G., Batalla, J., Dobre, C., Panagiotakis, S., & Pallis, E. (2016). Big Data and Cloud Computing: A Survey of the State-of-the-Art and Research Challenges. In Advances in Mobile Cloud Computing and Big Data in the 5G Era (pp. 23-41). Academic Press.

Solomon, M. R. (2014). *Consumer Behaviour: Buying, Having, and Being*. Prentice Hall.

Statista. (2017). Retrieved from https://www.statista.com

Surbhi, S. (2018). *Difference Between E-Commerce and M-Commerce.* Retrieved from https://keydifferences.com/author/surbhi/page/70

Tarasewich, P. (2003). Designing Mobile Commerce Applications. *Communications of the ACM, 46.*

Tiwari, R., & Buse, S. (2007). *The Mobile Commerce Prospects: A Strategic Analysis of Opportunities in the Banking Sector*. Hamburg University Press.

Turban, E., King, D., & Wang, J. (2003). *Introduction to E-Commerce*. Prentice Hall.

Vanathi, B., Shanmugam K., Rhymend, V., & Uthariaraj, V.R. (2016). Enhancing Secure Transaction and User Authentication Method Based on Fingerprint Mechanism Using Fuzzy Logic Amalgam Encryption for PIN Distribution Process in M-Commerce. *Asian Journal of Information Technology.*

Varshney, U., & Vetter, R. (2002). Mobile Commerce: Framework, Applications and Networking Support. *Mobile Networks and Applications*, *7*(3), 185–198.

Wang, J. J., Song, Z., Lei, P., & Sheriff, R. E. (2005). Design and Evaluation of M-Commerce Applications. Academic Press.

Wang, Y. S., & Liao, Y. W. (2007). The Conceptualization and Measurement of M-Commerce User Satisfaction. *Computation. Human Behaviour*, *23*(1).

Wu, J. H., & Wang, S. C. (2005). What Drives Mobile Commerce? An Empirical Evaluation of the Revised Technology Acceptance Model. *Information & Management*.

Xu, G., & Gutierrez, J. A. (2006). An Exploratory Study of Killer Applications and Critical Success Factors in M-Commerce. *Journal of Electronic Commerce in Organizations*.

Zhang, L., Zhu, J., & Liu, Q. (2012). *A meta-analysis of mobile commerce adoption and the moderating effect of culture*. Academic Press.

Chapter 17
Emerging Challenges for Digital Resources Transformation:
An Overview of Web Citation Analysis

Suganya E.
Bharathiar University, India

Vijayarani S.
Bharathiar University, India

ABSTRACT

Web citation analysis is emerging as an important subject of research in web mining, information retrieval, library science, etc. Scientific publications form a significant part of the research. The quality of the publication is determined by the citation which is to a published or an unpublished source. Citation analysis is used to evaluate the corresponding significance or an impression of an author or publication which is assessed by several times that an author or publication has been cited by other related works. It is useful in ascertaining the impression of a research article. It is useful in learning more about an area of knowledge. The main objective of this chapter is to provide knowledge about web citation analysis. A brief overview of web citation index, citation styles, citation-based metrics, and research challenges are discussed.

INTRODUCTION

A citation is a reference to the source of information used in research, which enables researchers to access another source to further their learning in the given field of study. Nowadays resources are being digitally transformed and made available on the internet and increasingly being used by researchers. It is used to ascertain information about the author, contents, and publication. Research is honestly mentioned, paraphrased or the essential content is summarized. Failure to cite sources is considered plagiarism. Researchers search for published researches, which is relevant to their research problems and use those researches as a base for arguments made in their research. Scholars, researchers, practitioners, and oth-

DOI: 10.4018/978-1-7998-8587-0.ch017

ers, who study those researches and also to identify the research gaps, drawbacks, and limitations, in the existing approaches. The fundamental reason for analyzing citations is to direct readers to authentic sources of relevant information that have been reported. Citation analysis helps researchers to trace the genealogy of their ideas and acknowledge pioneers and peers. The analysis also helps in knowing about the methods employed and equipment used in previous researches. This helps in making a critical observation of those researches and taking corrective measures, if necessary, in future researches (Harinarayana, 2010). Citation helps in validating the claims and arguments of the researcher. Furthermore, it highlights the originality of the research in the context of previous researches and, in other words, when the research does not have citations, it can be examined as plagiarism.

Digital citation analysis is undergoing major transformation and is defined as the analysis of information from citation indexes to determine the acclaim and the impact of distinguishing articles, authors, and publications. To evaluate citation analysis using significant measures like frequency of the citations, H-index, i10 index, and so on. Digital citation analysis is a bibliometrics technique, which is used to find patterns in scholars' publication practice like how often an author or publication is cited or to find networks in scholarly communication. It is very useful to identify top journals on a particular topic. There are several citation applications are available such as BibMe, Citation Machine, EasyBib, OttoBib, and Cite.com.

The recommendation of similar articles to the research scholars is known as research paper recommendation which can be digitally transformed and available to researchers worldwide over the internet. Some of the applications of research paper recommendation systems are collecting relevant information from the same domain and to use this information to provide insightful recommendations to the users (Masashi, 2018). For instance, a research scholar working on a project based on heart disease, the relevance can be mapped based on the domain, authors, and the overall context. To provide relevant recommendations, the most important part of the system is to analyze the similarity between the searched query and the contents in the digital database (Chengzhi, 2020).

BACKGROUND

The background study of this chapter is discussed in table 1 which contains eleven literature studies related to web citation analysis. Many of the authors analyzed the web citations with different parameters and obtained results with greater accuracy. Nowadays researchers and academicians give importance to their publications with citations because that proves the quality of their research work. The authors interested to analyze digital web citations since 1999 but in this chapter given the literature studies from 2003 and recent related works are discussed. The background study discussed existing methods and techniques used by different authors at different times.

Table 1. Related works for digital web citation

Author	Title	Techniques	Inference
Seth Porter (2020)	A Citation Analysis of the Woodrow Wilson School Master's Students Research Output	Citation analysis; collection development; teaching& learning	The author has analyzed the resources of Woodrow Wilson School Princeton Universities MPA/MPP (Master's in Public Affairs/ Master's in Public Policy) curriculum and the policy workshop reports from 2014-2018. Based on the analysis, 5.56% of the resources were inappropriate. (Porter, 2020)
Jonathan Frome (2019)	Describing the Game Studies Canon: A Game Citation Analysis	Citation Analysis, Scientometrics	The authors have analyzed game studies research using 580 articles from two primary journals. They identified the games in which familiarity is the most significant to understand previous research (Jonathan Frome, 2019). Finally, the authors concluded that the most frequently cited games of game citation.
ZehraTaşkın et al. (2018)	A Content-based Citation Analysis Study based on Text Categorization	Content-based citation analysis, qualitative research evaluation, text categorization	The authors analyzed the content-based citations for Turkish citation styles. They considered 423 peer-reviewed articles, 101019 sentences, and 12881 related references, which are published in library and information science literature in Turkey. They divided the citations into four different categories i.e. meaning, purpose, shape, and array-based on the content. They achieved 90% success rate for the citation classes (Al, 2018)
Giovanniet al. (2017)	The Closer the Better: The similarity of Publication Pairs at Different Co-Citation Levels	Similarity Measures	The authors investigated the closeness of sets of articles, which were co-cited at divergent co-citation steps of the journal, section, article, sentence, bracket, and paragraph. Their results indicated that the textual closeness shared references, shared authorship, proximity at publication time rise at co-citation level gets lower (from journal to bracket). The authors compared results from four journals over the years 2010-2015. This study established that the similarity was the result from journal to article co-citation; change at every level involves a rise in closeness. This is seen from section to paragraph and paragraph to sentence/bracket levels (Giovanni Colavizza, 2017).
Jeong et al. (2016)	Applying Content-based Similarity Measure to Author Co-Citation Analysis	Author Co-citation Analysis (ACA); similarity measure; Word2Vec; content analysis	The authors introduced a new approach to ACA by the proposed content-based similarity measure The study adopted Word2Vec as the measure of author similarity. The authors also conducted an in-depth network analysis of author maps. Although the dataset is limited to JASIST, their method can be applied to other disciplines. As a follow-up study, the authors planned to extend network analysis of all cited authors and construct the author map with all cited authors. They also planned to identify the relationships between authors by analyzing the sources and conduct various statistical analyses such as factor analysis to verify their results (Yoo Kyung Jeong, 2016).
Zhang et al. (2014)	Content-Based Citation Analysis: The Next Generation of Citation Analysis	Content Analysis, Computational Linguistics/ Natural Language Processing, Citation Motivation Classification, Citation Summarization, Retrieval, Citation Recommendation/ Prediction, Knowledge Graph Mining	The authors described a complete outline of CAA research as to its philosophical details, methodological processes, and various applications. The study highlighted how raised computational competencies and freely obtainable complete text resources had unlocked this part of research to infinite prospects such as deeper citation analysis, more accurate citation prediction, and increased knowledge discovery (Ying Ding, 2014).
Jeong et al.(2014)	Content-based author co-citation analysis	Author co-citation analysis Citation content analysis Bibliometrics Information science Citation analysis	The authors examined a novel methodology for quantifying the similarity among two cited authors in a research paper by citing sentences in the complete article. They introduced the content-based ACA method and compared the traditional ACA method in the area of information science by using electronically available issues of JASIST, a key journal on Information Science. The results of this paper showed that the proposed method revealed more precise subject areas than the existing method i.e. traditional ACA (Jeong, 2014).
Kevin et al.(2013)	Improving the Accuracy of Co-citation Clustering Using Full Text	Co-citation weighting, co-citation clustering	The authors studied the effect of citation proximity of co-citation cluster based on accuracy. They used 2007 to 2013 years documents, which included 270521 documents. The results explored the traditional approach and proposed approach which computing the proximity among reference pairs which were split into pair wise relationships. The authors observed that the proposed approach solved by 9-20% over the traditional approach based on bibliographic information (Kevin W. Boyack H. S., 2013).
Kevin et al. (2010)	Co-Citation Analysis, Bibliographic Coupling, and Direct Citation: Which Citation Approach Represents the Research Front Most Accurately?	Co-Citation Analysis, Bibliographic Coupling, Direct Citation, and A Bibliographic Coupling-Based Citation-Text Hybrid Approach	The authors identified a huge corpus that had 2.15 million research papers and produced cluster solutions by three traditional citation-based methods approaches bibliographic coupling, direct citation, co-citation analysis, and one-hybrid approach. They introduced an innovative approach to compare the accuracy of cluster solutions. The authors compared the existing methods, observed that the test of accuracy revealed that bibliographic coupling slightly outperformed co-citation analysis; the direct citation was by far the minimum accurate mapping method. The authors considered the very large size of the corpus and the specificity of the accuracy measures used (Kevin W. Boyack H. S., 2010).
Belaet al. (2009)	Citation Proximity Analysis (CPA) - A new approach for identifying related work based on Co-Citation Analysis	Citation Proximity Index (CPI)	This paper presented an approach for identifying similar documents that can be used to assist scientists to find works related to their research. The authors compared the existing approaches like co-citation analysis or keyword base Citation Proximity Analysis (CPA) and bibliographic coupling. Experimental results showed that CPA gave higher precision and the possibility to identify related sections within documents (Beel, 2009)
Hsuanet al. (2003)	Constructing a patent citation map using bibliographic coupling: A study of Taiwan's high-tech companies	Bibliographic coupling analysis	The authors used bibliographic coupling analysis for high-tech electronics companies in Taiwan and found the relationships among other companies, industries so on. The results were shown in a plot of a patent citation map which is used to realistically display the association between the groups. Finally, this experiment showed greater relationships between companies in the semiconductor sector. The distinction between industries increased was more ambivalent, and, in some cases, it even overlapped (MU-Hsuan Huang, 2003).

RESEARCH METHODOLOGY

The following research methodology is adopted for this study to investigate the digital resources transformation. This section discussed digital citation index, various digital citation databases, digital bibliography, references and citations, different digital citation styles, digital citation-based metrics for digital citation analysis, co-citation analysis, and bibliographic coupling. Significant research challenges for digital citation analysis and future directions are described in this section.

DIGITAL CITATION INDEX

An index is considered as a reflection and validation of the quality of a journal as it lists down the articles contained in it (YP, 2012). A citation index is a type of bibliographic index and it is defined as an index of citation among publications. It permits the users to establish new documents cite previous documents easily (Citation Index, 2009). The first citation index of papers published in academic journals of Science Citation Index (SCI). Thereafter, it was prolonged to contain the Social Sciences Citation Index (SSCI), Arts, and Humanities Citation Index (A&HCI). Giles et al. assisted an algorithm for citation extracting and grouping for several digital academic and scientific documents. This process led to the development of new establishments to automate citation indexing for the public such as Google Scholar, CiteSeerX, and Cora/Rexa (Garfield, 2020).

DIGITAL CITATION INDEXING DATABASES/SERVICES

There are several publishers of general-purpose academic citation indexes: Institution for Scientific Information (ISI), Scopus, Citeseer, Google Scholar, EBSCOhost, Web of Science (WOS), PubMed, and Mendeley. The most common and major citation databases are ISI and Elsevier. Web of Science and Scopus are subscription-based academic citation indexes. CiteSeer and Google Scholar are freely available online. PubMed is open-access and subject-specific citation indexing.

Institute for Scientific Information

Citation indexing has long been conquered by the ISI. It was founded by Eugene Garfield in 1960. It was developed by Thomson Scientific & Healthcare in 1992 and became known as Thomson ISI. It was a part of the Academic Property & Science business of Thomson Reuters until 2016, when the IP & Science business was sold, becoming Clarivate Analytics. ISI was re-established to enclose scientific and academic research group in 2018 February. It publishes the citation indexes in both print and soft copy of the documents that are publicly accessed over the web in the name of Web of Science (WOS). WOS offers access to several databases namely SCI, SSCI, A&HCI, Index Chemicus, Current Chemical Reactions, Conference Proceedings Citation Index: Science and Conference Proceedings Citation Index: Social Science and Humanities.

Scopus

It is a major multidisciplinary abstract and citation database of peer-reviewed related works and sources from the web with smart tools that are used for tracking, analyzing, and visualizing the research easily. It was launched in 2004. It is provided by Elsevier that includes R&D performance, professional education, information analytics solutions, and various digital tools in strategic research management, clinical decision support, scientific, technical, and medical information.

Figure 1. Home Page of Scopus
(Scopus, 2020)

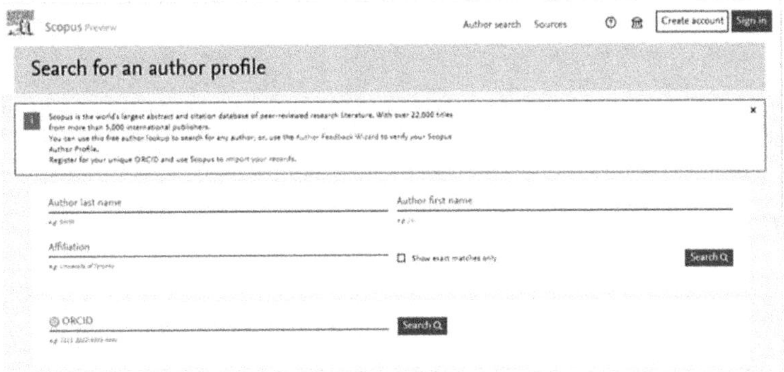

It is published by Scopus and is available only in online mode. Scopus allows the user to create a list of researches the researcher has undertaken by searching by the author using the field "Authors" on the main search page. Alternatively, "Author Search" from the top tab options can be run. Both options might involve manual sorting and displaying related documents as a list to the researcher in concern. Once the user has generated a list of publications by an author, he or she can select the items and then "View citation overview" to view graphs and summary data that illustrate the citation activity related to the author's publications (Bosman, 2006). It uses h-index, SNIP, and SJR indicators. Figure 1 represents the home page of the Scopus citation database.

CiteSeer

CiteSeer also called CiteSeer^{x} which is the first automated citation indexing framework. It was launched in 2007. It is both a citation engine and a digital library for academic and scientific research, mostly in the areas of information science and computer science. CiteSeer is established on the Small Search engine now called Bizseer, which offers citation, related document retrieval, citation graph analysis, and further scientific literature. Research publications in Economics (RePec) provide databases in economics and other discipline-specific indexes (Giles CL, 1998).CiteSeer aims to improve the dissemination andaccess to academic and scientific literature. It has automated information extraction and crawling features. Figure 2 represents the home page of the CiteSeer citation database.

Figure 2. Home Page of CiteSeer^x Citation Database
(CiteSeerX, 2020)

Google Scholar

Figure 3. Home Page of Google Scholar
(Google Scholar, 2020)

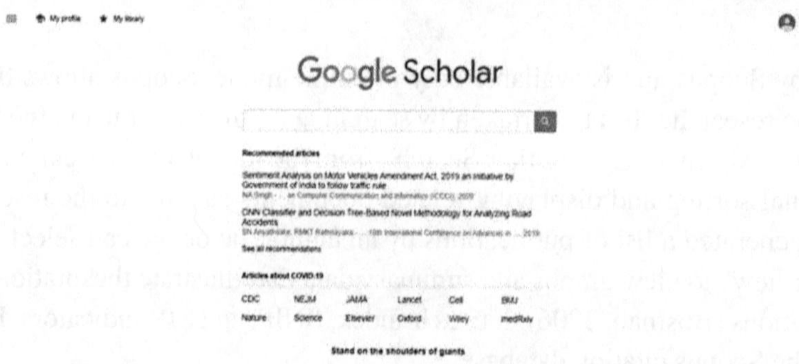

It was launched in 2004. Google Scholar (GS) index contains utmost technical reports, peer-reviewed online academic journal papers, conference papers, abstracts, books, theses, preprints, dissertations, and other scholarly literature. It provides an easy way to cite and search for scholarly literature across a range of regulations and sources. Even though restricted to the latest articles and GS is a publicly available web search engine. GS is commonly commended for its speed. As with general Google search, Google Scholar brings the most relevant results to the top of the result list. *Publish* or *Perish* software facilitates searching of Google Scholar and determines bibliometrics values without a Google Scholar Author Profile.Figure3 shows the home page of Google Scholar.

Web of Science

Web of Science, previously known as Web of Knowledge, from 1900 to the present it has indexing coverage. ISI produced WOS, it is a subscription-based online scientific indexing service, and now Clarivate Analytics handles it. Previously, WOS was named as Science business and Intellectual Property of Thomson Reuters. WOS provides access to several databases that allow assessment in the depth of specialized subfields in science and academic regulations that reference cross-disciplinary research (Drake, 2005).

Figure 4. Home Page of Web of Science
(Web of Science, 2020)

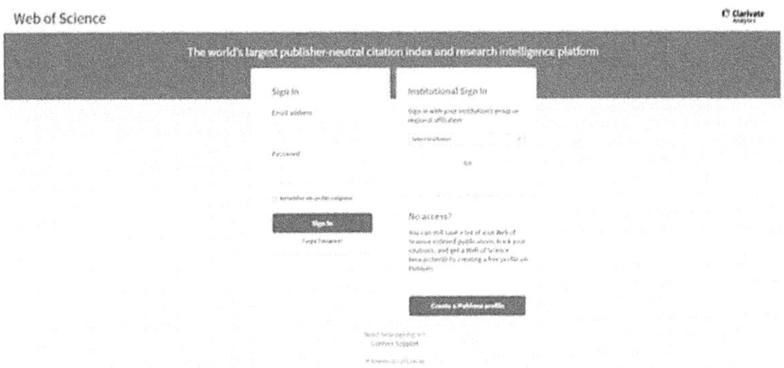

Figure4 shows the home page of Web of Science which consists of several online databases such as Conference Proceedings Citation Index (CPCI), SCI, SCIE, Emerging Sources Citation Index (ESCI), SSCI, A&HCI, Index Chemicus, Current Chemical Reaction, and Book Citation Index. CPCI includes the conference proceedings, which were produced by Clarivate Analytics. SCI was launched in 1964, SCIE is Thomson Reuters, and now using Clarivate Analytics launched the expanded version of SCI. ESCI in 2015. Academic journals in the discipline of Social Science are included in SSCI.A&HCI covered multiple subjects such as Language, Linguistics, History, Arts, Philosophy, Classical works, Humanities, Architecture, Poetry, Oriental Studies, Music, Radio, Religion, Television, and Theater. It also includes social and natural science and provides access to current and retrospective bibliographic information and cited references. Index Chemicus covers more than 100 organic chemistry journals. It offers researchers to access recent bibliographic and structural information published all over the world about innovative organic compounds.

PubMed

PubMed is a publicly accessing search engine and also mainly MEDLINE database of abstracts and references on biomedical and life science topics. PubMed is one of several databases under (National Center for Biotechnology Information) NCBI's Entrez retrieval system. It offers links and access to the integrated molecular biology databases managed by NCBI, which contains DNA, genome-mapping data, Online Mendel an Inheritance in Man, protein sequences, and 3-D protein structuresFigure5 shows the home page of the PubMed citation database.

Figure 5. Home Page of PubMed
(PubMed, 2020)

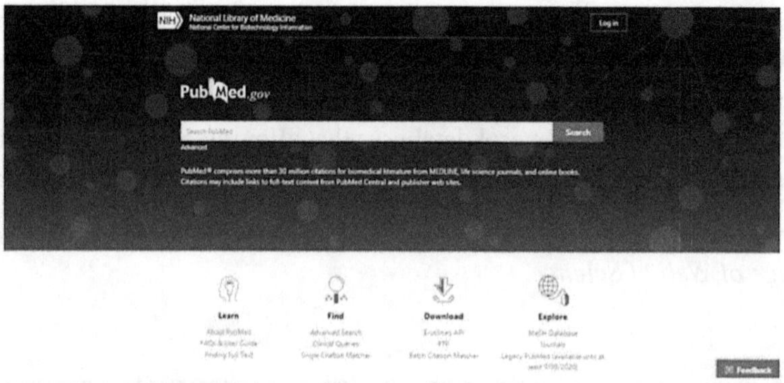

EBSCOhost

Figure 6. Home page of EBSCO
(EBSCO, 2020)

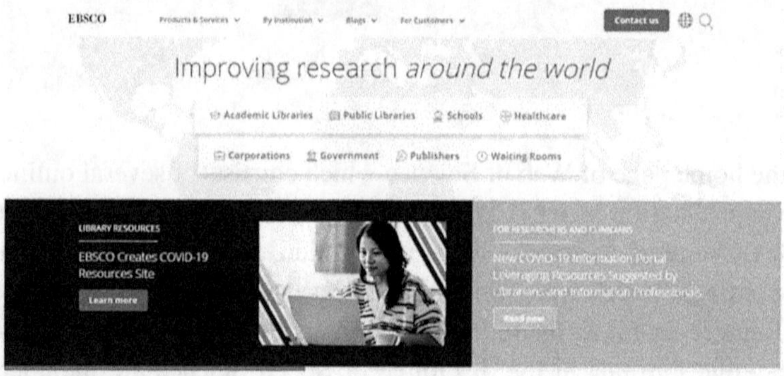

EBSCOhost is an energetic reference system accessible online and it provides multiple proprietary to standard full-text databases from prominent information providers. It also provides several subscription databases, which provide access to newspapers, magazines, scholarly journals, and trade publications. Its databases cover multiple subjects and academic disciplines. It is one of the best reference database services. Figure6 shows the EBSCO home page. EBSCOhost provides 375 full-text databases for a fee-based online research service, an array of historical digital archives, subject indexes, point-of-care medical references, and a collection of e-books.

Mendeley

It is a software called Mendeley desktop, which was launched by Elsevier to share and handle the research papers and references. It is used to discover research data and collaborate online. The users can store citation information on its servers to collect the document copies. Mendeley offers to the users 2 GB free web storage space on registration and it can be charged for upgradation.

Figure 7. Home Page of Mendeley
(Mendeley, 2020)

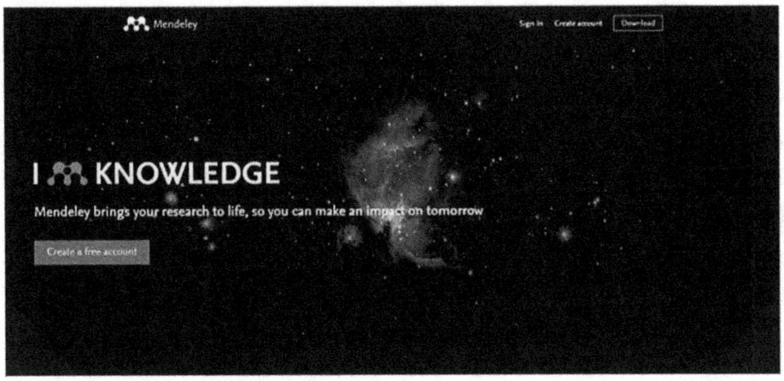

Figure7 shows the Mendeley home page. Mendeley combines a Desktop, a PDF, and a reference management application available for Windows and macOS. It also provides Android and iOS, with Mendeley Web, an online social network for researchers.

DIGITALBIBLIOGRAPHY, REFERENCES, AND CITATION

Bibliography

- The bibliography is a list of references, which is to acknowledge the work of authors that have been used in research. It is shown at the end of the manuscript/article.
- It is usually provided in alphabetical order, whether the author has referred to and cited the work or not.
- This includes all sources that to use to do any research. Bibliographies are repeatedly used in Turabian and Chicago citation styles.
- Within the body of the paper, it has a corresponding footnote.

References

- References are the bibliographic information that leads to the source that to have cited in among the text.
- This is a list of the sources to have cited.
- The references come at the deadline of the paper.
- In APA style, this is not a list of "works consulted." Every source that is listed in references also needs to be cited in the heart of the paper.
- It is arranged alphabetically by the author's last name.

Citation

- Citation is a way to acknowledge the work of others that you have used in your research.

- A specific source that to mention in the body of the paper.
- Inside the text, the researcher mentions in alphabets or numbers the reference that is described with the same alphabet or number at the end of your manuscript.
- The format of the citation may change depending on the style you use (e.g. MLA and APA) and the way that you weave the citation into your writing
- The researcher has to use that style to cite the references in his work.
- Name of the author(s), Year of publication, Page number, or page range is considered as the basic elements of the citation.
- If the authors directly mention a source he/she must include the page number exactly in their citation or it is incomplete.

DIGITAL CITATION STYLES

A citation is when one research paper denotes another paper. Citations are important because they show the credit that authors give to the work and ideas of others. Those who review a research count the citations to it because the number is indicative of its significance and its influence on other researches. A citation style dictates the information, which is necessary for a citation. It sometimes rests on the academic discipline. There are many different citation styles. Some of them are APA, MLA, Chicago/Turabian, etc.

APA Style

APA (American Psychological Association) style is used for researches in Education, Psychology, and Sciences. This style calls for three different types of information to be incorporated in in-text citations. They are the author's last name and date of publication of research, which must match the corresponding entry in the reference list exactly. The third piece of information is page number, which appears only in a citation to a direct quotation.

For Example:

... (Merton 1957)

"Merton, R.K. (1957). Priorities in scientific discovery: A chapter in the sociology of science. American Sociological Review, 22(6), 635–659."

MLA Style

MLA (Modern Language Association) style is used for researches in Humanities. The MLA style is one of the most popular and simplest forms used to attribute information.

For Example:

... (Merton) or Merton concluded that ...

"[21] Merton, R.K. Priorities in scientific discovery: A chapter in the sociology of science. American Sociological Review, 22(6), 635–659, 1957."

Table 2. Examples of Citation Based Metrics for Digital Resources Transformation

Metrics	Description
Citation Count	Citation Count is the quantity of times a paper is cited by other works. Sometimes, it is considered to indicate the quality and influence of the article. The occurrence of citations of a respective research paper, count of total citation of an author per paper, and count of average citation of the paper in a journal are analyzed using the citation count. Citation counts are correlated with other measures of scholarly/scientific performance and impact.
Citation Impact	A publication that received an average quantity of citations is called citation impact. It is computed by the formula of total no. of citations divided by the total no. of publications. This formula is mainly used for calculating the citation impact of a set of documents
h-Index	h-index is a factor that determines the quantity of the impact and quality of the published work of a researcher's/author's output h-index is sometimes called the Hirsch index or Hirsch number as it was first developed by Hirsh (Hirsch, 2005). A researcher/author by an index of h has published h papers and each of them has been cited in other papers as a minimum of h times. (Hirsch JE 2005) For example, if a researcher's h-index is 20, he/she 20 papers cited 20 times or more. If your h-index is 25, you have 25 papers cited 25 times or more.
i10 Index	It is the quantity of publications that have been cited a minimum of 10 times. This is a very simple and straight forward measure, which is used only in Google Scholar. For example, if the i10 index is 12, the researcher has 12 papers that have been cited 12 times or more. If your i10 index is 10, you have 10 papers cited 10 times or more (Noruzi, 2016).
g-index	g-index is an index for quantifying the efficiency in science, based on publication records. It is an author-level metric calculated based on the distribution of citations received by a given researcher's publications (Alireza Noruzi 2016). An article has obtained a quantity of citations, which are in descending order, and the articles are, ranked using the g-index. It is a unique leading amount where the best g articles received together as a minimum g^2(g square)citations. For instance, A g-index of 20 means that an academic has published at least 20 articles and of them all together has received at least 400 citations. Another example of g-index is when an academic has published 20 papers and if 15 of them have no citations, and the remaining five have 350, 32, 13, 2, and 3 citations respectively, it will be a g-index of 20.
CiteScore	CiteScore is a journal-ranking metric, which assigns percentile ranking within the journal's subject category. It is a brand-new product from Elsevier and used uses citation data from the Scopus database to rank journals.
SNIP	SNIP stands for Source Normalized Impact each article. It is used to measure the average citation impact by calculating citations based on the total amount of citations in a subject area using Scopus data. It is computed as the amount of citations given in the present year to the past three years' publications.
SJR	SJR stands for SCImago Journal Rank. This indicator is used to measure the scientific authority of scholarly journals (Eduardo 2014). It is the quantity of citations received by a journal and the prominence of the journals from where such citations come from. It offers the substitution to the average citations or impacts factor per an article in a period of two years, which is abbreviated as "Cites per Doc. (2y)".

Chicago/Turabian Style

Chicago or Turabian style is generally used for researches in Business, History, and Fine Arts. This style uses notes to cite sources and/or to provide a relevant explanation.

For Example:

"…"21

"[21] Merton, R.K. Priorities in scientific discovery: A chapter in the sociology of science. American Sociological Review, 22(6), 635–659, 1957."

DIGITAL CITATION BASED METRICS FOR CITATION ANALYSIS

Citation-based metrics are used to measure the impact of the publication, author, institutions, and countries. Some of these metrics are citation count, citation impact, h-index, i10 index, g-index, CiteScore, Source Normalized Impact per Paper (SNIP), and SCImago Journal Rank (SJR), which are given in table 2.

Several metrics are used to rank journals, researchers, articles, universities, and countries.

Ranking the Journal

Journal ranking is commonly used in academics. Journals are ranked based on the number of times their papers or articles are cited in other journals by other authors. It is a measure of evaluating the journal and its impact and quality. Journal level metrics help in determining journal status. The ranking of the journal is based on the journal impact factor, which is the average amount of citations (in all articles), a journal has received over a certain period.

Ranking the Researchers

Researchers are ranked based on the quantity of times their articles are cited in other published articles. To evaluate the researchers the metrics are very useful for their appointment, occupation, and grant decisions. A researcher level ranking that is achieving recognition is the h index.

Ranking the Articles

It is an accurate evaluation of the eminence and impact of a certain section of an article citation counts. However, ranking the article metric is rarely examined because gathering the article citations is a complex and inefficient process.

Ranking Universities and Countries

Some databases rank universities and countries based on their overall research output through criteria such as citable documents like the article, book, etc., citations per document, and total citations. These metrics help to define which country and the university has the best scientific research outcome. For instance, Scimago Research Group releases annual reports of the institution and country-wise rankings (Eduardo García-Pachón, 2014).

BIBLIOGRAPHIC COUPLING

Documents are bibliographically coupled if they cite one or more documents in common. When two works refer to the common work(s), the relationship between two refereeing document is called bibliographic coupling. The coupling strength is higher when the two works have more citations in common. The Coupling shows the similarity of the subject matter of the two works. Bibliographic coupling useful in a wide variety of fields since it helps the researchers to find researchers that are related to theirs. The term 'bibliographic coupling' was introduced by MM Kessler in the paper published in 1963 and has been embraced in the work of the information scientist Eugene Garfield

Figure 8. Bibliographic Coupling

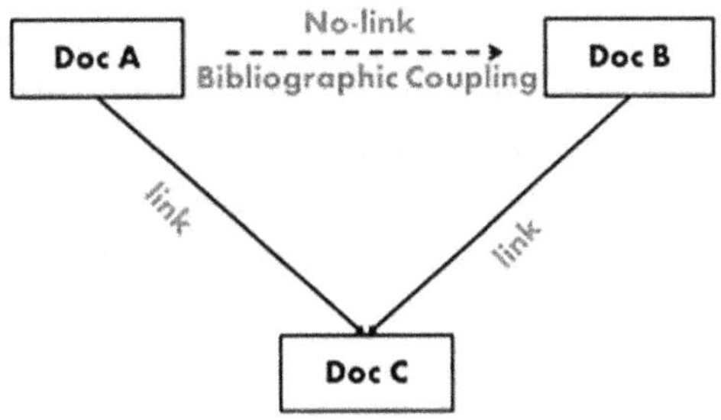

Figure 8 illustrates that documents A and B cite document C. They may be said to be related, even though they do not directly cite each other. Bibliographic coupling is used to find the relationship between two subjects and two different articles. It helps researchers for finding suitable topics for their research.

CO-CITATION ANALYSIS

Co-citation is a popular similarity measure used to establish a similarity between two documents. It is denoted as the frequency with which two documents are cited together by other documents. Figure 9illustrates documents both B and C are cited by document A., they may be said to be related to one another, even though they do not directly reference each other. If any other items cite B and C, they have a stronger relationship.

Figure 9. Co-Citation Analysis

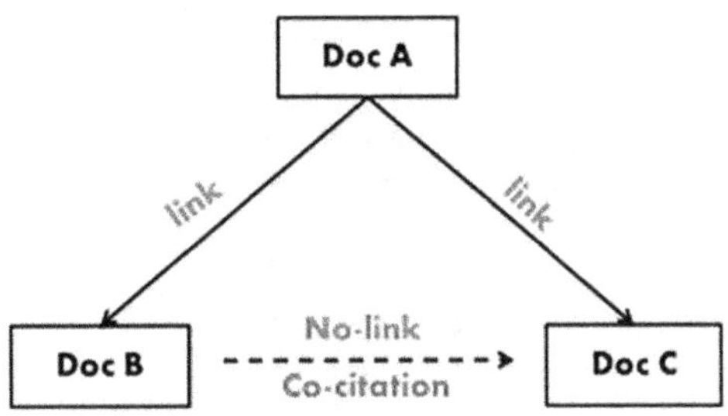

Co-citation is defined as the frequency with which two documents are cited together. The strength of co-citation between two cited documents can be easily determined from a citation index such as Scientific Citation Index (SCI). The number of identical citing documents defines the strength of co-citation between the two cited papers.

Co-citation Levels

The co-citation hierarchy has six levels, namely journal, article, section, paragraph, sentence, and bracket level. Journal level co-citation is considered the level of co-citation and bracket-level citation is considered the lowest of all.

1. Journal: Publications co-cited within the same journal; that is, the articles are co-cited within the same journal if they are cited in the same journal in the same year.
2. Article: Publications are co-cited within the same article.
3. Section: Publications are co-cited within the same section – some header in an article identifies a logical unit of the publication.
4. Paragraph: Publications are co-cited within the same paragraph in an article. Paragraphs are usually identified with some layout expedient such as indentation or interlinear space.
5. Sentence: Publications co-cited within the same sentence in an article.
6. Bracket: Publications are co-cited at the same location in an article. They are often delineated with brackets or parentheses.

Co-citation Analysis vs. Bibliographic Coupling (CCA vs. BC)

Figure 10. BC

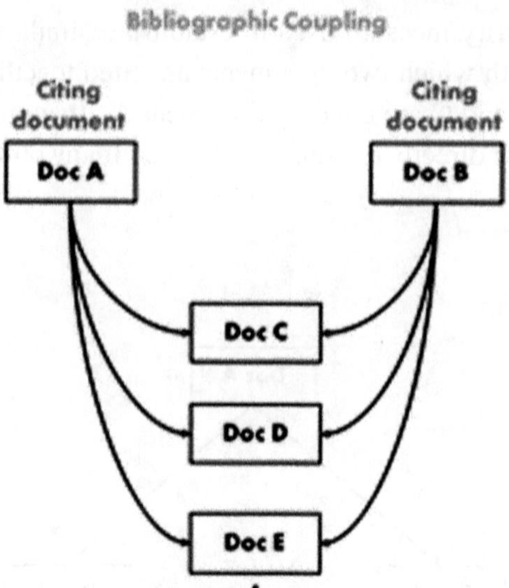

Documents are bibliographically coupled if they cite one or more documents in common. Figure 10shows documents A and B are related because they both cite documents C, D, and E. Here documents A and B are called citing documents, documents C, D, and E are called cited documents. Figure 11 documents

C, D, and E cited both documents A and B. Here documents C, D, and E are called citing documents and documents A and B are known as cited documents.

Figure 11. CCA

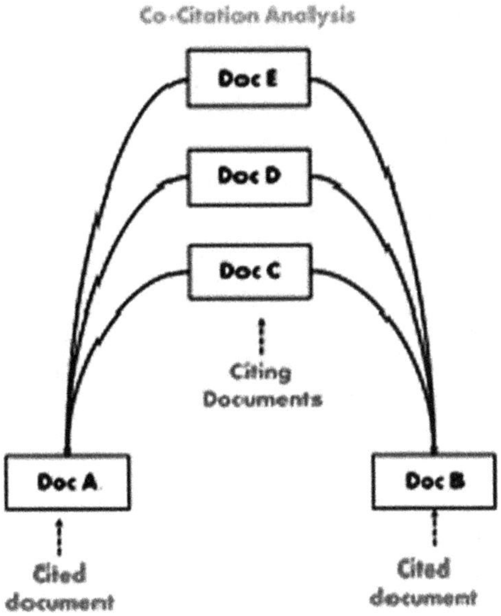

Although bibliographic coupling and co-citation are suitable for identifying related documents, they serve different purposes. While bibliographic coupling is a backward-looking perspective, co-citation is a forward-looking perspective. However, both methods often deliver unsatisfying results, since they make use only of the bibliography at the end of the document without analyzing the pattern of citations. Since these methods are system-instinctive, it is not possible to conclude in which part of a related document the content of interest can be found.

Author Co-citation Analysis

The main purpose of Author Co-citation Analysis (ACA) is to map scientific domains by pointing out the relationship of co-cited authors (McCain, 1990). ACA has been widely used in bibliometrics as an analytical method in analyzing the intellectual structure of science studies. It can be used to identify authors from the same or similar research fields. However, such analysis method relies heavily on statistical tools to perform the analysis and requires human interpretation. Digital Citation Database is a data warehouse used for storing citation indices of publications. As most researchers are interested in scientific publications from certain research areas, identifying authors from the same research area becomes one of the most important knowledge for most researchers. To achieve this, ACA (White, 1981) can be applied to identify inter-relationships between authors. An analytical method has been traditionally used to trace the intellectual structure in science studies. ACA assumes that two authors are correlated if the frequency that they are cited together by later works is high. Hence, if the frequency of two authors cited together by the same publication is very high, these two authors will belong to the same or similar research field.

RESEARCH CHALLENGES FOR DIGITAL CITATION ANALYSIS

- The citing author has either partly or fully used the ideas in the cited work. The citing author used all the cited documents.
- Sometimes, citations are received for the wrong reasons also. It has been shown by many studies that authors have the habit of giving citations to spurious works also.
- Studies often show that not all good works are cited. The number of Citations, among other reasons, also rests on the availability/accessibility of the documents to the authors. The non-availability of documents may have a negative impact on the citation analysis.
- When two papers are co-cited, it does not guarantee a relationship between their contents.
- It is not difficult to see that not all the papers cited in an article are of equal importance in the context of the citing work. This might have a destructive impression on the overall results.
- If researchers can take this as a challenge, they can detect self-citations. Then, they can find whether they have referred to the content of the previous paper or not.
- The author can intentionally cite papers of whom they know in their publications. This way they can also claim more citations for their papers.
- Some citation databases are not updated frequently. It leads to the problem of citation count differing from one index to another index (Satish Muppidi, 2018).
- Most of the papers are not in open access, which receives limited number of citations only because the readers did not spend money to search their relevant papers they find and open access papers.

SOLUTION AND RECOMMENDATIONS FOR DIGITAL CITATION ANALYSIS

In digital citation analysis, shows all works are cited but we do not know the exact reason behind their citations. If one author received more citations, what is the sign of the author's work? Whether it was a positive sign or a negative sign. This could be lead to take a negative impact on the particular author. Digital citations will be managed properly by digital citation databases and must be updated frequently. Digital citation databases will be eliminated self-citations or show the difference between self-citations and other authors' citations. This will be very useful to the author or publisher to evaluate an article or journal with good quality. As if an author has more self-citations than other citations, in this case how will be evaluating an article have good quality. Co-citations of two papers does not promise their relationship among them because authors may wrongly give co-citations. Hence, content-based digital citation analysis is required to encounter these kinds of problems. The journals are checked all the references are cited or not they did not spend time to check reference relevancy.

FUTURE RESEARCH DIRECTIONS

In the future, content-based citation analysis is the next generation of digital citation analysis and it is very significant to do digital citation analysis. Hence, citation purpose, citation meaning, and citation classes are going to be identified using content-based digital citation analysis. Based on the literature review, many authors analyzed the journal articles and conference papers from the same journal or similar templates. To consider all the templates of articles by performing content-based digital citation analysis is still a challenging task.

Digital resources transformation of citation databases and Journals are review and analyze the citations yearly once for calculating cite score and impact factor. Digital citations are dynamically change day by day hence analyze the citations frequently will be helpful to the authors and researchers. In the future, if content-based citation analysis to be done yearly once that shows the impact of citation meaning based on the content. Journals are struggled to check each references are cited in the article hence in the future, automatically check all the references are cited in the article also check the citation style. Besides, if this work is possible automatically check whether the references of an article are cited or not. In content-based citation analysis, able to check the references, paper title whether the paper title is related to an article or not this will be helpful for identifying irrelevant resources. Some of the author given irrelevant reference to their friends and families for the purpose of citation, which leads to false counts of citations. For instance, one author requests his/her friend to cite paper from various field they may claim false count of citations count, which means he/she actually did not support his/her point scientifically this may create a false impression of their creditability. In future, paper title of the references will be checked in initial stage for instance, if all paper titles of the references are related to the paper title or content then perform further analysis.

CONCLUSION

Digital Citations transformation are an essential part of an academic dissertation, project, or scientific work. The most time-consuming task for any scholar is to discover suitable citations for any work. This study discussed a detailed review of the digital citation index and digital citation analysis. The existing methods are explained in the literature review section that contains related work from 2003 also recent related works are discussed. Digital citation databases are significant for the authors easily checks their citations of ever paper with year. In past decades, journals are struggled to calculate the citations manually but now more number of digital citation indexing databases are available. In this chapter, we discussed most commonly used digital citation indexing databases like Google Scholar, Web of Science, ISI, Scopus, EBSCO, Citeseer, PubMed, and Mendeley are used to evaluate and compute the research impact and quality of the research. There are various styles for citations available but most commonly used citation styles are discussed with example which helps to understand easily. In digital citation analysis citation metrics are significant to evaluate the citations based on the citation metrics journals are computed their impact factor. Various digital citation metrics are discussed in this chapter. Co-citation analysis and bibliographic coupling are explained. Furthermore, recent research challenges and solutions of the issues, recommendations and future directions are given for researchers who are interested in digital citation analysis.

The current research is about digital resources transformation and web citation analysis which forms a part of citation analysis is an emerging area of research in information retrieval, library science, etc. The authors focused on various benefits of citation analysis and examined the challenges encountered in previous studies. This chapter is very useful for researchers, scientists, and professors because the citation is essential for their innovative ideas. If they got more citations means their idea must be a booming and interesting research area of more people. In this chapter, recent research challenges and issues are discussed. Based on that solutions and recommendations are also clearly explained. Digital citation analysis is a booming topic in the research and academic field. The academic community publishes millions of research articles each year, the literature search is becoming a more challenging and time-consuming task. This is significant and more efficient for the researchers, scientists, and students to claim the importance and quality of their work. Most of the research quality evaluated using digital citation analysis with significant parameters.

ACKNOWLEDGMENT

The authors thank the University Grants Commission (UGC), New Delhi (Official Memorandum No.F1-17.1/2016/RGNF-2015-17-SC-TAM-20541)for the financial support under Rajiv Gandhi National Fellowship for this research work.

REFERENCES

Al, Z. T. (2018). A Content-Based Citation Analysis Study Based on Text Categorization. *Scientometrics*, 335–357.

Beel, B. G. (2009). Citation Proximity Analysis (CPA) – A New Approach For Identifying Related Work Based on Co-Citation Analysis. In *International Conference on Scientometrics and Informetrics (ISSI'09)* (pp. 571–575). Academic Press.

BibMe. (2020). Retrieved from BibMe: https://www.bibme.org/style

Bosman, J. (2006). *Scopus Reviewed and Compared*. Utrecht University Library.

Chengzhi, M. S. (2020). A review of citation recommendation: From textual content to enriched context. *Scientometrics*, 1445–1472.

Citation Index. (2009, August 1). Retrieved from Edutech wikki: http://edutechwiki.unige.ch/en/Citation_index

Citation Machine. (2020). Retrieved from Citation Machine: https://www.citationmachine.net/apa

Cite.com. (2020). Retrieved from Cite.com: https://www.cite.com/

CiteSeerX. (2020). Retrieved from Solr: http://citeseerx.ist.psu.edu/index;jsessionid=341AE6933E128F38AB58BE43AA718916

Drake, M. A. (2005). *Encyclopedia of Library and Information Science*. Taylor & Francis Group.

EasyBib. (2020). Retrieved from EasyBib: https://www.easybib.com/mla8/source

EBSCO. (2020). Retrieved from EBSCO: https://www.ebsco.com/

Eduardo García-Pachón, R. A.-J. (2014). A Comparison of the Impact Factor and the SCImago Journal Rank Index in Respiratory System Journals. *Archivos de Bronconeumologia*, 263–310. PMID:24315384

Garfield, E. (2020). *The concept of citation indexing*. Retrieved from Clarivate Web of Science: https://clarivate.com/webofsciencegroup/essays/concept-citation-indexing/

Giles, C. L. (1998). CiteSeer: An Automatic Citation Indexing System. In *ACM Conference on Digital Libraries* (pp. 89-98). ACM.

Giovanni Colavizza, K. W. (2017). The Closer the Better: Similarity of Publication Pairs at Different Co-Citation Levels. *Journal of the Association for Information Science and Technology*, 1–17.

Google Scholar. (2020). Retrieved from Google Scholar: https://scholar.google.co.in/

HarinarayanaN. S. (2010). Retrieved from http://epgp.inflibnet.ac.in/epgpdata/uploads/epgp_content/library_and_information_science/informetrics_&_scientometrics/limitations_of_bibliometrics_and_scientometrics/et/334_et_m16.pdf

Hirsch, J. E. (2005). An index to quantify an individual's scientific research output. *The Proceedings of the National Academy of Sciences (PNAS)*, 16569-16572.

Jeong, Y. K., Song, M., & Ding, Y. (2014). Content -Based Author Co-Citation Analysis. *Journal of Informetrics*, *8*(1), 197–211. doi:10.1016/j.joi.2013.12.001

Jonathan Frome, P. M. (2019). Describing the Game Studies Canon: A Game Citation Analysis. DiGRA, 1-21.

Kevin, W., & Boyack, H. S. (2010). Co-Citation Analysis, Bibliographic Coupling, and Direct Citation: Which Citation Approach Represents The Research Front Most Accurately? *Journal of the American Society for Information Science and Technology*, 2389–2404.

Kevin, W., & Boyack, H. S. (2013). Improving the Accuracy of Co-Citation Clustering Using Full Text. *Journal of the American Society for Information Science and Technology*, 155–165.

Masashi, K. Y. (2018). Citation Recommendation Using Distributed Representation of Discourse Facets in Scientific Articles Share on. In *Proceedings of the 18th ACM/IEEE on Joint Conference on Digital Libraries*, (pp. 243-251). Academic Press.

McCain, K. W. (1990). Mapping authors in intellectual space: A technical overview. *Journal of the American Society for Information Science*, *41*(6), 433–443. doi:10.1002/(SICI)1097-4571(199009)41:6<433::AID-ASI11>3.0.CO;2-Q

Mendeley. (2020). Retrieved from Elsevier: https://www.mendeley.com/homepage-2-1?interaction_required=true&adobe_mc_sdid=SDID%3D66587ECF3B1E404B-1A7F944D87B75458%7CMCORGID%3D4D6368F454EC41940A4C98A6%40AdobeOrg%7CTS%3D1602154074

Mu. (2003). Constructing a Patent Citation Map Using Bibliographic Coupling: A Study of Taiwan's High-Tech Companies. *Scientometrics*, 489–506.

Noruzi, A. (2016). *Impact Factor, h-index, i10-index and i20-index of Webology*. Webology.

OttoBib. (2020). Retrieved from OttoBib: https://www.ottobib.com/

Porter, S. (2020). A Citation Analysis of the Woodrow Wilson School Master's Students Research Output. *Collection Management*, 1–5. doi:10.1080/01462679.2020.1742835

PubMed. (2020). Retrieved from National Library of Medicine: https://pubmed.ncbi.nlm.nih.gov/

Satish Muppidi, D. K. (2018). Challenges in Citation Analysis. *International Journal of Pure and Applied Mathematics*, 27–31.

Scopus. (2020). Retrieved from Scopus: https://www.scopus.com/sources?zone=&origin=NO%20ORIGIN%20DEFINED

Web of Science. (2020). Retrieved from Clarivate: https://clarivate.com/webofsciencegroup/solutions/web-of-science/

White, H. D., & Griffith, B. C. (1981). Author co-citation: A literature measure of intellectual structure. *Journal of the American Society for Information Studies*, *32*(3), 163–171. doi:10.1002/asi.4630320302

Ying Ding, G. Z. (2014). Content-Based Citation Analysis: The Next Generation of Citation Analysis. *Journal of the Association for Information Science and Technology*, *65*(9), 1820–1833. doi:10.1002/asi.23256

Yoo Kyung Jeong, M. S. (2016). Applying Content-Based Similarity Measure to Author Co-Citation Analysis. In *IConference*. iSchools.

YP, B. (2012). Indexed journal: What does it mean? Lung India: Official Organ of Indian Chest Society.

Compilation of References

A Global Perspective of Mobile Commerce. (2016). IAB-Global-Mobile-Commerce-Report.

Abbasi, W. A. K. (2013, April 25). Pakistan's e-banking - past, present and future. *Business Recorder*. https://fp.brecorder.com/2013/04/201304251178401/

Abed, S., Al-Mutairi, M., Al-Watyan, A., Al-Mutairi, O., AlEnizy, W. & Al-Noori, A. (2019). An automated Security Approach of Video Steganography–Based LSB using FPGA Implementation. *Journal of Circuits, Systems and Computers, 28*(5). doi:10.1142/S021812661950083X

Abreu, P. H. C. (2018). Perspectivas para a gestão do conhecimento no contexto da Indústria 4.0. *South American Development Society Journal, 4*(10), 126. doi:10.24325/issn.2446-5763.v4i10p126-145

Accenture. (2013). *Closing the Gap HowTech-Savvy Advisors Can Regain Investor Trust*. Retrieved from https://www.accenture.com/t20150707t195225__w__/us-en/_acnmedia/accenture/conversion-assets/dotcom/documents/global/pdf/industries_5/accenture-cm-awams-pov-gen-d-advisor-summary-final-mar2013-web.pdf

Ackoff, R. L. (1999). From data to wisdom. In *Ackoff's Best* (pp. 170–172). John Wiley & Sons.

Adapa, S. (2011). Global E-banking Trends. In M. A. Sarlak & A. A. Hastiani (Eds.), *E-Banking and Emerging Multidisciplinary Process: Social, Economical and Organizational Models* (pp. 1–16). IGI Global. doi:10.4018/978-1-61520-635-3.ch001

Aghaei, S., Nematbakhsh, M. A., & Farsani, H. K. (2012). Evolution of the world wide web: From web 1.0 to web 4.0. *International Journal of Web & Semantic Technology, 3*(1), 1–10. doi:10.5121/ijwest.2012.3101

Agwu, E. (2018). The role of e-banking on operational efficiency of banks in Nigeria. *Basic Res J Bus Manag Acc, 6*(1), 1–10. doi:10.2139srn.3122498

Akaichi, J. (2017). *Sentiment Classification ch076*. . doi:10.1155/2020/7403128

Akhlaq, M. A. (2011). Internet banking in Pakistan: Finding complexities. *Journal of Internet Banking and Commerce, 16*(1), 1–14.

Akram, U., Kaleem Khan, M., Tanveer, Y., Mehmood, K., & Ahmad, W. (2018). How website quality affectsonline impulse buyingModerating effects of sales promotion andcredit card use. *Asia Pacific Journal of Marketing and Logistics, 30*(1), 235–256. doi:10.1108/APJML-04-2017-0073

Akter, S., Michael, K., Uddin, M. R., McCarthy, G., & Rahman, M. (2020). Transforming usiness using Digital Innovations: The Application of AI, Blockchain, Cloud and Data Analytics. *Annals of Operations Research*. Advance online publication. doi:10.100710479-020-03620-w

Al Amoush, A. B., & Sandhu, K. (2020a). Digital Transformation of Learning Management Systems at Universities: Case Analysis for Student Perspectives. *Digital Transformation and Innovative Services for Business and Learning*, 41-61. doi:10.4018/978-1-7998-5175-2.ch003

Al Amoush, A. B., & Sandhu, K. (2020b). A Study of Digital Learning Management Systems in Developing Countries: Instructors' Perspectives. *Digital Transformation and Innovative Services for Business and Learning*, 80-101. doi:10.4018/978-1-7998-5175-2.ch005

Alasadi, S., & Bhaya, W. (2017). Review of Data Preprocessing Techniques in Data Mining. *Journal of Engineering and Applied Sciences (Asian Research Publishing Network)*, *12*, 4102–4107.

Al-Assaf, G., & Al-Malki, A. M. (2014). Modelling the macroeconomic determinants of workers' remittances: The case of Jordan. *International Journal of Economics and Financial Issues*, *3*(4), 514–526.

Alberto, F., Francisco, H., Oscar, C., Maria, J. J., & Francesco, M. (2019). Evolutionary Fuzzy Systems for Explainable Artificial Intelligence: Why, When, What for, and Where to. *IEEE Computational Intelligence Magazine*, *14*(1), 69–81. doi:10.1109/MCI.2018.2881645

Albright, S., & Winston, W. (2015). *Business Analytics: Data Analysis and Decision Making*. Cangage Learning.

Alcaraz, C., Chiquiar, D., & Salcedo, A. (2012). Remittances, schooling, and child labor in Mexico. *Journal of Development Economics*, *97*(1), 156–165. doi:10.1016/j.jdeveco.2010.11.004

Alejandro, B. A., Natalia, D. R., Javier, D. S., Adrien, B., Siham, T., Alberto, B., Salvador, G., Sergio, G. L., Daniel, M., Richard, B., Raja, C., & Francisco, H. (2019, December). *Explainable Artificial Intelligence (XAI): Concepts, Taxonomies, Opportunities and Challenges toward Responsible AI. IEEE International Conference on Fuzzy Systems*, New York, NY.

Altan, Z. (Ed.). (2020). *Applications and approaches to object oriented software design: Emerging research and opportunities*. Engineering Science Reference, an imprint of IGI Global. doi:10.4018/978-1-7998-2142-7

Álvarez, Y., Pérez, D., & Solana, P. (2013). Contribución de la web 2.0 al desempeño organizacional en las empresas del sector turismo. *Puente Revista Científica*, *7*(2), 7–13.

Al, Z. T. (2018). A Content-Based Citation Analysis Study Based on Text Categorization. *Scientometrics*, 335–357.

Ambler, T., & Barrow, S. (1996). The employer brand. *Journal of Brand Management*, *4*(3), 185–206. doi:10.1057/bm.1996.42

Amina, A., & Mohammed, B. (2018). Peeking Inside the Black-Box: A Survey on Explainable Artificial Intelligence. *IEEEE Access*, *6*(1), 52138–52160.

Ammar, M., Russello, G., & Crispo, B. (2018). Internet of Things: A survey on the security of IOT frameworks. *Journal of Information Security and Applications*, *38*, 8–27. doi:10.1016/j.jisa.2017.11.002

Amoros, J. E., Ciravegna, L., Mandakovic, V., & Stenholm, P. (2019). Necessity or opportunity? The effects of State fragility and economic development on entrepreneurial efforts. *Entrepreneurship Theory and Practice*, *43*(4), 725–750. doi:10.1177/1042258717736857

Amrani, A., & Ducq, Y. (2020). Lean practices implementation in aerospace based on sector characteristics: Methodology and case study. *Production Planning and Control*, *31*(16), 1–23. doi:10.1080/09537287.2019.1706197

Anderson, M., Toor, S., Rainie, L., & Smith, A. (2018). Public attitudes toward political engagement on social media. *Pew Research Center.* Retrieved from: https://www. pewinternet. org/2018/07/11/public-attitudes-toward-political engagement-on-social-media

Andersson, M., & Ekman, P. (2009). Ambassador networks and place branding. *Journal of Place Management and Development, 2*(1), 41–51. doi:10.1108/17538330910942799

Ang, J., Goh, C., Saldivar, A., & Li, Y. (2017). Energy-Efficient Through-Life Smart Design, Manufacturing and Operation of Ships in an Industry 4.0 Environment. *Energies, 10*(5), 610. doi:10.3390/en10050610

Anshari, M., Almunawar, M. N., Lim, S. A., & Al-Mudimigh, A. (2018). Customer relationship management and big data enabled: Personalization & customization of services. *Applied Computing and Informatics, 15*(2), 94–101. doi:10.1016/j.aci.2018.05.004

Antman, F. (2012). Gender, educational attainment, and the impact of parental migration on children left behind. *Journal of Population Economics, 25*(4), 1187–1214. doi:10.100700148-012-0423-y PMID:27616818

Anumala, S., & Reddy, B. K. K. (2007). *Benefits of e-CRM for banks and their customers: case studies of two Swedish banks* (Master's Thesis). Industrial marketing and e-commerce, Lulea tekniska universitet, Sweden.

App, S., Merk, J., & Büttgen, M. (2012). Employer branding: Sustainable HRM as a competitive advantage in the market for high-quality employees. *Management Review, 20*(1), 53–69.

Arham, A. F., Norizan, N. S., Khairuman, A., Hasim, M., Darson, M. D., & Faizal, N. S. M. (2018). Organizational restructuring: Lesson learned from tourism Malaysia. *International Journal of Academic Research in Business & Social Sciences, 8*(8), 42–49. doi:10.6007/IJARBSS/v8-i8/4431

Armstrong, J., & Franklin, T. (2008). *A review of current and developing international practice in the use of social networking (Web 2.0) in higher education.* Retrieved from: https://arthurmckeown.typepad.com/files/web-2.0-in-higher-education.pdf

Arora, J., & Narang, B. (2016). *Present and Future of Mobile Commerce: Introduction, Comparative Analysis of M Commerce and E Commerce, Advantages, Present and Future.* IGI Global.com.

Ashushrma. (2019). *Information security.* Geeks for geek. Retrieved from https://www.geeksforgeeks.org/e-commerce/

Ashwell, M. L. (2017). The digital transformation of intelligence analysis. *Journal of Financial Crime, 24*(3), 393–411. doi:10.1108/JFC-03-2017-0020

Asia, I. T. C. N. (2019). *ICT sector of Pakistan.* https://itcnasia.com/ict-sector-of-pakistan/

Awang, M. K., Labadu, N. L., & Campus, G. B. (2012). Transforming object oriented data model to relational data model. *New Comput. Archit. Appl, 2*(3), 402–409.

Backhaus, K. (2016). Employer Branding Revisited. *Organizational Management Journal, 13*(4), 193–201. doi:10.1080/15416518.2016.1245128

Backhaus, K., & Tikoo, S. (2004). Conceptualizing and researching employer branding. *Career Development International, 9*(5), 501–517. doi:10.1108/13620430410550754

Bahia, K., & Suardi, S. (2019). *Connected Society: The State of Mobile Internet Connectivity.* GSMA.

Bahrami, M., Ghorbani, M., & Arabzad, S. M. (2012). Information technology (IT) as an improvement tool for customer relationship management (CRM). *Procedia: Social and Behavioral Sciences, 41*, 59–64. doi:10.1016/j.sbspro.2012.04.008

Baiyere, A., Salmela, H., & Tapanainen, T. (2020). Digital transformation and the new logics of business process management. *European Journal of Information Systems, 29*(3), 238–259. doi:10.1080/0960085X.2020.1718007

Bala, B. K., & Kumar, A. B. (2017). The Combination of Steganography and Cryptography for Medical Image Applications. *Biomedical & Pharmacology Journal, 10*(4), 1793–1797. doi:10.13005/bpj/1294

Balasubramanian, S., Peterson, R. A., & Jarvenpaa, S. L. (2002). Exploring the Implications of M-Commerce for Markets and Marketing. *Journal of the Academy of Marketing Science, 30*(4), 348–361. doi:10.1177/009207002236910

Barclays. (2017). *From the archives: the ATM is 50.* Retrieved from https://home.barclays/news/2017/06/from-the-archives-the-atm-is-50/

Barnes, S. J. (2002, April). The Mobile Commerce Value Chain: Analysis and Future Developments. *International Journal of Information Management, 22*(2), 91–108. doi:10.1016/S0268-4012(01)00047-0

Barone, R., & Masciandaro, D. (2019). Cryptocurrency or usury? Crime and alternative money laundering techniques. *European Journal of Law and Economics, 47*(2), 233–254. doi:10.100710657-019-09609-6

Basole, R. C. (2016). Accelerating digital transformation: Visual insights from the API ecosystem. *IT Professional, 18*(6), 20–25. doi:10.1109/MITP.2016.105

Batra, S., & Juneja, N. (2013). M-Commerce in India: Emerging Issues. *International Journal of Advanced Research in IT and Engineering, 2*(2).

Bazhair, A., & Sandhu, K. (2015). Factors for the acceptance of enterprise resource planning (ERP) systems and financial performance. *Journal of Economics Business and Management, 3*(1), 1–10. doi:10.7763/JOEBM.2015.V3.146

Beel, B. G. (2009). Citation Proximity Analysis (CPA) – A New Approach For Identifying Related Work Based on Co-Citation Analysis. In *International Conference on Scientometrics and Informetrics (ISSI'09)* (pp. 571–575). Academic Press.

Belfkih, A., Duvallet, C., & Sadeg, B. (2017). The Internet Of Things For Smart Ports Application To The Port Of Le Havre. *Proceedings of IPaSPort, 2017*(May). https://www.researchgate.net/publication/316668793_The_internet_of_things_for_smart_ports_application_to_the_port_of_le_havre

Bennett, R. (1983). Management Research. Management Development Series, 20. Geneva: International Labour Office.

Berghaus, S., & Back, A. (2016). Stages in Digital Business Transformation: Results of an Empirical Maturity Study. *MCIS 2016 Proceedings. 22.* Retrieved from https://aisel.aisnet.org/mcis2016/22

Bernhard W. & Roland V. (2019, October) *A Survey on Explainable Artificial Intelligence (XAI): towards Medical XAI.* IEEEE Access.

Berthelon, M. E., & Kruger, D. I. (2011). Risky behavior among youth: Incapacitation effects of school on adolescent motherhood and crime in Chile. *Journal of Public Economics, 95*(1), 41–53. doi:10.1016/j.jpubeco.2010.09.004

Berthon, P., Ewing, M., & Hah, L. L. (2005). Captivating company: Dimensions of attractiveness in employer branding. *WORLD (Oakland, Calif.), 24*(2), 173–192. doi:10.1080/02650487.2005.11072912

Berz, K., Chin, V., & Maguire, A. (2019). *Come Out a Winner in Retail Banking*. The Boston Consulting Group BCG.

Bézivin, J., Soley, R. M., & Vallecillo, A. (2011). Model-Driven Interoperability: MDI 2010. In J. Dingel & A. Solberg (Eds.), *Models in Software Engineering* (Vol. 6627, pp. 145–149). Springer Berlin Heidelberg., doi:10.1007/978-3-642-21210-9_14

Bhalla, P. (2020). *What is ecommerce and how it operates*. Retrieved from https://www.shiprocket.in/blog/s

Bhatia, R., Kapoor, S., & Arai, K. (2020). Advances in Information and Communication*: Proceedings of the 2020 Future of Information and Communication Conference (FICC)*, Volume 1. Springer.

Bhatti, T. (2015). Exploring Factors Influencing the Adoption of Mobile Commerce. *Journal of Internet Banking and Commerce, 12*(3).

Bhuvaneswari, V., & Porkodi, R. (2014). *The internet of things (IoT) applications and communication enabling*. Paper presented at the meeting of the 2014 International Conference on Intelligent Computing Applications, Coimbatore, India.

BibMe. (2020). Retrieved from BibMe: https://www.bibme.org/style

Bignon, V., Caroli, E., & Galbiati, R. (2011). *Stealing to survive: Crime and income shocks in 19th century France*. Cepremac.

Binuyo, A. O., & Aregbeshola, R. A. (2014). The impact of information and communication technology (ICT) on commercial bank performance: Evidence from South Africa. *Problems and Perspectives in Management, 12*(3), 59–68.

Blackman, J. (2019). Deutsche Telekom, Nokia proclaim 5G slicing for industrial IOT after Hamburg port tests. *Enterprise IOT insight.* Retrieved from https://enterpriseIOTinsights.com/20190626/channels/news/dt-nokia-proclaim-5g-slicing-for-industrial-IOT

Blaikie, N. (2003). Analyzing quantitative data: From description to explanation. *Sage (Atlanta, Ga.).*

Blen, M. K., Devinder, K., Ali, A. B., Vijaya, K. D., Ahmad, Y. J., Jack, D. Z., & Robert, P. M. (2019). Evolving Rule-Based Explainable Artificial Intelligence for Unmanned Aerial Vehicle. *IEEEE Access, 7*(1), 17001–17016.

Blummer, B., & Kenton, J. M. (2015). *Improving student information search, A metacognitive approach.* Chandos Publishing.

Bondarouk, T., Ruël, H., Axinia, E., & Arama, R. (2014). What Is the Future of Employer Branding Through Social Media? Results of the Delphi Study into the Perceptions of HR Professionals and Academics. In Social Media in Human Resources Management (pp. 23–57). doi:10.1108/S1877-6361(2013)0000012006

Bond, M., Marín, V. I., Dolch, C., Bedenlier, S., & Zawacki-Richter, O. (2018). Digital transformation in German higher education: Student and teacher perceptions and usage of digital media. *International Journal of Educational Technology in Higher Education, 15*(1), 48. doi:10.118641239-018-0130-1

Bosman, J. (2006). *Scopus Reviewed and Compared.* Utrecht University Library.

Boumans, W. (2019). *A comprehensive meta model for the current data landscape.* Academic Press.

Bowles, M. S., & Bowles, M. S. (2004). *Relearning to e-learn: Strategies for electronic learning and knowledge.* Academic Monographs.

Boyd, D. M., & Ellison, N. B. (2007). Social network sites: Definition, history, and scholarship. *Journal of Computer-Mediated Communication, 13*(1), 210–230. doi:10.1111/j.1083-6101.2007.00393.x

Brenner, L., & Meyll, T. (2020). Robo-advisors: A substitute for human financial advice? *Journal of Behavioral and Experimental Finance, 25*, 1–8. doi:10.1016/j.jbef.2020.100275

Brodsky, L., & Oakes, L. (2017). *Data sharing and open banking.* Retrieved from https://www.mckinsey.com/~/media/McKinsey/Industries/Financial%20Services/Our%20Insights/Data%20sharing%20and%20open%20banking/Data-sharing-and-open-banking.ashx

Brown, R. (Ed.). (2010). *Higher education and the market.* Routledge. doi:10.4324/9780203849002

Brunetti, F., Matt, D. T., Bonfanti, A., De Longhi, A., Pedrini, G., & Orzes, G. (2020). Digital transformation challenges: Strategies emerging from a multi-stakeholder approach. *The TQM Journal*, *32*(4), 697–724. doi:10.1108/TQM-12-2019-0309

Brunetto, Y., & Farr-Wharton, R. (2002). Using social identity theory to explain the job satisfaction of public sector employees. *International Journal of Public Sector Management*, *15*(7), 534–551. doi:10.1108/09513550210448571

Brymer, R. A., Molloy, J. C., & Gilbert, B. A. (2014). Human Capital Pipelines. *Journal of Management*, *40*(2), 483–508. doi:10.1177/0149206313516797

Bryndin, E. (2018). System Synergetic Formation of Society 5.0 for Development of Vital Spaces. *Annals of Ecology and Environmental Science*, *2*(4), 12–19.

Bulfin, S., Johnson, N. F., & Bigum, C. (2015). *Critical perspectives on technology and education*. Springer. doi:10.1057/9781137385451

Bunmark. (2018). *Fintech Insights*. Retrieved from https://www.burnmark.com/uploads/offerings/Burnmark_Monthly_Fintech_Insights1.pdf

Burnes, B. (2004). Kurt Lewin and the Planned Approach to Change: A Re-appraisal. *Journal of Management Studies*, *41*(6), 977–1002. doi:10.1111/j.1467-6486.2004.00463.x

Buterin, V. (2015). *The Value of Blockchain Technology*. Retrieved from https://ethereum.github.io/blog/2015/04/13/visions-part-1-the-value-of-blockchain-technology/

Butler, T., & Hackney, R. (2015). Understanding digital eco-innovation in municipalities: An institutional perspective. *Proceedings of ECIS 2015*.

Callcenterhelper. (2018). *The History of the Call Centre*. Retrieved from https://www.callcentrehelper.com/the-history-of-the-call-centre-15085.htm

Camacho, A., & Mejia, D. (2013). *Las externalidades de los programas de transferencias condicionadas sobre el crimen: El caso de familias en acción en Bogotá*. IDB Working Paper 406. Institutions for Development Sector. Washington, DC: Inter-American Development Bank.

Cambridge Dictionary. (2020). *Remittance*. Retrieved June 10, 2020 from https://dictionary.cambridge.org/dictionary/english/remittance

Camilleri, M. A., & Camilleri, A. C. (2017). Digital learning resources and ubiquitous technologies in education. *Technology, Knowledge, and Learning*, *22*(1), 65–82. doi:10.100710758-016-9287-7

Cardoso, G., & Araújo, V. (2009). Out of information and into communication. Networked communication and Internet usage. *Worldwide internet: Changing societies, economies and cultures, 23*.

Carey, K., & Helfert, M. (2016). Improving the Front End of Innovation: The Case of Mobile Commerce Services. In *International Conference on HCI in Business, Government and Organizations*. Springer International Publishing.

Carlan, V., Sys, C., Vanelslander, T., & Roumboutsos, A. (2017). Digital innovation in the port sector: Barriers and facilitators. In Competition and regulation in network industries (pp. 1–23). doi:10.1177/1783591717734793

Carnevale, J. B., & Hatak, I. (2020). Employee Adjustment and Well-Being in the Era of COVID-19: Implications for Human Resource Management. *Journal of Business Research*, *116*, 183–187. Advance online publication. doi:10.1016/j.jbusres.2020.05.037 PMID:32501303

Carpentier, M., Van Hoye, G., Stockman, S., Schollaert, E., Van Theemsche, B., & Jacobs, G. (2017). Recruiting nurses through social media: Effects on employer brand and attractiveness. *Journal of Advanced Nursing*, *73*(11), 2696–2708. doi:10.1111/jan.13336 PMID:28494103

Carpentier, M., Van Hoye, G., & Weng, Q. (2019). Social media recruitment: Communication characteristics and sought gratifications. *Frontiers in Psychology*, *10*, 1669. doi:10.3389/fpsyg.2019.01669 PMID:31379686

Carraz, R., & Harayama, Y. (2018). Japan's Innovation Systems at the Crossroads: Society 5.0. In Panorama: Insights into Asian and European Affairs. Digital Asia, 33-45.

Castells, M., Roca, M., Sancho, T., & Tubella, I. (2007). La transición a la sociedad red (No. Sirsi i9788434442719). Barcelona: Ariel.

Castells, M. (2006). *The theory of the network society*. Great Britain by MPG Books Ltd.

Cerit, M. (2019). Dünyada ve Türkiye' de açık bankacılık: Bankacılığın geleceği. *Fintech Istanbul*, 11-40. https://bkm.com.tr/wp-content/uploads/2015/06/Dunyadaveturkiyedeacikbankacilik.pdf

Chalmers, J., & Reuter, J. (2015). Is Conflicted Advice Better Than No Advice? *NBER Working Paper Series*, 18158.

Chanias, S., Myers, M. D., & Hess, T. (2019). Digital transformation strategy making in pre-digital organizations: The case of a financial services provider. *The Journal of Strategic Information Systems*, *28*(1), 17–33. doi:10.1016/j.jsis.2018.11.003

Chanida, P., & Vichai, R. (2019). Material Cost Prediction for Jewelry Production Using Deep Learning Techniqu. *Engineering Journal (New York)*, *23*(6), 145–160.

Charbonnier-Voirin, A., & Vignolles, A. (2015). Marque employeur interne et externe : Un état de l'art et un agenda de recherche. *Revue Française de Gestion*, *41*(246), 63–82. doi:10.3166/rfg.246.63-82

Chatwal, T. (2019). Digitalization of Higher Education in India: A Boon Or A Bane. *Research Journal of Humanities and Social Sciences*, *10*(4), 1083–1085. doi:10.5958/2321-5828.2019.00178.5

Chauhan, K., Jani, S., Thakkar, D., Dave, R., Bhatia, J., Tanwar, S., & Obaidat, M. (2020). *Automated Machine Learning: The New Wave of Machine Learning*. ICIMIA. doi:10.1109/ICIMIA48430.2020.9074859

Chavan, J. (2013). Internet banking - Benefits and challenges in an emerging economy. *International Journal of Research in Business Management*, *1*(1), 19–26.

Chedrawi, C., Harb, B., & Saleh, M. (2019). The E-Banking and the Adoption of Innovations from the Perspective of the Transactions Cost Theory: Case of the Largest Commercial Banks in Lebanon. In Y. Baghdadi & A. Harfouche (Eds.), *ICT for a Better Life and a Better World The Impact of Information and Communication Technologies on Organizations and Society* (Vol. 30). Springer. doi:10.1007/978-3-030-10737-6_10

Chengzhi, M. S. (2020). A review of citation recommendation: From textual content to enriched context. *Scientometrics*, 1445–1472.

Chen, H., & Beaudoin, C. E. (2016). An empirical study of a social network site: Exploring the effects of social capital and information disclosure. *Telematics and Informatics*, *33*(2), 432–435. doi:10.1016/j.tele.2015.09.001

Chen, Y. Y. K., Jaw, Y. L., & Wu, B. L. (2016). Effect of digital transformation on organizational performance of SMEs: Evidence from the Taiwanese textile industry's web portal. *Internet Research*, *26*(1), 186–212. doi:10.1108/IntR-12-2013-0265

Child, J. (2015). *Organization: Contemporary Principles and Practice*. Wiley. doi:10.1002/9781119176862

Chioda, L., De Mello, J. M. P., & Soares, R. (2012). *Spillovers from conditional cash transfer programs: Bolsa família and crime in urban Brazil.* Department of Economics PUC-Rio.

Choi, A. J. (2014, November). Internet of things: Evolution towards a hyper-connected society. In *2014 IEEE Asian Solid-State Circuits Conference (A-SSCC)* (pp. 5-8). IEEE. 10.1109/ASSCC.2014.7008846

Choi, H. R., Kim, H. S., Park, B. J., Park, N. K., & Lee, S. W. (2003). An ERP approach for container terminal operating systems. *Maritime Policy & Management, 30*(3), 197–210. doi:10.1080/0308883032000089549

Choi, S. Y., & Whinston, A. B. (1999). The future of e-commerce: Integrate and customize. *Computer, 32*(1), 133–138. doi:10.1109/2.738310

Chopra, S., & Meindl, P. (2016). Supply Chain Management (Global Edition). Academic Press.

Chung, S. A., Park, S., & Lee, S. (2017). The era of hyper-connected society and the changes in business activities: Focusing on information blocking and acquisition activities. *International Journal of Management and Applied Science, 3*(4), 16–21.

Cirani, S., Ferrari, G., Picone, M., & Veltri, L. (2019). *Internet of things : Architectures, protocols and standards (First).* John Wiley & Sons Ltd.

Citation Index. (2009, August 1). Retrieved from Edutech wikki: http://edutechwiki.unige.ch/en/Citation_index

Citation Machine. (2020). Retrieved from Citation Machine: https://www.citationmachine.net/apa

Cite.com. (2020). Retrieved from Cite.com: https://www.cite.com/

CiteSeerX. (2020). Retrieved from Solr: http://citeseerx.ist.psu.edu/index;jsessionid=341AE6933E128F38AB58BE43AA718916

Clarke, I. (2008). Emerging Value Propositions for M-Commerce. *The Journal of Business Strategy, 25*, 2.

Clegg, S. R., Kornberger, M., & Pitsis, T. (2016). *Managing & Organizations: An Introduction to Theory and Practice.* SAGE.

Clegg, S., Hudson, A., & Steel, J. (2003). The emperor's new clothes: Globalisation and e-learning in higher education. *British Journal of Sociology of Education, 24*(1), 39–53. doi:10.1080/01425690301914

Clement, J. (2018). *Daily social media usage worldwide 2012-2018.* Retrieved from https://www.statista.com/statistics/433871/daily-social-media-usage-worldwide/

Clement, J. (2019). *Largest online population Countrywide.* Statistia reports.

Clement, J. (2020). *Number of mobile app downloads.* Statista reports.

Clement, J. (2020). *Statistics & Facts, Internet usage worldwide.* Statistia reports.

Cohen, A., Alhuraish, I., Robledo, C., & Kobi, A. (2020). A statistical analysis of critical quality tools and companies' performance. *Journal of Cleaner Production, 255*, 120221. doi:10.1016/j.jclepro.2020.120221

Collins Dictionary. (2020). *Remittance.* Retrieved June 10, 2020 from https://www.collinsdictionary.com/dictionary/english/remittance#:~:text=A%20remittance%20is%20a%20sum%20of%20money%20that%20you%20send%20to%20someone

Conole, G. G. (2013). MOOCs as disruptive technologies: strategies for enhancing the learner experience and quality of MOOCs. *Revista de Educación a Distancia*, (39).

Cook, S., & Daniels, J. (1994). *Designing object systems: Object-oriented modelling with Syntropy*. Prentice Hall.

Cotlier, M. (2000). *Wide Wireless World, Catalog Age*. New Canaan.

Cramer, D. (2003). *Advanced quantitative data analysis*. McGraw-Hill International.

Currency Rate Investor. (2020). Retrieved from https://btc.currencyrate.today/usd

Cziesla, T. (2014). A literature review on digital transformation in the financial service industry. *Proceedings of BLED 2014*.

Dahlström, P., Desmet, D., & Singer, M. (2017). *The seven decisions that matter in a digital transformation: A CEO's guide to reinvention*. Retrieved May 28, 2020, from https://www.mckinsey.com/business-functions/digital-mckinsey/our-insights/the-seven-ecisions-that-matter-in-a-digital-transformation

Danesi, M. (2004). *Messages, signs, and meaning: A basic textbook in semiotics and communication theory* (3rd ed.). Canadian Scholars' Press Inc.

Daniel, H., & Mark, A. E. (2018) *Explainable A.I.: the promise of Genetic Programming Multi-run*. 2018 International Conference on Machine Learning and Data Engineering (iCMLDE), Malvern, UK.

Daniel, E. (1999). Provision of electronic banking in the UK and the republic of Ireland. *International Journal of Bank Marketing*, *17*(2), 72–82. doi:10.1108/02652329910258934

Dannenberg, M., & Kellner, D. (1998). The bank of tomorrow with today's technology. *International Journal of Bank Marketing*, *16*(2), 90–97. doi:10.1108/02652329810206743

Daqar, M., & Smoudy, A. (2019). The role of artificial intelligence on enhancing customer experience. *International Review of Management and Marketing*, *9*(4), 22–31. doi:10.32479/irmm.8166

Davenport, T. H., & Redman, T. C. (2020). *Digital Transformation Comes Down to Talent in 4 Key areas*. Retrieved from https://store.hbr.org/product/digital-transformation-comes-down-to-talent-in-4-key-areas/H05N4Y

David, G. (2017). *Explainable Artificial Intelligence (XAI)*. Retrieved from https://www.darpa.mil/attachments/XAIProgramUpdate.pdf

Davis, F. D. (1989). Perceived usefulness, perceived ease of use, and user acceptance of information technology. *Management Information Systems Quarterly*, *13*(3), 319–340.

De Freitas, S., & Oliver, M. (2005). Does E-learning Policy Drive Change in Higher Education?: A case study relating models of organizational change to e-learning implementation. *Journal of Higher Education Policy and Management*, *27*(1), 81–96. doi:10.1080/13600800500046255

Dean, Y. (2008). International migration, remittances and household investment: Evidence from Philippine migrants' exchange rate shocks. *Economic Journal. Revue Economique et Sociale*, *118*(528), 591–630.

Deepa, B. (2020). *Advanced Machine Learning for Enterprise IoT Modeling*. Springer. doi:10.1007/978-3-030-44407-5_5

Delgaty, L. (2013). A critical examination of the time and workload involved in the design and delivery of an e-module in postgraduate clinical education. *Medical Teacher*, *35*(5), e1173–e1180. doi:10.3109/0142159X.2012.737963 PMID:23151211

Deloitte Sights. (2019). *The value of online banking channels in a mobile-centric world*. Retrieved from https://www2.deloitte.com/us/en/insights/industry/financial-services/online-banking-usage-in-mobile-centric-world.html

Deloitte Touche Tohmatsu (Firm). (2018). *The Fourth Industrial Revolution is here: are you ready?* Author.

Demirguc-Kunt, A., Lopez, E., Martinez, M., & Woodruff, C. (2011). Remittances and banking sector breadth and depth: Evidence from Mexico. *Journal of Development Economics*, *95*(2), 229–241. doi:10.1016/j.jdeveco.2010.04.002

Dennys, C. A. M., & Ricardo, A. S. F. (2018, December). Predicting the direction, maximum, minimum and closing prices of daily Bitcoin exchange rate using machine learning techniques. *Applied Soft Computing*, *75*(1), 596–606.

Denzin, N. K., & Lincoln, Y. S. (2018). The SAGE Handbook of qualitative Research. SAGE.

Deshmukh, S. P., Deshmukh, P., & Thampi, G. (2013). Transformation from E-Commerce to M-Commerce in Indian Context. International Journal Computational Science, 10(4).

Dickson, B. (2016). How Blockchain Can Change the Future of IOT. *Venture-Beat.* Retrieved from https://venturebeat.com/2016/11/20/how-blockchain-can-change-the-future-of-IOT/

Dietvorst, B. J., Simmons, J. P., & Massey, C. (2018). Overcoming algorithm a version: People will use imperfect algorithms if they can (even slightly) modify them. *Management Science*, *64*(3), 1155–1170. doi:10.1287/mnsc.2016.2643

Dijk, J. V. (2012). *The network society* (3rd ed.). Academic Press.

Dominik, S., Tobias, H., Florian, L., Michael, D., Andreas, S., & Elisabeth, A. (2019, September) *Relevance-based Feature Masking: Improving Neural Network based Whale Classification through Explainable Artificial Intelligence.* INTERSPEECH, Graz, Austria.

Dong, X., Gabrilovich, E., Heitz, G., Horn, W., Lao, N., Murphy, K., Strohmann, T., Sun, S., & Zhang, W. (2014). Knowledge vault: a web-scale approach to probabilistic knowledge fusion. *Proceedings of the 20th ACM SIGKDD international conference on Knowledge discovery and data mining.* 10.1145/2623330.2623623

Dong, X., Gang, X., Li, Y., Guo, X., & Lv, Y. (2013). Intelligent ports based on Internet of Things. *Proceedings of 2013 IEEE International Conference on Service Operations and Logistics, and Informatics, SOLI 2013*, 292–296. 10.1109/SOLI.2013.6611428

Drake, M. A. (2005). *Encyclopedia of Library and Information Science.* Taylor & Francis Group.

Drath, R., & Horch, A. (2014). Industrie 4.0: Hit or Hype? *IEEE Industrial Electronics Magazine*, *8*(2), 56–58. doi:10.1109/MIE.2014.2312079

Dreher, S. (2014). Social media and the world of work. *Corporate Communications*, *19*(4), 344–356. doi:10.1108/CCIJ-10-2013-0087

Duarte, P., Costa e Silva, S., & Ferreira, M. B. (2018). How convenient is it? Delivering online shopping convenience to enhancecustomer satisfaction and encourage e-WOM. *Journal of Retailing and Consumer Services*, *44*, 161–169. doi:10.1016/j.jretconser.2018.06.007

Dube, S., & Scott, E. (2017). A Survey of the University Students' Perspectives about Using Digital Technologies in Education: Zimbabwean Case. *IAFOR Journal of Education*, *5*(1), 123–139. doi:10.22492/ije.5.1.07

Dube, T., Njanike, K., Manomano, C., & Chiriseri, L. (2011). Adoption and use of SMS/mobile banking services in Zimbabwe: An exploratory study. *Journal of Internet Banking and Commerce*, *16*(2), 1–15.

EasyBib. (2020). Retrieved from EasyBib: https://www.easybib.com/mla8/source

Ebert, C., & Duarte, C. H. C. (2018). Digital Transformation. *IEEE Software*, *35*(4), 16–21. doi:10.1109/MS.2018.2801537

EBSCO. (2020). Retrieved from EBSCO: https://www.ebsco.com/

Eckenrode. (2006). *Building a more responsive banking industry: The bell is ringing but are banks salivating?* The Tower Group.

Econsultancy & Adobe. (2017). *Digital Intelligence Briefing: 2017 Digital Trends*. Retrieved from https://econsultancy.com/reports/digital-intelligence-briefing-2017-digital-trends/

Eden, R., Sedera, D., & Tan, F. (2014). Sustaining the Momentum: Archival Analysis of Enterprise Resource Planning Systems (2006–2012). *Communications of the Association for Information Systems, 35*. Advance online publication. doi:10.17705/1CAIS.03503

Edo, A. (2019). The impact of immigration on the labor market. *Journal of Economic Surveys, 33*(3), 922–948. Advance online publication. doi:10.1111/joes.12300

Eduardo García-Pach6n, R. A.-J. (2014). A Comparison of the Impact Factor and the SCImago Journal Rank Index in Respiratory System Journals. *Archivos de Bronconeumologia*, 263–310. PMID:24315384

Edwards, M. R. (2009). An integrative review of employer branding and OB theory. *Personnel Review, 39*(1), 5–23. doi:10.1108/00483481011012809

Eger, L., Mičík, M., Gangur, M., & Řehoř, P. (2019). Employer Branding: Exploring Attractiveness Dimensions in a Multicultural Context. *Technological and Economic Development of Economy, 25*(3), 519–541. doi:10.3846/tede.2019.9387

Eger, L., Mičík, M., & Řehoř, P. (2018). Employer branding on social media and recruitment websites: Symbolic traits of an ideal employer. *E+M. Ekonomie a Management, 21*(1), 224–237. doi:10.15240/tul/001/2018-1-015

Ehsan, H., & Saman, H. (2019, March). CNNpre d: CNN-based stock market prediction using a diverse set of variables. *Expert Systems with Applications, 129*(1), 273–285.

Eisenhardt, K. M. (1989). Building Theories from Case Study Research. *Academy of Management Review, 14*(4), 532–550. doi:10.5465/amr.1989.4308385

Eisenhardt, K. M., & Graebner, M. E. (2007). Theory building from cases: Opportunities and challenges. *Academy of Management Journal, 50*(1), 25–32. doi:10.5465/amj.2007.24160888

El Zoghbi, E., & Aoun, K. (2016). Employer Branding and Social Media Strategies. In F. Ricciardi & A. Harfouche (Eds.), *Information and Communication Technologies in Organizations and Society Past, Present and Future Issues* (pp. 277–283). Springer International Publishing Switzerland.

Electron, J. (2012). *Introduction to the Special Issue Mobile Commerce: The Past, Present, and Future of Mobile Commerce*. Research Int.

Elving, W. J., Westhoff, J. J., Meeusen, K., & Schoonderbeek, J.-W. (2012). The war for talent? The relevance of employer branding in job advertisements for becoming an employer of choice. *Journal of Brand Management, 20*(5), 355–373. doi:10.1057/bm.2012.21

Eren, B. A. (2020). The Role of Internet Banking in the Presentation and Marketing of Financial Services and Products in a Digital Environment. In K. Sandhu (Ed.), *Digital Innovations for Customer Engagement, Management, and Organizational Improvement* (pp. 162–183). IGI Global. doi:10.4018/978-1-7998-5171-4.ch009

Ernst & Young. (2018). *Open Banking Opportunity Index*. Retrieved from https://www.ey.com/en_gl/open-banking-opportunity-index

Ernst & Young. (2019). *EY- Eighth Annual global bank risk management survey*. Retrieved from https://www.ey.com/Publication/vwLUAssets/ey-eighth-annual-global-eyiif-bank-risk-management-survey/$FILE/ey-eighth-annual-global-eyiif-bank-risk-management-survey.pdf

Evans, E. (2003). *Domain-Driven Design*. Pearson Education.

Ewing, M. T., Pitt, L. F., de Bussy, N. M., & Berthon, P. (2002). Employment branding in the knowledge economy. *International Journal of Advertising*, *21*(1), 3–22. doi:10.1080/02650487.2002.11104914

Fajnzylber, P., Lederman, D., & Loayza, N. (1998). *Determinants of crime rates in Latin America and the world, an empirical assessment*. World Bank. doi:10.1596/0-8213-4240-1

Farooq, M. S., Salam, M., Fayolle, A., Jaafar, N., & Ayupp, K. (2018). Impact of service quality on customer satisfaction in Malaysia airlines: A PLS-SEM approach. *Journal of Air Transport Management*, *67*, 169–180. doi:10.1016/j.jairtraman.2017.12.008

Fatanti, M. N., & Suyadnya, I. W. (2015). Beyond user gaze: How Instagram creates tourism destination brand? *Procedia: Social and Behavioral Sciences*, *211*, 1089–1095. doi:10.1016/j.sbspro.2015.11.145

Featherman, M. M., Wells, J. D., & Campbell, D. E. (2010). *The Effect of Perceived Novelty on the Adoption of Information Technology Innovations: A Risk/Reward Perspective*. Elsevier publications.

Felix, P. (2018). Prospects and challenges of electronic banking in Ghana: The case of Zenith Bank Sunyani. *International Journal of Advances in Management, Economics and Entrepreneurship*, *1*(1), 6–14.

Fella, G., & Gallipoli, G. (2008). *Education and crime over the life cycle*. Working Paper 630. London: Queen Mary University of London.

Fernández-Cavia, J., Rovira, C., Gómez, L., Gascó, M., Pedraza, R., Bonilla, S., . . . Martín, S. (2010). Propuesta de diseño de una plantilla multidisciplinar para el análisis y evaluación de webs de destinos turísticos. In *VIII Congreso Turismo y Tecnologías de la Información y las Comunicaciones Turitec 2010* (pp. 1–18). Universidad de Málaga.

Fernández-Cavia, J., Díaz-Luque, P., Huertas, A., Rovira, C., Pedraza-Jimenez, R., Sicilia, M., ... Máguez-González, M. I. (2013). Marcas de destino y evaluación de sitios web: Una metodología de investigación. *Revista Latina de Comunicación Social*, *68*, 622–638. doi:10.4185/RLCS-2013-993

Fernández-Cavia, J., Rovira, C., Díaz-Luque, P., & Cavaller, V. (2014). Web Quality Index (WQI) for official tourist destination websites. Proposal for an assessment system. *Tourism Management Perspectives*, *9*, 5–13. doi:10.1016/j.tmp.2013.10.003

Ferreira, N. M. (2019). *Ecommerce-advantages-and-disadvantages*. Retrieved from https://www.oberlo.com/blog/20-

Ferreira, C. M., & Serpa, S. (2018). Society 5.0 and Social Development: Contributions to a Discussion. *Management and Organizational Studies*, *5*, 26–31. doi:10.20944/preprints201811.0108.v1

Figueroa-Armijos, M., & da Motta Veiga, S. (2019). Predictors of Early-Career Self-Employment among Millennials in the Digital Economy: The Role of The Great Recession. *Proceedings of the 52nd Hawaii International Conference on System Sciences*. 10.24251/HICSS.2019.546

Financial Stability Board (FSB). (2017). *Artificial intelligence and machine learning in financial services: Market developments and financial stability implications*. Retrieved from https://www.fsb.org/wp-content/uploads/P011117.pdf

Firdausi, A., Shaik, N., & Tiwari, G. (2020). *What is E-Commerce and how it operates*. Emerging Trends in Business.

Forristal, L. J. (2012). Using YouTube videos of anthropology of tourism pioneer Valene Smith's work and philosophy to balance the tourism curriculum. *Journal of Teaching in Travel & Tourism, 12*(1), 91–104. doi:10.1080/15313220.2012.650098

Fowler, M. (1997). *Analysis patterns: Reusable object models*. Addison Wesley.

Fowler, M., & Rice, D. (2005). *Architektura systemów zarządzania przedsiębiorstwem: Wzorce projektowe* (P. Koronkiewicz & P. Rajca, Trans.). Helion.

Fox, S. (2005). *The state of online banking*. PEW Internet & American Life Project. http://www.pewInternet.org/pdfs/PIP_Online_Banking_2005.pdf#search='The%20State%20of%20Online%20Banking%20Pew

Fredette, J., Marom, R., Steiner, K., & Witters, L. (2012). The promise and peril of hyperconnectivity for organizations and societies. *The global information technology report, 2012*, 113-119.

Fueyo, C. (2015). *E-réputation corporate : influence de la voix digitale des employés via l'e-contenu de leur « Profil » sur les réseaux sociaux professionnels ; application au secteur automobile*. Université Toulouse 1 Capitole.

Fukuda, K. (2020). Science, technology and innovation ecosystem transformation toward society 5.0. *International Journal of Production Economics, 220*(2), 107460. Advance online publication. doi:10.1016/j.ijpe.2019.07.033

Fukuyama, M. (2018) .Society 5.0: Aiming for a New Human-Centered Society. *Japan Spotlight*, 47-50.

Furst, S. A., Reeves, M., Rosen, B., & Blackburn, R. S. (2004). Managing the life cycle of virtual teams. *The Academy of Management Executive, 18*(2), 6–20. doi:10.5465/ame.2004.13837468

Galazova, S. S., & Magomaeva, L. R. (2019). The transformation of traditional banking activity in digital. *International Journal of Economics and Business Administration, 7*(2), 41–51. doi:10.35808/ijeba/369

Gallarza, M. G., Saura, I. G., & García, H. C. (2002). Destination image: Towards a conceptual framework. *Annals of Tourism Research, 29*(1), 56–78. doi:10.1016/S0160-7383(01)00031-7

Gao, J., Huang, C., Su, J., & Xie, Q. (2019). Examining the Factors Behind the Success and Sustainability of China's Creative Research Group: An Extension of the Teamwork Quality Model. *Sustainability, 11*(4), 1195. doi:10.3390u11041195

Gao, Y. H. Z., & Chen, Y. J. X. (2018). Exploring hidden factors behind online food shopping from Amazon reviews: A topic mining approach. *Journal of Retailing and Consumer Services, 42*, 161–168. doi:10.1016/j.jretconser.2018.02.006

García-Fernández, J., Gálvez-Ruíz, P., Fernández-Gavira, J., Vélez-Colón, L., Pitts, B., & Bernal-García, A. (2018). The effects of service convenience and perceived quality on perceived value, satisfaction and loyalty in low-cost fitness centers. *Sport Management Review, 21*(3), 250–262. doi:10.1016/j.smr.2017.07.003

Garfield, E. (2020). *The concept of citation indexing*. Retrieved from Clarivate Web of Science: https://clarivate.com/webofsciencegroup/essays/concept-citation-indexing/

Gärtner, C. (2020). *Smart HRM*. Springer. doi:10.1007/978-3-658-29431-1

Gerald, F., & San, J. (2018, November) *Developing Transparent Credit Risk Scorecards More Effectively: An Explainable Artificial Intelligence Approach. International Conference on Data Analytics*, Athens, Greece.

Ghose, S., & Dou, W. (1998). Interactive functions and their impacts on the appeal of Internet presence sites. *Journal of Advertising Research, 38*(2), 29–43.

Gibbert, M., Ruigrok, W., & Wicki, B. (2008). What Passes As A Rigorous Case Study? *Strategic Management Journal, 29*(13), 1465–1474. doi:10.1002mj.722

Gilani, H., & Cunningham, L. (2017). Employer branding and its influence on employee retention: A literature review. *The Marketing Review*, *17*(2), 239–256. doi:10.1362/146934717X14909733966209

Gil, E. (2017). Nuevos activismos sociales en la era digital: De las masas al crowd. *Politica y Sociedad*, *54*(1), 191–209.

Giles, C. L. (1998). CiteSeer: An Automatic Citation Indexing System. In *ACM Conference on Digital Libraries* (pp. 89-98). ACM.

Gil-Gomez, H., Guerola-Navarro, V., Oltra-Badenes, R., & Lozano-Quilis, J. N. (2020). *Customer relationship management: digitaltransformation and sustainable business modelinnovation*. Economic Research-Ekonomska Istraživanja., doi:10.1080/1331677X.2019.1676283

Gioia, D. A., Corley, K. G., & Hamilton, A. L. (2013). Seeking Qualitative Rigor in Inductive Research. *Organizational Research Methods*, *16*(1), 15–31. doi:10.1177/1094428112452151

Giovanni Colavizza, K. W. (2017). The Closer the Better: Similarity of Publication Pairs at Different Co-Citation Levels. *Journal of the Association for Information Science and Technology*, 1–17.

Girod, S. J. G., & Karim, S. (2017). Restructure or reconfigure? *Harvard Business Review*. Retrieved May 28, 2020, from https://hbr.org/2017/03/restructure-or-reconfigure

Gladden, M. (2019). Who Will Be the Members of Society 5.0? Towards an Anthropology of Technologically Posthumanized Future Societies. *Soc. Sci*, *8*(148), 1–39. doi:10.3390ocsci8050148

Glaser, B. G., & Strauss, A. L. (1967). *The discovery of grounded theory : strategies for qualitative research*. Aldine Transaction.

Globe Newswire. (2020). *Global Mobile Wallet Industry to 2028 - Flourishing m-Commerce Industry, Proliferation of Smartphones and Internet Penetration, Driving Growth*. Research and Markets.

Goh, K., & Kauffman, R. (2013). Firm strategy and the Internet in U.S. commercial banking. *Journal of Management Information Systems*, *30*(2), 9–40. doi:10.2753/MIS0742-1222300201

Goldratt, E. (1980). Optimized production timetable: a revolutionary program for industry. *APICS 23rd Annual Conference Proceedings*, 14–17.

Gölzer, P., & Fritzsche, A. (2017). Data-driven operations management: Organisational implications of the digital transformation in industrial practice. *Production Planning and Control*, *28*(16), 1332–1343. doi:10.1080/09537287.2017.1375148

Gomes, S. B., Santoro, F. M., & Mira da Silva, M. (2020). An Ontology for BPM in Digital Transformation and Innovation. *International Journal of Information System Modeling and Design*, *11*(2), 52–77. doi:10.4018/IJISMD.2020040103

Google Scholar. (2020). Retrieved from Google Scholar: https://scholar.google.co.in/

Government of Japan. (2016). *The 5th Science and Technology Basic Plan*. Available online: https://www8.cao.go.jp/cstp/english/basic/5thbasicplan.pdf

Government of Pakistan. Board of Investment. (2019). *Foreign Investment*. http://boi.gov.pk/ForeignInvestmentinPakistan.aspx

Government of Pakistan. Bureau of Statistics. (2017). *Provisional Summary Results of 6th Population and Housing Census - 2017*. https://bytesforall.pk/

Government of Pakistan. Ministry of Finance. (2019). *Economic Survey of Pakistan 2018-19*. http://www.finance.gov.pk/survey/chapters_18/overview_2018-19.pdf

Government of Pakistan. State Bank of Pakistan (2020). Retrieved from https://www.sbp.org.pk/

Graham, B. Z., & Cascio, W. F. (2018). The employer-branding journey : Its relationship with cross-cultural branding, brand reputation, and brand repair. *Management Research: Journal of the Iberoamerican Academy of Management, 16*(4), 363–379. doi:10.1108/MRJIAM-09-2017-0779

Greenport. (2016). 'Smart' and sustainable ports. *Greenport.* Retrieved from https://www.greenport.com/news101/Projects-and-Initiatives/smart-and-sustainable-ports

Gupta, G. (2019, June). Education and Digital Economy: Trends, Opportunities and Challenges. In *Proceedings of the 2019 4th International Conference on Machine Learning Technologies* (pp. 88-92). 10.1145/3340997.3341013

Guttag, J. (2013). *Introduction to computation and programming using Python.* Academic Press.

Haffke, I., Kalgovas, B., & Benlian, A. (2017). The transformative role of bimodal it in an era of digital business. In *Proceedings of 50th Hawaii International Conference on System Sciences* (pp. 5460–5469). 10.24251/HICSS.2017.660

Hall, S. (2020). *What is digital transformation?* https://enterprisersproject.com/what-is-digital-transformation

Hamel, G. (2000). *Leading the revolution.* Harvard Business School Press.

Hamilton, S. (1997). E-commerce for the 21st century. *Computer, 30*(5), 44–47.

Ha, N. M., & Luan, N. V. (2018). The effect of employers' attraction and social media on job application attention of senior students at pharmaceutical universities in Vietnam. *International Journal of Business and Society, 19*(2), 473–491.

Hanizan, H. S., Din, R., Hafiza, A. S., Rukhiya, A., & Noor, M. S. (2017). A Review of Artificial Intelligence Techniques in Image Steganography Domain. *Journal of Engineering Science and Technology*, 106-116.

Harayama, Y. (2017). Society 5.0: Aiming for a New Human-centered Society. Collaborative Creation through Global R&D Open Innovation for Creating the Future. *Hitachi Review, 66*(6), 8-13. https://www.hitachi.com/rev/archive/2017/r2017_06/pdf/p08-13_TRENDS.pdf

HarinarayanaN. S. (2010). Retrieved from http://epgp.inflibnet.ac.in/epgpdata/uploads/epgp_content/library_and_information_science/informetrics_&_scientometrics/limitations_of_bibliometrics_and_scientometrics/et/334_et_m16.pdf

Harrigan, P., Soutar, G., Choudhury, M. M., & Lowe, M. (2015). Modelling CRM in a social media age. *Australasian Marketing Journal, 23*(1), 27–37. doi:10.1016/j.ausmj.2014.11.001

Hartl, E., & Hess, T. (2017). The role of cultural values for digital transformation: Insights from a Delphi study. In *Proceedings of AMCIS 2017* (pp. 1–10). Retrieved May 28, 2020, from http://aisel.aisnet.org/cgi/viewcontent.cgi?article=1369&context=amcis2017

Hasiri, S. M. A., & Afghanpour, M. (2016). Investigation of the factors affective on the loyalty of customers in banking industry in the framework of the model of personality characteristics of personnel (Case Study: Sepah Bank in Mazandaran Province). *Procedia Economics and Finance, 36*, 490–501. doi:10.1016/S2212-5671(16)30072-7

Hassan, Y., Martin, F., & Iazza, G. (2004): *Diseño Web Centrado en el Usuario: Usabilidad y Arquitectura de la Información.* Retrieved from https://www.upf.edu/hipertextnet/numero-2/diseno_web.html

Hausberg, J. P., Liere-Netheler, K., Packmohr, S., Pakura, S., & Vogelsang, K. (2019). Research streams on digital transformation from a holistic business perspective: A systematic literature review and citation network analysis. *Journal of Business Economics, 89*(8-9), 931–963. doi:10.100711573-019-00956-z

Hayden, T., & Webster, T. (2014). *The Mobile Commerce Revolution: Business Success in a Wireless World.* Que Publishing.

Heavin, C., & Power, D. J. (2018). Challenges for digital transformation - towards a conceptual decision support guide for managers. *Journal of Decision Systems, 27*(sup1), 38–45. doi:10.1080/12460125.2018.1468697

He, H., & Harris, L. (2020). The Impact of Covid-19 Pandemic on Corporate Social Responsibility and Marketing Philosophy. *Journal of Business Research, 116*, 176–182. doi:10.1016/j.jbusres.2020.05.030 PMID:32457556

Heilig, L., Lalla-Ruiz, E., & Voß, S. (2017). Digital transformation in maritime ports: Analysis and a game theoretic framework. *NETNOMICS: Economic Research and Electronic Networking, 18*(2–3), 227–254. doi:10.100711066-017-9122-x

Heinz, J., Thomann, M., & Fischer, P. (2017). Ladders to M-commerce Resistance: A Qualitative Means-end Approach. *Computers in Human Behavior, 73*(2), 362–374.

Hellenic Shipping News. (2019). Internet Of Things On Course To The Ports. *Hellenic Shipping News.* Retrieved from https://www.hellenicshippingnews.com/internet-of-things-on-course-to-the-ports/

Hendry, C. (1996). Understanding and Creating Whole Organizational Change Through Learning Theory. *Human Relations, 49*(5), 621–641. doi:10.1177/001872679604900505

Hennies, M., & Raudjärv, M. (2015). Industry 4.0. Introductory thoughts on the current situation. *Estonian Discussions on Economic Policy, 23*(2). Advance online publication. doi:10.2139srn.2708757

Herbert, L. (2017). *Digital transformation: Build your organizations future for the innovation age*. Bloomsbury Publishing Plc.

Hernández-Nieves, E., Hernández, G., Gil-González, A. B., Rodríguez-González, S., & Corchado, J. M. (2020). Fog computing architecture for personalized recommendation of banking products. *Expert Systems with Applications, 140*, 1–10. doi:10.1016/j.eswa.2019.112900

Hesse, A. (2018). Digitalization and leadership: How experienced leaders interpret daily realities in a digital world. In *Proceedings of the 51st Hawaii International conference on System Sciences* (pp. 1865-1863). 10.24251/HICSS.2018.234

Hess, T., Matt, C., & Wiesbock, F. (2016). Options for Formulating a Digital Transformation Strategy. *MIS Quarterly Executive, 15*(2), 123–139.

Hiltz, S. R., & Turoff, M. (1978). *The Network Nation Reading*. Addison-Wesley.

Hiltz, S. R., & Turoff, M. (2005). Education goes digital: The evolution of online learning and the revolution in higher education. *Communications of the ACM, 48*(10), 59–64. doi:10.1145/1089107.1089139

Hirsch, J. E. (2005). An index to quantify an individual's scientific research output. *The Proceedings of the National Academy of Sciences (PNAS)*, 16569-16572.

Hoenig, T. M., & Morris, C. S. (2012). *Restructuring the banking system to improve safety and soundness*. Federal Deposit Insurance Corporation and Federal Reserve Bank of Kansas City.

Holbeche, L., & Matthews, G. (2012). Engaged: Unleashing your organization's potential through employee engagement. San Francisco, CA: Jossey-Bass.

Holm, S., Thees, O., Lemm, R., Olschewski, R., & Hilty, L. M. (2018). An agent-based model of wood markets: Scenario analysis. *Forest Policy and Economics, 95*, 26–36. doi:10.1016/j.forpol.2018.07.005

Hong, K. S., & Songan, P. (2011). ICT in the changing landscape of higher education in Southeast Asia. *Australasian Journal of Educational Technology, 27*(8). Advance online publication. doi:10.14742/ajet.893

Horwitz, L. (2019). Autonomous shipping charts new waters on the intelligent edge. *Cisco.* Retrieved from https://www.cisco.com/c/en/us/solutions/internet-of-things/autonomous-shipping.html?dtid=osscdc000283

Hou, W., & Perkowski, M. (2019). *A Novel Machine Learning Algorithm to Reduce Prediction Error and Accelerated Learning Curve for Very Large Datasets.* IEEE. doi:10.1109/ISMVL.2019.00025

Hozdi'c, E. (2015). Smart Factory for Industry 4.0: A Review. *International Journal of Modern Manufacturing Technologies, 7.* 28-35. Avaliable at: https://media.nature.com/full/naturecms/uploads/ckeditor/attachments/8431/InsideView_Display_-_Hitachi_-_Nature_-_Dec_21_2017_-_LH.PDF

Huang, S. M. (2003). Mobile Commerce: The Convergence of E-Commerce and Wireless Technology. *International Journal of Services Technology and Management, 4*(3), 302–322.

Huertas, A., & Fernández, J. (2006). Ciudades en la web: Usabilidad e interactividad de las páginas oficiales de los destinos turísticos. In *VI Congreso Turismo y Tecnologías de la Información y las Comunicaciones Turitec* (pp. 403–421). Málaga: Universidad de Málaga.

Huiru, W., Jinhui, S., Jianying, F., Huiru, F., Zhijian, Z., & Weisong, M. (2018). An agent-based modeling and simulation of consumers' purchase behavior for wine consumption. *IFAC-PapersOnLine, 51*(17), 843–848. doi:10.1016/j.ifacol.2018.08.089

Hussain, F., Hussain, R., Hassan, S. A., & Hossain, E. (2020). *Machine Learning in IoT Security: Current Solutions and Future Challenges.* IEEE. doi:10.1109/COMST.2020.2986444

Iansiti, M., & Lakhani, K. R. (2020). *Competing in the Age of AI. Strategy and Leadership When Algorithms and Networks Run the World.* Harvard Business Review Press.

India has largest diaspora population in world: UN. (2016, January 15). *The Tribune.* https://www.tribuneindia.com/news/nation/india-has-largest-diaspora-population-in-world-un/183731.html

Information and Communication Technology. (n.d.). *Free On-Line Dictionary of Computing.* Retrieved June 10, 2020 from https://foldoc.org/Information+and+Communication+Technology

Institute of Chartered Shipbrokers (ICS). (2007). *Port and Terminal Management.* London: Witherbys Publishing Limited.

International Telecommunication Union (ITU). (2012). *Overview of the Internet of things.* Retrieved from https://handle.itu.int/11.1002/1000/11559

Internet of Business. (n.d.a). Semtech LoRa geolocation helps Irish Port of Cork track shipping assets. *Internet of Business.* Retrieved from https://internetofbusiness.com/semtech-lora-irish-port-cork/

Internet of Business. (n.d.b). Port of Hamburg turns to Internet of Things to track pollution. *Internet of Business.* Retrieved from https://internetofbusiness.com/port-hamburg-IOT-pollution/

Internet World Stats. (2018). *World Internet Users and 2018 Population Stats.* https://www.internetworldstats.com/stats.htm

Ireland, C., & Bowers, D. (2015). *Exposing the Myth: Object-Relational Impedance Mismatch is a Wicked Problem.* http://oro.open.ac.uk/43318/1/download.php_articleid%3Ddbkda_2015_2_10_50020

Islam, S., & Jahan, N. (2018). Digitalization and Education System: A Survey. *International Journal of Computer Science and Information Security, 16*(1).

Ithiri, M. D. (2013). *Corporate restructuring and its effects on Kenya Commercial Bank performance* (Master's Thesis). Kenyatta University, Kenya.

Iwano, K., Yasunori, K., Yosuke, T., & Satoru, B. (Eds.). (2017). Future Services & Societal Systems in Society 5.0. Tokyo: Center for Research and Development Strategy, Japan Science and Technology Agency.

Jacob, B. A., & Ludwig, J. (2010). *The effects of family resources on children's outcomes.* Working Paper. Ann Arbor, MI: University of Michigan.

Jacobs, F. R., & Chase, R. B. (2018). Operations and supply chain management. New York NY: McGraw-Hill/Irwin.

Jacobs, F. R., Berry, W. L., Whybark, D. C., & Vollmann, T. E. (2011). *Manufacturing planning and control for supply chain management.* McGraw Hill Higher Education.

Jain, V., & Kumar, S. (2020). *Sentiment Recognition in Customer Reviews Using Deep Learning.* doi:10.4018/978-1-7998-0414-7.ch077

Jain, E. (2020). Digital Employability Skills and Training Needs for the Indian Healthcare Industry. In *Opportunities and Challenges in Digital Healthcare Innovation* (pp. 113–130). IGI Global. doi:10.4018/978-1-7998-3274-4.ch007

Jain, E., & Madan, M. (2017). An empirical study on acceptance of video on demand services in Indian market. *International Journal of Indian Culture and Business Management, 14*(4), 375–392. doi:10.1504/IJICBM.2017.084353

Jain, E., & Yadav, A. (2017). Marketing and Technology: Role of Technology in Modern Marketing. *IOSR Journal of Business and Management, 19*(5), 49–53. doi:10.9790/487X-1905064953

Jasny, M., Zeigler, T., Kraska, T., Roehm, U., & Binnig, C. (2020). DB4ML - An In-Memory Database Kernel with Machine Learning Support. *Sigmoid ACM Conference.* 10.1145/3318464.3380575

Jeong, Y. K., Song, M., & Ding, Y. (2014). Content -Based Author Co-Citation Analysis. *Journal of Informetrics, 8*(1), 197–211. doi:10.1016/j.joi.2013.12.001

Jewendah, S. (2018). How artificial intelligence is changing the banking sector –a case study of top four Commercial Indian Banks? *International Journal of Management, Technology and Engineering, 8*(7), 525–530.

Jianwei, E., Jimin, Y., & Haihong, J. (2019, May). A novel hybrid model on the prediction of time series and its application for the gold price analysis and forecasting. *Physica A, 527*(1), 1–16.

Jonathan Frome, P. M. (2019). Describing the Game Studies Canon: A Game Citation Analysis. DiGRA, 1-21.

Jones, D., Snider, C., Nassehi, A., Yon, J., & Hicks, B. (2020). Characterising the Digital Twin: A systematic literature review. *CIRP Journal of Manufacturing Science and Technology, 29,* 36–52. doi:10.1016/j.cirpj.2020.02.002

Jun, J., & Yeo, E. (2016). Entry of fintech firms and competition in the retail payments market. *Asia-Pacific Journal of Financial Studies, 45*(2), 159–184. doi:10.1111/ajfs.12126

Kagermann, H., Wahlster, W. & Helbig, J. (2013). *Securing the future of German manufacturing industry - Recommendations for implementing the strategic initiative Industrie 4.0.* Final Report of the Industrie 4.0 Working Group.

Kagermann, H. (2015). Change Through Digitization-Value Creation in the Age of Industry 4.0. In H. Albach, H. Meffert, A. Pinkwart, & R. Reichwald (Eds.), *Management of Permanent Change.* Springer Gabler. doi:10.1007/978-3-658-05014-6_2

Kagochi, J., & Kiambigi, M. (2012). Remittances' influence on housing construction demand in Sub-Saharan Africa: The case of Kenya. *African Development Review, 24*(3), 255–265. doi:10.1111/j.1467-8268.2012.00321.x

Kaminski, J. (2011). Theory applied to informatics – Lewin's Change Theory. *CJNI: Canadian Journal of Nursing Informatics, 6*(1). http://cjni.net/journal/?p=1210

Kane, G. C. (2015). Strategy, Not Technology, Drives Digital Transformation. *MIT Sloan Management Review*, 1–25.

Kang, T. J. (2017). *HMM completes pilot blockchain voyage with reefer-laden boxship*. Retrieved from https://lloydslist.maritimeintelligence.informa.com/LL111275/HMM-completes-pilot-blockchainvoyage-with-reeferladen-boxship

Kanter, R. M., Stein, B., & Jick, T. (1992). *The Challenge of Organizational Change*. The Free Press.

Kaplan, A. M., & Haenlein, M. (2010). Users of the world, unite! The challenges and opportunities of Social Media. *Business Horizons*, *53*(1), 59–68. doi:10.1016/j.bushor.2009.09.003

Kapoor, K., Dwivedi, Y. K., & Williams, M. D. (2013). In Role of Innovation Attributes in Explaining Intention and Adoption: A Case of the IRCTC Mobile Ticketing Application in the Indian Context. *UK Academy for Information Systems Conference Proceedings*.

Kapoor, V. (2010). Employer Branding : A Study of Its Relevance in India. *IUP Journal Of Brand Management*, *7*(1/2), 51–75.

Karnitis, G., & Arnicans, G. (2015). Migration of Relational Database to Document-Oriented Database: Structure Denormalization and Data Transformation. *2015 7th International Conference on Computational Intelligence, Communication Systems and Networks*, 113–118. 10.1109/CICSyN.2015.30

Kasapoğlu, Ö. A., & Tayalı, H. A. (2012). Transformation of Job Shop to Flow Shop in an Era of Global Crises. *Proceedings of the 10th International Logistics & Supply Chain Congress*, 112–116. Retrieved from https://papers.ssrn.com/sol3/papers.cfm?abstract_id=2919847

Kashive, N., Khanna, V. T., & Bharthi, M. N. (2020). Employer branding through crowdsourcing: Understanding the sentiments of employees. *Journal of Indian Business Research*, *12*(1), 93–111. doi:10.1108/JIBR-09-2019-0276

Kashmari, A., Nejad, A. H. G., & Nayebyazdi, A. (2016). Impact of electronic banking innovations on bank deposit market share. *Journal of International Bank Commerce*, *12*(1), 1–12.

Kats, R. (2017). *Mobile Commerce Daily*. Academic Press.

Kauffman, R., Liu, J., & Ma, D. (2015). Competition, cooperation and regulation: Understanding the evolution of the mobile payments technology ecosystem. *Electronic Commerce Research and Applications*, *14*(5), 372–391. doi:10.1016/j.elerap.2015.03.003

Kaufman, I., & Horton, C. (2015). *Digital marketing: integrating strategy and tactics with values*. Routledge Taylor & Francis Group.

Kaur, R., & Singh, S. (2016). Mobile Commerce: Indian Perspectives. *International Journal of Innovative Research in Computer and Communication Engineering, 4*.

Kaur, H., & Bath, A. K. (2019). Digital transformation strategies in different areas: A review. *International Journal of Scientific and Technology Research*, *8*(12), 348–351.

Kaur, N., Sahdev, M. S. L., Sharma, M., & Siddiqui, L. (2020). Banking 4.0: The influence of artificial intelligence on the banking industry & how AI is changing the face of modern day bank. *International Journal of Management*, *11*(6), 577–585. doi:10.34218/IJM.11.6.2020.049

Kaur, R., & Malhotra, H. (2016). *Securing Transactions and Payment Systems for M-Commerce*. IGI Global Publishing.

Keen, P. G., & Mackintosh, R. (2001). *The Freedom Economy: Gaining the M-Commerce Edge in the Era of the Wireless Internet*. McGraw-Hill Professional.

Keidanren (Japan Business Federation). (2016). *Toward realization of the new economy and society. Reform of the economy and society by the deepening of "Society 5.0"*. http://www.keidanren.or.jp/en/policy/2016/029_outline.pdf

Kevin, W., & Boyack, H. S. (2010). Co-Citation Analysis, Bibliographic Coupling, and Direct Citation: Which Citation Approach Represents The Research Front Most Accurately? *Journal of the American Society for Information Science and Technology*, 2389–2404.

Kevin, W., & Boyack, H. S. (2013). Improving the Accuracy of Co-Citation Clustering Using Full Text. *Journal of the American Society for Information Science and Technology*, 155–165.

Khan, S. (2009). *Adoption issues of internet banking in Pakistani' firms* (Unpublished Master Thesis). Lulea University of Technology, Lulea.

Khokhar, F. (2016). *E-Commerce challenges: The Story of Online Groceries*. Academic Press.

Kim, D., & Adler, H. (2011). *Student's use of hotel mobile Apps: Their effect of brand loyalty*. Retrieved from: http://scholarworks.umass.edu/cgi/viewcontent.cgi?article1/41242&contex t1/4gradconf hospitality

Kirkpatrick, L. A., & Brooke, C. F. (2010). *A simple guide to SPSS for version 17*. John- David Hague.

Kishtainy, N. (Ed.). (2018). *The Economics Book: Big Ideas Simply Explained*. Dorling Kindersley.

Kissel, P., & Büttgen, M. (2015). Using social media to communicate employer brand identity: The impact on corporate image and employer attractiveness. *Journal of Brand Management*, *22*(9), 755–777. doi:10.1057/bm.2015.42

Kithinji, A. K., Mwangi, M., Litondo, K., & Ogutu, M. (2017). Bank restructuring and financial performance. *International Journal of Economics. Commerce and Management*, *5*(10), 84–98.

Knox, S., & Freeman, C. (2006). Measuring and Managing Employer Brand Image in the Service Industry. *Journal of Marketing Management*, *22*(7–8), 695–716. doi:10.1362/026725706778612103

Kocianski, S. (2017). The Open Banking Report: How banks can leverage open APIs and maintain their retail banking dominance. *Business Insider*. Retrieved from https://www.businessinsider.com/open-banking-report-2017-4

Köseoğlu, M. C., & Solmaz, M. S. (2019). *Green Port Approach: A Comparative Assessment Criterion of Turkey and the World Green Port*. doi:10.18872/0.2019.2

Kotarba, M. (2018). Digital transformation of business. *Foundations of Management*, *10*(1), 123–142. doi:10.2478/fman-2018-0011

Kourouthanassis, P. E., & Giaglis, G. (2012). Introduction to the Special Issue Mobile Commerce: The Past, Present, and Future of Mobile Commerce Research. *International Journal of Electronic Commerce*, *16*(4), 5–18.

Krishna, G. J., & Ravi, V. (2016). Evolutionary computing applied to customer relationship management: A survey. *Engineering Applications of Artificial Intelligence*, *56*, 30–59. doi:10.1016/j.engappai.2016.08.012

Krishnamurthy, S. (2020). The Future of Business Education: A Commentary in the Shadow of the Covid-19 Pandemic. *Journal of Business Research*, *117*, 1–5. doi:10.1016/j.jbusres.2020.05.034 PMID:32501309

Kshetri, N. (2017). Can Blockchain Strengthen the Internet of Things? *IT Professional*, *19*(4), 68–72. doi:10.1109/MITP.2017.3051335

Kubina, M., & Lendel, V. (2015). Successful application of Social CRM in the Company. *Procedia Economics and Finance*, *23*, 1190–1194. doi:10.1016/S2212-5671(15)00487-6

Kumar, S. (2017). Not Just for Crypto- cash: How Blockchain Tech Could Help Secure IOT. *IOT Agenda*. Retrieved from https://internetofthingsagenda.techtarget.com/blog/IOT-Agenda/Not-just-for-cryptocash-How-blockchain-tech-could-help-secure-IOT

Kumar, B. (2020). Secure Data Communication with Cryptography and Steganography. *International Journal of Electrical Engineering and Technology*, *11*(3), 164–172.

Kuoppamäki, S. M., Wilska, T. A., & Taipale, S. (2017). Ageing and consumption in Finland: The effect of age and life course stage on ecological, economical, and self-indulgent consumption among late middle-agers and young adults between 1999 and 2014. *International Journal of Consumer Studies*, *41*(5), 457–464. doi:10.1111/ijcs.12353

Kyaw, N. Y. (2020). Next Generation of E-Commerce's Impacts on Myanmar Business Era. *International Journal of Scientific and Research Publications*, *10*(05), 690–699. doi:10.29322/IJSRP.10.05.2020.p10179

Lamba, J., & Jain, E. (2020). Covid-19 Pandemic–Bountiful for MSMES and Indian Economy. *Purakala Journal*, *31*(33), 89–94.

Larivière, B., Bowen, D., Andreassen, T. W., Kunz, W., Sirianni, N. J., & Vossf, C. (2017). Service encounter 2.0: An investigation into the roles of technology, employees and customers. *Journal of Business Research*, *79*, 238–246. doi:10.1016/j.jbusres.2017.03.008

Lasi, H., Fettke, P., Kemper, H. G., Feld, T., & Hoffmann, M. (2014). Industry 4.0. *Business and Information Systems Engineering*, *6*(4), 239–242.

Laudon, K. C., & Traver, C. G. (2001). *E-commerce: Business, technology, society*. Addison-Wesley.

Laudon, K., & Traver, C. (2006). *E-Commerce Essentials*. Pearson Publication.

Laukkanen, T., & Kiviniemi, V. (2010). The role of information in mobile banking resistance. *International Journal of Bank Marketing*, *28*(5), 372–388. doi:10.1108/02652321011064890

Leberecht, T. (2012). *Shaping the values of our connected world*. Retrieved from https://www.weforum.org/agenda/2012/11/shaping-the-values-of-our-connected-world

Ledford, J. L. (2009). *Search engine optimization bible*. John Wiley & Sons.

Leshob, A., Bourgouin, A., & Renard, L. (2018). *Towards a Process Analysis Approach to Adopt Robotic Process Automation*. IEEE. doi:10.1109/ICEBE.2018.00018

Lewin, K. (1947a). Frontiers in group dynamics. In D. Cartwright (Ed.), *Field Theory in Social Science*. Social Science Paperbacks.

Lewin, K. (1947b). Group decisions and social change. In T. M. Newcomb & E. L. Hartley (Eds.), *Readings in Social Psychology*. Henry Holt.

Lexis Nexis. (2016). *True Cost of Fraud Study*. Annual Report.

Lichtenstein, B. B. (2000). Self-organized transitions: A pattern amid the chaos of transformative change. *The Academy of Management Executive*, *14*(4), 128–141. doi:10.5465/ame.2000.3979821

Lievens, F., & Slaughter, J. E. (2016). Employer Image and Employer Branding: What We Know and What We Need to Know. *Annual Review of Organizational Psychology and Organizational Behavior*, *3*(1), 407–440. doi:10.1146/annurev-orgpsych-041015-062501

Li, F. (2018). The digital transformation of business models in the creative industries: A holistic framework and emerging trends. *Technovation*. Advance online publication. doi:10.1016/j.technovation.2017.12.004

Lin, K., Shyu, J., & Ding, K. (2017). A Cross-Strait Comparison of Innovation Policy under Industry 4.0 and Sustainability Development Transition. *Sustainability*, *9*(5), 786. doi:10.3390u9050786

Linnainmaa, J. T., Melzer, B., & Previtero, A. (2018). *The Misguided Beliefs of Financial Advisors.* Kelley School of Business Research Paper, No. 18-9.

Lissaneddine, Z. (2019). *Management de la marque employeur via les réseaux sociaux numériques : Cas des centres de la relation client au Maroc.* Cadi Ayyad University.

Liu, B., Guo, W., Niu, D., Luo, J., Wang, C., Wen, Z., & Xu, Y. (2020). GIANT: Scalable Creation of a Web-scale Ontology. *Proceedings of the ACM.* 10.1145/3318464.3386145

Liu, C., Feng, Y., Lin, D., Wu, L., & Guo, M. (2020). *Iot based laundry services: an application of big data analytics, intelligent logistics management, and machine learning techniques.* International Journal of Production. doi:10.1080/00207543.2019.1677961

Liu, Z., Chen, W., Zhang, C., Yang, C., & Cheng, Q. (2020). Intelligent scheduling of a feature-process-machine tool supernetwork based on digital twin workshop. *Journal of Manufacturing Systems.* Advance online publication. doi:10.1016/j.jmsy.2020.07.016

Li, Y. M., & Yeh, Y. S. (2010). *Increasing trust in mobile commerce through design aesthetics.* Computer Human Behaviour.

Lloyd, S. (2002). Branding from the inside out. *Business Review Weekly, 24*(10), 64–66.

Lochner, L. (2011). *Non-production benefits of education: Crime, health, and good citizenship.* NBER Working Paper 16722. Cambridge, MA: National Bureau of Economic Research.

Lochner, L. (2004). Education, work, and crime: A human capital approach. *International Economic Review, 45*(3), 811–843. doi:10.1111/j.0020-6598.2004.00288.x

Lockard, C., Shiralkar, P., Dong, X., & Hajishirzi, H. (2020). Web-scale Knowledge Collection. *Proceedings of the 13th International Conference on Web Search and Data Mining.* 10.1145/3336191.3371878

Loftus, A. (2019). How Industrial IOT will Disrupt the Shipping Industry. *IOT Evolution.* Retrieved from https://www.IOTevolutionworld.com/smart-transport/articles/442702-how-industrial-IOT-will-disrupt-shipping-industry.htm

Lourenço, C. J. S., Dellaert, B. G. C., & Donkers, B. (2020). Whose Algorithm Says So: The Relationships Between Typeof Firm, Perceptions of Trust and Expertise, and the Acceptance of Financial Robo-Advice. *Journal of Interactive Marketing, 49*, 107–124. doi:10.1016/j.intmar.2019.10.003

Lui, A., & Lamb, G. W. (2018). Artificial intelligence and augmented intelligence collaboration: Regaining trust and confidence in the financial sector. *Information & Communications Technology Law, 27*(3), 267–283. doi:10.1080/13600834.2018.1488659

Lukango, I. (2018). *Fintech, Inclusive Growth and Cyber Risks: A Focus on the MENAP and CCA Region.* IMF Working Paper. Retrieved from https://www.imf.org/~/media/Files/Publications/WP/2018/wp18201.ashx

Luo, X., Tong, S., Fang, Z., & Qu, Z. (2019). Frontiers: Machines vs. Humans: The Impact of Artificial Intelligence Chatbot Disclosure on Customer Purchases. *Marketing Science, 38*(6), 937–947. doi:10.1287/mksc.2019.1192

Lu, Y., Liu, C., Wang, K. I. K., Huang, H., & Xu, X. (2020, February 1). Digital Twin-driven smart manufacturing: Connotation, reference model, applications and research issues. *Robotics and Computer-integrated Manufacturing, 61*, 101837. doi:10.1016/j.rcim.2019.101837

Machekhina, O. N. (2017). Digitalization of education as a trend of its modernization and reforming. *Revista Espacios, 38*(40).

MacKnight. (2017). *Banks say social media is important – but how many are engaging?* The Banker. Retrieved from https://www.thebanker.com/Transactions-Technology/Banks-say-social-media-is-important-but-how-many-are-engaging?ct=true

Madden, G., Banerjee, A., Rappoport, P. N., & Suenaga, H. (2017). E-Commerce Transactions, the Installed Base of Credit Cards, and the Potential Mobile E-Commerce Adoption. *Applied Economics.*

Makanyeza, C., & Makuwaza, P. (2015). *The adoption of electronic banking technology: Challenges and opportunities in Zimbabwe's banking sector.* Paper presented at International Research Conference on Research, Technology and Innovation for Development in Africa, Chinhoyi University of Technology, Zimbabwe.

Malar, D. A., Arvidsson, V., & Holmstrom, J. (2019). Digital Transformation in Banking: Exploring Value Co-Creation in Online Banking Services in India. *Journal of Global Information Technology Management, 22*(1), 7–24. doi:10.1080/1097198X.2019.1567216

Maldonado, S. (2015). *Analítica web: Medir para triunfar.* ESIC.

Manda, M. I., & Backhouse, J. (2018). Inclusive digital transformation in South Africa: an institutional perspective. In *Proceedings of the 11th International Conference on Theory and Practice of Electronic Governance* (pp. 464-470). 10.1145/3209415.3209486

Mangold, W. G., & Miles, S. J. (2007). The employee brand: Is yours an all-star? *Business Horizons, 50*(5), 423–433. doi:10.1016/j.bushor.2007.06.001

Manhas, P. S., Manrai, L. A., & Manrai, A. K. (2016). Role of tourist destination development in building its brand image: A conceptual model. *Journal of Economics, Finance and Administrative Science, 21*(40), 25–29. doi:10.1016/j.jefas.2016.01.001

Manjula, K. A., & Karthikeyan, P. (2019). Gold Price Prediction using Ensemble based Machine Learning Techniques. *Proceedings of the Third International Conference on Trends in Electronics and Informatics.* 10.1109/ICOEI.2019.8862557

Marakarkandy, B., Yajnik, N., & Dasgupta, C. (2017). Enabling internet banking adoption: An empirical examination with an augmented technology acceptance model (TAM). *Journal of Enterprise Information Management, 30*(2), 263–294. doi:10.1108/JEIM-10-2015-0094

Marathe, S. (2018). Digitalization in education sector. *International Journal of Trend in Scientific Research and Development,* 51-56.

Marcum, D. (2014). The digital transformation of information, education, and scholarship. *International Journal of Humanities and Arts Computing, 8*(supplement), 1–11. doi:10.3366/ijhac.2014.0095

Marimuthu, M., & Roseline, A. (2020). A study on Consumer Perception Towards e-wallet. *Our Heritage, 68*(17), 283–288.

Marler, J. H., & Fisher, S. L. (2013). An evidence-based review of e-HRM and strategic human resource management. *Human Resource Management Review, 23*(1), 18–36. doi:10.1016/j.hrmr.2012.06.002

Martinez, F. (2019). Process excellence the key for digitalisation. *Business Process Management Journal, 25*(7), 1716–1733. doi:10.1108/BPMJ-08-2018-0237

Martinis, A., Papadatou, A., & Kabassi, K. (2019). An analysis of the electronic presence of national parks in Greece. In V. Katsoni & M. Segarra-Oña (Eds.), *Smart Tourism as a Driver for Culture and Sustainability* (pp. 433–449). Springer. doi:10.1007/978-3-030-03910-3_30

Martin, J. (1978). *The wired society*. Prentice-Hall.

Martins, P., Sá, F., Morgado, F., & Cunha, C. (2020). *Using machine learning for cognitive Robotic Process Automation (RPA)*. IEEE. doi:10.23919/CISTI49556.2020.9140440

Masashi, K. Y. (2018). Citation Recommendation Using Distributed Representation of Discourse Facets in Scientific Articles Share on. In *Proceedings of the 18th ACM/IEEE on Joint Conference on Digital Libraries*, (pp. 243-251). Academic Press.

Mastercard. (2020). *Mobil ve Dijital Çözümler*. Retrieved from https://www.mastercard.com.tr/tr-tr/issuers/products-and-solutions/digital-commerce-solutions.html

Maswaure, F., & Choga, F. (2016). Electronic banking uptake in Zimbabwe. *Journal of Business and Management*, *18*(4), 80–82.

Matt, C., Hess, T., & Benlian, A. (2015). Digital transformation strategies. *Business & Information Systems Engineering*, *5*(57), 339–343. doi:10.100712599-015-0401-5

Mavaza, T. (2019). E-banking adoption by Zimbabwe banks: An exploratory study. *PM World Journal*, *8*(11), 1–10.

Mavhiki, S., Nyamwanza, T., & Shumba, L. (2015). Impact of mobile banking on traditional banking practices in Zimbabwe. *International Journal of Economics. Commerce and Management*, *3*(1), 1–13.

McAteer, I., Ibrahim, A., Zheng, G., Yang, W., & Valli, C. (2019). Integration of Biometrics and Steganography: A Comprehensive Review. *Technologies*, *7*(34), 1–22. doi:10.3390/technologies7020034

McCain, K. W. (1990). Mapping authors in intellectual space: A technical overview. *Journal of the American Society for Information Science*, *41*(6), 433–443. doi:10.1002/(SICI)1097-4571(199009)41:6<433::AID-ASI11>3.0.CO;2-Q

McCartney, G., Butler, R., & Bennett, M. (2008). A strategic use of the communication mix in the destination image-formation process. *Journal of Travel Research*, *47*(2), 183–196. doi:10.1177/0047287508321201

McFarland, L. A., & Ployhart, R. E. (2015). Social media: A contextual framework to guide research and practice. *The Journal of Applied Psychology*, *100*(6), 1653–1677. doi:10.1037/a0039244 PMID:26052712

McKinsey & Company. (2015). *Manufacturing's next act: Industry 4.0 is more than just a flashy catchphrase. A confluence of trends and technologies promises to reshape the way things are made*. Available at: https://www.mckinsey.com/~/media/McKinsey/Business%20Functions/Operations/Our%20Insights/Manufacturings%20next%20act/Manufacturings%20next%20act.ashx

Megargel, A., Shankararaman, V., & Reddy, S. K. (2018). Real-Time Inbound Marketing: A Use Case for Digital Banking. In Handbook of Blockchain, Digital Finance, and Inclusion, Volume 1 (pp. 311–328). doi:10.1016/B978-0-12-810441-5.00013-0

Mendeley. (2020). Retrieved from Elsevier: https://www.mendeley.com/homepage-2-1?interaction_required=true&adobe_mc_sdid=SDID%3D66587ECF3B1E404B-1A7F944D87B75458%7CMCORGID%3D4D6368F454EC41940A4C98A6%40AdobeOrg%7CTS%3D1602154074

Merriam Webster Dictionary. (2020). *Remittance*. Retrieved June 10, 2020 from https://www.merriam-webster.com/dictionary/remittance

Mhlanga, K. (2019). *ZB embarks on $20 Million I.T boost programme*. Retrieved May 29, 2020, from https://www.eyetrodigital.com/2019/05/08/zb-embarks-on-20-million-i-t-boost-programme/

Mhlanga, D., & Moloi, T. (2020). COVID-19 and the Digital Transformation of Education: What Are We Learning on 4IR in South Africa? *Education in Science*, *10*(7), 180.

Mičík, M., & Mičudová, K. (2018). Employer Brand Building: Using Social Media and Career Websites to Attract Generation Y. *Economia e Sociologia*, *11*(3), 171–189.

Miles, M. B., Huberman, A. M., & Saldana, J. (2014). Qualitative Data Analysis: A Methods Sourcebook. In The SAGE Handbook of Applied Social Research Methods. SAGE.

Moreno, M. (2015). *Cómo triunfar en las redes sociales*. Ediciones Gestión.

Moroko, L., & Uncles, M. D. (2008). Characteristics of successful employer brands. *Journal of Brand Management*, *16*(3), 160–175. doi:10.1057/bm.2008.4

Morrar, R., Arman, H., & Mousa, S. (2017). The Fourth Industrial Revolution (Industry 4.0): A Social Innovation Perspective. *Technology Innovation Management Review*, *7*(11), 12–20. doi:10.22215/timreview/1117

Mosley, R. (2014). *Employer brand management : Practical lessons from the world's leading employers*. Wiley.

Mu. (2003). Constructing a Patent Citation Map Using Bibliographic Coupling: A Study of Taiwan's High-Tech Companies. *Scientometrics*, 489–506.

Mueller, B., & Renken, U. (2017). Helping employees to be digital transformers: The Olympus connect case. In *Proceedings of ICIS 2017* (pp. 1–19). Academic Press.

Munro, M. (2018). The complicity of digital technologies in the marketization of UK higher education: Exploring the implications of a critical discourse analysis of thirteen national digital teaching and learning strategies. *International Journal of Educational Technology in Higher Education*, *15*(1), 11. doi:10.118641239-018-0093-2

Musa, M. S. (2014). Customers' adoption of electronic banking: An investigation on the commercial banking industry in Zimbabwe. *International Journal of Economics, Commerce and Management*, *2*(7), 1–13.

Musavi, S. A., & Hashemi, M. R. (2018). *A Method for Ontology-based Architecture Reconstruction of Computing Platforms*. ArXiv Preprint ArXiv:1811.02748.

Nakanishi, H. (2019). Modern society has reached its limits. Society 5.0 will liberate us. *World Economic Forum Annual Meeting*. https://www.weforum.org/agenda/2019/01/modern-society-has-reached-its-limits-society-5-0-will-liberate-us/

Nambisan, S. (2017). Digital entrepreneurship: Toward a digital technology perspective of entrepreneurship. *Entrepreneurship Theory and Practice*, *41*(6), 1029–1055. doi:10.1111/etap.12254

Nassaji, H. (2015). Qualitative and descriptive research: Data type versus data analysis. *Language Teaching Research*, *19*(2), 129–132. doi:10.1177/1362168815572747

Nave, D. (2002). How to compare six sigma, lean and the theory of constraints. *Toc-Cga.Org*, *35*(3), 73–80. Retrieved from http://www.toc-cga.org/upload/reference/3.pdf

Ndlovu, I., & Siyavora, A. (2014). Impact of internet banking on the Zimbabwean banking sector an application of the multinomial logit modelling. *International Journal of Economics, Commerce and Management*, *2*(8), 1–17.

Neaman, R. (2017). *Empowerment is the key to a connected society*. Retrieved from: https://www.computerweekly.com/opinion/Empowerment-is-the-key-to-a-connected-society

Neelam. (2020). *Mobile Commerce - Its Advantages, Limitations, Future, Case study*. Retrieved from www.geocities.ws/neelam21582

New York. (2020). *Global Interior Car Accessories Industry*. Globe Newswire Report. Retrieved from https://www.reportlinker.com/p05899775/

Nguyen, Q. C., Næs, T., Almøy, T., & Varela, P. (2018). Portion size selection as related to product and consumer characteristics studied by PLS path modelling. *Food Quality and Preference*, *79*, 1–10.

Nicoletta, R., & Servidio, R. (2012). Tourists' opinions and their selection of tourism destination images: An affective and motivational evaluation. *Tourism Management Perspectives*, *4*, 19–27. doi:10.1016/j.tmp.2012.04.004

Nicoletti, B. (2014). *Mobile Banking, Evolution or Revolution?* Palgrave McMillian.

Nielsen. (2016). *Securing Transactions and Payment Systems for M-Commerce*. IGI Global.

Nielson. (2016). *The Science Behind What Will Happen Next*. Annual Report.

Niranjanamurthy, M., Kavyashree, N., Jagannath, S., & Chahar, D. (2013). Analysis of E-Commerce and M-Commerce: Advantages, Limitations and Security Issues. *International Journal of Advanced Research in Computer and Communication Engineering*, 2360–2370.

Noble, D. F. (1998). Digital diploma mills: The automation of higher education. *Science as Culture*, *7*(3), 355–368. doi:10.1080/09505439809526510

Norfazlina, G., Akma, A. S. S., Adrina, S. N., & Noorizan, M. M. (2016). Customer information system satisfaction and task productivity: The moderating effect of training. *Procedia Economics and Finance*, *37*, 7–12. doi:10.1016/S2212-5671(16)30085-5

Noruzi, A. (2016). *Impact Factor, h-index, i10-index and i20-index of Webology*. Webology.

NPD. (2020). *Distribution of retail website visits and orders worldwide as of 1st quarter, by device*. Press Release by Dublin/PRNewswire.

Nyoka, C. (2015). Banks and the fallacy of supervision: The case for Zimbabwe. *Banks and Bank Systems*, *10*(3), 8–17.

O'Neil, E. J. (2008). Object/relational mapping 2008: Hibernate and the entity data model (edm). *Proceedings of the 2008 ACM SIGMOD International Conference on Management of Data*, 1351–1356. 10.1145/1376616.1376773

Obukhova, A., Merzlyakova, E., Irina, E., & Karakulina, K. (2020). *Introduction of digital technologies in the enterprise*. IEEE. https://ui.adsabs.harvard.edu/abs/2020E3SWC.15904004O/abstract

Ojelabi, R. A., Afolabi, A. O., Oyeyipo, O. O., Tunji-Olayeni, P. F., & Adewale, B. A. (2018). Data exploration of social client relationship management (CRM 2.0) adoption in the Nigerian construction business. *Data in Brief*, *18*, 1471–1476. doi:10.1016/j.dib.2018.04.037 PMID:29900328

Olifrov, A., Makoveichuk, K., Zhytnyy, P., Filimonenkova, P., & Petrenk, S. (2018). *Models of process for governance of enterprise IT and personal training for digital Economy*. IEEE. doi:10.1109/PTES.2018.8604166

Oliveira, B., & Casais, B. (2019). The importance of user-generated photos in restaurant selection. *Journal of Hospitality and Tourism Technology*, *10*(1), 2–14. doi:10.1108/JHTT-11-2017-0130

OMG.org. (2016, October). *MetaObject Facility*. https://www.omg.org/spec/MOF

OMG.org. (2017, December). *About the Unified Modeling Language Specification Version 2.5.1*. https://www.omg.org/spec/UML/

OMG.org. (2019, December). *About the Semantics Of Business Vocabulary And Rules Specification Version 1.5.* https://www.omg.org/spec/SBVR/

Onday, O. (2019). Japan's Society 5.0: Going Beyond Industry 4.0. *Bus. Econ. J., 10*(2), 2–7. doi:10.4172/2151-6219.1000389

Orense, M., & Rojas, O. (2010). *SEO Cómo triunfar en buscadores.* ESIC.

Osmundsen, K., Iden, J., & Bendik, B. (2018). *Digital transformation: Drivers, success factors, and implications*, Paper presented at the 12th Mediterranean Conference on Information Systems (MCIS), Corfu, Greece.

Otken, A. B., & Okan, E. Y. (2016). The Role of Social Media in Employer Branding. In Entrepreneurship, Business and Economics (Vol. 13/1, pp. 245–260). doi:10.1007/978-3-319-27570-3_20

Otto, A., & Li, X. (2020). Product sequencing in multiple-piece-flow assembly lines. *Omega (United Kingdom), 91*, 102055. doi:10.1016/j.omega.2019.03.013

OttoBib. (2020). Retrieved from OttoBib: https://www.ottobib.com/

Overby, S. (2020). *What is digital transformation?* https://enterprisersproject.com/what-is-digital-transformation

Overseas Pakistanis remit $7.4 billion in first four months of FY19. (2018, November 9). *The News.* https://www.thenews.com.pk/latest/391754-overseas-pakistanis-remit-74-billion-in-first-four-months-of-fy19

Panel, I. L. (2002). Digital transformation: A framework for ICT literacy. Educational Testing Service, 1-53.

Panneerselvam, M. K. (2013). Mobile Commerce – A Mode of Modern Business. *Asia Pacific Journal of Marketing & Management Review, 2*(7), 141–149.

Panori, A., Kakderi, C., Komninos, N., Fellnhofer, K., Reid, A., & Mora, L. (2020). Smart systems of innovation for smart places: Challenges in deploying digital platforms for co-creation and data-intelligence. *Land Use Policy*, 104631. doi:10.1016/j.landusepol.2020.104631

Papamarkos, G., Zamboulis, L., & Poulovassilis, A. (2015). *Xml Databases.* School of Computer Science and Information Systems, Birkbeck College, University of London. http://www.dcs.bbk.ac.uk/~sven/adm08/xmlDBs.pdf

Park, S. B., Ok, C. M., & Chae, B. K. (2016). Using Twitter data for cruise tourism marketing and research. *Journal of Travel & Tourism Marketing, 33*(6), 885–898. doi:10.1080/10548408.2015.1071688

Pavel, C., & Vlad, F. (2016). Trends in the Evolution of Mobile Commerce. *Quaestus, 8*, 38.

Pelosi, M. J., Poudel, N., Lamichhane, P., & Soomro, D. B. (2018). Steganography System with Application to Crypto-Currency Cold Storage and Secure Transfer, Advances in Science. *Technology and Engineering Systems Journal, 3*(2), 271–282. doi:10.25046/aj030232

Permana, Tulus, & Situmorang. (2019). Combination of One Time Pad Cryptography Algorithm with Generate Random Keys and Vigenere Cipher with EM2B Key. *ICMASES.* doi:10.4108/eai.3-8-2019.2290723

Persaud, A., & Azhar, I. (2012). Innovative mobile marketing via smartphones. *Marketing Intelligence & Planning, 30*(4).

Peters, T., & Waterman, R. H. (1982). *In search of excellence: Lessons from America's best run companies.* Harper & Row.

Pettigrew, A. M. (1973). *The politics of organizational decision making.* Tavis-took.

Phan, D. D., & Douglas, R. V. (2010). A model of customer relationship management and business intelligence systems for catalogue and online retailers. *Information & Management, 47*(2), 69–77. doi:10.1016/j.im.2009.09.001

Piccoli, G., Lui, T. W., & Grün, B. (2017). The impact of IT-enabled customer service systems on service personalization, customer service perceptions, & hotel performance. *Tourism Management, 59*, 349–362. doi:10.1016/j.tourman.2016.08.015

Pidaparthy, U. (2011). *How colleges use, misuse social media to reach students.* CNN Tech.

Pierre, X., & Tremblay, D.-G. (2012). Améliorer l'implication et la rétention des agents dans les centres d'appels: Agir sur les pratiques de gestion. *Recherches En Sciences de Gestion, 91*(4), 17. doi:10.3917/resg.091.0017

Pikkarainen, T., Pikkarainen, K., Karjaluoto, H., & Pahnila, S. (2004). Consumer acceptance of online banking: An extension of the technology acceptance model. *Internet Research, 14*(3), 224–235. doi:10.1108/10662240410542652

Platt, D., & Gebbie, T. (2018). Can agent-based models probe market microstructure? *Physica A, 503*, 1092–1106. doi:10.1016/j.physa.2018.08.055

Poduval, V., Koul, A., Rebello, D., Bhat, K., & Wahul, R. M. (2020). Cloud based Secure Storage of files using Hybrid Cryptography and Image Steganography. *International Journal of Recent Technology and Engineering, 8*(6), 665–667. doi:10.35940/ijrte.F7227.038620

Polikarpova, E. V., Shipelik, O. V., & Krylova, I. V. (2020, May). Digitalization of Education: Save the Human. In *International Scientific Conference "Digitalization of Education: History, Trends and Prospects" (DETP 2020)* (pp. 652-658). Atlantis Press.

Popomaronis, T. (2016). Think Great Innovation Drives Mobile Commerce? It's Actually This. *Forbes.*

Port of Amsterdam. (2016). A mooring pile that tells you how it's doing. *Port of Amsterdam News.* Retrieved from https://www.portofamsterdam.com/en/news-item/mooring-pile-tells-you-how-its-doing

Port of Rotterdam. (2018). The port is getting smarter and smarter. *Port of Rotterdam News.* Retrieved from https://www.portofrotterdam.com/en/news-and-press-releases/the-port-is-getting-smarter-and-smarter

Port of Rotterdam. (2019). How Rotterdam is using blockchain to reinvent global trade. *Port of Rotterdam News.* Retrieved from https://www.portofrotterdam.com/en/news-and-press-releases/how-rotterdam-is-using-blockchain-to-reinvent-global-trade

Port of San Diego. (n.d.). On Track to Meet 2020 Goal. *Port of San Diego What we do.* Retrieved from https://www.portofsandiego.org/environment/energy-sustainability/climate-action-plan

Porter, S. (2020). A Citation Analysis of the Woodrow Wilson School Master's Students Research Output. *Collection Management*, 1–5. doi:10.1080/01462679.2020.1742835

Postal and Telecommunications Regulatory Authority of Zimbabwe. (2019). *Abridged postal and telecommunications sector performance report third quarter 2019.* http://www.potraz.gov.zw/wp-content/uploads/2019/12/Abridged-Sector-Performance-report-3rd-Q-2019-hmed-final.pdf

Pozza, I. D., Goetz, O., & Sahut, J. M. (2018). Implementation effects in the relationship between CRM & its performance. *Journal of Business Research, 89*, 391–403. doi:10.1016/j.jbusres.2018.02.004

Pradeep, H. G., Niranjanamurthy, M., Amulya, M. P., & Dayananda, P. (2020). Coronavirus – COVID-19 before and after solution through web application and App. *International Journal of Advanced Science and Technology, 29*(5s), 27–41.

Pramanik, S., & Bandyopadhyay, S. K. (2019). Image Steganography Using Wavelet Transform and Genetic Algorithm. *International Journal of Innovative Research in Advanced Engineering, 1*, 1-4.

Pramanik, S., Bandyopadhyay, S. K., & Ghosh, R. (2020). Signature Image Hiding in Color Image using Steganography and Cryptography based on Digital Signature Concepts. *2020 2nd International Conference on Innovative Mechanisms for Industry Applications (ICIMIA)*, 665-669.

Pramanik, S., Singh, R.P., & Ghosh, R. (2019). A New Encrypted Method in Image Steganography. *Indonesian Journal of Electrical Engineering and Computer Science, 14*(3), 1412–1419. .v13.i3 doi:10.11591/ijeecs

Pramanik, S., & Bandyopadhyay, S. K. (2014). Hiding Secret Message in an Image, - International Journal of Innovative Science. *Engineering & Technology, 1*(3), 553–559.

Pramanik, S., & Raja, S. S. (2020). A Secured Image Steganography using Genetic Algorithm. *Advances in Mathematics: Scientific Journal, 9*(7), 4533–4541.

Pramanik, S., & Singh, R. P. (2017). Role of Steganography in Security Issues. *International Conference on Advance Studies in Engineering and Sciences*, 1225-1230.

Pramanik, S., Singh, R. P., & Ghosh, R. (2020). *Application of bi-orthogonal wavelet transform and genetic algorithm in image steganography*. Multimed Tools Appl. doi:10.100711042-020-08676-1

Prasetyo, Y. A., & Arman, A. A. (2017). Group management system design for supporting society 5.0 in smart society platform. *2017 International Conference on Information Technology Systems and Innovation (ICITSI)*, 398-404. doi:10.1109/icitsi.2017.8267977

Prime Minister Japan and his Cabinet. (2017). *Prime Minister Shinzo Abe at CeBIT Welcome Night*. Avaliable at:http://japan.kantei.go.jp/97_abe/statement/201703/1221682_11573.html

PubMed. (2020). Retrieved from National Library of Medicine: https://pubmed.ncbi.nlm.nih.gov/

Quaratino, L., & Mazzei, A. (2018). Managerial strategies to promote employee brand consistent behavior. *EuroMed Journal of Business, 13*(2), 185–200. doi:10.1108/EMJB-02-2017-0008

Ragalutu, H., Ibrahim, N., & Madokala, M. (2019). Existence and role of character education in the middle of digitalization of education 4.0. *Science Proceedings Series, 1*(2), 140–143. doi:10.31580ps.v1i2.802

Rainie, H., & Wellman, B. (2012). *Networked: The new social operating system* (Vol. 419). MIT Press. doi:10.7551/mitpress/8358.001.0001

Raj, A., & Reshma, M. (2020). Impact of Digitalisation and Visual Communication on Education: A Study among Moodubidire City based Degree College Students. *CLIO An Annual Interdisciplinary Journal of History, 6*(1), 465–473.

Rana, G., & Sharma, R. (2019). Assessing Impact of Employer Branding on Job Engagement: A Study of Banking Sector. *Emerging Economy Studies, 5*(1), 7–21. doi:10.1177/2394901519825543

Rangone, A. (2020). *Innovation and Technology: The Age of the Digital Enterprise*. Springer. doi:10.1007/978-3-030-31768-3

Rasheed, A., San, O., & Kvamsdal, T. (2020). Digital twin: Values, challenges and enablers from a modeling perspective. *IEEE Access: Practical Innovations, Open Solutions, 8*, 21980–22012. doi:10.1109/ACCESS.2020.2970143

Ratti, B. (2018). Geographic Knowledge. Paradigm of Society 5.0. *Journal of Research and Didactics in Geography, 1*, 123-26.

Ray, P. P. (2018). A survey on Internet of Things architectures. *Journal of King Saud University - Computer and Information Sciences, 30*(3), 291–319. doi:10.1016/j.jksuci.2016.10.003

Ray. (2013). *Four studies on the adoption of social media by financial advisors and investors.* Retrieved from https://www.socialmediatoday.com/content/four-studies-adoption-social-media-financial-advisors-and-investors

Reddy, S., & Reinartz, W. (2017). Digital transformation and value creation: Sea change ahead. *GfKMarketing Intelligence Review, 9*(1), 10–17. doi:10.1515/gfkmir-2017-0002

Regis, P., Jean-Philippe, P., & Celine, H. (2018, July) *Learning Fuzzy Relations and Properties for Explainable Artificial Intelligence. IEEE International Conference on Fuzzy Systems*, Rio de Janeiro, Brazil.

Reis, J., Amorim, M., Melão, N., & Matos, P. (2018, March). Digital transformation: a literature review and guidelines for future research. In *World conference on information systems and technologies* (pp. 411-421). Springer. 10.1007/978-3-319-77703-0_41

Reserve Bank of India Annual Report. (2018). Retrieved from https://www.rbi.org.in/Scripts/AnnualReportPublications.aspx?year=2018

Reuters. (2017). *World's first ATM machine turns to gold on 50th birthday.* Retrieved from https://www.reuters.com/article/us-atm-anniversary/worlds-first-atm-machine-turns-to-gold-on-50th-birthday-idUSKBN19I166

Richard, K. & Raghu N. K. (2019, May) *An Application of Combinatorial Methods for Explainability in Artificial Intelligence and Machine Learning.* National Institute of Standards and Technology, Gaithersburg, MD.

Rigby, M. J. (2019). Ethical dimensions of using artificial intelligence in health care. *AMA Journal of Ethics, 21*(2), 121–124. doi:10.1001/amajethics.2019.121

Ritter, T., & Geersbro, J. (2018). Multidexterity in customer relationship management: Managerial implications & a research agenda. *Industrial Marketing Management, 69*, 74–79. doi:10.1016/j.indmarman.2018.01.019

Robbins, S., & Judge, T. (2011). Organizational Behaviour. Academic Press.

Rojers, J. P. (2018). Digital transformation, business model innovation and efficiency in content industries: A review. *International Journal of Computational Intelligence Systems, 7*, 59–70.

Romao, M., Costa, J., & Costa, C. J. (2019). *Robotic Process Automation: A Case Study in the Banking Industry.* CISTI. doi:10.1109/ACCESS.2020.2974934

Romli, A., Mazlina, A. M., Aziman, A., & Fatinatul, N. Z. (2018). *ePAL Apps: Enhancing Parenting Literacy in a Smart Society 5.0.* Paper presented at International University Carnival on e-Learning (IUCEL).

Rooney, S. A., & Rooney, J. J. (2005). Lean glossary. *Quality Progress, 38*(6), 41–47.

Rossato, C., & Castellani, P. (2020). The contribution of digitalisation to business longevity from a competitiveness perspective. *The TQM Journal, 32*(4), 617–645. doi:10.1108/TQM-02-2020-0032

Rouse, M. (2019). *ICT (Information and Communications technologies).* https://searchcio.techtarget.com/definition/ICT-information-and-communications-technology-or-technologies

Royakkers, L., Timmer, J., Kool, L., & van Est, R. (2018). Societal and ethical issues of digitization. *Ethics and Information Technology, 20*(2), 127–142. doi:10.100710676-018-9452-x

Ruchira, R., & Prakhar, K., & B., B. (2018) *A Survey on Stock Market Prediction using Artificial Intelligence Techniques. International Conference on Smart Systems and Inventive Technology (ICSSIT 2018)*, Kattankulathur, Chennai.

Rupeika-Apoga, R., Zaidi, H. S., Thalassinos, E. Y., & Thalassinos, I. E. (2018). Bank stability: The case of Nordic and non-Nordic banks in Latvia. *International Journal of Economics & Business Administration, 6*(2), 39–55. doi:10.35808/ijeba/156

Ruth, M. J. B. (2019). Counterfactuals in Explainable Artificial Intelligence (XAI): Evidence from Human Reasoning. *Proceedings of the Twenty-Eighth International Joint Conference on Artificial Intelligence (IJCAI-19).*

Rybarczyk, G., Banerjee, S., Starking-Szymanski, M. D., & Shaker, R. R. (2018). Travel and Us: The Impact of Mode Share on Sentiment Using Social Media And GIS. *Journal of Location Based Services.*

Sadeh, N. (2003). *M-Commerce: Technologies, Services, and Business Models* (C. A. Long, Ed.). John Wiley and Sons.

Sahu, S., Pathardikar, A., & Kumar, A. (2018). Transformational leadership and turnover. *Leadership and Organization Development Journal, 39*(1), 82–99. doi:10.1108/LODJ-12-2014-0243

Salgues, B. (2018). *Society 5.0: Industry of the Future, Technologies, Methods and Tools.* ISTE Ltd.

Sarif, S. M. (2017). Society 5.0 Qalb with Tawhidic Paradigm. *Journal of Education and Social Sciences, 8*, 208–217.

Satish Muppidi, D. K. (2018). Challenges in Citation Analysis. *International Journal of Pure and Applied Mathematics*, 27–31.

Schein, E. H. (1996). Kurt Lewin's change theory in the field and in the classroom: Notes toward a model of managed learning. *Systems Practice, 9*, 27–47. https://doi.org/10.1007/BF02173417

Schein, E. H. (2010). *Organizational Culture and Leadership* (4th ed.). Wiley.

Schlager, T., Bodderas, M., Cachelin, J. L., & Maas, P. (2011). The influence of the employer brand on employee attitudes relevant for service branding: An empirical investigation. *Journal of Services Marketing, 25*(7), 497–508. doi:10.1108/08876041111173624

Schmidt, J., Drews, P., & Schirmer, I. (2016). End-users' perspective on digitalization: A study on work order processing in the German banking industry. *Proceedings of AMCIS 2016.*

Schneiderman, C. (2001). Are you billing in real-time. *Telecommunications, 35*(7), 71–72.

Schwab, K. (2016). *The 4th Industrial Revolution: What It Means, How to Respond.* Retrieved from: https://www.ge.com/news/reports/the-4th-industrial-revolution-what-it-means-how-to-respond

Schwartz, E. S., & Mark, M. (2020). Rational Pricing of Internet Companies. *Financial Analysts Journal*, (January), 2019.

Schwertner, K. (2017). Digital transformation of business. *Trakia Journal of Sciences, 15*(Suppl.1), 388–393. doi:10.15547/tjs.2017.s.01.065

Schwiderski-Grosche, S., & Knospe, H. (2002). *Future mobile networks: Ad-hoc access based on online payment with smartcards.* Conference paper of Personal, Indoor and Mobile Radio Communications.

Scopus. (2020). Retrieved from Scopus: https://www.scopus.com/sources?zone=&origin=NO%20ORIGIN%20DEFINED

Scott, J. E. (2007). An e-transformation study using the technology-organization-environment framework. In *Proceedings of BLED 2007* (p. 55). Academic Press.

Scott, S. V., van Reenen, J., & Zachariadis, M. (2017). The long-term effect of digital innovation on bank performance: An empirical study of swift adoption in financial services. *Research Policy, 46*(5), 984–100. doi:10.1016/j.respol.2017.03.010

Seenivasan, E. (2020). Retail banking services – role of channel of distribution in delivery system. *International Journal of Multidisciplinary Educational Research, 9*(2-3), 93–99.

Senn, J. A. (2000). The Emergence of M-Commerce. *Computer, 33*(12), 148–150.

Serpanos, D. (2018). The Cyber-Physical Systems Revolution. *Computer, 51*(3), 70–73. doi:10.1109/MC.2018.1731058

Sharma, C. (2016). *Mobile Commerce Statictics.* Retrieved from hhttp://www.ecbilla.com/blogs/mobile-ecommerce-statistics-2016.html

Sharma, S., & Verma, H. V. (2018). Social Media Marketing: Evolution and Change. In Social Media Marketing (pp. 19–36). Academic Press.

Sharma, A., Adhikary, A., & Borah, S. (2020). Covid-19's Impact on Supply Chain Decisions: Strategic Insights for NASDAQ 100 Firms using Twitter Data. *Journal of Business Research, 117*, 443–447.

Shende, V., & Kulkarni, M. (2020). Application of Machine Learning in Cryptography. *International Journal of Advanced Trends in Computer Science and Engineering.* doi:10.30534/ijatcse/2020/149932020

Sheth, J. (2020). Impact of Covid-19 on Consumer Behavior: Will the Old Habits Return or Die? Journal of Business Research. *Journal of Business Research, 117*, 280–283.

Shim, B., Choi, K., & Suh, Y. (2012). CRM strategies for a small-sized online shopping mall based on association rulesand sequential patterns. *Expert Systems with Applications, 39*(9), 7736–7742. doi:10.1016/j.eswa.2012.01.080

Shimura, T., Yoshikawa, M., & Uemura, S. (1999). Storage and Retrieval of XML Documents Using Object-Relational Databases. In T. J. M. Bench-Capon, G. Soda, & A. M. Tjoa (Eds.), *Database and Expert Systems Applications* (Vol. 1677, pp. 206–217). Springer Berlin Heidelberg. doi:10.1007/3-540-48309-8_19

Shiroishi, Y., Uchiyama, K., & Suzuki, N. (2018). Society 5.0: For Human Security and Well-Being. *IEEE Xplore, 51*(7), 91–95.

Šilingas, D., & Butleris, R. (2009). Towards implementing a framework for modeling software requirements in MagicDraw UML. *Information Technology and Control, 38*(2).

Silver, L. (2019). *Smartphone Ownership Is Growing Rapidly Around the World, but Not Always Equally.* Pew Research Center.

Simser, J. (2015). Bitcoin and modern alchemy: In code we trust. *Journal of Financial Crime, 22*(2), 156–169. doi:10.1108/JFC-11-2013-0067

Singh, N., & Agarwal, S. (2019). *Encumbrances in M-Commerce: A Demographic context.* Taylor and Francis Group.

Singh, S. K., Rathore, S., & Park, J. H. (2020). BlockIoTIntelligence: A Blockchain-enabled Intelligent IoT Architecture with Artificial Intelligence. *Future Generation Computer Systems, 110*, 721–743. doi:10.1016/j.future.2019.09.002

Sivertzen, A.-M., Nilsen, E. R., & Olafsen, A. H. (2013). Employer branding: Employer attractiveness and the use of social media. *Journal of Product and Brand Management, 22*(7), 473–483. doi:10.1108/JPBM-09-2013-0393

Sjardin, B., Massaron, L., & Boschetti, A. (2016). *Large Scale Machine Learning with Python.* Academic Press.

Skinners, C. (2018). *Open banking has arrived, whether you like it or not.* Chris Skinner's blog. Retrieved from https://thefinanser.com/2018/10/open-banking-arrived-whether-like-not.html

Skobelev, P.O., & Borovick, Yu., S. (2017). On the way from Industry 4.0 to Industry 5.0: from digital manufacturing to digital society. *International Scientific Journal Industry 4.0, 6*, 307-311.

Skourletopoulos, G., Mavromoustakis, C., Mastorakis, G., Batalla, J., Dobre, C., Panagiotakis, S., & Pallis, E. (2016). Big Data and Cloud Computing: A Survey of the State-of-the-Art and Research Challenges. In Advances in Mobile Cloud Computing and Big Data in the 5G Era (pp. 23-41). Academic Press.

Ślęzak, D., Glick, R., Betliński, P., & Synak, P. (2018). A new approximate query engine based on intelligent capture and fast transformations of granulated data summaries. *Journal of Intelligent Information Systems*, *50*(2), 385–414. doi:10.100710844-017-0471-6

Smith, B. (1998). *Basic concepts of formal ontology*. Academic Press.

Smith, B. C. (1985). The Limits of Correctness. *SIGCAS Comput. Soc.*, *14-15*(1-4), 18–26. doi:10.1145/379486.379512

Snyder, H. (2019). Literature review as a research methodology: An overview and guidelines. *Journal of Business Research*, *104*, 333–339. doi:10.1016/j.jbusres.2019.07.039

Sohn, S. (2017). Consumer processing of mobile online stores: Sources and effects of processing fluency. *Journal of Retailing and Consumer Services*, *36*, 137–147. doi:10.1016/j.jretconser.2017.01.008

Solmaz, M. S. (2012). *In the context of the maritime security, evaluation of the ISPS Code port security implementation's effectiveness and Turkey's implementations* (Doctoral dissertation). Retrieved from Council of Higher Education Thesis Center. (318754)

Solmaz, M. S., & Koray, M. (2020). Blockchain Technology in Maritime Transportation and Management. Handbook of Research on the Applications of International Transportation and Logistics for World Trade, 483-499. doi:10.4018/978-1-7998-1397-2.ch026

Solomon, M. R. (2014). *Consumer Behaviour: Buying, Having, and Being*. Prentice Hall.

Sönmez, S. (2016). *Blockchain nedir?* Retrieved from https://www.dunyahalleri.com/blok-zinciri-blockchain-nedir

Soomro, T. R., & Hussain, M. (2019). Social Media-Related Cybercrimes and Techniques for Their Prevention. *Applied Computer Systems*, *24*(1), 9–17. doi:10.2478/acss-2019-0002

Sousa, R. D., Karimova, B., & Gorlov, S. (2020). Digitalization as a New Direction in Education Sphere. In *E3S Web of Conferences* (Vol. 159, p. 09014). EDP Sciences.

Sowa, J. F. (2000). Ontology, Metadata, and Semiotics. In B. Ganter & G. W. Mineau (Eds.), *Conceptual Structures: Logical, Linguistic, and Computational Issues* (Vol. 1867, pp. 55–81). Springer Berlin Heidelberg. doi:10.1007/10722280_5

Srinivasan, G. (2012). *Single piece transportation*. Retrieved from https://nptel.ac.in/courses/110/106/110106044/

Stankov, U., Lazic, L., & Dragicevic, V. (2010). The extent of use of basic Facebook user-generated content by the national tourism organizations in Europe. *European Journal of Tourism Research*, *3*(2), 105–113.

Statista. (2017). Retrieved from https://www.statista.com

Statista. (2020a). *Global smartphone sales to end users 2007-2020*. Retrieved from https://www.statista.com/statistics/263437/global-smartphone-sales-to-end-users-since-2007

Statista. (2020b). *Size of the chatbot market worldwide, in 2016 and 2025*. Retrieved from https://www.statista.com/statistics/656596/worldwide-chatbot-market/

Surbhi, S. (2018). *Difference Between E-Commerce and M-Commerce*. Retrieved from https://keydifferences.com/author/surbhi/page/70

Suseendran, G., Chandrasekaran, E., Akila, D. & Kumar, A.S. (2020). Banking and FinTech (Financial Technology) Embraced with IoT Device. *Data Management, Analytics and Innovation*, 197-211.

Swan, M. (2017). Anticipating the economic benefits of blockchain. *Technology Innovation Management Review*, *7*(10), 6–13. doi:10.22215/timreview/1109

Swanson, D. J., & Creed, A. S. (2014). Sharpening the Focus of Force Field Analysis. *Journal of Change Management*, *14*(1), 28–47. doi:10.1080/14697017.2013.788052

Tajfel, S., & Turner, S. (1987). The social identity theory of intergroup behaviour. In S. Worchel & W. Austin (Eds.), *Psychology of intergroup relations* (2nd ed., pp. 7–24). Nelson-Hall.

Takahashi, T. (2018). Behavioral Economics of Addiction in the Age of a Super Smart Society: Society 5.0. *Oukan Journal of Transdisciplinary Federation of Science and Technology, 12*, 119–122.

Talón-Ballestero, P., González-Serrano, L., Soguero-Ruiz, C., Muñoz-Romero, S., & Rojo-Álvarez, J. L. (2018). Using big data from customer relationship management information systems to determine the client profile in the hotel sector. *Tourism Management*, *68*, 187–197. doi:10.1016/j.tourman.2018.03.017

Tanniru, M. R., Xi, Y., & Sandhu, K. (2020). Leadership to Advance Innovation for Digital Healthcare Transformation. *Leadership, Management, and Adoption Techniques for Digital Service Innovation,* 1-24. doi:10.4018/978-1-7998-2799-3.ch001

Tanwar, K., & Kumar, A. (2019). Employer brand, person-organisation fit and employer of choice: Investigating the moderating effect of social media. *Personnel Review*, *48*(3), 799–823. doi:10.1108/PR-10-2017-0299

Tapera, J. (2014). An analysis of the impact of mobile phone-based products on the provision of financial services to the individual Zimbabwean customer. *International Journal of Economics, Commerce and Management*, 2(5), 1–21.

Tarasewich, P. (2003). Designing Mobile Commerce Applications. *Communications of the ACM*, *46*.

Tayalı, H. A. (2016). A Literature Review on Production Scheduling with the Drum-Buffer-Rope Technique. *16th International Symposium for Production Research*, 1085–1090. Retrieved from https://papers.ssrn.com/sol3/papers.cfm?abstract_id=2919846

Taylor, K. (2015). *Connected health: how digital technology is transforming health and social care*. Deloitte Centre for Health Solutions.

Terrar, D. (2015). *What is digital transformation? Agile elephant*. Retrieved June 1, 2020, from http://www.theagileelephant.com/what-is-digital-transformation/

Thakur, R. (2018). Customer engagement and online reviews. *Journal of Retailing and Consumer Services*, *41*, 48–59. doi:10.1016/j.jretconser.2017.11.002

The Business Times. (2020). *FBC goes digital, closes five branches*. Retrieved May 30, 2020, from https://businesstimes.co.zw/fbc-goes-digital-closes-five-branches/

The Enterprisers Project. (2020). *What is digital transformation?* https://enterprisersproject.com/what-is-digital-transformation

The Financial Brand. (2018). *The four pillars of digital transformation in banking*. https://thefinancialbrand.com/71733/four-pillars-of-digital-transformation-banking-strategy/

The Herald. (2020). *Stanbic enhances digital banking*. Retrieved May 28, 2020, from https://www.herald.co.zw/stanbic-enhances-digital-banking/

The Independent. (2016). *ZBFH: A turnaround success story for 2015.* Retrieved May 27, 2020, from https://www.theindependent.co.zw/2016/08/19/zbfh-turnaround-success-story-2015/

The News International. (2020, June 12). *Economic Survey 2019-2020.* https://www.thenews.com.pk/print/671294-economic-survey-2019-2020

The Standish Group International, Inc. (2015). *Chaos Report 2015.* https://www.standishgroup.com/sample_research_files/CHAOSReport2015-Final.pdf

Theoharides, C. (2013). Manila to Malaysia, Quezon to Qatar: International migration and the effects on origin-country human capital. Job Market Paper. Department of Economics and Ford School of Public Policy. Ann Arbor, MI: University of Michigan.

Thietart, R., & Forgues, B. (1995). Chaos theory and organization. *Organization Science, 6*(1), 19–31.

Thupae, R. (2018). *Machine Learning Techniques for Traffic Identification and Classification in SDWSN.* IEEE.

Timmons, J. A., & Spinelli, S. (2007). *New venture creation: Entrepreneurship for the 21st century* (7th ed.). Mcgraw-Hill/Irwin.

Tiwari, R., & Buse, S. (2007). *The Mobile Commerce Prospects: A Strategic Analysis of Opportunities in the Banking Sector.* Hamburg University Press.

Tokareva, E. A., Smirnova, Y. V., & Orchakova, L. G. (2019). Innovation and communication technologies: Analysis of the effectiveness of their use and implementation in higher education. *Education and Information Technologies, 24*(5), 3219–3234. doi:10.100710639-019-09922-2

Tomaszuk, D. (2010). Document-oriented triplestore based on RDF/JSON. *Studies in Logic, Grammar and Rhetoric,* (22), 130.

Transforming our World: The 2030 Agenda for Sustainable Development. (2015). https:// sustainabledevelopment.un.org/content/documents/21252030%20Agenda%20for%20Sustainable%20Development%20web.pdf

Travkina, E., & Alexandra, M. (2019). Modern types of Financial innovations in the conditions of digitalization of the global banking system. *Advances in Economics, Business and Management Research, 85,* 18–22.

Trivedi, J. (2019). Examining the customer experience of using banking chatbots and its impact on brand love: The moderating role of perceived risk. *Journal of Internet Commerce, 18*(1), 91–111. doi:10.1080/15332861.2019.1567188

Tuomi, I. (2013). Open educational resources and the transformation of education. *European Journal of Education, 48*(1), 58–78. doi:10.1111/ejed.12019

Turban, D. B., & Cable, D. M. (2003). Firm reputation and applicant pool characteristics. *Journal of Organizational Behavior, 24*(6), 733–751. doi:10.1002/job.215

Turban, E., King, D., & Wang, J. (2003). *Introduction to E-Commerce.* Prentice Hall.

Ufuk, Ç., & Çağatay, B. (2017, June). The Prediction of Precious Metal Prices via Artificial Neural Network by Using RapidMiner. *The Journal of Operations Research, Statistics, Econometrics and Management Information Systems, 5*(1), 45–54.

Umran Alrubaee, A., Cetinkaya, D., Liebchen, G., & Dogan, H. (2020). A Process Model for Component-Based Model-Driven Software Development. *Information (Basel), 11*(6), 302. doi:10.3390/info11060302

United Nations Conference on Trade and Development (UNCTAD). (2018). *Review of Maritime Transport*. Retrieved from doi:10.18356/fd502c06-en

United Nations Conference on Trade and Development (UNCTAD). (2019). *Review of Maritime Transport*. Retrieved from https://unctad.org/en/PublicationsLibrary/rmt2019_en.pdf

Vakulenko, Y., Shams, P., Hellström, D., & Hjort, K. (2019). Online retail experience and customer satisfaction: The mediating role of last mile delivery. *International Review of Retail, Distribution and Consumer Research*, *29*(3), 306–320. doi:10.1080/09593969.2019.1598466

Van Dijk, J. A. G. M. (1991). De Netwerk-maatschappij, Sociale aspecten van nieuwe media [The network society, social aspects]. *Digital Media*, ▪ ▪ ▪, 163.

Vanathi, B., Shanmugam K., Rhymend, V., & Uthariaraj, V.R. (2016). Enhancing Secure Transaction and User Authentication Method Based on Fingerprint Mechanism Using Fuzzy Logic Amalgam Encryption for PIN Distribution Process in M-Commerce. *Asian Journal of Information Technology.*

Vanhanen, J., Lehtinen, T. O. A., & Lassenius, C. (2018). Software engineering problems & their relationship to perceived learning & customer satisfaction on a software capstone project. *Journal of Systems and Software*, *137*, 50–66. doi:10.1016/j.jss.2017.11.021

Varshney, U., & Vetter, R. (2002). Mobile Commerce: Framework, Applications and Networking Support. *Mobile Networks and Applications*, *7*(3), 185–198.

Veit, D., Clemons, E., Benlian, A., Buxmann, P., Hess, T., Kundisch, D., Leimeister, J. M., Loos, P., & Spann, M. (2014). Geschäftsmodelle: Eine Forschungsagenda für die Wirtschaftsinformatik. *Wirtschaftsinformatik*, *56*(1), 55–64. doi:10.100711576-013-0400-4

Verhoef, P. C. (2019). Digital Transformation: A Multidisciplinary Reflection and Research Agenda. *Journal of Business Research*. Advance online publication. doi:10.1016/j.jbusres.2019.09.022

Verhoef, P. C., Broekhuizen, T., Bart, Y., Bhattacharya, A., Dong, J. Q., Fabian, N., & Haenlein, M. (2019). Digital transformation: A multidisciplinary reflection and research agenda. *Journal of Business Research*.

Vezina, S., & Belanger, A. (2019). Impacts of education and immigration on the size and skills of the future workforce. *Demographic Research*, *41*, 331–366. doi:10.4054/DemRes.2019.41.12

Von Leipzig, T., Gamp, M., Manz, D., Schöttle, K., Ohlhausen, P., Oosthuizen, G., Palm, D., & von Leipzig, K. (2017). Initialising customer-orientated digital transformation in enterprises. *Procedia Manufacturing*, *8*, 517–524. doi:10.1016/j.promfg.2017.02.066

Vo, X. V., Nguyen, H. H., & McMillan, D. (2018). Bank restructuring and bank efficiency: The case of Vietnam. *Cogent Economics and Finance*, *6*(1), 1–17. doi:10.1080/23322039.2018.1520423

Wallace, E., & de Chernatony, L. (2009). Exploring brand sabotage in retail banking. *Journal of Product and Brand Management*, *18*(3), 198–211. doi:10.1108/10610420910957825

Wamba, S. F., Kamdjoug, J. R. K., Bawack, R. E., & Keogh, J. G. (2020). Bitcoin, Blockchain and Fintech: A systematic review and case studies in the supply chain. *Production Planning and Control*, *31*(2-3), 115–142. doi:10.1080/09537287.2019.1631460

Wang, J. J., Song, Z., Lei, P., & Sheriff, R. E. (2005). Design and Evaluation of M-Commerce Applications. Academic Press.

Wang, Y. S., & Liao, Y. W. (2007). The Conceptualization and Measurement of M-Commerce User Satisfaction. *Computation. Human Behaviour*, *23*(1).

Wanga, Y., Kung, L., & Byrd, T. (2018). *Big data analytics: Understanding its capabilities and potential benefits for healthcare organizations*. Elsevier. doi:10.1016/j.techfore.2015.12.019

Wang, Y., & Wu, Z. (2020). Model construction of planning and scheduling system based on digital twin. *International Journal of Advanced Manufacturing Technology*, *109*(7), 2189–2203. doi:10.100700170-020-05779-9

Waweru, S. W., & Maina, S. (2019). Corporate restructuring and organization performance of national police service in Kenya. *International Academic Journal of Human Resource and Business Administration*, *3*(6), 55–70.

Weare42. (n.d.). The smartest container this planet has even seen. *We are 42*. Retrieved from https://weare42.io/about/

Web of Science. (2020). Retrieved from Clarivate: https://clarivate.com/webofsciencegroup/solutions/web-of-science/

Wei, B., Sun, J., & Wang, Y. (2018). A Knowledge Engineering Approach to UML Modeling (S). *SEKE*, 60–63.

Weick, K., & Quinn, R. (1999). Organisational change and development. *Annual Review of Psychology*, *50*(1), 361–386.

Weill, P., & Woerner, S. L. (2018). Is your company ready for a digital future? *MIT Sloan Management Review*, *59*(2), 21–25.

Wellman, B., Quan-Haase, A., Boase, J., Chen, W., Hampton, K., Díaz, I., & Miyata, K. (2003). The social affordances of the Internet for networked individualism. *Journal of Computer-Mediated Communication, 8*(3).

Wellman, B. (2001). Physical place and cyberplace: The rise of personalized networking. *International Journal of Urban and Regional Research*, *25*(2), 227–252. doi:10.1111/1468-2427.00309

Wesley, G. Y. Y., & Suliadi, S. (2019, January). Data Mining Technique in Precious Metal Price Forecasting. *Advances in Computing and Intelligent System*, *1*(1), 1–16.

Wessel, L. K., Baiyere, A., Ologeanu-Taddei, R., Cha, J., & Jensen, T. B. (2020). Unpacking the Difference between Digital Transformation and IT-enabled Organizational Transformation. *Journal of the Association for Information Systems*.

White, H. D., & Griffith, B. C. (1981). Author co-citation: A literature measure of intellectual structure. *Journal of the American Society for Information Studies*, *32*(3), 163–171. doi:10.1002/asi.4630320302

Wikhamn, W. (2019). Innovation, sustainable HRM and customer satisfaction. *International Journal of Hospitality Management*, *76*, 102–110. doi:10.1016/j.ijhm.2018.04.009

Winston, W. L., & Albright, S. C. (2019). *Practical management science : includes Microsoft Office Excel 2007 applications* (6th ed.). Cengage.

Wojciech, S., Thomas, W., & Klaus-Robert, M. (n.d.). Explainable artificial intelligence: Understanding, visualizing an interpreting deep learning models. *ITU Journal: ICT Discoveries*.

Wong, G., Greenhalgh, T., Westhorp, G., Buckingham, J., & Pawson, R. (2013). RAMESES publication standards: Meta-narrative reviews. *BMC Medicine*, *11*(1), 20. doi:10.1186/1741-7015-11-20 PMID:23360661

Woodruff, C., & Zenteno, R. (2007). Migration networks and micro-enterprises in Mexico. *Journal of Development Economics*, *82*(2), 509–528. doi:10.1016/j.jdeveco.2006.03.006

Woodside, A. G. (2020). Interventions as experiments: Connecting the dots in forecasting and overcoming pandemics, global warming, corruption, civil rights violations, misogyny, income inequality, and guns. *Journal of Business Research*, *117*, 212–218.

World Bank Group. (2017). *The Global Findex Database 2017*. Retrieved from https://globalfindex.worldbank.org/

World Internet Project. (2012). *International Report* (4th ed.). Retrieved from: http://www.worldinternetproject.net/_files/_Published/_oldis /770_2012wip_report4th_ed.pdf

World Maritime News. (2018). Port of Rotterdam Teams Up with IBM to Build Smart Port of the Future. *World Maritime News*. Retrieved from https://worldmaritimenews.com/archives/242383/port-of-rotterdam-teams-up-with-ibm-to-build-smart-port-of-the-future/

World Maritime News. (2019). Port of Rotterdam: New IOT Platform Put into Operation. *World Maritime News*. Retrieved from https://worldmaritimenews.com/archives/270275/port-of-rotterdam-new-IOT-platform-put-into-operation/

Worldbank. (2019a). *Databank*. Retrieved from https://data.worldbank.org/indicator/NY.GDP.MKTP.CD

Worldbank. (2019b). *Databank*. Retrieved from https://data.worldbank.org/topic/trade

Wu, J. H., & Wang, S. C. (2005). What Drives Mobile Commerce? An Empirical Evaluation of the Revised Technology Acceptance Model. *Information & Management*.

Xiao, P. (2018). *Designing embedded systems and IOT with the ARM Mbed*. John Wiley & Sons Ltd.

Xu, G., & Gutierrez, J. A. (2006). An Exploratory Study of Killer Applications and Critical Success Factors in M-Commerce. *Journal of Electronic Commerce in Organizations*.

Xu, M., Wu, H., Feng, G., Zhang, X., & Ding, F. (2020). Broadcasting Steganography in the Blockchain. In H. Wang, X. Zhao, Y. Shi, H. Kim, & A. Piva (Eds.), Lecture Notes in Computer Science: Vol. 12022. *Digital Forensics and Watermarking. IWDW 2020*. Springer.

Yalçin, N., & Köse, U. (2010). What is search engine optimization: SEO? *Procedia Social and Behavioral Sciences, 9*(July), 487–493.

Yasin, M., Liébana-Cabanillas, F., Porcu, L., & Kayed, R. N. (2020). The role of customer online brand experience in customers' intention toforward online company-generated content: The case of the Islamic onlinebanking sector in Palestine. *Journal of Retailing and Consumer Services, 52*, 1–11. doi:10.1016/j.jretconser.2019.101902

Yazıcı, S. (2019). *Dünyada ve Türkiye' de açık bankacılık: Bankacılığın geleceği*. Fintech Istanbul. Retrieved from https://bkm.com.tr/wp-content/uploads/2015/06/Dunyadaveturkiyedeacikbankacilik.pdf

Yıkılmaz, İ., Sağbaş, M., & Karabal, C. (2020). Pandemi Döneminden Çıkışta Çevik Soğuk Tedarik Zinciri Yönetimin Önemive Aşı Takip Sistemi Uygulaması, Anadolu 5. *Uluslararasi Sosyal Bilimler Kongresi*, 577-591.

Yin, J. H. J., Fen, G. M., Mughal, F., & Iranmanesh, V. (2015). Internet of Things: Securing Data Using Image Steganography. *2015 3rd International Conference on Artificial Intelligence, Modelling and Simulation (AIMS)*, 310-314.

Yin, R. K. (2009). Case study research : design and methods. In Applied social research methods series: 5 (4th ed.). SAGE Publications, Inc.

Ying Ding, G. Z. (2014). Content-Based Citation Analysis: The Next Generation of Citation Analysis. *Journal of the Association for Information Science and Technology, 65*(9), 1820–1833. doi:10.1002/asi.23256

Yin, R. K. (1994). *Case study research : Design and methods*. SAGE Publications.

Yoo Kyung Jeong, M. S. (2016). Applying Content-Based Similarity Measure to Author Co-Citation Analysis. In *IConference*. iSchools.

Yordming, R. (2017). Teachers' perspective towards digital teaching tools in Thai EFL classrooms. *International Journal of Languages. Literatura y Lingüística*, *3*(2), 45–48.

Younus, Z. S., & Younus, G. T. (2020). Video Steganography using Knight Tour Algorithm and LSB Method for Encrypted Data. *J. Intell. Syst.*, *29*(1), 1216–1225. doi:10.1515/jisys-2018-0225

Yousefikhah, S. (2017). Sociology of innovation: Social construction of technology perspective. *AD-Minister*, 31–43. doi:10.17230/ad-minister.30.2

YP, B. (2012). Indexed journal: What does it mean? Lung India: Official Organ of Indian Chest Society.

Yüksel, S., Dinçer, H., & Emir, Ş. (2017). Comparing the performance of Turkish deposit banks by using DEMATEL, GreyRelational Analysis (GRA) and MOORA approaches. *World Journal of Applied Economics*, *3*(2), 26–47. doi:10.22440/wjae.3.2.2

Żeliński, J. (2019). Synthesis of MOF, MDA, PIM, MVC, and BCE Notations and Patterns. In *Applications and Approaches to Object-Oriented Software Design: Emerging Research and Opportunities*. IGI Global. https://www.igi-global.com/book/applications-approaches-object-oriented-software/235699

Zhang, L., Zhu, J., & Liu, Q. (2012). *A meta-analysis of mobile commerce adoption and the moderating effect of culture*. Academic Press.

Zhang, H., Zhao, L., & Gupta, S. (2018). The role of online product recommendations on customer decision making and loyalty in social shopping communities. *International Journal of Information Management*, *38*(1), 150–166. doi:10.1016/j.ijinfomgt.2017.07.006

Zhang, N. (2017). Agent-based modelling of consumer purchased behavior considering website quality. *5th International Conference on Mechatronics, Materials, Chemistry and Computer Engineering (ICMMCCE 2017)*. 10.2991/icmmcce-17.2017.105

Zhanhong, H., Junhao, Z., Hong-Ning, D., & Hao, W. (2019). *Gold Price Forecast based on LSTM-CNN Model*. International Conference on Cyber Science and Technology Congress, Gjøvik, Norway.

Zhou, G., Zhang, C., Li, Z., Ding, K., & Wang, C. (2020). Knowledge-driven digital twin manufacturing cell towards intelligent manufacturing. *International Journal of Production Research*, *58*(4), 1034–1051. doi:10.1080/00207543.2019.1607978

Zimmerman, D. W. (2005). The A-Theory of Time, The B-Theory of Time, and 'Taking Tense Seriously'. *Dialectica*, *59*(4), 401–457. doi:10.1111/j.1746-8361.2005.01041.x

About the Contributors

Kamaljeet Sandhu is an active, experienced researcher, who is passionate about research in Digital Innovation and Strategy, Business Analytics, Digital Health, AI, IoT, Cryptocurrency, Blockchain, Cloud Computing, IT Startup, FinTech, Cybersecurity, Accounting, Corporate Governance and CSR, Supply Chain, ERP, SMEs, and Entrepreneurship. The editor held multiple leadership positions including Senior Research Fellow at the University of South Australia, and Senior Academic position in Canada at the University of Northern British Columbia, and in Australia that include University of Wollongong, Charles Darwin University, Deakin University, and in Fiji at the University of South Pacific. As a PhD Principal Supervisor, the editor has supervised and mentored several PhD research students to successful completion, and students have successfully gained academic and research appointments at international universities and other organizations. Dr. Sandhu's PhD students' research is funded by international government and industry scholarships. The editor has multidisciplinary experience working across different faculties such as business, accounting, finance, management, economics, IT and IS, software, and computer science.

* * *

Tasneem Aamir is an Assistant Professor at the Department of Computer Science and Engineering, Truba Institute, Bhopal, India. She is a learning enthusiast and passionate about teaching and igniting young minds for the betterment of technical education and society. She finds pleasure in content writing and has worked with eminent publishers like IGI Global Publishers, Springer etc. She has specializations in Technical Writing, Machine Learning, Big Data and the Internet of Things.

Bülent Akkaya received his Bachelor's degree in Teaching English Department in 2006 in Kocaeli University and received his master's degree in 2013 in Business Administration Department in Celal Bayar University. In 2018, he holds his PhD in Business Administration Management with a specialization in Management field from İzmir Katip Çelebi University. He has been working as Dr. Lecturer in the Department of Office Management-Executive Assistant of Manisa Celal Bayar University in Turkey since 2013. His research interests comprise networks and partnerships in diverse disciplines. He has been working on motivation in organization, distance management, dynamic capabilities, agile leadership, organizational agility, industry 4.0, Leadership 5.0, Society 5.0 and quality of management in contemporary enterprises. He worked as researcher in four projects and as executive in a project. He published many articles, books and book chapters both in Turkish and English.

Cristina Callejón-Gómez is a PhD candidate from the University of Malaga. She has worked in several Digital Marketing companies, focusing on the field of the tourism sector.

Shawni Dutta is placed as a lecturer in Bhawanipur Education Society College, Kolkata. Currently, she is working on Machine learning techniques. Her research interests include Recommender Systems, Medical Fields, Steganography, and many more. She has published an enormous number of publications. She has also received awards at an international level.

Soumi Dutta is an Associate Professor and Assistant HOD of the Department of Computer Application at the Institute of Engineering & Management, India. She has completed her Ph.D. from the Department of CST, IIEST, Shibpur. She received her B.Tech. in IT and her M.Tech. in CSE securing 1st position(Gold medalist), both from Techno India Group. Her research interests Data Mining, Information Retrieval, Online Social Media Analysis, Micro-Blog Summarization, Spam Filtering Sentiment Analysis, and Clustering of Micro-Blogging Data. She was the editor in CIPR 2020, IEMIS 2020,CIPR2019, IEMIS2018 Springer Conferences for, special issue 2 volumes in IJWLTT (IGI Global) . She is TPC member in various international conferences such as - SEAHF, DSMLA, ARIAM, CIPR. She is peer reviewer in different international journal such as - Journal of King Saud University - Computer and Information Sciences, Springer, Elsevier etc. She is the member of several technical functional bodies such as IEEE, MACUL, SDIWC, ISOC, ICSES, IEEE WIE. She has published several papers in reputed journals and conferences. She has recently published 2 patents on System and Method for Solar Powered Washing Machine for Industrial Purposes and Sensor Based Artificial Limb for Physically Challenged People.

Mufaro Dzingirai is a PhD candidate in Business Management at Midlands State University and a lecturer in the Department of Business Management, Midlands State University. He received his Master of Commerce in Strategic Management and Corporate Governance degree from Midlands State University in 2016. He was hired as a teacher by the Ministry of Education from 2014 to 2016. In 2013, he received the MSU Book Prize. His research interests include Higher Education, Strategy, Management, Finance, and Entrepreneurship.

Maryam Ebrahimi has working experience as an assistant professor at some universities and a senior researcher in several industries. She is currently an independent researcher in Germany. Her post-doctoral research was in the area of Information Systems Management funded by the Alexander von Humboldt Foundation, Germany. She has oriented her studies towards systems science in business management. Her interest is the use of modeling and simulation methodologies for the purpose of policymaking. A few of her publications are 'hybrid simulation approach for technological innovation policymaking in developing countries' and 'modeling and simulation techniques for improved business processes'.

Mostapha El Idrissi is a PhD in strategic management at Hassan II University Morocco. His research is focused on inter-organisational strategies and in particular on collaborations between competitors "co-opetition". His research areas include also entrepreneurship, SME, open innovation, proximity and innovation.

Younès El Manzani holds a Doctorate in Management Studies from the Jean Moulin Lyon 3 University and the Cadi Ayyad University as a part of a joint Ph.D. He is an assistant professor at the Institut supérieur de management (ISM-IAE), Versailles Saint-Quentin en Yvelines university. Attached to the research laboratory LAREQUOI, his research addresses topics related to strategic management, quality management, innovation management, and entrepreneurship.

Berrin Arzu Eren is Assistant Professor at Ufuk University in Ankara/Turkey. She received her MA from the Faculty of Business Administration at Istanbul Bilgi University and she holds PhD degree in Anadolu University Marketing Science. Her fields of work are service marketing, financial marketing, customer relationship management, and sales management. She had 13 years of banking experience and she managed Garanti Bank BBVA's several branches in Ankara and Istanbul.

Ramkrishna Ghosh is an Assistant Professor in the Department of Information Technology, Haldia Institute of Technology. He is pursuing Ph. D. from Kalinga Institute of Industrial Technology, Bhubaneswar. He has published many journals of international repute. His research interest is Wireless Sensor Network. He has authored various books on programming languages like C/C++ and Java.

Ayse Gunsel works in Kocaeli University, Turkey as Associated Prof.

Esha Jain is Ph.D., UGC-NET, MBA, and has more than 13 years of work experience including both the Industry and Academics. A Certified Technical Analyst (in Stock Market) from Government of NCT of Delhi and Government of India, and Amazon Trained E-commerce Specialist, she has also qualified a module of Financial Markets with Distinction organized by (NSE) National Stock Exchange of India. She has also achieved a Statement of Accomplishment with Distinction in the certification course on 'Personal and Family Financial Planning' from the University of Florida. An awardee of 'Eminent Educationist Award', 'Asia Pacific Gold Star Award', 'Young Woman Educator and Scholar Award', 'Excellence Award 2017', she was also selected for "Rajiv Gandhi Education Excellence Award" and 'Bharat Vidya Shiromani Award'. She is the Resource Person for Various Faculty Development Programmes in the field of Academics, Research, and SPSS. She is also awarded 27 Honors and Awards, including 15 Best Research Paper Awards and a Dean Committee Choice Award in various International Conferences of repute. She has been invited by IIM Indore for review of 'Institutional Development Plans (IDPs)' under the World Bank-supported Madhya Pradesh Higher Education Quality Improvement Project (MPHEQIP) to be submitted to Department of Higher Education, Government of Madhya Pradesh, and also took webinar sessions for Financial Management and Taxation Management (PG level) of Sikkim Manipal University Distance Learning Education. She has taken modules of Chartered Institute of Management Accountants (CIMA), London, UK, and certified by the Institute of Chartered Accountants of India (ICAI) for conducting 'Investor Awareness Programmes' in institutions and organizations. She has published five (5) patents with the Government of India. More than 70 of her research papers are published in various International Journals and Conference Proceedings of repute as well as authored two (2) books, one is on 'Foreign Exchange Management' & other one is on 'Principles of Management with text and cases' under reputed Brands and also contributed chapters in another book on 'Corporate Social Responsibility'. She has also presented around 80 research papers and cases at various national and international conferences as well as has chaired various National and International Seminars and Conferences as Session Chair, Keynote Speaker and Panelist in Panel Discussions. She has also associated 12 various International Journals as Editorial Board Member, Academic Advisor, Research Paper

Reviewer & Editor-in-Chief. She is also an External Examiner for evaluating Ph.D. Thesis for Jain University, Bengaluru, and Pune University.

Ashwini J is a freelance consultant, trainer and faculty in the area of management. Her area of expertise is in the field of Information Technology, Human Resource Management and Sociology. Her research areas include Organization Behaviour, Organization Development and Digital marketing.

Jonika Lamba is a Research Scholar at the School of Management, The NorthCap University, Gurugram, India. Her areas of interest include stock markets, accounting, auditing, technologies, and taxation.

Zakaria Lissaneddine holds a PhD in Human Resources Management from Cadi Ayyad University. He is an assistant professor at National School of Business & Management - Meknès and a member of Laboratory of Studies and Research in Entrepreneurship, Management and Control of Enterprises (LEREMCE) at Moulay Ismaïl University, his research activities are specifically about employer branding, digital marketing, social media and qualitative methods.

Zeynep Orman is Assoc. Prof. of Computer Science, Istanbul University-Cerrahpasa.

Digvijay Pandey is a lecturer, Department of Technical Education, Research Scholar, IET Lucknow, India.

Sabyasachi Pramanik is a Professional IEEE Member. He obtained his B. Tech (Electronics & Telecommunication Engineering), from Haldia Institute of Technology, India. He obtained his M. Tech and Ph.D. in Computer Science and Engineering from Sri Satya Sai University of Technology and Medical Sciences, Madhya Pradesh in the area of Image Steganography. His area of interests is Steganography, Artificial Intelligence, and Computational Intelligence. He is presently working as Assistant Professor, Department of Computer Science and Engineering, Haldia Institute of Technology, West Bengal, India. He has authored and co-authored over 30 papers in SCI / SCOPUS / SPRINGER Journals and IEEE / Springer Conference proceedings in areas of Steganography, Computational Intelligence and Image Processing. He has authored a book on Wireless Sensor Network. He is currently editing 6 books from publishers like Wiley, IGI Global, Springer and CRC Press, etc. He is on the editorial board of over 20 journals and serving as a Technical Committee Member of various international conferences. He is also a reviewer of several Springer/Elsevier/IGI Global and Inderscience journals. He is also a Keynote speaker and Session Chair for various international conferences.

Ranjith P V, Associate Professor, CMS Business School, Jain (deemed to be university), Bangalore, is an academician in the field of management for the last two decades. His areas of teaching include Quantitative Techniques and Research Applications in the field of management. His research areas include Service Quality, Consumer Behaviour, and Operations Effectiveness.

Tansif ur Rehman has a PhD in European Studies. He has also completed 56 Certification/Credit Courses, 11 Miscellaneous Diplomas, 08 Government of Pakistan Trainings, 04 Certification Courses and Diploma (Languages) - Deutsch, English, Italian, and Russian. He has several publications and has over 20 years teaching as well as 14 years research experience.

María-Mercedes Rojas-de-Gracia earned her PhD degree from University of Málaga. She is a Professor of the Department of Economics and Business Administration, University of Málaga (Spain). Her lines of research consist on the study of destination image and family vacation decision making. Currently, she is working on the study of Destination Image through the use of social media.

Debabrata Samanta is presently working as Assistant Professor, Department of Computer Science, CHRIST (Deemed to be University), Bangalore, India. He obtained his B.Sc. (Physics Honors), from Calcutta University; Kolkata, India. He obtained his MCA, from the Academy of Technology, under WBUT, West Bengal. He obtained his PhD in Computer Science and Engg. from National Institute of Technology, Durgapur, India, in the area of SAR Image Processing. His areas of interest are SAR Image Analysis, Video surveillance, Heuristic algorithm for image classification, Deep Learning Framework for Detection and Classification, Blockchain, Statistical Modelling, Wireless Adhoc Network, Natural Language Processing,V2I Communication. He is the owner of 17 Indian Patents. He has authored and coauthored over 134 research papers in international journal (SCI/SCIE/ESCI/Scopus) and conferences including IEEE, Springer and Elsevier Conference proceedings. He has received "Scholastic Award" at 2nd International conference on Computer Science and IT application, CSIT-2011, Delhi, India. He has published 9 books, available for sale on Amazon and Flipkart.

Murat Selçuk Solmaz is an Assistant Professor Doctor at Piri Reis University, Faculty of Engineering, Industrial Engineering Department. He completed his master program in 2004 and doctoral program in 2012 at Istanbul University, Institute of Marine Sciences and Management. His professional and research experience includes maritime security, maritime safety, port management and maritime transportation management.

Bhavna Taneja an Assistant Professor at Amity University, Jharkhand, India. She has done her PhD in Management, and Master of Business Administration with a specialisation in Finance and Marketing. She has experience of over 18 years in the education sector.

Halit Tayali is assistant professor at Istanbul University School of Business, the Department of Production and Operations Management.

Aparna J Varma, Associate Professor, Dept of MBA, GSSSIETW, Mysore, is an academician in the area of management for the past decade. Her teaching is in Marketing, Human Resources and Quantitative Techniques. Her area of research interest includes Services Marketing, Retail Management Consumer Behaviour, and Learning & Development.

İbrahim Yikilmaz is a research assistant of The Management and Organization Department at Kocaeli University. He is an academician and PhDC in Management and Organization field. He has completed his master's degrees at Ankara Yıldırım Beyazıt University Management and Organization (2018) and TODAIE (Institute of Public Administration For Turkey And The Middle East) Public Administration (2016) Master Programs and graduated from Turkish War Academy as a System Engineer in 2009. Before being a research assistant, he was working as a manager in several public organizations (Turkish Armed Forces, Maltepe Municipality, and Aydın Metropolitan Municipality) especially in the field of strategic management. He is mostly focused on Entrepreneurship, Management Strategies, Organizational

Behavior, Digital Transformation, and Agile Organizations as the subjects. He has scientific papers and articles published in national and international congresses and journals in the field of strategic management. English is fluent and at a professional level, Russian and Chinese are at pre-intermediate level. ORCID: 0000-0002-1051-0886.

Jaroslaw Zelinski, as a lecturer in 2005–2012, permanently cooperated with the Information Systems Department of the Maritime University of Gdynia. Since 2014, he has been a lecturer at the Faculty of Information Technology in Management Techniques at the University of Information Technology and Management under the auspices of the Polish Academy of Sciences, since 2016 he has been a PhD student at the Institute of System Research of the Polish Academy of Sciences. The subject of lectures are system analysis and systems logic projects for business, formalised business and system analysis aimed at optimising the work of the organisation, organisational aspects of business continuity management, developing requirements for management support software.

Index

P

R

S

T

U

V

W

Z

Premier Reference Source
Emerging GIS Applications for Emergency and Disaster Management

Premier Reference Source
Managerial Strategies and Green Solutions for Project Sustainability

Premier Reference Source
Comparative Approaches to Using R and Python for Statistical Data Analysis

Premier Reference Source
Solutions for High-Touch Communications in a High-Tech World

www.ingramcontent.com/pod-product-compliance
Lightning Source LLC
LaVergne TN
LVHW062116300926
849161LV00010B/2469